Creating Literacy Instruction for All Students in Grades 4 to 8

Thomas G. Gunning

Central Connecticut State University, Adjunct Professor
and
Southern Connecticut State University, Emeritus

Boston   New York   San Francisco
Mexico City   Montreal   Toronto   London   Madrid   Munich   Paris
Hong Kong   Singapore   Tokyo   Cape Town   Sydney

To my granddaughter:

Paige Gunning

Series Editor: Aurora Martínez-Ramos
Editorial Assistant: Katie Freddoso
Senior Marketing Manager: Elizabeth Fogarty
Editorial-Production Administrator: Karen Mason
Editorial-Production Services: Helane M. Prottas
Photo Research: Helane M. Prottas/Posh Pictures

Cover Coordinator: Linda Knowles
Cover Designer: Susan Paradise
Composition and Prepress Buyer: Linda Cox
Manufacturing Buyer: Megan Cochran
Electronic Composition: Dayle Silverman/Silver Graphics

For related titles and support materials, visit our
online catalog at www.ablongman.com.

Between the time Website information is gathered and then published, it is not unusual for
some sites to have closed. Also, the transcription of URLs can result in unintended typographical errors. The publisher would appreciate notification where these errors occur so that they
may be corrected in subsequent editions.

Library of Congress Cataloging-in-Publication Data

Gunning, Thomas G.
  Creating literacy instruction for all students in grades 4 to 8/Thomas G. Gunning.
      p. cm.
  Includes bibliographical references and index.
  ISBN 0-205-35684-2
      1. Reading (Elementary) 2. Reading (Middle school) 3. English language—Composition
and exercises—Study and teaching (Elementary) 4. English language—Composition and exer-
cises—Study and teaching (Middle school)   I. Title

LB1573.G934 2003
372.6--dc21

                                                                                2003041777

Printed in the United States of America
10 9 8 7 6 5 4 3 2 1   RRD-IND   08 07 06 05 04 03

Brief Contents

Special Features

Contents

Teaching Phonics, High-Frequency Words, and Syllabic Analysis 74

Building Vocabulary 118

5 Comprehension: Theory and Strategies *176*

6 Comprehension: Text Structures and Teaching Procedures 232

7 Reading and Writing in the Content Areas and Study Skills 270

8 Reading Literature 324

9 Approaches to Teaching Reading 362

10 Writing and Reading 392

11 Diversity in the Classroom 434

12 Creating and Managing a Literacy Program 454

Preface

Teaching literacy is in large measure a matter of making choices: Should you use basal readers or children's books, or both? Should you teach children to read whole words or to sound out words letter by letter, or both? Should you have three reading groups or four, or no groups? The answers depend on your personal philosophy, your interpretation of the research, the level at which you are teaching, the kinds of students you are teaching, community preferences, and the nature of your school's or school district's reading program.

This book has been written to help you discover approaches and techniques that fit your teaching style and your teaching situation. Its aim is to present as fairly, completely, and clearly as possible the major approaches and techniques that research and practice have indicated to be most effective. This book also presents the theories behind the methods, so you will be free *to choose, adapt, and/or construct* those approaches and techniques that best fit your style and teaching situation.

According to Howard Gardner, the multiple intelligence theorist, the purpose of education is to "enhance understanding" (Harvey, 2002). He recounts the story of his daughter who, despite being an A student in physics, was dismayed when she was unable to explain the physics behind a coin toss. Taking Gardner's remarks and his daughter's experience to heart, I have attempted in this text to build understanding. Understanding can lead to more effective teaching. The text also explains cognitive development, differences between the Spanish and English writing systems, and other topics that will foster a deeper understanding of teaching techniques.

Although the text emphasizes approaches and techniques, methods are only a portion of the equation. Reading is not just a process; it is also very much a content area. What students read does matter, and, therefore, I have provided recommendations for specific children's books and other reading materials.

Appendix A lists more than 800 high-quality children's books by grade level. The basic premise of this book is that the best reading programs are a combination of effective techniques and plenty of worthwhile reading material.

Because children differ greatly in their backgrounds, needs, and interests, the book offers a variety of suggestions for both techniques and types of books to be used. The intent is to provide you with sufficient background knowledge of teaching methods, children's books, and other materials to enable you to create effective instruction for all the children you teach, whether they are rich or poor; bright, average, or slow; with disabilities or without; urban or suburban; or from any of the diverse cultural and ethnic groups that compose today's classrooms.

This book also recognizes that reading is part of a larger language process; therefore, considerable attention is paid to oral language development, writing and the other language arts, especially as these relate to reading instruction. Whether reading or writing is being addressed, emphasis is on making the student the center of instruction. For instance, activities are recommended that allow students to choose writing topics and reading materials. Approaches that foster a personal response to reading are also advocated. Just as you are encouraged by this text to create your own reading instruction, students must be encouraged to create their own literacy.

Because of the impact of the standards movement and related assessment issues, a full chapter is devoted to assessment (Chapter 2). Lists of standards and assessment suggestions are provided at the end of each chapter on instructional techniques. Appendix B contains a series of informal measures of key skills

With classrooms becoming increasingly diverse, the emphasis has been placed on helping struggling readers and writers and English language learners. Chapters 3–11 conclude with a "Help for Struggling Readers and Writers" section. Emphasis has also been placed on programs of intervention and the role of the classroom teacher in working with struggling readers and writers. This text endorses the viewpoint that a well-prepared classroom teacher is capable of effectively instructing most struggling readers and writers. To prevent problems, the text stresses providing students with carefully planned direct instruction in both reading and writing.

To assist you as you construct a framework for teaching reading and writing, a number of features that readers and reviewers found most valuable have been included.

■ Each chapter begins with an **Anticipation Guide,** which invites you to take inventory of your current ideas and opinions about chapter topics. Review your answers to this guide after reading the chapter, and note how your ideas may have changed.

ANTICIPATION GUIDE

*F*or each of the following statements, put a check under "Agree" or "Disagree" to show how you feel. Discuss your responses with classmates before you read the chapter.

	Agree	Disagree
1 If students in grade four and beyond are still weak in phonics, they should be given a highly structured phonics program.	___	___
2 Phonics rules have so many exceptions that they are not worth teaching.	___	___
3 Phonics is hard to learn because English is so irregular.	___	___
4 The natural way to decode a word is sound by sound or letter by letter.	___	___
5 Memorizing is an inefficient way to learn new words.	___	___
6 Syllabication is not a very useful skill because you have to know how to decode a word before you can put it into syllables.	___	___

USING WHAT YOU KNOW

*B*y the time they reach fourth grade, most students have mastered basic phonics. However, there will be some students whose knowledge of phonics is inadequate. As a middle grade or middle school teacher, it would be helpful for you to have some basic knowledge of phonics and also know some techniques that you might use to help these students. Some students will have mastered basic phonics but will have difficulty applying these skills to multisyllabic

■ **Using What You Know** is a brief introduction to each chapter that helps you relate your prior knowledge and the information presented in previous chapters to the chapter you are about to read.

LESSON 5.5 Presenting QAR

To provide practice with making inferences at all levels, have students infer character traits based on the character's actions, because authors typically let a character's actions show what kind of a person the character is.

Step 1. Introducing the concept of QAR

Introduce the concept by writing on the board a paragraph similar to the following:

> Andy let the first pitch go by. It was too low. The second pitch was too high. But the third toss was letter high. Andy lined it over the left fielder's outstretched glove.

Ask a series of literal questions: "Which pitch did Andy hit? Where did the ball go? Why didn't Andy swing at the first pitch? The second pitch?" Lead students to see that the answers to these questions are "in the book."

Next, ask a series of questions that depend on the readers' background: "What game was Andy playing? What do you think Andy did after he hit the ball? Do you think he scored a run? Why or why not?" Show students that the answers to these questions depend on their knowledge of baseball. Discuss the fact that these answers are "in my head."

Step 2. Extending the concept of QAR

After students have mastered the concept of "in the book" and "in my head," extend the in-the-book category to include both "right there" and "putting it together." Once students have a solid working knowledge of these, expand the in-my-head category to include both "on my own" and "writer and me." The major difference between these two is whether the student has to read the text for the question to make sense. For instance, the question "Do you think Andy's hit was a home run?" requires knowledge of baseball and information from the story. The question "How do you feel when you get a hit?" involves only experience in hitting a baseball.

Step 3. Providing practice

Provide ample opportunity for guided and independent practice. Also refine and extend students' awareness of sources for answers and methods for constructing responses.

■ Additional model teaching **Lessons** have been provided that encompass nearly every area of literacy instruction.

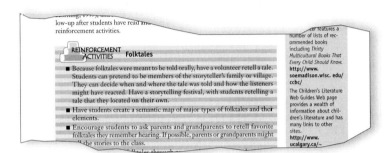

■ Key strategies, such as analyzing unknown words or summarizing a paragraph, which students can use to become independent learners, are outlined step by step and highlighted by the heading **Student Strategies.**

Applying the variability strategy to vowel correspondences

Because there is no way to predict on the basis of spelling whether ow will represent /ow/ (cow) or /ō/ (snow) or oo will represent a short (book) or long (boot) sound, you need to teach students to check whether the sounds they construct create a real word. If not, have them try the other major pronunciation of ow or oo. Model this process for your students.

1. Sound out the word as best you can.
2. After sounding out the word, ask yourself, "Is this a real word?" If not, try sounding out the word again. (Applying the variability principle to a word containing ow, a student might try the long-vowel pronunciation first. If that did not work out, he or she would try the /ow/ (cow) pronunciation. If there is a chart of spellings available, students can use it as a source of possible pronunciations.)
3. Read the word in the sentence. Ask yourself, "Does this word make sense in the sentence?" If not, try sounding it out again.
4. If you still cannot sound out a word so that it makes sense in the sentence, try context, skip it

■ Practice and application activities have been identified as **Reinforcement Activities.** Activities that involve reading and writing for real purposes have been stressed.

low-up after students have read and reinforcement activities.

REINFORCEMENT ACTIVITIES   Folktales

■ Because folktales were meant to be told orally, have a volunteer retell a tale. Students can pretend to be members of the storyteller's family or village. They can decide when and where the tale was told and how the listeners might have reacted. Have a storytelling festival, with students retelling a tale that they located on their own.
■ Have students create a semantic map of major types of folktales and their elements.
■ Encourage students to ask parents and grandparents to retell favorite folktales they remember hearing. If possible, parents or grandparents might the stories to the class.

features a number of lists of recommended books including *Thirty Multicultural Books That Every Child Should Know.* http://www. soemadison.wisc. edu/ ccbc/

The Children's Literature Web Guides Web page provides a wealth of information about children's literature and has many links to other sites. http://www. ucalgary.ca/~

Raw fish is his men.
This is the tale of a whiskered . . .

The next page shows the rest of the seal and the word *Seal.* Listed in the Children's Reading List are some more titles that may be used to reinforce initial consonants.

CHILDREN'S READING LIST   Recommended books for reinforcing initial consonants

When using alphabet books, be on the lookout for confusing presentations. In one book, the words tiger, thin, and the are used to demonstrate the sound usually represented by the letter t. However, th in thin represents a different sound than that heard at the beginn

Amery, H. (1997). *Usborne farmyard tales, alphabet book.* London: Usborne. Reinforces the target letter with an alliterative sentence and question.
Calmenson, S. (1993). *It begins with an A.* New York: Hyperion. Rhyming riddles challenge the reader to guess objects whose names begin with letters A to Z.
Cohen, N. (1993). *From apple to zipper.* New York: Macmillan. Rhyming text, with illustrations that form the letters they represent.
Ellwand, D. (1996). *Emma's elephant & other favorite animal friends.* New Y

■ **Children's Reading Lists** appear in all chapters as a resource for titles that reinforce the particular literacy skills being discussed.

■ To help make the descriptions of teaching techniques come alive, examples of good teaching practices have been placed throughout the book in a feature entitled **Exemplary Teaching.** All are true-life accounts; many have been drawn from the memoirs of gifted teachers, while others were garnered from newspaper reports or the author's observations.

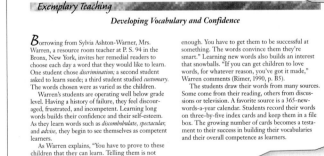

Exemplary Teaching

Developing Vocabulary and Confidence

*B*orrowing from Sylvia Ashton-Warner, Mrs. Warren, a resource room teacher at P. S. 94 in the Bronx, New York, invites her remedial readers to choose each day a word that they would like to learn. One student chose *discrimination;* a second student asked to learn suede; a third student studied *customary.* The words chosen were as varied as the children.

Warren's students are operating well below grade level. Having a history of failure, they feel discouraged, frustrated, and incompetent. Learning long words builds their confidence and their self-esteem. As they learn words such as *discombobulate, spectacular,* and *advise,* they begin to see themselves as competent learners.

As Warren explains, "You have to prove to these children that they can learn. Telling them is not

enough. You have to get them to be successful at something. The words convince them they're smart." Learning new words also builds an interest that snowballs. "If you can get children to love words, for whatever reason, you've got it made," Warren comments (Rimer, 1990, p. B5).

The students draw their words from many sources. Some come from their reading, others from discussions or television. A favorite source is a 365-new-words-a-year calendar. Students record their words on three-by-five index cards and keep them in a file box. The growing number of cards becomes a testament to their success in building their vocabularies and their overall competence as learners.

■ Marginal annotations throughout the text provide the reader with interesting, practical, handy advice and guidance. Because of the movement toward inclusive classrooms, suggestions for teaching students of varying abilities—including students with reading or learning disabilities—are presented in the body of the text and in marginal annotations with the heading **Adapting Instruction for Struggling Readers and Writers.** Suggestions are also made throughout the text for assisting students who are still acquiring English. Marginal annotations for these students are entitled **Adapting Instruction for English Language Learners.** Other headings include **Using Technology, Involving Parents,** and **Building Language.** There are also many untitled annotations on specific topics that elaborate on the text discussion. Key terms are highlighted in the text and appear, with their definitions, in the margin.

Failure to comprehend might be caused by a problem at any level of reading (Collins & Smith, 1980):

■ Words may be unknown or may be known but used in an unfamiliar way.
■ Concepts are unknown.
■ Punctuation is misread.
■ Words or phrases are given the wrong emphasis.
■ Paragraph organization is difficult to follow.
■ Pronouns and antecedent relationships are confused. Relationships among ideas are unclear.
■ Relatio

ADAPTING INSTRUCTION for *STRUGGLING READERS and WRITERS*
Research on metacognitive processes suggests that poor readers find it especially difficult to monitor or repair their reading. They often read materials that are far beyond their instructional levels. Over-

---

do with relationships between speakers and listeners. In Hispanic cultures, for example, it is customary to avert one's eyes when speaking to persons in authority. However, for many cultural groups, the opposite is true. Students learning English should learn the cultural expectations of the language along with vocabulary and syntax.

Adapt lessons to meet the needs of English learners. For example, when teaching phonics, start with sound–symbol relationships that are the same in both languages. For Spanish-speaking children, you might start with long *o*, since that sound is common in both English and Spanish. Before teaching elements that are not present in Spanish—short *i*, for instance—make sure that these elements have been introduced in the ELL class. For easily confused auditory items—long *e* and short *i*, for example—provide added auditory-discrimination exercises. Also use the items in context or use real objects or pictures to illustrate them. When discussing shoes, for example, point to them.

When teaching a reading lesson, examine the text for items that might cause problems. Pay attention to the following items:

ADAPTING INSTRUCTION for *ENGLISH LANGUAGE LEARNERS*
Because of limited English, ELLs may have difficulty fully explaining what they know about a selection they have read. They may mispronounce words whose meanings they know. The key element is whether students are getting meaning from these words, not whether they are pronouncing them correct-

---

USING TECHNOLOGY
National Clearinghouse for English Language Acquisition provides a wealth of information on bilingual education and includes excellent links to useful sites.
http://www.ncela.gwu.edu/

Dr. Mora's Web site is also an excellent source of information about bilingual education.
http://coe.sdsu.edu/people/jmora/

BUILDING LANG

word *cow*, the student may have to search his lexicon for the Spanish equivalent of *cow, vaca*. The extra step slows down the reading.

Use cooperative learning and peer tutoring strategies. Working with peers provides excellent opportunities for ELLs to apply language skills. In a small group, they are less reluctant to speak. In addition, they are better able to make themselves understood and better able to understand others.

Also plan strategic use of the students' native language. Use that level of English that students are familiar with. However, for developing complex concepts, use the students' native language, if possible, or ask another student to provide a translation. That way the student doesn't have the burden of trying to understand difficult concepts expressed in terms that may be hard to understand.

Use a language-experience approach. A language-experience approach avoids the problem of unfamiliar syntax and vocabulary because students read selections that they dictate. Some students might dictate stories that contain words in both English and their native tongue. This should be allowed and could be an aid as the student makes the transition to English.

---

http://www.resourceroom.net/OGLists/wordlists.asp.

INVOLVING PARENTS
Parents might want to know what to do if their children ask for help with a word. Having them simply tell their children unknown words is the safest, least frustrating approach (Topping, 1989). But in some situations, you may want to have them encourage their children in the use of specific strategies.

will help students pick up reading skills. Such an approach is ineffective and wasteful. Start where students are. Build on what they have learned. Also make sure that instruction is functional and contextual. Teach students the skills that they need in the context of real reading and writing. One way of doing that is to look at the materials students are about to read and to note the essential decoding skills needed to read that material. Teach students skills that they are lacking. For instance, in a science article about electricity, the words *circle, circuit, certain, certificate,* and *ceramic* are used. You might write the word *circle* on the chalkboard and *circuit* under it. Pointing to *circle*, have students read it and then use this known word to read *circuit*. If they have difficulty with *cuit*, tell them that *cu* represents a /k/ sound. They should then be able to read the *it* part of the word and put the syllables together. Then using *certain* as the known word, have students use their knowledge of *ce* in *certain* to read *certificate* and *ceramic*. If students have difficulty with *certain*, write the word *her* on the board and have them relate the first part of *certain* to *her*. Have them note that both words have an /er/ sound. Then encourage them to read the rest of the syllables. Provide help as necessary. Help students to see that *ceramic* begins in the same way as *certain* and *certificate*. Using this knowledge, they should be able to work out the pronunciation of *ceramic*. But provide help as needed. The lesson assumes that students know the words' meanings.

BUILDING LANGUAGE
Keep a file of pictures and artifacts that might be used to help explain a topic. For instance, maintain a file of minerals that might include pictures of minerals or actual samples. When you mention the mineral, hold up an illustration of it or the real mineral. This helps all learners, but is especially helpful to ELLs. Your picture file might be electronic and stored on your hard drive or a disk.

English and their native tongue. This should be allowed and could be an aid as the student makes the transition to English.

Although students are learning to read in English, they should still be encouraged to read in their native tongue if they are literate in that language. In the classroom library, include books written in the various languages of English learners. Because Spanish is spoken by a large proportion of the U.S. population, a number of books are published in Spanish, including both translations and original works. Most of the major educational and children's book publishers offer translations of favorite books.

Fortunately, ELLs have several strategies they can use to foster comprehension. One strategy is the use of cognates. Cognates are words that are descended from the same language or form. The word for *electricity* in Spanish is *electricidad*. Seeing the word *electricity*, the Spanish-speaking reader realizes that it means the same thing as *electricidad*. Native speakers of Spanish may not realize how many Spanish words have English cognates. You might model the process by demonstrating how cognates help you to read Spanish words. A listing of common cognates is presented in Figure 4.7.

laries and it also allows them to obtain the meanings of words not in their listening vocabularies. And it helps them with their spelling.

▞ ESSENTIAL STANDARDS

Fourth through eighth grades
Students will
- use context to derive the meanings of unknown words.
- use knowledge of homophones, homographs, synonyms, antonyms, and idioms to determine the meanings of words.
- use knowledge of word origins and derivations to determine the meanings of words.
- expand their vocabularies.
- use dictionaries, including electronic ones, and glossaries to derive the meanings and pronunciations of words.

- An **Essential Standards** section lists specific literacy curriculum goals so students and professors can focus on key objectives.

ings and pronunciations of words.
- use morphemic analysis to derive the meanings of words. At each level, they will be able to use increasingly sophisticated morphemic elements.
- identify the meanings of words that have multiple meanings.

▞ ASSESSMENT

Through observation, note whether students are learning the skills and strategies they have been taught. Watch to see what they do when they come across an unfamiliar word. Do they attempt to use context? Do they attempt to apply morphemic analysis strategies? Do they have a working knowledge of morphemic elements that have been introduced? When all else fails, do they use the dictionary or glossary as an aid? Do they know when to use which strategy? Are they able to integrate strategies? To enhance your observation, take advantage of selections that contain words that lend themselves to a particular strategy and see how well students do. For instance, if the selection has especially rich context clues, see whether students were able to make use of the clues. You might question them orally or

- **Assessment** sections provide specific focus on evaluation issues and ideas for individual chapters.

Benchmark passage: *Treasure Island* by Robert Lo...
The red glare of the **torch**, lighting up the **interior** of the blockhouse, showed me the worst of my **apprehensions realized**. The **pirates** were in **possession** of the house and stores; there was the **cask** of **cognac**, there were the

▞ ACTION PLAN

1. Become a acquainted with national, state, and local standards and expectations.
2. Set standards or goals for your program. Translate goals or standards into measurable objectives.
3. Align materials and instructional activities with your objectives.
4. Align assessment with objectives and instruction. For each objective, you need formal and/or informal assessment devices so that you can tell whether objectives are being achieved.
5. Begin assessment by finding out where students are and what their strengths and needs are. This can be done with an IRI, or other devices.
6. Screen students for specials needs. Students identified as being struggling should be given diagnostic tests that can be used to plan intervention programs.
7. Monitor students' progress on an ongoing ...ortfolio of students' work.

depth. Involve students in the assessment process. Guide them so they can self-assess. Involve them in the setting of standards and creation of rubrics. Make adjustments in the program as required.
8. At year's end, administer an outcomes measure. This could be another form of the IRI or other measures that you administered at the beginning of the year. As part of your assessment, use information yielded by district-required or state or national tests.
9. Do not overtest. Don't give a test if it is not going to provide useful information or if you are not going to use the information. Make sure that students are tested on the appropriate level.
10. Make sure that there is a match between students' reading levels and the materials that they read. Obtain readability information from appropriate sources and put a leveling system into place. Make sure that in determining difficulty ...judgment as well

- **Action Plan,** at the end of each chapter, lists specific steps that students might take to implement the assessment and teaching suggestions discussed in the chapter.

- Each chapter concludes with a brief **Summary** and activities designed to extend the student's understanding of key concepts and provide suggestions for practical applications in a section entitled **Extending and Applying.** In a feature entitled **Developing a Professional Portfolio,** students are provided with suggested activities

to help them create and maintain a portfolio, which might be used as a device for documenting and assessing their professional development. **Developing a Resource File,** provides practical suggestions for assembling assessment and instructional activities and materials.

ORGANIZATION OF THE TEXT

The text's organization has been designed to reflect the order of the growth of literacy. Chapter 1 stresses constructing a philosophy of teaching reading and writing. Chapter 2 presents techniques for evaluating individuals and programs so that readers come to see assessment as an integral part of instruction. Chapter 3 discusses basic decoding strategies, including phonics, syllabic analysis, and high-frequency words. Chapter 4 presents advanced word-recognition skills and strategies: morphemic analysis, dictionary skills, and techniques for building vocabulary. Chapters 5 and 6 are devoted to comprehension: Chapter 6 emphasizes comprehension strategies that students might use; Chapter 7 focuses on text structures and teaching procedures and covers application of comprehension skills in the content areas. Chapter 8 takes a step beyond comprehension by focusing on responding to literature and fostering a love of reading.

Chapters 3 through 8, which emphasize essential reading strategies, constitute the core of the book. Chapters 9 through 12 provide information on creating a well-rounded literacy program. Chapter 9 describes approaches to teaching reading. Chapter 10 explains the process approach to writing and discusses how reading and writing are related. Chapter 11 suggests how previously presented strategies might be used with children from diverse cultures and those with special needs or who are struggling with reading. Chapter 12 pulls all the topics together in a discussion of principles for organizing and implementing a literacy program. Also included in the final chapter is a section on technology and its place in a program of literacy instruction.

This text, designed to be practical, offers detailed explanations, and often examples of application, for every major technique or strategy. Numerous suggestions for practice activities and reading materials are also included. I hope that this book will furnish you with an in-depth knowledge of literacy methods and materials so that you will be able to construct lively, effective reading and writing instruction for all the students you teach.

SUPPLEMENTS FOR INSTRUCTORS AND STUDENTS

Instructor's Manual with Test Bank and Transparency Masters: For each chapter, the instructor's manual features a series of Learner Objectives, a Chapter Overview, suggestions for Before, After, and During Reading, a list of suggested Teaching Activities, and suggestions for Assessment. There is a Test Bank, which contains an assortment of multiple-choice, short essay, and long essay questions for each chapter. This supplement has been written completely by the text author, Tom Gunning.

ALLYN AND BACON SUPPLEMENTS FOR LITERACY

In addition to the supplements available with *Creating Literacy Instruction for All Students in Grades 4 to 8*, Allyn and Bacon offers an array of student and instructor supplements on the overall topic of literacy. All are available with this textbook.

Allyn & Bacon Digital Media Archive for Literacy: This CD-ROM offers still images, video clips, audio clips, weblinks, and assorted lecture resources that can be incorporated into multimedia presentations in the classroom.

Professionals in Action: Literacy Video: This 90-minute video consists of 10- to 20-minute segments on Phonemic Awareness, Teaching Phonics, Helping Students Become Strategic Readers, Organizing for Teaching with Literature, Discussions of literacy and brain research with experts. The first four segments provide narrative along with actual classroom teaching footage. The final segments present, in a question-and-answer format, discussions by leading experts in the field of literacy.

Allyn & Bacon Literacy Video Library: Featuring renowned reading scholars Richard Allington, Dorothy Strickland and Evelyn English, this three-video library addresses core topics covered in the Literacy classroom: reading strategies, developing literacy in multiple intelligences classrooms, developing phonemic awareness, and much more.

VideoWorkshop for Reading: A new way to integrate video for maximized learning! This total teaching and learning system includes quality classroom video footage on an easy-to-use CD-ROM plus a Student Learning Guide and an Instructor's Teaching Guide—both with textbook-specific Correlation Grids. The result? A program that brings textbook concepts to life with ease and that helps students understand, analyze, and apply the objectives of the course. VideoWorkshop is not sold separately and is available only as a FREE value-pack option with this textbook. (Special package ISBN required from your representative.)

Allyn & Bacon PowerPoint Presentation for Elementary Reading Methods: Available on the Web at http://www.ablongman.com/ppt. This PowerPoint presentation includes approximately 100 slides that cover a range of reading topics: assessment, building vocabulary, comprehension instruction and theory, developing literacy programs, diversity and special needs, reading and learning to read, using literature, and emergent early literacy, among others.

Allyn & Bacon Transparency Package for Reading Methods: This set includes 100 full-color transparencies that cover a myriad of reading topics.

CourseCompass Content for Elementary Reading Methods: CourseCompass, powered by Blackboard, is the most flexible online course management system on the market today. By using this powerful suite of online tools in conjunction with Allyn & Bacon's preloaded textbook and testing content, you can create an online presence for your course in under 30 minutes. You can find course objectives, lecture outlines, quizzes, essay activities, tests and a glossary of key terms in reading that you can adapt for your course. In addition, you will find weblinks providing access to a wealth of resources in the field of reading. Log on at http://www.coursecompass.com and find out how you can get the most out of this dynamic teaching resource.

Research Navigator™ Guide for Education with Access Code: Designed to help students select and evaluate research from the Web to find the best and most credible information available. The booklet contains:

- A practical and to-the-point discussion of search engines
- Detailed information on evaluating online sources
- Citation guidelines for Web resources

- Web activities for Education
- Web links for Education
- A complete guide to Research Navigator™ (access code required)

Allyn & Bacon's new Research Navigator™ is the easiest way for students to start a research assignment or research paper. Complete with extensive help on the research process and three exclusive databases of credible and reliable source material including EBSCO's ContentSelect Academic Journal Database, *New York Times* Search by Subject Archive, and "Best of the Web" Link Library. Research Navigator™ helps students make the most of their research time quickly and efficiently. Each Research Navigator Guide contains an access code allowing individual users entry into this wonderful resource for research assistance.

Allyn & Bacon LiteracyZone SuperSite (Access code required) (http://www.ablongman.com/literacy) A website with a wealth of information for pre-service and in-service teachers—whether you want to gain new insights, pick up practical information, or simply connect with one another! It includes State Standard Correlations; Teaching Resources; Ready-to-Use Lesson Plans and Activities for All Grade Levels; Subject-specific Web links for further research and discovery; Information in A&B professional titles to help you in your teaching career; Up-to-date "In the News" features and Discussion Forum, and much more.

Speak with your representative about obtaining these supplements for your class!

ACKNOWLEDGMENTS

I am indebted to Aurora Martínez, acquisitions editor at Allyn and Bacon, who provided thoughtful suggestions as well as support and encouragement. I am also grateful to Beth Slater and Katie Freddoso, editorial assistants at Allyn and Bacon, for their patient and timely assistance.

My wife, Joan, offered both thoughtful comments and continuous encouragement. I deeply appreciate her loving assistance.

T. G.

Creating Literacy Instruction for All Students in Grades 4 to 8

1

The Nature of Literacy and Today's Students

ANTICIPATION GUIDE

Complete the anticipation guide below. It will help to activate your prior knowledge so that you interact more fully with the chapter. It is designed to probe your attitudes and beliefs about important and sometimes controversial topics. There are often no right or wrong answers; the statements will alert you to your attitudes about reading instruction and encourage you to become aware of areas where you might require additional information. At the end of the chapter, you might respond to the anticipation guide again to see if your answers have changed in light of what you have read. For each of the following statements, put a check under "Agree" or "Disagree" to show how you feel. Discuss your responses with classmates before you read the chapter.

		Agree	*Disagree*
1	Before students are taught to comprehend main ideas, they should learn to understand details.	_____	_____
2	Reading should not be fragmented into a series of subskills.	_____	_____
3	Oral reading should be accurate.	_____	_____
4	The best way to develop proficient readers is to have students read lots of well-written books.	_____	_____
5	Reading short passages and answering questions about them provide excellent practice.	_____	_____
6	Mistakes in oral reading should be ignored unless they change the sense of the passage.	_____	_____

USING WHAT YOU KNOW

This chapter provides a general introduction to literacy instruction in grades four through eight. Before reading the chapter, examine your personal knowledge of the topic so that you will be better prepared to interact with the information. Sometimes, you may not realize what you know until you stop and think about it. Think over what you know about the nature of reading. What do you think reading is? What do you do when you read? What do you think the reader's role is? Is it simply to receive the author's message, or should it include

Using What You Know is designed to activate your prior knowledge on the general topic of the chapter. Sometimes, we don't realize that we already know something about a topic until we stop and think about it. By activating your prior knowledge, you will be better prepared to make connections between new information contained in this chapter and what you already know. When working with students, be sure to activate their prior knowledge before they read a selection.

some personal input? How about writing? What processes do you use when you write?

How would you go about fostering reading and writing proficiency in today's students? What do you think the basic principles of a literacy program should be? What elements have worked especially well in programs with which you are familiar?

THE NATURE OF READING

Which of the following students is the better reader?

> Adela's oral reading was flawless. She read smoothly and without hesitation. She also read with expression. However, when asked to retell the selection, she seemed disconcerted and was only able to supply a few disjointed details. Suspecting that maybe Adela was a bit nervous about reading orally and that was why she failed to comprehend the selection, the teacher asked her to read a selection silently. However, she was still only able to supply a few unrelated details. Her comprehension was no better when she was asked questions about the selection.
>
> Julio, on the other hand, mumbled his way through the selection. He stumbled over several words before finally pronouncing them correctly. His oral reading was hesitant and choppy and delivered in a singsong monotone. Surprisingly, when asked to retell the story, he recounted all the major events in proper order.

■ **Reading** is a process in which we construct meaning from print.

Although lacking in oral reading fluency, Julio is the better reader. Despite reading in fits and starts, he was able to construct an adequate meaning from what he read. Despite the smoothness with which she pronounced the words in the selection, Adela was unable to construct an adequate meaning. In a sense, Adela did not read the passage. **Reading** is first and foremost the construction of meaning from printed words. The true test of reading is not how well you pronounced the words but how well you used the words to construct meaning.

Importance of Language

Although it appears to be a visual perceptual task, reading is primarily a language activity. Persons who have lost their sight become better readers than those who have lost their hearing. Being cut off from the main source of learning language, children who are hearing impaired don't typically reach the same level of reading achievement as those who are visually impaired. Without language, there would be no reading. Reading is very much a language activity and, ultimately, our ability to read is limited by our language skills. We can't read what we can't understand. Even if we can pronounce words we don't understand because of superior phonics skills, we are not reading. Reading is a process in which we construct meaning from print. Without meaning, there is no reading.

Role of Cognitive Development

In a theory that has become a keystone for instruction, Vygotsky distinguished between actual and potential development. Actual development is a measure of the level at which a student is developing. In a sense, it is a measure of what the student has learned up to that point. Potential development is a measure of what the student might be capable of achieving. The difference between the two is known as the **zone of proximal development.** As explained by Vygotsky (1978), the zone of proximal development is "the distance between the actual developmental level as determined by independent problem solving and the level of potential development as determined through problem solving under adult guidance or in collaboration with more capable peers" (p. 84). In other words, the zone of proximal development is the difference between what a student can do on his or her own and what the student can do with help.

Focusing on the importance of interaction with adults or knowledgeable peers, Vygotsky's theory is that students learn through expert guidance. In time, they internalize the concepts and strategies employed by their mentors and so, ultimately, are able to perform on a higher level. The support, guidance, and instruction provided by an adult is known as **scaffolding** (Bruner, 1975, 1986).

Ideally, instruction should be pitched somewhat above a student's current level of functioning. Instruction and collaboration with an adult or more capable peers will enable the student to reach the higher level and ultimately function on that level. Instruction and interaction are key elements. The overall theories of evaluation and instruction presented in this book are grounded in the concepts of actual and potential development and the zone of proximal development.

Vygotsky's theories have held up well over the years. Many of his conclusions have been verified by recent research (Berk, 1997). However, Vygotsky neglected

> Because of the importance of language, suggestions for fostering language development have been included in the marginal notes entitled Building Language.

> ■ The **zone of proximal development** is the area between independent performance and potential as determined through problem solving under guidance of an adult or more capable peer.

> ■ **Scaffolding** refers to the support and guidance provided by an adult that helps a student function on a higher level.

*E*xpert guidance helps students improve their reading and writing.

the importance of other ways of learning. Students can and do learn through non-verbal imitation and self-discovery.

Importance of Experience

Although based on language, reading is also experiential. One class was reading a story that took place in a laundromat. None of the students had ever been to a laundromat or even heard of one, so they found the story confusing. Reading is not so much getting meaning from a story as it is bringing meaning to it. The more the reader brings to a story, the more she or he will be able to take away. For example, the child who plays on a Little League team will get much more out of one of John Tunnis's reissued tales or one of Matt Christopher's works from having actually been there. Such a student can empathize with the main character who makes a crucial error. In this instance, reading evokes an emotional response as well as an intellectual one.

Importance of the Students' Culture

How do you use reading and writing? How is literacy used in the culture in which you were raised? Taylor and Dorsey-Gaines's (1988) book, *Growing Up Literate: Learning from Inner-City Families,* would be especially valuable if you have limited experience with inner-city families or if you plan to teach in the inner city or are now teaching there.

Living as we do in a multicultural, pluralistic society, it is important for us to explore and understand the literacy histories of our pupils. We have to ask such questions as these: In students' culture(s), how are reading and writing used? What values are placed on them? What are the ways in which the students have observed and participated in reading and writing? Is literacy in their environment primarily a group or an individual activity? Given this information, the school should build on the children's experiences and develop and reinforce the skills and values important to their culture(s) as well as those important to the school.

THE READER'S ROLE IN THE READING PROCESS

What is the reader's role in the reading process? In the past, it was defined as being passive, getting the author's meaning. Today, reading requires a more active role—the reader must construct meaning from text. The model of transmission of information in which the reader was merely a recipient has given way to transactional theory, a two-way process involving a reader and a text:

■ **Transaction** refers to the relationship between the reader and the text in which the text is conditioned by the reader and the reader is conditioned by the text.

> Every reading act is an event, or a **transaction,** involving a particular reader and a particular pattern of signs, a text, and occurring at a particular time in a particular context. Instead of two fixed entities acting on one another, the reader and the text are two aspects of a total dynamic situation. The "meaning" does not reside ready-made "in" the text or "in" the reader but happens or comes into being during the transaction between reader and text. (Rosenblatt, 1994, p. 1063)

In her study of how students read a poem, Rosenblatt (1978) noted that each reader was active:

> He was not a blank tape registering a ready-made message. He was actively involved in building up a poem for himself out of his responses to text. He had to draw on his past experiences with the verbal symbols. . . . The reader was not only paying atten-

tion to what the words pointed to in the external world, to their referents; he was also paying attention to the images, feelings, attitudes, associations, and ideas that the words and their referents evoked in him. (p. 10)

The type of reading, of course, has an effect on the transaction. The reader can take an efferent or an aesthetic **stance.** When reading a set of directions, a science text, or a math problem, the reader takes an **efferent** stance, the focus being on obtaining information that can be carried away (*efferent* is taken from the Latin verb *efferre*, "to carry away"). In the **aesthetic** stance, the reader pays attention to the associations, feelings, attitudes, and ideas that the words evoke.

Does it make any difference whether reading is viewed as being transmissional, transactional, or somewhere in between? Absolutely. If reading is viewed as transmissional, students are expected to stick close to the author's message. If reading is viewed as transactional, students are expected to put their personal selves into their reading, especially when encountering literature. From a transactional perspective, building background becomes especially important because it enriches the transaction between reader and text. Personal response and interpretation are at the center of the reading process. The reader's role is enhanced when a transactional view prevails.

■ **Stance** refers to the position or attitude that the reader takes. The two stances are aesthetic and efferent.

■ **Efferent** refers to a kind of reading in which the focus is on obtaining or carrying away information from the reading.

■ **Aesthetic** is a type of reading in which the reader focuses upon experiencing the piece: the rhythm of the words, the past experiences these call up (Rosenblatt, 1978, p. 10).

APPROACHES TO READING INSTRUCTION: WHOLE VERSUS PART LEARNING

Just as there are philosophical differences about the role of the reader, there are differences in approaches to teaching reading. On one end of the continuum are those who espouse a subskills, or bottom-up, approach, and on the other end are those who advocate a **holistic,** top-down approach. In between are the interactionists. Where do you fit on the continuum? Go back to the anticipation guide at the beginning of the chapter. Take a look at how you answered the six statements. If you agreed with only the odd-numbered ones, you are a bottom-up advocate. If you agreed with only the even-numbered statements, you are a top-downer. If your answers were mixed, you are probably an interactionist.

■ **Holistic** refers to the practice of learning through the completion of whole tasks rather than fragmented subskills and fragments of reading and writing.

Bottom-Uppers

In the **bottom-up approach,** children literally start at the bottom and work their way up. First, they learn to comprehend details. Next, they learn to comprehend main ideas and then inferences. As Carnine, Silbert, and Kameenui (1990) explain: "Our position is that many students will not become successful readers unless teachers identify the essential reading skills, find out what skills students lack, and teach those skills directly" (p. 3).

Bottom-up procedures are intended to make learning to read easier by breaking complex tasks into their component skills. Instruction proceeds from the simple to the complex. In essence, there are probably no 100 percent bottom-uppers among reading teachers. Even those who strongly favor a skills approach recognize the importance of higher-level strategies.

■ **Bottom up** refers to a kind of processing in which meaning is derived from the accurate, sequential processing of words. The emphasis is on the text rather than the reader's background knowledge or language ability.

Bottom-up theorists claim that when reading, we process nearly every word and virtually every letter in the words. Samuels (1994) concludes that novice readers process words letter by letter but that experienced readers may process words holistically or break words down into their components. Context fosters both speed and accuracy of word recognition.

■ **Top-down processing** refers to deriving meaning by using one's background knowledge, language ability, and expectations. The emphasis is on the reader rather than the text.

■ **Interactionists** hold the theoretical position that reading involves processing text and using one's background knowledge and language ability.

Top-Downers

A **top-down approach,** as its name indicates, starts at the top and works downward. Learning to read is seen as being similar to learning to speak; it is holistic and natural through immersion. Subskills are not taught because it is felt they fragment the process and make learning to read more abstract and difficult (K. Goodman, 1986). One of the most influential models of reading is that proposed by Ken Goodman (1994). According to Goodman, readers use their background knowledge and knowledge of language to predict and infer the content of print. In Goodman's model, students use three cuing systems: semantic, syntactic, and graphophonic. Semantic cues derive from our past experiences, so that we construct meaning by bringing our background of knowledge to a story. Syntactic cues derive from our knowledge of how the structure of language works. Graphophonics cues refer to our ability to sound out words or recognize them holistically. Based on their use of these cues, students predict the content of the text, confirm or revise their predictions, and reread if necessary.

Interactionists

Most practitioners tend to be more pragmatic than either strict top-downers or dyed-in-the-wool bottom-uppers and borrow practices from both ends of the continuum. These **interactionists** teach skills directly and systematically, but they also provide plenty of opportunities for students to experience the holistic nature of reading and writing by having them read whole books and write for real purposes. As Gough (1985), a leading advocate of an interactive approach, described the reading process,

> Linguistics knowledge is skillfully combined with visual information to reconstruct the meaning intended by the author. But skilled readers, when seriously reading, not only succeed in extracting meaning from the printed page, they can (and I believe do) also succeed in accurately recognizing virtually every single word on that page . . . for while highly predictive context can and does facilitate word recognition, proving a strictly "bottom-up" model wrong, most words are not predictable and so can only be read bottom-up. (p. 688)

In a top-down approach, background knowledge and language are emphasized. In a bottom-up approach, the characteristics of the text and the skills needed to read the text are stressed. In an interactive approach, both the reader and the text are considered. Difficult text for which the reader has little background will demand more bottom-up processing as you piece together what the text is saying. What do you do when you read a very difficult text? You read slowly, perhaps stopping to look at illustrations or diagrams. You may pause when you come to technical terms. You might even begin to mouth each word if the text is very difficult. When reading a text about familiar topics, you will make greater use of top-down processes as you bring your background knowledge to bear on the topic. If the topic is a very familiar one, you might be able to skim through the text and still construct an adequate meaning.

Fostering reading development by arranging for students to read high-quality books is a top-down approach. Fostering reading development by carefully and explicitly teaching skills is a bottom-up approach. Combining strategy instruction with wide reading and instruction in skills and strategies is an interactive approach.

 ## IMPORTANCE OF LITERACY MODELS

Why is it important to be aware of different models of teaching reading? For one thing, it is important that you formulate your own personal beliefs about reading and writing instruction. These beliefs will then be the foundation for your instruction. They will determine the goals you set, the instructional techniques you use, the materials you choose, the organization of your classroom, the reading and writing behaviors you expect students to exhibit, and the criteria you use to evaluate students. For instance, whether you use children's books or a basal, how you teach comprehension, and whether you expect flawless oral reading or are satisfied if the student's rendition is faithful to the sense of the selection will depend upon your theoretical orientation (DeFord, 1985).

Having a theoretical orientation helps in another way. It provides a means of examining what you do in your teaching. You may find that you are not walking your talk—your practices might not fit in with your beliefs. According to Ross (cited in DeFord, 1985), the ability to implement your beliefs is dependent on the clarity of those beliefs and your ability to see a connection between them and what you do in your classroom.

> To clarify one's philosophy of teaching, ask: "What are my instructional practices and why am I doing what I'm doing?" Examining your practices should help you uncover your beliefs.

> **USING TECHNOLOGY**
> Controversies such as "Is reading top down or bottom up?" are often explored on the Web sites of professional organizations, such as the International Reading Association's Web site: **http://www.ira.org**

APPROACH TAKEN BY THIS TEXT

This book draws heavily on research in cognitive psychology, combines an interactionist point of view with a holistic orientation, and takes an integrated approach. In an integrated approach, reading is considered an active, constructive process, with the focus on the reader, whose experiences, cultural background, and point of view will play a part in her or his comprehension of a written piece. The focus is on cognitive processes or strategies used to decode words and understand and remember text: using phonics and context to decipher unknown words, activating one's knowledge of a topic, predicting meaning, summarizing, and visualizing.

Stress is also placed on teaching strategies in context and holistically applying them to children's books, periodicals, ads and other real-world materials, and content area text-

*E*xtensive reading is necessary for growth in literacy.

books. There is also an emphasis on integrating reading, writing, listening, and speaking with content areas and the performing and visual arts. This text recommends systematic, direct instruction in the context of extensive reading, writing, discussion, and listening. It recommends a balanced approach in which systematic instruction and immersion in reading and writing play complementary roles.

SCIENTIFICALLY BASED LITERACY INSTRUCTION

Because reading achievement has remained essentially unchanged since the 1970s and because the gap between the reading achievement of the poor and middle-class students is substantial, there has been a call in federal regulations for programs that are scientifically based. In federal regulations, scientific evidence is interpreted as meaning studies in which Method A has been compared with Method B and/or a control group and found to be statistically superior.

The International Reading Association (2002) uses the term *evidence-based* rather than *scientifically based*. *Evidence-based* is a broader term and includes qualitative studies as well as the more scientifically based studies that include comparison of experimental and control groups.

> In its simplest form, the term "evidence-based reading instruction" means that a particular program or collection of instructional practices has a tested and proven record of success. That is, there is reliable, trustworthy, and valid evidence to suggest that when the program or the practices are used with a particular group of children, the children can be expected to make adequate gains in reading achievement. (p. 1)

As a teacher, you should become acquainted with the major findings of literacy research so that you can construct a literacy program that is based on research and so you can assess whether new techniques or materials that you are thinking about trying are supported by research. You should also assesses the research base to see if it is applicable to your students and your situation. A technique that works well on a one-to-one basis may not be effective with small groups. Of course, research doesn't answer all the instructional questions that arise. You need to become a teacher-researcher so that you can test out methods and materials and have a better basis for selecting those that are most effective in your situation. You also need to assess all aspects of your program with a view to replacing or improving elements that aren't working and adding elements that are missing.

Insofar as possible, the suggestions made in this text are evidence-based. However, in some instances they are based on personal experience or the experience of others. Teaching literacy is an art as well as a science.

STANDARDS MOVEMENT

To raise the achievement of all students but especially those who are struggling with reading, the United States has embarked on a campaign to raise the literacy levels of all its students. Billions of dollars have been poured into intervention programs, summer school, after-school instruction, and research. Never before

USING TECHNOLOGY
To find the results of the latest National Assessment in reading and other areas, consult: National Center for Educational Statistics: **http://nces.ed.gov/ nationsreportcard/**

USING TECHNOLOGY
What Is Evidence-Based Reading Instruction? Available online at **http://www.reading. org/positions/ evidence_based. html,** this paper provides a summary of a position statement of the International Reading Association.

USING TECHNOLOGY
Research reported in the *Report of the National Reading Panel* has been judged to be scientifically based. The report contains many of the basic principles of teaching reading. The report is free and may be ordered at **http://www. nationalreadingpanel. org/Publications/**

has there been such an intense commitment to "leaving no child behind." The commitment has a standards and an assessment component. The logic behind standards is that once there is "broad agreement on what students should know and be able to do, then everything else in the system (i.e., assessments, professional development, materials, school structures) could be directed toward achieving these standards. It was a systemic approach that included *all* elements rather than the piecemeal approach of the past" (Valencia & Wixson, 2001, p. 204.)

All states are required to have standards. In many instances, literacy standards are based on the broad goals of national organizations such as the International Reading Association and the National Council of Teachers of English (1996). Students are assessed in terms of state or district standards. In addition, beginning in 2005–2006 all public school students in grades three through eight must be assessed in reading on a yearly basis. Students, especially those who have fallen behind, are expected to show an improvement. Otherwise, schools that fail to make adequate progress in closing the gap will be penalized. Because of the overwhelming concern with standards, assessment, and lifting the levels of the lowest performing students, these themes will be emphasized throughout this text.

The standards movement has provided schools with the opportunity to reexamine their literacy programs. Because the standards movement has set high expectations for all students to achieve, it has led to increased focus on underachieving readers. Classroom teachers and specialists are working together to help students who were previously not given the assistance they needed. It has also caused teachers to teach important skills that were previously neglected. For instance, in Illinois, standards require students to be able to read informational text, an area that was being overlooked (Ogle & Fogelberg, 2001).

However, standards are controversial. Some standards have been criticized as too vague or too general, others as so specific that they include requirements for the way the standards should be taught. Even more controversial, however, are the assessment measures that go along with standards and the consequences of not meeting standards. The tests tend to become the curriculum. Teachers emphasize those areas that are tested. As one teacher put it, "If it is not being tested, it is not being taught" (Hoffman, Assaf, & Paris, 2001, p. 489); other important areas are neglected. In addition, an inordinate amount of time may be spent preparing for the test. Good teaching and a solid curriculum lead to a natural improvement in achievement and test scores. Langer (1999) found that students in schools where teachers incorporated skills assessed on state standards-based tests into the curriculum did better than schools where teachers focused on test preparation.

Based an National Assessment results, some 37 percent of fourth graders read below a basic level. For children living in poverty, the figure is 60 percent. A basic level indicates partial mastery of skills required for fourth grade reading (Barton, 2001).

USING TECHNOLOGY

Standards for Education **http://edstandards. org/Standards. html** offers a wealth of information about curriculum frameworks and standards and provides links to each state so you can examine your state's standards.

Based on their review of standards, Valencia and Wixson (2001) concluded that standards-based reform is a way to "address the inequities of the past and raise the ceiling for all" (p. 210).

READ. WRITE. THINK **http://www. readwritethink.org/ site_features.html** Features a listing of IRA/NCTE standards and lessons geared to those standards. An outstanding site.

A READING AND WRITING PROGRAM FOR TODAY'S STUDENTS

The world is growing ever more complex, and so the demands for literacy are increasing. Functioning in today's global society requires a higher degree of literacy than did functioning in yesterday's preinformation superhighway society. Requirements for tomorrow's citizens will be higher yet. Today's and tomorrow's readers need to be selective and efficient. Bombarded with information, students must be able to select the information that is important to them. They must also be efficient.

What kind of program will help meet the literacy needs of today's students? That is a question that the remainder of this book will attempt to answer. However, when all is said and done, the ten principles discussed below, if followed faithfully, should make a difference in determining such a program.

1. *Students become proficient readers by reading.* Learning to read is a little like learning to drive a car—instruction and guidance are required. In addition to instruction and guidance, novice readers, like novice motorists, require practice. They must read a variety of fiction and nonfiction books, newspapers, and magazines to become truly skilled. In a way, each book or article makes a student a better reader. As Hirsch (1987) pointed out, students must have a broad background in a variety of areas in order to be able to understand much of what is being written and said in today's world. For example, a student who has read the fable "The Boy Who Cried Wolf" will have the background necessary to understand a story that includes the sentence "Frank cried wolf once too often." Reading is not simply a matter of acquiring and perfecting skills, it also requires accumulating vocabulary, concepts, experiences, and background knowledge.

To provide the necessary practice and background, **trade books** are an essential component of a reading program. Unfortunately, large numbers of students are alliterate: They *can* read, but they *do* not, at least not on a regular basis. In a recent study, only 44 percent of a large sample of fourth-graders reported reading on a daily basis; however, 60 percent of these same children watched three or more hours of television each day (Mullis, Campbell, & Farstrup, 1993). Responding to a reading attitude questionnaire, the Motivation to Read Profile (Gambrell, Codling, & Palmer, 1996), 17 percent of the students reported that they would rather clean their rooms than read, 10 percent said that people who read are boring, and 14 percent stated that they would spend little time reading when they grew up.

It is not surprising that those who do the most reading on their own are the most proficient readers (Anderson, Wilson, & Fielding, 1988; Applebee, Langer, & Mullis, 1988; Mullis, Campbell, & Farstrup, 1993). While it is true that better readers read more partly because reading is easier for them, Anderson, Wilson, and Fielding's (1988) analysis of data suggests a cause–effect relationship. Students are better readers because they read more.

The case for including trade books in a reading program is a compelling one. First, as just noted, those who read more, read better. Second, research suggests that students who read widely and are given some choice in what they read have a more favorable attitude toward reading (Cline & Kretke, 1980).

■ **Trade books** are books that are published for the general reading public as opposed to educational materials that are designed for schools. Trade books include children's books, young adult books, and adult books. Trade books are sold to libraries and in bookstores and through general catalogs.

*S*tudents do their best when they feel involved and have interesting materials and activities.

Exemplary Teaching

Fostering Reading

*T*aking over a failing middle-school in Boston, Principal Thomas P. O'Neill, Jr., instituted a self-selected reading period for ten minutes at the end of the school day. He also instituted 10 minutes of read-alouds at the beginning of the school day. Not only did the day get off to a better start and end on a high note, but reading scores began an upward climb. The read-alouds in the morning gave students ideas for their self-selected reading at the close of the school day. The self-selected reading in the afternoon was often continued on the bus ride home and, later at home. (O'Donnell, 1997)

In addition, all types of students—able readers, at-risk children, bilingual students—benefit from an approach that incorporates children's books. Based on their review of research, Tunnell and Jacobs (1989) concluded that programs using trade books achieve dramatic levels of success and are particularly effective with disabled and uninterested readers. Trelease (2001) has a two-part formula for becoming a better reader:

- The more you read, the better you get at it; the better you get at it, the more you like it; the more you like it, the more you do it.
- The more you read, the more you know; and the more you know, the smarter you grow. (p. 3)

Using trade books in the reading program not only leads to an opportunity for a greater enjoyment of reading but also builds skill in reading. In addition, allowing some self-selection should produce students who can and do read. To assist you in choosing or recommending books for your students, lists of appropriate books are presented throughout the text along with a description of several extensive lists of leveled books (see Chapter 2). Chapter 2 also describes a number of devices for leveling or assessing the difficulty level of books. Appendix A presents more than 800 titles listed by suggested grade level.

2. *Reading should be easy—but not too easy.* Think about it this way: If students find reading difficult, they will acquire a distaste for it and will simply stop reading except when they have to. Because of inadequate practice, they will fall farther behind, and their distaste and avoidance will grow. In addition, students will be unable to apply the strategies they have been taught, and learning will be hampered if the text is too difficult (Clay, 1993a). As Fry (1977a) put it years ago, make the match. Give students a book that they can handle with ease. Research by Berliner (1981) and Gambrell, Wilson, and Gantt (1981) suggested that students do best with reading materials in which no more than 2 to 5 percent of the words are difficult for them.

3. *Instruction should be functional and contextual.* Do not teach skills or strategies in isolation—teach a word-attack skill because students must have it to decipher words. For example, teach the prefix *pre-* just before the class reads a selection about prehistoric dinosaurs. Students learn better when what they are being taught has immediate value. Suggestions for lessons that are both functional and contextual are presented throughout this book.

4. *Make connections.* Build a bridge between students' experiences and what they are about to read. Help them see how what they know is related to the story or article. Students in Arizona reading about an ice hockey game may have no experience either playing or watching the sport. However, you could help create a bridge of understanding by discussing how hockey is similar to soccer, a sport with which they probably are familiar. You should also help students connect new concepts to old concepts. Relate reading, writing, listening, and speaking—they all build on each other. Reading and talking about humorous stories can expand students' concept of humor and remind them of funny things that have happened to them. They might then write about these events. Also build on what students know. This will make your teaching easier, since you will be starting at the students' level. It will also help students make a connection between what they know and what they are learning.

5. *Promote independence.* Whenever you teach a skill or strategy, ask yourself: How can I teach this so students will eventually use it on their own? How will students be called on to use this skill or strategy in school and in the outside world? When you teach students how to summarize, make predictions, or use context or another skill or strategy, teach so that there is a gradual release of responsibility (Pearson & Gallagher, 1983). Gradually fade your instruction and guidance so that students are applying the skill or strategy on their own. Do the same with the selection of reading materials. Although you may discuss ways of choosing books with the class, you ultimately want students to reach a point where they select their own books.

6. *Believe that all students can become proficient readers and writers.* Given the right kind of instruction, virtually all students can learn to read. There is increasing evidence that the vast majority of students can learn to read at least on a basic level.

In virtually every elementary and middle school classroom, there are a number of struggling readers and writers. Classroom teachers estimate that as many as one student out of four is reading more than one year below grade level (Baumann, Hoffman, Duffy-Hester, & Ro, 2000). Teachers also report that their greatest challenge is working with struggling readers. Fortunately, today's teachers have a strong commitment to helping struggling readers (Baumann, Hoffman, Duffy-Hester, & Ro, 2000). Although classroom teachers receive support from specialists, they usually bear the primary responsibility for helping struggling readers. However, all of today's basal and anthology reading programs offer suggestions and materials for helping struggling readers.

Given the large number of struggling readers and writers in today's elementary and middle schools, this text has numerous suggestions for helping these students and concludes each instructional chapter with a section entitled "Help for Struggling Readers and Writers," which discusses steps classroom teachers might take to help underachieving students.

7. *The literacy program should be goal oriented and systematic.* In keeping with the current concern for articulating and teaching to high standards, this text

---

ADAPTING INSTRUCTION for *STRUGGLING READERS and WRITERS*

Classroom teachers are taking increased responsibility for helping struggling readers and writers. Suggestions for working with struggling readers and writers are made throughout the text.

provides suggested grade-by-grade content standards for each of the major instructional areas: phonics and other word analysis skills and strategies, vocabulary, comprehension, reading in the content areas, study skills, and writing. These objectives are presented at the end of each appropriate chapter in a panel entitled "Essential Standards."

8. *Build students' motivation and sense of competence.* Students perform at their best when they feel competent, view a task as being challenging but doable, understand why they are undertaking a task, are given choices, feel a part of the process, and have interesting materials and activities. For many students, working in a group fosters effort and persistence. Students also respond to knowledge of progress. They work harder when they see that they are improving, and they are also energized by praise from teachers, parents, and peers, especially when that praise is honest and specific (Schunk & Zimmerman, 1997; Sweet, 1997; Wigfield, 1997). The aim of a literacy program is to produce engaged readers and writers. Engaged readers and writers are motivated, are knowledgeable, and have mastered key strategies. They also do well when working with others (Guthrie & Wigfield, 1997).

9. *Ongoing assessment is an essential element in an effective literacy program.* Teachers need to know how students are progressing so they can give extra help or change the program, if necessary. Assessment need not be formal. Observation can be a powerful assessment tool. However, assessment should be tied in to the program's standards and should result in improvement in students' learning. In each chapter in which instructional objectives are stated, suggestions are made for assessing those objectives. Suggestions for assessment can also be found in annotations in the margins and in Chapter 2. In addition, there are several assessment instruments in Appendix B.

10. *Build students' language proficiency.* Reading and writing are language based. Students' reading levels are ultimately limited by their language development. Students can't understand what they are reading if they don't know what the words mean or get tangled up in the syntax of the piece. One of the best ways to build reading and writing potential is to foster language development. In study after study, knowledge of vocabulary has been found to be the key element in comprehension. Students' listening level has also been found to be closely related to students' reading level. The level of material that a student can understand orally is a good gauge of the level that a student can read with understanding. While fostering language development is important for all students, it is absolutely essential for students who are learning English as a second language.

Language development need not be a separate teaching area. Build language into activities that you are already conducting. For instance, during discussions of text that students have read, use prompts that help students expand their responses. Plan activities such as Think-Pair-Share that foster discussion. In Think-Pair-Share, students think on their own about a question or problem raised in class, pair up with another student to discuss possible answers or solutions, and then meet with another pair of students to share responses. After sharing in groups of four, one person from each group then reports to the whole class. Think-Pair-Share is an excellent technique for discussing ideas and developing language. Students develop language as they discuss one-to-one, in groups of four, and then before the whole class. The technique is especially effective when the teacher provides prompts to students who are reporting the results of their group's discussion to the whole class. These prompts help children construct more fully developed responses (Fowler, et al., 2002).

HIGHLY EFFECTIVE TEACHERS

In the 1960s, the U.S. Department of Education spent millions of dollars in an attempt to find out which method of teaching reading was the best (Bond & Dykstra, 1967; Graves & Dykstra, 1997). More than a dozen approaches were studied. There was no clear winner. No one method was superior in all circumstances. What the researchers did find was that the teacher was key. Teachers using the same methods got differing results. Some teachers were simply more effective than others.

What are the characteristics of effective teachers? During the 1990s, a number of top researchers visited the classes of teachers judged to be highly effective. Their students read more books and wrote more stories. Virtually all read on or above grade level. Their writing skills were surprisingly advanced. They also enjoyed school. On many occasions observers watched in surprise as students skipped recess so they could continue working on an activity. Their work was more appealing to them than play.

Caring and High Expectations

Perhaps the most outstanding characteristic of highly effective teachers is that they cared for their students and believed in them (Pressley, Allington, Wharton-McDonald, Block, & Morrow, 2001). They were genuinely convinced that their students could and would learn and acted accordingly. The highly effective teachers realized that high expectations are in the same category as good intentions; they need to be acted on. High expectations were accompanied by the kind of instruction that allowed students to live up to the high expectations. Highly effective teachers were also superior motivators. The teachers created a feeling of excitement about the subject mater or skill areas they teach (Ruddell, 1995).

Balanced Instruction

Although nearly all teachers now believe in balancing holistic reading and writing activities with direct instruction in skills, the most effective teachers were better at integrating skills instruction and actual reading and writing (Pressley, et al., 2001). When students evidenced a need for instruction, teachers were quick to conduct a minilesson. Key skills were taught directly and thoroughly but were related to the reading and writing that students were doing. Highly effective teachers used a variety of techniques. Techniques were matched to students' needs. Hands-on activities were prominent. However, the activities were minds-on and had legitimate learning goals.

Extensive Instruction

Effective teachers used every opportunity to reinforce skills. Wherever possible, connections were made between reading and writing and between reading and writing and content area concepts. Often students would develop or apply science and social studies concepts in their writing.

Scaffolding

Exemplary teachers scaffold students' responses. Instead of simply telling students answers, teachers use prompts and other devices to help the students reason their way to the correct response.

Classroom Management

Highly effective teachers were well organized. Routines were well established and highly effective. The core of their management was building in students a sense of responsibility. Students learned to regulate their own behavior. One of the things that stood out in the rooms of highly effective classes was the sense of purpose and orderliness. There was a 90–90 rule: 90 percent of the students were engaged in productive activity 90 percent of the time. The greatest proportion of time was spent with high-payoff activities. When students composed illustrated booklets, for instance, the bulk of their time was spent researching and composing the booklets. Only a minimum of time was spent illustrating them.

Students learned how to work together. The classroom atmosphere was one of cooperation rather than competition. Effort was emphasized. Praise and reinforcement were used as appropriate. Students were also taught to be competent, independent learners. They were taught strategies for selecting appropriate level books, for decoding unfamiliar words, and for understanding difficult text. Their efforts were affirmed, so that they would be encouraged to continue using strategies. "Jonathan, I liked the way you previewed that book before selecting it to read. Now you have a better idea of what is about and whether you'll enjoy reading it."

High-Quality Materials

The best teachers used the best materials. Students listened to and read classics as well as outstanding contemporary works from children's literature. There was a decided emphasis on reading. Classrooms were well stocked with materials, and time was set aside for various kinds of reading: group, partner, and individual.

ACTION PLAN

In order to make the text as practical as possible, each chapter concludes with an Action Plan that provides specific suggestions for applying each of the key concepts and assessment and teaching suggestions discussed in the chapter.

1. Construct a personal philosophy of teaching literacy. Note the effect that your philosophy of teaching literacy would have on your approach to teaching, your assessment methods, grouping practices, and choice of learning activities and materials.

2. Create a plan for becoming an effective teacher. What steps will you take to create a high-quality program and to continue to develop your ability to teach literacy?

Matching of Materials and Tasks to Student Competence

Highly effective teachers gave students materials and tasks that were somewhat challenging but not overwhelming. Teachers carefully monitored students and made assignments on the basis of students' performance. If the book students were reading seemed to have too many difficult words and concepts, students were given an easier book. If they mastered writing a brief paragraph, they were encouraged to write a more fully developed piece. However, they were provided with the assistance and instruction needed to cope with more challenging tasks.

SUMMARY

1. Reading is an active process in which the reader constructs meaning from text.

2. In Vygotsky's view, social interaction is an important factor in children's cognitive and language development. More knowledgeable others can help students operate on a higher level of development.

3. Living as we do in a pluralistic society, it is important for the school to build on the literacy activities that are prominent in students' cultures.

4. The type of reading being done can help determine whether the reader takes primarily an efferent or an aesthetic stance.

5. Reading can be viewed as holistic, which is a top-down approach. Reading can also be viewed as composed of a number of subskills, which is a bottom-up approach. A third approach is to describe reading as a balanced interaction between top-down and bottom-up processes, which is the position that this book takes.

6. By creating clear expectations for students and teachers, the standards movement is designed to improve the reading and writing performance of all students, but especially those who are struggling. Although it is bringing additional resources to struggling readers, the standards movement has been criticized because it may lead to teaching to standards-based tests and result in the neglect of important literacy skills.

7. Widespread reading and functional instruction commensurate with students' abilities are essentials of an effective reading program. Also necessary is instruction that helps students make connections and fosters independence. Believing that virtually every student can learn to read and building students' motivation and sense of competence are important factors in an effective literacy program, as are setting goals; systematic, direct instruction; ongoing assessment; and building students' language proficiency. However, a highly effective teacher is the key to effective instruction.

EXTENDING AND APPLYING

1. Analyze your beliefs about teaching reading. Make a list of your major beliefs. Are you a top-downer, a bottom-upper, or an interactionist? Now make a list of your major teaching and reinforcement activities. Do they fit your philosophy? If not, what changes might you make?

2. To find out more about the thinking behind setting literacy goals for students in the middle grades, read the joint position statement issued by the International Reading Association and the National Middle School Association, which can be found at http://www.reading.org/positions/supporting_young_adolesc.html

3. Find out what your state's literacy goals or standards are. Most state departments of education list this information on their Web sites. If so, what are they? How are they assessed?

4. Analyze your activities as you teach a reading lesson or observe a class being taught. Classify the instructional activities as being top down, bottom up, or interactive. Also, note the reactions of the students to the activities. Do they find them interesting? Do they seem to be learning from them?

DEVELOPING A PROFESSIONAL PORTFOLIO

Many school systems require applicants to submit a portfolio. Some also require new teachers to complete portfolios as part of the evaluation process. Even if a portfolio is not required in your situation, creating and maintaining one provides you with the opportunity to reflect on your ideas about teaching and your teaching practices. It will help you get to know yourself better as a teacher and so provide a basis for improvement. To assist you in creating a portfolio, each chapter will contain suggestions for working on your portfolio.

Set up a professional portfolio. The portfolio should highlight your professional preparation, relevant experience, and mastery of key teaching skills. Using the list compiled in Item 1 of Extending and Applying, draw up a statement of your philosophy of teaching reading and writing.

DEVELOPING A RESOURCE FILE

As you read about various teaching and assessment procedures in the text, collect resources that will help you implement the procedures and assessments. The resources might be a list of books for reading out loud or a list of Web sites for developing vocabulary. For this chapter, you might collect articles that have helpful suggestions for setting up a literacy program.

2

Evaluation

ANTICIPATION GUIDE

*F*or each of the following statements related to the chapter you are about to read, put a check under "Agree" or "Disagree" to show how you feel. Discuss your responses with classmates before you read the chapter.

		Agree	*Disagree*
1	Nationwide achievement tests are essential for the assessment of literacy.	_____	_____
2	Setting high standards and assessing student achievement on those standards is a good way to improve the quality of reading and writing instruction.	_____	_____
3	Most writing assessments are too subjective.	_____	_____
4	Today's students take too many tests.	_____	_____
5	The community has a right to know how its schools are doing.	_____	_____
6	Observation yields more about a student's progress in reading and writing than a standardized test does.	_____	_____

USING WHAT YOU KNOW

*E*valuation is an essential part of literacy learning. It is a judgment by teachers, children, parents, administrators, and the wider community as to whether instructional goals have been met. Evaluation also helps teachers determine what is and what is not working so that they can plan better programs. Self-evaluation gives students more control over their own learning.

What kinds of experiences have you had with evaluation? How has your school work been assessed? Do you agree with the assessments, or do you think they were off the mark? Keeping in mind the current emphasis on balanced reading and writing processes and integration of language arts, what might be some appropriate ways to evaluate the literacy development of today's students?

THE NATURE OF EVALUATION

■ **Evaluation** is the process of using the results of tests, observations, work samples, or other devices to judge the effectiveness of a program. A program is evaluated in terms of its objectives. The ultimate purpose of evaluation is to improve the program.

In evaluation, we ask, "How am I doing?" so that we can do better. **Evaluation** is a value judgment. We can also ask, "How is the education program doing?" and base our evaluation on tests, quizzes, records, work samples, observations, anecdotal records, portfolios, and similar information. The evaluation could be made by a student while reviewing her or his writing folder or by parents as they look over a report card. The evaluator could be a teacher, who, after examining a portfolio or collection of a student's work and thinking over recent observations of that student, concludes that the student has done well but could do better.

Evaluation should result in some kind of action. The evaluator must determine what that action should be, based on her judgment. The student may decide that he has been writing the same type of pieces and needs to branch out, the parents might decide that their child must study more, and the teacher might choose to add more self-selected reading time to the program.

The Starting Point

Evaluation starts with a set of goals. You cannot tell if you have reached your destination if you do not know where you were headed. For example, a teacher may decide that one of her goals will be to instill in children a love of reading. This is a worthy goal, but it is lacking in many programs. How will the teacher decide whether the goal has been reached, and what will the teacher use as evidence? The goal has to be stated in terms of a specific objective that includes, if possible, observable behavior—for example, students will voluntarily read at least twenty minutes a day or at least one book a month. The objective then becomes measurable, and the teacher can collect information that will provide evidence as to whether it has been met.

■ **Standards** are statements of what students should know and be able to do.

A composite set of standards is available from the Mid-Central Regional Educational Laboratory (MCREL, 2001). *Content standards and benchmarks for K–12 education.* Available online at **http://www.mcrel.org/ standards-benchmarks/.** Composite goals are also available from New Standards (National Center on Education and the Economy & The University of Pittsburgh, 1997).

The Standards Movement

Along with standards have come assessment devices for measuring students' progress toward meeting those standards. All states are required to have standards in at least reading and math. All public school students in grades three through eight must be assessed on state reading and math standards on a yearly basis beginning in 2005–2006 (U.S. Department of Education, 2002). Students, especially those who have fallen behind, are expected to show "adequate yearly progress." By the school year 2013–2014, all students are expected to be proficient in both reading and math. Students in poorly performing schools may transfer to a better school or will be eligible for additional assistance such as tutoring.

Setting and assessing standards have resulted in some positive educational benefit. Teachers report that as a result of standards, the curriculum is more challenging, students are working harder, expectations for students are on the rise, and students are reading more (Editorial Projects in Education, 2001). On the minus side, teachers also report that state tests are dictating what is taught and too much time is spent preparing for tests.

For more information about No Child Left Behind, see the Department of Education Web site at **http://www.nclb.gov/**

High-Stakes Testing

In 1999, the Board of Directors of the International Reading Association announced its opposition to high-stakes testing. As its name suggests, a **high-stakes test** is one in which an important decision will be based on the outcome of a single test. The decision might be whether the student passes or fails or is placed in a special program. The IRA is not opposed to assessment or testing. It is opposed to making critical decisions based on a single test. It is also opposed to the undue influence that high-stakes testing may have on what is taught in the schools. As the IRA Board of Directors commented, "Our central concern is that testing has become a means of controlling instruction as opposed to a way of gathering information to help students become better readers" (p. 257).

> ■ A **high-stakes test** is one in which the results are used to make important decisions such as passing students, graduating students, or rating a school.

Instead of being used to assess how well students are doing and providing information for program improvement, high-stakes tests have the potential to dictate curriculum. Instead of teaching what their community has judged to be important, educators might teach what is tested. This has the effect of narrowing the curriculum. Knowing, for instance, that students will be tested on persuasive writing in the eighth grade, teachers in the middle grades overemphasize writing persuasive pieces and neglect other kinds of writing. A great deal of time is also spent writing to a prompt because that is the way students will be assessed on the state tests. To combat the misuse of tests, the International Reading Association has made the following recommendations:

Teachers should

- construct rigorous classroom assessments to help outside observers gain confidence in teacher techniques.
- educate parents, community members, and policy makers about classroom-based assessment.
- teach students how tests are structured, but not teach to the test.

An essential component of evaluation is improvement of the instructional program. Once strengths and weaknesses are noted, steps should be taken to build on the strengths and repair the weak spots. For example, if you find that students' ability to interpret graphs is weak, you would make plans to improve that area. As the Board of Directors of the International Reading Association (1999) commented, "Assessment involves the systematic and purposeful collection of data to inform actions. From the viewpoint of educators, the primary purpose of assessment is to help students by providing information about how instruction can be improved" (p. 258). The final step in evaluation is to improve the program and the achievement of each of your students.

Three Perspectives of Evaluation

Evaluation has three perspectives: self, collaborative others, and society (Short, 1990). The self is the student. The collaborative others are all those who work with the student, including the teacher, peer editor, learning team, and discussion groups. Society includes the parents, the community at large, and officials of the school or school district. Each group may have a different purpose for evaluating and may require different types of evidence. The school board, for instance, may want information on how the students in the district are doing as compared with students in other districts; students may note that they are not doing well on science and social studies tests; and teachers may observe that students are having difficulty applying comprehension strategies to expository text. The students and teacher are using information as cues to improving students' immediate performance. The school board is more concerned with how the district's students are performing as compared with similar schools or how the performance of this year's students compares to that of past students or whether standards are being met.

Because students, teachers, parents, and school boards have differing perspectives, they need different kinds of evaluation information. Although results of norm-referenced tests are frequently used by school boards and state departments of education as a basis for evaluation, they have limited usefulness for teachers. **Norm-referenced tests** rank students' performance by comparing them to a representative sample of students—the norm group—who took the test. Authentic measures are more helpful because they provide insight into students' learning strategies.

Authentic Assessment

Changing views of reading and writing have created a need for alternative methods of **assessment.** Alternative forms of assessment are often called **authentic assessment.** The word *authentic* is used because these assessment procedures "reflect the actual learning and instructional activities of the classroom and out-of-school worlds" (Hiebert, Valencia, & Afflerbach, 1994, p. 11). In authentic assessment, students retell or summarize whole texts, as opposed to the kind of objective testing in which students respond to multiple-choice questions asked about short paragraphs. Observations, think-alouds, holistic scoring of writing, anecdotal records, and assembling and evaluating a portfolio are also examples of authentic assessment. Even large-scale assessments are becoming more authentic. Many state and national assessments now use longer passages and ask for constructed responses in which students respond in writing.

Some kinds of assessment practices are not very helpful to teachers. For instance, using norm-referenced tests, which compare one student with another or one school district with another, has fostered competition and a focus on high scores. The emphasis should be on developing each student's abilities to the fullest. If administrators and teachers are being judged by test results, there will be a natural tendency to gear instruction to the test. If the assessment measures only a portion of the curriculum, the portion not measured may be neglected. Worse, the format of the test may influence instruction. For example, if the test features short paragraphs with multiple-choice responses, the instructional reading program will tend to emphasize that format. Valuable instructional time that could have been devoted to reading literature and developing higher-order thinking skills may be allotted instead to low-level exercises designed to help students achieve higher scores. Moreover, the population most likely to be subjected to these lower-level activities is remedial

■ **Norm-referenced tests** are ones in which students are compared with a representative sample of students who are the same age or are in the same grade.

■ **Assessment** is the process of gathering data about an area of learning through tests, observations, work samples, or other means.

■ **Authentic assessment** involves using tasks that are typical of the kinds of reading or writing that students perform in school and out.

and at-risk because the pressure to show improvement in the performance of these students is greatest (Herman, 1992).

However, when assessment is authentic and when students are judged on their ability to read whole selections and to respond by composing a written response, assessment practices can be very helpful. Teachers then emphasize these more holistic activities. As a result of holistic writing assessment in California, for instance, teachers began requiring their students to write more frequently and to attempt a greater variety of writing genres (Herman, 1992). However, there is danger even with these more realistic measures. If the assessment requires writing in response to a prompt, students may spend too many classroom hours writing to prompts of the same type tested.

*O*bservations often reveal more information about students' progress than do traditional paper-and-pencil tests.

Product versus Process Measures

Authentic assessment emphasizes process rather than product. Product assessment is concerned with what the student has learned. Process assessment seeks to find out how the student learns. Product measures are the number of correct answers on a quiz, the score on a norm-referenced test, the final copy of a composition, or the number of books read. They help teachers assess students' current and past levels of achievement. They provide information on students' reading and writing levels and abilities, the kinds of materials they can read, the kinds of writing they can do, and how well they can spell. Knowing where each student is, the teacher can plan instruction and activities that build on what students have already accomplished.

Process measures include observing students to see what strategies they use to arrive at a particular answer, to compose a piece of writing, or to study for a test. These measures seek to answer such questions as How do students prepare to read an assignment? Do they reread or use some other strategy when the material they are reading doesn't make sense? Do students select, organize, and elaborate information as they read? If so, how? Having this kind of insight, the teacher is able to redirect errant thought processes, correct poorly applied strategies, or teach needed strategies. Actually, both process and product measures provide useful information. Knowing where a child is and how he or she got there, the teacher is better prepared to map out a successful journey.

Questions to Be Asked

Essentially, evaluation is the process of asking a series of questions. Specific questions depend on a program's particular goals and objectives. However, some

One danger in evaluation is the temptation to gather too much information. Be economical. Do not waste time gathering information you are not going to use.

general questions that should be asked about every literacy program include the following:

- What is the level of student's language development?
- Where are students in their literacy development?
- At what level are they reading?
- Are they reading up to their ability level?
- How well do they comprehend what they read?
- How adequate are students' reading vocabularies?
- What comprehension and word-analysis strategies do students use?
- Do students know how to study?
- What are their attitudes toward reading?
- Do they enjoy a variety of genres?
- Do they read on their own?
- How well do they write?
- What kinds of writing tasks have they attempted?
- Are students' reading and writing improving?
- Which students seem to have special needs in reading and writing?
- Are these special needs being met?

Answers to these essential questions help teachers plan, revise, and improve their reading and writing programs. The rest of this chapter explores a number of techniques for gathering the assessment information necessary to answer them. Both traditional and alternative means will be used.

PLACEMENT INFORMATION

■ An **informal reading inventory (IRI)** is an assessment device in which a student reads a series of selections that gradually increase in difficulty. The teacher records errors and assesses comprehension in order to determine levels of materials that a student can read.

The first question the classroom teacher of reading has to have answered is Where are the students? If they are reading, assessment begins with determining the levels at which they are reading. One of the best placement devices is an **informal reading inventory (IRI).** In fact, if properly given, it will tell just about everything a teacher needs to know about a student's reading. It will also supply useful information about language development, work habits, interests, and personal development.

Informal Reading Inventory

An informal reading inventory is a series of graded selections beginning at the very easiest level—preprimer—and extending up to eighth grade or beyond. Each level has two selections; one is silent and the other oral. Starting at an easy level, the student continues to read until it is obvious that the material has become too difficult.

An IRI yields information about four levels: independent, instructional, frustration, and listening capacity. The **independent level,** or the free-reading level, is the point at which students can read on their own without teacher assistance.

The **instructional level** refers to the point at which students need assistance because the material contains too many unknown words or concepts or their background of experience is insufficient. This is also the level of materials used for teaching. Material at the **frustration level** is so difficult that students cannot read it even with teacher assistance. The fourth level is listening capacity, the highest level at which students can understand what has been read to them. **Listening capacity** is an informal measure of ability to comprehend spoken language. Theoretically, it is the level at which students should be able to read if they have all the necessary decoding skills. In practice, a small percentage of students have listening deficiencies, so a listening test might underestimate their true capacity. Younger students also tend to read below capacity because they are still acquiring basic reading skills. As students progress through the grades, listening and reading levels grow closer together (Sticht & James, 1984).

The first informal reading inventories were constructed by teachers and were created using passages from basal readers. This was a good idea because it meant that there was an exact match between the material the student was tested on and the material the student would be reading. Because constructing informal reading inventories is time consuming, most teachers now use commercially produced informal reading inventories (see Table 2.1). However, informal reading inventories are available for basal reading programs.

Informal reading inventories can also be geared to trade books. If, for instance, your program emphasizes the reading of trade books, you might designate

- The **independent level** is the level at which a student can read without any assistance. Comprehension is 90 percent or higher and word recognition is 99 percent or higher.

- The **instructional level** is the level at which a student needs teacher help. Comprehension is 75 percent or higher and word recognition is 95 percent or higher.

- The **frustration level** is the level at which reading material is so difficult that the student can't read it even with help. Frustration is reached when either word recognition is 90 percent or lower or comprehension is 50 percent or lower.

- **Listening capacity** is the highest level at which students can understand material that is read to them with 75 percent comprehension.

TABLE 2.1 Commercial reading inventories

Name	Publisher	Grades	Added Skill Areas
Bader Reading and Language Inventory	Merrill	1–12	phonics, language, spelling, emergent literacy
Basic Reading Inventory	Kendall/Hunt	1–8	emergent literacy
Classroom Reading Inventory	McGraw-Hill	1–8	spelling
Ekwall/Shanker Reading Inventory	Allyn & Bacon	1–12	emergent literacy, word analysis, reading interests
English-Español Reading Inventory for the Classroom	Prentice Hall	1–12	emergent literacy (has an English-only version)
Informal Reading Thinking Inventory	Harcourt	1–11	
Qualitative Reading Inventory III	Scott, Foresman	1–12	
Spanish Reading Inventory	Kendall/Hunt	1–4	
Stieglitz Informal Reading Inventory	Allyn & Bacon	1–8	emergent literacy

certain titles as benchmark books and construct questions or retelling activities based on these books. Benchmark books can be used to place students and check their progress. Sets of benchmark books and accompanying questions are available from basal reader publishers. Or you can construct your own. This chapter lists benchmark books that can be used to judge the difficulty level of children's books. These books can also be used as the basis for an informal reading inventory.

■ Determining Placement Levels

Placement levels are determined by having students read two selections, one orally and one silently, at appropriate grade levels. The percentages of oral-reading errors and comprehension questions answered correctly at each level are calculated. This information is then used to determine placement levels. Quantitative data for determining levels are contained in Table 2.2.

The listening portion of the inventory provides only an approximate indication of children's capacity. It would tend to be inaccurate with youngsters who have difficulty paying attention or who lack good listening skills or who are still learning English.

To be at the independent level, a reader must have both 99 percent word recognition and 90 percent comprehension. At the instructional level, the reader must have at least 95 percent word recognition and at least 75 percent comprehension. The frustration level is reached when word recognition drops to 90 percent or comprehension falls to 50 percent. Even with 80 percent comprehension and 90 percent word recognition, readers are at the frustration level because they are encountering too many words that they cannot decode. Listening capacity is the level at which students can understand 75 percent of the material that is read to them.

Standards for determining levels, marking symbols, types of misreadings that are counted as errors, and administration procedures vary, depending on the source consulted. The standards used in this book are taken from Johnson, Kress, and Pikulski (1987) and seem to be the most widely used.

Some placement devices use lower standards, such as 90 to 95 percent word recognition. It is strongly advised that you stick to the 95 to 98 percent word recognition standard. Research indicates that students do best when they can read at least 95 to 98 percent of the words (Berliner, 1981; Biemiller, 1994; Gambrell, Wilson, & Gantt, 1981). It is also important that the examiner adhere to strict standards when marking word reading errors. Enz (1989) found that relaxing IRI standards resulted in a drop in both achievement and attitude. Students placed according to higher standards spent a greater proportion of time on task, had a higher success rate, and had a more positive attitude toward reading.

■ Administering the Word-List Test

Rather than guessing at which grade level to begin the inventory, a teacher can administer a word-list test to locate an approximate starting point. This test consists

TABLE 2.2	Quantitative criteria for IRI	
Level	Word Recognition in Context (%)	Average Comprehension (%)
Independent	99	90–100
Instructional	95–98	75–89
Frustration	≤90	≤50
Listening capacity		75

TABLE 2.3   Word-list marking symbols

Word	Teacher Mark	Meaning
the	✓	Correct
was	✓'	Incorrect response or repeated error
have	_o_	No response
dog	_boy_ / _dog_	Mispronunciation
are	_dk_	Don't know

Increasingly, classroom teachers are administering informal reading inventories. The *Classroom Reading Inventory* (Silvaroli & Wheelock, 2001), which is a streamlined inventory, was specifically designed to be given by classroom teachers and takes approximately twelve minutes to administer.

of a series of ten to twenty words at each grade level. Students read the words in isolation, starting with the easiest and continuing until they reach a level where they get half or more of the words wrong. In a simplified administration of the test, students read the words from their copy of the list and the teacher marks each response on her or his copy as being right or wrong.

In a diagnostic administration, the teacher uses three-by-five cards to flash the words for one second each. When students respond correctly, the teacher moves on to the next word. If the answer is incorrect or if students fail to respond, the teacher stops and lets them look at the word for as long as they wish (within reason). While students examine the missed word, the teacher writes down their response or marks a symbol in the flash (timed) column. If students make a second erroneous response, it is written in the second, or untimed, column. Symbols used to mark word-list tests are presented in Table 2.3. A corrected word-list test is shown in Figure 2.1.

Although used to indicate the starting level for the IRI, a word-list test can yield valuable information about students' reading, especially if a diagnostic administration has been used. By comparing flash and untimed scores, teachers can assess the adequacy of students' sight vocabulary (their ability to recognize words immediately) and their proficiency with decoding. Teachers can note which decoding skills students are able to use and which must be taught. Looking at the performance depicted in Figure 2.1, it is clear that the student has a very limited sight vocabulary. The flash col-

FIGURE 2.1

A Corrected Word-List Test

	Flash	Untimed
1. brief	✓	
2. special	_sp–_	_speckled_
3. passenger	_pass_	_passer_
4. settler	_settle_	✓'
5. wreck	_wick_	✓
6. discovery	_disk_	_discuss_
7. cause	✓	
8. invitation	_in–_	_invit_
9. distant	_dis_	_distan_
10. stroll	_stole_	✓
11. escape	_escap_	✓
12. famous	✓	
13. adventure	_add_	_avenue_
14. breathe	_breath_	✓
15. pilot	_pile_	✓
16. judge	✓	
17. claim	✓	
18. several	_seven_	_seventh_
19. squirt	✓	
20. voyage	_dk_	
Percent correct	30%	55%

umn shows that the student recognized few of the words immediately; the un-timed column gives an overall picture of the student's ability to apply decoding skills. When given time, the student was able to figure out six words that he was unable to read immediately. An analysis of errors shows that he was able to read most of the single-syllable words immediately and was able to decode the three-syllable words that he missed at sight. However, he had considerable difficulty with multi-syllabic words, even when he was given time to decode them. He misread words such as *special*, *adventure*, and *invitation*, which incorporate patterns not found in single-syllable words: *-cial*, *-tion*, and *-ture*.

■ Administering the Inventory

The informal reading inventory is started at the level below the student's last perfect performance on the flash or timed portion of the word-list test. If that perfect performance was at the fourth-grade level, the inventory is started at the third-grade level.

An IRI is like a directed reading lesson, except that its main purpose is to assess a student's reading. To administer an IRI, first explain to the student that she will be reading some stories and answering some questions so that you can get

TABLE 2.4   Oral-reading symbols

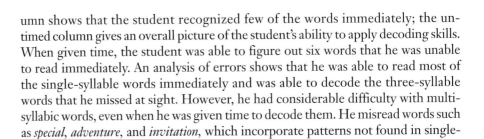

	Marking	Meaning
Quantitative errors	the fer~~ocio~~us dog *(fierce)*	Mispronounced
	the fer~~ocious~~ dog	Omitted word
	the (ferocious) dog	Asked for word
	the big ^ dog *bad*	Inserted word
Self-correction	the ~~big~~ dog *bad ✓*	Self-corrected (not counted as error)
Qualitative errors	I hit the ball⊗ and George ran.	Omitted punctuation
	The ‖ferocious dog	Hesitation (one line per each second)
	<u>the ferocious dog</u>	Repetition (one line per each repetition)
	Good morning! ↑	Rising inflection
	Are you reading? ↓	Falling inflection
	W x W	Word-by-word reading
	HM	Head movement
	FP	Finger pointing
	PC	Use of picture clue

some information about her reading. Before each selection is read, have the student read its title and predict what it will be about (Johns, 1997). Doing this will help the student set a purpose for reading, and it will give you a sense of the student's prediction ability and background of experience.

The student reads the first selection orally. This is one of the few times in which reading orally without having first read the selection silently is valid. As the student reads, use the symbols shown in Table 2.4 to record her performance. Although many different kinds of misreadings are noted, only the following are counted as errors or **miscues:** mispronunciations, omissions, insertions, and words supplied by the examiner because the student asked the examiner to read them or apparently could not read them on her own. Self-corrected errors are not counted. Hesitations, repetitions, and other qualitative misreadings are noted but not counted as errors. A corrected inventory selection is shown in Figure 2.2.

After the student finishes reading aloud, ask the series of comprehension questions that accompany the selection or ask for an oral retelling (see pp. 47–49 for information on administering a retelling). Then, introduce a silent selection on the same level. Just as with the oral selection, allow a very brief preparation phase

■ A **miscue** is an oral reading response that differs from the expected (correct) response. The term *miscue* is used because miscue theory holds that errors are not random but are the attempts of the reader to make sense of the text.

FIGURE 2.2

Oral Selection

Oral Selection   **156 words**

The Hatchet Fish

The hatchet fish is a‖strange looking sea creature *(create)*. It has a thin *(tin)* hatchet-

shaped body. But the strangest thing about the hatchet fish is its eyes.

One (type) of hatchet fish has large eyes that point|upwards. This hatchet

fish lives|deep in the water. Because they point upwards, the eyes of the

deep water hatchet fish help it to spot fish or bugs swimming above it.

The hatchet fish's unusual *(usual)* eyes help it to hunt down other sea creatures *(creeps)*.

Even stranger than the deep water hatchet fish is the flying hatchet

fish. Flying hatchet fish live near the surface *(sure)* of the water and feed‖on

insides✓ insects. If an insect tries to fly out of their reach, they‖chase it. Speeding

through the water, they shoot up into the air. Then by flapping their large

fins, they glide *(guide)* through the air. They can't fly very far. But often they fly far

enough to catch a meal *(metal✓)*.

0.95
149) 156

95% accuracy rate

corrects some words that are misread

choppy, poor expression

fails to process all the parts of words

TABLE 2.5	Silent-reading symbols
Symbol	**Meaning**
HM	Head movement
FP	Finger pointing
LM	Lip movement
SV	Subvocalizing

Some inventories recommend counting all miscues as errors. Others suggest counting only those that disrupt the meaning or flow of the passage. It is easier and quicker to count all misreadings but to make note of whether or not they fit the sense of the passage. Deciding whether a miscue is significant is subjective. If standards are too lenient, the student being assessed may end up being placed with a text that is too difficult.

BUILDING LANGUAGE

When students are responding orally to informal reading questions, note the level and quality of their language and use your observations to plan a program of language development.

and have the student make a prediction. During the silent reading, note finger pointing, head movement, lip movement, and subvocalizing. Symbols for these behaviors are given in Table 2.5. Ask comprehension questions when the student finishes reading. Proceeding level by level, continue to test until the student reaches a frustration level—that is, misreads 10 percent or more of the words or misses at least half the comprehension questions.

When the frustration level has been reached, read to the student the oral and silent selections at each level beyond the frustration level until the student reaches the highest level at which she or he can answer 75 percent of the comprehension questions. This is the student's listening capacity, and it indicates how well the student would be able to read if she or he had the necessary word-recognition skills and related print-processing skills. For children who have limited language skills or background of experience or deficient listening skills, you may have to backtrack and read selections at the frustration level and below. Because students will already have been exposed to the lower-level selections, you will have to use alternative selections to test listening comprehension.

After administering the inventory, enter the scores from each level on the inventory's summary sheet (see Figure 2.3). Word-recognition scores are determined by calculating the percentage of words read correctly on each oral selection (number of words read correctly divided by number of words in the selection). If the student made 5 miscues in a 103-word selection, the word recognition score would be 98/103 = 95.1 percent.

Comprehension is calculated by averaging comprehension scores for the oral and silent selections at each level. Using the numbers on the summary sheet, determine the placement levels. Refer to the criteria in Table 2.2.

■ **Interpreting the Inventory**

After determining the student's levels, examine her or his performance on the inventory to determine word-recognition and comprehension strengths and weaknesses. What kinds of phonics skills can the student use? Is the student able to decode multisyllabic words? Could the student read words that have prefixes or suffixes? Did the student use context? Did the student integrate the use of decoding skills with context? How did the student's word recognition compare with her or his comprehension? How did the student handle literal and inferential questions? How did comprehension on oral passages compare with comprehension on silent passages? You can also note the quality of the student's responses as she or he answered questions and the way the student approached the tasks. What level of language did the student use to answer questions? What was the student's level of confidence and effort as she or he undertook each task? Through careful observation, you can gain insight into the student's reading processes. For example, you may observe the student decoding unfamiliar words sound by sound or using a combination of context and phonics to handle difficult words. Strengths and weaknesses as well as immediate needs can be noted on the IRI summary sheet.

FIGURE 2.3

Informal Reading Inventory Summary Sheet

Word-List Scores

Inventory Scores

Level	Flash	Untimed	Word recognition (in context)	Comprehension (oral)	Comprehension (silent)	Comprehension (avg.)	Listening capacity
PP	100						
P	100						
1	100						
2	100		100	90	100	95	
3	90	100	99	90	90	90	
4	90	100	98	80	90	85	
5	80	90	96	80	70	75	
6	65	75	91	60	50	55	
7	50	60	88	50	40	45	75
8	30	40					50

Levels

Independent   _3_

Instructional   _5_

Frustration   _7_

Listening capacity   _7_

Strengths and weaknesses

Strong language development and background knowledge

Difficulty with multisyllabic words and words with affixes

■ Miscue Analysis of IRIs

Students use three cueing systems to decode printed words: syntactic, semantic, and phonic (graphophonic). In other words, they use their sense of how language sounds (syntax), the meaning of the sentence or passage (semantics), and phonics to read. To determine how they are using these systems, analyze their word-recognition errors, or miscues, with a modified **miscue analysis.** On a sheet similar to the one in Figure 2.4, list the students' miscues. Try to list at least ten miscues, but do not analyze any that are at or beyond the frustration level. Miscues can be chosen from the independent and instructional levels and from the buffer zone between the instructional and frustration levels (91 to 94 percent word recognition). Also list the correct version of each error. Put a check in the syntactic column if the miscue is syntactically correct—that is, if it is the same part of speech as the word in the text or could be used in that context. Put a check in the semantic column if the miscue makes sense in the sentence. In the graphic column, use a check to show whether the miscue is graphically and/or phonically similar to the

■ **Miscue analysis** is the process of analyzing miscues in order to determine which cueing systems or combination of cueing systems the student is using: semantic, syntactic, or graphophonic.

FIGURE 2.4

Miscue Analysis

Name: _____   Date: _____

Miscue	Text	Syntactic similarity	Semantic similarity	Graphic similarity	Beginning	Middle	End	Nonword	Self-correction
dust	dusty	—	—	✓	✓	✓	—		
southern	southwestern	✓	✓	✓	✓	—	✓		
saddles	settlers	✓	—	—	✓	—	—		
pouring	plowing	✓	—	✓	✓	—	✓		
threw	tossed	✓	✓	—	✓	—	—		
blanged	blanketed	✓	—	✓	✓	—	✓	✓	
fires	fierce	—	—	—	✓	—	—		
power	powerful	—	✓	✓	✓	✓	—		
grinds	grains	—	—	✓	✓	—	✓		
thinnest	tiniest	✓	—	—	—	—	✓		
destroyed	darkened	✓	—	—	✓	—	—		
middle	midday	—	—	✓	✓	✓	—		
create	creature	—	—	✓	✓	✓	—		
—	type	—	—	—	—	—			
upward	upwards	✓	✓	✓	✓	✓	—		
usual	unusual	✓	—	✓	—	✓	✓		
creeps	creatures	✓	—	—	✓	✓	—		
sure	surface	—	—	—	—	—	—		
insides ✓	insects	—	—	—	✓	—	—		✓
guide	glide	✓	—	✓	—	✓	✓		
metal ✓	meal	✓	—	✓	✓	—	✓		✓
soup	soil	✓	—	—	✓	—	—		
Totals		13	4	12	17	8	8	1	2
Numbers of miscues analyzed		22	22	22				22	22
Percentage		59	18	55				5	9

text word. It is similar if it contains at least half the sounds in the text word. Also use a check to show whether the beginning, middle, and end of the miscue are similar to the text word. Put a check in the nonword column if the miscue is not a real word. Also indicate corrected miscues with a check in the self-correction column.

Tally each column (as shown in Figure 2.4) and convert tallies to percentages. After tallying the columns, examine the numbers to see whether the student is reading for meaning. Miscues that make sense in the context of the selection, self-corrections, and absence of nonwords are positive signs. They show that the student is reading for meaning. Conversely, the presence of nonwords is a negative sign, as are miscues that do not fit the sense of the passage or the syntax.

Also compare the tallies to see whether the cues are being used in balanced fashion or whether one is being overused or underused. The student could be overusing phonics and underusing semantic context, or vice versa. Draw tentative conclusions about the strategies that the student uses in his or her word recognition. Double-check those conclusions as you observe the student read in the classroom.

As you can see from Figure 2.4, fewer than 20 percent of this student's miscues fit the context semantically. Moreover, one of them was a nonword, and the student had only two self-corrections. All indications are that the student is failing to use context clues and is not reading for meaning. The student makes heavy use of phonics, especially at the beginning of words, but must also integrate his or her use of phonics with syntactic and semantic cues. The student also needs to improve his or her use of syllabic analysis skills, especially for the endings of words. The student does not seem to be processing words fully.

IRIs require training and practice to administer and interpret. In the past, they were generally administered by the school's reading specialist. However, increasingly, classroom teachers are administering IRIs. To make the best possible use of time, classroom teachers might give a streamlined version of an IRI in which they give the full word list test but only administer the oral passages of the inventory and don't administer the listening portion of the IRI. It will also save time if an inventory that contains brief passages is given. Giving a shortened inventory reduces its reliability, so results should be regarded as being tentative and verified by observation of the student's performance reading books at the estimated instructional level.

Even if you, as a classroom teacher, never formally administer an IRI, it is still essential that you be familiar with the concept. Knowing the IRI standards for instructional and other levels, you have a basis for evaluating your students' reading performance. If students have difficulty orally reading more than five words out of a hundred, or if their oral and written comprehension seem closer to 50 percent than 75 percent, you may have to check the material they are reading to see whether it is too difficult. On the other hand, if both word recognition and comprehension in everyday reading tasks are close to perfect, you may want to try more challenging materials.

As students struggle with difficult words, you may also want to conduct a mental miscue analysis. By closely observing miscues, you can sense whether stu-

Generally, IRIs are given at the beginning of the school year to obtain placement information, when a new student enters the class, or whenever a student's placement is in doubt. They may also be given as pretests and posttests and are often more sensitive indicators of progress than norm-referenced tests.

dents might need added instruction in using context, using phonics, or integrating the two.

Running Records

■ The **running record** is an assessment device in which a student's oral reading errors are noted and classified in order to determine whether the material is on the appropriate level of difficulty and to see which reading strategies the student is using.

Similar to the informal reading inventory and based on K. S. Goodman's (1974) theory of analyzing students' miscues to determine what strategies they are using to decode words, the **running record** has become a popular device for assessing students' progress. Like the IRI, the running record is administered individually. However, only an oral-reading sample is obtained. The running record has two major purposes: to determine whether students' reading materials are on the proper level and to obtain information about the word-recognition processes students are using. To get a fuller assessment of comprehension, some teachers supplement the administration of a running record by having students retell the selection.

Running records are administered according to a standard format in which students' errors and corrections are recorded on a separate sheet. As adapted for use by classroom teachers, running records may be recorded (as long as the fair-use provision of the copyright laws is adhered to or permission is obtained from the publisher) on a photocopy of the text that the student is using (Learning Media, 1991). To assess whether materials are on a suitable level of difficulty and to determine how well the student makes use of previously presented strategies, take a running record on a text that the student has recently read. To assess the student's ability to handle challenging materials and apply strategies independently, take a running record on material that the student has not read. If the book or article is very brief, take a running record of the whole piece. If the text is lengthy, select a sample of 100 to 200 words. As the student reads orally, record her or his performance with symbols, such as those presented in Table 2.6. However, you

▌To simplify the administration of running records, use IRI marking symbols and record miscues on photocopies of the selection.

▌Running records provide indirect evidence of comprehension. "Observation of how a child reads a text—including phrasing, expression, and use of a variety of clues, checking to be sure all sources of information fit to determine when attempts don't make sense—provide evidence of comprehension" (Fountas, 1999, p. 11).

*R*unning records help teachers monitor students' progress.

TABLE 2.6	Running record symbols	
Symbol	**Text**	**Example**
Words read correctly are marked with a check mark.	Janice kicked the ball.	✓ ✓ ✓ ✓
Substitutions are written above the line.	A barn owl hooted.	✓ *big* ✓ ✓ *barn*
Self-corrections are marked *SC*.	A barn owl hooted.	✓ *big* |*sc* ✓ ✓ *barn*
A dash is used to indicate no response.	I saw her yesterday.	✓ ✓ ✓ — *yesterday*
A dash is used to indicate an insertion of a word. The dash is placed beneath the inserted word.	We spotted the van.	✓ ✓ ✓ *large* ✓ —
A *T* is used to indicate that a child has been told a word.	Her cat ran away yesterday.	✓ ✓ ✓ ✓ *T* *yesterday*
The letter *A* indicates that the child has asked for help.	A large moose appeared.	✓ ✓ ✓ *A* *appeared*
At times, the student becomes so confused by a misreading that it is suggested that she or he "try that again" (coded TTA). Brackets are put around the section that has been misread, the whole misreading is counted as one error, and the student reads it again for a new score.	The deer leaped over the fence.	[✓ ✓ *landed* ✓ ✓ *field*] *TTA* *leaped* *fence*
A repetition is indicated with an *R*. Although not counted as errors, repetitions are often part of an attempt to puzzle out a difficult item. The point to which the student returns in the repetition is indicated with an arrow.	The deer leaped over the fence.	✓ ✓ *landed*|*sc* ✓ ✓ *field*|*sc.* *R* *leaped* *fence*

may use the IRI symbols if you are more familiar with them. After taking a running record, record the number of words in the selection, number of errors made, error rate, number of self-corrections made, and the accuracy rate.

Clay (1993a) accepts 90 percent as an adequate accuracy rate; however, 95 percent seems more realistic. Word recognition is emphasized in a running record, so comprehension is not directly checked. However, you may ask the student to retell the story if you wish to obtain information about comprehension.

It is essential that you analyze a student's miscues in order to determine what strategies she or he is using. As you examine the student's miscues, ask the following questions:

- Is the student reading for meaning? Do the student's miscues make sense?
- Is the student self-correcting miscues, especially those that do not fit the meaning of the sentence? Is the student using meaning cues?
- Is the student using word analysis cues (phonics, syllabic analysis, morphemic analysis)? Are the student's miscues similar in appearance and sound to the target word?
- Is the student using graphics cues such as illustrations, maps, and diagrams?
- Is the student integrating cues? Is the student balancing the use of meaning and word analysis cues?
- Based on the student's performance, what strategies does she or he need to work on?

For detailed information on analyzing and interpreting running records, see Clay (1993a, 2000) or P. Johnston (1997).

Group Inventories

Because of the time involved, it may be impractical to administer individual IRIs. However, you may choose to administer a group reading inventory. Information about constructing and administering group reading inventories can be found in *Informal Reading Inventories* (2nd ed.) by Johnson, Kress, & Pikulski (1987). Some reading series contain group reading inventories. There are also three tests that function as group inventories: the Degrees of Reading Power, the Scholastic Reading Inventory, and STAR.

■ Degrees of Reading Power (DRP)

Composed of a series of passages that gradually increase in difficulty, the Degrees of Reading Power assesses overall reading ability by having students choose from among five options the one that best completes a portion of the passage from which words have been omitted. Each passage has nine deletions.

As in a traditional IRI, the passages gradually increase in difficulty and encompass a wide range of difficulty so that slow, average, and superior readers' ability may be appropriately assessed. Instead of yielding a grade-level score, the assessment provides a DRP score. The DRP score indicates what level of material the student should be able to read. A complementary readability formula is used to indicate the difficulty level of books in DRP units. Approximate grade equivalents of DRP units are presented in Table 2.7. The main purpose of the DRP is to match students with books that are on their levels.

TABLE 2.7	Comparison of readability levels				
Grade Equivalent	**DRP**	**Lexile**	**Guided Reading**	**Reading Recovery**
First Grade	34–43	200–400	A–I	1–17
Grade 2a	44–45	400–500	J–K	18–20
Grade 2b	46–47	400–500	L–M	
Grade 3	48–49	500–700	N–P	
Grade 4	50–51	700–800	Q–S	
Grade 5	52–53	800–900	T–V	
Grade 6	54–55	900–1000	W–X	
Grade 7	56–57	1000–1100	Y	
Grade 8	58–59	1000–1100	Z	

■ The Scholastic Reading Inventory

The Scholastic Reading Inventory, which also uses a modified cloze procedure, yields lexile scores. Lexile units range from about 70 to 1700+. A score of 70 to 200 is about mid-first grade. A score of 1700 would be the level at which difficult scientific journals are written. Approximate grade equivalents of lexile units are presented in Table 2.7.

■ STAR

STAR (Advantage Learning Systems), which is administered and scored by a computer and so doesn't require valuable teacher time, has a branching component. The program is set so that if students give correct answers they are given higher-level passages, but are given lower-level passages if they respond incorrectly. The STAR uses a modified cloze procedure. Students need a reading vocabulary of 100 words in order to be able to take STAR. Testing time is ten minutes or less.

NORM-REFERENCED VERSUS CRITERION-REFERENCED TESTS

Norm-Referenced Tests

Many traditional tests provide some sort of comparison. In a **norm-referenced test,** students are compared with a representative sample of others who are the same age or in the same grade. The scores indicate whether students did as well as the average, better than the average, or below the average. The norm group typically includes students from all sections of the country, from urban and nonurban areas, and from a variety of racial or ethnic and socioeconomic groups. The group is chosen to be representative of the nation's total school population. However, norm-referenced tests can result in unfair comparisons. Urban schools, for example, should only be compared with other urban schools.

■ **Norm-referenced tests** are those in which students' performance is compared with a norm group, which is a representative sampling of students.

Norm-referenced tests provide information generally desired by school boards, policymakers, and the public at large. Ease and efficiency of administration and objectivity are appealing factors.

■ Norm-referenced tests are sometimes called **standardized tests.** However, the two terms have different meanings. *Standardized* means that a test is given under a set of standard conditions. Tests are standardized so that all students taking the test do so under the same set of circumstances. All norm-referenced tests are standardized, but not all standardized tests are norm-referenced.

Because norm-referenced tests yield comparative results that are generally used by school boards, school administrators, and the general public, they provide one source of information to assess the effectiveness of the school program. Classroom teachers can also make use of the data to complement information from quizzes, informal tests, and observations. Reading scores indicate an approximate level of achievement. If a measure of academic aptitude has been administered, results can be examined to see whether students are reading up to their expected or anticipated level of achievement. If they are not, the teacher can explore the problem.

The tests can also be used as a screening device. Very high-scoring students may be candidates for a gifted or enriched reading program. Low-scoring students may benefit from input from the reading or learning-disabilities specialist, especially if there is a marked difference between capacity and performance. Subtest scores of individuals can also be analyzed for patterns of strengths and weaknesses. A high-vocabulary, low-comprehension score, for example, is often a sign that a student needs extra instruction in the use of comprehension strategies. A low-vocabulary, high-comprehension score might indicate the need for language development. Occasionally, norm-referenced tests yield surprises. Sometimes students, because of shyness or other factors, hide their talents. Norm-referenced tests occasionally spotlight a student whose abilities have gone unnoticed.

Some school districts have as a goal that all students will be reading on grade level according to the results of a norm-referenced test. This is the same thing as saying that everyone will be at least average. However, norm-referenced tests are created in such a way that half the students in a typical group will score below average. Even if students' scores improve, this won't make the goal achievable. Test publishers periodically renorm their tests so that if scores generally improve, the norms are set higher (Harcourt Educational Measurement, 2000).

Norm-referenced tests have a number of weaknesses. Because they are multiple choice, they don't assess reading the way it is taught or used, and guessing is a factor. They also invite competition and comparison. According to some theorists the most serious problem with standardized tests is that "they are often considered to be the single or at least the most important determinate of students' achievement" (Salinger, 2001, p. 394). When documenting students' progress, teachers tend to use information garnered from standardized tests, even if they have data gathered through informal methods. It is as though teachers don't trust their own judgments (Johnston & Rogers, 2001). To offset this, teachers need to be more careful and systematic with their classroom assessments.

This book does not recommend administering norm-referenced tests. However, in many school systems, their administration is mandated. If information from these tests is available, you should make use of it along with other sources of data.

Criterion-Referenced Tests

■ A **criterion-referenced test** is one in which the student's performance is compared to a criterion, or standard.

In contrast to a norm-referenced test, a **criterion-referenced test** compares students' performance with some standard, or criterion. For instance, the criterion on a comprehension test might be answering 80 percent of the questions correctly. The informal reading inventory is criterion-referenced; a student must have at least 95 percent word recognition and 75 percent comprehension to be on the instructional level, for example. Tests that accompany basal readers also tend to be criterion-referenced. Many have a passing score, which is the criterion. Most state tests and the National Assessment of Educational Progress (NAEP) tests are criterion-referenced. The major weakness of criterion-referenced tests is that, all too often, the criterion is set arbitrarily. No one tests it to see whether average students usually answer 80 percent of the items correctly, for example, or whether 80 percent comprehension is adequate in most instances. Sometimes the criterion is set too high. For instance, the NAEP test has been criticized for having standards that are unrealistically high. Although America's fourth-graders outscored every country but Finland on an international test (Elley, 1992), according to NAEP test results, only 67 percent of fourth-graders read at or above the basic level and only 24 percent read at or above the proficient level (Barton, 2001).

A second major shortcoming of criterion-referenced tests is that all too often they do not assess reading skills and strategies in the way students actually use them. For instance, comprehension might be assessed as in norm-referenced tests, with brief passages and multiple-choice questions. Despite these limitations, criterion-referenced tests are generally more useful to teachers than are norm-referenced tests. They indicate whether students have mastered particular skills and so are useful for making instructional decisions.

JUDGING ASSESSMENT MEASURES

Reliability

To be useful, tests and other assessment instruments, whether criterion- or norm-referenced, must be both reliable and valid. **Reliability** is a measure of consistency, which means that if the same test were given to the same students a number of times, the results would be approximately the same. Reliability can also be thought of as generalizability. In observations and other informal approaches to assessment, it means that similar findings have been found by different judges and at different times (Johnston & Rogers, 2001). One way of increasing reliability is by training observers. Another is to have several observations. Reliability is usually reported as a coefficient of correlation and ranges from 0.00 to 0.99 or −0.01 to −0.99. The higher the positive correlation, the more reliable the test. For tests on which individual decisions are being based, reliability should be in the 0.90s.

A test that is not reliable is of no value. It is the equivalent of an elastic yardstick—the results of measurement would be different each time.

Validity

In general, **validity** means that a test measures what it says it measures: vocabulary knowledge or speed of reading, for instance. Ultimately, it means that a particular test will provide the information needed to make a decision, such as placing a student with an appropriate level book or indicating specific strengths and weaknesses in comprehension (Farr & Carey, 1986). Johnston and Rogers (2001) contend

■ NAEP has been assessing students in grades four, eight, and twelve since 1969. Carefully constructed, the NAEP tests in reading and writing are highly regarded and are the standard against which other tests are evaluated.

■ **Reliability** is the degree to which a test yields consistent results. In other words, if you took the test again, your score would be approximately the same.

■ Whether assessment is formal or informal, through observation or paper-and-pencil testing, reliability is essential. As Farr (1991) observes, "If a test or other means of assessment is not reliable, it's no good. . . . If you stand on the bathroom scale and it registers 132 lbs. one morning, but it's 147 the next morning, and 85 the morning after that, you conclude it's time for a new set of bathroom scales. . . ." (p. 4).

■ **Validity** is the degree to which a test measures what it is supposed to measure or the extent to which a test will provide information needed to make a decision. Validity should be considered in terms of the consequences of the test results and the use to which the test results will be put.

that unless an assessment practice helps to improve students' learning, it should not occur. Reading tests need content validity, meaning that skills and strategies tested must be the same as those taught. Calfee and Hiebert (1991) define validity with the following question: "Does assessment match what I have taught and the way I have taught it?" (p. 282).

To check for **content validity,** list the objectives of the program and note how closely a particular test's objectives match them. The test selections should be examined, too, to see whether they reflect the type of material that the students read. Also, determine how reading is tested. If a test assesses skills or strategies that you do not cover or assesses them in a way that is not suitable, the test is not valid for your class.

Closely tied to validity are the consequences or uses to which the assessment will be put. If the test assesses only a narrow part of the curriculum, it will be detrimental and thus invalid (Joint Task Force on Assessment, 1994). Assessment measures should also be fair to all who take them. There should be no biased items, and the content should be such that all students have had an equal opportunity to learn it.

■ **Content validity** means that the tasks of an assessment device are representative of the subject or area being assessed.

REPORTING PERFORMANCE

There are two primary ways of reporting scores: norm-referenced and criterion-referenced. In norm-referenced reporting, a student's performance is compared with that of other students. In criterion-referenced reporting, a student's performance might be described in terms of a standard or expected performance or in terms of the student's goals.

Norm-Referenced Reporting

Tests and other assessment measures yield a number of possible scores. To interpret results correctly, it is important to know the significance of each score. Here are commonly used test scores:

■ A **raw score** is the number of correct answers or points earned on a test.

■ The **percentile rank** is the point on a scale of 1 to 99 that shows what percentage of students obtained an equal or lower score. A percentile rank of 75 means that 75 percent of those who took the test received an equal or lower score.

■ A **grade equivalent score** indicates the score that the average student at that grade level achieved.

- **Raw score.** A raw score represents the total number of correct answers. It has no meaning until it is changed into a percentile rank or other score.
- **Percentile rank.** A percentile rank tells where a student's raw score falls on a scale of 1 to 99. A score at the first percentile means that the student did better than 1 percent of those who took the test. A score at the fiftieth percentile indicates that the student did better than half of those who took the test. A top score is the ninety-ninth percentile. Most norm-referenced test results are now reported in percentiles; however, the ranks are not equal units and should not be added, subtracted, divided, or used for subtest comparison.
- **Grade equivalent score.** The grade equivalent score characterizes a student's performance as being equivalent to that of other students in a particular grade. A grade equivalent score of 5.2 indicates that the student correctly answered the same number of items as the average fifth-grader in the second month of that grade. Note that the grade equivalent score does not tell on what

level the student is operating; that is, a score of 5.2 does not mean that a student is reading on a fifth-grade level. Grade equivalent scores are more meaningful when the test students have taken is at the right level and when the score is not more than a year above or a year below average. Because grade equivalent scores are misleading and easily misunderstood, they should be used with great care or not at all.

- **Normal curve equivalents.** Normal curve equivalents (NCEs) rank students on a scale of 1 through 99. The main difference between NCEs and percentile ranks is that NCEs represent equal units and so can be added and subtracted and used for comparing performance on subtests.

- **Stanine.** Stanine is a combination of the words *standard* and *nine*. The stanines 4, 5, and 6 are average points, with 1, 2, and 3 being below average and 7, 8, and 9 above average. Stanines are useful when making comparisons among the subtests of a norm-referenced test.

- **Scaled scores.** Scaled scores are a continuous ranking of scores from the lowest levels of a series of norm-referenced tests—first grade, for example— through the highest levels—high school. They start at 000 and end at 999. They are useful for tracking long-term reading development through the grades. Lexiles, DRP units, and grade equivalents are also examples of scaled scores.

Grade equivalents and other scaled scores rise over time. However, percentiles, stanines, and normal curve equivalents may stay the same from year to year. If they do, this means that the student is making average progress in comparison with others. For instance, if a student is at the thirty-fifth percentile in third grade and then tests at the thirty-fifth percentile in fourth grade, that means that his relative standing is the same. He continues to do better than 35 percent of the students who took the test. However, if he moves to a higher percentile, this means that he outperformed students who started off with similar scores. If he scores at the fortieth percentile in fourth grade, it means that he is moving up in the relative standings. Now he is doing better than 40 percent of those who took the test.

For additional information about tests, see the *Fifteenth Mental Measurements Yearbook* (Plake, Impara, & Spies, 2003) or *Tests in Print VI* (Murphy, Plake, Impara, & Spies, 2002), which lists more than 4,000 tests. You might also consult the Buros Institute, which specializes in test information: http://www.unl.edu/buros/ or the ERIC site for assessment: http://ericae.net/.

Criterion-Referenced Reporting

Criterion-referenced results are reported in terms of a standard, or criterion. For example, the student answered 80 percent of the comprehension questions correctly. Two types of standards now being used in authentic assessment are the benchmark and the rubric, which are descriptive forms of criterion-referenced reporting.

■ Benchmarks

A **benchmark** is a written description of a key task that students are expected to perform. For instance, a benchmark for word recognition might be "Uses both context and phonics to identify words unknown in print." If adapted to fit your curriculum,

> Grade equivalent scores, which have been opposed by the International Reading Association, are relatively valid when pupils are tested on their instructional level and when extrapolations are limited to a year or two beyond the target grade level.

> ■ A **normal curve equivalent** is the rank on a scale of 1 through 99 that a score is equal to.

> ■ A **stanine** is a point on a nine-point scale, with 5 being average.

> ■ A **scaled score** is a continuous ranking from 000 to 999 of a series of norm-referenced tests from the easiest to the highest-level test.

> ■ A **benchmark** is a standard of achievement or written description of performance against which a student's achievement might be assessed.

the Essential Standards presented in the instructional chapters could be used to create benchmarks. Information on expected level of performance should be added, however.

Benchmarks are useful because they provide a concrete description of what students are expected to do. They provide students, teachers, parents, and administrators with an observable framework for assessing accomplishments and needs. Using benchmarks, the teacher can assess whether the student has mastered key skills and strategies and is ready to move on. Opportunities for assessing benchmark behaviors include observing during shared reading, story discussions, drama, writing activities, and student conferences. Parent conferences during which parents provide information about the child's reading and writing at home offer additional sources of data.

■ Rubrics

A **rubric** is a written description of what is expected in order to meet a certain level of performance and is usually accompanied by samples of several levels of performance. For assessing a piece of writing, such samples show the characteristics of an excellent, average, fair, and poor paper. A writing rubric is presented in Table 2.8. Although rubrics are typically used in the assessment of writing tasks, they can also be used to assess combined reading and writing tasks, portfolios, presentations, and projects.

In addition to their use as scoring guides, rubrics can be powerful teaching tools (Popham, 2000). Carefully constructed rubrics describe the key tasks that students must complete or the main elements that must be included in order to produce an excellent piece of work. This helps both the teacher and student focus on key skills. To be effective, rubrics should contain only three to six evaluative criteria so that students and teachers do not get sidetracked by minor details. More important, each evaluative criterion must encompass a teachable skill. For instance, evaluative criteria for a story might include an exciting plot, believable characters, an interesting setting, and the use of vivid language.

Creating a rubric. To develop a rubric, first identify the key characteristics or traits of the performance or piece of work to be assessed. For a rubric for a friendly letter, the key traits might include interesting content, chatty style, correct letter format, and correct mechanics. If available, examine finished products to see what their major traits are. Write a definition of each trait. What exactly is meant by "interesting content," "chatty style," "correct letter format," and "correct mechanics"? Develop a scale for the characteristics. It is usually easiest to start with the top performance. If you have examples of students' work, sort them into piles: best, worst, and middle. Look over the best pieces and decide what makes them the best. Look at the poorest and decide where they are deficient. Write a description of the best and poorest performances. Then fill in the middle levels. For the middle levels, divide the remaining papers into two or more piles from best to worst depending upon how many levels you wish to have. However, the more levels you create, the more difficult it becomes to discriminate between adjoining

---

When setting up benchmarks, it is important not to set up too many tasks.

■ A **rubric** is a description of the traits or characteristics of standards used to judge a process or product.

USING TECHNOLOGY
The Staff Room for Ontario's Teachers: Rubrics
http://www.odyssey. on.ca/~elaine.coxon/ rubrics.htm
Contains links to an impressive variety of rubrics covering virtually every subject. Provides excellent links for information about portfolios, including electronic ones.

Rubistar
http://rubistar. 4teachers.org/
Provides generic rubrics in a format that can be customized and printed out.

TABLE 2.8   Rubric for assessing writing

	Level 4 Most Successful	Level 3 Upper Half	Level 2 Lower Half (Basic)	Level 1 Least Successful (Skill Failure)
Content	Shows clear understanding of content. Develops the topic with appropriate detail in each paragraph.	Generally understands content. At least two paragraphs used. Details relate clearly to topic sentence.	Appears to understand the topic. If using more than one paragraph, relation to overall topic may be weak.	Some misunderstanding of topic. Usually only one paragraph. Includes material not related to topic.
Organization	Organization and sequence of ideas are clear and relate to one another in development of the overall topic.	Clear organization and sequences of detail. Relationship of paragraphs to major topic not fully developed.	Basically sequential. Some weakness in relating paragraph details to topic sentences.	Lacks coherence. Sequencing of ideas may be incorrect.
Sentence structure	Uses correct sentence structure, descriptive words, and phrases. Expands sentence patterns. Makes few grammatical errors.	Basic sentence patterns correct. Some difficulty with expanded sentence patterns and grammar.	Uses simple sentences. Errors in grammar when more complex structure is attempted. Some run-on and sentence fragments.	Uses basic simple sentences. Errors in noun–verb agreement. Infrequent use of modifiers.
Mechanics	Capitalization, punctuation, and spelling are generally correct.	Few problems with capitalization, punctuation, and spelling.	Errors in capitalization, punctuation, and spelling.	Frequent errors in capitalization, punctuation, and spelling of words.
Word choice	Vocabulary includes some words usually used at a higher level.	Average for grade level. Vocabulary words used correctly.	Simple vocabulary words used, some incorrectly.	Poor word choice.

From *The Writing Handbook* (p. 19) by the Reading and Communications Arts Department, 1983, Hartford, CT: Hartford Public Schools. Reprinted by permission of the Hartford Board of Education.

levels. You may find that four suffice. Evaluate your rubric. Use the following checklist to assess your rubric:

■ Does the rubric measure the key traits in the student performance?
■ Are differences in the levels clearly specified?
■ Does the rubric clearly specify what students are required to do?
■ Can the rubric be used as a learning guide by students?
■ Can the rubric be used as an instructional guide by the teacher? (Chicago Public Schools, 2000)

Discuss the rubric with students and invite feedback. Through helping with the creation of the rubrics, students form a better idea of what is expected in the task being assessed and also feel more willing to use the rubric because they had a hand

Students should participate in the creation of rubrics. Through helping with the creation of the rubrics, students form a clearer idea of what is expected in their writing. In one study, students used these rubrics to assess their own writing. They also took part in peer evaluation sessions in which the rubric was used to judge their writing. As a result of creating and using the rubric, students' writing of persuasive pieces showed a significant improvement (Boyle, 1996).

In some assessments, students are given materials on grade level to read and respond to. Because as many as one student in four will be reading significantly below grade level (Gunning, 1982), this practice is unfair to underachieving youngsters. Lower-achieving readers should be provided with at least some items that are on their instructional level. Test publishers support the concept of functional level testing and offer guidelines for out-of-level assessment. A general practice is to use the teacher's estimate or a quick locator test provided by the publisher to obtain a rough estimate of the child's reading level and to test the child on that level.

■ **Functional level testing** is the practice of assigning students to a test level on the basis of their reading ability rather than their grade level.

in its construction. When fourth-graders used cooperatively created rubrics to assess their writing (Boyle, 1996), their persuasive pieces showed a significant improvement.

Try out the rubric, revise it, and then use it. As you use the rubric with actual pieces of students' work, continue to revise it.

One source of rubrics might be the key standards for a grade. Teachers can align their rubrics with key state or local standards (Skillings & Ferrell, 2000). To ease her students into using rubrics, Ferrell modeled the process. She also had students create rubrics for everyday activities such as picking the best restaurant. After students caught on to the idea of creating rubrics, she involved them in creating rubrics for basic writing tasks. To keep the rubrics simple, the class had just three levels: best, okay, not so good. Later the class created rubrics for more complex tasks. Sample rubrics can be found at the following Web sites:

The State of Colorado (2000) has developed an online set of general, holistic scoring rubrics designed for the evaluation of various writing tasks. http://www.cde.state.co.us/cdeassess/as_rubricindex.htm

Chicago Public Schools (1999) maintain an extensive electronic list of analytic and holistic scoring rubrics that span the broad array of subjects represented from kindergarten through high school. http://intranet.cps.k12.il.us/Assessments/Ideas_and_Rubrics/ ideas_and_rubrics.html

FUNCTIONAL LEVEL ASSESSMENT

The typical class will exhibit a wide range of reading ability. Just as students need appropriate levels of materials for instruction, they should have appropriate levels of materials for testing. Most literacy tests cover a limited range. For instance, a general reading test designed for sixth-graders will mostly have selections on a sixth-grade level, a selection or two on a fifth-grade level, and a few selections beyond the sixth-grade level. A sixth-grader reading on a second-grade level should not be given a sixth-grade reading test. It would be frustrating to the student and would yield misleading results. The student should take a test that includes material on his level of reading ability. This might mean giving the student a test designed for third grade but which includes second-grade material. Similarly, a sixth-grade-level test would probably not be appropriate for a sixth-grader reading on a high school level. It would probably lack an adequate ceiling and so would underestimate the student's true reading ability. Students should be tested at their **functional level,** which is not necessarily their grade level. Students reading significantly above or below grade level should be given out-of-level tests unless the tests they are taking cover a wide range of levels. Giving students a test at the wrong level results in erroneous, invalid information. This is true whether norm-referenced, criterion-referenced, or other assessment is being used.

Unfortunately, students are not always assessed on the appropriate level. Some state tests, for instance, set their test passages and items at grade level. For instance, the sixth-grade test is written at a sixth-grade level. Although this may seem logical, it fails to provide for students reading below grade level. A sixth-grader reading on a third-grade level may not be able to read a single passage on the state proficiency test. The student is denied the opportunity to show what he knows and can do. The test is also damaging to his self-concept and attitude toward school and himself as learner. Tests that are being given to a wide range of students should have sufficient "bottom" so that there are below-level passages that below-level readers can handle. In NAEP reading tests, an attempt is made to include some passages that can be read by the least proficient readers. The fourth-grade NAEP test, for instance, contains some selections written on a second-grade level (National Assessment Governing Board, 2001). If the test is lacking in sufficient bottom, students reading below the level of the easiest passage should be given out-of-level tests. Otherwise, the tests yield invalid, misleading results (Gunning, 2001). The state of Oregon adminsters three levels of tests for each grade assessed (Oregon Department of Education, 2001). Teachers use past performance, observations, and other sources to determine which level to administer. In addition, a locator test is available. Locator tests provide estimates of reading levels. Because students are taking tests more closely tailored to their achievement levels, the tests more precisely measure student proficiency in relation to the state's standards. However, the standards are not compromised by giving some students lower-level tests. The tests overlap. Students taking a lower-level test must get more items correct in order to meet a standard.

Grade equivalent measures, lexiles, and DRPs can be used with out-of-level testing. However, out-of-level norms should be used to report percentile and stanine scores, because these scores involve comparing students who are in the same grade.

Administering the right level test means that you need to know students' approximate reading levels. Approximate reading levels may be obtained from teacher judgment, IRIs, running records, observing which level of materials the students can handle, or administering a locator test. Federal and state regulations are calling for a wider inclusion of students in high-stakes tests, including some students who were previously excused. This will entail making fuller use of functional level testing.

> Obtaining a valid assessment of the ability and performance of English Language Learners is a problem. ELLs can obtain conversational proficiency in two years or less. However, it may take five years or more for ELLs to learn enough academic English so that they can do as well on tests of academic proficiency as native speakers of English do (Cummins, 2001).

OTHER METHODS OF ASSESSMENT

Retelling

Retelling has the potential for supplying more information about a student's comprehension than simply asking questions does. In a retelling, a student is asked to do what the name suggests: The student may retell a selection that has been read to her or him or one that she or he has read. The student may do this orally or in writing. In addition to showing what the reader comprehended, retelling shows what she or he added to and inferred from the text (Irwin & Mitchell, 1983). Free from the influence of probes or questions, retelling demon-

> ■ **Retelling** is the process of summarizing or describing a story that one has read. The purpose of the retelling is to assess comprehension.

Being less time consuming, informal retellings are more practical for the classroom teacher. Of course, shy children may not perform up to their ability.

strates the student's construction of text and provides insight into her or his language and thought processes. It shows how the student organizes and shapes a response. The teacher can also assess the quality of language used by the student in the retelling.

To administer a retelling, explain to the student what she or he is supposed to do: Read a selection orally or silently or listen to one read aloud. It may be a narrative or expository piece. Tell the student that she or he will be asked to retell the story in her or his own words. Use neutral phrasing, such as "Tell me about the story that you read."

If a student stops before retelling the whole selection, encourage her or him to continue or elaborate. When the student is finished, ask questions about any key elements that were not included in the retelling.

■ Evaluating Retellings

As the student retells the selection, record it on audiocassette and/or jot down brief notes on the major events or ideas in the order in which the student relates them. Note any recalls that were not spontaneous but were elicited by your questions. Tape recording provides a full and accurate rendition of the retelling but is time consuming.

Retellings can be scored numerically by giving students credit for each major unit that they retell. However, this is a laborious process. Far less time consuming but still useful is noting the major units in the retelling in one column, comments about it in a second column, and a summary and recommendations in a third. Because the main purpose of the retelling is to gain insight into students' reading processes, draw inferences about students' overall understanding of the selection and their ability to use strategies to construct the meaning of the piece. A sample retelling is presented in Figure 2.5.

■ Written Retellings

As an alternative to a strictly written response, you might invite students to use whatever form they want to retell a selection: semantic map or web, story map, outline, flow chart, diagram, or other graphic organizers. Students, might also respond by drawing an illustration of the story.

Written retellings can be timesavers, as the teacher can assess the class as a group. Using holistic scoring, the teacher can also assess the quality of the response. It is important to keep in mind that, whether oral or written, the mode of expression will affect the information students convey. Students may have good knowledge of a selection but find it difficult to express their ideas orally and/or in writing. To obtain a better picture of that knowledge, the teacher might have a class discussion after students have completed their written retellings and compare impressions garnered from the discussion with those from the written versions.

Structured written retellings. In a structured written retelling, the teacher might ask students to read a whole selection and write answers to a series of broad questions. The questions are constructed to assess students' ability to understand major aspects of the text, such as characters, plot, and setting. The questions can also be framed to provide some insight into the strategies students are using. They are scored and analyzed by the teacher.

FIGURE 2.5

Evaluation of an Oral Retelling

Name of student: _Jamie S._

	Retelling	Comments	Summary and Recommendations
Excerpt from Ben and Me	Mouse by the name of Amos said that Ben Franklin took credit for his ideas.	Starts with overall gist of the story.	Got overall gist of story but not some of the important details.
	Mouse was oldest in family. Had to help family during one cold winter.	Comprehended Amos's motivation.	
	Found some cheese and a cap to sleep in.	Most events are in order but these are not.	
	Saw Ben Franklin. Franklin had a cold but was trying to write.		
	Amos told him that fireplace wasted a lot of heat. Told him about a stove that could be put in the middle of the room.	Failed to mention Franklin's sayings: Waste not want not. Failed to make inference that Amos claimed to be source for sayings.	Background knowledge about Ben Franklin is somewhat limited. Did not realize that Franklin was famous for his sayings.
	Franklin built the stove and told Amos how much he liked it. Called it the Franklin stove.		
	Gave Amos bread and cheese each week for the rest of his life.	Failed to mention contract drawn up between Franklin & Amos. Did not seem to realize that food was given in payment for Amos's help.	Average performance. Although Jamie got the overall gist of the story, he didn't make the connection between the proverbs and Franklin's actions. Discussing proverbs and their meanings should help. Would also help if visualized the scenes: the mouse shaking hands with Franklin after signing the contract, for instance. Might also help to discuss the humor of a mouse becoming Franklin's advisor and the impact of telling history from the point of view of a mouse.

Think-Aloud Protocols

Think-alouds are used to show readers the thought processes students use as they attempt to construct meaning. During a think-aloud, the reader explains her thought processes while reading a text. These explanations might come after each sentence, at the end of each paragraph, or at the end of the whole selection. Students'

■ **Think-alouds** are procedures in which students are asked to describe the processes they are using as they engage in reading or another cognitive activity.

thoughts might be expressed as "news bulletins or play-by-play accounts" of what students do mentally as they read (Brown & Lytle, 1988, p. 96).

■ Informal Think-Alouds

Whereas formal think-aloud procedures might be too time consuming, informal think-alouds can be incorporated into individual and small-group reading conferences and classroom activities. For example, the teacher might simply ask students to share their thoughts on a difficult passage or question or to tell what strategies they used. Think-aloud questions can include the following:

- Tell me how you figured out that hard word.
- Tell me how you got the answer to that question.
- What were you thinking about when you read that selection?
- Pretend that you are an announcer at a sports game. Tell me play by play what was going on in your mind as you read that sentence (or paragraph) (Brown & Lytle, 1988).
- What do you think will happen next in the selection? What makes you think that?
- How did you feel when you read that passage? What thoughts or pictures were going through your mind?

Think-alouds may also be expressed in writing. In their learning logs, students can note the difficulties they encountered in hard passages and describe the processes they used to comprehend the selections. In follow-up class discussions, they can compare their thought processes and strategies with those of other students (Brown & Lytle, 1988). A simple way for students to keep track of perplexing passages is to have students record comprehension problems on sticky notes and place them next to the passages.

*A*s part of an informal think-aloud, students might be asked to discuss strategies they used to read a difficult passage.

Observation

Teachers learn about students "by watching how they learn" (Y. M. Goodman, 1985, p. 9). As "kidwatchers," teachers are better able to supply the necessary support or ask the kinds of questions that help students build on their evolving knowledge.

■ Opportunities for Observations

Observations can be made any time students are involved in reading and writing. Some especially fruitful opportunities for observation include reading and writing conferences (What are the students' strengths and weaknesses in these areas? What is their level of development? How might their progress in these areas be characterized?) and sustained silent reading (Do students enjoy reading? Are they able to select appropriate materials? What kinds of materials do they like to read?). Other valuable observation opportunities include author's circle, literature circle, and sharing periods in general (Australian Ministry of Education, 1990).

Anecdotal Records

Certain kinds of highly useful information will not appear in students' written work or show up on a retelling, checklist, quiz, or end-of-book test. This information is best captured in an **anecdotal record,** which is a kind of field note or description of a significant bit of student behavior. It is an observational technique long used by both anthropologists and teachers. Good teachers constantly engage in kidwatching but seldom record their observations, trusting instead to memory. But memory can be fragile and deceptive. Bush and Huebner (1979) cautioned, "The record keeping is an absolute necessity because teachers may forget previous behaviors as new ones appear (psychological principle of recency), they may misinterpret if they jump to conclusions with insufficient data, or they may let one situation analysis overshadow numerous others" (p. 333).

> ■ An **anecdotal record** is the recording of the description of a significant incident in which the description and interpretation are kept separate.

Almost any observation that can shed light on a student's literacy endeavors is a suitable entry for an anecdotal record, including notes on strategies, miscues, interests, interactions with others, and work habits (Rhodes, 1990). The anecdotal record should be "recordings of what the child said or did—not interpretations" (Bush & Huebner, 1979, p. 355). Interpretation comes later and is based on several records and other sources of information. It is important to keep in mind that when recording observations of strategy use, the way in which strategies are used may vary according to the nature of the task—the type of story being read, its relative difficulty, and the purpose for reading it. Therefore, it would be helpful to record several observations before coming to a conclusion (Tierney, Readence, & Dishner, 1995). In going over anecdotal records, the teacher should ask what this information reveals about the student and how it can be used to plan her or his instructional program.

> ■ Teachers may resist keeping anecdotal or other written records because they believe that they will remember the important things that the student does. However, memories are fallible. They may remember only the good things or not so good things that a student does and thus fail to obtain a balanced view of the pupil.

To keep track of observations and anecdotal records, you might keep a notebook that has a separate section for each student. Or you might use a handheld computer to record observations, which then can be downloaded into a database, class management, or assessment management software, such as Learner Profile (Sunburst), which allows you to record and organize observations and other data in terms of standards or objectives.

Ratings

■ **Rating** is the process of estimating the quality of a learning process or product.

A structured and efficient way to collect data is through the use of **ratings.** Ratings generally indicate the "degree to which the child possesses a given trait or skill" (Bush & Huebner, 1979, p. 353). The three kinds of ratings are checklists, questionnaires, and interviews. Checklists can use a present–absent scale (a student has the trait or does not have it) or one that shows degrees of involvement. The present–absent scale might be used for traits for which there is no degree of possession, such as knowing one's home address and telephone number. The degree scale is appropriate for traits that vary in the extent to which they are manifested, such as joining in class discussions. Figure 2.6 shows a sample observation checklist designed to assess voluntary reading.

Questionnaires

■ A **questionnaire** is an instrument in which a subject is asked to respond to a series of questions on some topic.

A good example of a reading attitude **questionnaire** is the Elementary Reading Attitude Survey (ERAS) (McKenna & Kerr, 1990). It includes twenty items designed to measure how students feel about recreational and school reading. The questionnaire addresses such areas as how students feel when they read a book on a

---

FIGURE 2.6

Observation Checklist for Voluntary Reading

Name of student: _____   Date: _____

	Never	Seldom	Occasionally	Frequently
Reads during free time	_____	_____	_____	_____
Visits the library	_____	_____	_____	_____
Reads books on a variety of topics	_____	_____	_____	_____
Recommends books to others in the class	_____	_____	_____	_____
Talks with others about books	_____	_____	_____	_____
Checks out books from the library	_____	_____	_____	_____

rainy Saturday and how they feel about reading in school. Students respond by circling one of four illustrations of the cartoon cat Garfield, which range from a very happy to a very sad cat. Another questionnaire that might be used is the Reading Survey section of the MRP (Motivation to Read Profile), which can be found in the March 1996 issue of *The Reading Teacher.* The Survey probes two aspects of reading motivation: self-concept as a reader and value of reading.

> Thanks to the generosity of the authors and the cartoon Garfield's creator, Jim Davis, ERAS has not been copyrighted and was presented, ready to duplicate, in the May 1990 issue of *The Reading Teacher.*

Questionnaires can provide information about reading interests, study habits, strategy use, and other areas in reading and writing. They can be forced-choice like ERAS or open-ended and requiring a written response. Questionnaires assessing study habits and skills might cover such topics as how students go about studying for a test, where they study, and how much time they spend doing homework each night.

Interviews

Interviews are simply oral questionnaires. Their advantage is that the teacher can probe a student's replies, rephrase questions, and encourage extended answers and so obtain a wide range of information. An interview can focus on such topics as a student's likes and dislikes about a reading group, preferences with respect to reading materials, and reasons for these attitudes. A good example of an interview is the Conversational Interview section of the Motivation to Read Profiles (Gambrell, Codling, & Palmer, 1996). The Conversational Interview, which complements the Reading Survey, consists of a series of questions about a student's reading interests and habits and possible influences on those habits.

> ■ An **interview** is the process of asking a subject a series of questions on a topic.

One kind of interview, the process interview, provides insight about the strategies students are using and also helps students become aware of their processes

Exemplary Teaching

Ongoing Assessment

*T*o make her instruction as fruitful as possible, Pat Loden bases her instruction on ongoing assessment of students (Morrow & Asbury, 2001). Each day she focuses on two students to assess. During the day she carefully observes these students and records her observations. She keeps running records of their reading, assesses their retellings, and notes their use of reading strategies. She also has a conference with them and goes over their reading logs. In their reading logs, they record titles and authors of books read and their reading goals for the week. During whole-class activities she makes sure to direct questions to them and notes their responses. She also observes the two focus students as they work independently. She

keeps a file on each student and uses the files when planning instruction, when making decisions about placing students in guided reading groups, and before holding conferences with students. Loden also keeps records of conferences she holds during writing workshop. During the conferences she asks questions that help reveal students' thought processes as they write and the strategies they use. Emphasis throughout the assessment is to obtain a deeper understanding of where students are and what processes and strategies they are using so individual and group instructional activities can be planned to further foster their development.

USING TECHNOLOGY

The National Center for Research on Evaluation, Standards, and Student Testing provides information on assessment. **http://cresst96.cse. ucla.edu/**

National Center on Educational Outcomes provides information on assessing students who have disabilities. **http://www.coled.umn. edu/nceo/**

Self-assessment is essential because this is how students determine whether their learning goals are being met. If goals aren't being met, then students need to take corrective action. As such, self-assessment is a key element in the learning process.

(Jett-Simpson, 1990). The process interview is best conducted informally on a one-to-one basis, but if time is limited, you might ask for written responses to your questions or hold sessions with small groups. Possible process interview questions include the following, which are adapted from Jett-Simpson (1990). Only one or two of these questions should be asked at one sitting.

1. When you come to a word you don't know, what do you do?
2. How do you choose something to read?
3. Where do you read or study at home?
4. When a paragraph is confusing, what do you do?
5. How do you check your reading?
6. What do you do to help you remember what you've read?

Questionnaires, interviews, conferences, and ratings completed by students have a common weakness. Their usefulness depends on students' ability and willingness to supply accurate information. Students may give answers that they think the teacher wants to hear. Information gathered from these sources, therefore, should be verified with other data.

SELF-EVALUATION

The ultimate evaluation is, of course, self-evaluation. Students should be involved in all phases of the evaluation process and, insofar as possible, take responsibility for assessing their own work. To self-assess, students reflect on their learning, assemble portfolios of their work, list their achievements, and, with the guidance of the teacher, put together a plan for what they hope to achieve (Ahlmann 1992). Questionnaires and self-report checklists are especially useful for this. Figure 2.7 shows a self-report checklist with which students can assess their use of strategies in learning from text.

In some classes, students complete exit slips on which they talk about what they have learned that day or raise questions that they did not have time to raise in class or were reluctant to raise. Learning logs and journals might perform a similar function. As an alternative, the teacher and the class might design a form on which students tell what they learned in a certain class and list questions that they still have. In reading and writing conferences, part of the discussion should center on skills mastered and goals for the future and how those goals might be met. These conferences, of course, should be genuinely collaborative efforts so that students' input is shown to be valued.

Some teachers have students keep a record of their reading or what they have done that day. As part of the record keeping, students might assess books read and activities completed, including statements that tell how they benefited. Portfolios, which are described later in this chapter, also offer opportunities for self-assessment.

As students engage in a literacy task, they should assess their performance. After reading a selection, they might ask themselves: How well did I understand this se-

FIGURE 2.7

Student's Self-Report Checklist on Strategies for Learning from Text

	Usually	Often	Sometimes	Never
Before reading, do I				
1. Read the title, introductory paragraph, headings, and summary?	_____	_____	_____	_____
2. Look at photos, maps, charts, and graphs?	_____	_____	_____	_____
3. Think about what I know about the topic?	_____	_____	_____	_____
4. Predict what the text will be about or make up questions that the text might answer?	_____	_____	_____	_____
During reading, do I				
5. Read to answer questions that the teacher or I have made up?	_____	_____	_____	_____
6. Stop after each section and try to answer my questions?	_____	_____	_____	_____
7. Use headings, maps, charts, and graphs to help me understand the text?	_____	_____	_____	_____
8. Try to make pictures in my mind as I read?	_____	_____	_____	_____
9. Reread a sentence or get help if I don't understand what I am reading?	_____	_____	_____	_____
10. Use context or the glossary if I don't understand what I am reading?	_____	_____	_____	_____
After reading, do I				
11. Review the section to make sure that I know the most important information?	_____	_____	_____	_____
12. Try to organize the information in the text by creating a map, chart, time line, or summary?	_____	_____	_____	_____

lection? Do I need to reread or take other steps to improve my comprehension? After completing a piece of writing, they should also evaluate their performance. If a rubric has been constructed for the piece of writing, they should assess their work in terms of the rubric.

Logs and Journals

Reading logs and response journals can also be a part of students' self-evaluation as well as a source of information for the teacher. Reading logs contain a list of books read and, perhaps, a brief summary or assessment. Response journals provide students with opportunities to record personal reactions to their reading. Both reading logs and response journals offer unique insights into students' growing ability to handle increasingly difficult books, their changing interests, and personal involvement with reading.

Conferences

Just as with interviews, conferences can be an excellent source of assessment information. During writing conferences, you might ask questions such as, "What do you like best about writing? What kind of writing do you like to do? What is easy for you in writing? What is hard for you? What are some things that you might do to become an even better writer than you are now?" During reading conferences, ask, "What do you like best about reading? Do you have any favorite authors? Who are they? What is easy for you in reading? What is hard for you? What might you do to become a better reader?"

In this era of mandated, high-stakes assessment, informal measures are more important than ever. High-stakes tests can tend to narrow the curriculum and lead to teaching to the test. What's more they generally fail to yield information that is useful to teachers. Using observation, think-alouds, samples of students' work, and other informal measures can broaden the curriculum and yield useful information for teachers. As the prestigious Rand Reading Study Group notes, "the power of high-stakes assessments over instruction can be somewhat mitigated if teachers have available alternative assessment options that give them more information" (Snow, 2002, p. 55).

EVALUATING WRITING

Holistic Scoring

■ **Holistic scoring** is a process for sorting or ranking written pieces on the basis of an overall impression of the piece. Sample pieces (anchors) or a description of standards (rubric) for rating the pieces might be used as guides.

What captures the essence of a piece of writing—its style, its theme, its development, its adherence to conventions, its originality? The answer is all of these elements and more. Because of the way the parts of the piece work together, it must be viewed as a whole. In **holistic scoring,** instead of noting specific strengths and weaknesses, a teacher evaluates a composition in terms of a limited number of general criteria. The criteria are used "only as a general guide . . . in reaching a holistic judgment" (Cooper & Odell, 1977, p. 4). The teacher does not stop to check the piece to see whether it meets each of the criteria but simply forms a general impression. The teacher can score a piece according to the presence or absence of key elements. There may be a scoring guide, which can be a checklist or a rubric. (A holistic scoring guide in the form of a rubric is shown in Table 2.8.) The teacher should also use anchor pieces along with the rubric to assess compositions. Anchor pieces, which may be drawn from the work of past classes or from the compositions that are currently being assessed, are writing samples that provide examples of beginning, developing, proficient and superior pieces. The teacher decides which of the anchor pieces a student's composition most closely resembles.

■   Applying Holistic Scoring

Before scoring the pieces, the teacher should quickly read them all to get a sense of how well the class did overall. This prevents setting criteria that are too high or too low. After sorting the papers into four groups—beginning, developing, proficient and superior—the teacher rereads each work more carefully before confirming its placement. If possible, a second teacher should also evaluate the papers. This is especially important if the works are to be graded.

Analytic Scoring

Analytic scoring involves analyzing pieces and noting specific strengths and weaknesses. It requires the teacher to create a set of specific scoring criteria. Instead of overwhelming students with corrections, it is best to decide on a limited number of key features, such as those that have been emphasized for a particular writing activity. Spandel and Stiggins (1997) suggest the following six characteristics: ideas, organization, voice, word choice, sentence fluency, and conventions. Although more time consuming than holistic scoring, analytic scoring allows the teacher to make constructive suggestions about students' writing. An analytic scoring guide for a friendly letter is presented in Figure 2.8.

■ **Analytic scoring** is a type of scoring that uses a description of major features to be considered when assessing the piece.

FIGURE 2.8

Analytic Scoring Guide for a Friendly Letter

Name of student: _____   Date: _____

	Beginning	Developing	Proficient	Superior
Content				
Has a natural but interesting beginning.	_____	_____	_____	_____
Includes several topics of interest.	_____	_____	_____	_____
Develops each topic in sufficient detail.	_____	_____	_____	_____
Shows an interest in what's happening to the reader.	_____	_____	_____	_____
Has a friendly way of ending the letter.	_____	_____	_____	_____
Style				
Has a friendly, natural tone.	_____	_____	_____	_____
Form				
Follows friendly letter form.	_____	_____	_____	_____
Indents paragraphs.	_____	_____	_____	_____
Is neat and legible.	_____	_____	_____	_____
Mechanics				
Begins each sentence with a capital.	_____	_____	_____	_____
Uses correct end punctuation.	_____	_____	_____	_____
Spells words correctly.	_____	_____	_____	_____

When reviewing students' papers, there is a tendency to note all errors. However, students do their best when comments are positive and when there is emphasis on one or two areas, such as providing more detail or use of more vivid language. This is especially effective when instruction is geared to the areas highlighted and students revise targeted areas in their compositions (Dahl & Farnan, 1998).

Using a Combination of Techniques

In some cases, a combination of holistic and analytic scoring works best. Holistic scoring guards against the teacher's becoming overly caught up in mechanics or stylistics and neglecting the substance of the piece. Analytic scoring provides students with necessary direction for improving their work and becoming more proficient writers. Whichever approach is used, it is important that criteria for assessment be clearly understood. As Dahl and Farnan (1998) note, "When writers lack specific standards and intentions, their ability to reflect on and evaluate their writing is severely compromised. It is not surprising that if writers do not know what they want to accomplish with a particular writing, it will be difficult for them to judge whether they have created an effective composition" (p. 121).

PORTFOLIOS

■ A **portfolio** is a collection of work samples, test results, checklists, or other data used to assess a student's performance.

Artists, photographers, designers, and others assemble their work in **portfolios** for assessment. Portfolios are now being used in a somewhat modified fashion to assess the literacy growth of elementary and middle school students. Portfolios have a number of advantages. First, they facilitate the assessment of growth over time. Because they provide the teacher with an opportunity to take a broad look at a student's literacy development, they are an appropriate method for assessing holistic approaches. Portfolio assessment can also lead to changes in the curriculum and teaching practices. In Au's (1994) study, for instance, teachers began emphasizing the revision phase of writing when portfolio assessment helped them see that they were neglecting that area. Teachers in Kentucky reported that portfolios were the key element in a program designed to improve writing (Stecher, Barron, Kaganoff, & Goodwin, 1998).

Types of Portfolios

There are five kinds of portfolios, each performing different functions and containing different kinds of materials: showcase, evaluation, documentation, process, and composite (Valencia & Place, 1994). Like the traditional portfolio used by artists to display their best works, the showcase is composed of works that students have selected as being their best. The focus in the evaluation portfolio is on obtaining representative works from key areas. The samples included might be standardized—that is, based on a common text or a common topic—so that results are comparable across students. A documentation portfolio is designed to provide evidence of students' growth and so might contain the greatest number and variety of work samples. The process portfolio is designed to show how students work, so it includes samples from various stages of a project along with students' comments about how the project is progressing. A composite portfolio contains elements from two or more types of portfolios. For instance, a portfolio designed for district evaluation might contain showcase and process items.

Writing Samples

Collecting representative pieces from several types of writing assignments gives the teacher a broad view of a student's development. Including pieces written at different times of the year allows the teacher to trace the student's growth. Rough drafts as well as final copies illustrate the student's writing progress and indicate how well the student handles the various processes. Each student might include in her or his portfolio lists of pieces written, major writing skills learned, and current goals. Both student and teacher should have access to the portfolio and should agree on which pieces should be included. Teacher and student should also agree on how to choose what goes into the portfolio.

To help students reflect on their learning and make wise choices about the included pieces, you might have them explain their choices by completing a self-evaluative statement. The statement can be a brief explanation with the heading "Why I Chose This Piece." Initially, reasons for inclusion and comments tend to be vague (Tierney, Carter, & Desai, 1991). However, through classroom discussions and conferences, you should help students explore criteria for including certain pieces rather than others—it tells a good story, it has a beginning that grabs the reader, it has many interesting examples, it seems to flow, and so on.

Reading Samples

Some teachers use portfolios primarily to assess writing. If you wish to use portfolios to assess reading, include samples of reading. Samples to be included depend on the goals of the program. Valencia (1990) cautioned, "If the goals of instruction are not specified, portfolios have the potential to become reinforced holding files for odds and ends . . . " (p. 339). If a goal of reading instruction is to teach students to visualize, drawings of reading selections might be included. If you have been working on summaries, you may want to see sample summaries. A list of books read might be appropriate for a goal of wide reading. Running records or informal reading inventories might be included to demonstrate fluency, word recognition in context, comprehension, or overall reading development.

At certain points, reading and writing will converge—written summaries of selections and research reports using several sources might count toward both reading and writing goals. Other items that might be placed in the portfolio are checklists, quizzes, standardized and informal test results, learning logs, written reactions to selections, and graphic organizers.

You also need to decide how you will rate the portfolios and whether your assessment of the portfolios will be used as a grade. If they are used as a grade, how will you decide what kind of portfolio constitutes an A, a B, a C, and so on? A rubric might be used for this purpose.

Reviewing Portfolios

To check on students' progress, periodically review their portfolios. Farr and Farr (1990) suggested that this be done a minimum of four times a year. In order

A portfolio can demonstrate the power of a reader and a writer. Unbeknownst to the teacher, a student may read dozens or hundreds of books or be a budding author. A reading log or sampling of written pieces should reveal this (Tierney, Carter, & Desai, 1991).

Portfolios have the potential for demonstrating students' growth. As you assess folders, note the areas in which students have done especially well. Also note areas of weakness. In addition, portfolios provide information that shows class as well as individual needs. If the class as a whole is evidencing difficulty with the mechanics of writing, that might be an area in your curriculum that needs special attention.

Giving students a say in portfolio decisions helps them maintain a sense of ownership (Simmons, 1990). It also fosters a more positive attitude and encourages students to take risks in their writing (Johnson, 1995).

Portfolios are most useful when goals are clearly stated and specific criteria are listed for their assessment. It is essential, of course, that goals and criteria be understood by students (Snider, Lima, & DeVito, 1994).

to make the best use of your time and to help students organize their work, you might have them prepare a list of the items included in the portfolio. The portfolio should also contain a list of students' learning objectives. Students might write a cover letter or fill out a form summarizing work they have done, explaining which goals they feel they have met, which areas might need improvement, and what their plans for the future are. A sample portfolio evaluation form is presented in Figure 2.9.

Before you start to review a portfolio, decide what you want to focus on. It could be number of books read, changes in writing, or effort put into revisions. Your evaluation should, of course, consider the student's stated goals; it is also important to emphasize the student's strengths. As you assess the portfolio, consider a variety of pieces and look at the work in terms of its changes over time. Ask yourself: What does the student's work show about her or his progress over the time span covered? What might she or he do to make continued progress?

To save time and help you organize your assessment of the portfolio, you may want to use a checklist that is supplemented with personal comments. A sample port-

FIGURE 2.9

Portfolio Evaluation by Student

Name: _____   Date: _____

Portfolio Evaluation

What were my goals in reading for this period?

What progress toward meeting these goals does my portfolio show?

What are my strengths?

What are my weaknesses?

What are my goals for improving as a reader?

How do I plan to meet those goals?

What were my goals in writing for this period?

What progress toward meeting these goals does my portfolio show?

What are my strengths as a writer?

What are my weaknesses?

What are my goals for improving as a writer?

How do I plan to meet these goals?

What questions do I have about my writing or my reading?

folio review checklist is presented in Figure 2.10. Because the objective of evaluation is to improve instruction, students should be active partners in the process. "It follows that . . . assessment activities in which students are engaged in evaluating their own learning help them reflect on and understand their own strengths and needs, and it instills responsibility for their own learning" (Tierney, Carter, & Desai, 1991, p. 7).

Portfolios can be passed on from grade to grade and can even be used as part of a districtwide assessment system. Teachers in Orange County, Florida, place both

INVOLVING PARENTS

Parents may feel uncomfortable or even threatened by portfolios. When portfolios are explained, parents prefer them to standardized tests (Tierney, Carter, & Desai, 1991). Tierney, Carter, and Desai (1991) suggested sitting down with parents and explaining the portfolio process to them. This not only helps parents understand the process, it also helps them to see what their role might be.

FIGURE 2.10

Portfolio Review Checklist

Name of student: _____   Date: _____

Voluntary Reading
  Number of books read   _____
  Variety of books read   _____
  Strengths   _____
  Needs   _____

Reading Comprehension
  Construction of meaning   _____
  Extension of meaning   _____
  Use of strategies   _____
  Quality of responses   _____
  Strengths   _____
  Needs   _____

Writing
  Amount of writing   _____
  Variety of writing   _____
  Planning   _____
  Revising   _____
  Self-editing   _____
  Content   _____
  Organization   _____
  Style   _____
  Mechanics   _____
  Strengths   _____
  Needs   _____

Comments: _____
_____
_____

*T*eachers periodically review students' portfolios with them.

■ In Kentucky, teachers reported that the portfolio system was the most influential factor in determining their instructional practices (Stecher, Barron, Kaganoff, & Goodwin, 1998). They also credited the portfolio system with helping them to become better teachers and their students better writers.

core and supplementary items in students' portfolios. Core items provide consistency and feature (1) a reading development checklist that includes questions about the students' comprehension, word-recognition strategies, and attitudes toward reading; (2) writing samples, including rough drafts; (3) a list of books that students have read; and (4) a test of reading comprehension. The reading development checklist and list of books read could be added to each year, as both are indicators of students' continuous progress. The checklist highlights mastery of strategies; the book list provides insight into students' changing interests and indicates what kinds of materials they are able to handle. Optional elements include students' self-assessments, pages from learning logs or response journals, teacher notes from reading or writing conferences, or "other measures a teacher or student felt would illustrate the growth of the student as a language learner" (Matthews, 1990, p. 421). Ultimately, all sources of information should be integrated to obtain the fullest possible picture of the student, group, and program.

BASAL READER ASSESSMENT

Today's basal readers and literature anthologies offer a variety of assessment devices. Tests that accompany each selection or skills checks contained in workbooks can be used as part of a paper-and-pencil formative assessment. There are also numerous suggestions for ongoing, informal assessment through observation or use of checklists. In some instances, these suggestions are accompanied by corrective techniques: For instance, if students have difficulty making inferences, the teacher is provided with a reteaching lesson (Cooper, et al., 2001). There are also numerous suggestions for self-assessment by students: "What parts of the selection were difficult for me? Why?" (Cooper, et al., 2001). End-of-theme tests are also available, as are benchmark tests designed to be given quarterly. Portfolio systems are also part of the assessment package. One program also includes weekly lessons on test-taking skills (Flood, et al., 2001).

ASSESSING ENGLISH LANGUAGE LEARNERS

Under No Child Left Behind legislation, the academic progress of every child in grades three through eight will be tested in reading and math, including those learning English. All English language learners (ELLs) will be tested annually to measure how well they are learning English. States and individual schools will be held accountable for results.

Apart from state and federal regulations, it is essential that you have information about ELLs' proficiency in their first language. Students who can read in another language will have learned basic concepts of reading. They will have acquired knowledge of basic phonics and comprehension strategies. You can build on this knowledge. It is also essential you have information about the students' proficiency in oral and written English. If students are weak in understanding English, you can plan a literacy program that develops oral language.

Key questions include the following:

- What is the student's proficiency in speaking her or his first language?
- What is the student's proficiency in speaking English?
- What is the student's proficiency in reading in the first language?
- What is the student's proficiency in reading in English?
- What is the educational background of the student?

The ESL or bilingual specialist should be able to provide information about the students' proficiency in their first language and also their knowledge of English. If this information is not available, use informal techniques to assess the students' proficiency in reading and writing their first language. Ask students to bring in books in their native tongue, read them to you, and then retell the selection in English. Also ask them to bring in a piece of writing that they have done in their native language, read it to you, and then retell it in English. Based on the ease with which they read and the level of their writing, you can judge whether they are literate in their first language, even if you don't know the language.

> **ADAPTING INSTRUCTION for *ENGLISH LANGUAGE LEARNERS***
> English-only assessments underestimate students' ability until they have been exposed to English for at least five years (Cummins, 2001).

ASSESSING MATERIALS

Just about the most important instructional decision you will make is selecting the appropriate level of materials for your students. Choose a level that is too easy and students will be bored and unchallenged. Select material that is too difficult and they will be discouraged, have their academic self-concepts demolished, and fail to make progress. Perhaps, worst of all, they will learn to hate reading (Juel, 1994). As noted earlier, students should know at least 95 percent of the words in the materials they are asked to read and should have about 75 percent comprehension.

Publishers of school materials generally provide reading levels for their texts. Using a formula or subjective leveling scale, they estimate that the material is at, for example, a fifth- or eighth-grade level, which means that the average fifth- or eighth-grader should be able to read it. Some publishers of children's books also sup-

■ **Readability** is the difficulty level of a selection. A formula may be used to estimate readability by measuring quantitative factors such as sentence length and number of difficult words in the selection. A leveling system may use a number of qualitative factors to estimate the difficulty of the text. Best results are obtained by assessing both qualitative and quantitative factors.

ply **readability** levels. If no readability level is indicated for a book that you wish to use, you might check Appendix A, which contains more than 800 leveled titles, or you can consult one of the following sources.

ATOS (Advantage-TASA Open Standard)

ATOS is a new computerized formula that uses number of words per sentence, characters per word, and average grade level of words and analyzes the entire text to estimate the readability of a book and provide a grade-level equivalent. ATOS scores for more than 40,000 trade books are available from Renaissance Learning, the creators of Accelerated Reading, at their Web site: http://www.renlearn.com. Click on Quizzes and enter the title of the book for which you would like to have an ATOS score. ATOS scores are expressed in grade equivalents. If the text for which you want a readability estimate is not available, contact Renaissance Learning. They may have the ATOS score. If you provide sample passages for the book, the company will provide an ATOS score for you.

Lexile Scale

The lexile scale is a two-factor computerized formula that consists of a measurement of sentence length and word frequency. The lexile scale ranges from about 70 to 1700+, with 70 being very easy beginning reading material and 1700 being very difficult reading material of the type found in scientific journals. Table 2.7 provides approximate grade equivalents for lexile scores. A software program for obtaining readability estimates, the *Lexile Analyzer*, is available from MetaMetrics. However, lexile scores for about 25,000 books are available on line at http://www. lexile.com/.

Degrees of Reading Power

Because it uses a fill-in-the-blank format, the DRP distorts the reading process somewhat.

The Degrees of Reading Power measures sentence length, number of words not on the Dale List of words known by fourth-graders, and average number of letters per word (Touchstone Applied Science Associates, 1994). Compilations of readability levels expressed in DRP units for content area textbooks can be found on the following Web site: http://www.tasaliteracy.com. DRP readabilities for trade books are available on a piece of easy-to-use software, *BookLink*. DRP units range from 15 for the easiest materials to 85 for the most difficult reading material. Table 2.7 provides approximate grade equivalents for DRP scores.

Other Readability Formulas

If you are unable to get a readability level from one of these sources, or if you prefer to assess the readability of the text yourself, there are a number of formulas you can apply. One of the easiest to use is the Fry Graph. The Fry Graph bases its estimate on two factors: sentence length and number of syllables in a word. Number of syllables in a word is a measure of vocabulary difficulty. In general, the more syllables a word has, the harder it tends to be. The Fry Readability Graph (Fry, 1977b) is presented in Figure 2.11. A formula that counts the number of hard words but is

FIGURE 2.11

Fry Graph for Estimating Readability

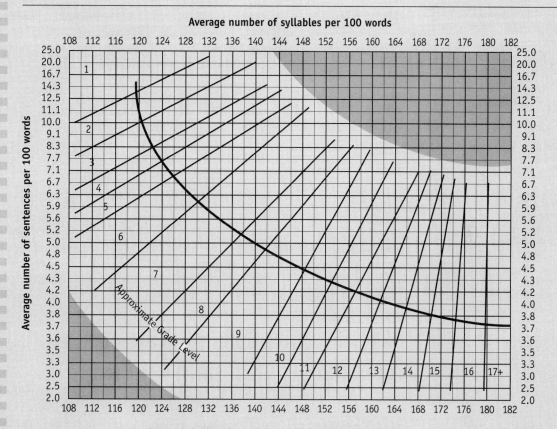

Average number of syllables per 100 words

Expanded Directions for Working Readability Graph

1. Randomly select three (3) sample passages and count out exactly 100 words each, beginning with the beginning of a sentence. Do count proper nouns, initializations, and numerals.

2. Count the number of sentences in the 100 words, estimating length of the fraction of the last sentence to the nearest one-tenth.

3. Count the total number of syllables in the 100-word passage. If you don't have a hand counter available, an easy way is to simply put a mark above every syllable over one in each word, then when you get to the end of the passage, count the number of marks and add 100. Small calculators can also be used by pushing numeral 1, then the + sign for each word or syllable when counting.

4. Enter graph with *average* sentence length and *average* number of syllables; plot dot where the two lines intersect. Area where dot is plotted will give you the approximate grade level.

5. If a great deal of variability is found in syllable count or sentence count, putting more samples into the average is desirable.

6. A word is defined as a group of symbols with space on either side; thus, *Joe, IRA, 1945,* and *&* are each one word.

7. A syllable is defined as a phonetic syllable. Generally, there are as many syllables as vowel sounds. For example, *stopped* is one syllable and *wanted* is two syllables. When counting syllables for numerals and initializations, count one syllable for each symbol. For example, *1945* is four syllables, *IRA* is three syllables, and *&* is one syllable.

Fry's Readability Graph: Clarifications, Validity, and Extension to Level 17 by E. Fry, 1977, *Journal of Reading, 21,* p. 249.

relatively easy to use is the Primary Readability Formula, which can be used to assess the difficulty level of materials in grades one to four and is found in *Assessing and Correcting Reading and Writing Difficulties*, 2nd ed. (Gunning, 2002). *The New Dale-Chall Readability Formula* (Chall & Dale, 1995), which also counts the number of hard words, is recommended for grades three and up.

One problem with readability formulas is that they are mechanical and so do not consider subjective factors, such as the density of concepts, use of illustrations, or background required to construct meaning from the text. Readability formulas should be complemented by the use of the subjective factors incorporated in a leveling system (Gunning, 2000b). A leveling system uses subjective or qualitative factors to estimate the difficulty level of materials.

Leveling Systems

Leveling systems consider subjective factors and can be used along with or instead of formulas. The most widely used leveling system is one adapted by Fountas and Pinnell (1996) and Pinnell and Fountas (1999, 2002). They have compiled a list of almost 14,000 leveled books for students in kindergarten through grade eight. Books are leveled from A through Z, with A being very beginning reading and Z being eighth-grade reading. Books in Appendix A have been leveled according to both quantitative as well as qualitative factors.

However, you may wish to use books that have not been leveled, or you may not have access to a listing of leveled books. In that case, you need to be able to level books on your own. To level books, consider key subjective factors and compare passages from the book you are leveling to passages from benchmark books. *The Qualitative Assessment of Text Difficulty* (Chall, Bissex, Conard, & Harris-Sharples, 1996) provides benchmark passages and directions for leveling both fictional and informational books. Or you might use the Basic Leveling Index, which is explained below.

■ The Basic Leveling Index

The Basic Leveling Index uses both quantitative and qualitative factors to level books. Subjected to extensive tryouts, it has been used to level several thousand books and compares favorably with other leveling systems (Gunning, 1998b, 2000b). Tryouts suggest that it is more accurate than readability formulas or subjective leveling systems used alone.

Using the basic leveling system with beginning reading books. Beginning reading books are more difficult to level than are upper grade books because they encompass a very wide range of difficulty. Beginning books range from those that have just an illustrated word or sentence or a page to those that are composed of brief chapters. However, there are very few trade books on a first-grade level that are appropriate for older students. In fact, a computer search of 50,000 books turned up just one. *Water Dance* (Locker, 2002) is the only book for middle grade students listed as being on a first-grade level. Fortunately, a number of educational publishers have created books for older students reading on a beginning reader level. For a listing, see Chapter 11. The benchmark book, *The Tug* (Sims, 1999), is drawn from a reading series for older struggling readers and is on a mid-first-grade level.

    Leveling books works best when those leveling the books are carefully trained. Otherwise, it is prone to error. To get a more reliable and more accurate estimate, use a quantitative measure along with the qualitative ones.

    If possible, use the Fry Graph, one of the other formulas mentioned, or obtain a readability score from one of the sources mentioned earlier in the chapter. Use the objective readability as an estimate. Compare 100-word passages from the book you are assessing with the benchmark books or passages. Find the passage that is most like the one you are assessing. Pay particular attention to difficulty level of vocabulary, complexity of ideas, and sentence complexity. Be conservative. If undecided between the fourth- and fifth-grade levels, go with the more difficult level. It does not hurt students to read a book that is on the easy side; it can be very frustrating for them to cope with a book that is too hard. If the book is very brief and has 100 words or fewer, assess the entire book. If the book is longer, assess three sample passages chosen from near the beginning, middle, and end of the book, but avoid using the first page as a sample. Average the three readability levels that you obtain. Also consider the qualitative factors listed in Figure 2.12. In the light of the comparison with the benchmark passages and qualitative factors, you might decide that the objective readability estimate is accurate or you might move it up or down a level.

FIGURE 2.12

Estimating Difficulty of Materials

Objective level (estimate yielded by formula) _____

Background required to read text	familiar	limited amount	considerable
Difficulty and density of concepts	easy	average	challenging
Difficulty of vocabulary	easy	average	challenging
Complexity of language	easy	average	challenging
Degree of interest of content	high	average	low
Use of graphics and other aids	high	average	low

When compared with benchmark passages or books, what level(s) do the sample passages from the text seem to be most like?

Passage 1 _____
Passage 2 _____
Passage 3 _____
Average   _____

Estimated difficulty level of text (objective and subjective factors) _____

Listed on the next few pages are descriptions of levels and benchmark passages. The Primary Readability Formula (Gunning, 2002), the *New Dale-Chall Readability Formula* (Chall & Dale, 1995), and qualitative factors were used to estimate readability. Words not on the high-frequency word list from the Primary Readability Formula are boldfaced for passages on a first- and second-grade readability level. Words not on the Dale list of words known by fourth-graders are boldfaced for passages on grade three and above.

■ Grade 1

To read beginning first-grade level books, students would need to know high-frequency words and some short-vowels patterns. Middle first-grade level would require an expanded knowledge of high-frequency words and knowledge of all short-vowel patterns. End-of-first-grade books would require knowledge of all types of single-syllable words and a few easy multisyllabic words. The benchmark passage is on a mid-first-grade level.

Benchmark passage: The Tug by Matt Sims

Bob put on his cap and got in his **van.** He went to the **dock** in his van. When he got to the dock, he saw that Sam was in the van.

"Sam, I did not let you in the van," said Bob. "I have to go to my job on the **tug.** You will have to go to the tug with me."

Bob saw Gus. Gus was his boss on the tug. "Gus, Sam is with me. Can he go on the tug?" said Bob.

"No, he can not go on the tug," said Gus. "I do not like dogs." (pp. 2-5)

■ Grade 2

There are nearly 200 books for older students reading on a second-grade level. However, most of these are series books. At this level, books are usually divided into short chapters. Readers would need a grasp of basic vowel patterns. Texts have a number of multisyllabic words.

Benchmark books:
Amazing Rescues by George Shea
Sitting Bull by Lucille Recht Penner
Shoeshine Girl by Clyde Bulla

Benchmark passage: Shoeshine Girl by Clyde Bulla

On **Monday** morning Sarah Ida packed her things, and Aunt Claudia took her to the **station.** Rossi came along in the **taxi.** "You'll be riding all day," she said. "I made you some cupcakes so you won't get **hungry.**"

They waited for the train. All at once, Sarah Ida looked up and Al was there!

"Why aren't you at the stand?" she asked. "You'll miss a lot of **customers.**"

He looked a little **embarrassed.** "I just thought I'd take a few minutes to see you off."

The train came in.

Aunt Claudia and Rossi said good-by. Al said, "You get on, and I'll help you with your things." (Bulla, 1975, p. 82)

■ **Grade 3**

Sentence length continues to increase, as does the number of mutlisyllabic words.

Benchmark books:
Man from the Sky by Avi
Blubber by Judy Blume
Courage of Sarah Noble by Alice Dalgliesh

Benchmark passage: *Courage of Sarah Noble* by Alice Dalgliesh

Now they had come to the last day of the journey. The Indian trail had been narrow, the hills went up and down. **Sarah** and her father were tired, and even **Thomas** walked **wearily.**

By late afternoon they would be going home. Home? No, it wasn't really home, just a place out in the **wilderness.** But after a while it would be home. **John Noble** told Sarah it would be. His voice kept leading her on.
"Now we must be about two miles away."
"Now it is surely a mile . . . only a mile."

■ **Grade 4**

Sentences are somewhat longer. Vocabulary is somewhat more advanced and includes words such as *glistened, delicate,* and *veil,* which might not be in some fourth-graders' listening vocabulary. Greater use of figurative language.

Benchmark books:
Help I'm a Prisoner in the Library by Eth Clifford
Little House in the Big Woods by Laura Ingalls Wilder
Charlotte's Web by E. B. White

Benchmark passage: *Charlotte's Web* by E. B. White

The next day was foggy. Everything on the farm was dripping wet. The grass looked like a magic carpet. The **asparagus** patch looked like a silver forest.

On foggy mornings, **Charlotte's** web was truly a thing of beauty. This morning each thin **strand** was **decorated** with dozens of tiny beads of water. The web **glistened** in the light and made a pattern of **loveliness** and mystery, like a **delicate veil. Lurvy,** who wasn't **particularly** interested in beauty, noticed the web when he came with the pig's breakfast. He noted how clearly it showed up and he noted how big and carefully built it was. And then he took another look and saw something that made him set his pail down. There, in the center of the web, neatly **woven** in block letters, was a message.

■ **Grade 5**

Vocabulary becomes more advanced, with the use of a greater number of words that may not be in readers' listening vocabularies. Introduces experiences that readers may not be familiar with.

Benchmark books:
Great Brain by John D. Fitzgerald
My Side of the Mountain by Jean C. George
Fear Place by Phyllis Naylor

Benchmark passage: Fear Place by Phyllis Naylor

Doug didn't know why he felt a **vague** sense of **discomfort,** like some **unpleasant** memory tapping at the side of his head. No, he thought **fiercely.** He was doing too well. No unpleasant thoughts now, thank you.

The **muscles** in Doug's legs carried him easily with each **stride.** He forced himself to think **positively, concentrating** on his **strength.** He didn't even bother to rest at the next place the ground leveled out, but moved on around the curve of the mountain, inching down steep, rocky **troughs chiseled** out by water, then making his way through a long **maze** of rocky outcrops.

■ Grade 6

Sentences are longer and more complex. Vocabulary is definitely more advanced. Concepts are becoming more abstract and density of concepts has increased. Selections require increased ability to comprehend complex characters and situations.

Benchmark books:
Caddie Woodlawn by Carol Ryrie Brink
Phantom Toll Booth by Norton Juster
Wolves of Willoughby Chase by Joan Aiken

Benchmark passage: *Wolves of Willoughby Chase* by Joan Aiken

Sylvia was an **orphan,** both her parents having been carried off by a fever when she was only an **infant.** She lived with her Aunt **Jane,** who was now becoming very aged and **frail** and had written to Sir **Willoughby** to **suggest** that he take on the care of the little girl. He had agreed at once to this **proposal,** for Sylvia, he knew, was **delicate,** and the country air would do her good. Besides, he welcomed the idea of her gentle **companionship** for his rather **harum scarum Bonnie.** Aunt Jane and Sylvia shared a room at the top of a house.

■ Grade 7

Sentences are longer and more complex. Greater proportion of advanced vocabulary. Plots are more complicated. Selections require increased ability to comprehend complex characters and situations.

Benchmark books:
Alice in Wonderland by Lewis Carroll
Jungle Book by Rudyard Kipling
Incredible Journey by Sheila Burnford

Benchmark passage: Incredible Journey by Sheila Burnford

This journey took place in a part of **Canada** which lies in the northwestern part of the great **sprawling province** of **Ontario.** It is a **vast** area of **deeply** wooded **wilderness**—of endless chains of lonely lakes and rushing rivers. Thousands of miles of country roads, rough timber lanes and **unmapped** trails snake across its length and **breadth.** It is a country of **far-flung,** lonely farms and a few widely scattered small towns and villages, of lonely **trappers' shacks** and logging camps. Most of its industry comes from the great **pulp** and paper companies who work their timber **concessions** deep in the very heart of the forests; and from the mines, for it is rich in **minerals.**

■ **Grade 8**

Language is becoming increasingly literary and includes an increased number of difficult words.

Benchmark books:
The Hobbit by J. R. R. Tolkien
Planet of Junior Brown by Virginia Hamilton
Treasure Island by Robert L. Stevenson

Benchmark passage: *Treasure Island* by Robert Loius Stevenson

The red glare of the **torch,** lighting up the **interior** of the blockhouse, showed me the worst of my **apprehensions realized.** The **pirates** were in **possession** of the house and stores; there was the **cask** of **cognac,** there were the

ACTION PLAN

1. Become a acquainted with national, state, and local standards and expectations.
2. Set standards or goals for your program. Translate goals or standards into measurable objectives.
3. Align materials and instructional activities with your objectives.
4. Align assessment with objectives and instruction. For each objective, you need formal and/or informal assessment devices so that you can tell whether objectives are being achieved.
5. Begin assessment by finding out where students are and what their strengths and needs are. This can be done with an IRI, or other devices.
6. Screen students for specials needs. Students identified as being struggling should be given diagnostic tests that can be used to plan intervention programs.
7. Monitor students' progress on an ongoing basis. Maintain a portfolio of students' work. On a quarterly basis, assess students in more depth. Involve students in the assessment process. Guide them so they can self-assess. Involve them in the setting of standards and creation of rubrics. Make adjustments in the program as required.
8. At year's end, administer an outcomes measure. This could be another form of the IRI or other measures that you administered at the beginning of the year. As part of your assessment, use information yielded by district-required or state or national tests.
9. Do not overtest. Don't give a test if it is not going to provide useful information or if you are not going to use the information. Make sure that students are tested on the appropriate level.
10. Make sure that there is a match between students' reading levels and the materials that they read. Obtain readability information from appropriate sources and put a leveling system into place. Make sure that in determining difficulty levels that you use subjective judgment as well as objective data.

pork and bread, as before; and, what tenfold **increased** my **horror,** not a sign of any **prisoner.** I could only judge that all had **perished,** and my heart **smote** me sorely that I had not been there to **perish** with them. There were six of the **buccaneers,** all told; not another man was left alive. Five of them were on their feet. . . .

Verifying Readability Levels

The true measure of the difficulty level of a book is the proficiency with which students can read it. Note how well students are able to read books that have been leveled. Based on your observation of students' performance, be prepared to change the estimated difficulty level.

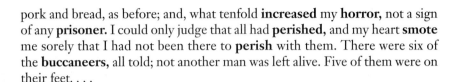

SUMMARY

1. Evaluation entails making a subjective judgment about the quality of students' work or the effectiveness of a program or some component of it. It is based on data from tests, work samples, and observations. An evaluation is made in terms of goals and objectives and should result in some sort of action to improve deficiencies that are noted or to build on strengths.

2. The standards movement is an attempt to improve the quality of education by setting high but clear standards for all. If assessment and instruction are aligned with the standards, education should be more effective. A controversial component of the standards movement is high-stakes testing. Although testing can highlight needs and result in more resources being allocated to struggling readers, there is concern that high-stakes testing may result in a narrowing of the curriculum by encouraging teaching to the test and spending too much time on test preparation.

3. Placement information is necessary to indicate where the student is on the road to literacy. The informal reading inventory is one of the best sources of such information. It taps word recognition and comprehension and yields information about language development and thought processes. It also yields information on four reading levels: independent, instructional, frustration, and listening capacity.

4. In norm-referenced tests, students are compared to a representative sample of students who are the same age or in the same grade. Scores are reported in a variety of ways: raw scores, percentile ranks, grade equivalent scores, stanines, normal curve equivalents, and scaled scores.

5. In criterion-referenced tests, students' performance is assessed in terms of a criterion or standard. Because they indicate whether students have mastered a particular skill or strategy, these tests tend to be more valuable than norm-referenced tests for planning programs. Because neither norm-referenced nor criterion-referenced tests are adequate for today's balanced instruction and student-centered assessment in reading and writing, there has been a strong push for authentic assessment. In authentic assessment, students read whole texts and construct responses. Portfolios and observation are widely used components of authentic assessment.

6. Benchmarks and rubrics offer ways of holistically indicating performance. The benchmark is a written description of a key task that students would be expected to perform. Rubrics provide descriptions of expected or desirable performances as well as unsatisfactory ones.

7. Students should be given tests designed for the level on which they are reading. Tests that are too easy or too hard are invalid and yield erroneous information.

8. Assessment is beginning to catch up with evolving theories of reading and writing instruction. Oral and written retellings, think-alouds, obser-

vations, anecdotal records, questionnaires, interviews, and ratings are growing in popularity.

9. Holistic evaluation of writing is based on the premise that, to capture the essence of a piece, it is necessary to consider it as a whole and assess it by forming an overall impression. However, analytic assessment of key elements of the piece provides information that the teacher can use to make specific suggestions to the writer.

10. Portfolios provide a means of assembling a broad range of assessment data. They can include work samples, a list of books read, results of observations, test scores, and other information.

11. A number of objective readability formulas and several subjective leveling systems are used to estimate the difficulty level of texts. Because formulas neglect such factors as background needed to read a text and leveling systems rely on subjective judgment, it is strongly recommended that both objective and subjective factors be used when estimating the readability of books.

EXTENDING AND APPLYING

1. Examine the assessment devices in a basal or literature anthology. Evaluate their content validity and format. Note whether all major areas of reading have been covered, whether guessing is a factor, and whether the devices have been tested and give information on validity and reliability.

2. Create a portfolio system for evaluation. Decide what kinds of items might be included in the portfolio. Also devise a checklist or summary sheet that can be used to keep track of and summarize the items.

3. Find out what the standards are for your state, how they are assessed, and how test results are used. Check the American Federation of Teachers Web site to find out how your state's standards are rated at: http://www.aft.org/edissues/standards/. Explain how you would implement the standards for the grade that you teach or plan to teach.

4. Administer an informal reading inventory or running record to at least one student. Based on the results of the assessment, draw up a list of the student's apparent strengths and needs.

DEVELOPING A PROFESSIONAL PORTFOLIO

Place in your portfolio any checklists, rubrics, or other similar assessment devices that you have devised and used. Reflect on the effectiveness of these devices.

DEVELOPING A RESOURCE FILE

Keep a file of observation guides, checklists, sample tests, think-aloud protocols, questionnaires, sample tests, rubrics, and other assessment devices that might be useful. For a wealth of information about literacy assessments, go to the Southwest Educational Development Laboratory Web site at: http://www.sedl.org/reading/rad.

3

Teaching Phonics, High-Frequency Words, and Syllabic Analysis

*F*or each of the following statements, put a check under "Agree" or "Disagree" to show how you feel. Discuss your responses with classmates before you read the chapter.

	Agree	*Disagree*
1 If students in grade four and beyond are still weak in phonics, they should be given a highly structured phonics program.	_____	_____
2 Phonics rules have so many exceptions that they are not worth teaching.	_____	_____
3 Phonics is hard to learn because English is so irregular.	_____	_____
4 The natural way to decode a word is sound by sound or letter by letter.	_____	_____
5 Memorizing is an inefficient way to learn new words.	_____	_____
6 Syllabication is not a very useful skill because you have to know how to decode a word before you can put it into syllables.	_____	_____

USING WHAT YOU KNOW

*B*y the time they reach fourth grade, most students have mastered basic phonics. However, there will be some students whose knowledge of phonics is inadequate. As a middle grade or middle school teacher, it would be helpful for you to have some basic knowledge of phonics and also know some techniques that you might use to help these students. Some students will have mastered basic phonics but will have difficulty applying these skills to multisyllabic words. They will be able to read words such as *car*, *pen*, and *her*, but will stumble over the word *carpenter*, even though it is made up of familiar word parts. And they will have difficulty with words such as *future* and *nation*, which contain word parts such as *–ture* and *–tion*, which only occur in multisyllabic words. These students need instruction in syllabic analysis. Even achieving readers may need some instruction with advanced multisyllabic patterns.

Some readers can decode all the words, but their decoding is slow and labored. They may spend so much mental energy decoding words that comprehension suffers. They need activities that help their word recognition to become automatic and their reading to become fluent.

This chapter will be more meaningful if you first reflect on what you already know about phonics, syllabic analysis, and fluency. Think about how you use phonics and syllabic analysis to sound out strange names and other unfamiliar words. Think about how you might teach phonics and syllabic analysis, and ask yourself what role phonics and syllabic analysis should play in a reading program.

PHONICS ELEMENTS

■ **Phonics** is the study of speech sounds related to reading.

Before discussing how to teach **phonics,** it is important to know the content of phonics. Knowing the content, you are in a better position to decide how to teach phonics elements and in what order these elements might be taught.

The content of phonics is fairly substantial. Depending on the dialect, English has forty or more sounds; however, many of them, especially vowels, may be spelled in more than one way. As a result, students have to learn more than one hundred spellings. The number would be even greater if relatively infrequent spellings were included, such as the *eigh* spelling of /ā/ in *neighbor* or the *o* spelling of /i/ in *women.*

▌When infrequent spellings are included, there are more than 300 spellings of the forty-plus sounds of English. Many of these infrequent spellings occur in words borrowed from other languages, as in the long *a* spelling of *exposé* and *beret.*

*T*he purpose of learning phonics is to enable students to decode words that are in their listening vocabularies but that they fail to recognize in print.

Consonants

There are twenty-five consonant sounds in English (see Table 3.1). Some of the sounds are spelled with two letters (*ch*urch and *sh*ip) and are known as **digraphs,** but these two letters represent just one sound. The most frequently occurring digraphs are *sh* (*sh*op), *ch* (*ch*ild), *-ng* (si*ng*), *wh* (*wh*ip), *th* (*th*umb), and *th* (*th*at). Common digraphs are listed in Table 3.2.

Some groups of consonants represent two or even three sounds (*stop, strike*). These are known as **clusters** or blends and are listed in Table 3.3. Most clusters

TABLE 3.1	Consonant spellings		
Sound	**Initial**	**Final**	**Model Word**
/b/	barn	ca*b*, ro*b*e	ball
/d/	deer	ba*d*	dog
/f/	fun, *ph*oto	lau*gh*	fish
/g/	gate, *gh*ost, *gu*ide	ra*g*	goat
/h/	house, *wh*o		hat
/hw/	whale		whale
/j/	jug, *g*ym, sol*di*er	a*ge*, ju*dge*	jar
/k/	can, kite, *qu*ick, *ch*aos	ba*ck*, a*ch*e	cat, key
/l/	lion	mai*l*	leaf
/m/	me	hi*m*, co*mb*, autu*mn*	man
/n/	now, *kn*ow, *gn*u, *pn*eumonia	pa*n*	nail
/p/	pot	to*p*	pen
/r/	ride, *wr*ite		ring
/s/	sight, *c*ity	bu*s*, mi*ss*, fa*ce*	sun
/t/	time	ra*t*, jump*ed*	table
/v/	vase	lo*ve*	vest
/w/	we, *wh*eel		wagon
/y/	yacht, on*i*on		yo-yo
/z/	zipper	ha*s*, bu*zz*	zebra
/ch/	chip, *c*ello, ques*ti*on	ma*tch*	chair
/sh/	ship, *s*ure, *ch*ef, ac*ti*on	pu*sh*, spe*ci*al, mi*ssi*on	sheep
/th/	thin	brea*th*	thumb
/th̲/	this	brea*the*	the
/zh/	a*z*ure, ver*si*on	bei*ge*, gara*ge*	garage
/ŋ/		si*ng*	ring

Although there are forty sounds in English, there are only twenty-six letters. This explains some of the variability in the spelling system.

■ If you look at the consonant chart in Table 3.1, you will notice that some of the sounds are spelled with two letters. The sound /f/ is usually spelled with *f* as in *fox* but may also be spelled with *ph* or *gh,* as in *photograph.* When two letters are used to spell a single sound, these double letters are known as **digraphs** (*di,* "two"; *graphs,* "written symbols").

■ A **cluster** is composed of two or more letters that represent two or more sounds, such as the *br* in *broom.* Clusters are sometimes called "blends." Because it is difficult to hear the separate sounds in a cluster, this element poses a special difficulty for many students.

TABLE 3.2 Common consonant digraphs

Correspondence	Examples	Correspondence	Examples
ch = /ch/	chair, church	sh = /sh/	shoe, shop
ck = /k/	tack, pick	(s)si = /sh/	mission
gh = /f/	rough, tough	th = /th/	there, them
kn = /n/	knot, knob	th = /th/	thumb, thunder
ng = /ŋ/	thing, sing	ti = /sh/	station, action
ph = /f/	phone, photograph	wh = /w/	wheel, where
sc = /s/	scissors, scientist	wr = /r/	wrench, wrestle

are composed of *l, r,* or *s* and another consonant or two. Because they are composed of two or more sounds, clusters pose special problems for students. Novice readers have a difficult time discriminating separate sounds in a cluster and often decode just the first sound, the /s/ in /st/, for example.

TABLE 3.3 Common consonant clusters

Initial Clusters							
With *l*	Example Words	With *r*	Example Words	With *s*	Example Words	Other	Example Words
bl	blanket, black	br	broom, bread	sc	score, scale	qu	queen, quick
cl	clock, clothes	cr	crow, crash	sch	school, schedule	tw	twelve, twin
fl	flag, fly	dr	dress, drink	scr	scream, scrub		
gl	glove, glue	fr	frog, from	sk	sky, skin		
pl	plum, place	gr	green, ground	sl	sled, sleep		
sl	slide, slow	pr	prince, prepare	sm	smoke, smile		
				sn	snake, sneakers		
				sp	spider, spot		
				st	star, stop		
				sw	sweater, swim		

Final Clusters					
With *l*	Example Words	With *n*	Example Words	Other	Example Words
ld	field, old	nce	prince, chance	ct	fact, effect
lf	wolf, self	nch	lunch, bunch	mp	jump, camp
lk	milk, silk	nd	hand, wind	sp	wasp, grasp
lm	film	nk	tank, wink	st	nest, best
lp	help	nt	tent, sent		
lt	salt, belt				
lve	twelve, solve				

Vowels

English has about sixteen vowel sounds. (The number varies somewhat because some dialects have more than others.) Each vowel sound has a variety of spellings. For example, /ā/, which is commonly referred to as long *a*, is usually spelled *a-e*, as in *late*; *a* at the end of a syllable, as in *favor*; or *ai* or *ay*, as in *train* and *tray*. We can say then that the vowel sound /ā/ has four main spellings, two of which are closely related: *ay* appears in final position, and *ai* is found in initial and medial positions; so these two spellings work together.

All the other vowel sounds are similar to /ā/ in having two to four major spellings. Considering correspondences in this way makes vowel spellings seem fairly regular. It is true that /ā/ and other vowel sounds can each be spelled in a dozen or more ways, but many of these spellings are oddities. For instance, the *Random House Dictionary* (Flexner & Hauck, 1994) lists nineteen spellings of /ā/: *ate, Gael, champagne, rain, arraign, gaol, gauge, ray, exposé, suede, steak, matinee, eh, veil, feign, Marseilles, demesne, beret,* and *obey*. Many of these are in words borrowed from other languages.

TABLE 3.4	Vowel Sound	Major Spellings	Model Word
Short Vowels	/a/	rag, happen, have	cat
	/e/	get, letter, thread	bed
	/i/	wig, middle, event	fish
	/o/	fox, problem, father	mop
	/u/	bus	cup
Long Vowels	/ā/	name, favor, say, sail	rake
	/ē/	he, even, eat, seed, bean, key, these, either, funny, serious	wheel
	/ī/	hide, tiny, high, lie, sky	nine
	/ō/	vote, open, coat, bowl, old, though	nose
	/ū/	use, human	cube
Other Vowels	/aw/	daughter, law, walk, off, bought	saw
	/oi/	noise, toy	boy
	/o͝o/	wood, should, push	foot
	/o͞o/	soon, new, prove, group, two, fruit, truth	school
	/ow/	tower, south	cow
	/ə/	above, operation, similar, opinion, suppose	banana
r Vowels	/ar/	far, large, heart	car
	/air/	hair, care, where, stair, bear	chair
	/i(ə)r/	dear, steer, here	deer
	/ər/	her, sir, fur, earth	bird
	/or/	horse, door, tour, more	four

■ **Short vowels** are the vowel sounds heard in *cat, pet, sit, hot,* and *cut.*

■ **Long vowels** are the vowel sounds heard in *cake, sleep, pie, boat,* and *use.*

TABLE 3.5 Common rimes			A chart of vowels and

	Vowel Sound	Rimes	
Short Vowels	/a/	-ab, -ack, -ad, -ag, -am, -amp, -an, -and, -ang, -ank, -ant, -ap, -ash, -ask, -ast, -at, -atch	
	/e/	-ead, -eck, -ed, -ell, -elt, -en, -end, -ent, -ess, -est, -et	
	/i/	-ick, -id, -ig, -ill, -im, -in, -ing, -ink, -ip, -ish, -iss, -it	
	/o/	-ob, -ock, -od, -og, -op, -ot	
	/u/	-ub, -uck, -ud, -udge, -uff, -ug, -um, -ump, -un, -unch, -ung, -unk, -us, -ust, -ut	
Long Vowels	/ā/	-ace, -ade, -age, -ake, -ale, -ame, -ane, -ape, -ate, -aid, -ail, -ain, -aste, -ate, -ave, -ay	
	/ē/	-e, -ea, -each, -ead, -eak, -eal, -eam, -ean, -ee, -eep, -eet	
	/ī/	-ice, -ide, -ie, -ife, -ike, -ile, -ime, -ind, -ine, -ipe, -ite, -ive, -y	
	/ō/	-o, -oe, -oke, -old, -ole, -oll, -one, -ope, -ow, -own	
	/ū/	-ute	
Other Vowels	/aw/	-alk, -all, -aught, -aw, -awl, -awn, -ong, -ought	
	/oi/	-oil, -oy	
	/o͝o/	-ood, -ook, -ould	
	/o͞o/	-ew, -oo, -ool, -oom, -oon, -oot, -ue, -oup	
	/ow/	-ouch, -ound, -our, -ouse, -out, -ow, -owl, -own	
r Vowels	/air/	-air, -are, -ear	
	/ar/	-ar, -ard, -ark, -art	
	/ər/	-ir, -ird, -irt, -urt	
	/e(ə)r/	-ear, -eer	
	/i(ə)r/	-ire	
	/or/	-oar, -ore, -ort, -orn	

Note: Rimes containing few examples have been omitted. Because of dialect variation, some rimes (-og, for instance) may have more than one pronunciation. Depending upon onset, some rimes will vary in pronunciation: *mash* vs. *wash,* for example.

■ The **onset** is the initial part of a word, the part that precedes a vowel. The onset could be a single consonant (*c*+*at*), a digraph (*sh*+*eep*), or a cluster (*tr*+*ip*). A word that begins with a vowel, such as *owl* or *and*, does not have an onset.

■ The **rime** is the part of a word that rhymes and refers to the *ook* in *look* or the *ow* in *cow*.

their major spellings is presented in Table 3.4. Note that the chart lists twenty-one vowel sounds and includes *r* vowels, which are combinations of *r* and a vowel and so, technically, are not distinct vowels.

Onsets and Rimes

The **onset** is the consonant or consonant cluster preceding the rime: *b-, st-, scr-*. The **rime** is the pattern's vowel and any consonants that follow it: *-at, -op, -een*. Rimes, which are also known as phonograms and word families, are highly predictable. When considered by itself, *a* can represent several sounds. However, when followed by a consonant, it is almost always short (*-at, -an, -am*). A list of common rimes is contained in Table 3.5.

TEACHING PHONICS TO OLDER STUDENTS

Although most students will have mastered basic phonics before they reach the middle grades or middle school, a number of older students will be deficient in this area. Some may only need instruction in a few advanced vowel patterns or may have difficulty with multisyllabic words. A few may have difficulty with more basic elements such as consonants or consonant clusters. Some students may be literate in their language but are learning to read in English. Because of the needs of older struggling readers and ELL, you should have an overview of basic phonics and a command of some basic techniques for teaching decoding skills to older students.

Virtually all older struggling readers will have learned some phonics. However, seeing that their students lack essential decoding skills, some teachers are tempted to start from the beginning and review all phonics, including initial consonants. This is a poor practice. Besides wasting time, it further undermines struggling readers' damaged self-concept by unnecessarily forcing them to go over material that they recognize as being designed for younger students. It is essential that you determine how much phonics students know and build on that knowledge. You can use the Word Pattern Survey and Syllable Survey in Appendix B to determine a starting point. You can also use the results of the word lists test of an informal reading inventory and the passages.

An approach known as word building is recommended for older struggling readers. Word building is a convenient, economical way to teach basic phonics and has been tried out successfully with a number of older disabled readers. Word building presents phonics in rimes or patterns: for example, *-ame* in *came, game,* and *name,* or *-ark* in *bark, dark,* and *mark*. Patterns can be presented in a number of ways. A word-building approach helps students note the onset and the rime in each word (Gunning, 1995). Students are presented with a rime and then add onsets to create words. Next, students are provided with onsets and add rimes. Because some students have difficulty with rimes (Bruck, 1992; Juel & Minden-Cupp, 2000), rimes are broken down into their individual sounds after being presented as wholes. After introducing the rime *-ame* as a whole, the teacher would highlight its individual sounds: /ā/ and /m/. This fosters awareness of the individual sounds in words, an awareness that older struggling readers often lack. Lesson 3.1 describes how the rime *-ound* might be presented.

> Although onsets and rimes seem to be natural units of language, some students may have to process individual sounds before being able to group them into rimes. They may need to learn *a* = /a/ and *t* = /t/ before learning the *-at* rime.

> **ADAPTING INSTRUCTION for *STRUGGLING READERS and WRITERS***
> Struggling readers may have been through a number of programs and may have been taught a variety of decoding strategies, some of which may conflict with each other (Stahl, 1998). Focus on the teaching of a few strategies and meet with other professionals in the school to discuss and implement the use of a consistent set of strategies.

 LESSON 3.1 **Word-building pattern**

Step 1. Building words by adding onsets

To introduce the *-ound* pattern, write *ound* on the board and ask the class what letter would have to be added to *ound* to make the word *found*. As you add *f* to *ound*, carefully enunciate the /f/ and the /ound/ and then the whole word. Have several volunteers read the word. Then write *ound* underneath *found* and ask the group what letter should be added to *ound* to make the word *sound*. As you add *s* to *ound*, carefully enunciate /s/ and /ound/ and then the whole word. Have the word *sound* read by volunteers. The word *found* is then read, and the two words are contrasted. Ask students how the two are different. Other high-frequency -*ound* words are formed in the same way: *pound, bound, hound, ground.* (Students often have difficulty with clusters such as the *gr* at the beginning of *ground.* To help them see that the cluster is composed of two sounds as well as two letters, have students form *round* and then form *ground* by adding a *g* to *round.*) After the words have been formed, have students tell what is the same about all the words. Have students note that all the words end in the letters *o-u-n-d*, which make the sounds heard in *ound.* Then have them tell which letters make the /ou/ sound and which make the /n/, and /d/ sounds in *ound.* Calling attention to the individual sounds in *ound* will help students discriminate between the -*ound* and other /ou/ patterns. It should also help students improve perception of individual sounds in words and so help improve their reading and spelling.

Step 2. Building words by adding rimes to onsets

To make sure that students have a thorough grasp of both key parts of the word—the onset and the rime—present the onset and have students supply the rime. Write *f* on the board and have students tell what sound it stands for. Then ask them to tell what should be added to *f* to make the word *found.* After adding *ound* to *f*, say the word in parts—/f/ /ou/ /n/ /d/—and then as a whole. Pointing to *f*, say the sound /f/. Pointing to *ou*, say /ou/, pointing to *n*, say /n/ and pointing to *d*, say /d/. Running your hand under the whole word, say, "found." Show *sound, pound, hound*, and *ground* being formed in the same way. After all words have been formed, have students read them.

Step 3. Providing mixed practice

Realizing that they are learning words that all end in the same way, students may focus on the initial letter and fail to take careful note of the rest of the word, the rime. After presenting a pattern, mix in words from previously presented patterns and have students read these. For example, after presenting the -*ound* pattern, you might have students read the following words: *found, south, sound, mound, mount, pound, pout* (assuming that the other -*ou* patterns have been previously taught). This gives students practice in processing all the letters in the words and also reviews patterns that have already been introduced.

Step 4. Creating a model word

Create a model word. This should be a word that is easy and can be depicted. Construct a chart on which model words are printed and depicted with a photo or illustration. For the -*ound* pattern, the word *hound* might be used. Students can keep the chart in their notebooks and use it to help them decipher difficult words that incorporate patterns that have already been taught. Explain to students that if they come across a word that contains *ound* and forget how to say it, they can use their model words chart to help them figure it out. Explain that the model word *hound* has a picture that shows the word. In case they forget how to say the model word, the picture will help them.

Step 5. Guided practice

Under the teacher's direction, the class might read sentences that contain *-ound* words or they might create group or individual experience stories about favorite sounds.

Step 6. Application

Students read stories and/or create pieces using *-ound* words and real-world materials such as a lost and found sign and a Mounds candy bar wrapper. Also have students read words such as *bound* and *wound* (past of *wind*), which incorporate the pattern but which were not presented. As students encounter words such as *boundary* and *foundry*, encourage them to use the known *ound* element in the word to help them decode the whole word.

Step 7. Writing and spelling

Dictate some useful *-ound* words (*bound, found, round, sound, pound, ground*) and have students spell them. When dictating the words, stretch out their pronunciations (/f/ – /ou/ – /n/ – /d/) and encourage students to do the same so that they can better perceive the individual sounds. After students have attempted to spell the words, have them check their attempts against correct spellings placed on the board or overhead. Students should correct any misspellings. Encourage students to use *–ound* words in their writing.

Step 8. Extension

Students learn other *-ou* patterns: *-out, –oud*.

Step 9. Assessment and review

Note whether students are able to read words containing *-ound*. Note in particular whether they are able to decode *–ound* words that have not been taught. Note, too, whether students are spelling *-ound* words in their writing.

> **ADAPTING INSTRUCTION for *STRUGGLING READERS and WRITERS***
>
> Struggling readers often fail to process all the letters in a word and so misread it. To help students match all the sounds and letters in a word, try this activity. Say a word (*snack*), stretching out its sounds as you do so: "sssnnnaaakkk." Have students repeat the word and *explain* how many sounds they hear. Show a card that has the word written on it. Match up the sounds and their spellings. Have students tell why there are five letters but only four sounds. Have students find another word with the same vowel sound, spell the word from dictation, and meet it in their reading (Gaskins et al., 1996–1997).

If students have difficulty with consonants, present them through a word-building approach. As students form patterns, focus on the consonants that they are having difficulty with. For example, if students are having difficulty with *m* = /m/, have them form words by adding *m* to rimes. Writing *e* on the board, have them form the word *me*. Writing *an* on the board, have them form the word *man*. Writing *ad* on the board, have them form the word *mad*. Emphasize the sound of /m/ and lead them to see that *m* represents the sound /m/. Have them read food labels that contain *m* words: *milk, mustard, mayonnaise, marshmallows, margarine*. Have them suggest other words that begin with *m*. Write these on the board and read them together. Do the same with digraphs, such as *sh* and *ch*, and clusters such as *br* and *sl*, if students are having difficulty with these. Whenever possible, use real words materials such as signs and labels. These are more mature. Also consider using programs specifically designed for older struggling readers. A number of literacy programs for older students are described in Chapter 11.

■ Sorting

One activity that is especially useful in deepening students' understanding about phonics elements is sorting (Bear, 1995). Sorting forces students to analyze the elements in a word and select critical features as they place the words in piles. Through sorting, students classify words on the basis of sound and spelling and construct an understanding of the spelling system. They also enjoy this active, hands-on, non-threatening activity.

Students should sort only elements and words that they know. This allows them to construct basic understandings of the spelling system. Although they may be able to read *cereal, cycle, circle, cab, cob,* and *cub,* they may not realize that when *c* is followed by *e, i,* or *y,* it usually has an /s/ sound but when folowed by *a, o,* or *u,* it usually has a /k/ sound. Sorting helps them come to these understandings.

Words can also be sorted according to whether they have long or short vowels, begin with single consonants or clusters, or any other element that students need to study.

Sorts can be open or closed. In a closed sort, the teacher provides the basis for sorting the cards. In an open sort, students decide the basis for sorting the cards.

Major Word Patterns

ADAPTING INSTRUCTION for *ENGLISH LANGUAGE LEARNERS*

Both Chinese- and Spanish-speaking youngsters have difficulty with long *e.* When working with these youngsters, start with long *o.*

A listing of major word patterns is presented in Table 3.6. The sequence of presentation would be similar to the order in which the elements are listed: short-vowel patterns, followed by long-vowel patterns, followed by other vowel and *r*-vowel patterns. However, within each grouping, patterns are presented in alphabetical order. Do not present the patterns in alphabetical order. Start with the easiest and most useful patterns. When teaching short *a* patterns, begin with the *-at* pattern, for instance. When introducing patterns, do not present every word that fits the pattern. Present only words that students know, and present only words that they will be likely to meet in the near future. It's better for them to attain a good grasp of a few high-frequency pattern words rather than have an uncertain knowledge of a large number of pattern words. It also saves time to introduce just the important words. It is not necessary to teach every pattern. For instance, after five or six short *-a* patterns have been introduced, help students to generalize that all the patterns contain a short *-a* sound and help them apply this to short *-a* words from patterns that have not been introduced. Words from low-frequency patterns such as *-ab, -ag, -aft,* and *-ax* might be presented in this way.

Familiar words are easier to decode. A student who has been taught the *-at* pattern may have little difficulty with the high-frequency words *cat, that,* and *sat* but may falter when encountering *chat, drat,* and *mat.*

Also teach only those patterns that students don't know. Use the Word Pattern Survey in Appendix B to assess students' knowledge of patterns.

Teaching Vowel Generalizations

"When two vowels go walking, the first one does the talking." Recited by millions of students, this generalization is one of the best known of the vowel rules. It refers to the tendency for the first letter in a digraph to represent the long sound typically

TABLE 3.6 Major word patterns

Short Vowels

-ab	-ack	-ad	-ag	-am	-amp	-an	-and	-ang	-ank
cab	back	bad	bag	*ham	camp	an	and	bang	*bank
tab	jack	dad	rag	jam	damp	can	band	gang	sank
*crab	pack	had	tag	slam	*lamp	fan	*hand	hang	tank
	sack	mad	wag	swam	stamp	man	land	*rang	blank
	*tack	*sad	drag			*pan	sand	sang	thank
	black	glad	*flag			tan	stand		
	crack					plan			
	stack					than			

-ap	-at		-ed	-ell	-en	-end	-ent	-ess	-est
cap	at		*bed	*bell	den	end	bent	guess	best
lap	bat		fed	fell	hen	bend	dent	less	nest
*map	*cat		led	tell	men	lend	rent	mess	pest
tap	fat		red	well	pen	mend	sent	bless	rest
clap	hat		shed	yell	*ten	*send	*tent	*dress	test
slap	pat		sled	shell	then	tend	went	press	*vest
snap	rat			smell	when	spend	spent		west
trap	sat			spell					chest
wrap	that								guest

-et	-ead	-ick	-id	-ig	-ill	-im	-in	-ing
bet	dead	kick	did	big	bill	dim	in	king
get	head	lick	hid	dig	fill	him	fin	*ring
jet	lead	pick	kid	*pig	*hill	skim	*pin	sing
let	read	sick	*lid	wig	kill	slim	sin	wing
met	*bread	click	rid	twig	pill	*swim	tin	bring
*net	spread	*stick	skid		will		win	sting
pet	thread	thick	slid		chill		chin	thing
set		trick			skill		grin	
wet		quick			spill		skin	
							spin	
							thin	
							twin	

-ink	-ip	-it	-ob	-ock	-op	-ot
link	dip	it	job	dock	cop	dot
pink	lip	bit	mob	*lock	hop	got
*sink	rip	fit	rob	rock	*mop	hot
wink	tip	*hit	sob	sock	pop	lot
blink	zip	kit	*knob	block	top	not
clink	chip	sit		clock	chop	*pot
drink	flip	knit		flock	drop	shot
stink	*ship	quit		knock	shop	spot
think	skip	split			stop	
	trip					
	whip					

continued

TABLE 3.6 Major word patterns *(continued)*

Short Vowels

-ub	-uck	-ug	-um	-ump	-un	-unk	-us (s)	-ust	-ut
cub	*duck	bug	bum	bump	bun	bunk	*bus	bust	but
rub	luck	dug	hum	dump	fun	hunk	plus	dust	cut
sub	cluck	hug	yum	hump	gun	junk	us	just	hut
tub	stuck	mug	*drum	*jump	run	sunk	fuss	*must	*nut
*club	struck	*rug	plum	lump	*sun	shrunk	muss	rust	shut
scrub	truck	tug		pump	spun	*skunk		trust	
		chug		thump		stunk			
				stump					

Long Vowels

-ace	-ade	-age	-ake	-ale	-ame	-ape	-ate	-ave	-ail
*face	fade	age	bake	pale	came	ape	ate	*cave	fail
race	made	*cage	*cake	sale	game	*cape	date	gave	jail
place	grade	page	lake	tale	*name	tape	*gate	save	mail
space	*shade	rage	make	*scale	same	scrape	hate	wave	*nail
	trade	stage	rake		tame	grape	late	brave	pail
			take		blame	shape	mate		sail
			wake		shame		plate		tail
			flake				skate		snail
			shake				state		trail
			snake						

-ain	-ay		-ea	-each	-eak	-eal	-eam	-ean	-eat
main	bay		pea	each	*beak	deal	team	*bean	eat
pain	day		sea	beach	leak	heal	*dream	lean	beat
rain	*hay		*tea	*peach	peak	meal	scream	mean	neat
brain	lay		flea	reach	weak	real	stream	clean	*seat
chain	may			teach	creak	*seal			cheat
grain	pay			bleach	sneak	squeal			treat
*train	say				speak	steal			wheat
	way				squeak				
	gray								
	play								

-ee	-eed	-eel	-eep	-eet		-ice	-ide	-ile	-ime
*bee	deed	feel	beep	*feet		*mice	hide	mile	*dime
see	feed	heel	deep	meet		nice	ride	pile	lime
free	*seed	kneel	*jeep	sheet		rice	side	*smile	time
knee	weed	steel	keep	sleet		slice	wide	while	chime
tree	bleed	*wheel	peep	sweet		twice	*bride		
	freed		weep				slide		
	speed		creep						
			sleep						
			steep						
			sweep						

TABLE 3.6 Major word patterns *(continued)*

Long Vowels

-ine	-ite	-ive	-ie	-ind	-y		-o, -oe	-oke	-ole
fine	bite	dive	die	find	by		go	joke	hole
line	*kite	*five	lie	kind	guy		*no	poke	mole
mine	quite	hive	pie	*mind	my		so	woke	*pole
*nine	white	live	*tie	blind	dry		doe	broke	stole
pine		drive			fly		hoe	*smoke	whole
					*sky		toe	spoke	
					try				
					why				

-one	-ope	-ose	-ote	-oad	-oat	-ow	-old		u-e
bone	hope	hose	*note	load	boat	bow	old		use
cone	nope	*nose	vote	*road	coat	low	cold		fuse
*phone	*rope	rose	quote	toad	*goat	tow	fold		*mule
shone	slope	chose	wrote		float	blow	hold		huge
		close				glow	*gold		
		those				grow	sold		
						slow	told		
						*snow			

Other Vowels

-all	-aw	-au	-oss	-ost	-ought		-oil	-oy
*ball	caw	fault	boss	cost	ought		*boil	*boy
call	jaw	*caught	loss	*lost	*bought		soil	joy
fall	paw	taught	toss	frost	fought			toy
hall	*saw		*cross		brought			
wall	claw							
small	draw							
	straw							

-oud	-our	-out	-ound	-ow	-own		-ood	-ook	-ould
loud	our	out	bound	ow	down		good	*book	*could
*cloud	*hour	*shout	found	bow	gown		hood	cook	would
proud	sour	scout	*hound	*cow	town		*wood	hook	should
	flour	spout	mound	how	brown		stood	look	
			pound	now	clown			took	
			round	plow	*crown			shook	
			sound						
			wound						
			ground						

continued

TABLE 3.6	Major word patterns *(continued)*

r Vowels

-air	-are	-ear, ere	-ar	-ard	-ark	-art	-ear
fair	care	*bear	*car	*card	bark	art	*ear
*hair	hare	pear	far	guard	dark	part	dear
pair	share	there	jar	hard	mark	*chart	fear
chair	scare	where	star		park	smart	hear
	spare				*shark		year
	*square				spark		clear

-eer	-or	ore	-orn	-ort
*deer	*or	more	born	*fort
cheer	for	*sore	*corn	port
steer	nor	tore	torn	sort
		wore	worn	short
				sport

*May be used as model words.

From *Assessing and Correcting Reading and Writing Difficulties* (2nd ed.) by T. Gunning, 2002. Boston: Allyn & Bacon. Reprinted by permission of Allyn & Bacon.

associated with that letter: For example, *ea* in *team* represents long *e*, and *ai* in *paid* represents long *a*. Although heavily criticized because, as expressed, it applies only about 50 percent of the time, it can be helpful (Gunning, 1975; Johnston, 2001).

About one word out of every five has a double vowel, or digraph; however, the generalization does not apply equally to each situation. For some spellings—*ee*, for example—it applies nearly 100 percent of the time. The letters *ea*, however, represent at least four different sounds (as in *bean*, *bread*, *earth*, and *steak*). Moreover, the generalization does not apply to such vowel–letter combinations as *au*, *aw*, *oi*, *oy*, and *ou*.

This generalization about digraphs should not be taught as a blanket rule because it has too many exceptions. Instead, it should be broken down into a series of minigeneralizations in which the most useful and most consistent correspondences are emphasized. These minigeneralizations include the following:

> A number of vowel combinations are not used to spell long vowels:
>
> *au* or *aw* = /aw/ *fault, saw*
>
> *oi* or *oy* = /oy/ *toil, toy*
>
> *oo* = /o͞o/ *moon*
>
> *oo* = /o͝o/ *book*
>
> *ou* or *ow* = /ow/ *pout, power*

Instances where the double vowels usually represent a long sound.

- The letters *ai* and *ay* usually represent long *a*, as in *way* and *wait*.
- The letters *ee* usually represent long *e*, as in *see* and *feet*.
- The letters *ey* usually represent long *e*, as in *key*.
- The letters *oa* usually represent long *o*, as in *boat* and *toad*.

Instances where the double vowels regularly represent a long sound or another sound.

- Except when followed by *r*, the letters *ea* usually stand for long *e* (*bean*) or short *e* (*bread*).
- The letters *ie* usually stand for long *e* (*piece*) or long *i* (*tie*).

- The letters *ow* usually stand for a long *o* sound (*snow*) or an /ow/ sound (*cow*).

The minigeneralizations could also be taught as patterns, such as *seat, heat, neat,* and *beat* or *boat, goat,* and *float*. Whichever way they are taught, the emphasis should be on providing ample opportunities to meet the double vowels in print. Providing exposure is the key to learning phonics. Generalizations and patterns draw attention to regularities in English spelling, but actually meeting the elements in print is the way students' decoding skills become automatic; they can then direct fuller attention to comprehension.

Most vowel rules are not worth teaching because they have limited utility, have too many exceptions, or are too difficult to apply. However, the following generalizations are relatively useful (Gunning, 1975):

- *Closed syllable generalization.* A vowel is short when followed by a consonant: *wet, but–ter.* This is known as the closed syllable rule because it applies when a consonant "closes," or ends, a word or syllable.
- *Open syllable generalization.* A vowel is usually long when it is found at the end of a word or syllable: *so, mo–ment.* This generalization is known as the open syllable rule because the word or syllable ends with a vowel and so is not closed by a consonant.
- *Final* e *generalization.* A vowel is usually long when it is followed by a consonant and a final *e: pine, note.*

> One of the few generalizations that students make use of in their reading is the final *-e* generalization. When they reach the orthographic stage of reading, students make use of final *e* as part of a larger pattern: *-age, -ate, -ive.*

Vowel generalizations should be taught inductively. After experiencing many words that end in *e* preceded by a consonant, for example, students should conclude that words ending in a consonant plus *e* often have long vowels. Students might also discover this by sorting words that end in final *e* and words that don't.

The real payoff from learning generalizations comes when students group elements within a word in such a way that they automatically map out the correct pronunciation most of the time. For example, when processing the words *vocal, token,* and *hotel* so that the first syllable is noted as being open (*vo–cal, to–ken, ho–tel*) and the vowel is noted as being long, students are able to decode the words quickly and accurately. This is a result of many hours of actual reading. However, it is also a process that can be taught (Glass, 1976).

> The best way to "learn" generalizations is to have plenty of practice reading open and closed syllable words, final *e* words, and other words covered by generalizations.

Because none of the vowel generalizations applies 100 percent of the time, students should be introduced to the variability principle. They need to learn that digraphs and single vowels can represent a variety of sounds. If they try one pronunciation and it is not a real word or does not make sense in context, then they must try another. A student who read "heevy" for *heavy* would have to try another pronunciation, because *heevy* is not a real word. A student who read "deed" for *dead* would need to check to see whether that pronunciation fits the context of the sentence in which the word was used. Although *deed* is a real word, it does not make sense in the sentence "Jill's cat was dead"; so the student would try another pronunciation. This strategy needs to be taught explicitly, and students must have plenty of opportunity for practice. To sound out a word, they should be taught the general steps outlined in the Student Strategy that follows.

Because there is no way to predict on the basis of spelling whether ow will represent /ow/ (*cow*) or /ō/ (*snow*) or oo will represent a short (*book*) or long (*boot*) sound, you need to teach students to check whether the sounds they construct create a real word. If not, have them try the other major pronunciation of ow or oo. Model this process for your students.

 Applying the variability strategy to vowel correspondences

1. Sound out the word as best you can.
2. After sounding out the word, ask yourself, "Is this a real word?" If not, try sounding out the word again. (Applying the variability principle to a word containing *ow*, a student might try the long-vowel pronunciation first. If that did not work out, he or she would try the /ow/ (*cow*) pronunciation. If there is a chart of spellings available, students can use it as a source of possible pronunciations.)
3. Read the word in the sentence. Ask yourself, "Does this word make sense in the sentence?" If not, try sounding it out again.
4. If you still cannot sound out a word so that it makes sense in the sentence, try context, skip it, or get help.

Introducing Syllabic Analysis Early

Long words pose problems for students. Although students might know the words *in* and *ant*, they have difficulty reading the word *instant*. Most multisyllabic words are composed of known word parts or patterns. After teaching several short-vowel patterns, present two-syllable words composed of those patterns. For instance, after students have studied the short *-a* and short *-i* patterns, present words such as *rabbit*, *napkin*, *distant*, and *instant*. When students encounter multisyllabic words, prompt them to use their knowledge of word parts to figure out the words. Also build words. After students have learned a word such as *swim*, have them make words that contain *swim: swims, swimming, swimmer* so they get used to reading words that contain suffixes.

USING WORD ANALYSIS REFERENCES

Good evidence for the integration of context and phonics cues comes from reading sentences containing a word whose pronunciation depends on its meaning. Good readers can read the following sentences without difficulty: "The does have no antlers, but the bull does." "He wound the bandage around the wound" (McCracken, 1991, p. 91).

Students should have references that they can use to help them read and spell unfamiliar words (Pinnell & Fountas, 1998). These references could include dictionaries, illustrated charts of model words, lists of patterns and other words, a chart listing the steps in decoding a difficult word, and a talking word processor or talking electronic dictionary so that students could type in an unknown word and have it pronounced.

USING AN INTEGRATED APPROACH

Although phonics, context clues, and vocabulary are treated as separate topics in this book, students make use of all three when they face an unknown word. In fact, they make use of their total language system. When students decode words, four processors are at work: orthographic, phonological, meaning, and context (Adams,

1990; 1994). The orthographic processor is responsible for perceiving the sequences of letters in text. The phonological processor is responsible for mapping the letters into their spoken equivalents. The meaning processor contains one's knowledge of word meanings, and the context processor is in charge of constructing a continuing understanding of the text. The processors work simultaneously and both receive information and send it to the other processors. Therefore, phonics instruction must be viewed as being part of a larger language process. Phonics is easier to apply when context clues are used, and, in turn, it makes those clues easier to use. Students who are adept decoders will be able to recognize more words and so will have more context to use. Moreover, greater knowledge of the world, larger vocabularies, and better command of language increase students' ability to use phonics. If a student has a rich vocabulary, there is a better chance that the word he or she is decoding will be recognized by his or her meaning processor. Even if the word is not known, the student will have a better chance of deriving its meaning from context if most of the other words in the passage are known and if his or her background knowledge of the concepts in the passage is adequate.

To be most effective, therefore, phonics instruction should be presented in context and practiced and applied through extensive reading, which enables students to connect phonics instruction with its functioning as part of a total language system. Extensive reading also provides practice for phonics skills so that students' decoding becomes so effortless and automatic that they can devote full attention to comprehension, which is what reading is all about.

TEACHING PHONICS TO ENGLISH LANGUAGE LEARNERS

If students have learned decoding skills in their native language, some of what they have learned should transfer to English. For instance, regardless of which language they have learned to read in, they should have the basic concept of decoding words. The degree to which specific skills transfer would depend on their orthographic and phonological similarities between the languages. Spanish, for instance, is a highly regular language. For the most part, each sound has just one spelling. However, Spanish is more syllabic than English. It has relatively few single-syllable words. It is also more highly inflected. For instance, inflected endings are used to show gender in Spanish: *señor, señora,* or *señorita.* This, of course, adds to the number of syllables. Spanish has fewer homographs. Words that are spelled the same but have different meanings are differentiated by accent marks. For instance, *si* means "if" but *sí* means "yes." The word *te* means "you," but the word *té* means "tea." However, as noted in Table 10.1 in Chapter 10, Spanish lacks short *i* and a number of other vowels. It also lacks a number of consonants. Although Spanish has beginning *l* (*clear*) and *r* (*bring*) clusters, it lacks *s* clusters (*stop, sweet*). When teaching Spanish-speaking students English phonics, start, insofar as possible, with elements that are the same in both languages. You might start with long *o*, because it has approximately the same sound in both English and Spanish and the same spelling in words like *go, no,* and *so.* Spanish has vowel sounds that are similar to short *o* (*hot*), short *e* (*pet*), long *a* (*day*), long *e* (*we*), and long double *o* (*too*), but the spellings generally differ. There is less opportunity for transfer for languages

With the help of the ESL or bilingual teacher, find out what literacy skills students possess in their native language. Then build on these skills. For instance, students may have a good command of phonics. Show the student how she might use this in English.

such as Greek and Russian, which have a different alphabet, or for nonalphabetic languages such as Chinese or Vietnamese.

When English language learners read English words, they may pronounce them in terms of their native language. For instance, a native speaker of Spanish may pronounce *mitt* as *meet*. This reading should be counted as accurate if the student realizes that the word he read is something that is worn on the hand.

STRATEGY INSTRUCTION

> Do not ask students to "look for the little word in the big word." This may work sometimes but would result in a misleading pronunciation in a word like *mother*. Besides, there are many words that don't have "little words" in them.

> Pronounceable word part and analogy strategies should be integrated with the use of context clues. There are some situations in which context simply does not work. There are others in which neither pronounceable word part nor analogy will work.

ADAPTING INSTRUCTION for *STRUGGLING READERS and WRITERS* Word analysis skills are interdependent. For instance, sight words are easier to learn if students know basic phonics. Analogies can only be used on a limited basis if there are few comparison words in the student's store of known words. Therefore, struggling readers often have difficulty in several areas of word analysis and so need broad-based instruction (Ehri & McCormick, 1998).

The ultimate value of phonics instruction is that it provides students with the keys for unlocking the pronunciations of unknown words encountered in print. For instance, a student who has studied both the *-ode* and the *-ire* patterns but has difficulty with the words *strode* and *spire*, even though these are in his listening vocabulary, needs strategies for decoding those words. In addition to context, there are two powerful decoding strategies that the student might use: pronounceable word part and analogy (Gunning, 1995).

To apply the pronounceable word part strategy, a student who is having difficulty with a word seeks out familiar parts of the word. You might prompt the student by pointing to *spire* and asking, "Is there any part of the word that you can say?" If the student fails to see a pronounceable word part, cover up all but that part of the word (*ire*) and ask the student if he can read it. Once the student reads the pronounceable part, he adds the onset (*sp*) and says the word *spire*.

If a student is unable to use the pronounceable word part strategy, try the analogy strategy. With the analogy strategy, the student compares an unknown word to a known one. For instance, the student might compare the unknown word *spire* to the known word *tire*. The teacher prompts the strategy by asking, "Is the word like any word that you know?" If the student is unable to respond, the teacher writes the model word *tire*, has the student read it, and then compares *spire* to *tire*. Or the teacher might refer the student to a model words chart.

When students reconstruct a word using the pronounceable word part or analogy strategy, they must always make sure that the word they have constructed is a real word. They must also make sure it fits the context of the sentence. The pronounceable word part strategy should be tried before the analogy strategy because it is easier to apply and is more direct. Although students may have to be prompted to use the strategies, they should ultimately apply the strategies on their own.

STUDENT strategies Word recognition

To cue the use of word recognition strategies, the student should ask one or more of the following questions when encountering an unknown word in print:

1. Is there any part of this word that I can say?
2. Is this word like any word I know?
3. What word would make sense here?

Building Independence

When a student has difficulty with a printed word, you may be tempted to supply the word or give some unhelpful admonition, such as "You know that word. We had it yesterday." Size up the word. Think of the skills the student has, the nature of the word, and the context in which it appears. Then ask the question from the Student Strategy (change the "I" to "you") that will prompt the use of the cue that seems most likely to work. (Of course, if you feel the student has no chance of working out the word, supply two options by asking, "Would *speck* or *speak* fit here?" By giving students a choice of two words, one of which is the answer, you provide students with the opportunity to apply a skill and you also preserve their self-confidence.) Helping students apply decoding strategies provides them with a powerful tool that empowers them as readers. Encouraging them to work out words also affirms your faith in them and builds their confidence.

If a student is reading orally in a group situation, do not allow another student to correct her or him. This robs the student of her or his academic self-concept and also of the opportunity to apply strategies. If a student misreads a word and does not notice the error, do not immediately supply a correction or even stop the reading. Let the student continue to the end of the sentence or paragraph; there is a good chance that she or he will notice the misreading and correct it. If the student does correct the misreading, make sure that you affirm this behavior: "I like the way you went back and corrected your misreading. You must have seen that the word _____ didn't make sense in the sentence."

If the student does not self-correct a misreading, you have two choices. If the error is a minor one, such as *this* for *that* or *the* for *these*, which does not change the meaning of the sentence, ignore it. If the misreading does not fit the sense of the sentence, use a prompt that will help the student correct the misreading:

- If the misreading does not make sense, ask, "Does _____ make sense in that sentence?"
- If the misreading is not a real word, ask, "Does that sound right?"
- If the misreading makes sense but does not fit phonically, say, "*Grim*" makes sense in the sentence, but the word in the sentence ends with *e*. How would that change the pronunciation of the vowel in *grim*? (Clay, 1993). (Prompt for a pronounceable word part or analogy if you think it necessary).

Periodically, model the process of using strategies to figure out a word. Using a think-aloud, show how you go about seeking a pronounceable word part or using an analogy strategy.

> If other prompts don't work and you believe the student can't decode a word, give the students a choice between two responses: "Is the word (incorrect response) or (correct response)?" This helps students think about what strategies might be used.

> Additional word analysis strategies can be found in Chapter 4.

HIGH-FREQUENCY WORDS

Close your book and on a separate piece of paper spell the word *once*. As you write the word, try to be aware of the processes you are using. Did your lips move? As you wrote the word, did you sound it out? A small number of words, such as *of* and *once*, and, to a lesser extent, *were* and *some*, are said to be irregular. Their spellings don't do a good job of representing their sounds. Because these words are irregular, at one time it was thought that the best way to learn them was to memorize them visually. They were put on cards and studied. Because it is believed that they were memorized visually, they became known as **sight words.** However, more recent research indicates that even irregular words are learned phonologically. That's why when you wrote the word *once*, chances are you said the word, at least subvocally, and then said the sounds of the word as you spelled each sound. There is also an element of visual memory involved. Otherwise, you may have spelled *once* as *wuns*.

A list of **high-frequency** words is presented in Table 3.7. Note that these are all common words. Ironically, the words that appear most frequently tend to have the most irregular spellings, mainly because they are some of the oldest words in the language. Over the years, English evolved so that, in many instances, spellings no longer do a very good job of representing pronunciations.

Table 3.7 gives 200 high-frequency words in order of their frequency of appearance. The list is drawn from a compilation of words that appear in books and other materials read by school children (Zeno, Ivens, Millard, & Duvvuri, 1995). These 200 words would make up about 60 percent of the words in continuous text. For example, the most frequently occurring word *the* would appear about 2 percent of the time.

By fourth grade, nearly all students will have mastered the list of high-frequency words in Table 3.7. This list is typically learned in first grade by achieving readers. However, the most seriously disabled of the struggling readers may not have learned all the high-frequency words, and English language learners may still be acquiring them. Before teaching high-frequency words to students, assess them to make sure that they need help with them. When teaching high-frequency words, limit the number being taught to three or four. Choose words that students will soon be meeting in print. Select words that are different in appearance. Presenting *put* and *but* or *where, when,* and *were* together is asking for trouble, as students are almost sure to confuse them.

Take full advantage of phonic regularities, such as initial and final consonant correspondences. Also, seek out commonalties of words. For instance, when teaching *at* as a high-frequency word, also teach *that* and show how the two are related; have students note that *that* contains the pronounceable word part *at*. Except for dramatically irregular words like *of* and *one*, help students match up spellings and sounds. For *were*, help students see that *w* represents /w/ and *ere* represents /er/ as in *her*. For the word *some*, match *s* with /s/, note that *o* is a very unusual way of spelling /u/, and match *m* with /m/. Encourage students to spell out the words and provide opportunities for them to meet the words in many contexts so they form a visual image of the words in addition to making phonological connections. As students are learning exception words such as *know* or *sure*, they also need to be taught specific distinguishing features of these words.

Because high-frequency words are such a prominent part of just about everything that students read, it is important that they learn to recognize them rapidly. The idea behind rapid recognition of words is that the human mind has only so much mental-processing ability and time. If students get caught up trying to sound out words, they lose the memory of what they are attempting to read.

■ A **sight word** is one that is recognized immediately. However, the term *sight words* also refers to words that occur with high frequency and words that are learned through visual memorization. Only a small number of words can be learned through visual memory. The vast majority of words are learned through phonics.

■ **High-frequency words** are words such as *the, of,* and *them* that appear in printed material with a high rate of occurrence.

TABLE 3.7 High-frequency words

1. the	41. which	81. made	121. also	161. name
2. of	42. their	82. over	122. around	162. should
3. and	43. said	83. did	123. another	163. home
4. a	44. if	84. down	124. came	164. give
5. to	45. will	85. way	125. three	165. air
6. in	46. do	86. only	126. word	166. line
7. is	47. each	87. may	127. come	167. mother
8. you	48. about	88. find	128. work	168. set
9. that	49. how	89. use	129. must	169. world
10. it	50. up	90. water	130. part	170. own
11. he	51. out	91. little	131. because	171. under
12. for	52. then	92. long	132. does	172. last
13. was	53. them	93. very	133. even	173. read
14. on	54. she	94. after	134. place	174. never
15. are	55. many	95. word	135. old	175. am
16. as	56. some	96. called	136. well	176. us
17. with	57. so	97. just	137. such	177. left
18. his	58. these	98. new	138. here	178. end
19. they	59. would	99. where	139. take	179. along
20. at	60. other	100. most	140. why	180. while
21. be	61. into	101. know	141. things	181. sound
22. this	62. has	102. get	142. great	182. house
23. from	63. more	103. through	143. help	183. might
24. I	64. two	104. back	144. put	184. next
25. have	65. her	105. much	145. years	185. below
26. not	66. like	106. good	146. different	186. saw
27. or	67. him	107. before	147. number	187. something
28. by	68. time	108. go	148. away	188. thought
29. one	69. see	109. man	149. again	189. both
30. had	70. no	110. our	150. off	190. few
31. but	71. could	111. want	151. went	191. those
32. what	72. make	112. sat	152. tell	192. school
33. all	73. than	113. me	153. men	193. show
34. were	74. first	114. day	154. say	194. always
35. when	75. been	115. too	155. small	195. until
36. we	76. its	116. any	156. every	196. large
37. there	77. who	117. same	157. found	197. often
38. can	78. now	118. right	158. still	198. together
39. an	79. people	119. look	159. big	199. ask
40. your	80. my	120. think	160. between	200. write

Adapted from *The Educator's Word Frequency Scale* by S. M. Zeno, S. H. Ivens, R. T. Millard, & R. Duvvuri, 1995. Brewster, NY: Touchstone Applied Science Associates.

Knowing how to spell and/or sound out a word partially or fully helps students learn and remember new words (Ehri, 1991), but time spent discussing known definitions may be wasted (Kibby, 1989).

They need automaticity, the ability to process words effortlessly and automatically (Laberge & Samuels, 1974). Students who are able to recognize words rapidly have ample attention and mental energy left to comprehend what they are reading. Ultimately, because of lots of practice, most of the words that skilled read-

Two factors are involved in rapid recognition of words: accuracy and automaticity (Samuels, 1994). To reach an effective level of accuracy, students must actively process words and process virtually every letter. Students need varying amounts of time to reach a high level of accuracy. Once they have reached an acceptable level of accuracy, they seem to gain automaticity at similar rates (Samuels, 1994). Students who seem to take longer to become fluent readers may not have achieved accuracy.

ers meet in print, although learned through phonics, are processed as rapid recognition words. Only when they meet strange names or unfamiliar words do they resort to decoding words.

Teaching High-Frequency Words

When presenting high-frequency words, emphasize activities that reflect this purpose. Use phonics to help students accurately decode words—accuracy must come first. As Samuels (1994) notes, accuracy precedes automaticity, or rapid recognition. Use of knowledge of patterns and individual correspondences facilitates accurate recognition. Once accuracy has been achieved, stress rapid recognition.

As you gradually introduce added phonics skills, include high-frequency words as part of your instruction. For instance, when teaching the consonant cluster *bl*, use the high-frequency words *black* and *blue* as examples. When studying short *a*, present the high-frequency words *am*, *an*, and *at*. Being able to relate the printed versions of these words with their sounds gives students another way to process them, which aids memory and speed of processing. Use the steps listed in Lesson 3.2 as a framework for presenting high-frequency words.

LESSON 3.2 — High-frequency words

Step 1. Develop understanding of the words

This step is only necessary if students do not have an adequate understanding of the words being presented. Since high-frequency words are among the most common in the language, they will be in the listening vocabularies of the majority of students. However, some high-frequency words may be unknown to English Language Learners.

Step 2. Present printed words in isolation

There are actually few words in which phonics cannot be used at least partially. These include such irregular words as *one, once,* and *of.*

Write each word to be learned on the chalkboard, or present each one on a large card. Although students may not be able to read the words, they may know parts of them. Build on any part they know. This will make the task of learning the word easier, as students will be faced with learning only a portion of the word rather than the whole word; it also helps them connect new knowledge with old knowledge. If students know only initial consonant correspondences, build on that knowledge: Emphasize the *y* = /y/ in *you* and the *f* = /f/ in *for.* If they know initial and final consonants, talk about the *c* = /k/ and *n* = /n/ in *can.* If they know word patterns, make use of those: Help them use their knowledge of *-an* to read *man* and their knowledge of *-op* to read *stop.* Present these elements as ways of perceiving and remembering sight words, but do not turn the sight word lesson into a phonics lesson. For words that are highly irregular, such as *of*, *one*, and *once*, simply stress their spellings. Do not attempt to discuss any phonics elements.

After all the words have been introduced, have students read them chorally and individually. Distribute cards containing the words so that each student has a set. If long cards are used, the reverse side might contain the word used in a sentence.

Step 3. Present printed words in context

On the chalkboard, story paper, or overhead transparency, present the high-frequency words in context. Underline the target words so that they stand out. Take care to use each word in the same sense in which students will most likely see it. For instance, if the high-frequency word *water* is going to be a verb in an upcoming story, show it as a verb. In composing sample sentences, except for the target high-frequency words, use words already taught so that students can concentrate their efforts on the new ones. Actually, using high-frequency words that have already been taught is a good way to review them. Read the sentences to the students, and then have them read in unison as you sweep your hand under the words. Later, individual volunteers can read the sentences.

Step 4. Practice

Provide ample practice for high-frequency words. Practice could be in the form of maze worksheets on which students choose from three words the one that correctly completes the sentence:

through
We walked thought the open door.
though

Step 5. Application

Have students create experience stories or read easy selections that contain target high-frequency words. Experience stories naturally contain a high proportion of sight words. Easy selections also provide an opportunity for students to meet sight words in context.

Step 6. Assessment and review

Observe students as they read to see how well they do when they encounter high-frequency words.

> **USING TECHNOLOGY**
>
> Talking CD-ROM books that highlight the words that are being read are a good way to build up students' rapid recognition of high-frequency words, especially if the student reads the story several times. It is crucial that students read along as the words are being highlighted. To test themselves, students might turn down the sound and see if they can read the words as they are being highlighted.

> There is some disagreement about how expert readers recognize words. Ehri (1994) theorizes that they are recognized holistically because the word's letters and pronunciation have become bonded through repeated encounters, thus providing an access route which leads instantaneously from the word's graphic representation to the word's pronunciation. Gough and Hillinger (1980) believe that readers process words phonologically, but the processing is so rapid that recognition appears to be instantaneous.

Finding books that reinforce high-frequency words and basic patterns and that are mature enough for older struggling readers is a problem. One source of books for older struggling readers that reinforce both high-frequency words and basic decoding patterns is High Noon Reading (Academic Therapy Publications).

■ **Fluency** is freedom from word identification problems that might hinder comprehension in silent reading or the expression of ideas in oral reading.

■ **Automaticity** refers to tasks that can be performed without attention or conscious effort.

■ **Accuracy** means being able to pronounce or sound out a word and also knowing the word's meaning.

Fluency is sometimes equated with phrasing, smoothness, and expressiveness as well as rate, accuracy, and automaticity (Worthy & Broadus, 2001).

BUILDING FLUENCY

Students who struggle with decoding skills may read in slow, halting fashion. If labored reading persists, comprehension will suffer. Students will expend so much effort decoding that they won't be able to devote mental energy to understanding what they read.

Students who have struggled with reading and have not engaged in much voluntary reading may also lack fluency, even though their word attack skills are adequate. Because they are reading below grade level, some students may have found themselves reading materials that were too difficult. They might never have experienced reading material that was relatively easy for them, so they never built up the kind of reading speed that comes with reading easy materials. These students have simply not put in enough practice time. They need to read lots of material on their independent level.

Students need to become fluent as well as accurate readers. Although often equated with smoothness of oral reading, **fluency** has been defined as "freedom from word identification problems that might hinder comprehension in silent reading or the expression of ideas in oral reading; **automaticity**" (Harris & Hodges, 1995, p. 85). Fluency has two components: **accuracy** and automaticity. Students are accurate readers if they can recognize the words. They have automaticity if they recognize the words rapidly. Students can be accurate but slow decoders. One way of judging fluency is by noting students' rate of silent reading and their comprehension. If they can read at a reasonable pace, then they probably are able to recognize the words rapidly. If they can answer questions about what they read, their word recognition is probably accurate. Another way of assessing fluency is through having students read a selection orally. If they misread a number of words, this indicates that accuracy is a problem. It also may be an indication that the material is beyond their instructional level. If they read word by word and seem to need to sound out an excessive number of words, then automaticity is an issue.

Phrasing of Text

Fluency is more than just accuracy and speed in reading; it also includes proper phrasing. Word-by-word reading is frequently caused by giving students material that is too difficult so that they literally have to figure out just about every word. It also can be caused by a lack of automaticity. Students have to stop and decode a large proportion of words because they don't recognize them immediately. Word-by-word reading should fade out as students improve their decoding skills and as their skills become automatic. If word-by-word reading persists even though word recognition is adequate and automatic, model reading orally in logical phrases and have students read selections in which phrases are marked so that they have practice reading in meaningful chunks.

Comprehension is also an element in fluency. Students' phrasing and expressiveness should be noted. Does their reading indicate an understanding of what they are reading? Understanding what one reads is important for proper expression. Of course, it is essential that students be given material that is on the appropriate level. Given material that is too difficult, even the best readers become dysfluent.

Accuracy and speed of reading have to be balanced. An overemphasis on accuracy will lead to a decrease in reading speed. Do not insist on 100 percent accuracy (Samuels, 1994). An overemphasis on oral reading will decrease reading speed. Students will also get the wrong idea about reading. They will begin to see reading as an oral performance activity in which they are expected to pronounce each word correctly. This could carry over into students' silent reading and so hinder comprehension. When students read orally, their purpose should be to convey the meaning of the passage rather than to render accurate pronunciation of each word.

Less fluent readers comprehend less. In a study of oral fluency among fourth-grade readers, the more fluent readers had better comprehension (Pinnell et al., 1995). Although they had 94 percent accuracy, the least fluent readers read much more slowly. Their average reading speed was just 65 words per minute. Fluent readers in fourth grade read between 126 and 162 words a minute.

The foundation for fluency is to build solid word analysis skills (Wolf & Katzir-Cohen, 2001) and to monitor for meaning. Struggling readers need to check themselves as they read by asking: Do the words that I am reading match the letters? Do the words make sense?

In addition to prompting students to monitor for meaning, activities that foster rapid recognition of high-frequency words will foster fluency, as will wide reading of books at the students' independent level. This reading need not be oral. In fact, silent reading provides more realistic practice. At all levels, silent reading is recommended for building fluency. As they read books in which nearly all the words are known, students' ability to recognize the words faster should increase. Like any other complex behavior, reading requires substantial practice before it becomes automatic and seemingly effortless. If students persist in reading in a labored, halting fashion, the material is probably too difficult. Try material that is easy, and gradually move up to more difficult selections. Students, especially if they are younger, might also be encouraged to read the same selections a second, a third, or even a fourth time.

A first step in building fluency is to model the process. As you read orally, you are modeling the process of smooth, expressive reading. As you read orally to students, explain the techniques that you use: how you read in phrases, how you use your voice to express the author's meaning, how you read at a pace that listeners can keep up with but that isn't too fast.

The ability to read orally with expression is, in part, a public speaking skill. Its goal is to convey meaning to others rather than to construct meaning. Oral reading should be preceded by silent reading. Readers need to construct a good understanding of the text so they can then read it orally in such a way as to convey their interpretation of the text. If you wish to promote oral reading skills, use drama and poetry to provide practice. Students don't mind reading a script

Except when working with very beginning readers, the initial reading of a selection should almost always be silent. While discussing a selection read silently, students might read orally a favorite part, dramatize dialogue, or read a passage out loud to provide support for a point they are making.

ADAPTING INSTRUCTION for *ENGLISH LANGUAGE LEARNERS* Reading along with a taped version of a story fosters fluency, as does simply reading the story several times. Taped versions, however, are especially helpful for students whose reading speed is extremely slow and for students who are still learning English (Blum et al., 1995; Dowhower, 1987).

When students are asked to read orally, they should have a chance to read silently first and should be asked to read in such a way as to convey what the author meant. Students will then have to think about the meaning and emphasize the meaning of what they read. Model the process frequently.

TABLE 3.8 Reading rate in words per minute

Instructional Reading Level	Oral Reading	Silent Reading
Grade 1	55	55
Grade 2	85	85
Grade 3	115	130
Grade 4	135	155
Grade 5	145	185
Grade 6	150	205
Grade 7–8	150	225

Adapted from Powell (1980); cited in Lipson and Wixson (1997) and Harris and Sipay (1990).

Unrehearsed oral reading in which students take turns reading (round robin) can be painful for struggling readers, who are embarrassed by their mistakes, and good readers, who are bored by slow, choppy reading.

over and over again if they are going to dramatize it. Students are also motivated to read accurately and expressively if they are reading to others. Having older students read to young students—fifth-graders reading to second-graders—provides students with a reason to read a selection over and over again. Choral reading of selections also promotes oral fluency (McMaster, 1998). Collections of poetry and drama, including reader's theater selections, that might be used for repeated reading can be found in Chapter 9.

Because oral reading is used to measure fluency, there is a tendency to overemphasize oral reading as a way of fostering fluency. However, silent and oral reading are different tasks. Oral reading focuses the reader's attention on pronouncing words correctly. Silent reading stresses constructing meaning, which is the essence of reading. Silent reading also provides students the opportunity to work out troublesome words on their own without feeling rushed or embarrassed because people are listening to them struggle.

Silent reading is faster and more efficient. Readers can skip unnecessary words or sections. Beyond second grade level reading, silent reading speed should exceed oral reading (see Table 3.8). If students are reading at a very slow pace, try to determine why and take corrective action. If the material is too difficult—if they miss more than five words out of one hundred—obtain materials on the appropriate level. If they are having difficulty decoding words, work on decoding skills. If they have mastered decoding skills but are reading in a slow or labored fashion, work on fluency. They may also be very anxious readers who feel they have to read each word carefully.

Repeated Readings

A popular technique for fostering fluency is through **repeated reading** (Samuels, 1979). Repeated reading helps students achieve accuracy and rapid recognition of high-frequency words. In one study, slow-reading students doubled their reading speed after just seven weeks of repeated reading training (Dowhower, 1987). In another study, students enjoyed the fluency exercises so much that after the experiments were concluded, they asked for additional repeated reading sessions (Rashotte & Torgesen, 1985).

Rereadings are effective because students meet high-frequency words over and over, and these become part of their automatic recognition vocabulary (Dowhower, 1987). However, this means that selections chosen should be on the same approximate level and should be on the students' instructional level. Lesson 3.3 lists some suggested steps for a repeated reading lesson.

Repeated Reading

LESSON 3.3

Step 1. Introducing repeated readings

Explain the reasons behind repeated readings. Discuss how we get better when we practice. Explain to students that they will be practicing by reading the same story over and over again. Tell students that this will help them read faster and better.

Step 2. Selecting a passage

Select or have the students choose short, interesting selections of approximately 100 words. Make sure that books are on the students' instructional level.

Step 3. Obtaining an initial timing

Obtain a baseline reading and accuracy rate. Have students read a selection orally. Time the reading and record the number of words read correctly. If students take more than two minutes to read the selection and make more than five errors out of 100 words (not counting missed endings), the selection is too hard. If students make only one or two errors and read the selection at 85 words per minute or faster, the selection is too easy. If students can read 100 words a minute or close to it, repeated reading is probably a waste of instructional time (Dowhower, 1987). They would be better off with self-selected reading.

Step 4. Rereading

Go over the students' miscues with them. Help them read these words correctly. Also help them with phrasing problems or any other difficulties they may have had. Then direct them to reread the selection until they feel they can read it faster and more smoothly. Practice can take one of three forms: (1) reading the selection to oneself, (2) listening to an audiotape or viewing the selection on a CD-ROM while reading the selection silently and then reading the selection without the aid of the tape or CD, (3) reading the selection to a partner. If students' reading speed is very slow, below 50 words per minute, they will do better reading along with a person or taped or CD version (Dowhower, 1987). After they reach speeds of 60 words per minute, they can practice without the tape or CD. Initially, students with very low reading rates will need lots of practice to reach 85 words per minute. But as the reading rate increases, they won't need as many practice readings. Once they get used to the procedure, four or five rereadings should provide optimal returns for time spent. Additional rereadings would provide diminishing returns.

Step 5. Evaluating the reading

Students read the selections to you or to a partner. The number of word recognition errors and the reading speed are recorded. Students are informed of their progress. A chart, as in Figure 3.1, might be constructed to show the degree of improvement. The goal is to have students read at least 85 words per minute. Students should practice until they reach that standard. Errors in word recognition should also decrease. However, do not insist on perfect word recognition. Setting a standard of 100 percent accuracy leads students to conclude that reading is a word-pronouncing rather than a meaning-constructing activity. It also slows the reading rate. Afraid of making a mistake, students will read at a slow-but-sure pace (Samuels, 1988).

FIGURE 3.1

Speed of Reading Chart

If you read the same words over and over, you will read faster and better. On this sheet, show how long it took you to read 100 words. Blacken one block for each 10 seconds of time you took. For the first time that you read the story, blacken the blocks under number 1. For the second time, blacken the blocks under number 2, and so on. Write down the number of mistakes that you make on the lines at the bottom.

Number of Times I Read the Story

	1	2	3	4	5	6	7	8	9	10
(2 minutes) 120										
110										
100										
90										
80										
70										
(1 minute) 60										
50										
40										
30										
20										
10										

Time (in seconds)

Number of mistakes ___ ___ ___ ___ ___ ___ ___ ___ ___ ___

From *Assessing and Correcting Reading and Writing Difficulties* (2nd ed.) by T. Gunning, 2002. Boston: Allyn & Bacon. Reprinted by permission of allyn & Bacon.

■ Variations on Rereading

Instead of working with a teacher, students may work in pairs. However, explain and model the procedure first. One student reads while the other charts her progress. Then they switch roles. Show students how to time the reading and count errors. To make the charting easier, have students check 100-word samples only. Students might read a selection that contains more than 100 words, but only 100 words should be used for charting reading rate. Students may hurry through a selection to obtain a fast time. Explain to students that they should read at a normal rate. On occasion have students read a song or a poem instead of the usual reading selections. Because of their rhythm, narrative poems and songs lend themselves to a rapid reading.

Repeated Reading versus Wide Reading

Both repeated reading and wide reading are effective approaches for building fluency (Hiebert, 2002). However, wide reading has a key advantage. Wide reading, especially if informational text is being read, is a more effective way to build background and vocabulary (Hiebert, 2002). If students read five selections rather than reading one selection five times, they are encountering five times as many ideas and five times as many vocabulary words. Background knowledge and vocabulary form the foundation for reading. Perhaps the best solution is to balance a limited amount of rereading with extensive reading of informational text on the appropriate level of challenge.

Reading to Others

An excellent device for fostering oral fluency is to arrange for students to read to younger pupils. Discuss with them the importance of being able to read smoothly and with expression. Demonstrate for them how books should be read to younger students and provide them with guided practice. Also help them select suitable books, ones that are interesting but aren't too long. Also have students create taped books. Having taped books in your class library helps make them accessible to struggling readers. Creating tapes fosters fluency. Students must practice so they can read accurately and with proper expression. Invite struggling as well as achieving readers to create tapes. Struggling readers can create tapes for books that they have read and enjoyed (Worthy, Broadus, Ivy, 2001).

Modelled Techniques for Building Fluency

Reading along with a taped or CD-ROM version of a selection can build oral fluency. Paired reading, which is also known as Duolog Reading (Topping, 1998), can also be effective in building oral fluency. The teacher, a parent, or a helper student who is a more proficient reader teams up with a student. The student chooses the book to be read. The book selected is one that would be a little too difficult for the student to read on his own. After a brief discussion of the title and cover illustration, the helper and student simultaneously read the book out loud. During this dual reading, the helper adjusts her reading rate so it matches that of the student. When the student feels that he can read a portion of the text on his own, he signals the helper by raising his left hand. When he wants the helper to resume reading with him, he raises his right hand. The helper automatically provides assistance when the student stumbles over a word or is unable to read the word within five seconds (Topping, 1987; 1989). As an alternative to paired reading, the teacher, parent, or tutor may take turns reading the selection. At first, the teacher might do most of the reading. The student would read any words that he could. As the student becomes more proficient, he can read larger segments. All of these techniques provide a model of phrasing and expression that students might then incorporate into their silent reading.

SYLLABIC ANALYSIS

By fourth grade, about half the words in texts are multisyllabic; by sixth grade, the figure is more than 80 percent. As students move up through the grades, the ability to decode multisyllabic words becomes increasingly more important. However, not all students will need instruction in syllabic analysis. To assess students' ability to decode multisyllabic words, note how they handle polysyllabic words that they encounter. You can also administer the Syllable Survey in Appendix B. Teach syllable patterns according to students' needs. Some students may have difficulty only with a few advanced patterns. Others may need extensive instruction in **syllabication.**

Syllabic analysis is deceptively difficult. Surprisingly, in one study students who had no difficulty reading single-syllable words read *letter* as *later, weeding* as *wedding, cabbage* as *cab bag,* and *ribbon* as *rib bahn,* the last two errors being nonwords (Gunning, 2001). In 20 percent of the multisyllabic words, students omitted at least one syllable. An analysis of students' errors has a number of implications for instruction. These include:

- Students should be taught and prompted to process all the syllables in a word.
- Students need to be taught to see patterns in words. Students who can read *let* and *her* but read *letter* as *later* are not seeing the familiar *et* pattern.
- Students need to be flexible in their decoding of words. If one pronunciation doesn't work out, they should be prepared to try another. This ties in with reading for meaning. Pronouncing *even* as *ev-en,* the student should note that this is not a word and so should try a long pronunciation: *e-ven.*
- Students should integrate context and syllabic analysis. A number of students read *wedding* for *weeding* in the sentence: "Amy was weeding her garden," which indicates failure to use context. A number of other students read the sentence as "Amy was watering her garden," which suggests that although they used context they failed to process the whole word.
- Students need to be reminded to use the orthographic aspects of phonics. Many students had difficulty with words containing final *e* markers and digraphs.

■ **Syllabication** is the division of words into syllables. In reading, words are broken down into syllables phonemically, according to their sound (*gen e rous, butt er*) rather than orthographically, according to the rules governing end-of-line word division (*gen er ous, but ter*).

ADAPTING INSTRUCTION for *STRUGGLING READERS and WRITERS*

Some students have difficulty decoding multisyllabic words even though they are able to decode single-syllable words. These students may not realize that they can apply their single-syllable skills to the decoding of multisyllabic words. Having them seek out known parts in multisyllabic words helps them make use of what they know.

Students did not make use of the final *e* marker that indicates a soft *g* in *cabbage* or the digraph *ai* in *contain* that indicates a long *a*. When presenting syllable patterns, it may be helpful to review the single-syllable elements that make up those patterns.

■ Students should also be taught that sometimes an element in a multisyllabic word is not read in the same way as when it appears in a single-syllable word. For instance, many students read the *car* in *carrots* as though it were the word *car*. Students also need to know that often the pronunciation of an element changes when it is in a multisyllabic word. Because of reduced stress, the *on* in *ribbon* has a schwa rather than a short-*o* pronunciation. Many students pronounced it as though it had a short-*o* pronunciation and ended up with the nonword *ribbahn*. Students need to be flexible in their pronunciation of the syllables in mulitsyllabic words and should also be using context as an aid.

■ Elements such as *tion* and *ture* as in *mention* and *future*, which occur only in multisyllabic words, need a careful introduction, frequent review, and a great deal of practice.

Generalization Approach to Teaching Syllabic Analysis

Sort the following words. You can have a question mark category for words that don't seem to fit a pattern.

spider	super	magnet	clever
even	flavor	bitter	custom
rabbit	hotel	tiger	over
supper	music	fever	elbow
pepper	pupil	wagon	future

How did you sort the words? One way of sorting them would be by sounds. All the words with long vowels in the first syllable are placed in one column; all the words with short vowels in the first syllable are put in a second column. You can also sort them by sound and spelling. Notice that the syllables that end in a consonant seem to be short and those that end in a vowel seem to be long. You might also note that the long vowels were followed by one consonant and short vowels were followed by two consonants. However, there were two exception words: *wagon*, and *clever*. Sorting is a way of helping students make discoveries about words. Through sorts of this type, help them discover one of the most sweeping generalizations in phonics: the open and closed vowel syllables, which states that syllables that end in a vowel are generally long and those that end in a consonant are short.

The two approaches to teaching syllabication are generalization and pattern. Sorting is an excellent way to help students discover or reinforce their knowledge of generalizations or patterns in syllabication. In the generalization approach, students learn general rules for dividing words into syllables. The generalizations listed below seem to be particularly useful (Gunning, 1975). These should be presented in the following order, which reflects both their frequency of occurrence and approximate order of difficulty:

1. *Easy affixes: -ing, -er, -ly.* Most prefixes and suffixes form separate syllables: *un-safe, re-build, help-ful, quick-ly.* Except for *s* as a plural marker, affixes generally are composed of a vowel and consonant(s). Thus, they are syllables in themselves: *play-ing, re-play.*

2. *Compound words.* The words that make up a compound word usually form separate syllables: *sun-set, night-fall.*

3. *Two consonants between two vowels.* When two consonants appear between two vowels, the word generally divides between them: *win-ter, con-cept.* The place of division is often an indication of the pronunciation of the vowel. The *i* in *winter;* the *o* in the first syllable of *concept,* and the *e* in the second syllable of *concept* are short. Note that all three vowels are in closed syllables—that is, syllables that end in consonants: *win, con, cept.* Closed syllables often contain a short vowel. (The *e* in winter is not short because it is followed by *r.*) Note, too, that digraphs are not split: *broth-er, with-er.*

4. *One consonant between two vowels.* When one consonant appears between two vowels, it often becomes a part of the syllable on the right: *ma-jor, e-vil.* When the single consonant moves to the right, the syllable to the left is said to be open because it ends in a vowel. If a syllable ends in a vowel, the vowel is generally long. In a number of exceptions, however, the consonant becomes a part of the syllable on the left: *sev-en, wag-on.*

5. *le.* The letters *le* at the end of a word are usually combined with a preceding consonant to create a separate syllable: *cra-dle, ma-ple.*

6. *Two vowels together.* A limited number of words split between two vowels: *i-de-a, di-al.*

It is important to keep in mind that syllabication is designed to help students decode an unfamiliar word by separating it into its syllabic parts and then recombining the parts into a whole. It is not necessary for students to divide the word exactly right, which is a highly technical process. All that matters is whether students are able to arrive at the approximate pronunciation.

Pattern Approach to Teaching Syllabic Analysis

Knowing syllabic generalizations is one thing; applying them is quite another. Research (Gunning, 1975) and experience suggest that many students apparently do not apply syllabic generalizations. When faced with unfamiliar, multisyllabic words, they attempt to search out pronounceable elements or simply skip the words. These students might fare better with an approach that presents syllables in patterns (Cunningham, 1978).

In a pattern approach, students examine a number of words that contain a syllable that has a high frequency. For example, dozens of words that begin with a consonant and are followed by a long *o* could be presented in pattern form. The advantage of this approach is that students learn to recognize pronounceable units

---

Students often confuse open and closed syllables. They tend to read open syllables such as those occurring in *even* and *noticed* as closed syllables: *ev-en, not-iced.*

Putting words into syllables can be a challenging task because it's sometimes difficult to tell where one syllable ends and another begins. Even the experts disagree. If you look up the word *vocational,* for instance, you will see that Merriam-Webster dictionaries divide it into syllables in one way and Thorndike-Barnhart dictionaries syllabicate it in another way.

ADAPTING INSTRUCTION for STRUGGLING READERS and WRITERS

When working with struggling readers, especially those who have been unsuccessful with a particular program or approach, try using a new approach and also new materials. Struggling readers don't want to work with a program or text that they associate with failure (Stahl, 1998).

in multisyllabic words and also to apply the open-syllable generalization in a specific situation. The pattern could be introduced with a one-syllable word contrasted with multisyllabic words to make it easier for students to grasp, for example:

so
soda
total
local
vocal
motel
hotel
notice

The steps to follow in teaching a syllabication lesson using the pattern approach are presented in Lesson 3.4. Schwa *a*, as in *above*, a high-frequency pattern, is introduced.

LESSON 3.4   Syllabication using the pattern approach

Step 1. Introducing the schwa *a* pattern

Write the word *go* on the board, and have students read it. Then write *ago* under it, and have students read it. Contrast *go* and *ago* by pointing to the sound that each syllable makes. To help students perceive the separate syllables in *ago*, write them in contrasting colors or underline them. Then have students read *ago*. Present the words *away*, *alone*, *awake*, and *asleep* in the same way. As students read the separate syllables in each word, point to each one. Note similarities among the words.

Step 2. Formulating a generalization and selecting a model word

Lead students to see that *a* at the beginning of a word often has the schwa sound /uh/. Since schwa, according to most systems of categorizing speech sounds, occurs only in multisyllabic words, provide students with a multisyllabic model word for the *a* spelling of schwa. Tell students that *ago* is the model word for this pattern. If they forget the pattern or have difficulty with a schwa *a*, they can use the model word to help them. If you have a model words chart, add *ago* to it. If you do not have a model words chart, you may wish to start one.

Step 3. Guided practice

For guided practice, have students read a second set of schwa *a* words: *around*, *along*, *alive*, *across*, *about*. Also have students search out schwa *a* words in a reading selection so they can see this pattern in context. Have students complete exercises similar to the following:

▌Why might students who can read elements in single-syllable words have difficulty with those same elements in multisyllabic words? The students may have difficulty locating the known element in a polysyllabic word. For instance, *par* is a single-syllable word that appears as an element in *partial*, *parcel*, and *particle* but has a different identity in *parade* and *paradise*. As Shefelbine (1990) notes, "Identifying patterns of syllables requires more developed and complex knowledge of letter and spelling patterns than the knowledge needed for reading single syllable words" (p. 225).

Make words by putting together two of the three syllables in each row. Write the words on the lines.

sleep	a	read
a	go	play
head	a	next
over	a	round
a	long	lamp

Underline the word that fits the sense of the sentence better.

Toads and frogs look (*alike, away*).

Do you know how to tell them (*alive, apart*)?

Toads like to live in gardens that are (*alive, alone*) with bugs.

Toads eat an (*amazing, awakening*) number of bugs.

A toad can flick its tongue so fast that a bug would have a hard time getting (*awake, away*). (Gunning, 1994)

Step 4. Application

Have students read selections—stories, informational pieces, and/or real-world materials—that contain schwa *a* words.

Step 5. Assessment and review

Note students' ability to read multisyllabic words that follow the pattern introduced. Also note what they do when they encounter multisyllabic words. Are they able to use strategies to decode the words? Review and reteach as necessary.

■ Additional Practice Activities for Multisyllabic Words

When students decode polysyllabic words, do not insist upon exact syllable division. All that should be expected is that the student break polysyllabic words into smaller units so that she or he can pronounce each one and then put the units back together again to form a whole word.

- Have students read or sing song lyrics in which the separate syllables of multisyllabic words are indicated.
- Make available books in which difficult words are put into syllables and phonetically respelled.
- Write words on the board, syllable by syllable. After writing the first syllable, have students read it and guess what the word might be. Then write the second syllable. Have them read the first syllable again and combine it with the second syllable. Continue until the whole word has been written.
- Encourage students to bring in multisyllabic words that they have noticed in their reading and which they were able to pronounce. They might write their words on the board and have the other students read them.
- When introducing new words that have more than one syllable, write the words on the board and encourage students to read them. Provide help as needed.
- Use software, such as *Word Parts* (Sunburst), that challenges students to

build words by combining syllables and use multisyllabic words to compose poems, riddles, and stories.

- To help students differentiate between open and closed syllables, have them read contrasting word pairs (*super, supper; biter, bitter*) or complete sentences by selecting one of two contrasting words: Although the dog looked mean, it was not a (*biter, bitter*). We had chicken and mashed potatoes for (*super, supper*).

Multisyllabic Patterns

In approximate order of difficulty, the major multisyllabic patterns are:

- Easy affixes: *play-ing, quick-ly*
- Compound words: *base-ball, any-one*
- Closed-syllable words: *rab-bit, let-ter*
- Open-syllable words: *ba-by, ti-ny*
- *e* marker words: *es-cape, do-nate*
- Vowel digraph words: *a-gree, sea-son*
- Other patterns: *cir-cle, sir-loin*

Major syllable patterns and example words for the patterns are presented in Table 3.9.

Combining the Generalization and Pattern Approaches

Although the pattern approach is highly effective and builds on what students know, students sometimes are unable to see patterns in words. In these instances, they should try applying generalizations. In his research, Shefelbine (1990) found that instruction in open (*mo-, ta-, fi-*) and closed (*-at, -em, -in*) syllables and affixes (*un-, pre-, -less, -ful*) was especially helpful. After teaching a number of open-syllable patterns, you might have students construct a generalization about the pattern, such as, "Syllables that end in a vowel are often long (*ta ble*). After teaching a number of closed-syllable patterns, you might have students construct a generalization about the pattern, such as, "Syllables that end in a consonant are often short (*hap py*)."

To apply generalizations, students should identify the first syllable by locating the first vowel and note whether the syllable is open (followed by one consonant or digraph) or closed (followed by two or more consonants). Students should say the first syllable and then proceed in this same way, syllable by syllable. After they have pronounced all the syllables, they should attempt to say the word, making any adjustments necessary. Prompt students as needed. If students misread an open syllable as a closed one, for instance, reading *no-tice* as *not-ice*, ask them to tell where the vowel is so they can see that the vowel should be ending the syllable and should be long (Shefelbine & Newman, 2000). Often vowel sounds are reduced when they appear in multisyllabic words, as in *educate*, where the *u* has a schwa

> Some students have difficulty telling where one syllable ends and another starts. Teaching students to see syllable patterns should help. They can also use a generalization approach.

> Students need not be able to pronounce every syllable. Often, if they find a key syllable or two that they can pronounce, they can use this to reconstruct the whole word.

TABLE 3.9 Common syllable patterns

Compound-Word Pattern

some	day	out	sun
someone	daylight	outside	sunup
sometime	daytime	outdoor	sundown
something	daybreak	outline	sunfish
somehow	daydream	outgrow	sunlight
somewhere		outfield	sunbeam

Schwa *a* Pattern

a	a
ago	around
away	along
alone	alive
awake	apart
among	across
asleep	about

High-Frequency Patterns

en	o	er
pen	go	her
open	ago	under
happen	over	ever
enter	broken	never
twenty	spoken	other
plenty	frozen	farmer

ar	at	it
car	mat	sit
garden	matter	sitter
sharpen	batter	bitter
farmer	chatter	kitten
marker	clatter	kitchen
partner	scatter	pitcher

in	is(s)	un
win	miss	under
winter	mister	until
window	mistake	hunter
dinner	sister	thunder
finish	whisper	hundred

be	re	or
became	remind	order
beside	report	morning
below	reward	corner
begin	refuse	forty
belong	receive	before

a	y = /ē/	ey	ble
pay	sunny	turkey	able
paper	funny	monkey	table
baby	dusty	money	cable
famous	shady	honey	bubble
favorite			mumble

i	ur	um	
tie	fur	sum	
tiger	furry	summer	
spider	hurry	number	
tiny	turkey	pumpkin	
title	turtle	stumble	
Friday	purple	trumpet	

ic(k)	et	et	im
pick	let	ticket	swim
picnic	letter	pocket	swimmer
attic	better	rocket	chimney
nickel	lettuce	bucket	limit
pickle	settle	magnet	improve
chicken	metal	jacket	simple

Short-Vowel Patterns

ab	ad	ag
cab	sad	bag
cabin	saddle	baggy
cabbage	paddle	dragon
rabbit	shadow	wagon
habit	ladder	magazine
absent	address	magnet

an	ap
can	nap
candy	napkin
handy	happy
handle	happen
giant	captain
distant	chapter

ent	el
went	yell
event	yellow
prevent	elbow
cement	elephant
invent	jelly
experiment	welcome

TABLE 3.9 Common syllable patterns *(continued)*

ep	es(s)	ev	ub	uc(k)	ud
pep	less	seven	rub	luck	mud
pepper	lesson	several	rubber	lucky	buddy
peppermint	address	never	bubble	bucket	study
September	success	clever	stubborn	chuckle	puddle
shepherd	yesterday	every	subject	success	huddle
separate	restaurant	level	public	product	sudden

ea	ea		uf	ug	up
sweat	treasure		stuff	bug	pup
sweater	measure		stuffy	buggy	puppy
weather	pleasure		muffin	ugly	supper
feather	pleasant		suffer	suggest	upper
leather	threaten		buffalo	struggle	puppet
meadow	wealthy				

id	ig	il	us	ut	uz
rid	wig	pill	muss	but	fuzz
riddle	wiggle	pillow	mustard	button	fuzzy
middle	giggle	silver	muscle	butter	puzzle
hidden	signal	silly	custom	clutter	muzzle
midnight	figure	building	customer	flutter	buzzer
			discuss	gutter	buzzard

ob	oc	od
rob	doc	cod
robber	doctor	body
problem	pocket	model
probably	chocolate	modern
hobby	rocket	product
gobble	hockey	somebody

Long-Vowel Patterns

ol	om	on	ade	ail/ale
doll	mom	monster	parade	detail
dollar	momma	monument	invade	female
volcano	comma	honest	lemonade	airmail
follow	common	honor	centigrade	trailer
holiday	comment	concrete		
jolly	promise	responsible		

			ain	ate
			obtain	hesitate
			explain	hibernate
			complain	appreciate

op	ot	age	ea	ea	ee	e
shop	rot	cabbage	sea	eat	bee	equal
shopper	rotten	bandage	season	eaten	see	secret
chopper	gotten	damage	reason	beaten	beetle	fever
popular	bottom	message	beaver	repeat	needle	female
opposite	bottle	baggage	eagle	leader	indeed	even
copy	robot	garbage	easily	reader	succeed	

		ide	ire	ize	ise	ive
		side	tire	prize	wise	drive
		beside	entire	realize	surprise	arrive
		divide	require	recognize	exercise	alive
		decide	admire	memorize	advise	survive
		provide	umpire	apologize	disguise	beehive

continued

TABLE 3.9　Common syllable patterns *(continued)*

ope	one	u	ture	ou	ou	ow
hope	phone	use	future	round	mountain	power
antelope	telephone	music	nature	around	fountain	tower
envelope	microphone	human	adventure	about	surround	flower
telescope	xylophone	museum	creature	announce	compound	allow
				amount	thousand	allowance

Other Vowel Patterns

al	au	au	aw	oo	ove	u
also	cause	caution	draw	too	prove	Sue
always	saucer	faucet	awful	bamboo	proven	super
already	author	sausage	awesome	shampoo	improve	student
altogether	August	daughter	drawing	cartoon	approve	studio
although	autumn	auditorium	crawling	raccoon	remove	truly
walrus	audience		strawberry	balloon	movements	tuna

oi	oy			tion	tion	sion	y = /ī/
point	joy			action	question	conclusion	try
poison	enjoy			addition	mention	confusion	reply
disappointment	destroy			station	suggestion	occasion	supply
noisy	royal			invention	exhaustion	explosion	deny
avoid	loyal			information	indigestion	persuasion	magnify
moisture	voyage						

From *Assessing and Correcting Reading and Writing Difficulties* (2nd ed.) by T. Gunning, 2002. Boston: Allyn & Bacon. Reprinted by permission of Allyn & Bacon.

Instead of, or along with, the traditional strategy for decoding multisyllabic words presented on the previous page, students might use the pronounceable word part or analogy strategy.

pronunciation. Explain to students that they should not just pronounce syllables but should change pronunciations if they have to so they can "read the real word" (Shefelbine & Newman, 2000).

Whether you teach using generalizations, patterns, or, as this book recommends, a combination of approaches, students must have a plan of attack or strategy when facing an unfamiliar multisyllabic word. Students can use the steps in the following traditional Student Strategy on their own.

 Attacking multisyllabic words

1.　See whether the word has any prefixes or suffixes. If so, pronounce the prefix, then the suffix, and then the remaining part(s) of the word. If the word has no prefix or suffix, start with the beginning of the word and divide it into syllables (as explained on previous pages). Say each syllable.

2.　Put the syllables together. If the word does not sound like a real word, try other pronunciations until you get a real word.

3. See if the word makes sense in the sentence in which it appears. If it does not, try other pronunciations.

4. If nothing works, use a dictionary or ask the teacher.

Syllabic analysis might be used to shore up weak phonics skills. Some older students may be weak in basic phonics. They have some basic knowledge of phonics but are unable to decode a word here and there. Since these students will also need instruction in syllabic analysis, you might combine the two. Realizing that they are being taught skills that were meant for younger students, older students might be resentful of phonics instruction or embarrassed by it. If they have some skills in single-syllable phonics, but just need some review, you might review phonics elements that they are having difficulty with as you provide instruction in syllabic analysis. When presenting a new multisyllabic pattern, you might take a little time to review the single-syllable pattern on which it is based. For instance, when teaching the *-oy* pattern, you introduce it by presenting the word *joy* and build on that. If students are sometimes having difficulty with single-syllable *-oy* words, you might spend some time reviewing that pattern before moving to *enjoy* and other multisyllabic words. Older students will appreciate being given work that is more mature, and you will be making good use of limited instructional time.

Using the Pronounceable Word Part and Analogy Strategies

The pronounceable word part and analogy strategies recommended for decoding single-syllable words may also be used to decode multisyllabic words. For instance, if students are having difficulty with the word *silver*, they might look for a pronounceable word part such as *il* and add /s/ to make *sil*. They would then say *er*, add /v/ to make *ver* and reconstruct the whole word. In many instances, saying a part of the word—the *sil* in *silver*, for example—is enough of a clue to enable students to say the whole word. If the pronounceable word part strategy does not work, they may use an analogy or compare/contrast strategy, in which students employ common words to help them sound out the syllables in a multisyllabic word that is in their listening but not their reading vocabulary. For instance, faced with the word *thunder*, the student works it out by making a series of comparisons. The first syllable is *thun*, which is similar to the known word *sun*, and the second syllable is *der*, which is similar to the known word *her*. Putting them together, the student synthesizes the word *thunder*.

As students read increasingly complex materials and meet a higher proportion of polysyllabic words, their ability to perceive the visual forms of syllables should develop naturally. As with phonics skills, the best way to practice dealing with polysyllabic words is through a combination of instruction and wide reading.

KEEPING INSTRUCTION FUNCTIONAL

A variety of word lists for practice with both single-syllable words and multisyllabic words can be found at **http://www. resourceroom.net/ OGLists/wordlists.asp.**

INVOLVING PARENTS

Parents might want to know what to do if their children ask for help with a word. Having them simply tell their children unknown words is the safest, least frustrating approach (Topping, 1989). But in some situations, you may want to have them encourage their children in the use of specific strategies.

Teachers in the upper grades are sometimes inclined to provide struggling readers with a complete course in phonics or syllabic analysis. They hope that starting over will help students pick up missing skills. Such an approach is ineffective and wasteful. Start where students are. Build on what they have learned. Also make sure that instruction is functional and contextual. Teach students the skills that they need in the context of real reading and writing. One way of doing that is to look at the materials students are about to read and to note the essential decoding skills needed to read that material. Teach students skills that they are lacking. For instance, in a science article about electricity, the words *circle, circuit, certain, certificate,* and *ceramic* are used. You might write the word *circle* on the chalkboard and *circuit* under it. Pointing to *circle*, have students read it and then use this known word to read *circuit*. If they have difficulty with *cuit*, tell them that *cu* represents a /k/ sound. They should then be able to read the *it* part of the word and put the syllables together. Then using *certain* as the known word, have students use their knowledge of the *cer* in *certain* to read *certificate* and *ceramic*. If students have difficulty with *certain*, write the word *her* on the board and have them relate the first part of *certain* to *her*. Have them note that both words have an /er/ sound. Then encourage them to read the rest of the syllables. Provide help as necessary. Help students to see that *ceramic* begins in the same way as *certain* and *certificate*. Using this knowledge, they should be able to work out the pronunciation of *ceramic*. But provide help as needed. The lesson assumes that students have heard the words and know their meanings.

One lesson that students will have to learn as they work out the pronunciation of multisyllabic words is that they might have to adjust the pronunciation of some of the elements. For instance, a student pronouncing *certificate* as *sir-tif-ih-kate* would have to adjust the pronunciation of the last syllable to produce a real word.

HELP FOR STRUGGLING READERS AND WRITERS

Struggling readers and writers do best when given a systematic program in word analysis skills (Foorman et al., 1998). Although most students will grasp word analysis skills regardless of the approach used to teach them, at-risk learners need direct, clear instruction (Snow, Burns, & Griffin, 1998). For students who are struggling with decoding, this text recommends word building. Also, use spelling to reinforce phonics. Dictating and having students spell pattern words helps them to focus on the individual sounds and letters in the pattern words and provides another avenue of learning. Most important of all, encourage students to read widely. Struggling readers often need much more practice than do achieving readers. Reading books on their level that apply patterns they have been taught is the best possible practice.

For syllabic analysis, use the pattern approach. One advantage of this approach is that it reviews basic phonics as new elements are being introduced. For instance, when introducing the *aw* multisyllabic pattern, the teacher automatically reviews the *aw* element, as in *law*. This is helpful to struggling readers, who often have gaps in their skills. Shefelbine (1990) found that 15 to 20 percent of the students in the fourth- and eighth-grade classes that he tested had difficulty with multisyllabic words, and some students were still experiencing problems with single-syllable phonics, especially vowel elements.

 ## ESSENTIAL STANDARDS

Grades four and beyond
Students will

- use a full range of phonics skills to decode words.
- use a full range of syllabic analysis skills and patterns to decode words.
- use pronounceable word part, analogy, and contextual strategies to decode words.
- integrate the use of contextual and word analysis strategies.
- read with accuracy, fluency, and expression at an appropriate rate (see Table 3.8).

 ## ASSESSMENT

Assessment should be ongoing. Through observation, note whether students are learning the skills and strategies they have been taught. Watch to see what they do when they come across an unfamiliar word. Do they attempt to apply pronounceable word part, analogy, or context strategies? When they read, what phonics elements are they able to handle? What phonics elements pose problems for

 ### ACTION PLAN

1. Assess students' knowledge of word analysis skills and strategies.
2. Construct or adapt a program for development of word analysis skills and strategies based upon students' needs.
3. Introduce needed phonics and syllabication skills and strategies in functional fashion.
4. Provide ample practice and application opportunities.
5. Develop fluency through modeling, instruction, wide reading, and rereading.
6. Plan a systematic program. However, provide on-the-spot instruction when the need arises.
7. For English language learners, plan a program that takes into consideration word analysis knowledge that they already possess in their native language and areas that might pose problems.
8. Monitor students' progress and make necessary adjustments.

them? In addition to observation, you might use the Word Pattern Survey to assess students' knowledge of major phonics patterns and the Syllable Survey in Appendix B to get a sense of students' ability to handle multisyllabic words. Chapter 2 contains additional assessment suggestions, including using a running record.

SUMMARY

1. By the time they reach fourth grade, most students have mastered basic phonics. However, there will be some students whose knowledge of phonics is inadequate. The most efficient approach to take with these students is to use a pattern approach such as word building.

2. Along with phonics, students should use semantic and syntactic clues and their general knowledge to decode words. Along with context clues, students should be taught how to use two powerful word identification strategies: pronounceable word part and analogy.

3. High-frequency words are frequently appearing words. These include some words such as *of* and *once* that have irregular spellings. Although irregular, these words are learned through phonologi-cal and spelling connections. Because they occur so frequently, students should be given extra practice with them so that they can be recognized rapidly.

4. Fluency is "freedom from word identification problems that might hinder comprehension in silent reading or the expression of ideas in oral reading." Fluency is fostered by providing a solid foundation in word analysis skills and numerous opportunities to read materials on the appropriate level of challenge.

5. In syllabication, words are broken up into parts primarily based on sound patterns. Syllabication may be taught through generalizations or patterns or some combination of the two.

EXTENDING AND APPLYING

1. Read over the pronunciation key of a dictionary. Notice the spellings given for the consonant sounds and the vowel sounds. Check each of the sounds. Are there any that are not in your dialect? The following words have at least two pronunciations: *dog* ("dawg" or "dog"), *roof* ("ro͞of" or "ro͝of"), *route* ("root" or "rowt"). How do you pronounce them?

2. Examine the word analysis component of a program such as High Noon Reading (Academic Therapy), the SIPPS: Challenge Level, Polysyllabic Decoding (Developmental Studies Center) or, Fast Track Reading, Word Work Strand (Wright Group). What is its approach to teaching phonics and syllabic analysis? Are the lessons and activities functional and contextual? Is adequate practice provided? What is your overall evaluation of the word analysis program in this series?

3. Using the word-building (pattern) approach described in this chapter, plan a lesson in which a phonics or a syllabic analysis element is introduced. State your objectives and describe each of the steps of the lesson. List the materials that might be used to reinforce or apply the element taught. Teach the lesson and evaluate its effectiveness.

4. Working with a small group of struggling readers, note which strategies they use when they encounter difficult words. Providing the necessary instruction and prompts, encourage them to use the pronounceable word part, analogy, and context strategies.

DEVELOPING A PROFESSIONAL PORTFOLIO

Document your knowledge of and ability to teach word analysis skills. Include a sample word analysis lesson that you have taught and your reflection on it. Keep a record of any inservice sessions or workshop sessions on word analysis that you have attended.

DEVELOPING A RESOURCE FILE

Maintain a list of materials and activities that you might use to provide students with opportunities to practice and apply word analysis skills. Focus on materials and activities that would be appropriate for older students. Include helpful Web sites and software.

4

Building Vocabulary

*F*or each of the following statements, put a check under "Agree" or "Disagree" to show how you feel. Discuss your responses with classmates before you read the chapter.

	Agree	*Disagree*
1 Vocabulary words should be taught only when students have a need to learn them.	_____	_____
2 All or most of the difficult words in a selection should be taught before the selection is read.	_____	_____
3 Building vocabulary leads to improved comprehension.	_____	_____
4 The best way to build vocabulary is to study a set number of words each week.	_____	_____
5 Using context is the easiest way to get the meaning of an unfamiliar word.	_____	_____
6 The best way to learn about roots, prefixes, and suffixes is to have a lot of experience with these word parts.	_____	_____
7 Using the dictionary as a strategy to get the meanings of unfamiliar words is inefficient.	_____	_____

USING WHAT YOU KNOW

*C*hapter 3 explained techniques for teaching children how to decode words that were in their listening vocabularies but which they might not recognize when they saw them in print. This chapter is also concerned with reading words. However, the focus in this chapter is on dealing with words whose meanings are unknown. In preparation for reading this chapter, explore your knowledge of this topic.

How many words would you estimate are in your vocabulary? Where and how did you learn them? Have you ever read a book or taken a course designed to increase your vocabulary? If so, how well did the book or the course work? What strategies do you use when you encounter an unknown word? How would you go about teaching vocabulary to an elementary or middle school class?

THE NEED FOR VOCABULARY INSTRUCTION

Most new words are formed by combining parts of old words or giving old words new meanings.

The latter part of this century has been witness to an explosion of knowledge; it is estimated that human knowledge doubles every ten years. Accompanying that explosion are new words invented to label new discoveries and concepts. The most up-to-date unabridged dictionary, *Random House Webster's Unabridged Dictionary of the English Language* (2nd ed.) (Steinmetz, 1999), which contains 2,500 pages and more than 315,000 entries, is a silent tribute to the richness of our language. For its latest printing, the editors added hundreds of new words, providing clear evidence that the English language is alive and thriving.

Even the largest dictionaries, however, contain only a small proportion of the words in the language, with many technical terms never making it into a general lexicon. When these terms are included in the count, the English language has approximately 5 million words (Landau, 1984).

Estimates of the number of words known by average first-graders vary widely from 2,500 to 24,000. However, 5,000 to 6,000 seems a reasonable figure.

This rich store of words allows us to transmit knowledge with precision and imagination. The abundance of new words also poses a challenge to students, who, to be fully literate, must acquire a larger vocabulary than has any preceding generation. Nagy and Anderson (1984) estimated that there are 110,000 words in printed school English when homographs and important people's names are included. Many of these words are relatively rare, however; approximately half would occur only once in a billion words of running text. Even so, students have a good chance of encountering some 55,000 words in their school-related reading.

With a vocabulary of just about 10,000 word families, upper elementary and middle students should be able to cope with most of the reading that they will be required to do. They won't know all of the words in every selection they read, but they will know enough to cope with most texts (Nation, 2002).

STAGES OF WORD KNOWLEDGE

Knowing a word's meaning is not an either/or proposition. Dale and O'Rourke (1971) posited four stages in word knowledge:

1. I never saw it before.
2. I've heard of it, but I don't know what it means.
3. I recognize it in context—it has something to do with _____.
4. I know it. (p. 3)

"M. F. Graves (1987) expanded these stages in learning words to six tasks:

Task 1: Learning to read known words. Learning to read known words involves sounding out words that students understand but do not recognize in print. It includes learning a sight vocabulary and using phonics and syllabication to sound out words.

Task 2: Learning new meanings for known words. Even a cursory examination of a dictionary reveals that most words have more than one meaning. A large part of expanding a student's vocabulary is adding new shades of meaning to words partly known.

Task 3: Learning new words that represent known concepts. Because the concept is already known, this really is little more than learning a new label.

BUILDING LANGUAGE

Students enjoy the challenge of learning long words. Actually, long words are easier to learn because their length makes them more distinctive.

Task 4: Learning new words that represent new concepts. As M. F. Graves (1987) observed, "Learning new words that represent new concepts is the most difficult word-learning task students face" (p. 169).

Task 5: Clarifying and enriching the meanings of known words. Although this task is accomplished when students meet known words in diverse contexts, Graves felt that more systematic, more direct involvement is called for. Teachers have to help students forge connections among known words and provide a variety of enrichment exercises to ensure greater depth of understanding.

Task 6: Moving words from receptive to expressive vocabulary. It is necessary to teach words in such a way that they appear in students' speaking and writing vocabularies. The ultimate test is whether students actually use newly learned words correctly. As Nagy and Scott (2000) comment, "Knowing a word means being able to do things with it. . . . Knowing a word is more like being able to use a tool than it is like being able to state a fact" (p. 273).

As can be seen from the six tasks just described, word knowledge is often a question of degree. The person who uses a CD burner on a regular basis has a better knowledge of the words *CD burner* than does one who has simply seen the device advertised. Instruction needs to be devoted to refining as well as to introducing vocabulary and concepts.

> A key task for ELL is learning the English labels for concepts that they possess in their native language.

> It is difficult to say when a word is learned. Some concrete words may be learned instantaneously; others may be learned slowly, after repeated encounters. In time, words take on a greater depth of meaning as they conjure up more associations.

SEVEN PRINCIPLES OF DEVELOPING VOCABULARY

Developing vocabulary is not simply a matter of listing ten or twenty words and their definitions on the board each Monday morning and administering a vocabulary quiz every Friday. In a sense, it is a part of living. Children learn their initial 5,000 to 6,000 words by interacting with parents and peers, gradually learning labels for the people, objects, and ideas in their environment. As children grow and have additional experiences, their vocabularies continue to develop. They learn *pitcher, batter, shortstop,* and *home run* by playing or watching softball or baseball. They learn *gear shift, brake cable, kick stand,* and *reflector* when they begin riding a bicycle. They learn *magnify, microscope, slide, stage, stage clips, high-power objective, low-power objective, coarse,* and *fine adjustment* as they use a microscope in science.

Building Experiential Background

The first and most effective step that a teacher can take to build vocabulary is to provide students with a variety of rich experiences. These experiences might involve taking students to a weather station, factory, planetarium, museum, or office. Working on projects, conducting experiments, handling artifacts, and other hands-on activities also build a background of experience.

Not all activities can be direct. Viewing computer simulations and demonstrations, films, videotapes, filmstrips, and special TV shows helps build experience, as do discussing, listening, and reading. The key is to make the activity as concrete as possible.

■ Talking Over Experiences

Although experiences form the foundation of vocabulary, they are not enough; labels or series of labels must be attached to them. A presurvey and postsurvey of visitors to a large zoo found that people did not know much more about the animals after leaving the park than they did before they arrived. Apparently, simply looking at the animals was not enough; visitors needed words to define their experiences.

■ Learning Concepts versus Learning Labels

■ A **label** is simply a name for a concept. Students may use labels without really understanding the meanings behind the labels.

For maximum benefit, it is important that experiences be discussed. It is also important to distinguish between learning **labels** and building concepts. For example, the words *petrol* and *lorry* would probably be unfamiliar to American students preparing to read a story set in England. The students would readily understand them if the teacher explained that to the British *petrol* means "gasoline" and *lorry* means "truck." Since the concepts of gasoline and truck are already known, it would simply be a matter of learning two new labels. If the word *fossil* appeared in the selection, however, and the students had no idea what a fossil was, the concept would have to be developed. To provide a concrete experience, the teacher might borrow a fossil from the science department and show it to the class while explaining what it is and relating it to the children's experiences. Building the **concept** of a fossil would take quite a bit more teaching than would learning the labels *petrol* and *lorry*.

■ A **concept** is a general idea, an abstraction derived from particular experiences with a phenomenon. In our rush to cover content, we may not take the time necessary to develop concepts thoroughly; thus students may simply learn empty labels for complex concepts such as *democracy* or *gravity*.

Over time, our expanding background of experience allows us to attach richer meaning to words. For example, *love, truth, justice,* and *freedom* mean more to us at age twenty than they did at age ten, and even more as we approach thirty or forty. In many instances, when dealing with abstract terms, students know the forms of words but not the concepts behind them. A student may have heard and seen the word *independence* many times but have no real idea of what it means. The student may not even realize that as she or he grows and develops, her or his own independence is gradually being gained. The student must learn the concept behind the label; otherwise, the word will be literally meaningless.

Relating Vocabulary to Background

The second principle of vocabulary development is relating vocabulary to students' background. It is essential to relate new words to experiences that students may have had. To teach the word *compliment*, the teacher might mention some nice things that were said that were complimentary. Working in pairs, students might compose compliments for each other.

Gipe (1980) devised a background-relating technique in which students are asked to respond to new words that require some sort of personal judgment or observation. For example, after studying the word *beacon*, students might be asked, "Where have you seen a beacon that is a warning sign?" (p. 400). In a similar vein, Beck and McKeown (1983) asked students to "Tell about someone you might want to eavesdrop on," or "Describe the most melodious sound you can think of" (p. 624). Carr (1983) required students to note a personal clue for each new word. It could be an experience, object, or person. One student associated a local creek with *murky*; another related *numbed* to how one's hands feel when shoveling snow.

Building Relationships

The third principle of developing vocabulary is showing how new words are related to each other. For example, students may be about to read a selection on autobiographies and biographies that includes the unfamiliar words *accomplishment*, *obstacles*, and *nonfiction*, as well as *autobiography* and *biography*. Instead of simply presenting these words separately, demonstrate how they are related to each other. Discuss how autobiography and biography are two similar types of nonfiction, and they often describe the subject's accomplishments and some of the obstacles that he or she had to overcome.

Other techniques for establishing relationships include noting synonyms and antonyms, classifying words, and completing graphic organizers. These techniques are covered later in this chapter.

Developing Depth of Meaning

The fourth vocabulary-building principle is developing depth of meaning. The most frequent method of teaching new words is to define them. Definitions, however, may provide only a superficial level of knowledge (Nagy, 1988). They may be adequate when new labels are being learned for familiar concepts, but they are not sufficient for new concepts. Definitions also may fail to indicate how a word should be used. The following sentences were created by students who had only definitional knowledge. Obviously, they had some understanding of the words, but it was inadequate.

The *vague* windshield needed cleaning.
At noon we *receded* to camp for lunch.

Words may have subtle shades of meanings that dictionary definitions may not quite capture. Most students have difficulty composing sentences using new words when their knowledge of the words is based solely on definitions (McKeown, 1993). Placing words in context (Gipe, 1980) seems to work better, as it illustrates use of words and thereby helps to define them. However, in order for vocabulary development to aid in the comprehension of a selection, both the definition and the context should reflect the way the word is used in the selection the students are about to read.

Obviously, word knowledge is a necessary part of comprehension. Ideas couched in unfamiliar terms will not be understood. However, preteaching difficult vocabulary has not always resulted in improved comprehension. In their review of the research on teaching vocabulary, Stahl and Fairbanks (1986) found that methods that provided only definitional information about each word to be learned did not produce a significant effect on comprehension; nor did methods that gave only one or two exposures to meaningful information about each word. For vocabulary instruction

When concerned about comprehension, choose a few key terms for intensive teaching. The words should be taught so well that pupils don't have to pause when they encounter them.

to have an impact on comprehension, students must acquire knowledge of new words that is both accurate and enriched (Beck, McKeown, & Omanson, 1987). Experiencing a newly learned word in several contexts broadens and deepens understanding of it. For instance, the contexts *persistent detective*, *persistent salesperson*, *persistent pain*, and *persistent rain* provide a more expanded sense of the word *persistent* than might be conveyed by a dictionary or glossary definition.

One way of developing depth of meaning for abstract terms is through simulation. When children are about to encounter abstract concepts such as *democracy* and *republic*, have them form groups, each of which sets up a governing structure for a mythical country; then have the students in each group describe their form of government to the rest of the class. Note on the chalkboard the main features of each type and compare them. Then introduce *democracy* and *republic*. Ask students again to discuss the types of government they set up; also discuss what type of government the United States has. Many will undoubtedly be surprised to learn that they live in a republic. Although they probably have heard the word, some will begin to understand this conceptually complex term for the first time.

Presenting Several Exposures

Although students may derive only a vague idea of a word's meaning after a single exposure, additional incidental exposures help clarify the meaning. Over a period of time, many words are acquired in this way.

Frequency of exposure is the fifth principle of vocabulary building. Beck, McKeown, and Omanson (1987) suggested that students meet new words at least ten times; however, Stahl and Fairbanks (1986) found that as few as two exposures were effective. It also helps if words appear in different contexts so that students experience their shades of meaning. Frequent exposure or repetition of vocabulary is essential to comprehension because of limitations of attention and memory. Fifth-graders reading a selection about the brain that uses the new words *lobe* and *hemisphere* may not recall the words if the teacher has discussed them only once. Although the students may have understood the meanings of the words at the time of the original discussion, when they meet them in print they are vague about their definitions and must try to recall what they mean. Because they give so much attention to trying to remember the meanings of the new words, they lose the gist of the fairly complex passage. Preteaching the vocabulary did not improve their comprehension because their reading was interrupted when they failed to recall the words' meanings immediately or their knowledge of the words was too vague.

*W*ebs are useful for developing and organizing concepts.

Even if the students do recognize the words, their recognition may be slower because they have seen the words only once before. Slowness in accessing the meanings of words from one's mental dictionary can hinder comprehension (Samuels, 1994). This discouraging situation does have a positive side. Although limited exposure may not help immediate compre-hension, the long-term payoff is that students should gain some knowledge of words even from just a single, brief encounter. Perhaps it is enough to move the word from the I-never-saw-it stage to the I've-heard-of-it plateau. Added encounters may bring added knowledge until the word moves to the I-know-it stage.

> Vocabulary knowledge is the most important predic-tor of reading comprehen-sion (Davis, 1968; Thorndike, 1973).

Creating an Interest in Words

Generating interest in words can have a significant impact upon vocabulary de-velopment. In their experimental program, Beck and McKeown (1983) awarded the title of "Word Wizard" to any student who noted an example of a taught word outside of class and reported it to the group. Students virtually swamped their teachers with instances of seeing, hearing, or using the words as they worked toward gaining points on the Word Wizard Chart. On some days, every student in the class came in with a Word Wizard contribution. Teachers also reported that the students would occasionally cause a minor disruption—for example, at an assembly when a speaker used one of the taught words and the entire class buzzed with recognition (p. 625).

> A useful resource for word play activities is *Wordworks: Exploring Language Play* by Bonnie von Hoff Johnson. Golden, CO: Fulcrum Publishing.

Teaching Students How to Learn New Words

The seventh and last principle of vocabulary development is promoting independ-ent word-learning skills. Teaching vocabulary thoroughly enough to make a dif-ference takes time. If carefully taught, only about 400 words a year can be introduced (Beck, McKeown, & Omanson, 1987). However, students have to learn thousands of words, so teachers also have to show them how to use such tools of vocabu-lary acquisition as context clues, morphemic analysis, and dictionary skills. Vocabulary instruction must move beyond the teaching of words directly as a primary activity. Because students derive the meanings of many words incidentally, without in-struction, another possible role of instruction is to enhance the strategies readers use when they do learn words incidentally. Directly teaching such strategies holds the promise of helping students become better independent word learners (Kameenui, Dixon, & Carnine, 1987).

Depending on the nature of the words to be learned and the students' back-ground knowledge, vocabulary development represents two related but somewhat different cognitive tasks: establishing associations and developing conceptual knowl-edge (Baumann, Kameenui, & Ash, 2003). To learn associations between a known concept and a new label for that concept, students don't have to do much more than hear or use the label several times or use mnemonic devices to help them re-member the words. Intensive instruction is not required.

However, depending on its complexity, a concept might require considerable instruction. Conceptual learning is a far more demanding cognitive task. Such words as *democracy, photosynthesis, personality, state, government, emigration, fossils,* and *poverty* would require experience or extensive explanation and discussion before under-standing was achieved. The new word becomes a label for the concept. Of course,

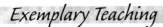

How to Create an Interest in Words

*I*n his first year at an elementary school in Harlem, sixth-grade teacher Herbert Kohl (1967) was having a difficult time reaching his students until a boy named Ralph called a boy named Alvin "psyches." The following interchange ensued:

"Ralph, what does *psyches* mean?"

An embarrassed silence.

"Do you know how to spell it?"

Alvin volunteered. "S-i-k-e-s."

"Where do you think the word came from? Why did everybody laugh when you said it, Ralph?"

"You know, Mr. Kohl, it means, like crazy or something."

"Why? How do words get to mean what they do?"

Samuel looked up at me and said: "Mr. Kohl, now you're asking questions like Alvin. There aren't any answers. You know that."

"But there are. Sometimes by asking Alvin's kind of questions you discover the most unexpected things. Look." I wrote *psyche*, then *cupid*, on the blackboard.

"That's how *psyche* is spelled. It looks strange in English, but the word doesn't come from English. It's Greek. There's a letter in the Greek alphabet that comes out *psi* in English. This is the way *psyche* looks in Greek."

Some of the children spontaneously took out their notebooks and copied the Greek.

"The word *psyche* has a long history. *Psyche* means mind or soul for the Greeks, but it was also the name of a lovely woman who had the misfortune to fall in love with Cupid, the son of Venus, the jealous Greek goddess of love . . ." (pp. 23–24).

Enthralled by Kohl's explanation, the students learned a series of words related to *psyche*—*psychological, psychic, psychotic,* and *psycho-somatic*—with relative ease and demanded to learn more. The class became "word-hungry."

having the label does not guarantee understanding the concept behind the label. Students can tell what state they live in without knowing what a state is.

Concepts are organized into networks. For instance, if I say "cake," chances are you will say something like "ice cream" or "chocolate" or "party." These don't define what a cake is but present associations or experiences that you might have with cake. Of course, the more experiences we have with cake, the more associations we have constructed. Because our concepts are stored in networks, conceptual words are best presented in frameworks that show how they are related to other concepts and also how they are related to students' background of knowledge. Unfamiliar concepts are best learned when they are presented within the context of known concepts or words. That way they become part of the network. That's one reason why simply presenting words in unrelated lists is the least effective way to present new vocabulary.

TECHNIQUES FOR TEACHING WORDS

Dozens of techniques are available for introducing and reinforcing new vocabulary. Those discussed here follow all or some of the seven principles presented above.

Graphic Organizers

Graphic organizers are semantic maps, pictorial maps, webs, and other devices that allow students to view and construct relationships among words. Because they are visual displays, they allow students to picture and remember word relationships.

■ A **graphic organizer** is a diagram used to show the interrelationship among words or ideas.

■ Semantic Maps

Suppose that your students are about to read an informational piece on snakes that introduces a number of new concepts and words. For example, it states that snakes are reptiles, a concept that you believe will be new to the class. You have scheduled an article about alligators and crocodiles for future reading. Wouldn't it be efficient if you could clarify students' concept of snakes and also prepare them to relate it to the upcoming article? There is a device for getting a sense of what your students know about snakes, helping them organize their knowledge, and preparing them for related concepts: semantic mapping, or, simply, mapping.

A **semantic map** is a device for organizing information graphically according to categories. It can be used for concepts, vocabulary, topics, and background. It may also be used as a study device to track the plot and character development of a story or as a prewriting exercise. Mapping may be presented in a variety of ways but is generally introduced through the following steps (Heimlich & Pittelman, 1986; Johnson & Pearson, 1984):

■ A **semantic map** is a graphic organizer that uses lines and circles to organize information according to categories.

1. *Introduce the concept, term, or topic to be mapped.* Write the key word for it on the chalkboard, overhead transparency, or chart paper.
2. *Brainstorm.* Ask students to tell what other words come to mind when they think of the key word. Encourage them to volunteer as many words as they can. This may be done orally, or students may write their lists and share them. If the new words that you plan to teach are not suggested, present them and discuss them.
3. *Group the words by category, discussing why certain words go together.* Encourage students to supply category names.
4. *Create the class map, putting it on a large sheet of paper so that the class can refer to it and add to it.*
5. *Once the map has been finished, discuss it.* Encourage students to add items to already established categories or to suggest new categories.
6. *Extend the map.* As students discover, through further reading, additional new words related to the topic or key word, add these to the chart.

Inspiration (Inspiration Software) or similar software can be used to create graphic organizers.

Lesson 4.1 shows, in abbreviated form, how a map on *snakes* was produced by a class of fifth-graders.

Semantic mapping

Step 1.

The teacher writes the word *snakes* on the board and asks the class to tell what words come to mind when they think of snakes.

Step 2.

Students suggest the following words, which are written on the chalkboard: *poisonous, rattlesnakes, nonpoisonous, garter snakes, sneaky, king snakes, dangerous, frightening, deserts, rocky places,* and *forests.* No one mentions *reptiles,* which is a key word in the article students are about to read. The teacher says that he would like to add that word and asks students if they know what a reptile is. One student says reptiles are cold-blooded. This word is also added to the list.

Step 3.

Words are grouped, and category names are elicited. Students have difficulty with the task, so the teacher helps. He points to the words *forests* and *deserts* and asks what these tell about snakes. The class decides that they tell where snakes live. The teacher then asks the class to find another word that tells where snakes live. Other words are categorized in this same way, and category labels are composed. The map in Figure 4.1 is created.

Step 4.

Students discuss the map. Two of them think of other kinds of snakes—water moccasins and boa constrictors—which are added. During the discussion, the teacher clarifies concepts that seem fuzzy and clears up misconceptions. One student, for instance, thinks that all snakes are poisonous.

Step 5.

Students read to find out more information about snakes. They refer to the map, which is displayed in the front of the room, to help them with vocabulary and concepts. After reading and discussing the selection, students are invited to add words or concepts they learned. The following are added: *dry, smooth skin; scales; vertebrae;* and *flexible jaws.*

Step 6.

A few weeks later, the class reads a selection about helpful snakes. The map is reviewed before reading the story and then expanded to include new concepts and vocabulary.

Actively involving students aids both their understanding of concepts and retention. In one project in which maps were used to help portray complex concepts, students failed to show improvement. Analysis revealed that the instructors were doing much of the map making. Having minimal involvement in the process, students received minimal benefit (Santa, 1989).

After students have grasped the idea of mapping, they can take a greater share of responsibility for creating maps. The sequence listed below gradually gives students ownership of the technique (Johnson & Pearson, 1984).

1. Students cooperatively create a map under the teacher's direction.
2. Students begin assuming some responsibility for creating maps. After a series of items has been grouped, they might suggest a category name.
3. Students are given partially completed maps and asked to finish them. They can work in groups or individually.

FIGURE 4.1

Semantic Map on Snakes

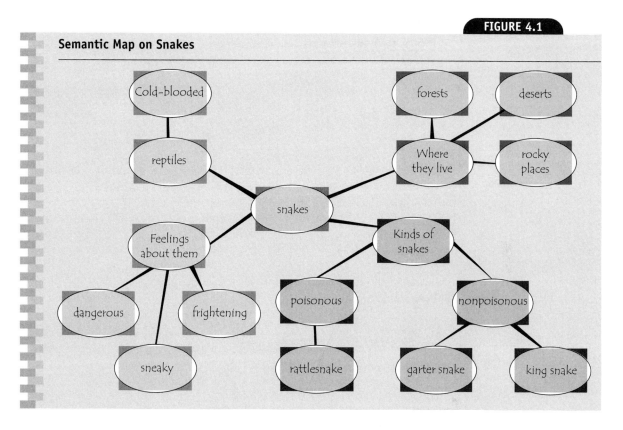

4. The teacher supplies the class with a list of vocabulary words. Working in groups, students use the list to create maps.

5. Working in groups or individually, students create their own maps.

■ Pictorial Maps and Webs

Pictorial and mixed pictorial–verbal maps work as well as, and sometimes better than, purely verbal maps. A **pictorial map** is a map that uses pictures along with words. For some words or concepts, teachers may want to use a more directed approach to constructing semantic maps. After introducing the topic of the planet Mars, the teacher might discuss the characteristics in a **web,** which is a simplified map. A web does not have a hierarchical organization, and it is especially useful for displaying concrete concepts (Marzano & Marzano, 1988). A web is displayed in Figure 4.2.

■ Semantic Feature Analysis

Semantic feature analysis uses a grid to compare words that fall in a single category. For example, it could be used to compare different mammals, means of transportation, tools, sports, and so on. In constructing a semantic feature analy-

■ A **pictorial map** uses drawings, with or without labels, to show interrelationships among words or concepts.

■ A **web** is another name for a semantic map, especially a simplified one.

■ A **semantic feature analysis** is a graphic organizer that uses a grid to compare a series of words or other items on a number of characteristics.

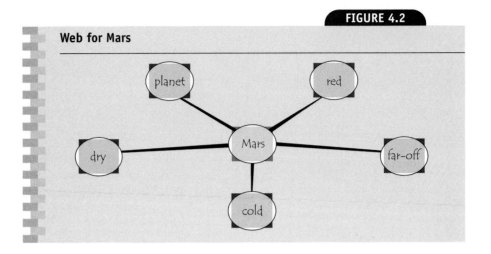

FIGURE 4.2

Web for Mars

sis, complete the steps outlined in Lesson 4.2, which are adapted from Johnson and Pearson (1984).

Semantic feature analysis
LESSON 4.2

Step 1.

Announce the topic, and ask students to give examples. In preparation for reading a story about boats, ask students to name different kinds of boats.

Step 2.

List the boats in the grid's left-hand column.

Step 3.

Ask students to suggest characteristics or features that boats have. List these in a row above the grid.

Step 4.

Look over the grid to see if it is complete. Have students add other boats or their qualities. At this point, you might suggest additional kinds of boats or added features of boats.

Step 5.

Complete the grid with the class. Put a plus or minus in each square to indicate whether a particular kind of boat usually has the quality or characteristic being considered. If unsure, put a question mark in the square. Encourage students to discuss items about which they may have a question—for example, whether hydrofoils sail above or through the water. As students become proficient with grids, they may complete them independently.

Step 6.

Discuss the grid. Help students get an overview of how boats are alike as well as of how specific types differ.

Step 7.

Extend the grid. As students acquire more information, they may want to add other kinds of boats and characteristics.

Eventually, students should compose their own grids. Through actively creating categories of qualities and comparing items on the basis of a number of features, students sharpen their sense of the meaning of each word and establish relationships among them. A sample of a completed grid is shown in Figure 4.3.

■ Venn Diagram

Somewhat similar in intent to the semantic feature analysis grid is the **Venn diagram** (Nagy, 1988), in which two or three concepts or subjects are compared. The main characteristics of each are placed in overlapping circles. Those traits that are shared are entered in the overlapping area and individual traits are entered in the portions that do not overlap. In discussing crocodiles and alligators, the teacher might encourage students to list the major characteristics of each, noting which belong only to the alligator and which belong only to the crocodile. A Venn diagram like that in Figure 4.4 could then be constructed. After they grasp the concept, students should be encouraged to construct their own diagrams. Because this activity requires active comparing and contrasting, it aids both understanding and memory.

■ A **Venn diagram** is a graphic organizer that uses overlapping circles to show relationships between words or other items.

FIGURE 4.3

Semantic Feature Analysis

BOATS	On water	Under water	Above water	Paddles, oars	Sails	Engines
Canoe	+	–	–	+	–	–
Rowboat	+	–	–	+	–	–
Motorboat	+	–	–	?	–	+
Sailboat	+	–	–	?	+	?
Submarine	–	+	–	–	–	+
Hydrofoil	–	–	+	–	–	+
Hovercraft	–	–	+	–	–	+

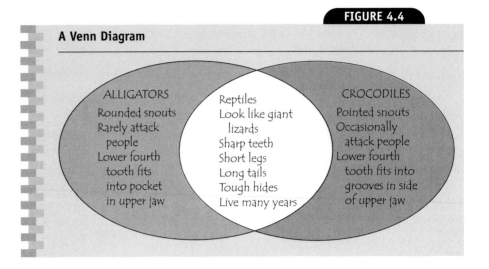

FIGURE 4.4

A Venn Diagram

ALLIGATORS
Rounded snouts
Rarely attack
   people
Lower fourth
   tooth fits
   into pocket
   in upper jaw

Reptiles
Look like giant
   lizards
Sharp teeth
Short legs
Long tails
Tough hides
Live many years

CROCODILES
Pointed snouts
Occasionally
   attack people
Lower fourth
   tooth fits into
   grooves in side
   of upper jaw

Dramatizing

Although direct experience is the best teacher of vocabulary, it is not possible to provide it for all the words that have to be learned. Dramatization can be a reasonable substitute. Putting words in the context of simple skits adds interest and reality.

Dramatizations can be excerpted from a book or created by teachers or students. They need not be elaborate; a simple skit will do in most instances. Here is one dramatizing the word *irate*.

Student 1: Hey, Brian, what's wrong? You seem really mad.

Student 2: Someone's eaten my lunch. They must have known my dad packed my favorite sandwich, peanut butter and banana with raisins. I'm boiling inside. I'm really irate.

Student 1: I'd be irate, too, if someone took my lunch. But before you blow your lid, calm down. Maybe you misplaced it. Say, isn't that your dad coming down the hall? And what's that in his hand? It looks like a lunch bag.

Another way of dramatizing words is to use a hinting strategy (Jiganti & Tindall, 1986). After a series of new words has been introduced and discussed, the teacher distributes to individuals or pairs of students cards on each of which is one of the new words. Each student or pair creates a series of sentences that contain hints to the identity of the target word. Hints for *exaggerate* can be found in the following paragraph:

I like being around Fred, but he tends to stretch the truth a little. The other day he caught a fairly large fish. But to hear him tell it, it sounded like a whale. When Fred catches five fish, he pretends that he really caught twenty. And when it's a little chilly, Fred says it's the coldest day of the year. I like Fred, but I wish he'd stick a little closer to the facts.

The new words are written on the chalkboard. Students read their hints, and the class then tries to figure out which of the new words they describe.

Exploring Word Histories

Knowing the histories of words helps students in three ways: It sheds light on their meanings and helps students remember them better and longer; it "can function as a memory device by providing additional context" (Dale & O'Rourke, 1971, p. 70); and it can spark an interest in words.

Large numbers of words and expressions are drawn from Greek and Roman mythology. Read Greek and Roman myths to students, or, if they are able, have them read some on their own. As a follow-up, discuss words that have been derived from them. After reading about one of Hercules' adventures, discuss what a herculean task might be. After reading about Mars, the god of war, ask what martial music is. Discuss, too, expressions that are drawn from Greek and Roman mythology: Achilles heel, Midas touch, Gordian knot, Pandora's box, and laconic reply. The books in the following Children's Reading List provide word histories.

> Find the origins of *boycott, pasteurized,* and *iridescent.* How would knowing the origins help your students understand the words?

CHILDREN'S READING LIST — Word histories

Graham-Barber, L. (1992). *Doodle Dandy: The complete book of Independence Day words.* New York: Avon.

Klausner, J. (1990). *Talk about English: How words travel and change.* New York: HarperCollins.

Sarnoff, J., & Ruffins, R. (1981). *Words: A book about the origins of everyday words and phrases.* New York: Scribner's.

Steckler, A. (1979). *101 words and how they began.* New York: Doubleday.

Terban, M. (1988). *Guppies in tuxedos: Funny eponyms.* New York: Clarion.

Terban, M. (1989). *Superdupers: Really funny real words.* New York: Clarion.

Once students have an awareness of word histories, have them explore the etymology of words. Students use their knowledge of words or a dictionary to note the etymology of a word. They then write a sentence telling how the word's origin and current meaning are connected. For the word *audition*, students note that it comes from a Latin word that means "hearing" and that an audition is a hearing for an actor or a singer or other entertainer. Since most school dictionaries and online dictionaries don't usually include etymologies, it would be necessary to acquire one that does. Students would also need instruction in interpreting the histories. Providing them with a brief history of English would also be helpful.

Enjoying Words

In school, words are used to instruct, correct, and direct. They should also be used to have fun, as one of the functions of language is to create enjoyment. Recite appropriate puns, limericks, and jokes to the children, and encourage them to share their favorites.

■ Crossword Puzzles

Crossword puzzles are excellent for reinforcing students' vocabulary. When creating them, also use previously introduced words. Puzzles are more valuable if they revolve around a theme—such as farm implements, the parts of the eye, or words that describe moods, for example. For younger readers, start out with limited puzzles that have only five to ten words and expand them as students gain in proficiency. *Worksheet Magic Plus* (Teacher Support Software) or a similar piece of software can be used to create crossword puzzle grids. Crossword and other puzzles can also be created at Web sites such as Puzzlemaker at http://puzzlemaker.school.discovery.com/. All you have to do is supply the words and definitions. Crossword puzzles and word games frequently appear in the following periodicals: *Cobblestone, Cricket, Highlights for Children, My Friend, National Geographic World, Ranger Rick, Sports Illustrated for Kids,* and Web sites such as those listed in Surfing the Net with Kids: Crossword Puzzles at http://www.surfnetkids.com/crossword.htm.

*T*hrough playing Scrabble and other word games, students develop an interest in words.

■ Riddles

Riddles are inherently interesting to youngsters, and they provide an enjoyable context for developing vocabulary. They can be used to expand knowledge of homonyms, multiple meanings, figurative versus literal language, and intonation as a determiner of word meaning (Tyson & Mountain, 1982). Homonyms can be presented through riddles such as the following:

> Why is Sunday the strongest day?
> (Because the other days are weak days.) (p. 171)

Multiple meanings might be reinforced through riddles of the following type:

> If you were locked in a concrete room with no windows or doors, and all you
> have with you is a bed and a calendar, how would you eat and drink?
> (Dates from the calendar and water from the bed springs.) (National Institute
> of Environmental Health Sciences, 2002)

Riddles containing figurative language can be used to provide practice with common figures of speech:

> Which moves faster: heat or cold?
> (Heat. Everybody can catch a cold.) (National Institute of Environmental
> Health Sciences, 2002)

Also, plan activities in which riddles and puzzles are not tied to a lesson, so that students can experience them just for the fun of it.

> **USING TECHNOLOGY**
> Challenging riddles that involve homophones can be found at the National Institute of Environmental Health Sciences Kids' Pages site, Homonyms by the Seashore, **http://www.niehs. nih.gov/kids/ quizseashore.htm.**

Discovering Sesquipedalian Words

Students enjoy the challenge of sesquipedalian words (Dale & O'Rourke, 1971). Composed of the Latin form *sesqui* ("one and one-half") and *ped* ("foot"), *sesquipedalian* means "foot and a half," or very long words. Long or obviously difficult words tend to be easier to learn than short ones because they are distinctive. Given the prestige and pride involved in learning them, students are also willing to put in more effort. Set up a sesquipedalian bulletin board. Encourage students to contribute to it. They can write the words, including the sentence context in which the words were used, on three-by-five cards, which can then be placed on the sesquipedalian bulletin board. Other students should be encouraged to read each word and see whether they can use context to determine its meaning. Then they can use the dictionary to check whether their guess is correct and learn how to pronounce the word. The ultimate aim is to have students become lifetime collectors of long and interesting words.

> Because they are distinctive, long words are often easier to remember than short ones.

Word of the Day

A good way to begin the day is with a new word. The word might tie in with the day, the time of year, or some special local or national event. Or choose a word related to a topic the students are studying. Select interesting, useful words. Write the word on the chalkboard, or put it on a special bulletin board. Read or write the context in which the word is used. Have students try to guess the meaning

Exemplary Teaching

Words of Fortune

*R*ealizing that the typical procedure of having students look up ten words in their dictionaries and then study the words and their definitions for a quiz each Friday was boring as well as ineffective, Marcus Zumwalt (2003) looked for a better approach, one that would motivate his students and use their energies to help them learn. He adapted charades and created the Words of Fortune. One student would act out the vocabulary word; the others would try to guess its identity. Despite Zumwalt's enthusiastic modeling of how words might be dramatized, the students, fearful of being embarrassed, were hesitant to volunteer.

Shyness disappeared when Zunwalt turned the activity into a game. Two teams were formed. The vocabulary words were put into a hat. Zumwalt pulled a word out of the hat and gave it to a performing student. The performing student had 30 seconds to act her word in such a way that her team would guess the word. The team that guessed the most words was declared the winner. With the focus placed on guessing the words and winning the game, the students lost their reluctance. They soon became exuberant partici-

pants. Scores on the weekly vocabulary tests shot up. The number of students achieving at least a B on the vocabulary tests doubled from 42 percent to 83 percent. Students didn't need to be urged to study for the weekly tests. They studied the words on their own so that they would be better prepared to participate in Words of Fortune.

The students were inspired and so was Zumwalt. As he commented,

> The nicest thing about Words of Fortune is that its success in my classroom has inspired me to seek out creative formats to teach other subjects. Creating enthusiasm for skills that my students see as boring is not an easy task. But sometimes beating out multiplication facts on a desk, graphing the flight distance of a paper airplane, and even pretending to engulf a table of imaginary pies in order to ingrain the word *glutton* can be moments that help your students to connect personally with the topic they are learning. (p. 441)

of the word. Provide a history of the word, and discuss why it's an important word. Encourage students to collect examples of the word's use. Working alone or in pairs, older students might present their own words of the day.

▌Labeling helps students visualize words. Information may be coded in words or images (Sadowski & Paivio, 1994), and if it can be coded into both, memory is enhanced.

Labeling

Labeling provides greater depth of meaning to words by offering at least second-hand experience and, in some instances, helps illustrate relationships. The parts of plants, the human body, an airplane, and many other items lend themselves to labeling. For instance, when students are about to read a true-life adventure about a pilot whose life was endangered when the flaps and ailerons froze, present a labeled diagram showing these and other airplane parts, such as fuselage, landing gear, aileron, stabilator, fin, rudder, and trim tab. A sample of such a labeled drawing is presented in Figure 4.5. Discuss each part and its function. Relate the parts to each other and show how they work together to make the plane fly. Ask students to picture the parts in operation during takeoff, level flight, turns, and landing. After the story has been read, give them drawings of a plane. Have them label the parts. Better yet, let them label their own drawings of a plane.

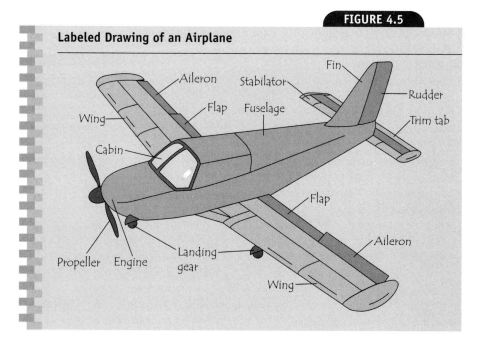

FIGURE 4.5

Labeled Drawing of an Airplane

Feature Comparison

Through questions that contain two newly learned words, students can compare major meanings (Beck & McKeown, 1983). For example, ask such questions as "Could a virtuoso be a rival?" and "Could a philanthropist be a miser?" (p. 624). Answering correctly is not the crucial point of this kind of activity. What is important is that students have the opportunity to discuss their responses so as to clarify their reasoning processes and their grasp of the meanings of the words.

Using Word-Building Reference Books

Dictionaries give definitions, illustrative sentences, and sometimes drawings of words. However, this is often not enough, especially for words that apply to concepts that are unknown or vague. For example, a dictionary definition of *laser* is not sufficient for a student who is reading a selection that assumes knowledge of both the operation and the uses of lasers. In contrast, an encyclopedia entry on lasers explains how they work, what their major uses are, and how they were invented. Encourage the use of the encyclopedia so that students eventually refer to it or other suitable references independently to clarify difficult words.

Predicting Vocabulary Words

The main purpose of studying vocabulary words before reading a selection is to improve comprehension. Two techniques that relate new vocabulary to the selec-

> **USING TECHNOLOGY**
>
> *The Way Things Work* (Dorling Kindersley), a CD-ROM program, uses explanations, labeled illustrations, and animations to show how dozens of technical devices work. Excellent for building background and vocabulary.

tion to be read are the predict-o-gram, which works only with fictional pieces, and possible sentences, which works best with informational text.

■ Predict-O-Gram

In a predict-o-gram, students organize vocabulary in terms of the story grammar of a selection (Blachowicz, 1977). Students predict which words would be used to describe the setting, the characters, the story problem, the plot, or the resolution. Both familiar and new words are chosen. Here's how the technique works: First, the teacher selects key words from the story. The words are written on the board and discussed to make sure students have some grasp of the meanings of the words. Students are then asked to predict which words the author would use to tell about the main parts of a story: the setting, the characters, the story problem, the plot, the resolution. The teacher asks the class to predict which words might fit in each part of the story grammar: "Which words tell about the setting? Which tell about the characters?" and so on. Once all the words have been placed, students might predict what the story is about. A completed predict-o-gram based on a chapter from *The Outside Shot* (Myers, 1984) is presented in Figure 4.6.

The predict-o-gram forces students to think about new vocabulary words in terms of a story that is to be read. It also helps students relate the words to each other. After the story has been read, students should discuss their predictions in terms of the actual content and structure of the story. They should also revise their predict-o-grams, which provides them with additional experience with the new words.

■ Possible Sentences

Possible sentences is a technique by which students use new vocabulary words to predict sentences that might appear in the selection to be read. Possible sentences has five steps (Moore & Moore, 1986):

1. *List key vocabulary.* The teacher analyzes the selection to be read and selects two or three concepts that are the most important. Vocabulary words from the selection that are essential to understanding those concepts are chosen. These words are listed on the board, pronounced by the teacher, and briefly discussed with the class.

FIGURE 4.6

Predict-O-Gram for *The Outside Shot*

Setting	Characters	Story Problem	Plot	Resolution
hospital	Eddie	problem therapy	response	Eddie
campus	Lonnie Jackson	sits around	basketball game	ball
gymnasium	Ann Taylor	budget	announced	hoop
physical therapy department	Mrs. Brignole		eight	
	athletes		losing	

2. *Elicit sentences.* Students use the words listed to compose sentences. They must use at least two words in each sentence and create sentences they feel might occur in the selection. It is suggested that the teacher model the creation of a sample sentence and the thinking processes involved. Students' sentences are written on the board even if not correct. Words may be used more than once. This step ends when all the words have been used in sentences or after a specified time.

3. *Read to verify sentences.* Students read the text to verify the accuracy of their possible sentences.

4. *Evaluate sentences.* After reading the selection, students evaluate their sentences. They discuss each sentence in terms of whether or not it could appear in the selection. Sentences are modified as needed.

5. *Create new sentences.* Students use the words to create new sentences. These sentences are also discussed and checked for accuracy of usage.

The value of the possible sentences technique is that, in addition to being motivational, it helps students use informational text to refine their knowledge of new words. Because students write the words, it also helps them put new words into their active vocabularies. Putting new words in sentences is difficult, so the teacher should provide whatever guidance is necessary.

Word Sorts

Word sorts is a useful activity when dealing with groups of related words. Sorting forces students to think about each word and to see similarities and differences among words. Students might sort the following words: *melancholy, weary, tired, sorrowful, exhausted, glad, contented, cheerful, delighted, unhappy, gloomy, overworked, dejected.* The sort could be open, which means that students would decide on categories, or it could be closed. In a closed sort, the teacher decides the categories: happy, sad, tired. After sorting the words, students would discuss why they sorted them the way they did.

Vocabulary Self-Collection Strategy (VSS)

When given the opportunity to personalize their learning, students become more involved. (Blachowicz & Fisher, 2000). A device that helps students personalize their learning is the vocabulary self-collection strategy (VSS) (Ruddell, 1992). In VSS each student chooses one word to learn. The word selected should be one that the student believes is important enough for the whole class to learn. The teacher also selects a word. Students record the printed sentence or oral context in which they discovered the word. Students also tell what they think the word means in the context in which it is found and explain why they think the class should learn the word.

Words are discussed and dictionaries and glossaries may be checked to make sure that the correct pronunciation and definition have been obtained. As the words and their possible meanings are discussed, the teacher might model the use of context clues and the dictionary. The teacher adds a word and the class list is reviewed. Words selected are recorded in vocabulary notebooks or study sheets.

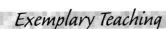

Developing Vocabulary and Confidence

*B*orrowing from Sylvia Ashton-Warner, Mrs. Warren, a resource room teacher at P. S. 94 in the Bronx, New York, invites her remedial readers to choose each day a word that they would like to learn. One student chose *discrimination;* a second student asked to learn suede; a third student studied *customary.* The words chosen were as varied as the children.

Warren's students are operating well below grade level. Having a history of failure, they feel discouraged, frustrated, and incompetent. Learning long words builds their confidence and their self-esteem. As they learn words such as *discombobulate, spectacular,* and *advise,* they begin to see themselves as competent learners.

As Warren explains, "You have to prove to these children that they can learn. Telling them is not enough. You have to get them to be successful at something. The words convince them they're smart." Learning new words also builds an interest that snowballs. "If you can get children to love words, for whatever reason, you've got it made," Warren comments (Rimer, 1990, p. B5).

The students draw their words from many sources. Some come from their reading, others from discussions or television. A favorite source is a 365-new-words-a-year calendar. Students record their words on three-by-five index cards and keep them in a file box. The growing number of cards becomes a testament to their success in building their vocabularies and their overall competence as learners.

Realizing that they are responsible for selecting a word for the whole class to study, students suddenly become word conscious and begin noticing words as possible candidates for selection. As students become more conscious of words, they begin acquiring new vocabulary words at an increased rate (Shearer, 1999). VSS is initiated after the text has been read because being familiar with the text helps students select words that are important.

Wide Reading

The most productive method for building vocabulary—wide reading—requires no special planning or extra effort (Nagy & Herman, 1987). Research (Herman, Anderson, Pearson, & Nagy, 1987) indicates that average students have between a one-in-twenty and a one-in-five chance of learning an unfamiliar word they meet in context. Those who read for twenty-five minutes a day at the rate of 200 words per minute 200 days of the year will encounter a million words (Nagy & Herman, 1987). About 15,000 to 30,000 of these words will be unfamiliar. Given just a one-in-twenty chance of learning an unfamiliar word from context, students should pick up between 750 and 1,500 new words. Of course, if they read more, they have even greater opportunity for vocabulary growth. If they read 2 million rather than 1 million words a year, they theoretically would double the number of new words they learn.

Many of today's informational books for young people contain glossaries or phonetic spellings of difficult words and provide definitions in context. Some also contain labeled diagrams of technical terms. Note how the following excerpt from

ADAPTING INSTRUCTION for STRUGGLING READERS and WRITERS

Many students who would benefit the most from wide reading seldom read for pleasure. Reading less, they fall farther behind their peers. One way for at-risk students to catch up is to read on their own.

a reader-friendly informational book entitled *Fish that Play Tricks* (Souza, 1998) provides both phonetic respelling and contextual definitions:

> The grouper is only one of more than 20,000 different species (SPEE-sheez), or kinds, of fish that live in waters around the world. All fish are cold-blooded, meaning they cannot make themselves much warmer than the temperature around them. Like you, fish are vertebrates (VUHR-tuh-brits), or animals with skeletons inside their bodies. The skeletons of some fish, such as sharks and rays, are made of cartilage, a flexible tissue. (p. 4)

In addition to encouraging wide reading of varied materials, teachers can also provide students with strategies for using context clues, morphemic analysis, and the dictionary to decipher unknown words. Sternberg (1987) found that average adults trained to use context clues were able to decipher seven times as many words as those who spent the same amount of time memorizing words and definitions. If students are taught to use such clues with greater efficiency, it should boost their vocabulary development as well. For instance, students reading the book *Fish that Play Tricks*, from which the excerpt above was taken, would benefit if they were helped to discover that many of the terms in the book are explained in context, and the explanatory context often begins with the word *or*. Modeling the use of context clues and guided practice should also prove to be helpful.

Almost any book that students read will help them improve their vocabularies. But some books do an especially good job of fostering word learning. In *Stealing Home* (Stolz, 1992), the main character's grandfather uses a number of big words, many of which are explained in context. Other books that are especially effective at building vocabulary are listed below.

ADAPTING INSTRUCTION for *STRUGGLING READERS and WRITERS*
The *Early Bird Nature Books* (Lerner) explore a variety of science topics in easy-to-read fashion and develop key vocabulary through previewing, context, and a glossary.

BUILDING LANGUAGE
High-quality books that are reasonably challenging are best for building vocabulary.

USING TECHNOLOGY
Talking software has the potential for use in developing vocabulary. For example, in *The New Kid on the Block* (Broderbund), viewers hear the poems read aloud as text is displayed on the screen with accompanying animation. When words or phrases are clicked on, they are dramatized.

CHILDREN'S READING LIST — Building vocabulary

DuTemple, L. A. (1998). *Moose*. Minneapolis: Lerner.

Frasier, D. (2000). *Miss Alaineus: A vocabulary disaster*. San Diego: Harcourt Brace.

Gibbons, G. (1990). *Weather words and what they mean*. New York: Holiday House.

Juster, N. (1961). *The phantom toll booth*. New York: Knopf.

Parson, A. (1997). *Electricity*. Chicago: World Book.

Souza, D. M. (1998). *Fish that play tricks*. Minneapolis: Carolrhoda.

Reading to Students

There are other methods for learning vocabulary besides direct instruction and wide reading. Reading to students is a significant source of new vocabulary (Elley, 1989). Even older students benefit from having stories read aloud to them. Sixth-graders showed a significant gain in vocabulary after having selections from a seventh-grade anthology read to them (Stahl, Richek, & Vandeiver, 1991). Reading aloud is especially effective when new words are discussed.

Beck and McKeown (2001) devised an approach in which a portion of the read-aloud was devoted to developing vocabulary. From each book, two to four words were selected. Words were selected that were probably unknown to students but which labeled concepts or experiences that would be familiar. These included words such as *reluctant, immense,* and *miserable.* The words were presented in the context of the story, discussed, and later used by the students. For the word *reluctant,* for instance, students talked about foods that they might be reluctant to eat or amusement park rides that they might be reluctant to go on.

Speaking and Writing

The ultimate aim of vocabulary development is to have students use new words in their speaking and writing. In-depth study of words and multiple exposures will help students attain sufficient understanding of words and how they are used so they will be able to employ them in their speech and writing. Students should be encouraged to use new words in the classroom so that they become comfortable with them and so feel confident in using them in other situations. Students should also be encouraged to use new words in their written reports and presentations. As part of preparing students for a writing assignment, teachers might highlight words that lend themselves to inclusion in the written pieces.

Students are often asked to use new words in sentences. This is a difficult, complex task. It takes time to get to know a word well enough in order to be able to use it in a sentence. Instead of having students write sentences using new words, have them complete sentence stems which prompt them to use the word appropriately and in a sentence which shows that they know the meaning of the word: The widow was grieving because _____. In order to complete the sentence, students will have to consider why a widow might grieve (Beck, McKeown, & Kucan, 2002).

If carefully designed, a completing sentences exercise can foster comprehension as well as word knowledge. In the following excerpt of a vocabulary exercise, which is drawn from the sixth-grade level of a literature program (Holt, Rinehart Winston, 2003), students complete each sentence by using examples or details that show they know the meaning of the italicized word. The words are drawn from the selection they read, "The Song of the Trees" (Taylor, 2003). In order to complete the sentences, students must draw details or examples from the selection.

1. Cassie thought Little Man was *finicky* because _____.
2. Mama's *dispute* with Mr. Andersen was_____.
3. The children wouldn't have *ambled* down the cow path if _____. (p. 2).

Using a Thesaurus

Students tend to use familiar, everyday words to express their thoughts. A thesaurus is an excellent tool to help them use a greater range of vocabulary by seeking out and using synonyms. In addition to helping students use a more varied vocabulary, a thesaurus can help students become aware of the shades of meanings of words and can acquaint them with new words for old meanings. By providing synonyms, a thesaurus can also clarify the meaning of the word being looked up. Many thesauruses also provide antonyms. Being provided with a word's opposites also clarifies the meaning of the word. Because most word processing programs have a thesaurus, using a thesaurus is convenient and easy.

To introduce a thesaurus, you may have students brainstorm synonyms for an overused word such as *said*. After listing the synonyms, show students how they can use a thesaurus to accomplish the same purpose. A good practice activity would be to provide students with a paragraph in which overused words are underlined and have them select synonyms for them. Stress the importance of finding the appropriate synonym. The synonym must match the meaning of the word according to the way it is being used. Initially, underline only those words that are relatively easy to find synonyms for. Once students have a basic grasp of how to use a thesaurus, show how it can be used to improve the wording of a written piece. Encourage them to use a thesaurus to provide a more varied vocabulary in their writing.

Introducing New Words

At a minimum, introduction of new words should include a definition of the word, the use of the word in a sentence or story context, an activity that relates the word to other words being introduced, and an activity that relates the word to the student's background. In the sixth-grade level of one basal series (Flood et al., 2001), the words are *participate, ordeals, grimaced, spat, encounter,* and *victorious* introduced with definitions in preparation for reading the selection *Ta-Na-E-Ka* (Whitebird, 2001). The words are also used in context and discussed. To help students relate the words to their backgrounds of experience, the following types of questions are asked:

- What school activities do you like to participate in?
- Have you ever had to go through something that you consider an ordeal?
- In what contest would you most like to be victorious? (Flood et al., p. 140D)

Adapting Basal Reader and Anthology Instruction

All basal readers and anthology programs introduce potentially difficult vocabulary beforehand. Typically, they provide definitions of the words and a story that puts the words in context. Generally, they also suggest added activities to enforce the words. However, basal readers do not do a particularly good job of selecting words to be taught. In a number of studies, researchers have shown that many of the words being introduced are already known by students (Ryder & Graves, 1994; Stallman et al., 1990). On the other hand, an examination of basal manuals suggests that, in many instances, words that are apparently difficult are not taught. When using a basal series or other program, use whatever resources are provided for teaching vocabulary, but you also need to look over the selection and decide which words your students are likely to have difficulty with and which of these words should be introduced. Also, if it is not a part of the introduction, make sure that you spend some time helping students see how the new words are related to each other and are related to students' backgrounds. Also provide differential instruction depending on the word learning tasks that your students face. For instance, in one basal series the words *sentries, cargo, revolutionary,* and *liberty* are given the same amount of coverage (Cooper & Pikulski, 2001). However, *sentries* and *cargo* represent associative learning. Students need only learn that *sentries* means the same thing as *guards* and that *cargo* is another word for *freight* or "things carried by a ship." *Liberty* and *revolutionary* are difficult concepts, and would require conceptual teaching.

Teaching Vocabulary to English Language Learners

Edguardo, a sixth-grader, is a conscientious, highly motivated student. Having attended a dual language school since kindergarten, he is reading on grade level in Spanish and is fluent in English. Although his decoding skills in English reading are on grade level, Edguardo has difficulty with comprehension. He feels overwhelmed when he meets a number of words that he doesn't know. As might be expected of an English language learner (ELL), Edguardo's English vocabulary is somewhat below grade level. Because he has had less opportunity to develop English vocabulary, Edguardo could benefit from a program of intensive vocabulary instruction. A general program of vocabulary development would be helpful. But even more effective would be a program designed to teach Edguardo and other students in similar circumstances the words that they are most likely to meet in their texts.

English learners know fewer English words than their native speaking peers and they also possess fewer meanings for these words (Verhallen & Schoonen, 1993). Ironically, English language learners rely more on their vocabulary knowledge than do native speakers of English when reading. Intensive instruction in vocabulary can make a difference. After two years of systematic instruction, English language learners closed the gap in vocabulary and comprehension that existed between their performance and that of native speakers by about 50 percent McLaughlin, et al., 2000). Taking part in a similar program that lasted for four years, language minority elementary school students in Holland made gains of one or two years beyond that made by a control group (Appel & Vermeer, 1996 as cited in McLaughlin et al., 2000). There were also encouraging gains in reading comprehension. The researchers concluded that language minority students can catch up to native speakers in vocabulary knowledge if they receive targeted vocabulary instruction for about four hours a week throughout the school year and if the instruction is carried out for all eight grades of elementary and middle school.

Knowing how words are stored in bilingual students' minds will help you plan ways to develop their vocabularies. Words learned in Spanish might not be stored in the same place as words stored in English so that *amigo* and *friend* do not share a storage location. Others believe that there is a single store so that *amigo* and *friend* are stored in the same location. A third possibility is that the first language

Expository text seems to lead to more word learning. Expository texts typically define words and provide examples and, sometimes, illustrations. Expository texts also elicit more interaction from parents and teachers (Schickedanz, 1999).

Using a thesaurus is a good way to learn new words. Checking the thesaurus to find a substitute for the word *ask,* students find such words as *inquire, query,* and *interrogate.* The words are relatively easy to learn because they have the common meaning "ask." Students simply have to learn the shades of meanings of the words.

words are linked to the second language words. When the student hears *friend*, she thinks first of the equivalent in her language: *amigo*. The fourth theory is that there are overlapping stores. Some words are linked; some are not. The most reasonable theory seems to be that there is overlap between the two stores (Cook, 2001). With some words, students might have to access the meaning in their native language first. With others they can access the meaning without going through a translation process. For young students, it is easier for them to learn a word through translation than it is through an explanation, definition, or even illustration. A young Spanish-speaking student will learn the word *cat* faster if you say it means "el gato" than she will if you show her a picture of a cat or point to a cat (Durgunoglu & Oney, 2000).

To promote full understanding provide translations of new vocabulary words. If you are unable to translate the words, enlist the services of a bilingual student, a parent, or a bilingual teacher. You might post key vocabulary words in both languages in a prominent spot. Also explore cognates.

Using Cognates

Cognates are words that are similar in both languages, have a common derivation, and a common meaning, although the pronunciation may differ. Some Spanish-English cognates have identical spellings as *color* (KOH-lor) and *chocolate* (choh-koh-LAH-teh) but, as you can see, do not have the same pronunciations. Others have similar spellings: *calendario, excelente, lista*. Still others have spellings that are similar but might not be similar enough to be recognized: *carro (car), crema (cream), difícil (difficult)*. A list of high-frequency cognates is presented in Figure 4.7. Spanish-speaking students may know some advanced English words without realizing it. For instance, the word *luna (moon)* would be known by very young Spanish-speaking children. However, *lunar*, as in *lunar landing*, is an advanced word for native speakers of English. Spanish developed from Latin. *Luna*, for instance, is a Latin word. Although English has thousands of words that it borrowed from Latin, English developed primarily from Anglo-Saxon. Our most basic words are derived from Anglo-Saxon. Words derived from Latin tend to be more advanced words. They are a more advanced way of expressing common concepts encapsulated by our most basic words. Although Spanish-speaking students have to learn most common English words from scratch, they have a running start on learning many of the more advanced words because a large proportion of these words are derived from Latin.

■ **Cognates** are words that are similar in both languages, have a common derivation, and a common meaning, although the pronunciation may differ.

FIGURE 4.7

High-Frequency Spanish Cognates

artista	famoso	música
autor	foto	necesita
bebé	favorito	nota
biografía	fruta	número
carácter	gigante	oficina
carro	gorila	página
causa	grado	papá
contento	hipopótamo	perfecta
describir	importante	rápido
diferente	insecto	teléfono
difícil	jirafa	tigre
elefante	mamá	tomate
enciclopedia	mágico	uniforme
eléctrica	mayo	vegetales
familia	minuto	zoológico

Explain to Spanish-speaking students that they know some of the harder words in English. You might use *lunar* as an example. This will affirm the value of the students' first language but will also provide them with a most valuable tool for learning English. Make use of this principle when introducing new vocabulary. For instance, when introducing *annual*, ask Spanish speaking students to tell you the word for *year (año)*. Help them to see that the word *annual* is related to *año*. Follow a similar approach for words like *arbor (árbol-tree), ascend (ascensor), grand (grande-big), primary (primero-first), rapidly (rapidamente-quickly), tardy (tarde-late)*.

Not having had the same opportunity to learn English as native speakers have, English learners understandably have a more limited store of English words. Experts agree that this is their main stumbling block on the road to literacy in English. They need a long-term, well-planned program of vocabulary development, which builds on their growing knowledge of English and their command of another language. In many instances, vocabulary development for them will simply consist of learning the English label for a familiar concept. In other instances, they might be able to use cognates to help them develop their English vocabulary.

A PLANNED PROGRAM

■ **A planned program** is one in which a certain amount of time is set aside each week for vocabulary instruction. Vocabulary may be preselected from materials students are about to read or from words they may need to understand content-area concepts.

Although young people apparently learn an amazing number of words incidentally, a **planned program** of vocabulary development is highly advisable. Research from as far back as the 1930s (Gray & Holmes, 1938, cited in Curtis, 1987) suggested that direct teaching is more effective than a program that relies solely on incidental learning. A more recent review of a number of research studies confirmed these results (Petty, Herold, & Stoll, 1968).

Based on their extensive investigations, Beck, McKeown, and Omanson (1987) opted for a program that includes both direct teaching and incidental learning of words and also differentiates among words. Words especially important to the curriculum are given "rich instruction." These words are chosen from basals, content-area texts, or trade books that are to be read by students and are selected on the basis of their importance in understanding the text, frequency of appearance in students' reading, and general usefulness. Rich instruction goes beyond simple definition to include discussion, application, and further activities. Words selected for rich instruction might be presented five to ten times or more. Less important words are simply defined and used in context. This process introduces words that become more familiar as students meet them in new contexts. Any remaining new words are left to incidental learning. Perhaps the most important feature of this program is that words are taught within the context of reading, as opposed to being presented in isolated lists.

Another important component of a planned vocabulary program is motivation. Students will try harder and presumably do better if they encounter intriguing words in interesting stories and if they can relate learning vocabulary to their personal lives. As Sternberg (1987) commented, "In most of one's life, one learns because one wants to or because one truly has to, or both" (p. 96).

A Balanced Blend

Vocabulary instruction should be a balanced blend of the planned and the incidental. The **incidental approach** capitalizes on students' immediate need to know words. It gives the program spontaneity and vitality. A planned approach ensures that vocabulary instruction is given the attention it deserves. Important words and techniques for learning words are taught systematically and in depth. Combining these two types of approaches should provide the best possible program.

REMEMBERING VOCABULARY

Most of this chapter has been devoted to a discussion of teaching new words. But learning the words is only part of the task—students must also remember them.

Organizing new words to show relationships helps students remember them. So does elaboration (Bradshaw & Anderson, 1982). Elaborating on, or expanding, sentences in which vocabulary words are used should aid students' recall. Consider the sentence "The Tigers were *defeated* ten to one." If you elaborate on *defeated* by asking why the Tigers were defeated by such a lopsided score, how they felt about being defeated, and how many times they have been defeated, the word becomes more vivid and will be remembered better.

Key Word Approach

Images can also be used to improve memory. In the **key word approach,** students create an image to form a link between the word they are learning and its meaning. The key word portrays the meaning of the word being learned and also incorporates a portion of it. For instance, for the word *educator,* the student might imagine a teacher named Ed. *Educator* begins with *ed-* and Ed is a teacher, so Ed portrays the meaning of *educator.* The student can make the image as vivid as possible. He or she may picture Ed wearing a bow tie and thick glasses pointing to math examples on a blackboard. Thus, when the student sees the word *educator,* he or she uses the word *Ed* to conjure up the image and is led to the meaning of the new word.

Because it involves creating an image of words' meanings, it also fosters a deeper understanding of words. Older students are encouraged to create their own key words and images. It is not necessary that the key words be whole words, because some vocabulary words do not lend themselves to this. The key words can show just the beginning letters—for instance, the key word for *pelican* might be *pet,* which contains the first two letters of *pelican;* a person with a pet pelican might be pictured. Children aged ten and younger may need to have the teacher create an image for them. The technique works even if the teacher constructs the interactive image (Pressley, Levin, & Miller, 1981). Lesson 4.3 describes how the key word approach might be used to present the words *antique, fortune,* and *messenger.*

■ **Incidental learning** occurs when vocabulary words are studied as they occur in the natural course of reading and writing. A balanced vocabulary program is both incidental and planned.

> **ADAPTING INSTRUCTION for ENGLISH LANGUAGE LEARNERS**
> Television, radio, lessons, lectures, discussions, and conversations are rich sources of new words. Set aside a few minutes each day to discuss new words that your pupils have heard. This could be especially helpful to students still learning English. They may have questions about pronunciation and shades of meaning.

■ The **key word approach** is a strategy in which students create images to help them associate a meaning with a new word.

LESSON 4.3 Key word approach

Step 1. Introducing the technique

If this is the first time the class has used the key word approach, the teacher explains that the class will be using a new way to learn vocabulary words. She tells the students that this method of learning words has been used with boys and girls their age, as well as with high school and college students and adults, and that it helped all these people remember new words longer.

Step 2. Demonstrating the technique

The teacher writes the word *tarpaulin* on the board and explains that it means a large piece of waterproof cloth. She tells the class that she is going to form a word and create a picture in her mind that will help her remember the word *tarpaulin* and its meaning. Then she explains that from the word *tarpaulin* she is going to form a word she already knows: *tar*. She says she is going to make a picture of the meaning of the word *tarpaulin* and put it together with the meaning of the word *tar*; she draws a giant mound of tar being covered by a tarpaulin because rain is beginning to fall. The teacher tells the class that when she sees the word *tarpaulin* in the future, she will think of the key word *tar* and use it to bring to mind the meaning of the word *tarpaulin* by recalling the picture.

Step 3. Presenting words and images

The teacher then presents the words *antique, fortune,* and *messenger*. She helps the class select *ant* as the key word for *antique*. In the interactive image, the ant could be seen rocking back and forth in an antique chair. For *fortune*, the key word is *fort*; the interactive image shows a fortune in gold and diamonds stored in a fort. The key word for *messenger* is *mess*. In the interactive image, a messenger delivers a package to a house that is a mess because it is full of packages that have not been put away.

Step 4. Guided application

The students then try out the technique themselves. The teacher says the vocabulary word *antique* and asks the class what the key word is. Repeating *ant*, the teacher asks the students to tell what picture they have formed and to tell what *antique* means. After the teacher has gone over the three words and is sure that the students have mastered the technique, she simply says each vocabulary word and directs the students to say the key word to themselves, call up the picture, and then the definition. Gradually, the teacher leads the students to the point at which they are able to use the technique independently.

Used originally to teach students foreign words, the key word approach has been successful in helping students retain associations between English words and their definitions (Pressley, Levin, & McDaniel, 1987).

Try the key word approach with several technical words that you have to learn. How well did the technique work? Would you introduce it to your students? Why or why not?

Step 5. Assessment and review

Through observation, discussions, and quizzes, note how effectively students are using the key word technique. Review the technique and reteach if necessary.

Besides being a research-based method for learning vocabulary, the key word approach is fun to use. Students enjoy choosing key words and creating images. They will also be surprised at how well the technique works. Eventually, students should adapt the key word technique and use it on their own as an independent study technique. To help them get to this stage, actively use the key word approach for several months, gradually leading students to a point where they can use it on their own. Because students are most likely to use a strategy when they see its value, have students compare their achievement on vocabulary tasks undertaken before and after the key word technique is used.

TEACHING SPECIAL FEATURES OF WORDS

Many words have special characteristics that have to be learned if the words are to be understood fully. Among such important features are homophones, homographs, figurative language, multiple meanings, connotation, and denotation.

Homophones

Homophones are words that are pronounced the same but differ in spelling and meaning and often have different origins as well: for example, *cheap* and *cheep* or *knew*, *gnu*, and *new*. In reality, homophones are more of a problem for spelling than for reading because context usually clarifies their meaning. In some instances, however, it is important to note spelling to interpret the meaning of a sentence correctly—for example:

He complements his wife.
The shed is dun.
To avoid being tackled, you must feint.

To build awareness of homophones, discuss riddles. Write a riddle on the chalkboard, and have students identify the word that has a homophone—for example, "What animal keeps the best time?" (a watchdog). Students might enjoy reading Fred Gwynne's books on homophones, such as *The King Who Rained* (1970), *Chocolate Moose for Dinner* (1988a), and *A Little Pigeon Toad* (1988b).

Homographs

Homographs are words that have the same spelling but different meanings and possibly different pronunciations—for example, *palm* (part of the hand or a tree) and

> ■ The combining form *phon* means "sound," so **homophones** are words that have the same sound but differ in meaning and often have different origins. They may or may not have the same spelling: *be, bee; him, hymn.*

> ▌ To convey the concept of homophones, you might have students translate sentences similar to the following that have been written in homophones: Aye gnu Gym wood bee hear. Dew ewe no hymn?

> ■ *Graph* is a combining form meaning "written element," so **homographs** are two or more words that have the same spelling but different meanings and different word origins. Homographs may have the same or different pronunciations: *bark* (dog), *bark* (tree); *bow* (ribbon), *bow* (front of a boat).

bat (a club or a mammal). They make spelling easier but reading more difficult. For instance, on seeing the word *page*, the reader must use context to decide whether the word means "a piece of paper" or "someone who attends a knight or runs errands for lawmakers." Homographs may share a single pronunciation or have different pronunciations. Homographs such as the following, which have two distinct pronunciations, can be particularly troublesome for students: *bass, bow, desert, dove, lead, minute, sewer,* and *sow.*

As students learn that a word may have two, three, or even more entirely separate meanings, stress the importance of matching meaning with context. Students may also need to learn an entirely new meaning, and perhaps a pronunciation, for a word that looks familiar. Reading the sentence "The neighbors had a terrible row," students will see that neither of the familiar meanings "paddle a boat" or "in a line" fits this sense of *row.* They must learn from context, a dictionary, or another source that the word's third meaning is "a noisy fight or quarrel." They will also need to learn that *row* in this context is pronounced /rau/.

Students will require extra help and reinforcement when learning homographs. Research indicates that learning a new meaning for an old word is more difficult than learning a new meaning for a new word (Tetewsky & Sternberg, 1986). Apparently, past learning interferes with new learning. It may be helpful to trace the etymology of some homographs. For example, the word *page* meaning "paper" comes from the Latin word *pagina,* "a sheet of writing." The word *page* meaning "someone who attends a knight" is derived from the Italian word *paggio,* which in turn comes from the Greek word *paidon,* for "boy" (Davies, 1986). Also, students might keep a dictionary of homographs they find in their reading, adding new meanings as they come across them. For example, reading the sentence "It was a beautiful bay horse," students might add for the word *bay* the meaning "reddish-brown" to "a body of water" and "make a barking sound."

Figurative Language

If taken literally, **idiomatic expressions** and figures of speech such as "catch her eye," "lose heart," and "save face" can be gruesomely frightening. However, language is replete with phrases in which words take on new meaning that is no longer literal. Sometimes, idiomatic expressions are not counted as difficult because they consist of easy words; in "catch her eye," for example, all the words are on a first-grade level (Harris & Jacobson, 1982). Because idiomatic phrases hinder comprehension in much the same way difficult vocabulary words do, they should be discussed before students read a selection in which they appear, especially if they might obscure the meaning of the reading.

Many students tend to interpret language literally and may have difficulty with figurative language. This is especially true for students who have a profound hearing loss and those whose native language is not English. It is important to make them aware that language is not always to be taken literally. As they grow in their ability to handle figurative expressions, they should be led to appreciate phrases that are especially apt and colorful. Students might also keep a dictionary

---

ADAPTING INSTRUCTION for *ENGLISH LANGUAGE LEARNERS*
Self Study Quizzes for ESL Students offers a variety of self-checking quizzes on common words, idioms, homonyms, and slang expressions. It also includes games and crossword puzzles. Although designed for ESL students, it could be used with native speakers of English: **http://www.aitech.ac. jp/~iteslj/quizzes/lb/ ho1.html.**

■ An **idiomatic expression** is one that is peculiar to a language and cannot be understood from the individual words making up the expression: for example, *call up* a friend.

▌ Students may not realize that figures of speech can be found in the dictionary, usually under the key word in the phrase. For instance, the expressions "big heart," "take to heart," and "with all one's heart" would be found under *heart.*

of idiomatic and figurative expressions. Some books of idioms are listed in the following Children's Reading List.

 Figurative language

Arnold, T. (2001). *More parts.* New York: Dial.

Christopher, M. (1996). *Baseball jokes and riddles.* Boston: Little, Brown.

Fakih, K. O. *Off the clock: A lexicon of time words and expressions.* New York: Ticknor & Fields.

Rosen, M. (1995). *Walking the bridge of your nose: Wordplay poems and rhymes.* Las Vegas, NV: Kingfisher.

Terban, M. (1990). *Punching the clock: Funny action idioms.* Boston: Clarion.

Terban, M. (1993). *It figures! Fun figures of speech.* New York: Scholastic.

Terban, M. (1998). *Scholastic dictionary of idioms.* New York: Scholastic.

Multiple Meanings

One study found that 72 percent of the words that appear frequently in elementary school materials have more than one meaning (Johnson, Moe, & Baumann, 1983). When teaching new meanings for old words, stress the fact that words may have a number of different meanings and that the context is the final determinant of meaning. Some words with apparently multiple meanings are actually homographs. For instance, *bark* means "a noise made by a dog," "the covering of a tree," and "a type of sailing ship." These are really three different words and have separate dictionary entries. Other examples for which there are diverse meanings associated with one word are *elevator* ("platform that moves people up and down," "place for storing grain," "part of airplane") and *magazine* ("periodical" and "building where arms and/or ammunition are stored"). Provide exercises that highlight the new meaning of an old word by asking questions specific to a definition: "What does a plane's elevator do? Why would a fort have a magazine?"

> When learning words having multiple meanings, students learn concrete and functional meanings first (The dog barked at me) followed by more abstract meanings (The coach barked out instructions for the team) (Asch & Nerlove, 1967).

Connotations

It is important to introduce the concept of **connotations** and **denotations** of words. Comparing words and noting connotations helps students to detect subtle shades of meaning (Dale & O'Rourke, 1971). For example, in comparing the synonyms *slender, skinny, lanky,* and *scrawny,* students find that although all refer to being thin, they are not interchangeable. *Scrawny* and *skinny* convey less favorable meanings than do *slender* and *lanky.* Provide students with opportunities to discriminate between synonyms, such as which word in the following pairs sounds better: *chuckle/guffaw; gossip/chat; request/demand.* Have students tell which word in each of the following pairs sounds worse: *scribbled/wrote; sip/slurp; muttered/said.* Encourage students to find

> ■ A **connotation** is a word's implied, suggested, or associated meaning or meanings. The **denotation** of a word is its explicit meaning.

words in their reading that have favorable and unfavorable connotations and discuss them.

LEARNING HOW TO LEARN WORDS

A key objective for a vocabulary-building program is to teach students how to learn words on their own. Three major skills for learning the meanings of unknown words are morphemic analysis, contextual clues, and dictionary usage.

Morphemic Analysis

■ **Morphemic analysis** is the examination of a word in order to locate and derive the meanings of the morphemes.

■ A **morpheme** is the smallest unit of meaning. The word *nervously* has three morphemes: *nerv(e)-ous-ly*.

One of the most powerful word-attack skills is **morphemic analysis.** As Nagy and Anderson (1984) noted, "for every word a child learns we estimate that there are an average of one to three additional words that should be understandable to the child, the exact number depending on how well the child is able to utilize context and morphology to induce meaning" (p. 304). Morphemic analysis is the ability to determine a word's meaning through examination of its prefix, root, and/or suffix. A **morpheme** is the smallest unit of meaning. It may be a word, a prefix, a suffix, or a root. The word *believe* has a single morpheme; however, *unbelievable* has three: *un-believ(e)-able. Telegraph* has two morphemes: *tele-graph.* Whereas syllabic analysis involves chunks of sounds, morphemic analysis is concerned with chunks of meaning.

     Unfortunately, morphemic analysis is woefully neglected (O'Rourke, 1974). Henry (1990) found that students knew very little about morphemic elements. Henry also found that both achieving students and students classified as learning disabled showed significant gains after instruction in morphemic analysis. Based on their research, White, Power, and White (1989) estimated that average students double their ability to use morphemic analysis after just ten hours of instruction.

> **ADAPTING INSTRUCTION for *STRUGGLING READERS and WRITERS***
>
> Learning-disabled students' knowledge of morphemic elements is especially poor. However, given systematic instruction, they make encouraging gains (Henry, 1990).

     Talk of prefixes, suffixes, root words, and compounds may conjure up images of memorizing lists of word elements; however, learning morphemes is a constructive, generative process. Children demonstrate the ability to construct morphemes as early as age two (Brown, 1973). The process continues into elementary school, where they refine their knowledge of past tense and third-person plural. Evidence that morphemic knowledge is constructive rather than imitative comes from the "mistakes" of young speakers—for instance, "We bringed our lunch to the zoo." The process is not simply a question of parroting what adults say because no adult would say "bringed." Rather, having heard *-ed* added to other words to indicate past tense, the child constructs a rule wherein *-ed* is added to all verbs, including *bring*, as a past tense marker. Later, the child refines the process and says *brought* instead of *bringed.*

     Morphemic analysis as a word-attack skill should build on this constructive element. Instruction must be generative and conceptual rather than mechanical and isolated. For example, students can use their knowledge of the familiar word *microscope* to figure out what *micro* means and to apply that knowledge to *microsecond, microwave, micrometer,* and *microbe.* By considering known words, they can generate a concept of *micro* and apply it to unknown words, which, in turn, enriches that concept (Dale & O'Rourke, 1971). The key to teaching morphemic analysis is to help students note prefixes, suffixes, and roots and discover their meanings. It is also essential that elements having a high transfer value be taught and that students be trained in transferring knowledge (Dale & O'Rourke, 1971).

■ Prefixes

In general, **prefixes** are easier to learn than suffixes (Dale & O'Rourke, 1964, cited in O'Rourke, 1974). According to Graves and Hammond (1980), there are relatively few prefixes, and they tend to have constant, concrete meanings and relatively consistent spellings. Prefixes are also more useful than suffixes in decoding words. When applying morphemic analysis, readers remove the prefix first to find the root, and the suffix next. However, in many instances, they might not need to remove the suffix to identify the root word (White, Power, & White, 1989). When learning prefixes and other morphemic elements, students should have the opportunity to observe each one in a number of words so that they have a solid basis for constructing an understanding of the element. Lesson 4.4 describes how the prefix *pre-* might be taught.

> ■ A **prefix** is an affix placed at the beginning of a word or root in order to form a new word: for example, *prepay.*

Prefixes

Step 1. Construct the meaning of the prefix

Place the following words on the board:

> pregame   prepay   preview   pretest   predawn

Discuss the meanings of these words and the places where students may have seen them. Note in particular how *pre-* changes the meaning of the word it precedes. Encourage students to construct a definition of *pre-*. Lead students to see that *pre-* is a prefix. Discuss, too, the purpose and value of knowing prefixes. Explain to students how knowing the meanings of prefixes will help them figure out unknown words. Show them how you would syllabicate words that contain prefixes, and how you would use knowledge of prefixes to sound out the words and determine their meanings.

Step 2. Guided practice

Have students complete practice exercises similar to the following:

> Fill in the blanks with these words containing prefixes: *preview, pregame, prepay, predawn, pretest.*

> To make sure they had enough money to buy the food, the party's planners asked everyone to _____.

> The _____ show starts thirty minutes before the kickoff.

> ▌The most frequently occurring prefixes include: *un-, re-, in-, im-, ir-, il-, dis-, en-, em-, non-, in-, im-* (meaning "into"), *over-, mis-, sub-, pre-, inter-, fore-, de-, trans-, super-, semi-, anti-, mid-, under-* (White, Sowell, Yanagihara, 1989).

The _____ of the movie made it seem more exciting than it really was.

Everyone got low marks on the spelling _____ because they had not been taught the words yet.

In the _____ quiet, only the far-off barking of a dog could be heard.

Step 3. Application

Have students read selections that contain the prefix *pre-* and note its use in real-world materials.

Step 4. Extension

Present the prefix *post-*, and contrast it with *pre-*. Since *post-* is an opposite, this will help clarify the meaning of *pre-*.

Step 5. Assessment and reteaching

Through observation, note whether students are able to use their knowledge of **affixes** to help them pronounce and figure out the meanings of unfamiliar words. Review common affixes from time to time. Discuss affixes that appear in selections that students are reading.

Scope-and-Sequence Chart. A scope-and-sequence chart based on an analysis of current reading programs is presented in Table 4.1. At each level, elements from earlier grades should be reviewed. Additional suffixes that students encounter in their reading should also be introduced.

■ Suffixes

The two kinds of **suffixes** are derivational and inflectional. **Derivational suffixes** change the part of speech of a word or change the function of a word in some way. Common derivational suffixes are presented in Table 4.2. Some of these suffixes form adjectives: *-al (musical), -less (helpless), -ous (joyous)*. Others form nouns: *-ance (resistance), -ence (occurrence), -ness (happiness)*. Still others change the function of a noun so that it indicates a person rather than a thing: *-er (farmer), -ist (artist)*. You may want to emphasize the following suffixes because they occur with the highest frequency: *-er, -(t)ion, -able, -ible, -al, -ial, -y, -ness, -ity (-ty), -ment, -ic, -ous (-ious), -en, -ive, -ful, less* (White, Sowell, & Yanagihara, 1989). **Inflectional suffixes** mark grammatical items and include plural *-s (boys)*, third-person singular *-s (he helps)*, present participle *-ing (hopping)*, past tense *-ed (hopped)*, past participle *-en (chosen)*, comparisons *-er* and *-est (taller, tallest)*, and the adverbial *-ly (quickly)*.

For the most part, students are already using inflectional suffixes widely in their oral language by the time they meet them in their reading. They simply have to become used to translating the letters into sounds. If they are reading for meaning and using syntactic as well as semantic cues, translating the letters into sounds should happen almost automatically. For example, children's grammatical sense will tell them that a /z/ sound is used in the italicized word in the following sentence: The two *boys* were fighting. Also, it is not necessary to teach students that *s* repre-

---

Prefixes are most useful when they contribute to the meaning of a word and can be added to other words. The prefix *un-* is both productive and easy to detect (*unafraid, unable, unhappy*), but the prefix *con* in *condition* is unproductive and difficult to detect (McArthur, 1992).

■ An **affix** is a morphemic element added to the beginning or ending of a word or root in order to add to the meaning of the word or change its function. Prefixes and suffixes are affixes: for example, *prepayment*.

■ A **suffix** is an affix added to the end of a word or a root in order to form a new word: for example, *helpless*.

■ A **derivational suffix** produces new words by forming derived words or words whose meanings have been added to: *happiness, penniless*.

■ An **inflectional suffix** changes the inflected ending of a word by adding an ending such as *s* or *ed* that shows number or tense: *girls, helped*.

TABLE 4.1		Scope-and-sequence chart for common prefixes						
Grade	Prefix	Meaning	Example	Grade	Prefix	Meaning	Example	
4	*dis-*	not	dishonest	5–6	*ex-*	out, out of	exhaust	
	dis-	opposite	disappear		*ex-*	former	explayer	
	re-	again	reappear		*inter-*	between	international	
	re-	back	replace		*mis-*	not	misunderstanding	
	un-	not	unhappy		*mis-*	bad	misfortune	
	un-	opposite	undo	6–7	*en-*	forms verb	enrage	
	under-	under	underground		*ir-*	not	irresponsible	
4–5	*im-*	not	impossible		*trans-*	across	transatlantic	
	in-	not	invisible	8	*anti-*	against	antiwar	
	pre-	before	pregame		*pro-*	in favor of	prowar	
	sub-	under	submarine		*sub-*	under	submarine	
					super-	above	supersonic	

sents /z/ at the end of some words: *friends, cars,* and so on. The sound is automatically translated. In the same way, students automatically pronounce the *-ed* correctly in the following words, even though three different pronunciations are represented: *called, planted,* and *jumped.* Exercises designed to have children identify which pronunciation each *-ed* represents—/d/, /id/, or /t/—are time wasters.

Suffixes are taught in the same way as prefixes. As can be seen from Tables 4.1 and 4.2, the definitions of prefixes and suffixes are sometimes vague. Although only one or two definitions are given in the tables, in reality, some affixes have four or five. To give students a sense of the meaning of each affix, provide experience with several examples. Experience is a better teacher than mere definition.

> Suffixes that change both spelling and pronunciation, such as in *sane* and *sanity,* are the hardest for students to deal with. Most students encountering the word *sanity* would be unable to relate it to *sane* (White, Power, & White, 1989).

TABLE 4.2		Scope-and-sequence chart for common derivational suffixes						
Grade	Suffix	Meaning	Example	Grade	Suffix	Meaning	Example	
4	*-able*	is; can be	comfortable	4–5	*-ian*	one who is in a certain field	musician	
	-al	having	magical					
	-ance	state of	allowance		*-ic*	of; having	gigantic	
	-en	made of	wooden		*-ish*	having the quality of	foolish	
	-ence	state of; quality of	patience		*-ive*	being	creative	
	-er	one who	painter	5–6	*-ian*	one who	guardian	
	-ful	full of; having	joyful		*-ist*	a person who	scientist	
	-ible	is; can be	visible		*-ity*	state of	reality	
	-ify	make	magnify		*-ize*	make	apologize	
	-less	without	fearless	6–7	*-age*	forms nouns	postage	
	-ment	state of	advertisement		*-ar*	forms adjectives	muscular	
	-ness	having	sadness		*-ess*	female	hostess	
	-or	one who	actor	7–8	*-ary*	forms adjectives	budgetary	
	-ous	having	curious		*-ette*	small	dinette	
	-(t)ion	act of	construction		*-some*	forms adjectives	troublesome	
	-y	being; having	dirty					

Suffixes, especially those that appear often, are worth teaching because they help students add words to their meaning vocabularies. The most frequently occurring derivational suffixes include: *-er, -tion (-ion), -ible (-able), -al (-ial), -y, -ness, -ity (-ty), -ment, -ic, -ous (-ious), -en, -ive, -ful, -less* (White, Sowell, & Yanagihara, 1989).

■ The **root** of a word is the part of the word that is left after all the affixes have been removed. A root is also defined as the source of present-day words. The Latin verb *decidere* is the root of the English verb *decide* (McArthur, 1992). The words *base, combining form, root,* and *stem* are sometimes used interchangeably but actually have different meanings. To keep matters simple, this text uses the word *root.*

■ Value of Affixes

About 80 percent of affixed words are analyzable (White, Power, & White, 1989). Having knowledge of high-frequency affixes should help fourth graders learn an additional 125 words a year. That figure would probably double for fifth-graders, since they would encounter more affixed words. By eighth grade, knowledge of affixes might enable students to learn 500 or more words that they wouldn't have learned without instruction in affixes.

■ Root Words

As students move through the grades, knowledge of morphemic elements becomes more important for handling increasingly complex reading material. As the reading becomes more abstract and therefore more difficult in every subject area, the number of words made up of **roots** and affixes becomes greater. Science, for instance, often uses Greek and Latin words and compounds (O'Rourke, 1974). As with prefixes and suffixes, roots that should be taught are those that appear with high frequency, transfer to other words, and are on the appropriate level of difficulty. For example, the root *cil (council),* meaning "call," should probably not be taught because it is difficult to distinguish in a word. Roots such as *graph (autograph), cred (incredible),* and *phon (telephone)* are easy to spot and appear in words likely to be read by elementary or middle school students. Roots that are good candidates for inclusion in a literacy program are shown in Table 4.3. The sequence is based on O'Rourke's research (1974) and an analysis of the roots found in current reading programs.

Teaching root words. Teach root words inductively, and take advantage of every opportunity to develop students' knowledge of them. For example, if stu-

---

TABLE 4.3   Scope-and-sequence chart for common roots

Grade	Root	Meaning	Example	Grade	Root	Meaning	Example
4	graph	writing	autograph	7	chrono	time	chronometer
	phon	sound	telephone		dict	say	dictate
	port	carry	import		hemi	half	hemisphere
	saur	lizard	dinosaur		manu	hand	manuscript
	tele	distance	telescope		mid	middle	midday
	vid, vis	see	visible		ped	foot	pedestrian
5	astro	star	astronaut	8	bio	life	biology
	cred	believe	incredible		geo	earth	geology
	duct	lead	conductor		micro	small	microscope
	tri	three	triangle		mono	one	monotone
6	aud	hearing	auditorium		semi	half, part	semisweet
	auto	self	autobiography		some	group	foursome
	bi	two	bicycle				
	ology	study of	geology				
	scrib, script	writing	inscription				
	therm	heat	thermometer				

dents wonder what a thermal wind is, discuss known words such as *thermos*, *thermostat*, and *thermometer*. Lead them to see that in all three words, *therm* has to do with heat; thus, thermal winds are warm winds. Choose elements to be taught from students' reading. If students read about dinosaurs, use the opportunity to introduce *tri*, *saurus*, *pod*, *ornitho*, and other roots. This often helps students use the name to identify the distinguishing characteristics of the creature. For example, *triceratops* uses three word parts to describe a dinosaur that has three horns, two of which are over the eyes: *tri*, "three"; *cerat*, "horn"; and *ops*, "eyes." Two of the parts also transfer to a number of other words: *tri* to *triangle*, *tripod*, etc., and *op* to *optical*, *optician*, *optometrist*, etc.

Scope-and-sequence charts for affixes and roots have been provided to give you a sense of when certain ones are usually presented. The real determinants, however, are the needs of the students and the demands of their reading tasks.

■ Morphemic Analysis For English Language Learners

Just as in English, Spanish has roots, prefixes, and suffixes. In fact, Spanish has more affixes than English does because Spanish nouns and adjectives have endings that show agreement in gender and number. However, there are many similarities between Spanish and English. A number of elements are identical in both languages or altered slightly. For instance, the prefixes *re-* and *sub-* are the same in both languages; so are the suffixes *-able* and *-ion*. The suffix *-tion* is slightly different in Spanish. It is spelled *ción* in Spanish but may also be spelled *-sión* or *-xión*. If students know prefixes, suffixes, and roots in Spanish, they can transfer some of this knowledge to English.

REINFORCEMENT ACTIVITIES   Morphemic analysis

- Provide students with several long words composed of a number of morphemic units, for example:

enrollment	improperly	transoceanic	unimaginable
disagreeable	prehistoric	photographer	disagreeable
misjudgment	irregularly	unfavorable	autobiographical
uncomfortable	disallowable	unpresidential	oceanographer

  Have them determine the morphemic boundaries and try to figure out what the words mean based on analysis of the units. Good sources of other words to analyze are the texts that students are encountering in class.

- Ask students to create webs of roots and affixes in which the element is displayed in several words (Tompkins & Yaden, 1986). A web of the root *loc* might look like Figure 4.8. As an alternative, students might create a more elaborate organizer in which the focus is on the meanings of the related words. A root, prefix, or suffix is placed in the center of the web. Meanings of the root are placed in circles connected to the center. Examples of the word's use that the student has seen or heard are placed in a second row of connecting circles. In a third circle, the student notes where the word was encountered. Students might also create a tree in which the root is in the

FIGURE 4.8

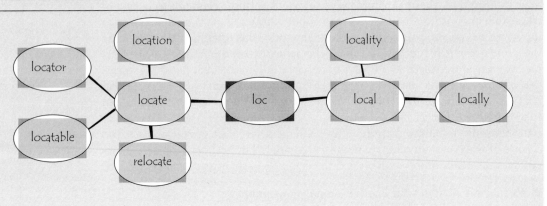

Web of the Root *loc*

location

locality

locator

locate

loc

local

locally

locatable

relocate

trunk and the large branches show words using the root and smaller branches growing out of the larger branches show where the word was used (Worthy, Broadus, & Ivy, 2001).

Included among the list of roots are combining forms. A combining form is a base designed to combine with another combining form (*tri + pod*) or a word (*tri + angle*). Combining forms differ from affixes because two combining forms can be put together to make a word but two affixes cannot. Although combining forms are not roots, they are included in with the roots because in most texts that is where they are presented (McArthur, 1992).

■ Students can incorporate roots and affixes into their everyday lives by constructing personal reactions. In a list like the following, have them underline the prefix *pro-* or *anti-* to show that they are for or against each item:

pro-   anti-   spinach
pro-   anti-   baseball
pro-   anti-   spiders
pro-   anti-   ice cream
pro-   anti-   rock music
pro-   anti-   snakes
pro-   anti-   chores
pro-   anti-   homework
pro-   anti-   pizza
pro-   anti-   bubble gum

■ To help students discover the underlying meanings and functions of affixes, have them sort words containing affixes in a variety of ways—according to whether the affix forms a noun (*narration*), an adjective (*natural*), or a verb (*terrify*)—and sort prefixes that indicate number (*mono-, bi-, tri-*), negation (*il-, im-, in-, un-, ir-*), size (*micro-, macro-, mega-*), etc. Sorting might also be used to help students to discover why some affixes are formed in a certain way. They might try sorting words ending in *-tion* or *-sion* or words ending in *-able* or *-ible* (Bear, Invernizzi, Johnston, & Templeton, 1996).

To see how effective sorting is, sort the following words and see what you discover about ending a word with *able* or *ible*: *agreeable, affordable, terrible, credible, profitable, possible, legible, breakable, saleable, acceptable, visible, plausible.*

■ Using root words, prefixes, and suffixes, let students create words that label a new creature, invention, or discovery. For example, a *quintocycle* would be a cycle with five wheels. A *monovideopod* would be a single walking eye.

■ Ask students to bring in examples of roots and affixes from periodicals, children's books, textbooks, signs, and labels or from spoken language. For example, a child who has recently been on an airplane may have noted the word *preboard*. Let the class determine the word's root and/or affix and discuss the word's meaning.

Contextual Analysis

Imagine that you are a fourth-grader who has never seen or heard the word *salutations*. What does the following passage indicate about its meaning?

"Salutations!" repeated the voice.
"What are they, and where are you?" screamed Wilbur. "Please, please, tell me where you are. And what are salutations?"
"Salutations are greetings," said the voice. "When I say 'salutations' it's just my fancy way of saying hello or good morning." (White, 1952, p. 35)

Not only does E. B. White define the word *salutations* in context in *Charlotte's Web*, but also he implies that its use is somewhat pompous. Of course, not all difficult words are explained with such care; in fact, in many instances, **contextual analysis** is not at all helpful (Schatz & Baldwin, 1986). Context determines the particular meaning of a word, but it may not reveal it (Deighton, 1959).

An informal survey of difficult words in children's periodicals, textbooks, and trade books indicates that definitions or usable **context clues** are supplied about one third of the time (Gunning, 1990). However, it is estimated that the average reader is able to use context successfully only between 5 and 20 percent of the time (Jenkins, Matlock, & Slocum, 1989; Nagy, Anderson, & Herman, 1987). Even when context clues are fairly obvious, students may fail to take advantage of them. Fortunately, students do become more proficient at using context clues as they progress through the grades. They also do significantly better with practice. Simply directing students to use context to get the meaning of an unfamiliar word is not effective. The directive has to be accompanied by practice and feedback to let them know whether their contextual guesses are correct (Carnine, Kameenui, & Coyle, 1984).

■ Processing Context Clues

Instruction in the use of context clues should make explicit the thinking processes involved. Sternberg and Powell (1983) postulated a three-step cognitive process in using context clues:

1. *Selective encoding.* Students separate relevant from irrelevant information, choosing only information that will help them construct a meaning for an unfamiliar word.

Even when contextual clues are as rich as they are in this excerpt from *Charlotte's Web*, some students still may not pick up the meaning of *salutations*. After the story has been read, write *salutations* and other words that had rich contextual clues on the board and ask the class what the words meant. This will give you a rough idea as to how well students were using context. Discussing the words and the context in which they appear would reinforce the meanings of the words and the use of contextual clues.

■ **Contextual analysis** is an attempt to derive the meaning of a word by examining the context in which the unknown word appears.

■ **Context clues** are bits of information in the surrounding text that might be used to derive the meaning of an unknown word. Context clues include appositives, restatement of the word's meaning, comparative or contrasting statements, and other items that might provide clues to the word's meaning.

Context clues should be used to complement phonics strategies and help students predict the pronunciations of words that are in their listening vocabularies but not in their reading vocabularies. However, context clues in this section are designed to help students derive the meanings of words that are not in the students' listening or reading vocabularies.

2. *Selective combination.* Students combine clues into a tentative definition.

3. *Selective comparison.* Students use their background of experience to help figure out the meaning of a word.

Here is how the three steps would be put to use to figure out the meaning of *brigantine* in this passage from Speare's (1958) *The Witch of Blackbird Pond:*

> On a morning in mid-April, 1687, the brigantine *Dolphin* left the open sea, sailed briskly across the Sound to the wide mouth of the Connecticut River and into Saybrook Harbor. Kit Tyler had been on the forecastle deck since daybreak, standing close to the rail, staring hungrily at the first sight of land for five weeks. (p. 5)

1. *Selective encoding.* What information in the sentence containing the unknown word will help me figure out what this word means? Is there any information in earlier sentences that will help? Is there any information in later sentences that will help?

Helpful clues include information about leaving the open sea, sailing, standing on a deck, and seeing land for the first time in five weeks. The fact that it was a morning in mid-April and Kit had been waiting since daybreak are not relevant clues.

2. *Selective combination.* When I think about all the information given about this unknown word, what does the word seem to mean?

When readers put all relevant clues together, they will see that *brigantine* is some kind of ship or boat. Because the passage states that the ship had been on the open sea and that it had a deck with a rail, readers might also infer that the ship was large.

3. *Selective comparison.* What do I know that will help me figure out the meaning of this word?

The helpfulness of contexts varies from those that provide no useful clues to those that supply explicit definitions or explanations. School texts, since their purpose is to instruct, generally provide explicit clues. Trade books vary in the helpfulness of the clues they provide. Informational children's books often provide helpful clues for key terms but not for the general vocabulary.

Using past experience, readers might realize that in the 1600s there were no engine-driven ships, so a brigantine is probably powered by sails. Once readers have used context to construct a tentative meaning for the unknown word, they should try substituting the tentative meaning for the word. If the meaning does not fit the sense of the sentence, they should revise their substitution, use the dictionary, or get help.

■ Types of Context Clues

Listed in the following paragraphs in approximate order of difficulty are eight main types of context clues. They have been drawn from a variety of materials that elementary or middle school students might read.

While you should discuss the different types of context clues, students need not be able to identify the specific type of context clue provided. It is more important that they direct their efforts toward figuring out the meaning of the unknown words.

1. *Explicit explanation or definition.* The easiest clue to use is a definition in context. For instance, the following passage from *The Wright Brothers at Kitty Hawk* (Sobol, 1961) gives a detailed, conceptual explanation of warping:

> "Why the wings are twisting!" exclaimed Bill Tate.
> "We call it warping," said Orville. "See the wings on the side? Their ends are turned upward and forward."

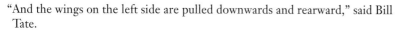

"And the wings on the left side are pulled downwards and rearward," said Bill Tate.

Orville let go of the rope. "Now, in front—"

"Hold on," said Bill Tate. "I'm not sure I understand what I saw."

"The warping is our idea for keeping the glider level," said Orville. Carefully he explained how it changed the way the wind pushed against the wings. (p. 24)

Explicit definitions are usually more concise, as in this excerpt from *Brown Bears* (Stone, 1998): "Brownies are omnivores (AHM-nih-vorz). Omnivores eat both plants and animals" (p. 14).

2. *Appositives.* Definitions are sometimes supplied in the form of appositives immediately after the difficult word: "On a clear summer morning, a pod, or group, of close to fifty dusky dolphins moves toward deeper water" (Souza, 1998, p. 27).

3. *Synonyms.* Finding a synonym sometimes takes some searching. It often appears in a sentence after the one that used the target word. In the following passage from *Little House on the Prairie* (Wilder, 1941), the synonym for *ague* is given in a preceding sentence: "Next day he had a little chill and a little fever. Ma blamed the watermelon. But next she had a chill and a little fever. So they did not know what could have caused their fever 'n' ague" (p. 198).

4. *Function indicators.* Sometimes context provides clues to meaning because it gives the purpose or function of the difficult word (Sternberg, 1987). In the following sentence, the reader gets an excellent clue to the meaning of *derrick* in a sentence that indicates what a derrick does: "The derrick lifted the glider into the sky" (Sobol, 1961, p. 27).

5. *Examples.* The example—lions—in the following passage would give the reader a sense of the meaning of predators: "Only 5 percent of cheetah cubs live to become adults. The remainder die from disease, starvation, or attacks from other predators, such as lions" (Thompson, 1998, p. 7).

6. *Comparison–contrast.* By contrasting the unknown word *opponents* with the known word *teammates* in the following passage, readers can gain an understanding of the unknown word: "You should always know where on the field your teammates and opponents are" (Rolfer, 1990, p. 46). Students must be able to reason that the word *opponents* is the opposite of *teammates*, however.

7. *Classification.* By noting similarities in items, some of which are known, readers can guess what an unknown word means. In the following sentence, they know from the word *town* and the earlier mention of Canada that places are being talked about; based on this conclusion, they can infer that *province*, the unknown word, is also a place: "Gordie was born on March 31, 1928, in the town of Floral, in the province of Saskatchewan" (Neff, 1990, p. 48). Because the sentence says that the town is in the province, they could infer that a province is larger than a town.

8. *Experience.* A main clue to the meaning of an unfamiliar word is students' background of experience. In the following passage, readers can use their own experience of being cut or injured together with imagining what it might be like to undergo the experience that is described; this will enable them to make an informed guess as to what the unfamiliar word *excruciating* means: "Suddenly, the hedge clippers caught a branch, and my left middle finger was pulled into the blades. I felt an excruciating pain. The tip of my finger was hanging by a thread" (Rolfer, 1990, p. 25).

■ Presenting Context Clues

Use of context should permeate the reading program from its very beginning. When emerging readers use phonics skills to try to decode words that are in their listening but not in their reading vocabulary, they should use context as well, both as an aid to sounding out and as a check to make sure they have decoded the words correctly. Context clues presented in this chapter are designed to help readers derive the meanings of unknown words—words that are not in the students' listening vocabularies. Although one hopes that over the years the use of context will become automatic, context clues should be taught explicitly. Using a direct teaching model, the teacher should explain what the clues are, why it is important to use context, and how they can be applied. Modeling use of clues, guided practice, and application are important elements in the process. Lesson 4.5 describes how context clues might be presented.

As your class studies context clues, encourage students to be alert to especially good clues that they encounter in their reading and bring these into class. Set aside a few minutes each day for a discussion of context clues, with one student reading the clue and the rest of the class attempting to use the clue to derive the meaning of the word.

 Context clues

Step 1. Explain context

Demonstrate the usefulness of context clues. Select five or six difficult words from a book the class is reading and show how context could be used to derive their meanings.

Step 2. Demonstrate Sternberg and Powell's (1983) three-step process

This can be done by asking the following questions:

What information in the selection will help me figure out what the unknown word means? (selective encoding)

When I put together all the information about the unknown word, what does the word seem to mean? (selective combination)

What do I know that will help me figure out the meaning of this word? (selective comparison)

Step 3. Try out the tentative meaning of the unknown word

Show students how they should try out the tentative meaning of the unknown word by substituting the meaning for the word and reading the sentence to see whether the substitution fits. Explain that if the tentative meaning does not fit the sense of the sentence, they should revise it.

Step 4. Model the process

Model the process of using context with a variety of words. Explain the thinking processes that you go through as you attempt to figure out their meanings and then try out these tentative meanings. Show, for example, how you might use examples as clues, use a comparison, search out synonyms, look for appositives, use your background of experience, or try a combination of strategies. Show, too, how you would use context and experience to construct a tentative meaning for the unknown word and then try out the meaning by substituting it in the sentence.

Step 5. Guided practice

Have students use context clues to figure out unfamiliar words in selected passages that provide substantial clues. Do one or two cooperatively. Then have students try their hands. Discuss the meanings of the unfamiliar words and the types of clues they used.

Step 6. Application

Encourage students to try using context clues in selections that they read. After the reading, talk over the meanings that they derived and the strategies they used. Ask how they went about determining what the unknown word meant, what clues they used, and how they decided on their definition of the unknown word.

Step 7. Assessment and review

Note how often and how well students apply context clues on their own. From time to time, check on their use of context. Provide additional instruction as needed.

> **USING TECHNOLOGY**
> Vocabulary Drill for Kids presents words in context. Students select from three options the one they think is the correct response: **http://www. edu4kids.com/lang1/.**

■ Subsequent Lessons in the Use of Context Clues

In a series of lessons, present other major context clues, emphasizing the thinking processes involved in using each one. After introducing all the types of clues appropriate for students' level, review them. However, instruction should be focused on using context clues effectively rather than on identification of types of clues. Draw sample sentences from children's periodicals, trade books, content-area texts, and the Internet, so that students can see that the skills have relevance and that context clues will help them analyze words. Most important, encourage students to get in the habit of using context to figure out the meanings of unfamiliar words. Instead of merely suggesting that they use clues, model the process from time to time to remind them about it. Also, encourage them to use the dictionary as a means of checking definitions derived by using context clues.

> Review context clues periodically. Whenever a selection is discussed, talk over passages that contained especially effective context clues so as to remind students to use context clues and also to refine students' usage of them.

Also integrate the use of context with morphemic and syllabic analysis. Note how morphemic analysis and context clues might be used to derive the meanings of *microbats* and *megabats*.

> Bats are the masters of the ultrasonic world. They are divided into two groups, the microbats and the megabats. Most microbats are insect eaters. All microbats rely on ultrasound to guide them when they fly and to help them find food and communicate with each other. The large, fruiteating megabats can make ultrasounds, too, but they do not use them when flying or searching for food. (Arnold, 2001)

An exercise that combines applying meanings of words and using context is one in which students choose from two words the one that best completes a sentence in which the target word is used in fairly explicit context.

> After weeks of arguing the two teammates softened their hardened hearts and agreed to an (amicable, antagonized) compromise that saved their friendship.

Students might be encouraged to work in small teams and compose sentences of this type. Groups could then test each other.

Dictionary Usage

Context, especially when combined with phonics and morphemic and syllabic analysis, is a powerful word-attack strategy, but some words defy even these four strategies. When all else fails, it is time for the student to consult the world's greatest expert on words, the dictionary.

■ Using Glossaries

Glossaries are included in the anthologies of major reading programs and content-area texts. Easier to use than dictionaries because they have only a limited number of words and definitions, glossaries are a useful tool and a good preparation for the dictionary.

■ Using Dictionaries

By fourth grade, students with average reading achievement are ready to use real dictionaries. They should, of course, use beginning dictionaries that are simplified so that the definitions are readable. Using a dictionary is a complex task. Care must be taken that students do not feel defeated by it. Landau (1984) cautioned:

> The skills required to use a dictionary are often taken for granted by adults; teachers, however, know very well that they must be taught and are not easily mastered by everyone. One's grasp of the alphabet must be secure, and more, one must grasp conceptually the sequential way in which alphabetizing is done. Even if the child can perform the operation of finding the word he seeks, if it is a great chore filled with false starts, he is likely to give up the battle. (p. 14)

To keep students from believing that looking up words is a great chore, teachers must provide them with systematic instruction in the process and tasks that are well within their grasp. For reading, students must have three major skills: locating the target word, finding the proper definition, and learning the pronunciation. For writing, determining correct spelling and usage is also important.

Locating the words to be looked up.   The first thing that students must realize is that words are arranged in alphabetical order—*a* to *z*—by first letter and then by second letter, and, if necessary, by third letter, and so on. From the beginning, train students to use guide words so that they do not adopt the time-wasting habit of simply thumbing through the *s*s or the *w*s page by page until they find the appropriate location. Explain that not all letters encompass the same number of

---

Model the use of the dictionary by letting students see how you use the dictionary to look up an unfamiliar word, check the spelling or pronunciation of a word, or use its style guide section to get information on a question of style.

words; for example, *c* words take up many more pages than *x*, *y*, and *z* words put together. Describe how the dictionary can be divided in such a way that each of the following groups of letters covers approximately one fourth of all the words: *a–d*, *e–l*, *m–r*, and *s–z*. Even after they have mastered alphabetical order, students may be confused as they search for some entry words. Entry words often exclude inflected forms. A student looking up *rallies* or *exporter*, for example, will have to look under *rally* or *export*.

Locating and understanding meanings.   Definitions are not the only way words are explained. Many dictionaries also include synonyms, illustrations, and phrases or sentences in which the word is used. Some give a word history for selected words and explain how words that are synonyms differ in meaning. For instance, *Webster's New World Dictionary* supplies a definition for *kiosk*, gives a history of the term, and includes a photo of a kiosk. For the word *model*, it presents a brief explanatory paragraph that contrasts *model* and *pattern*.

Demonstrate the various ways a dictionary explains words. Direct students to look up words that are accompanied by illustrations. Discuss the definition, illustration, synonym, and example, if given, for each one. Words likely to have illustrations include the following (this will vary from dictionary to dictionary): *manatee*, *lattice*, *isobar*, *ibex*, *hoe*, *heart*, and *funnel*. Choose examples that are at the appropriate level for your students and that would be helpful for them to know.

Once students have a good grasp of how to locate words and how to use the several kinds of defining and explanatory information, have them look up words. Choose words that students have a genuine need to know, such as hard words from a content-area text or children's book that they are reading. In the beginning, stress words that have just one or two meanings, like *edifice*, *egret*, or *cellist*.

As students grow in skill in using the dictionary, tell them that some words may have many meanings. Have them look up the following words and count the number of meanings given: *ace*, *bit*, *bowl*, *comb*, and *free*. Emphasize that context can help them choose the correct meaning for a word that has several definitions. Have them practice finding the correct meaning for each of several words that have just two or three distinct meanings:

Because I moved the camera, the photo was a bit *fuzzy*.
The blanket was warm and *fuzzy*.
The explorers packed up their *gear* and left.
Use second *gear* when going up a steep hill.

Homographs.   Have students note how homographs are handled in their dictionaries. Usually, they are listed as separate entries and numbered, as in Figure 4.9. For practice, students can use context to help them determine which definition is correct in sentences such as the following:

The doctor gave me medicine for my *sty*.
The king signed the paper and put his *seal* on it.
We landed on a small sandy *key*.

Do not make dictionary use so tiresome that students acquire genuine dislike of this tool. Looking up all one's vocabulary words is just the type of assignment that gives the dictionary a bad name. Make sure that tasks that students are required to do are not too complex. Asking students to use new words in sentences after looking them up is difficult. It often takes a number of experiences with a word before a student acquires enough feeling for it to use it in a sentence.

ADAPTING INSTRUCTION for *ENGLISH LANGUAGE LEARNERS*
For ELLs, a translation dictionary that contains English and their first language could be an invaluable aid. Students might use one of the many language translators found on the Web, such as Web-a-dex Language Translator: **http://www.web-a-dex.com/translate.htm.**

FIGURE 4.9

Homographs in a Dictionary

bay[1] (bā), a part of a sea or lake extending into the land. A bay is usually smaller than a gulf and larger than a cove. *noun.*

bay[2] (bā), **1** a long, deep barking, especially by a large dog: *We heard the distant bay of the hounds.* **2** to bark with long, deep sounds: *Dogs sometimes bay at the moon.* 1 *noun,* 2 *verb.*

bay[3] (bā), **1** reddish-brown. **2** a reddish-brown horse with black mane and tail. 1 *adjective,* 2 *noun.*

Scott, Foresman Beginning Dictionary (p. 51) by E. L. Thorndike & C. L. Barnhart, 1988, Glenview, IL: Scott, Foresman and Company. Copyright © 1988 by Scott, Foresman & Company. Reprinted by permission of Scott, Foresman and Company.

▌Build your pupils' skill in using dictionary phonetic respellings to get the correct pronunciations along with the meanings of unknown words. Just as it's easier to remember a person's name if you can pronounce it, so, too, it's easier to remember a new word if you can say it correctly.

Constructing the correct pronunciation. While reading a historical selection, one young girl pronounced the word *plagues* as /plā-jiz/. From context, she had a sense of what the word meant and so mispronouncing it did not interfere with her comprehension. Students do not have to be able to pronounce a word accurately to understand its meaning. Most of us have had the experience of discovering that for years we have been mispronouncing a word we see in print. Even so, being aware of the correct pronunciation means that students can make connections between the word they see in print and the word when spoken. For example, if they have read the word *quiche* but have no idea how to pronounce it, they will not recognize it as being the same word they saw in print when they hear it spoken. Not knowing how to pronounce a word also means that they will not be able to use it in speech. On the other hand, knowing how to pronounce a word is another aid to remembering it.

After students have acquired some skill in locating words and deriving appropriate meanings, introduce the concept of phonetic respellings. Display and discuss the pronunciation key contained in the dictionary your class is using. To avoid confusion, have all students use the same dictionary series, if possible, because different publishers use different keys. Help students discover what they already know about the key. Almost all the phonetic respellings of consonants will be familiar, except for, perhaps, *ng* in words like *sung*, which is signified by /ŋ/ in some systems. Short vowels, indicated by *a, e, i, o* (sometimes symbolized as /ä/), and *u*, will also be familiar. Inform the students that long vowels are indicated by a symbol known as a macron, as in /gōt/. Explain that the macron is a diacritical mark and that such marks are used to show pronunciation.

▌Merriam-Webster presents a number of vocabulary-building exercises. The site also provides pronunciations for words: **http://www.m-w.com/.**

Show how diacritical marks are used to indicate the pronunciation of *r* vowels. Other symbols that may have to be explained to students are the pronunciations of short and long double *o*, schwa, the vowel sounds heard in *paw, toy,* and *out,* and short *o* (in Merriam-Webster).

After providing an overview of the pronunciation key, concentrate on its segments so that students acquire a working knowledge of the system. In order of difficulty, these segments might include consonants and short vowels, long vowels, *r* vowels, short and long double *o*, other vowels, and schwa. After introducing each segment, have students read words using the elements discussed. Encourage the active use of the pronunciation key.

Once students have mastered phonetic respelling, introduce the concept of accent. One way to do this would be to say a series of words whose meaning changes according to whether the first or second syllable is accented: *record, present, desert, minute, object*. As you say the words, stress the accented syllable. Have students listen to hear which syllable is said with more stress. After the class decides which syllable is stressed, write the words on the board and put in the accent marks while explaining what they mean. Discuss how the change in stress changes the pronunciation, meaning, or use of each word. To provide guided practice, select unknown words from materials students are about to read and have students reconstruct their pronunciation. Discuss these reconstructions, and provide ample opportunity for independent application. Later, introduce the concept of secondary stress.

Dialects and variant pronunciations.   As students grow in their ability to use the dictionary, discuss **dialects** and variant pronunciations. Explain that people in various parts of the country have different pronunciations because of the regional or cultural dialect that they speak. Encourage respect for dialects, and show students how to select the pronunciation appropriate for the regional dialect that they speak. For instance, looking up the word *route*, students see that it has two pronunciations: /ro͞ot/, /rout/. Neither pronunciation is preferred; the appropriate pronunciation is the one that the student and the other members of her or his speech community use. Of course, not all possible pronunciations are listed in the

■ A **dialect** is a form of a language that differs from other forms of the same language in pronunciation, vocabulary, or grammar. Dialect varies by region, class, occupation, and age.

*I*llustrations in dictionaries and glossaries supplement verbal definitions.

USING TECHNOLOGY
Kids Click
**http://sunsite.
berkeley.edu/
KidsClick!/**
Click on Dictionaries.
Has links to online dictionaries that range
from regular to rhyming.

dictionary; just because a certain pronunciation is not listed does not mean that it is not acceptable.

Electronic dictionaries. Electronic dictionaries are far easier to use than book versions. Words are easier to look up. All the student need do is to type in the target word. Some electronic dictionaries accept misspelled words so that students looking up the spelling of a word can find it even if they can't spell it accurately. Speaking dictionaries also pronounce the word being looked up and read the definition, so students don't have to be able to use the pronunciation key before they can use the dictionary. Electronic dictionaries are also motivational: They're more fun to use than a traditional dictionary. Electronic dictionaries come in CD-ROM and handheld versions or are available on the Web. Handheld versions have the advantage of being small and portable. And some of the simpler models are not much more expensive than book versions.

■ The Dictionary as a Tool

Many school dictionaries include generous instructions for use, along with practice exercises. Use these selectively. Avoid isolated drill on dictionary skills. Concentrate on building dictionary skills through functional use—that is, show students how to use the dictionary, and encourage them to incorporate it as a tool for understanding language. For instance, when they have questions about word meaning, pronunciation, spelling, or usage, encourage them to seek help in the dictionary.

USING TECHNOLOGY
If possible, acquire a
CD-ROM or other electronic dictionary. The
advantages of an electronic dictionary are
that it locates the word
faster and is motivational. An electronic
dictionary may also read
the word and its definition. This is a help for
students whose reading
skills are limited.

One word of caution is in order: For word recognition, the dictionary should generally be used as a last resort. Looking up a word while reading a story interrupts the flow of the story and disturbs comprehension. Students should try context, phonics, and morphemic or syllabic analysis before going to the dictionary. Moreover, unless the word is crucial to understanding the story, they should wait until they have read the selection to look up the word. The dictionary is also a good check on definitions derived from context clues. After reading a story in which they used context clues, students should check their educated guesses against the dictionary's definitions.

REINFORCEMENT ACTIVITIES Dictionary usage

- Have students find out how the following words should be pronounced: *psalm, ptomaine, crepes, depot,* and *czar.*
- Have students use the dictionary to find out what the following sports are and tell which one(s) they might enjoy: *quoits, cricket, boccie, curling, biathlon, rugby,* and *billiards.*
- Ask students to determine from whose names the following words were created: *Braille, xylophone, boycott, silhouette,* and *gardenia.*
- Have students use the dictionary to determine which of the following are animals:

oryx	peccary	marten
okapi	parka	manatee
ocarina	parabola	marmoset
oboe	pagoda	marquee

- To give students guided practice in looking up words, have them answer questions similar to the following:

  Are all *nocturnal* animals dangerous?

  Would a *yurt* taste good?

  Would a *filigree* make a good pet?

  Have you ever been *reticent*?

  Could you use the word *bayou* to say good-bye to a friend?

- An excellent activity for helping students understand how the dictionary works is the dictionary builder at Word Central (Wordcentral.com). Students build a word by providing a definition, a part of speech, a history of the word, a sample sentence, and, if they wish, personal information. They can also have the word included in the site's listing of student-built words. Sample entries include such words as *enticon* (fabricated word) and *puffenglooper* (person who is never on task but always has a joke to tell).

USING TECHNOLOGY

Handheld electronic dictionaries are available from Franklin Electronic Publishers, Inc., One Franklin Plaza, Burlington, NJ, 08016-4907, 800-266-5626.

■ Contextual Redefinition

Contextual redefinition is an excellent technique for reviewing and integrating word analysis strategies. Contextual redefinition aids students in the use of context clues by contrasting definitions from words in isolation and words in context (Tierney & Readence, 2000). It also provides reinforcement for dictionary skills. An easy-to-implement but effective technique, it consists of four steps: (1) choosing hard words; (2) presenting words in isolation; (3) presenting words in context; (4) checking derived meanings against those provided by a dictionary. Lesson 4.6 shows the steps in a contextual redefinition.

 LESSON 4.6 **Contextual redefinition**

Step 1. Selecting hard words

Words are chosen that are important to an understanding of the selection and which may pose problems for students.

Step 2. Presenting words in isolation

Unfamiliar words are listed on the chalkboard or on a transparency. Volunteers are invited to pronounce them—they are given help if needed—and are asked to define the words. Because the words are presented in isolation, students must rely on morphemic analysis clues to define the words. Students are asked to provide reasons for their definitions. However, because they have little to go on, their proposed definitions may be far afield. Unless students spot the root word *viv*, a word such as *vivacious* might be defined as "having a lot of sounds" or "colorful." Encourage students to agree on one meaning for each word.

Step 3. Presenting words in context

Words are then presented in context. Ideally, this would be the context in which the words are used in the selection to be read: "In contrast to her more serious husband, Mary Todd Lincoln was a vivacious and colorful addition to the Washington scene" (Burchard, 1999, p. 49). However, if the context is not adequate, create your own sentence. Using the context, students make their best guesses about the meaning of each word. They might do this alone, in pairs, or in small groups. As in the previous step, they are expected to explain why they constructed a particular meaning. This provides an opportunity for students to share their reasoning processes. The group is again asked to agree on the best guess as to the target word's meaning.

Step 4. Checking the meaning in the dictionary

Students look up the word in the dictionary and discuss possible definitions with the group. The group chooses the most appropriate definition.

Contextual redefinition provides a natural opportunity to provide guided practice in three interrelated word identification skills: morphemic analysis, contextual analysis, and dictionary usage. In deriving the meaning of *vivacious*, students can use their knowledge of the root *viv* and the suffix *-ous*, the context clue, and the dictionary definition to arrive at a fuller, more precise understanding of *vivacious*.

SUPPLYING CORRECTIVE FEEDBACK

A student is reading and is suddenly stopped cold by an unknown word. What should the teacher do? If the student does not self-correct and the error is not substantive—the student says *this* for *that*—you may choose to do nothing. Sometimes an error is substantive and disturbs the sense of the sentence, but it is obvious that the student will not be able to work out the word using phonics, syllabication, context, or morphemic analysis. In such a case, you might supply the word as one of two options so the student is involved in the process: "Would *chat* or *champ* fit here?" If there is a chance that the student can use strategies to decode the word, pause briefly—about five seconds or so—to provide an opportunity for the student to work out the word (Harris & Sipay, 1990). If the student fails to work out the word but might be able to with a little help, try a **corrective cues hierarchy** (McCoy & Pany, 1986).

■ A **corrective cues hierarchy** is a series of corrective feedback statements arranged in order of utility and ease of application.

Applying a Corrective Cues Hierarchy

The following corrective cues hierarchy is adapted from McCoy and Pany (1986):

For words in the students' listening but not reading vocabulary

- *Strategy 1.* Seeking out a pronounceable word part and using it to reconstruct a word is often the simplest, most direct strategy and, in most instances, should be attempted first. When encountering an unknown word, the student should ask, "Is there any part of this word that I can say?" If that does not work, the student should try an analogy strategy, asking, "Is this word like any word I know?" If the word is a multisyllabic one, the student might need to reconstruct the word part by part. Once the word has been reconstructed, the student should verify the reconstruction by checking whether the word is real and fits the context of the sentence.

- *Strategy 2.* If the student is unable to use the pronounceable word part or analogy strategy to work out the pronunciation of the difficult word rapidly, encourage the use of context. The student should say "blank" for the unknown word and read to the end of the sentence and ask, "What would make sense here?"

For words not in the students' listening or reading vocabulary

- *Strategy 1.* The student should use context clues designed to help derive the meaning of an unknown word. The student should determine what information in the sentence containing the unknown word—and additional sentences, if necessary—helps her to figure out the word. The student should think about all the information given and about what she knows that might help in determining the meaning of the word. The student should then check to make sure that a real word has been constructed and that the word fits the context of the sentence.

- *Strategy 2.* If the meaning of the word is unknown and context does not help, the student should use morphemic analysis. The student should look for parts of the word whose meaning she knows and use those to construct the meaning of the word. The student should then reread the sentence, substituting the constructed word to see whether it fits the sense of the sentence. If neither contextual analysis nor morphemic analysis works, students should use a glossary or the dictionary.

Although the strategies are presented here in consecutive order, they may be applied in tandem. For instance, a student may use both morphemic analysis and context to derive the meaning of a word or may use context and pronounceable word parts or phonics and syllabication to reconstruct the pronunciation of a word.

Using Prompts

When students are having difficulty with a word, use a prompt to encourage the use of word analysis. Listed below are suggested prompting questions that you might ask students in order to cue the use of a particular strategy.

> As students are taught how to use word recognition strategies, they should also be taught when to apply them so that they can make the choice as to whether to try context, phonics, syllabic analysis, or morphemic analysis first. The corrective cues hierarchy depends on the nature of the word to be identified, and the student's background and ability to apply strategies.

> The six major word-attack skills are phonics, sight words, syllabication (covered in Chapter 3), morphemic analysis, context clues, and dictionary use. Each was presented separately; but they are applied in an integrated fashion. Context is used to act as a check on the results of the student's attempt to use one of the other strategies. If a word the student has reconstructed does not make sense, or if the definition selected by the dictionary does not quite fit the sense of the passage, this is a signal for the student to try again.

- *Pronounceable word part.* Is there any part of the word that you can say?
- *Analogy.* Is the word like any that you know?
- *Context.* What would make sense here? What would fit? Say "blank" for the word, and read to the end of the sentence. Then ask yourself, "What word would make sense here?"
- *Syllabic analysis.* How would you say the first syllable? The second syllable? The next syllable? What does the word seem to be?
- *Morphemic analysis.* Is there any part of the word that you know?
- *Dictionary or glossary usage.* Would the dictionary or glossary help?
- *Affirmation.* I like the way you used context (or another strategy) to help you figure out that word.

The probing prompt encourages the students to reflect on their knowledge of strategies and to select the most appropriate one.

- *Probing.* What could you do to help you figure out that word?

Using Think-Alouds

To assess students' use of word analysis skills and to provide guidance in their use, conduct a **think-aloud** (Harmon, 1998). In a think-aloud, students stop when they come to a difficult word and then give a description of what is going on in their minds as they try to figure out the word. Instead of providing direct instruction, the teacher offers neutral prompts that encourage students to explain their thinking: "Can you tell me what you are thinking? Can you tell me more?" Once you know what strategies students are using, you can then use the think-aloud as an instructional tool. You might use such prompts as: "Can you find clues to the word's meaning in other sentences of other parts of the article? What might help you to get the word's meaning? Would the glossary help?"

■ **Think-alouds** are procedures in which students are asked to describe the processes they are using as they engage in reading or another cognitive activity.

Guidance provided in a think-aloud is designed to help students apply and integrate strategies. It also helps build students' confidence in the use of word analysis strategies and helps build their sense of competence. If individual think-alouds are too time consuming, group think-alouds might be used instead. That way students learn from each other.

HELP FOR STRUGGLING READERS AND WRITERS

As struggling readers and writers make their way through the grades, they may master phonics only to find that they are having difficulty in reading because their background knowledge and vocabularies are limited. Having struggled with reading, poor readers generally read less and so meet and learn fewer new words and acquire less background information. With these students, it is essential to build background and related vocabulary. Spend more time building essential concepts and vocabulary before they read a selection. Also spend time after the selection has been read clarifying and deepening concepts. Try to help students see how new concepts are related to concepts they already know.

Encourage students to read widely, but be sure that they have lots of materials on their level. Also seek out reader-friendly informational books, such as books from the *Science Alive* (Crabtree) series, that do a particularly good job of building background and vocabulary.

Struggling readers often have poor concepts of themselves as learners. To build their self-concepts and vocabulary, plan a program of vocabulary development that introduces challenging words to them. They will appreciate learning "big" words. Also provide instruction in morphemics, context clues, and dictionary skills to help them to become independent word learners. A handheld speaking electronic dictionary can be a big help for struggling readers and writers. It allows them to obtain the pronunciation of words in their listening but not their reading vocabularies and it also allows them to obtain the meanings of words not in their listening vocabularies. And it helps them with their spelling.

ESSENTIAL STANDARDS

Fourth through eighth grades
Students will

- use context to derive the meanings of unknown words.
- use knowledge of homophones, homographs, synonyms, antonyms, and idioms to determine the meanings of words.
- use knowledge of word origins and derivations to determine the meanings of words.
- expand their vocabularies.
- use dictionaries, including electronic ones, and glossaries to derive the meanings and pronunciations of words.
- use morphemic analysis to derive the meanings of words. At each level, they will be able to use increasingly sophisticated morphemic elements.
- identify the meanings of words that have multiple meanings.

ASSESSMENT

Through observation, note whether students are learning the skills and strategies they have been taught. Watch to see what they do when they come across an unfamiliar word. Do they attempt to use context? Do they attempt to apply morphemic analysis strategies? Do they have a working knowledge of morphemic elements that have been introduced? When all else fails, do they use the dictionary or glossary as an aid? Do they know when to use which strategy? Are they able to integrate strategies? To enhance your observation, take advantage of selections that contain words that lend themselves to a particular strategy and see how well students do. For instance, if the selection has especially rich context clues, see whether students were able to make use of the clues. You might question them orally or

ACTION PLAN

1. Assess students' word knowledge.
2. Construct or adapt a program for vocabulary development based upon students' needs.
3. Gear instruction to the students' level of knowledge. Words that convey new concepts will need a greater degree of teaching than words that are simply labels for known concepts.
4. Develop a depth of meaning of a core of essential words rather than trying to cover a wide range of words.
5. Use graphic organizers, wide reading, games, sorting, self-collection of words, and other activities to provide practice and application.

6. Introduce morphemic analysis, contextual clues, and dictionary usage in functional fashion. Integrate use of skills.
7. Provide ample practice and application opportunities.
8. Help students to develop an interest in words.
9. Help English language learners recognize and take advantage of cognates. Be aware that ELLs have many concepts developed in their native language and may only be lacking English labels for the concepts.
10. Monitor students' progress and make necessary adjustments.

have them write down what they think the target words meant or do both. Having them write down meanings gives you an indicator of everyone's performance. Discussing responses gives you the opportunity to ask probing questions so that you can determine how they applied their strategies.

Also, note the quality of students' word knowledge. Is their vocabulary adequate for the materials they must read and the concepts they must learn? Are they acquiring new words at an adequate rate? Do they have an interest in words? Standardized tests often have a vocabulary section. If so, use these results as a possible indicator of the students' word knowledge. Note, however, whether the test required students to read the words or whether the words and definitions were read to students. Poor readers' vocabularies are underestimated if they have to read the vocabulary words. See Chapter 2 for limitations of standardized test results.

SUMMARY

1. Average first-graders know between 5,000 and 6,000 words and learn about 3,000 new ones each year. By the end of high school, students generally know more than 40,000 words. Having rich experiences and talking about them are important factors in learning new words. Also important are relating vocabulary to background, building relationships, developing depth of meaning, presenting numerous exposures, creating an interest in words, and promoting transfer. A variety of activi-

ties, such as graphic organizers and playing word games, can be used to develop word knowledge. The most powerful word learning activity is wide reading.
2. Words are learned through association or conceptualization or some combination of the two. Concepts and their labels are stored in neworks. At a minimum, introduction of new words should include a definition of the word, the use of the word in a sentence or story context, an activity

that relates the word to other words being introduced, and an activity that relates the word to the
student's background.

3. A planned program of vocabulary development is
advisable. Words chosen for intensive instruction
should be key words that will be encountered
again and again. Techniques that help students
remember new words include organizing the
words to show relationships, elaboration, and the
key word approach.

4. A carefully planned program of vocabulary development should include provision for teaching students how to learn words on their own through
the use of morphemic analysis, contextual analysis, and the dictionary.

EXTENDING AND APPLYING

1. Try using graphic devices, such as semantic feature analysis, a Venn diagram, or a semantic map,
to organize words that you are studying or in
which you are interested. Which of these devices
works best for you? Why?

2. Plan a program of vocabulary development.
Include a description of the class, your objectives,
the source of words, and the activities that you will
use to reinforce words and the techniques you will
use. Also tell how you will evaluate the program.

3. Choose four to six words from a chapter in a children's book. Then, using the steps detailed in this
chapter, create a vocabulary lesson. Teach the lesson to a group of students, and critique it. What
worked well? What might be changed?

4. Investigate one of the vocabulary-building Web
sites mentioned or one that you have discovered.
How might you use this site?

5. Using procedures explained in this chapter, create
a semantic map with an elementary school or
middle school class. Evaluate the map's effectiveness. In what ways did it help students? Did the
activity engage their attention?

DEVELOPING A PROFESSIONAL PORTFOLIO

Teach and record a morphemic analysis lesson. Select
elements that appear in students' texts and that have a
high degree of utility. Summarize the lesson and reflect
on its effectiveness.

DEVELOPING A RESOURCE FILE

Keep a list of children's books and Web sites that do a
particulary good job of developing vocabulary. Also collect riddles, jokes, and games that make learning words
fun.

5

Comprehension:
Theory and Strategies

ANTICIPATION GUIDE

*F*or each of the following statements related to the chapter you are about to read, put a check under "Agree" or "Disagree" to show how you feel. Discuss your responses with classmates before you read the chapter.

	Agree	*Disagree*
1 Reading comprehension is understanding the author's meaning.	_____	_____
2 The less one knows about a topic, the more one will learn by reading about it.	_____	_____
3 Comprehension is a social activity.	_____	_____
4 Knowledge of words is the most important ingredient in comprehension.	_____	_____
5 As students read, they should be aware of whether they are comprehending.	_____	_____
6 Before learning to draw inferences, the reader must master comprehension of literal details.	_____	_____
7 In comprehension instruction, the teacher should focus on the processes students use rather than on whether they obtain the right answers.	_____	_____

USING WHAT YOU KNOW

*I*n a sense, all the previous chapters have provided a foundation for this one, which is about comprehension. This chapter begins with a discussion of the nature of comprehension and goes on to describe the strategies used to obtain meaning from reading, with suggestions for teaching them. Comprehension is very much a matter of bringing your knowledge to the task. What do you know about comprehension? What strategies do you use as you try to understand what you read? What do you do when your comprehension goes astray? What tips for comprehension might you share with a younger reader?

THE PROCESS OF COMPREHENDING

Comprehension is the main purpose of reading. In fact, without it, there is no reading, since reading is the process of constructing meaning from print. Comprehension is a constructive, interactive process involving three factors—the reader, the text, and the context in which the text is read. For comprehension to improve, the interaction among all three factors must be taken into consideration. Readers vary in the amount and type of prior knowledge they possess, the strategies they use, their attitudes toward reading, and their work habits. Texts vary in genre, theme or topic, style, difficulty level, and appeal. The context includes when, where, and why a text is being read. Is it being read at home in preparation for a test the next day? Is it an antidote description printed on the can of a pesticide being read by a frantic parent whose child has sprayed himself with the substance? Or is it a novel being read for pleasure in an easy chair on a sunny day? Although the bulk of this chapter will discuss comprehension strategies, the use of these strategies will be affected by reader, text, and context factors.

Schema Theory

To gain some insight into the process of comprehension, read the following paragraph, which has been divided into a series of sentences. Stop after reading each sentence and ask yourself: "What did the sentence say? How did I go about comprehending it? What does this paragraph seem to be about?"

> A hoatzin has a clever way of escaping from its enemies.
> It generally builds its home in a branch that extends over a swamp or stream.
> If an enemy approaches, the hoatzin plunges into the water below.
> Once the coast is clear, it uses its fingerlike claws to climb back up the tree.
> Hoatzin are born with claws on their wings but lose the claws as they get older.

To make sense of the selection, you would have to rely heavily on the knowledge you bring to the text. One definition of comprehension is that it is the process of building a connection between what we know and what we do not know, or the new and the old (Searfoss & Readence, 1994). It is currently theorized that our knowledge is packaged into units known as schemata. A **schema** is the organized knowledge that one has about people, places, things, and events (Rumelhart, 1984). A schema may be very broad and general (for example, a schema for animals) or it may be fairly narrow (for example, a schema for Siamese cats).

■ A **schema** is a unit of organized knowledge. (The plural of *schema* is *schemata*.)

In R. C. Anderson's (1984) view, comprehension primarily involves activating or constructing a schema that accounts for the elements in a text, similar to constructing an outline of a script. For example, a script outline for buying and selling includes the following categories, which are known as slots: buyer, seller, merchandise, money, and bargaining (Rumelhart, 1980). Comprehending a story involves filling these slots with particular examples or instances. As a student reads about a character in a story who is purchasing a bicycle, her or his buyer schema is activated. The student fills in the buyer and seller slots with the characters' names. The bicycle is placed in the merchandise slot. The story says that the buyer got a good deal, so that is placed in the bargaining slot. The story may not say how the character paid for the bike—cash, check, charge card, or an IOU—but the reader may infer that it was with cash because in her or his buyer schema, goods are purchased with cash. A schema thus provides a framework for comprehending a story and making inferences that flesh it out. A schema also aids retention, as students use it to organize their reconstruction of the events.

In constructing the meaning of the selection on the hoatzin, you used various processes to activate the appropriate schema and fill the slots. In reading the first sentence, assuming that you did not know what a hoatzin is, you may have made a reasoned prediction that it was some kind of animal. The information in the first sentence was probably enough to activate your animal-survival-from-enemies schema. The slots might include type of animal, enemies, ability to flee, and ability to fight; guided by your schema, you may have been on the lookout for information to fill the slots. Integrating or summarizing the first three sentences made it possible for you to place "plunges into the water" into the ability to flee slot. You also did quite a bit of inferencing. When you read about the wings in the last sentence, you probably inferred that the hoatzin is a bird, even though it dives into the water. Thus you were able to fill in the type of animal slot. You probably also inferred that the hoatzin's enemies could not reach it in the water. You may have inferred, too, that the creature is not fierce, since it seems to prefer fleeing to fighting. These inferences enabled you to fill in the enemies and ability to fight slots. As you can probably see, comprehending the selection about the hoatzin was not so much a question of getting meaning from the text as it was bringing meaning to it or constructing meaning by transacting with the text.

Not only do readers have schemata for ideas and events, but also they have schemata for text structures, which help them organize information. For instance, a selection might have a main idea and details organization. A reader who realizes this can use the structure of the text to organize the information in his or her memory.

Although activating schemata is essential in reading, reading is more complex than simply filling slots. As they transact with text, proficient, active readers are constantly relating what they are reading to other experiences they have had, other information in the text they have read, and texts previously read. Their interest in the text plays a powerful role in the web of linkages that they construct (Hartman, 1994). A student captivated by the idea that a bird has claws on its wings might relate this text to passages that he or she has read or a TV show about unusual animals.

Situation Models

Comprehension can also be thought of as the construction of a mental or **situation model.** Schema theory provides a good description of what happens when the reader deals with objects or events for which she or he has a schema. But what happens when the reader is dealing with novel objects or events? Situation model

USING TECHNOLOGY
Because comprehension is dependent on what we know, one way to foster comprehension is to build background. Hundreds of sites that students might use to learn about a vast array of topics can be found in Polly, J. A. (2002). *The Internet Kids & Family Yellow Pages.* New York: McGraw-Hill.

■ A **situation model,** also known as a mental model, views comprehension as a "process of building and maintaining a model of situations and events described in text" (McNamara, Miller, & Bransford, 1991, p. 491). Schema theory describes how familiar situations are understood. Situation model theory describes how new situations are comprehended.

construction is a more inclusive theory of comprehension because it can handle both schema-based and novel activities (McNamara, Miller, & Bransford, 1991).

> Activating schemata is part of a situation model. As Zwaan and Graesser (1998) noted, "To construct situation models, readers must integrate information from the text with prior knowledge" (p. 197).

A situation model for fiction is the microworld that the reader has created and includes the characters, the setting, the plot, and the mental states of the characters (Graesser & Bertus, 1998). In creating a situation model of a piece of fiction, the reader keys in on the apparent main character and creates a mental model of the circumstances in which the character finds himself or herself. To help them construct meaning, readers also keep track of the who, when, where, and why of a story, although they are less aware of spatial elements (Zwaan, Radvansky, Hilliard, & Curiel, 1998).

Remembering and Learning

> Based on a situation model, you could take at least three steps to improve comprehension: build background, give students material on the appropriate level, and teach strategies, such as generating questions as they read, that would help them make connections.

Situation models also help us to understand how we learn from text. Learning from text is not the same thing as remembering or reproducing text (Kintsch, 1994). It is possible to recite verbatim all of what one has read but not be able to put that information to use or draw any conclusions based on the information. Akin to literal comprehension, remembering text means being able to reproduce the content of the text, either word by word or as a summary. Learning from text means being able to use or apply the text in some way. It involves a greater depth of comprehension and includes making inferences or taking a course of action based on what one has read. Following a written recipe or deciding which bicycle to buy based on reports in a consumer magazine are two examples of learning from text.

The situation model is a deeper level of understanding. The situation model integrates the reader's schema or background knowledge and information from the text. For instance, in reading about heart disease, a student may find out that blood turns purple when it cannot get rid of carbon dioxide through the lungs. But lacking background knowledge about the circulatory system, the student cannot infer why this is so and is therefore unable to construct a situation model. The student can recite the information that he has read but cannot explain it because he really doesn't understand it (Kintsch, 1994).

> Following directions is an example of a situation model of reading. It requires that students go beyond merely remembering information. They must also put the information to use.

A student who has knowledge of the circulatory system can create a situation model by combining information from the text with background information and infer why the blood was purple instead of red. Of course, had the text reviewed the operation of the circulatory system, the reader might then have had sufficient background knowledge to infer why the blood was purple. Or the teacher could have built the necessary background. Because comprehension is a combination of reader, text, and context, a well-written, very explicit text, building of necessary background, and instruction in the use of strategies can compensate for weak initial background.

Role of Reasoning

Reasoning is a key component in comprehension. Students may be called upon to infer character traits, judge a solution, analyze a situation, compare settings, draw conclusions, form concepts, apply a principle, or evaluate the credibility of information. Reasoning and background knowledge interact. Comprehension relies heavily on the reader's ability to use background knowledge to make inferences. Students who have a richer background and can make more connections between what they know and what they are reading have better comprehension and retention.

Role of Attention

Attention is also a factor in comprehension. Constructing meaning is hindered if the student is not reading actively and purposely: "Successful comprehension depends in part on readers' ability to allocate their limited attention efficiently and effectively to the most relevant pieces of information within the text and within memory" (van den Broek & Kremer, 2000, p. 7).

Another essential factor is the kind of comprehension the reader demands before moving on to the next sentence. Proficient readers establish referential and causal–logical relationships between the current and previously read sentences, whereas less effective readers might be satisfied with understanding each individual sentence and so fail to create connections between sentences.

Role of Interest

Interest has a positive impact on comprehension. When possible, students should be given some choice in what they read and how they read it.

> . . . teachers who provide meaningful choices and autonomy increase students' motivation to read and to expend effort to gain knowledge from text (Reeve, Bolt, & Cai, 1999). The explanation for the benefit of autonomy support for reading comprehension is that students become more active learners when teachers provide a minimal, but meaningful, choice in the topics, texts, activities, and strategies for learning. For example, when given a choice of two books for a comprehension activity, students will choose the one that interests them. This interest deepens the students' thinking and their use of strategies and background knowledge during reading. . . . High interest, derived from choice, leads to high comprehension. (Snow, 2002, p. 43)

Interest leads to deeper comprehension (Schiefele, 1999). This is true for selections in which the reader has a personal interest because of the topic being covered as well as selections that are interesting because of the way they are written.

COMPREHENSION STRATEGIES

Before you began reading this chapter, what did you do? Did you read the title? Did you ask yourself what you know about comprehension? As you read, did you question what the author was saying? Did you try to relate information in the text to your experience? Did you reread sections because you didn't quite understand what the author was saying or you were momentarily distracted? If you did any of these things, you were using reading strategies.

To help you understand strategies, think about the processes you use as you read. Because we are experienced readers, our strategies have become relatively automatic. Stop your reading from time to time and think about the processes you are using to comprehend what you are reading. Do this especially when you are reading difficult material. Strategies tend to become more conscious when the material is difficult because we have to take deliberate steps to comprehend it. One group of highly effective staff developers and classroom teachers tried out each strategy on their own reading before teaching it. They discovered that their comprehension as well as their understanding of strategies and ability to teach them to students improved.

> We tested the strategies on our reading. We became more conscious of our own thinking processes as readers. We realized that we could concentrate simultaneously on the text and our ways of thinking about it. What seems most extraordinary, however, was that by thinking about our own thinking—by being metacognitive (literally, to think about one's thinking)—we could actually deepen and enhance our comprehension of the text. (Keene & Zimmermann, 1997, p. 21)

According to a schema–situational model of comprehension, the reader plays a very active role in constructing an understanding of text. One way the active reader constructs meaning is by using **strategies.** Strategies are deliberate, planned procedures designed to help us reach a goal. Comprehension strategies include preparing, organizing, elaborating, rehearsing, and monitoring. There are also affective strategies (Weinstein & Mayer, 1986), in which motivation and interest play a role in the construction of meaning.

■ A **strategy** is a deliberate, planned activity or procedure designed to achieve a certain goal.

Preparational strategies are processes that readers use, such as surveying a text and predicting what it will be about, to prepare themselves to construct meaning. Using organizational strategies, readers construct relationships among ideas in the text, specifically between the main idea and supporting details. Paraphrasing, summarizing, clustering related words, noting and using the structure of a text, and creating semantic maps are also ways of organizing.

Elaborating involves building associations between information being read and prior knowledge or integrating them by manipulating or transforming information. Elaboration strategies include drawing inferences, creating analogies, visualizing, and evaluating, or reading critically. (Evaluating is discussed in Chapter 6.)

■ **Rehearsing** is studying or repeating something so as to remember it.

Rehearsing involves taking basic steps to remember material. Outlining, taking notes, underlining, testing oneself, and rereading are rehearsal strategies. Elaborating or organizing and rehearsing are often used in combination to learn complex material.

■ **Monitoring** is being aware of or checking one's cognitive processes. In reading comprehension, the reader monitors his understanding of the text.

Monitoring consists of being aware of one's comprehension and regulating it. Monitoring strategies include setting goals for reading, adjusting reading speed to difficulty of material, checking comprehension, and taking corrective steps when comprehension fails. (Some preparational strategies are actually a special set of monitoring strategies that are employed prior to reading.) See Table 5.1 for a listing of comprehension strategies.

A good summary description of what good readers do as they read is provided by the distinguished Rand Study Group (Snow, 2002):

> We know that students who are good comprehenders read for a purpose and actively monitor whether that purpose is being met. They notice when something they are reading is incongruous with their background knowledge or is unclear, then they take action to clarify their understanding, such as rereading or reading ahead. They may

TABLE 5.1	Major comprehension strategies		
Preparational Strategies	**Organizational Strategies**	**Elaboration Strategies**	**Metacognitive Strategies**
Previewing	Comprehending the main idea	Making inferences	Regulating
Activating prior knowledge	Determining important details	Imaging	Checking
Setting purpose and goals	Organizing details	Generating questions	Repairing
Predicting	Sequencing	Evaluating (critical reading)	
	Following directions		
	Summarizing		

also stop periodically when reading to summarize what they have read as a way to check their understanding. To further enhance comprehension, good comprehenders also use strategies that help them retain, organize, and evaluate the information they are reading. (p. 33)

Scaffolds for Comprehension

Kyleen Beers (2003) recalls giving her students a practice exercise for finding main ideas. A student by the name of Al raised his hand and said he didn't know what to do. Kyleen Beers explained that he was to find the main idea. But Al protested that he didn't know what the main idea was. As he put it, "Yeah, but how do I know what that is if I don't already know what the main idea is?" (p. 3) After reflecting on his dilemma, Beers realized that she needed to teach students the thinking skills that would enable them to compose or infer main ideas. However, based on her observations of students, she discovered that they used a variety of high-level skills in their everyday lives but weren't applying these to their reading.

The key to teaching students how to apply skills is direct instruction and providing needed scaffolds until they apply the strategies independently. You might provide direct instruction in a strategy and culminate the instruction with a list of steps that students can follow in order to apply the strategy.

Each comprehension strategy that is discussed is accompanied by a list of steps that provide students with specific suggestions for applying a strategy. Please feel free to modify the steps to fit your situation. It is also suggested that you post the steps in a prominent spot or even give students copies of the steps that they might place in their notebooks. You might also use an instructional procedure or technique that guides students through the necessary processing. For instance, the anticipation guide that begins each chapter is a scaffold that prods you to activate your prior knowledge and evaluate your knowledge of a topic. Using What You Know is a scaffold that helps you to activate prior knowledge. Think-alouds are a scaffold for virtually all the strategies.

Preparational Strategies

Preparational strategies include previewing, activating prior knowledge about a topic before reading, and predicting what a piece is about or what will happen in a story. Setting purposes and goals are also in this category.

In this text, strategies are presented according to cognitive or affective processes involved.

■ **Prior knowledge** is the background information that a reader brings to the text.

■ The **purpose** for reading is the question that the reader wants to answer or the information the reader is seeking. The **goal** for reading is the outcome the reader is seeking: to gain information, to prepare for a test, to learn how to put a toy together, to relax, etc.

■ **Previewing** can also be applied during reading. A reader may complete a section and then activate prior knowledge and make predictions for the upcoming section.

■ Activating Prior Knowledge

Because comprehension involves relating the unknown to the known, it is important that students become aware of what they know about a subject. The teacher should model the process. In preparation for reading an article about computers, the teacher should show the class how she previews and asks herself what she already knows about the subject and then decides what she would like to find out.

Before students read a selection, the teacher activates students' **prior knowledge** through questioning. This works best when both subject knowledge and personal knowledge are activated. For instance, before reading a story about poisonous snakes, the teacher asks students to tell what they know about poisonous snakes and also relate any personal knowledge they have about snakes. In one study, students who activated both subject knowledge (school-type knowledge) and personal knowledge prior to reading were better able to apply their knowledge and also had a more positive attitude (Spires & Donley, 1998). In time, students should be led to activate both subject and personal knowledge on their own, because much of their reading will be done without benefit of preparatory discussion or teacher assistance.

■ Setting Purpose and Goals

Although the teacher often sets the **purpose** for reading a piece by giving students a question to answer, students must be able to set their own purpose. This could fit in with activating prior knowledge. As readers activate knowledge about computers, they may wonder how the machines work, which could be a purpose for reading. Readers also have to decide their overall **goal** for reading—for pleasure, to gain information, or to study for a test—as each goal requires a different style of reading. Again, these are processes that the teacher should model and discuss. However, students should gradually take responsibility for setting purposes and goals.

■ Previewing

A strategy that helps readers set a purpose for reading is **previewing.** In previewing, also known as surveying, students read the title, headings, introduction, and summary and look at illustrations to get an overview of the selection. This preview orients them to the piece so that they have some sense of what it will be about. It can function as a kind of blueprint for constructing a mental model of the text and also activates readers' schemata. As readers preview, they ask themselves what they know about the subject. Previewing is often used with predicting: Information gathered from previewing can be used to make predictions.

■ Predicting

Powerful, but relatively easy to use, predicting activates readers' schemata because predictions are made on the basis of prior knowledge. Predicting also gives readers a purpose for reading and turns reading into an active search to see whether a prediction is correct. This strategy can and should be taught even before students can read on their own. Before reading a storybook aloud, the teacher should read its title, show the students one or more illustrations, and have them predict what they think the story might be about or what they think will happen. Consensus is not necessary. Each student should feel free to make her or his own prediction. However, the teacher might ask students to justify their predictions

For setting up predictions, Nessel (1987) suggested two questions that could be asked at the beginning or at crucial points in the story:

1. What do you think will happen? (e.g., What do you think *X* will do? How do you think this problem will be resolved?)

2. Why do you think so? (What have you experienced and what did you read in the story that leads you to make that prediction?) (p. 604)

The first question elicits the prediction; the second asks students to explain it to ensure that it is thoughtful and plausible. Students also must learn to be flexible so that they can alter a prediction if it proves to be off the mark.

In addition to teaching students what kinds of questions to ask, the teacher should show them the best sources of predictions: title, illustrations, introductory note, and first paragraph. Gradually, students can create their own predictions as they read. Predicting becomes an excellent device for enhancing comprehension when students are reading independently—ideally, it will become automatic. Predicting should also be a lifelong strategy. As they move into higher grades, students should use predicting as part of a study technique as well as for other sustained reading.

Part of being an effective user of strategies is knowing when and where to use a particular strategy. Making predictions requires prior knowledge. Students beginning to read about a topic for which they have little background information will have difficulty making reasonable predictions and so should use another strategy.

 Previewing and Predicting

- Read the title. What does the title suggest that the selection will be about?
- Read the introduction. What does the introduction say the selection will be about?
- Read the headings. What topics or subtopics will be discussed?
- Look over the illustrations. What information do they add?
- Read the summary. What are the key points that the selection covers?
- Based on my survey, what do I predict will happen? Or what do I think this selection will tell me?

Organizational Strategies

Organizational strategies are at the heart of constructing meaning. In contrast to preparational strategies, they are employed during reading as well as after reading. As students read, they form a situation model. Organizational strategies involve selecting important details and building relationships among them. For reading, this entails identifying the main idea of a passage and its supporting details and summarizing.

■ Comprehending the Main Idea

Deriving the main idea is at the core of constructing meaning from text, as it provides a framework for organizing, understanding, and remembering the essential details. Without it, students wander aimlessly among details. Being able to identify or compose main ideas is essential for summarizing, note taking, and outlining. (Although suggestions for teaching comprehension of main ideas and important details are presented separately in this chapter for the sake of clarity, these should be taught together.)

The **main idea** has been defined in a variety of ways (Cunningham & Moore, 1986). In this book, the main idea will be defined as a summary statement that includes the other details in a paragraph or longer piece; it is what all the sentences are about. Despite the importance of main ideas, little is known about how elementary or middle school students generate them.

Adept readers tend to use either a whole-to-part strategy, in which they draft or hypothesize the whole and confirm it by reading the parts, or a part-to-whole strategy, in which they note important parts, construct relationships among them, and compose a main idea statement (Afflerbach, 1990; Afflerbach & Johnston, 1986). The whole-to-part strategy fits best with a schema theory of comprehension; the part-to-whole strategy exemplifies the construction of a situation model.

Because of its complexity and importance, main idea comprehension has to be taught step by step. Instruction should include presenting underlying processes, one of which is classifying.

Classifying. Determining the main idea is partly a classification skill. The main idea statement is a category label for all or most of the details in the piece. The best way to convey the concept of a main idea and to provide instruction in its underlying cognitive process is to have students classify a series of objects or words (Baumann, 1986; Johnson & Kress, 1965; Williams, 1986b).

To demonstrate classifying, display a variety of objects, illustrations, or words and indicate how they might be sorted. For example, display an apple, orange, pear, banana, and book, and ask students to tell which go together. Discuss why the book does not belong. Put the objects in a box. Tell students you want to label the box so that you know what is in it and ask them what word you might use. Students can name other objects that might be put in the box, with a discussion of why they belong there. Follow a similar procedure with tools or other objects.

Once students have grasped the idea of classifying objects, have them classify words. First, give them lists of words that include labels. Model how you would go about choosing the category label. Tell students that you are looking for a word that tells about all the others. Read a series of related words that have been written on the board: *queen, ruler, president, chief, king.* Model how you would choose *ruler* as the label because it includes the other four words. After working through sev-

■ The **main idea** is the overall meaning or gist of a passage. It is what the passage is all about, a summary statement of its meaning.

BUILDING LANGUAGE

Have students work in pairs as they sort. Encourage them to discuss what things items have in common and ways in which they are different. This fosters language development.

eral sample series of words, have students complete exercises similar to the following. Make sure that all the words are known to students. For older students, select more challenging items.

oak	birch	elm	tree	pine
niece	cousin	uncle	aunt	relative
spice	pepper	cinnamon	clove	nutmeg

To vary the activity, include an item in the series that does not belong (*wood, oil, rice, gas, coal*) and have students identify it. Also, list a series of related items (*Earth, Mercury, Venus, Mars*) and let students supply a category label.

After students are able to categorize words with ease, have them categorize groups of sentences by identifying the one that tells about all the others. Call this the main idea sentence. To construct exercises of this type, locate brief paragraphs that have an explicitly stated main idea. Write the sentences in list form, and have students point out which sentence tells about all the others. Groups of sentences similar to the following can be used:

The car door locks were frozen.
Small children refused to venture from their warm homes.
It was the coldest day that anyone could remember.
The temperature was twenty below zero.
The lake was frozen solid.

Model the process of choosing the most inclusive sentence, thinking aloud as you choose it. Let students see that the process involves checking each sentence to determine which one includes all the others and then examining the other sentences to make sure that each one can be included under the main idea sentence. In your explanation, you might use the analogy of a roof. Explain that the main idea sentence is like a roof. The other sentences contain details that hold up the roof. They are like the walls that support a roof. As part of the process, explain how pointing out the inclusive sentence will help them find main ideas in their reading. After students have acquired a concept of an inclusive sentence, have students complete a series of similar exercises under your guidance.

Recognizing topic sentences. Once students have a sense of what a main idea is, begin working with brief paragraphs that contain an explicitly stated main idea, a sentence that tells about all the others. Explain that the main idea sentence is called a topic sentence because it contains the topic of the paragraph. It is often the first sentence of a paragraph, but may be last or in the middle. Move the topic sentence in a sample paragraph around to show students how it could make sense in a number of positions. Also point out how the details in a paragraph support the main idea.

Provide students with guided practice in locating topic sentences and supporting details in paragraphs. Locating supporting details is like proving a problem in math: If the details do not support the sentence chosen as the topic sentence, the student has probably not located the real topic sentence. Take practice paragraphs from children's periodicals, books, and textbooks. At first, select paragraphs

Although well-formed paragraphs might be used for initial instruction in main ideas, students should apply their strategies to informational trade books and texts. Authors do not begin each paragraph with a main idea. Often, the main idea is implied, and some paragraphs simply provide an introduction or additional information and lack a clear-cut main idea.

in which the main idea sentence comes first, as this is the easiest organizational pattern to understand. Students have more difficulty with paragraphs in which the topic sentence occurs last (Kimmel & MacGinitie, 1984). Also choose paragraphs that are interesting and well written. Students will then enjoy the activity more and will pick up incidental information. Using real books and periodicals also demonstrates that this is a practical activity, one students can use in their everyday reading. It also makes the practice more realistic because students will be working with the kinds of material they actually read rather than with paragraphs contrived for teaching the main idea. The following is an example of a paragraph that might be used:

> The largest members of the cat family are truly large. They range in size from about 6 feet to 12 feet long, measured from the tips of their noses to the tips of their tails. They weigh from 50 to 500 pounds, and are 22 to 44 inches tall at the shoulder. (Thompson, 1998, p. 26)

Presenting paragraphs that contain topic sentences makes sense in the beginning stages of instruction as it simplifies identifying the main idea, but you must emphasize that not all paragraphs contain topic sentences. In fact, most do not. Baumann and Serra (1984) found that only 44 percent of the paragraphs in elementary social studies textbooks had explicitly stated main ideas, and only 27 percent of the main ideas occurred in the opening sentence.

Even when the main idea is explicitly stated and is in the opening sentence, readers must still infer that the first sentence tells what the rest of the paragraph is about. Young readers and poor readers tend to select the first sentence as the topic sentence almost automatically (Gold & Fleisher, 1986). To prevent this, ask them to check by specifying the supporting details in this paragraph and to see whether all the other sentences support the first one (Duffelmeyer, 1985). If that is the case, the first sentence is the topic sentence. If not, the students should search for a sentence that does serve that function.

■ Selecting or Constructing the Main Idea

Most passages do not have an explicitly stated main idea, so it must be constructed. Students might use the following steps to select a stated main idea or construct a main idea if it is not stated:

1. Use the heading, title, or first sentence to make a hypothesis (careful guess) as to what the main idea is.
2. Read each sentence and see whether it supports the hypothesis. If not, revise the hypothesis.
3. If you can't make a hypothesis as to what the main idea is, see what all or most of the sentences have in common or are talking about.
4. Select a sentence or make a sentence that tells what all the sentences are about. (Post these steps or an adaptation of them.)

One problem that students have in recognizing or generating main ideas is a tendency to focus on a narrow statement of a single detail instead of on a broad statement that includes all the essential information in a paragraph (Williams, 1986a). As students work with paragraphs, you might use a series of prompts to help them identify what the paragraph is about. Start off by asking them what the general topic of the paragraph is, and then ask them to identify the specific topic and check whether all the details support it. For instance, using the following simple paragraph about robots, you might ask, "What is the general topic of the paragraph? What is the specific topic? What does the paragraph tell us about robots?"

> Robots help us in many ways. Robots work in factories. They help put cars and TVs together. In some offices, robots deliver the mail. And in some hospitals, robots bring food to sick people. A new kind of robot can mow lawns. And some day there may even be robots that can take out the trash and take the dog for a walk.

If students provide the correct specific topic, ask them to verify their response. The class should go over each sentence to determine whether it tells how robots help out. If, on the other hand, students supply a supporting detail rather than a statement of the specific topic, the teacher would have the class examine the detail to see if it encompassed all the other details in the paragraph. Lesson 5.1 presents suggestions for teaching the main idea.

LESSON 5.1 Determining the main idea and its supporting details

Step 1. Introducing the strategy

Explain what main ideas and supporting details are and why it is important to locate and understand them in reading. Give a clear definition of what a main idea is—it tells what the paragraph or section is all about. Provide examples of main ideas.

Step 2. Modeling the process

Show how you would go about determining a main idea and its supporting details. Starting off with well-constructed paragraphs, demonstrate the hypothesis strategy, because this is the strategy most frequently used by adept readers. Show students how you would use a title, heading, graphic clues, and the apparent topic sentence to predict the main idea. Then confirm or revise your hypothesis as you read and see whether the details support your hypothesized main idea. (Even if the main idea is directly stated, it is still necessary to use a hypothesis or other strategy because readers cannot be sure that the sentence is indeed a topic sentence until they read the rest of the paragraph.)

In subsequent lessons that tackle implied main idea paragraphs that have no titles or headings that could be clues to the main idea, you may have to use a part-to-whole strategy. Note the details in such a paragraph and then construct a main idea statement after seeing how the details are related or what they have in common. A part-to-whole strategy is best taught after students have

Comprehension instruction requires scaffolding. Teachers provide examples, modeling, explicit instruction, prompts, and discussions in helping students learn strategies (Dole, Duffy, Roehler, & Pearson, 1991). In time, the scaffolding is reduced and the students apply the strategies independently.

a firm grasp of the hypothesis-confirmation strategy. Model the process with a variety of paragraphs.

Step 3. Guided practice

Have students derive main ideas from brief, well-constructed paragraphs. If possible, choose paragraphs that cover familiar topics, as it is easier to construct main ideas when the content and vocabulary are known. Students face a double burden when they must grapple with difficult concepts and vocabulary while trying to construct a main idea. Although shorter paragraphs should be used in the beginning stages, have students gradually apply this skill to longer pieces, such as selections from content-area textbooks.

Step 4. Independent practice and application

Have students derive main ideas and supporting details in trade books, textbooks, periodicals, and other materials that they read on their own. From well-written, well-organized science or social studies textbooks or trade books, choose sections that convey an overall main idea or theme and develop it in several paragraphs. At first, choose pieces that have an explicitly stated main idea. Show students how you would use a hypothesis strategy to derive the main idea. For instance in an article about tsunamis in a sixth-grade science text, the heading is "Earthquakes on the Sea Floor" (Badders, 1999). Subheads include: "Tsunamis: What are They," "Destructive Walls of Water," and "Predicting Tsunamis." The article is accompanied by maps and charts of tsunamis. Using a selection with explicit headings and subheads similar to this one, show how you would survey the head and subheads to predict what the overall main idea of the selection is. Note that as you read the selection, the subheads provide specific main ideas that support the overall main idea or topic. The first section, which is under the heading "Tsunamis: What are They," tells what tsunamis are and how they are formed. The second subhead, which falls under the heading, "Destructive Walls of Water," tells about the damage that tsunamis can cause. The third section, which is under the heading, "Predicting Tsunamis," tells how tsunamis are predicted and tracked. Lead students to see that identifying main ideas will help them to get a sense of what a section will tell them. This, in turn, provides them with a way to organize the information in their minds by relating essential details to each main idea.

Guide students as they begin to use headings and graphics as an aid to constructing main ideas in content-area and other texts. Lead them to the point where they construct main ideas on their own.

Step 5. Assessment and reteaching

Observe students as they obtain main ideas from a variety of passages in texts and trade books. Note how well they can do the following:

_____ Identify the main idea and supporting details in a brief, well-constructed paragraph in which the main idea is directly stated in the first sentence.

▌Noting main ideas in longer sections is the ultimate payoff. This helps pupils better understand and remember information. Today's content-area texts make plentiful use of heads and subheads, which announce main ideas or can be used to construct them.

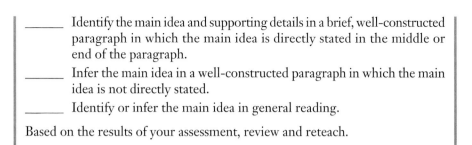

_____ Identify the main idea and supporting details in a brief, well-constructed paragraph in which the main idea is directly stated in the middle or end of the paragraph.

_____ Infer the main idea in a well-constructed paragraph in which the main idea is not directly stated.

_____ Identify or infer the main idea in general reading.

Based on the results of your assessment, review and reteach.

In a discussion with students, create a series of steps that they might use to locate or construct the main idea. Make a poster containing the steps and put it in a prominent place so students can refer to it while reading. (Use the steps listed below or an adaptation of them.)

STUDENT strategies Constructing the main idea

- Use the heading, title, or first sentence to predict what the main idea is.
- As you read the selection, see whether the details support your prediction. If not, revise your prediction.
- If you can't make a prediction as to what the main idea is, see what all or most of the details are talking about.
- Pick a sentence or make up a sentence that tells what the details are about.

Extending the ability to construct the main idea. Take advantage of discussions of selections that students have read and other naturally occurring opportunities to apply and extend the skill of constructing main ideas. Note how important details are related to the main idea of a selection. Also apply the concept to writing. Have students create and develop topic sentences on nonfiction subjects of their own choosing.

Graphic displays can help students identify the topic sentence and its supporting details. Use a simplified semantic map, which is sometimes called a spider web when the supporting details are equal, as shown in Figure 5.1. Use a linear display like that in Figure 5.2 when the piece has a sequential order, that is, when the ideas are listed in order of occurrence.

Main idea instruction is more appropriate for nonfiction than for fiction. Fiction has a theme rather than a main idea. Identifying a theme can be subtler and more complex than noting a main idea. Most children's fiction also has a central problem that gives coherence to the story (Moldofsky, 1983).

> As with other strategies, this one follows a gradual release of responsibility. As students grow in skill, they gradually take responsibility for their own learning.

> **BUILDING LANGUAGE**
> Having students talk about strategies they are using, especially when they describe specific instances of strategy use, develops academic language.

■ Reviewing the Strategy

Learning a strategy may take a month or more. In subsequent lessons, review and extend the strategy. To review the strategy, ask the following kinds of questions:

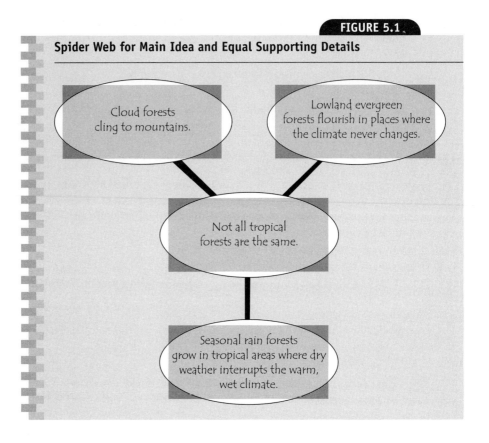

FIGURE 5.1

Spider Web for Main Idea and Equal Supporting Details

- What strategy are we learning to use? (main idea)
- How does this strategy help us? (Helps us understand and remember what we read. Helps us organize important details.)
- When do we use this strategy? (With nonfiction.)

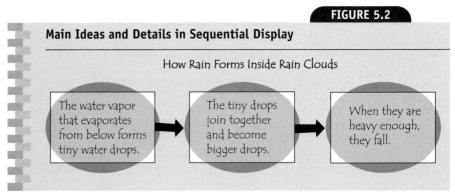

FIGURE 5.2

Main Ideas and Details in Sequential Display

Text *from Weather Words,* by G. Gibbons, 1990, New York: Holiday House.

■ How do we use this strategy? (Review the steps presented on p. 191.) Also ask students to tell about instances when they used the strategy on their own (Scott, 1998).

REINFORCEMENT ACTIVITIES   Main idea construction

■ Cut out newspaper headlines and titles of articles, and have students match them with the articles.

■ Have students classify lists of items.

■ When discussing selections that students have read, include questions that require them to identify and/or construct a main idea.

■ Determining the Relative Importance of Information

The ability to determine what is important in a selection is a key factor in comprehension as it keeps readers from drowning in a sea of details or having to cull out trivial information. Determining main ideas and the relative importance of information should be taught together. Determination of what is important in a selection is often dependent on the derivation of the main idea. Once they know the main idea, readers are in a better position to identify the relative importance of information and to construct a situation model of the text. For instance, once they know that the main idea of an article is how to use a video camera, they can assume that the steps in the process will be the important details. Readers have to ask themselves which details support or explain a selection's main idea or, if the article is especially rich in details, which are the most important. If an article cites twenty capabilities of lasers, readers might decide which five are most essential.

Adept readers will use textual clues to help determine which details are most important. A carefully written text might state which details are essential. Or the reader might note those details that are discussed first and given the most print. Minor details might be signaled by words such as *also*, as in the sentence "Laser readers are also used to check out books in many libraries and to check times in many competitive sports."

Expert readers also use text structure, relational terms, and repetition of words or concepts to determine importance. Relational terms and expressions such as "most important of all" and "three main causes" help readers determine important ideas. A repeated word or concept is an especially useful clue. The structure of the piece also gives clues as to which details are most essential (Afflerbach & Johnston, 1986). With a problem–solution organization, an adept reader will seek out the problem and solution and ignore extraneous descriptions or examples.

In addition to using textual clues, readers can use their schemata or background knowledge to determine what is important. A student who raises tropical fish would seek out certain kinds of information when reading about a new species, such as a description of the species, its habits, and where it is found. The purpose for reading is also a factor. A student who is contemplating buying a new tropical fish will realize that details on cost and care are significant.

Expert readers also use their beliefs about the author's intention to determine which details are essential and which are not (Afflerbach & Johnston, 1986). Expert readers are able to step back from the text and consider the author's purpose. If, for instance, the author is trying to establish that a certain point is true, the reader will seek out the details or examples the author provides as proof of the contention. Lesson 5.2 includes some steps that might be used to help students determine important information.

LESSON 5.2 Determining important details

Step 1. Introduction of strategy

Explain what is meant by "important details" and why being able to identify them is an essential skill. Display and discuss several short selections that contain both important and unimportant information, and help students discriminate between the two.

Step 2. Model the process

Determine important information in a sample paragraph. Show how you would use contextual clues: topic sentence, placement of ideas, and graphic aids. In another session, demonstrate how you might use knowledge of the topic or your purpose for reading.

Step 3. Guided practice

Provide guidance as students determine important information in a selection. Start with well-structured texts that supply plenty of clues and gradually work up to selections from their basal readers, content-area textbooks, library books, or periodicals. Ask students to justify their choice of important details, because this skill is somewhat subjective.

Step 4. Application

Have students note important ideas in materials that they read independently. The more experience students have with varied reading materials and the broader and deeper their knowledge base, the better prepared they will be to determine the relative importance of information. Set purposes that lead students to grasp essential information. Ask questions that focus on important information. By asking such questions, you will be modeling the kinds of questions that students should be asking themselves before, during, and after reading.

Step 5. Assessment and reteaching

During discussions of selections that have been read, ask questions that require selecting important details. Take note of students' performance. Ask the kinds of questions that provide insight into students' reasoning processes. Supply on-the-spot help if students need it. Also, plan reteaching lessons if needed.

■ Reviewing the Strategy

In subsequent lessons, review and extend the strategy. To review the strategy, ask the following kinds of questions:

- What strategy are we learning to use? (Understanding important ideas.)
- How does this strategy help us? (Helps us understand and remember important details. Keeps us from getting lost in too many details.)
- When do we use this strategy? (with nonfiction)
- How do we use this strategy? (Review the steps listed below.)

STUDENT strategies Determining important details

- Use the title, heading, and first sentence to make a hypothesis (careful guess) about what the main idea will be.
- Read the selection to see if I have chosen the right main idea. If not, change it.
- Choose the most important details. These will be details that support the main idea. The author might signal the most important details by using phrases like "most important of all" (Scott, 1998). (Post these steps or your adaptation of them.)

REINFORCEMENT ACTIVITIES Determining importance of information

- Have students predict the important ideas in a selection they are about to read.
- After they have read a selection, ask students to tell which ideas are most important.
- Encourage students to write newspaper stories. In most newspaper stories, the important information is provided in the first paragraph.

Sequencing. Because some details have to be comprehended and then remembered in a certain order, readers must organize them sequentially. These include historical or biographical events, steps in a process, and directions. Because the extra step of noting the sequence is involved, organizing sequential details often poses special problems, especially for younger readers. To introduce sequence, have students tell about some simple sequential activities in which they engage, such as washing dishes, playing a favorite game, or assembling a puzzle. Discuss the order of the activities, and place them on the chalkboard using cue words such as *first, second, next, then, before, last,* and *after.*

Place lists of other events on the chalkboard, and ask students to put them in order. Start with a series of three or four events for younger students and work up

To provide practice with the sequence of steps in a process, you might encourage students to read such books as *Howling Hurricanes* (Richards, 2002) or *Recycle! A Handbook for Kids* (Gibbons, 1992).

to six or seven items for more advanced readers. Encourage students to use their sense of the situation or the process to put the events in order. Show how cue words help indicate sequence.

After students have become adept at this activity, let them apply their skill to stories and articles. To help them become aware of the sequence of a story, have them map out the main events, showing how the story progresses to its climax and the resolution of a problem. Help students create causal links between events in a story, as this aids retention (McNamara, Miller, & Bransford, 1991). Two literary techniques that might make a story more appealing but cause the sequence to be more difficult to comprehend are flashback and *in medias res.* When a flashback occurs in a story, point it out and discuss why the author used it. Encourage students to try this technique in their writing. Also point out occurrences of *in medias res* and talk about why an author would use this technique.

For biographies and historical accounts, show students how to use dates to keep events in order. Show students books like *The World in the Time of Marco Polo* (Macdonald, 2001) and *Frederick Douglas* (Lutz, 2001), in which the authors use time lines or chronologies to help readers keep track of key events. When time lines have not been included in a selection, encourage students to create them to help keep a sequence of events in order. As students read about the steps in a process (e.g., a caterpillar becoming a butterfly or a bill becoming a law), have them note the sequence and visualize it if possible. Show them how they might use a graphic organizer to display a process or chain of events. Figure 5.3 presents a chain map showing how radar works.

Following directions.   Following directions is a natural outgrowth of sequencing. As students read directions, remind them to make use of cue words such as *first, next,* and *last.* Students can create mental models of directions by visually depicting the process, using an accompanying diagram or other illustration, or describing the steps. If possible, have students carry out the procedures outlined in the directions.

After techniques for understanding directions have been taught, students should be made responsible for reading and following directions. They should read the directions once to get an overview, and then a second time to find out exactly what they are to do. Encourage them to study any samples that are given; however, these samples should be examined after the directions are read, not before. Some

USING TECHNOLOGY

HyperHistory Online presents a variety of time lines for famous people and key events. **http://www. hyperhistory.com/ online_n2/ History_n2/a.html**

Being able to comprehend and follow directions is more important than ever. Many items that we purchase come unassembled. And many appliances have to be programmed. Downloading a file from the Internet or using a new program requires being able to follow sophisticated directions.

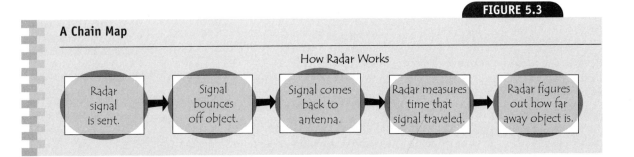

FIGURE 5.3

A Chain Map

How Radar Works

Radar signal is sent. → Signal bounces off object. → Signal comes back to antenna. → Radar measures time that signal traveled. → Radar figures out how far away object is.

students skip the directions and look only at the sample, and some do not even bother looking at the sample. They simply plunge ahead or ask the teacher what to do. If students ask what they are supposed to do, tell them to read the directions carefully. If they still fail to understand, have them tell you what they think they are to do, and then redirect their thinking as necessary.

Use printed directions for some classroom routines—for example, how to operate the computer or the tape recorder. Also, use directions that accompany real-world materials. Students might follow sets of printed directions for assembling a simple toy or a piece of furniture or using a new piece of software. Have them note how studying the illustration is an important part of following the directions.

 Following directions

- Read the directions to get an overview.
- Look at any pictures or diagrams that go along with the directions.
- Make sure all parts have been included.
- Get all necessary tools and materials or ingredients.
- Read and follow each step. Use any pictures or diagrams as an aid. (Post these steps or your adaptation of them.)

Other activities that provide natural practice in following directions are planting seeds, caring for classroom animals or plants, using a computer program, finding a site on the Web, and following recipes. The best thing about real-life exercises is that they are self-checking. A computer program that is not used correctly will flash an error message, recipes incorrectly followed result in inedible food, and devices improperly constructed do not work.

Summarizing

What is the most effective comprehension strategy of all? When five experts in learning examined the research on comprehension in order to discover which strategies seemed to have the greatest payoff and were the most solidly grounded in research, they listed summarization first (Pressley, Johnson, Symons, McGoldrick, & Kurita, 1989). Summarization, which builds on the organizational strategy of determining main ideas and supporting details, improves comprehension and increases retention. It is also a metacognitive means of monitoring, through which students can evaluate their understanding of a passage that they have just read. If a student has not comprehended a selection, she or he is almost certain to have difficulty summarizing it. Summarizing also helps students understand the structure of text. In writing a summary, students are brought face-to-face with the organization of a piece of writing. This should help them detect the underlying structure of the text, which is a key to understanding text and writing effective summaries (Touchstone Applied Science Associates, 1997).

BUILDING LANGUAGE

Demonstrate how you would explain a series of directions. Emphasize the use of signal words such as *first, second, last* and phrases such as "assemble all materials" and "next step" that occur frequently in directions. Have students give directions orally and in writing.

Use writing to support reading. Encourage students to write a series of directions for a favorite game or other activity. Have students work in pairs. The partners can check the clarity of each other's directions by trying them out and seeing whether they can follow them.

Although a complex skill, summarizing begins early. Students summarize when they describe a real event or retell a story.

*S*tudents should be taught strategies for reading to follow directions.

Summarizing is a complex skill that takes years to develop. Even college students may have difficulty summarizing. Young children realize that a summary is a retelling of material; however, they have difficulty determining what points should be included in a summary. The view of young students seems to be egocentric: They choose details that are personally interesting rather than selecting details that seem important from the author's point of view. Young students also have difficulty with the procedures necessary to summarize (Hidi & Anderson, 1986). They delete information but do not combine or condense details; they also tend to use a copy strategy. Until about fifth or sixth grade, students record details word for word in their summaries. Once they learn to put information into their own words, they begin combining and condensing.

In a study of fifth-grade students, K. K. Taylor (1986) found that proficient readers sift information and combine details as they read, using the title and organization of the material to help them. They have a good understanding of the demands of the task and see it in terms of searching out and constructing the most important ideas. They also monitor their work, checking their own written summaries against the original.

▌Present summarizing as a tool that students can use to share information and better comprehend and remember what they read (Touchstone Applied Science Associates, 1997). When teaching and applying summarization, use students' content-area texts so they can see how summarizing can be a learning aid.

Introducing summarizing.　Summaries need not be written. All of us make oral summaries of movie and book plots, events, conversations, and so on. Because writing summaries can be difficult (Brown & Day, 1983; Hare & Borchardt, 1984), teachers should first develop students' ability to summarize orally.

Retelling is a natural way to lead into summarizing. Some students tend to recount every incident in a story and give every detail about a topic. Help them structure their retellings so as to emphasize major events and main ideas. Ask questions like these: "What were the two most important things that the main character did? What were the three main things that happened in the story? What are the main things you learned about robots? What are the main ways in which robots are used?"

Teachers can model the process of summarizing by providing summaries of selections read, especially nonfiction, and of discussions and directions. As students read content-area material or informational texts, they can be directed to pay special attention to chapter summaries. Emphasize including the most important information in a summary. As students become proficient in extracting the most essential information, teach techniques for condensing information.

Certain activities can build summarizing or its underlying skills. Encourage students to use titles, illustrations, topic sentences, headings, and other textual clues. In K. K. Taylor's (1986) study, many students failed to use the title and topic sentence when composing their summaries, although both contained the main idea of the selection. Teach students how to read expository text. Ineffectual summarizers read such works as though they are fiction and so fail to note textual cues that could help them create better summaries (Taylor, 1986). Have students compose oral summaries of stories, articles, and class discussions. Also compose group summaries.

To create a group summary, read an informational article aloud and ask students what the most important points are. After listing the points on the board, have the class summarize them. Group summaries provide preparation for the creation of independent summaries (Moore, Moore, Cunningham, & Cunningham, 1986).

Summarizing can be an excellent device for checking comprehension. Encourage students to stop after reading key sections of expository text and mentally summarize the materials. Once they have some ability to identify relevant details, make use of structural cues, and identify and construct main ideas, they are ready for a more formal type of instruction in summarizing.

Ironically, because they often contain a greater number of interesting details, trade books and newspaper and magazine articles may be more difficult to summarize. Because they go into great detail, there are more details to sift through. As Harvey (1998) notes, "The most important ideas in well-written nonfiction are often deeply embedded in rich detail" (p. 83). Students may mistake interesting details for important details. Fascinated by the fact that roaches can make themselves as thin as a dime, one student judged that this was an essential detail in an article about roaches. Although it perhaps was one of the most interesting facts about roaches, it was not one of the most essential (Harvey, 1998). To overcome this tendency, Harvey listed information about jelly fish that she had found interesting in one column and then discussed with students which of the interesting bits of information was essential. After discussion, students were able to identify four key facts.

> Organizational strategies are effective. Whether it be creating main ideas, making semantic maps, or summarizing, just about any attempt to organize information results in better understanding and recall.

Presenting summarizing skills. When teaching summarizing, begin with shorter, easier text. Texts that are shorter and easier to comprehend are easier to summarize. Also, start off with narrative text, which is easier than expository text to summarize (Hidi & Anderson, 1986). Focus on the content rather than the form of the summaries. After students become accustomed to summarizing essential details, stress the need for well-formed, polished summaries. Because many students have great difficulty determining which details are important, have them list important details. Discuss these lists before they compose their summaries. Also have students create semantic maps before writing summaries. In addition to helping students select important information, such maps may help them detect important relationships among key ideas. In a study conducted with older students, those who constructed maps before summarizing used a greater number of cohesive ties than those who did not (Ruddell & Boyle, 1989).

Students should know why summarizing is important and how it might benefit them. Instruction should also focus on teaching and reinforcing summarization operations. According to Brown and Day (1983) and Rinehart, Stahl, and Erickson (1986), there are five such operations:

> Being able to determine relative importance of information is essential for summarizing. However, in addition to sifting out the important ideas, the summarizer must also synthesize those ideas into a coherent whole, which makes summarizing a difficult, complex skill (Dole, Duffy, Roehler, & Pearson, 1991).

1. Selecting or constructing the overall (main) idea
2. Selecting important information that supports the main idea
3. Deleting information that is not important or is repeated
4. Combining and condensing information
5. Polishing the summary

Lesson 5.3 shows the steps in summarization.

 Introduction to summarization

Step 1. Explaining the skill

Emphasize that a summary includes the most important ideas or information in a text. Students may have erroneous notions about summaries. For instance, they may tend to highlight the most interesting or the most difficult details, or sentences that are richly detailed (K. K. Taylor, 1986; Winograd, 1984). Give examples of summaries, and tell why they are useful and when they should be written.

Step 2. Modeling the process

Model the process of constructing a summary. In the beginning, focus on the first three operations: selecting or constructing the overall idea, selecting supporting details, and taking out details that are not important or repeated. Choose a brief, well-formed paragraph, such as the following:

> The New World turned out to be a good place to find new foods. Potatoes were first grown by the Incas of South America. Corn, a main food throughout America, was also first grown in Central or South America. The tomato is a third American food. It, too, was first grown in Central America. And if it hadn't been for America, there would be no vanilla ice cream. The vanilla bean was first grown in Mexico.

Explain that you will read it, and as you read, you will be asking yourself: "What is this paragraph all about?" Have students read the paragraph silently as you read it aloud. Then, think aloud. Demonstrate to students the process you use to select the overall idea and supporting details. Explain that the paragraph is all about foods that were first grown in America, so the first sentence of your summary will be "Many foods were grown first in America." Then, search out supporting details. Explain that since you are writing a summary, you want to write the details as briefly as possible; so you write, "Potatoes came from South America. Corn and tomatoes came from Central America. And the vanilla bean came from Mexico." Explain that the third operation is to take out unimportant or repeated details. Note for the students that you are not including the statement that corn was a main food because this detail is not important: It does not support the main idea but simply gives extra information. Note, too, that the detail that states "if it hadn't been for America, there would be no vanilla ice cream" is unimportant and therefore should be taken out.

Model the summarization of two or three additional brief but well-constructed paragraphs. As students catch onto the concept of summarization, involve them in the process. Have them help decide what the overall idea is and help choose important details. Have them help, too, with the wording of the summaries. Stress that the wording of summaries will vary from person to person, as will decisions about what to include and what to omit. As students become more adept at summarizing, model the processes of combining and condensing information and polishing summaries. Students should also be shown how to check their summaries against the original text to ensure that they are accurate and complete. A checklist that students can use to help them with their summaries is presented in Figure 5.4.

Step 3. Guided practice

Provide ample practice opportunities for students. Have them start with brief, well-constructed paragraphs about relatively familiar topics and gradually work up to more complex materials. For younger students and poorer readers, emphasis can be placed on oral summaries or retellings. Students who are struggling with summarizing might use text frames like that shown in Figure 5.5, in which the format of a general summary is provided. Aided by this structure, students only have to fill in the blanks with the specific elements.

Step 4. Independent practice and application

Have students summarize both fiction and nonfiction selections orally and/or in writing. Class discussions, demonstrations, stories read aloud, films, and other nonprint sources of information can and should be summarized.

Step 5. Extending the concept

For several lessons, review the concept of summarizing. Gradually provide students with somewhat longer paragraphs. Once they have a grasp of sum-

> Hidi and Anderson (1986) distinguish between reader-based and writer-based summaries. Reader-based summaries are written for the person reading the selection. They are longer, not as well formed, but easier to compose. Writer-based summaries are written for someone else and so are better written, but are more difficult to create. Initial efforts at summarizing might be focused on reader-based versions.

> Different prompts result in different responses. When Brady (1991), while eliciting summaries, asked what a paragraph was all about, students often responded by simply giving the topic: "horses." When Brady used the following prompt: "This paragraph tells us that . . ." responses went beyond merely providing the topic.

FIGURE 5.4

Student Checklist for Summaries

Put a check before the question if your answer is "yes."
Put an X if your answer is "no."

_____ Does the summary state the main idea?
_____ Is the main idea stated first?
_____ Does the summary state *all* the important ideas?
_____ Does the summary state *only* the most important information?
_____ Are details combined so that the summary is brief?
_____ Is the summary clear?

TextSense, Summary Writing (Touchstone Applied Science Associates, 1997) is a research-based, thorough program designed to develop the ability to compose summaries. It includes a series of lessons, sample summaries, and a program for assessing summaries.

marizing brief paragraphs, demonstrate how selections with several paragraphs can be summarized. This can be done in two phases. Students first write a summary of each individual paragraph; they then write a summary of the paragraph summaries. Once students have become adept at writing these two-part summaries, have them do this in one phase by composing the overall idea for the group of paragraphs and then including the most important ideas. Once students are able to write summaries of a series of paragraphs, have them summarize sections of texts.

Step 6. Assessment

Observe students as they summarize passages in texts and trade books. Note how well they can do the following:

_____ Include the most important information in an oral retelling but omit unimportant details.

_____ Include the most important information in a written retelling or summary but omit unimportant details.

_____ Write a concise summary.

_____ Write a concise, polished summary.

Summaries should have a practical payoff: preparation for a test or oral report, for instance.

■ Reviewing the Strategy

In subsequent lessons, review and extend the strategy. To review the strategy, ask the following kinds of questions:

To help students structure their summaries of fictional pieces, you might use story grammar, which is explained in the next chapter.

- What strategy are we learning to use? (Summarizing.)
- How does this strategy help us? (Helps us understand, select, and remember the most important information. Helps us organize the important information.)
- When do we use this strategy? (When we need to organize information. When we want to check to see whether we have understood what we read and whether we remember the most important information.)
- How do we use this strategy? (Review the steps listed on p. 203.)

Teaching a major strategy takes time. Wong and Wong (1986) spent two months teaching summarizing to learning disabled students. At the end of that time, all students were able to write summaries successfully.

FIGURE 5.5

A Sample Text Frame

Three main toxic hazards can be found in homes.

Asbestos is _____ . It can cause _____ .

Radon is _____ . It can cause _____ .

Household chemicals include _____ . They can cause _____ .

Text adapted from *Toxic Waste* (pp. 32–33), by S. D. Gold, 1990, New York: Crestwood House.

Summarizing

- Decide on the main idea.
- Choose important details that support the main idea.
- Take out details that are not important or which are repeated.
- Combine details and take out unneeded words or phrases.
- Fix up the summary so it reads smoothly.

> **ADAPTING INSTRUCTION for _STRUGGLING READERS and WRITERS_**
> Some students might do better with strategies that help them visualize information. They might find semantic maps and other graphic methods of organizing information to be especially helpful.

Elaboration Strategies

Elaboration is a generative activity in which the reader constructs connections between information from text and prior knowledge. Like organizational strategies, elaboration strategies are employed during reading but may also be put into operation after reading. The reader generates inferences, images, questions, judgments, and other elaborations. A powerful strategy, elaboration increased comprehension by 50 percent in a number of studies (Linden & Wittrock, 1981).

> ■ **Elaboration** refers to additional processing of text by the reader which may result in improved comprehension and recall. Elaboration involves building connections between one's background knowledge and the text or integrating these two sources through manipulating or transforming information.

■ Making Inferences

Although students have the cognitive ability to draw inferences, some do not do so spontaneously. A probable cause of this deficiency is a lack of background information about the topic or the failure to process information in the text that would foster drawing inferences. Or students may not realize that inferences are necessary. They might believe that only literal comprehension is called for (Westby, 1999). Two approaches enhance the ability to make inferences: building background and teaching specific strategies for making inferences. However, sustained instruction is required. When students were taught processes for making inferences, no significant change was noted until after four weeks of teaching. The effects were long-lasting, and, as a side benefit, literal comprehension improved (Dewitz, Carr, & Patberg, 1987).

There are two kinds of inferences: schema-based and text-based (Winne, Graham, & Prock, 1993). Schema-based inferences depend on prior knowledge. For instance, reading the sentence "They rode into the sunset," inferring that it was late in the day and the riders were heading west is schema-based. The reader uses her or his schema for the position of the sun to infer approximate time and direction. Schema-based inferences allow the reader to elaborate on the text by adding information that has been implied by the author. A text-based inference is one that requires putting together two or more pieces of information from the text. Reading that peanuts have more food energy than sugar and that a pound of peanut butter has more protein than thirty-two eggs but more fat than ice cream, the reader might put all this information together to infer that peanuts are nutritious but fattening.

> To make inferences, students must have access to the information necessary to make the inference. If students can't recall the information or can't recall enough of it, they won't be able to make an inference. Also important is being able to implement inference-making procedures such as combining several pieces of text information or combining text information and prior knowledge (Winne, Graham, & Prock, 1993).

Students should only be given text that they can decode with a fair degree of accuracy (95 percent) and at a reasonable speed (85 words per minute). If these conditions are not met, students might expend so much energy decoding text that they have little or no cognitive energy left for comprehension because they have expended all their cognitive resources on lower-level processes (Sinatra, Brown, & Reynolds, 2002).

Making inferences is the most important elaboration strategy. Much of the information in a piece, especially fiction, is implied. Authors show and dramatize rather than tell. Instead of directly stating that a main character is a liar, the author dramatizes situations in which the character lies. For instance, in *Last Summer with Maizon*, Jacqueline Woodson wrote:

> "Sure wish you weren't going away," Margaret said choking back tears for what seemed like the millionth time. They were sitting on the M train, crossing the Williamsburg Bridge, and Margaret shivered as the train passed over the water. The L train would have made the trip easier but the L train didn't go over the bridge and Maizon had wanted to ride over it once more before she left. (Woodson, 1991)

The reader can infer that Margaret is sad, and has been so for a while. The reader can also infer that Margaret and Maizon are close friends and that Margaret is sad because Maizon is moving away. The reader can infer that the story takes place in a city because the girls are riding subway trains. None of this is stated, so readers must use their schema for friendship and losing friends because they move away and also their schema for what cities are like. In a sense, the author erects the story's framework, and the reader must construct a fuller meaning by filling in the missing parts.

Activating prior knowledge helps students make inferences. For instance, if the teacher discusses the impact of having a friend move away before the students read *Last Summer with Maizon*, they will be much more likely to draw appropriate inferences from the passage previously cited. Asking questions that require students to make inferences also helps. It increases both their ability and their inclination to make inferences (Hansen, 1981).

Although above-average students make more inferences than average ones (Carr, 1983), below-average readers can be taught the skill. Hansen and Pearson (1982) combined activation of prior knowledge, direct instruction in an inference-making strategy, posing of inferential questions, and predicting to create a series of lessons in which poor readers improved to such an extent that their inferential comprehension became equal to that of good readers. Here is how Hansen and Pearson's prior knowledge–prediction strategy works:

1. The teacher reads the story and analyzes it for two or three important ideas.
2. For each important idea, the teacher creates a previous-experience question that elicits from students any similar experiences that they may have had. This is a have-you-ever question (Pearson, 1985).
3. For each previous-experience question, an accompanying prediction question is created. This is a what-do-you-think-will-happen question.
4. Students read the selection to check their predictions.
5. Students discuss their predictions. Inferential questions, especially those related to the key ideas, are discussed.

The following important ideas, previous-experience questions, and prediction questions were used in the study (Pearson, 1985, Appendix B):

Important idea number 1: Even adults can be afraid of things.

Previous-experience question: Tell something an adult you know is afraid of.

Prediction question: In the story, Cousin Alma is afraid of something even though she is an adult. What do you think it is?

Important idea number 2: People sometimes act more bravely than they feel.

Previous-experience question: Tell about how you acted some time when you were afraid and tried not to show it.

Prediction question: How do you think that Fats, the boy in the story, will act when he is afraid and tries not to show it?

Important idea number 3: Our experience sometimes convinces us that we are capable of doing things we thought we couldn't do.

Previous-experience question: Tell about a time that you were able to do something you thought you couldn't do.

Prediction question: In the story, what do you think Cousin Alma is able to do that she thought she couldn't do?

An important element of the technique is the discussion, with students' responses acting as a catalyst. One student's answer reminds others of similar experiences that they have had but do not think apply. For example, a girl mentioning that her uncle is afraid of snakes might trigger in another student the memory that his grandfather is afraid of dogs, even small ones. The teacher also emphasizes that students should compare their real-life experiences with events in the story.

Together with having background activated and being asked inferential questions, students should be taught a strategy for making inferences. Gordon (1985) mapped out a five-step process, which is outlined in Lesson 5.4.

 Making inferences

LESSON 5.4

Step 1. Explaining the skill

The teacher explains what the skill is, why it is important, and when and how it is used. This explanation might be illustrated with examples.

Step 2. Modeling the process

While modeling the process of making inferences with a brief piece of text written on the chalkboard, the teacher reveals her or his thinking processes: "It says here that Jim thought Fred would make a great center when he first saw him walk into the classroom. The center is usually the tallest person on a basketball team, so I inferred that Fred is tall." The teacher also models the process with several other selections, so students see that inferences can be drawn from a variety of materials.

Step 3. Sharing the task

Students are asked to take part in the inferencing process. The teacher asks an inferential question about a brief sample paragraph or excerpt and then answers it. The students supply supporting evidence for the inference from the selection itself and from their background knowledge. The reasoning processes involved in making the inference are discussed. The teacher stresses the need to substantiate inferences with details from the story.

Step 4. Reversing the process

The teacher asks an inferential question and the students supply the inference. The teacher provides the evidence. As an alternative, the teacher might supply the evidence and have the students draw an inference based on it. Either way, a discussion of reasoning processes follows.

Step 5. Integrating the process

The teacher just asks the inferential question. The students both make the inference and supply the evidence. As a final step, students might create their own inferential questions and then supply the answers and evidence. Basically, the procedure turns responsibility for the strategy over to students.

Step 6. Application

The students apply the process to texts and trade books.

Step 7. Assessment

Observe students as they make inferences in texts and trade books. Note how well they can do the following:

_____ Make an inference based on two or more pieces of information in the text.

_____ Make an inference based on information in the text and their own background knowledge.

_____ Find support for an inference.

_____ Make increasingly sophisticated inferences.

> **ADAPTING INSTRUCTION for _STRUGGLING READERS and WRITERS_**
>
> As Hansen and Pearson (1982) noted, poor readers are typically asked literal questions, so their inferential skills are underdeveloped. If carefully taught, lower-achieving readers can make inferences.

> Although making inferences is more difficult than literal comprehension, it isn't necessary that students master literal comprehension before they are instructed in making inferences. Both can and should be taught simultaneously.

■ Reviewing the Strategy

In subsequent lessons, review and extend the strategy. To review the strategy, ask the following kinds of questions:

- What strategy are we learning to use? (Making inferences.)
- How does this strategy help us? (Helps us to read between the lines, to fill in details that the author has hinted at but which she has not directly stated.)
- When do we use this strategy? (When we have to put together two or more pieces of information in a story. When the author has hinted at but not directly stated information.)
- How do we use this strategy? (Review the steps listed on the next page.)

STUDENT strategies — Summarizing

- As I read, ask myself, "What is the author suggesting here but not saying?"
- Put together pieces of information from the story with what I know.
- Make an inference or come to a conclusion.

Using QAR. Some students are text-bound and may not realize that answers to some questions require putting together several pieces of information from the reading or using their background of experience plus that information to draw inferences. Teachers frequently hear students lament that the answer is not in the book; those students do not know how to construct the answer from prior knowledge and textual content (Carr, Dewitz, & Patberg, 1989). Such readers may benefit from using QAR (question–answer relationship), in which questions are described as having the following four levels, based on where the answers are found (International Reading Association, 1988):

1. *Right there.* The answer is found within a single sentence in the text.
2. *Putting it together.* The answer is found in several sentences in the text.
3. *On my own.* The answer is in the student's background of knowledge.
4. *Writer and me.* A combination of information from the text and the reader's background is required to answer the question.

In a series of studies, Raphael (1984) observed that students' comprehension improved when they were introduced to the concept of QAR and given extensive training in locating the source of the answer. Initially, they worked with sentences and

As Alvermann and Phelps (1994) explain, the QAR progression is oversimplified. Readers do not begin by comprehending information that is right there, then move on to putting it together, and end up with on-my-own or writer-and-me responses. These processes operate simultaneously and interact with each other. However, QAR is a useful way of viewing the process of question answering.

*S*tudents learn to locate evidence for inferences they have made.

very short paragraphs, but they progressed to 400-word selections. Raphael (1986) recommended starting with two categories of answers: "in the book" and "in my head." This would be especially helpful when working with elementary students. "In the book" includes answers that are "right there" or require "putting it together." "In my head" items are "on my own" and "writer and me" answers. Based on Raphael's (1986) suggestions, QAR might be presented in the manner described in Lesson 5.5.

LESSON 5.5   Presenting QAR

Step 1. Introducing the concept of QAR

Introduce the concept by writing on the board a paragraph similar to the following:

> Andy let the first pitch go by. It was too low. The second pitch was too high. But the third toss was letter high. Andy lined it over the left fielder's outstretched glove.

Ask a series of literal questions: "Which pitch did Andy hit? Where did the ball go? Why didn't Andy swing at the first pitch? The second pitch?" Lead students to see that the answers to these questions are "in the book."

Next, ask a series of questions that depend on the readers' background: "What game was Andy playing? What do you think Andy did after he hit the ball? Do you think he scored a run? Why or why not?" Show students that the answers to these questions depend on their knowledge of baseball. Discuss the fact that these answers are "in my head."

Step 2. Extending the concept of QAR

After students have mastered the concept of "in the book" and "in my head," extend the in-the-book category to include both "right there" and "putting it together." Once students have a solid working knowledge of these, expand the in-my-head category to include both "on my own" and "writer and me." The major difference between these two is whether the student has to read the text for the question to make sense. For instance, the question "Do you think Andy's hit was a home run?" requires knowledge of baseball and information from the story. The question "How do you feel when you get a hit?" involves only experience in hitting a baseball.

Step 3. Providing practice

Provide ample opportunity for guided and independent practice. Also refine and extend students' awareness of sources for answers and methods for constructing responses.

> To provide practice with making inferences at all levels, have students infer character traits based on the character's actions, because authors typically let a character's actions show what kind of a person the character is.

> Students who are good decoders but poor comprehenders have problems with all kinds of comprehension, but have the most difficulty making inferences (Oakhill & Yuill, 1996).

Difficulties in making inferences.   Some students' responses to inference questions are too specific. In addition to knowing that they can use both text and background knowledge as sources of information, students need to learn to gather all the information that is pertinent (McCormick, 1992). They need to base their inferences on several pieces of textual or background information. Some students choose the wrong information on which to base their inferences, and others do not use the text at all. They overrely on prior knowledge or do not recall or use sufficient pertinent text to make valid inferences (McCormick, 1992). This is especially true of poor readers.

■ Imaging

Although readers rely heavily on verbal abilities to comprehend text, they also use imaging. According to a **dual coding** theory of cognitive processing, information can be coded verbally or nonverbally. The word *robot* for instance, can be encoded verbally. It can also be encoded visually as a mental picture of a robot. Because it can be encoded as a word or mental picture, it can be retrieved from memory either verbally or visually, so it is twice as memorable. In one research study, participants who encoded words visually remembered twice as many words as those who encoded the words just verbally (Schnorr & Atkinson, 1969).

> ■ **Dual coding** is the concept that text can be processed verbally and nonverbally. Nonverbal coding focuses on imaging.

Verbal processing seems especially well suited to abstract and sequential text and tends to be characterized by order, logic, and organization. Nonverbal processing, or **imaging,** tends to be more holistic, less bound by constraints of logic, and better for dealing with concrete aspects of reality. These systems can perform independently, in parallel, or in a complementary, integrated fashion in which verbal input can stimulate the creation of a nonverbal image and a nonverbal image can stimulate a verbal response (Gambrell & Javitz, 1993; Sadoski & Paivio, 1994). Creating mental images has been shown to have many benefits. It promotes the use of prior knowledge and improves the ability to make predictions and draw inferences. In addition to aiding overall comprehension, imaging aids retention.

> ■ **Imaging** refers to creating sensory representations of items in text.

For some passages, imaging is not just an aid to comprehension, it is the only way to grasp the author's meaning:

> The sea became a wildcat now, and the galleon her prey. She stalked the ship and drove her off course. She slapped at her, rolling her victim from side to side. She knocked the spars out of her and used them to ram holes in her sides. She clawed the rudder from its sternpost and threw it into the sea. She cracked the ship's ribs as if they were brittle bones. Then she hissed and spat through the seam. (Henry, 1947, p. 11)

The meaning of this passage is in seeing, hearing, and even feeling the ship being smashed by the storm. After students have read such a passage, encourage them to imagine the scene and tell what they see, hear, and feel. Talk over how the metaphor of the sea as a wildcat might influence how they sense the passage. Have them identify words that paint pictures in their minds and create sound effects in their imaginations.

Imaging is relatively easy to teach. In one study, students' comprehension increased after just thirty minutes of instruction (Gambrell & Bales, 1986). The increase was not large, but it was significant. When teaching students to create images, start with single sentences and then move on to short paragraphs and, later, longer

> ▌ One way of enhancing imaging is to read high-imagery selections to students and ask them to try to picture the main character, a setting, or a scene.

The aim for strategy instruction is to have it become automatic. As students become more proficient in the application of a strategy, make them responsible for its use (Sinatra, Brown, & Reynolds, 2002).

ADAPTING INSTRUCTION for *ENGLISH LANGUAGE LEARNERS*

Have students draw pictures of concepts or topics rather than use words to describe or talk about them. This works especially well with students who are still learning English or other students who might have difficulty expressing their ideas through words alone.

pieces. Have students read the sentence or paragraph first, and then ask them to form a picture of it.

Creating images serves three functions: fostering understanding, retaining information, and monitoring for meaning. If students are unable to form an image, or if it is incomplete or inaccurate, encourage them to reread the section and then add to the picture in their minds or create a new one. As a comprehension strategy, imaging can help students who are having difficulty understanding a high-imagery passage. For example, it might be effective for comprehending the following highly visual description:

> A comet is like a dirty snowcone. A comet has three parts: a head, coma, and tail. The head is made of ice, gases, and particles of rocks. The heads of most comets are only a few kilometers wide. As a comet nears the sun, gases escape from the head. A large, fuzzy, ball-shaped cloud is formed. This ball-shaped cloud is the coma. The tail is present only when the coma is heated by the sun. The tail is made of fine dust and gas. A comet's tail always points away from the sun. The tail can be millions of kilometers long. (Hackett, Moyer, & Adams, 1989, p. 108)

Imaging can also be used as a pictorial summary. After reading a paragraph similar to the one about comets, students can review what they have read by trying to picture a comet and all its parts. A next step might be to draw a comet based on their visual summary. They might then compare their drawing with an illustration in the text or an encyclopedia and also with the text itself to make sure that they have included all the major components.

Exemplary Teaching

Using Imaging

Creating images is a powerful strategy for enhancing both comprehension and memory of text. Maria (1990) encouraged fourth-graders to construct images to foster their understanding of a social studies passage that described an Iroquois village. Maria started the lesson by having students study a detailed drawing of an Iroquois village. After shutting their eyes and visualizing the scene, students discussed what they had seen. Their images varied.

Students were then directed to close their eyes as Maria described a scene laden with sensory images and asked image-evoking questions:

> You are at an Iroquois village in New York State about the year 1650. It is winter. Feel how cold you are. Feel the snow crunch under your feet. The wind is blowing. You can hear it and feel it right through

your clothes. See yourself walk through the gate into the village. See the tall fence all around the village. . . . (p. 198)

After discussing what they saw, heard, and felt, the students read a passage in their social studies textbook about life in an Iroquois longhouse. After each paragraph, they stopped and created images of what they had read and discussed the images. In the discussion, Maria asked questions that focused on the important details so that when students later created images on their own, they, too, would focus on these elements. The images that students created demonstrated that their comprehension was indeed enriched. Best of all, many of the students who responded were those who usually had little to say in class discussions.

Like other elaboration strategies, imaging should be taught directly. The teacher should explain and model the strategy; discuss when, where, and under what conditions it might be used; and provide guided practice and application. From time to time, the teacher should review the strategy and encourage students to apply it.

Questions that ask students to create visual images should become a natural part of postreading discussions. Auditory and kinesthetic or tactile imaging should also be fostered. Students might be asked to tell how the hurricane in the story sounded, or what the velvet seats in the limousine they read about felt like. In discussing images that students have formed, remind them that each of us makes our own individual picture in our mind. Ask a variety of students to tell what pictures they formed.

Whether used with fiction or nonfiction, imaging should follow these guidelines (Fredericks, 1986):

- Students create images based on their backgrounds. Images will differ.
- Teachers should not alter students' images but might suggest that students reread a selection and then decide whether they want to change their images.
- Students should be given sufficient time to form images.
- Teachers should encourage students to elaborate on or expand their images through careful questioning: "What did the truck look like? Was it old or new? What model was it? What color? Did it have any special features?"

Dramatizing fosters the creation of images. When called on to act out a scene in a play, readers can be asked to picture the scene and speaker and try to imagine how the words were spoken. To build imaging ability, students might act the part of a character in a selection the class has read and invite the other class members to guess who the character is. Characters could be historical figures (McMaster, 1998).

STUDENT strategies — Imaging

- As you read, put your self into the selection.
- Picture what is going on.
- Try to hear the sounds being described, smell the smells, and feel what's happening.

■ Question Generation

Accustomed to answering questions posed by teachers and texts, students enjoy composing questions of their own. In addition to being a novel and interesting activity, **question generation** is also an effective strategy for fostering comprehension. It transforms the reader from passive observer to active participant. It also encourages the reader to set purposes for reading and to note important segments of text so that questions can be asked about them and possible answers considered. Creating questions also fosters active awareness of the comprehension process. Students who create questions are likely to be more aware of whether they are understanding the text and are more likely to take corrective action if their comprehension is inadequate (Andre & Anderson, 1978–1979).

■ **Question generation** is a powerful strategy. Through creating questions, students' comprehension jumped from the fiftieth percentile to the sixty-sixth percentile and in some instances from the fiftieth to the eighty-sixth percentile (Rosenshine, Meister, & Chapman, 1996).

Question Generation

- As you read, ask yourself questions about what you are reading.
- After reading a section, see if you can answer your questions.
- If you can't answer your questions, go back and reread.
- After answering questions for one section, go on to the next section. Make up new questions.
- After you have finished reading the whole selection, put all the information together. Ask yourself, "What have I learned? How does this fit in with what I already know?"

■ **ReQuest** is a procedure in which the teacher and student(s) take turns asking and answering questions.

ReQuest. One of the simplest and most effective devices for getting students to create questions is **ReQuest,** or reciprocal questioning (Manzo, 1969; Manzo & Manzo, 1993). Although originally designed for one-on-one instruction of remedial pupils, ReQuest has been adapted for use with groups of students and whole classes. In ReQuest, the teacher and students take turns asking questions. ReQuest can be implemented by following the steps outlined in Lesson 5.6.

 ReQuest procedure

Step 1. Choose a text that is on the students' level but is fairly dense so that it is possible to ask a number of questions about it.

Step 2. Explain the ReQuest procedure to students. Tell them that they will be using a teaching technique that will help them better understand what they read. Explain that in ReQuest, they get a chance to be the teacher because they and you take turns asking questions.

Step 3. Survey the text. Read the title, examine any illustrations that are part of the introduction, and discuss what the selection might be about.

Step 4. Direct students to read the first significant segment of text. This could be the first sentence or the first paragraph but should not be any longer than a paragraph. Explain that as they read, they are to think up questions to ask you. Students can make up as many questions as they wish. Tell them to ask the kinds of questions that a teacher might ask (Manzo & Manzo, 1993). Read the segment with the students.

Step 5. Students ask their questions. The teacher's book is placed face down. However, students may refer to their texts. If necessary, questions are restated or clarified. Answers can be checked by referring back to the text.

Step 6. After student questions have been asked, ask your questions. Pupils' books are face down. You might model higher-level questioning by asking for responses that require integrating several details in the text. If difficult concepts or vocabulary words are encountered, they should be discussed.

Step 7. Go to the next sentence or paragraph. The questioning proceeds until enough information has been gathered to set a purpose for reading the remainder of the text. This could be in the form of a prediction: "What do you think the rest of the article will be about?" Manzo and Manzo (1993) recommended that the questioning be concluded as soon as a logical purpose can be set but no longer than ten minutes after beginning.

Step 8. After the rest of the selection has been read silently, the purpose question and any related questions are discussed.

Students enjoy reversing roles and asking questions. Initially, they may ask lower-level questions but with coaching and modeling will soon ask higher-level ones. ReQuest is especially effective with lower-achieving readers.

Other elaboration strategies include applying information that has been obtained from reading, creating analogies to explain it, and evaluating text (covered in Chapter 6). A general operating principle of elaboration is that the more readers do with or to text, the better they will understand and retain it.

Monitoring

As you were reading this chapter, did you reread a section because you didn't quite understand it? Did you go back and reread any sentences? Did you have an awareness of whether or not the text was making sense? Did you decide to use a particular strategy such as summarizing or questioning or imaging? If so, you were engaged in metacognition. Summarizing, inferring, creating images, predicting, and other strategies are valuable tools for enhancing comprehension. Knowing how to use them is not enough, however; it is also essential to know when and where to use them. For example, visualizing works best with materials that are concrete and lend themselves to being pictured in the imagination (Prawat, 1989). Predictions work best when the reader has a good background of knowledge about the topic. Knowing when and where to use these and other strategies is part of monitoring, which is also known as **metacognition,** or metacognitive awareness.

Monitoring also means recognizing what one does and does not know, which is a valuable asset in reading. If a reader mouths the words of a passage without comprehending their meaning and does not recognize his or her lack of comprehension, the reader will not reread the passage or take other steps to understand it; the reader is not even aware that there is a problem. "Metacognitive awareness is the ability to reflect on one's own cognitive processes, to be aware of one's own ac-

◼ **Metacognition** or metacognitive awareness means being conscious of one's mental processes.

tivities while reading, solving problems, and so on" (Baker & Brown, 1984, p. 353). A key feature of metacognitive awareness is knowing what one is expected to be able to do as a result of reading a selection. All of the other activities are examined in light of the desired outcome. Students will read a book one way if they are reading it as part of voluntary reading, another way if they are to evaluate it, and still another way if they are taking a test on it. Their criteria for success will depend on their specific goal for reading the text. A critical factor is the level of comprehension that students demand. Proficient readers generally demand a higher level of comprehension than do struggling readers.

An abstract ability, metacognition develops gradually; some types of awareness may not be present until students are in their teens. For example, in one study, both fourth- and eighth-graders were able to skim a passage, but it was not until eighth grade that the majority of students could describe how to skim (Kobasigawa, Ransom, & Holland, 1980, cited in Baker & Brown, 1984).

The four major aspects of metacognition in reading are knowing oneself as a learner, regulating, checking, and repairing (Baker & Brown, 1984; McNeil, 1987).

■ Knowing Oneself as a Learner

The student is aware of what he or she knows, his or her reading abilities, what is easy and what is hard, what he or she likes and dislikes. The student is able to activate his or her prior knowledge in preparation for reading a selection:

> I know that Theodore Roosevelt was a president a long time ago. Was it during the late 1800s or early 1900s? I'm not sure. I remember reading a story about how he was weak as a child and had bad eyesight. I'll read about him in the encyclopedia. I'll try *World Book* instead of *Encyclopedia Britannica*. *Encyclopedia Britannica* is too hard, but I can handle *World Book*.

■ Regulating

■ **Regulating** is a metacognitive process in which the reader guides his reading processes.

In **regulating,** the student knows what to read and how to read it and is able to put that knowledge to use. The student is aware of the structure of the text and how this might be used to aid comprehension. The student also understands the criterial task for what he or she will be expected to do as a result of reading this selection: retelling, writing a story, taking a test. He or she surveys the material, gets a sense of organization, sets a purpose, and then chooses and implements an effective strategy:

> Wow! This is a long article about Roosevelt. But I don't have to read all of it. I just need information about his boyhood. These headings will tell me which section I should read. Here's one that says "Early Life." I'll read it to find out what his childhood was like. After I read it, I'll take notes on the important points.

■ Checking

The student is able to evaluate his or her performance. He or she is aware when comprehension suffers because an unknown term is interfering with meaning or an idea is confusing. Checking also involves noting whether the focus is on important, relevant information and engaging in self-questioning to determine whether goals are being achieved (Baker & Brown, 1984):

> The part about Roosevelt's ancestors isn't important. I'll skim over it. I wonder what *puny* and *asthma* mean. I've heard of asthma, but I don't know what it is. This is confusing, too. It says, "He studied under tutors." What does that mean? Let's see if I have all this straight. Roosevelt's family was wealthy. He was sickly, but then he worked out in the gym until he became strong. He liked studying nature and he was determined. I don't know about his early schooling, though, and I ought to know what *asthma* and *puny* mean.

■ Repairing

In **repairing,** the student takes corrective action when comprehension falters. He or she is not only aware that there is a problem in understanding the text but does something about it:

> I'll look up *asthma, puny,* and *tutor* in the dictionary. Okay, I see that *tutor* means "a private teacher." Oh, yeah, it's like when my brother Bill had trouble with math and Mom got him a private teacher. Did Roosevelt have trouble in school? Is that why he had tutors? I'm still confused about his early schooling. I think I'll ask the teacher about it.

Failure to comprehend might be caused by a problem at any level of reading (Collins & Smith, 1980):

- Words may be unknown or may be known but used in an unfamiliar way.
- Concepts are unknown.
- Punctuation is misread.
- Words or phrases are given the wrong emphasis.
- Paragraph organization is difficult to follow.
- Pronouns and antecedent relationships are confused. Relationships among ideas are unclear.
- Relationships among paragraphs and sections are not established.
- The reader becomes lost in details. Key ideas are misinterpreted.
- The reader has inadequate prior knowledge, or a conflict exists between that knowledge and the text.

Repair strategies (Baker & Brown, 1984; Harris & Sipay, 1990) include the following:

- Rereading the sentence or paragraph may clear up a confusing point or provide context for a difficult word.
- Reading to the end of the page or section might provide clarification.
- Having failed to grasp the gist of a section, the student might reread the preceding section.

■ Repairing refers to taking steps to correct faulty comprehension.

ADAPTING INSTRUCTION for *STRUGGLING READERS and WRITERS*
Research on metacognitive processes suggests that poor readers find it especially difficult to monitor or repair their reading. They often read materials that are far beyond their instructional levels. Overwhelmed with difficult words and concepts, comprehension is literally beyond them.

- If there are specific details that a student cannot remember, she or he should skim back through the material to find them.
- The text may be difficult or require closer reading, so the student may have to slow down, adjusting his or her rate of reading.
- Consulting a map, diagram, photo, chart, or illustration may provide clarification of a puzzling passage.
- Using a glossary or dictionary will provide meaning for an unknown word.
- Consulting an encyclopedia or similar reference may clarify a confusing concept.

Figure 5.6 shows a series of questions that students might ask themselves if they encounter difficulties as they read. The questions provide prompts for the major repair strategies and should be posted in a prominent spot in the classroom.

Lookbacks. Students may not realize that they can look back at a text when they cannot recall a specific bit of information or do not understand a passage (Garner, Hare, Alexander, Haynes & Winograd, 1984). If students' overall comprehension of a passage is faulty, they will need to reread the entire passage. If, however, they have simply forgotten or misunderstood a detail, they may use the lookback strategy, skimming back over the text and locating the portion that contains the information they need.

To present the strategy, the teacher should explain why it is needed: It is not possible to remember everything (Garner, MacCready, & Wagoner, 1984). Therefore, it is often necessary to go back over a story. The teacher should then model the strategy by showing what he or she does when unable to respond to a question. The teacher should demonstrate how he or she skims through an article to find pertinent information and then uses that information to answer a difficult question. Guided practice and application opportunities should be provided. When stu-

---

FIGURE 5.6

Repair Strategies

What to Do When I Don't Understand

What is keeping me from understanding?

Should I read the sentence or paragraph again?

Will looking at maps, charts, photos, or drawings help?

Should I look up key words?

Should I keep on reading and see whether my problem is cleared up?

Should I slow down?

Should I ask for help?

dents are unable to respond to questions during class discussions or on study sheets or similar projects, remind them to use **lookbacks**. As they learn how to use lookbacks, students should discover when and where to use them. Lookbacks, for instance, are useful only when the information needed to answer the question is present in the text.

■ **Lookback** is a strategy that involves skimming back over a selection that has already been read in order to obtain information that was missed, forgotten, or misunderstood.

■ Instruction in Metacognitive Strategies

For most students, metacognitive awareness develops automatically over time; however, instruction is also helpful (Anthony, Pearson, & Raphael, 1989). In fact, it should be a part of every reading strategy lesson.

During each part of the lesson, the teacher should make explicit the cognitive processes involved. In the early stages, for instance, the teacher might model how he or she recalls prior knowledge, sets a purpose, decides on a reading strategy, executes the strategy, monitors for meaning, organizes information, takes corrective action when necessary, and applies knowledge gained from reading. Later, the teacher should discuss these elements with students, asking them what they know about a topic, how they plan to read a selection, and what they might do if they do not understand what they are reading. The ultimate aim is to have metacognitive processes become automatic. In the past, teachers have not made their thinking processes explicit. The teaching of reading now follows the novice–expert or master craftsperson–apprentice model. The student learns from the teacher's modeling and guidance as she or he progresses from novice reader and writer to expert.

Although teachers agree that strategies are important, they may not spend enough time teaching them. In one study, the teachers assessed and provided practice opportunities for students to use strategies but spent little time teaching students how to use strategies (Pressley, Wharton-McDonald, Mistretta-Hampston, & Echevarria, 1998).

One way of reminding students of metacognitive strategies is to make a list of those that have been introduced and place them in a prominent spot in the classroom. A sample list of metacognitive strategies appears in Figure 5.7. This list can be used with fiction or nonfiction. You may want to adapt the list so that it fits the needs of your class. You may also want to have two lists: one for fiction and one for nonfiction.

To reinforce the use of metacognition, ask process, as well as product, questions. Product questions get at the content of a story. You might ask who the main character is, what problem he had in the story, and how he felt. A process question attempts to uncover how a student arrived at an answer. After a student responds that the main character was angry, ask, "How do you know that?" Other process questions are "How did you figure out that word? How did you find the answer? What did you do when you realized that you had forgotten some main facts?"

Metacognitive awareness has to be built into virtually all reading instruction; "Any attempt to comprehend must involve comprehension monitoring" (Baker & Brown, 1984, p. 385). This monitoring need not be on a conscious level. The skilled reader operates on automatic pilot until some sort of triggering event signals that comprehension is not taking place. At that point, the reader slows down, focuses on the problem, and decides how to deal with it (Baker & Brown, 1984).

Students should monitor how effectively they apply new strategies, perhaps by using before-and-after comparisons. For instance, if they have learned to use predicting, they might note that it improves their comprehension and provides

ADAPTING INSTRUCTION for *STRUGGLING READERS and WRITERS*
Good readers have good monitoring skills and poor readers don't. Poor readers are less likely to detect lapses in comprehension and, when they do detect them, are less able to repair them. However, when instructed, poor readers can and do learn to become effective monitors (Palincsar et al.,1993).

FIGURE 5.7

Metacognitive Strategies

Thinking and Reading

Before reading

What does this selection seem to be about?

What do I already know about this subject?

What do I want to learn or find out?

Why am I reading this?

While reading

What am I learning or finding out?

Is the selection making sense?

If I'm having trouble understanding the selection, what can I do?

After reading

What have I learned or found out?

What questions do I still have?

How does what I read fit in with what I know?

deeper involvement in reading. Students might also discuss ways in which they have made especially good use of the strategy; if they were involved in preparing for a test, they could show how their performance improved. Thus, metacognition becomes a motivating device, as students are more likely to use a strategy if they are convinced of its value and have faith in their ability to employ it effectively (Schunk & Rice, 1987).

In addition to scheduling lessons devoted to teaching monitoring and fix-up strategies, be alert for opportunities to do on-the-spot teaching or reinforcement. When a student is reading orally and makes an error, do not immediately correct her or him. Give the student the opportunity to monitor her or his own reading and apply a fix-up strategy. In fact, if the miscue makes sense in the sentence, you might ignore it. If it changes the meaning of the sentence and the student does not correct it, ask questions like these: "Did that sentence make sense? What might you do to read the sentence correctly?" If the student cannot make the correction after a reasonable effort, supply the correct word by asking, "Would (unknown word) fit here?" or "Would (an incorrect response) fit?" However, it is important that students be given a chance to correct their errors. To develop monitoring and fix-up strategies, students need ample opportunity to apply them. They also need an environment in which they are not afraid to make mistakes.

To promote monitoring and use of repair strategies during silent reading, review these strategies from time to time. During times when it is not possible for students to get help with comprehension difficulties, have them make a note of problems they encounter. A sticky note might be put under the word or passage that poses a problem. As part of every postreading discussion, talk over any difficulties that students may have had while reading the text. Also make sure that the text is not too difficult for students. They will have difficulty monitoring for meaning if they are unable to construct a coherent situation model of the text (Paris, Wasik, & Turner, 1991).

To understand metacognition, try to become aware of the strategies that you use. When reading becomes difficult and comprehension breaks down, what repair strategies do you use?

> Because metacognition is a developmental process, young students are less adept than older readers. However, developmentally appropriate instruction in metacognitive processes is effective.

> In addition to being taught how to use strategies, students should learn why, where, and when to use them so as to acquire cognitive command of them.

STUDENT strategies   Checking and Repairing

- As you read, ask yourself, "Is this making sense? Do I understand what I am reading?"
- If you are not understanding what you are reading, reread it.
- If you still don't understand what you are reading, ask yourself why? If there are words you don't understand, look them up. Look at the charts, maps, and pictures to see if they will help. If nothing else works, ask for help.

Special Comprehension Strategies for Bilingual Readers

For bilingual students, reading and comprehending in their weaker or nondominant language is more difficult. One of the major obstacles is vocabulary. If they have recently learned to speak English, chances are they will encounter a greater number of unknown words than will their same-age English-speaking counterparts. Fortunately, successful bilingual readers do use a repertoire of strategies to aid themselves. For one thing, they seem to be more metacognitively aware. Apparently, the process of learning a second language has provided them with insights into language on an abstract level, as an object of study. They are more likely to notice problems in word recognition or comprehension. While using the same kinds of strategies (predicting, inferencing, monitoring, etc.) as their monolingual counterparts, they also use additional strategies: translating from one language to another and transferring information learned in one language to another.

Achieving bilingual readers see similarities between their native language and their new language. They use their native language as a source of help by activating prior knowledge in both languages and by translating when encountering a difficult passage, especially when they are in the earlier stages of learning English. Transferring, translating, and reflecting on text in their native or stronger language has the potential for improving comprehension (Jiménez, 1997).

> **ADAPTING INSTRUCTION for *ENGLISH LANGUAGE LEARNERS***
> When introducing selections to bilingual students, extra time needs to be spent building background and vocabulary. Providing students with high interest, readable, culturally relevant materials also provides a boost to motivation and comprehension (Jiménez, 1997).

Culturally diverse youngsters do especially well in cooperative learning situations.

BUILDING LANGUAGE

Model accountable talk by showing how you use facts and details or passages from a selection to back up your judgments. Use probes and prompts to coach students as they do the same. Discuss the difference between opinions that have no backing and those that are supported by facts or incidents.

SOCIAL–CONSTRUCTIVIST NATURE OF COMPREHENSION

According to Vygotsky (1978), learning is a social process. Directions and explanations provided by a more knowledgeable other are internalized by the learner and become part of his or her thinking. In similar fashion, when teacher and students or just students gather in groups and discuss a selection, they help each other construct meaning. Comprehension is still an individual task. Participants discuss their personal understandings of the text, but as they engage in an interchange of ideas, they may modify their understandings as they perceive the selection from other perspectives. This is especially true in their reading of literature, where understandings are enriched and broadened by discussion with others. However, even when reading informational texts, understandings are deepened and clarified through discussion. If the discussion includes processes of reading in which students explain how they comprehended a particular passage or what they did when a passage was confusing, understanding of reading processes is enhanced (Kucan & Beck, 1996).

The degree to which comprehension is fostered depends on the quality of the thinking and the ideas exchanged. The talk must be accountable (New Standards Primary Literacy Committee, 1999). It must go beyond mere opinion. Students must be prepared to back up a judgment about a literary piece by using passages from the text, for instance. For a conclusion drawn from a passage in a history text, they must cite supporting details. In this way, students learn to draw evidence from text, check facts, and reason with information. Teachers play a key role in modeling accountable talk and in shaping discussions so that student talk becomes accountable.

Reciprocal Teaching

■ **Reciprocal teaching** is a form of cooperative learning in which students learn to use four key reading strategies in order to achieve improved comprehension: predicting, questioning, summarizing, and clarifying.

In a **reciprocal teaching** situation, the group reads a story and then discusses it. Members of the group take turns leading the discussion. They use four tried-and-true techniques for building comprehension and for monitoring for meaning—predicting, question generating, clarifying, and summarizing (Palincsar & Brown, 1986).

Reciprocal teaching is based on four highly regarded learning principles: expert scaffolding, cooperative learning, guided learning, and Vygotsky's zone of proximal development.

1. *Predicting.* Students predict what information a section of text will present based on what they have read in a prior section. If they are just starting a selection, their prediction is based on illustrations, headings, or an introductory paragraph. They must activate their background knowledge to guess what the author is going to say next. Predicting makes them active readers and gives them a purpose for reading.

2. *Question generating.* Students must seek out the kinds of information in a text that provide a basis for well-formed questions. Not being able to formulate a question may be a sign that they have failed to understand the significant points in the text and so must reread or take other corrective action.

3. *Clarifying.* Students note words, concepts, expressions, or other items that hinder comprehension, and they ask for explanations during discussion.

4. *Summarizing.* The discussion leader, with or without the help of the group, retells the selection, highlighting the main points. This retelling reviews and integrates the information and is also a monitoring device. Inability to paraphrase is a sign that comprehension is poor and rereading is in order (A. L. Brown, 1985). Summarizing also becomes a springboard for making predictions about the content of the next section.

Using direct instruction, the teacher introduces reciprocal teaching over approximately a week's time but may take longer if necessary. Lesson 5.7 outlines the teacher's role in reciprocal teaching.

> In addition to fostering monitoring for meaning, the strategy known as clarifying introduces students to the idea that students can help each other (Rosenshine & Meister, 1994).

 Reciprocal teaching

Step 1. Introduce reciprocal teaching

Ask students whether they have ever wanted to switch places with the teacher. Tell them that they will be using a new method to help them read with better understanding and that each student will have a chance to lead a discussion of a story that the class has read. Outline for the students the four parts of the method: predicting what will happen; making up questions; clarifying, or clearing up details that are hard to understand; and summarizing.

Step 2. Explain the four basic parts

(a) Explain that predicting helps readers think what a story might be about and that it gives them a purpose for reading. Students will want to see whether their predictions are correct, so they will read with greater interest and understanding. Model the process, and give students a chance to try it out.
(b) Explain to students that asking questions will help them read with better understanding. Model the process by reading a selection and constructing questions. Emphasize the need to ask questions about the important parts of the selection, and provide guided practice in constructing some questions.
(c) Explain what clarifying is. Tell students that it is important to notice words or ideas that make it hard to understand a selection. Explain that clarifying hard parts of a selection will help them get more meaning out of what they are reading. Have them locate which words, sentences, or ideas in a sample selection need clarifying. Explain that what is clear to one person may not be clear to another.
(d) Explain why summarizing is an important skill. Tell students that summarizing a paragraph helps them concentrate on important points while reading. Demonstrate creating a summary for a model paragraph. Explain that if students summarize, they will better understand what they read and remember it longer.

Depending on students' age, ability, and previous experience with the strategies, the teacher might introduce the strategies all at once, one a day, or even one a week. It is not expected that students will become proficient in their use

> Some students may have difficulty composing questions. Supply these students with model questions. As they begin to catch onto the process, provide prompts or partial questions until they are able to create questions on their own.

or even fully understand them at this point. That will come when the strategies are applied in a reciprocal teaching lesson. At first, the teacher plays a major role in the application of reciprocal teaching, modeling the four strategies, making corrections, and providing guidance when necessary. Gradually, the students take more responsibility for leading discussions and applying the strategies.

The following is a sample reciprocal teaching lesson based on the reading of a selection about Daisy Low, the founder of the Girl Scouts of America.

(Lead-in question)

Carmen (student discussion leader): My question is, how did Daisy Low help people and animals?

Paula: She fed stray cats and dogs.

Frank: She got clothes for needy children.

(Clarification request)

Charles: I think we should clarify *needy.*

Ann: I think needy children need stuff, like clothes and maybe food.

Teacher: What would be another word for *needy?*

James: Poor. I think *poor* means the same thing as *needy.*

Teacher: Good answer. *Poor* and *needy* mean just about the same thing. I have another question. Why did Daisy put a blanket on the cow?

Paula: She was afraid it would get cold.

James: I think that should be clarified. Do cows get cold?

Teacher: Does anybody know? Did any of you ever live on a farm? How can we find out?

Paula: We could look in the encyclopedia.

John: My grandfather raised cows. He's visiting us. I could ask him.

Teacher: That's a great idea. You ask him and report back to us. Maybe your grandfather could come in and talk to the class about life on a farm. By the way, Carmen, do you feel that your question has been answered?

Carmen: I think the story tells about some more things that Daisy Low did to help people. Can anyone tell me what they were?

Ann: Yes, she started a children's group called Helping Hands.

Frank: And the first sentence says that she was the founder of the Girl Scouts in America.

Teacher: Those are good answers. Can you summarize this section of the story, Carmen?

(Summary)

Carmen: The paragraph tells about Daisy Low.

Teacher: That's right, Carmen. The paragraph tells us about Daisy Low. In a summary, you give the main idea and main details. What does the paragraph tell us about Daisy Low?

Carmen: She helped animals and children who were in need.

(Prediction)

Teacher: Very good, Carmen. What do you predict will happen next?

Carmen: I think the story will tell how Daisy Low started the Girl Scouts.

Teacher: Does anyone have a different prediction? Okay. Let's read the next section to see how our prediction works out. Who would like to be the leader for this section?

In reciprocal teaching, students learn key strategies by imitating and working along with the teacher.

During the session, the teacher provides guidance where needed and also models the four strategies. The teacher provides prompts and probes and models strategies as necessary. For instance, creating questions is difficult for many students. The teacher might show how she or he would go about creating a question, supply question words—*who, what, why, when, where,* and *how*— or use prompts to help students reformulate awkward questions. Ultimately, students should be able to apply the comprehension and strategy lessons they have learned. Research suggests that this does happen: Students who were trained in the use of the strategies were apparently able to apply them to their social studies and science reading; their rankings in content-area evaluations shot up from the twentieth to the fiftieth percentile (A. L. Brown, 1985).

An entire class can use reciprocal teaching if it is adapted in the following two ways. First, students use the headings to make two predictions about the content of the text they are about to read. Second, after reading a segment, they write two questions and a summary, as well as list any items that require clarification. The predictions, summaries, and clarification requests are discussed after the selection has been read. Even with these whole group adaptations, comprehension improved twenty percent after using the approach for just one month (Palincsar & Brown, 1986).

Why is reciprocal teaching so powerful? Reciprocal teaching leads students to a deeper processing of text. It may also change the way students read. It focuses their attention on trying to make sense of what they read, instead of just decoding words (Rosenshine & Meister, 1994).

Reciprocal teaching can be used with nonreaders, the major difference being that the teacher reads the selection to the students. The process can also be adapted to a peer-tutoring situation in which a good reader is trained in the strategies and works with a poor reader (Palincsar & Brown, 1986).

Questioning the Author

Another highly effective technique that emphasizes collaboration and discussion is Questioning the Author. Based on their research, McKeown, Beck, and Sandora (1996) found that fifth-graders weren't learning very much from their content-area texts. The researchers sought ways to help the students get more out of their reading. A program was set up in which students read brief segments of text and then responded to teacher queries so that they were cooperatively constructing meaning as they processed the text instead of reading the entire text and then answering questions. Students were told that sometimes the author's meaning wasn't clear, so they would have to ask themselves such questions as, "What is the author trying to say here?" Having students ask the author questions made reading a more active process. Rather than simply extracting information from text, readers would have to build a genuine understanding of the text. Beck, McKeown, Hamilton, and Kucan (1997) compared it to the difference between building a model ship and being given one. The student who has assembled a model ship knows a great deal more about its parts than the one who has simply looked at the model.

The teacher used general queries to get the discussion started and to keep it moving. Initiating queries included: "What is the author trying to say here? What is the author's message? What is the author trying to tells us?" Follow-up queries were designed to help the students construct meaning. If a passage didn't seem clear, the teacher might ask, "What did the author mean here? Did the author explain this clearly?" Questions could also be asked that helped connect ideas that had been read previously: "How does this connect to what the author told us before? How do these two ideas fit together?" Other kinds of questions lead students to seek reasons. "Does the author tell us why? Why do you think the author included this information?" Questions might also help students see how what they are learning relates to what they know: "How does this fit in with what you know?"

To structure the discussion so that it helps students construct meaning, the teacher uses six Questioning-the-Author moves: marking, turning back, revoicing, modeling, annotating, and recapping.

Marking. The teacher highlights a student's comment or idea that is important to the meaning being built. The teacher might remark, "You are saying that immigration was a good thing. It helped the United States grow and develop." Or the teacher might simply say, "Good point!"

Turning Back. The teacher turns students' attention back to the text so that they can get more information, fix up a misreading, or clarify their thinking: "Yes, I agree that people should have been pleased to have so many newcomers to build railroads and work in factories. But what does the author tell us about the way the newcomers were actually treated?"

Revoicing. The teacher helps students clearly express what they were attempting to say: "So what you're telling us is that the newcomers put up with hardships and worked long hours so that their children would have a better life."

Modeling. The teacher shows how he might go about creating meaning from text. He might show how he clarifies a difficult passage, draws a conclusion, visualizes a complex process, or uses context to derive the meaning of a difficult word. The teacher might say, "Here's what was going through my mind as I read that passage," or "Here's how I figured out what the author meant," or, "When an author explains how something works, I try to picture the steps in my mind."

ADAPTING INSTRUCTION for *STRUGGLING READERS and WRITERS*
Questioning the Author works with all students but has been especially successful with struggling readers and writers and students in urban schools.

For detailed information on how to conduct a Questioning-the-Author lesson, see *Questioning the Author, An Approach for Enhancing Student Engagement with Text* (Beck, McKeown, Hamilton, & Kucan, 1997). Newark, DE: International Reading Association.

Annotating. The teacher fills in information that is missing from a discussion but that is important for understanding key ideas. It might be information that the author failed to include: "The author tells us that factory goods were so cheap that people stopped making clothes and household items at home and bought them instead. What the author doesn't say is that more and more people became dependent on a job. Up to this time, they had raised their own food and made much of what they needed. Now they needed money to live."

Recapping. The teacher highlights key points and summarizes. "Now that we understand how immigrant parents sacrificed for their children, let's see whether the children benefited from all those sacrifices." Lesson 5.8 lists the steps in a Questioning-the-Author lesson.

 Questioning the author

LESSON 5.8

Step 1. Analyze the text and decide what you want students to know or understand as a result of reading the text. List two or three major understandings.

Step 2. Note any potential difficulties in the text that might hamper students' comprehension. This could be difficult vocabulary or concepts or needed background knowledge.

Step 3. Segment the text into readable blocks. A segment could be a single sentence or paragraph or several paragraphs. A block would generally encompass one major idea.

Step 4. In light of the understandings you wish students to attain and the possible difficulties in the text, plan your queries. Plan queries for each segment.

Step 5. Introduce the selection. Clarify difficult vocabulary and other hindrances to comprehension in a particular segment before that segment is read.

Step 6. Students read the first segment silently.

Step 7. Students and teacher discuss the first segment.

Step 8. Students go on to the next segment.

Step 9. At the conclusion, the class, with the teacher's help, sums up what they have read.

How well does Questioning the Author work? Examine the following slightly edited discussion. Note how students construct meaning and the depth of their thinking.

The class has just read a text segment about the presidency of James Buchanan, which stated that many people believed that he liked the South better than the North because he said that owning slaves should be a personal choice. The teacher began the discussion by posing a general query. After a student responded, the teacher asked a follow-up question.

Teacher: This paragraph that Tracy just read is really full of important information. What has the author told us in this important paragraph?

Laura: They think that Buchanan liked the South better because he said that it is a person's choice if they want to have slaves or not, so they thought that he liked the South better than the North.

Teacher: Okay. And what kind of problem then did this cause Buchanan when they thought that he liked the South?

Janet: Well, maybe less people would vote for him because like in Pennsylvania we were against slavery and might have voted for him because he was from Pennsylvania. But now since we knew that he was for the South, we might not vote for him again.

Jamie: I have something to add on to Janet's 'cause I completely agree with her. We might have thought that since he was from Pennsylvania and Pennsylvania was an antislavery state, that he was against slavery. But it turns out he wasn't.

Teacher: Just like someone whom you think is your best friend, and then all of a sudden you find out, oh, they're not. (pp. 113–114)

At this point, students read and then discuss another text segment.

INTEGRATION OF STRATEGIES

For the sake of clarity, the major comprehension strategies presented in this chapter have been discussed in isolation. However, it should be emphasized that reading is a holistic act. Often, several interacting strategies are being applied simultaneously. As Pressley, Borkowski, Forrest-Pressley, Gaskins, and Wiley (1993) explained,

> Strategies are rarely used in isolation. Rather, they are integrated into higher-order sequences that accomplish complex cognitive goals. For example, good reading may begin with previewing, activation of prior knowledge about the topic of a to-be-read text, and self-questioning about what might be presented in the text. These prereading activities are then followed by careful reading, reviewing, and rereading as necessary. General strategies (e.g., self-testing) are used to monitor whether subgoals have been accomplished, prompting the reader to move on when it is appropriate to do so or motivating reprocessing when subgoals have not been met. That is, good strategy users evaluate whether the strategies they are using are producing progress toward goals they have set for themselves. (p. 9)

Learning to use a strategy is a long process. Although researchers may get positive results after twenty lessons on predicting or summarizing, it may actually

Some theorists see reading as a holistic attempt to construct meaning rather than a problem-solving attempt to apply specific strategies (Kucan & Beck, 1996). This text views reading as a combination of the two: strategies, once learned, are ultimately applied in a holistic, integrated fashion.

USING TECHNOLOGY
Cool Sites for Kids presents dozens of sites on a variety of topics. These sites are good for applying comprehension strategies and are recommended by the American Library Association.
http://www.ala.org/alsc/children_links.html

take students many months to master a particular strategy (Pressley, 1994). In addition, strategies learned at one level may have to be refined when used at higher levels with more complex materials.

MAKING STRATEGY INSTRUCTION WORK

Strategy instruction works best when students evidence a need for a strategy, when the strategy taught is applied to a selection, when the teacher repeatedly models and explains the strategy, when the students have many opportunities to use the strategy, and when assessment is based on comprehension of the text and the use of the strategy (Duffy, 2002). The key element is the teacher's ability to adapt instruction to students' understanding and to provide a depth of instruction. In teaching deriving the main idea, for instance, the most effective teachers provided extensive modeling and adjusted guided practice to help students overcome shortcomings in their thinking. If students create a main idea that is too broad, teachers use prompts that help the students narrow their main idea. When students select details that are very interesting but do not encompass all the details in a selection, teachers use prompts to help students redirect their thinking.

IMPORTANCE OF AFFECTIVE FACTORS

Motivation is a key factor in strategy use. If students believe that the strategies they possess can help improve their performance, they are more inclined to use them. Believing that they have sufficient competency to complete the task motivates students to put forth the necessary effort (Gaskins, 1998; Pressley, Borkowski, Forrest-Pressley, Gaskins, & Wiley, 1990, 1993). As part of your program, be sure to call attention to students' successes. For instance, after students have done a good job comprehending a selection, discuss the strategies that they used. But also set aside time to help them with any difficulties that they are having. Overcoming difficulties is also motivational.

Being attentive, active, and reflective are key factors in strategy use. Provide students with a rationale for being attentive: the more attentive you are, the more you learn and remember. Attentiveness is enhanced by applying strategies covered here—surveying, predicting, inferring, and monitoring—all of which require active student involvement. Students are also more motivated and more involved when they are consulted and given choices and when they have the opportunity to collaborate with classmates. Reflection is also important. Taking time to think about what we have read improves comprehension and retention. Provide students with questions that require careful thinking about what they have read. And provide time for them to reflect (Gaskins, 1998).

Along with comprehension strategies, students also need to be taught self-regulatory behaviors. Having knowledge of strategies isn't of much value if students don't use them. Students need to be taught how to organize their time and how to go about completing assignments, especially those that are long range. See Chapter 7 for more information about self-regulatory behaviors.

 EXPLICIT VERSUS NONEXPLICIT INSTRUCTION OF STRATEGIES

Strategy instruction varies in its explicitness. Guided reading, for instance, focuses on having students and the teacher mutually construct a representation of the text. Strategies might not be explicitly taught. The assumption is that after repeated encounters students will infer that they should use these strategies on their own. Explicit teaching grew out of concern for struggling readers who might not pick up strategies without direct instruction. As Duffy (2002) explains, "explicit teaching is intentional and direct about teaching individual strategies on the assumption that clear and unambivalent information about how strategies work will put struggling readers in a better position to control their own comprehension; other approaches, on the other hand, emphasize quality interaction with text content but avoid explicit teacher talk designed to develop students' metacognitive awareness of when and how to use a particular strategy. . . . Many struggling readers cannot, by simply watching a teacher guide their reading, figure out what they are supposed to do on their own. Consequently, they remain mystified and do not achieve the desired 'inner control' (pp. 30–31).

In other approaches, the goal is student comprehension of text. In explicit teaching, the goal is students' mastery of strategies. Approaches in which the focus is on comprehension of text rather than mastery of strategies include the directed reading activity, directed reading-thinking activity, and KWL, which are covered in the next chapter.

 HELP FOR STRUGGLING READERS AND WRITERS

When explicitly taught strategies, poor readers typically do as well as average or even better-than-average readers. However, it is essential that struggling readers be given materials on their level. They should know at least 95 percent of the words and have 75 percent comprehension of materials used for instructional purposes. If given materials on a higher level than that, the material is so overwhelming that they are unable to apply strategies (Kletzien, 1991).

Intensive, step-by-step, explicit instruction is also part of the package. At the Benchmark School, which is a special school for disabled readers, students are taught one strategy at a time, with each strategy being taught for nearly two months. During that time, students have frequent reviews and use the strategy on a daily basis. A chart is displayed reviewing the steps of the strategy, and students discuss when, where, and how to use the strategy.

Strategy instruction is also made an integral part of the reading lesson. Along with building background and introducing new vocabulary, the teacher introduces or reviews a strategy that students are expected to use in their reading. After reading, the students discuss the selection and also talk over ways in which they used the strategy in their reading.

After a strategy has been thoroughly learned, a new strategy is introduced. The new strategy is related to the old, and students are shown how to use both together. Another key to success is to apply strategies to a variety of materials and especially to the content-areas, so that it generalizes (Gaskins, 1998). Two strategies that are especially helpful for struggling readers are self-questioning and summarizing. In addition to helping students become more active, they also serve as a self-check on understanding. If students can't summarize or answer questions that they have posed, this is a sign that they haven't understood what they have read and should lead to a rereading, using illustrations, or some other fix-up strategy.

ESSENTIAL STANDARDS

Fourth through eighth grades
Students will

- prepare for reading by previewing, activating prior knowledge, setting a purpose for reading, and deciding how a selection should be read.
- adjust rate and style of reading to purpose for reading and nature of the material being read.
- seek out main ideas and essential details as they read and demonstrate comprehension by orally summarizing a selection and by using graphic organizers and/or creating written summaries.
- make inferences, create images, and generate questions about their reading.
- make connections between what they have read and their own experiences.
- monitor their reading to see that it makes sense and use basic and advanced fix-up strategies if it doesn't.
- compare selections that they have read.
- follow increasingly complex written directions.
- apply information that they have gained through reading.

 ASSESSMENT

Assessment should be ongoing. Through observation, note the strategies students use before, during, and after reading. Note in particular what they do when they are stumped by a passage. During discussions, note the overall quality of their comprehension and the kinds of strategies they seem to be using. Occasionally, ask them how they were able to comprehend a difficult passage. Ask them to describe the strategies they used. For older students, you might ask them to submit a web of a selection or a written summary. Also, from time to time, have students mark confusing passages. Analyze the passages and discuss students' difficulties to get a

ACTION PLAN

1. Use comprehension test and quiz results, observations of students as they discuss selections, think-alouds, and written responses to assess students' comprehension strengths and weaknesses. Plan a program accordingly.
2. Use modeling, think-alouds, explanation, and explicit, direct instruction of strategies with lots of opportunities for practice, review and application. It might take weeks or even months for students to master a strategy.
3. Before students read selections, provide activities that help them to activate prior knowledge, set purpose and goals, preview the selection and predict based on their previews.
4. Teach and provide practice with strategies such as comprehending the main idea, determining important details, organizing details, and summarizing. Help students organize information.
5. Teach and provide practice with strategies, such as inferring, imaging, generating questions, and evaluating, that help students make connections between what they have read and their prior knowledge.
6. Provide instruction and activities that help students to become aware of their comprehension and to take corrective action when comprehension is inadequate.
7. Use approaches such as reciprocal teaching that make use of discussion and working together to construct meaning.
8. Model how you would integrate strategies. Also model how you go about selecting which strategies to use. Provide practice and application opportunities.
9. Adapt instruction for English language learners by spending added time building background and vocabulary. Also use culturally-relevant materials and draw on the students' background knowledge and strong metacognitive skills. Focus on the content of student responses rather than the way they express their answers.
10. Provide extra instruction for struggling readers. Make sure struggling readers are given materials on their level.
11. Monitor students' progress and revise the program as needed.

sense of the kinds of things that are hindering their comprehension. Also note how students do with different types of texts being read for different purposes. How well do students do when reading on a literal level? How well do they read when they have to organize, infer, or evaluate information?

SUMMARY

1. Comprehending involves activating a schema, which is an organized package or network of information. Comprehension can also be viewed as a process of constructing situation models. While processing text, the reader continually reconstructs or updates the situation model.
2. Major types of comprehension strategies include preparational, organizational, elaboration, and monitoring. Preparational strategies are activities in which a reader engages just before reading a selection. Organizational strategies involve selecting the most important details in a piece and constructing relationships among them. Elaboration strategies involve constructing relationships between prior knowledge and knowledge obtained from print. Monitoring strategies include being aware of oneself as a learner and of the learning task, regulating and planning comprehension activities, monitoring one's comprehension, and repairing it when it is faulty.

3. Reciprocal teaching is a well-researched technique that integrates predicting, question generating, clarifying, and summarizing. Questioning the Author breaks the text into brief segments to allow for intensive, collaborative construction of meaning. The focus is on text, rather than strategies.

4. Integrating strategies and establishing an environment conducive to learning foster comprehension. Students' motivation, willingness to pay attention, active involvement, and reflection also have an impact on comprehension.

EXTENDING AND APPLYING

1. In your own reading, try out for at least a week one of the strategies introduced in this chapter. Note its effectiveness. Did you encounter any difficulties implementing it?
2. To gain insight into the comprehension process, do a think-aloud with a partner as you read a challenging selection. What processes and strategies did you use? What difficulties, if any, did you experience? How did you cope with these difficulties?
3. Plan a direct instruction lesson for teaching one of the comprehension strategies. If possible, teach it and evaluate its effectiveness.
4. Obtain information about an older elementary school student's use of comprehension strategies.

Ask the student what she or he does to prepare for reading. Then ask what the student does if she or he is reading a selection and discovers that she or he does not understand it.

5. Introduce ReQuest, or the reciprocal teaching approach, or Questioning the Author to a group of elementary or middle school students or try it out with a group of classmates. What seem to be the advantages and disadvantages of the approach? (If you choose to try out reciprocal teaching or Questioning the Author, be aware that they will take some time. These are complex techniques with many parts but are highly effective and so worth the effort.)

DEVELOPING A PROFESSIONAL PORTFOLIO

Videotape a lesson in which you teach a comprehension strategy to a group of students. Describe the lesson and reflect on its effectiveness. Explain what you did in subsequent lessons to help students apply the strategy. Document progress that students you taught made in comprehension. Documentation might include completed graphic organizers, written summaries, or pre- and post-test results.

DEVELOPING A RESOURCE FILE

Keep a list of activities and techniques that foster comprehension. Also keep a list of books, periodicals, and Web sites that are especially effective for fostering comprehension strategies: books that lend themselves to imaging, books that lend themselves to creating questions, etc. Collect brief articles from periodicals, children's books, or other sources that might be used to provide practice with inferring, visualizing, or other strategies.

6

Comprehension: Text Structures and Teaching Procedures

*F*or each of the following statements related to the chapter you are about to read, put a check under "Agree" or "Disagree" to show how you feel. Discuss your responses with classmates before you read the chapter.

		Agree	*Disagree*
1	The structure of a piece of writing influences its level of difficulty.	_____	_____
2	Talking about the structure of a story ruins the fun of reading it.	_____	_____
3	How you ask a question is more important than what you ask.	_____	_____
4	Struggling learners should be asked a greater proportion of lower-level questions.	_____	_____
5	Students should play the most important role in class discussions.	_____	_____
6	Structured reading lessons usually work better than unstructured ones.	_____	_____
7	Critical (evaluative) reading skills have never been more important or more neglected.	_____	_____

USING WHAT YOU KNOW

*T*he emphasis in Chapter 5 was on learners and the strategies they might use to construct meaning. Of course, strategies have to be integrated with text, which has an effect on the types of strategies that can be applied. This chapter emphasizes the role of text, both narrative and expository, in comprehension. However, a number of teaching procedures are also explored, such as the use of questions and techniques for asking them, reading lessons, and the cloze procedure, which consists of supplying missing words. This chapter also includes a section on critical (evaluative) reading.

What do you already know about text structure? How might that knowledge improve your comprehension? What kinds of questions might foster comprehension? How should questions be asked? Think back on lessons that were used to introduce reading selections when you were in elementary or middle school. What procedures did the teacher use? What aspects of those procedures worked best?

NATURE OF THE TEXT

A text has both content and organization. Students are prepared for the content when the teacher activates schema or builds background; however, they also have to interact with the structure. Therefore, they develop another schema for organizational patterns. Knowledge of structure provides a blueprint for constructing a situational model of a story or informational piece. As students read, text is transformed into ideas or details known as propositions. **Propositions** are combined, deleted, and integrated so that a macrostructure is formed. The **macrostructure** is a running summary of the text. The propositions are organized according to their relative importance or hierarchy. A general statement would be toward the top of the hierarchy. Details are lower. A reader who is able to detect the main idea of a text and its supporting details will better understand and retain information in the text than will a reader who fails to use the text's organization. Likewise, a reader who has a good sense of story structure can use the structure of a story as a framework for remembering it (Gordon, 1989).

Narrative Text and Story Schema

Various **story grammars,** or schemes, are available for analyzing a story into its parts. Although each may use different terminology, they all tend to concentrate on setting, characters, and plot. Plot is divided into the story problem and/or the main character's goal, the principal episodes, and the resolution of the problem. In most story grammars, characters are included in the setting; however, as *setting* is a literary word that has long been used to indicate only time and place, it is used in that sense in this book. Different types of stories have different types of structures, and, as students progress through the grades, both stories and structures become more complex. Goals and motivations of major characters become more important. Settings may be exotic and include mood as well as time and place.

Narratives progress primarily in terms of the main character's goals. The reader comprehends the story in terms of the main character's attempts to resolve a problem or conflict. For instance, readers comprehend *The Barn* (Avi, 1994) in terms of Ben's goal of building a barn so that his father will be inspired to recover.

Narratives differ in their overall orientation. Some are action oriented. Mystery novels, such as the *Great Britain* (Fitzgerald) or *Encyclopedia Brown* (Sobol) series, tend to fall in this category. They stress actions. Others emphasize characters' consciousness and explore thoughts and feelings and motivations. *The Pinballs* (Byars, 1972), a story of children in a foster home, and *Charlotte's Web* (White, 1952) delve into the characters' emotions. In action-oriented narratives, the tale is composed of a series of episodes arranged in the order in which they hap-

---

■ A **proposition** is a statement of information. "Janice hit the ball" is a proposition; "Janice hit the red ball" is two propositions because it contains two pieces of information: Janice hit the ball. The ball is red.

■ **Macrostructure** is the overall organization of a selection. It refers to the main idea or overall meaning of the selection. Microstructure refers to the details of a selection.

■ A **story grammar** is a series of rules designed to show how the parts of a story are interrelated.

▌Bartlett (1932), a British psychologist, asked subjects to read and retell an Indian folk tale, which contained an unfamiliar structure. In the retelling, aspects of the tale were changed so that the reconstructed tale was more like that of a traditional English tale. Bartlett concluded that we tend to reinterpret tales in terms of our own experience.

pened. Little space is devoted to the psychological states of the main characters. The story is usually told from the perspective of a third-person narrator (Westby, 1999). More complex are stories that embody the consciousness of the characters. These are often told from the perspectives of several characters and are more complex because they require an understanding of human motivation. This involves understanding the actions of others in terms of their goals and plans (Bruce, 1980). Most books combine action and consciousness but emphasize one or the other.

What can be done to build a sense of story? The most effective strategy is to read aloud to students from a variety of materials, from kindergarten right through high school. Most children gain a sense of story simply from this exposure, but it is also helpful to highlight major structural elements. This can be done by discussing the story's setting, characters, plot, and main problem. Story structure can be used to guide discussions through questions such as the following (Sadow, 1982):

When and where does the story take place?
Who are the characters?
What problem does the main character face?
What does the main character do about the problem? Or what happens to the main character as a result of the problem?
How is the problem resolved?

These questions will help students create an understanding of action-oriented narratives. However, to promote understanding of consciousness-oriented narratives, it is necessary to ask questions about motives and feelings: Why did Marty lie to his parents? How do you think he felt about it? How would you feel if you lied to your parents? Consciousness-oriented narratives have a double level: the level of action and the level of thought and emotion. The student must be prepared to grasp both levels.

Asking what, how, and why questions fosters understanding. What questions generally assess literal understanding; why and how questions help the reader integrate aspects of the story and create causal or other relationships. Why questions also foster making inferences (Trabasso & Magliano, 1996).

Discussions should also include an opportunity for students to construct personal responses. The structure is the skeleton of a story. The reader's response is the heart of the piece.

Another technique for reinforcing story structure is having students fill out generic guide sheets. Students reading significantly below grade level found that guide sheets and maps based on story structure helped them better understand the selections they read (Cunningham & Foster, 1978; Idol & Croll, 1985). In their review of the research, Davis and McPherson (1989) concluded that **story maps** are effective because they require students to read actively to complete the maps and also require self-monitoring.

A generic story map based on McGee and Tompkins's (1981) simplified version of Thorndyke's (1977) story grammar is presented in Figure 6.1. As students meet increasingly complex stories, other elements can be added—for example, theme, conflict, and multiple episodes. Maps can be filled in by students

> **ADAPTING INSTRUCTION for *ENGLISH LANGUAGE LEARNERS***
> Some ESL students and also some native-speaking students may come from cultures that have different norms for storytelling. In some cultures, children only listen to stories. They don't tell them until they are teenagers (Westby, 1999).

■ **Story maps** provide an overview of a story: characters, setting, problem, goal, plot, and outcome.

FIGURE 6.1

A Generic Story Map

Setting　　Where does the story take place?

　　　　　　　When does the story take place?

　　　　　　　_____

　　　　　　　_____

Characters　Who are the main people in the story?

　　　　　　　_____

　　　　　　　_____

Problem　　What problems does the main character face?

　　　　　　　_____

　　　　　　　_____

Goal　　　What is the main character's goal?

　　　　　　　What is he or she trying to do?

　　　　　　　_____

　　　　　　　_____

Plot　　　What are the main things that happened in the story?

　　　　　　　_____

　　　　　　　_____

Outcome　　How was the story problem resolved?

　　　　　　　_____

　　　　　　　_____

working alone or in small groups, with each student having a different part to work on. They can also be used in the prereading portion of the lesson. The teacher might give students a partially completed map and ask them to finish it after reading.

■ Retelling

One of the best devices for developing both comprehension and awareness of text structure has been around since the dawn of speech but is seldom used in classrooms—**retelling.** It has proved to be effective in improving comprehension and providing a sense of text structure for average learners and learning-disabled students (Koskinen, Gambrell, Kapinus, & Heathington, 1988; Rose, Cundick, & Higbee, 1983); it also develops language skills. Combining questions with retelling enhances the effectiveness of the technique. This was especially true in Morrow's study when the questions prompted students whose retelling was flagging or helped students elaborate.

There are several steps that can be taken to enhance students' retellings. Before students read or listen to a story they will be asked to retell, explain to them they

■ **Retelling** is the process of telling a story that one has read or heard. Retelling is used to check comprehension or gain insight into a student's reading processes.

will be asked to retell it. If you will be focusing on a specific aspect of the retelling, inform them of this; if you will be focusing on plot and sequence, ask them to note the main things that happen in the story and then try to remember them in order (Morrow, 1997). Also, use props. For instance, when giving a book talk about *Tomás and the Library Lady* (Mora, 1997), they might have a map to show where Tomás lived, plastic or real fruits to show that he picked fruit, and library books to show that he went to the library to get books (Vardell, 2002). Other visual aids include drawing a series of pictures of the main episodes in the tale and using these as a way of structuring the story.

In time, retelling can be a learning strategy. Students can be encouraged to retell stories or informational selections in their heads to help them better understand and remember what they have read (Koskinen, Gambrell, Kapinus, & Heathington, 1988).

■ Writing Stories

Story structure can also be used as a framework for composing stories. Laura Pessah, a staff developer at P.S. 148 in New York City, introduced students to the fact that books have different patterns of development (Calkins & Harwayne, 1991). Students discovered that some are a series of snapshots; others are circular, as the ending returns to the beginning; still others embody contrasts. Studying these structures gave students ideas about how they might organize picture books they were creating. However, students should be encouraged to follow the dictates of their own imaginations. As Calkins and Harwayne noted, too strict an adherence to structure could limit individual visions. Fitzgerald (1989) cautioned, "Strict adherence

A retelling has several advantages over the question–answer discussion format. A retelling is more holistic. It avoids the fragmentation of questions and answers about specific parts of a story. A retelling helps students assimilate the concept of story structure (Morrow, 1985).

ADAPTING INSTRUCTION for *ENGLISH LANGUAGE LEARNERS*
Because they are still learning English, retelling a story will be more difficult for ELL students but could be a valuable tool for developing language. Model the process and provide prompts. Also, start with simple stories and work up to more complex ones.

Narrative structures are easier to understand for a number of reasons. Children acquire familiarity with narratives before coming to school. Narratives incorporate one or several sequences of events. A sequence of events is a more familiar system of organizing knowledge than are main idea-details or other more abstract structures. Narrative structures are similar to oral language (Graesser, Golding, & Long, 1991).

*W*riting stories helps students develop a greater awareness of narrative structure.

to a particular story structure could have a detrimental effect, resulting in formulaic stories" (p. 20).

Expository Text

Generally speaking, stories are easier to read than science articles, how-to features, and descriptions of historical events (Graesser, Golding, & Long, 1991). Students' schema for **expository text** develops later than that for narration. Expository text has a greater variety of organizational patterns, and, typically, young students have limited experience hearing and reading it. Narrative text is linear; there is generally an initiating event and a series of following episodes which lead to a climax or high point, a resolution of the story problem, and the ending. Because of its structure and linear quality, narrative text is generally more predictable than expository text.

Narrative and expository text are also based on different ways of thinking. We think in narrative fashion and logical–scientific style. Narrative texts are based on the more straightforward style of thinking, whereas expository text is based on the more complex logical–scientific style (Bruner, 1986). If students are presented with narrative text only, they tend to focus on linear thinking (Trussell-Cullen, 1994). A mix of narrative and expository text is needed to promote a full range of thinking and comprehension skills.

Expository text is generally harder to read than narrative text because there is no story grammar to provide the reader with the overall organization of the piece. Instead, the reader usually has to integrate details in order to compose or verify a main idea. Reading expository text requires a more advanced type of thinking than reading narrative text. Reading an expository selection demands seeing interactions among facts or ideas. Because the content in an expository piece might be unfamiliar, the reader must comprehend new facts, retain them in memory, and integrate them with other facts in the selection to create a schema and/or integrate them with what he knows about the topic. This places a greater demand on memory and cognitive processing than does the typical narrative selection (Westby, 1999).

One key to comprehension of expository text is understanding the **text's structure**—that is, the way the author has organized her or his ideas. The author may develop an idea by listing a series of reasons, describing a location, supplying causes, or using some other technique. Often, content dictates structure. In science texts, students expect to see both descriptive passages that tell, for example, what a nerve cell is or what an anteater looks like and explanatory paragraphs that tell how a nerve cell passes on impulses or how an anteater obtains food.

Knowledge of structure has a three-way payoff. It focuses attention on individual ideas, it provides a clearer view of the relationship among ideas, and it is a framework to aid retention of information (Slater & Graves, 1989). The reader can use text structure to organize information from the text and build a situation model.

■ Types of Expository Text Structure

Listed below are some of the most important types of text structure (Armbruster & Anderson, 1981; Meyer & Rice, 1984):

■ **Expository text** is writing that is designed to explain or provide information.

■ **Text structure** is the way a piece of writing is organized: main idea–details, comparison–contrast, problem–solution, etc.

ADAPTING INSTRUCTION for *ENGLISH LANGUAGE LEARNERS*

Students who are still learning English can transfer their ability to use text structure in their native language to the ability to use it in English. However, students must be proficient readers in their native language and proficient in reading English (Hague, 1989). A lack of proficiency in English "short circuits" the transfer process.

1. *Enumeration–description.* This type of structure is a listing of details about a subject without any cause–effect or time relationship among them. Included in this category are structures that describe, give examples, and define concepts. It uses no specific signal words except in pieces that provide examples, where *for example* and *for instance* may be used as signals.

2. *Time sequence.* This type of structure is similar to enumeration; however, time order is specified. Signal words include the following:

after	first	and then
today	next	finally
afterward	second	earlier
tomorrow	then	dates
before	third	later

3. *Explanation–process.* An explanation tells how something works, such as how coal is formed, how a diesel engine works, or how a bill becomes law. Sequence may be involved, but steps in a process rather than time order are stressed. An explanation structure may include some of the same signal words as those found in a time-sequence structure.

4. *Comparison–contrast.* This type of structure presents differences and/or similarities. Signal words and terms include the following:

although	similar	on the one hand
but	different	on the other hand
however	different from	

5. *Problem–solution.* A statement of a problem is followed by a possible solution or series of solutions. Signal words are *problem* and *solution.*

6. *Cause–effect.* An effect is presented along with a single cause or a series of causes. Signal words and terms include the following:

because	therefore	thus
cause	since	for this reason
effect	as a result	consequently

Some kinds of text structure can facilitate comprehension and retention. Readers understand more and retain information better from text written in cause–effect or comparison–contrast patterns than they do when the text is written in an enumeration–description frame (Pearson & Camperell, 1994):

> These structures apparently provide readers with additional schemata to help them understand and remember the information. . . . [A comparison–contrast structure] indicates that the information will be about opposing views. . . . Cause–effect structures indicate that the information will be about problems and solutions. . . .
> [Enumeration–description structures] are more loosely organized, however, and do not provide additional information. (p. 460)

When reading, students need to activate two kinds of schema: prior knowledge and text structure. The content of a text cannot be separated from the way that content is expressed. Teachers are "well advised to model for students how to figure out what the author's general framework or structure is and allow students to practice finding it on their own" (Pearson & Camperell, 1994, p. 463).

To foster awareness of paragraph organization, one teacher divides a bulletin board into six segments, one for each type of paragraph organization. Students are encouraged to bring in examples of different types of paragraphs. Before the teacher places the sample, she reads it aloud, and the class discusses in which category it should be placed (Devine, 1986).

Although cause–effect structure aids comprehension, it is one that elementary school students may be less familiar with (Richgels, McGee, & Slaton, 1989).

■ Teaching Expository Text Structure

One way to teach expository text structure is simply to have students read a variety of expository materials. This may include periodicals, trade books, content-area textbooks, recipes, sets of directions, and other real-world materials. Teachers should also read expository prose aloud to students.

Before preparing students to read an expository piece, examine it for content and structure. Usually, the two will go together. Purpose questions and discussion questions should also reflect both features. For example, a brief biography of Abraham Lincoln may highlight the main events of his life and use a time-sequence structure. You might instruct students to note these events and their dates to help keep them in order.

Direct instruction in the recognition of text patterns is also helpful. Text patterns should be introduced one at a time. Start off with well-organized, single paragraphs that reflect the structure being taught. Signal words used in that structure should be presented. To provide practice in the recognition of signal words, use a cut-up paragraph or article and have students recreate the piece by using signal words and the sense of the piece as guides. For instance, students might use dates to help them rearrange a chronologically organized piece. Or they might use the signal words *first*, *second*, *next*, and *last* to arrange sentences or paragraphs explaining a step-by-step process.

Gradually, work up to longer selections. Whole articles and chapters often use several text structures, and students should be aware of that. However, in many cases, a particular structure dominates.

Using graphic organizers.　As a postreading activity, students might fill in a time line, as in Figure 6.2, to capitalize on both content and structure. Or they may use a graphic organizer, in which concepts are written in circles, rectangles, or triangles, and interrelationships are shown with lines and arrows. Generally, the more important ideas are shown at the top of the display and subordinate concepts are

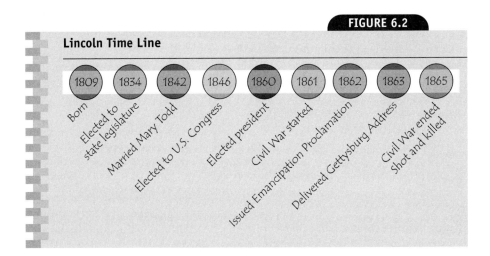

FIGURE 6.2

Lincoln Time Line

1809 — Born
1834 — Elected to state legislature
1842 — Married Mary Todd
1846 — Elected to U.S. Congress
1860 — Elected president
1861 — Civil War started
1862 — Issued Emancipation Proclamation
1863 — Delivered Gettysburg Address
1865 — Civil War ended; Shot and killed

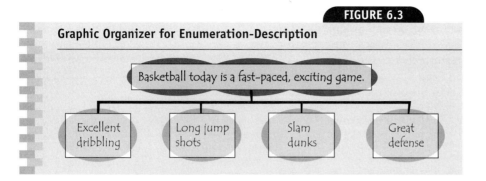

FIGURE 6.3

Graphic Organizer for Enumeration-Description

Basketball today is a fast-paced, exciting game.

| Excellent dribbling | Long jump shots | Slam dunks | Great defense |

shown at the bottom. The organizers can be constructed to reflect a variety of patterns (Sinatra, Stahl-Gemeke, & Berg, 1984; Sinatra, Stahl-Gemeke, & Morgan, 1986). After reading a selection, students complete an appropriate graphic organizer and, in so doing, organize the major concepts in a text and discover its underlying structural pattern. Graphic organizers for two major types of text structures, enumeration–description and time sequence, are presented in Figures 6.3 and 6.4.

STUDENT strategies   Using Text Structure

As you read, ask yourself these questions:
- How is the information organized?
- How can I use the organization of the text to help me organize the information so I can understand it better and remember it longer?
- Are there signal words? If so, how might I use them?

Using questions to make connections. Identifying the structure of a text is only a first step. The reader must then make two kinds of connections: internal (how ideas in the text are related to each other) and external (how text ideas are related to the reader's background) (Muth, 1987). The right kinds of questions can help

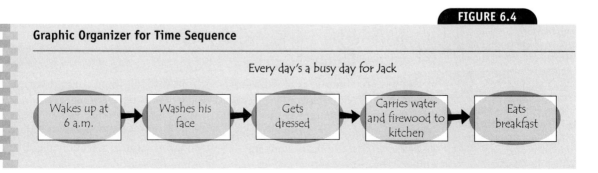

FIGURE 6.4

Graphic Organizer for Time Sequence

Every day's a busy day for Jack

| Wakes up at 6 a.m. | → | Washes his face | → | Gets dressed | → | Carries water and firewood to kitchen | → | Eats breakfast |

students detect relationships among ideas in a text. For instance, if the text has a cause–effect relationship, you can ask questions that highlight that relationship. Your questions can seek out causes or effects. Questions can also help the students relate ideas in the text to their own backgrounds. Here are some questions (adapted from Muth, 1987) that might be asked to help students who have read a piece about the process of rusting make internal connections:

> What causes rusting?
> What are some effects of rusting?
> Under what conditions does rusting take place fastest? Why?

These questions focus on external connections:

> What kinds of things rust in your house? Why?
> In what areas of the house do things rust? Why?
> What can be done to prevent rusting? Why would these preventive steps work?

Note that all these questions require students to establish internal or external cause–effect relationships. Questions can also be posed that facilitate establishing relationships in comparison–contrast, problem–solution, or other kinds of patterns. Once students have grasped the concept, have them create their own connection questions.

To help students incorporate structure in their writing, use frames in which students fill in the blanks with details or planning sheets which lead students step-by-step through the writing of a well-organized piece. Both of these are covered in detail in Chapter 10.

Writing for organization.   Another way to teach expository text structure is to encourage students to compose pieces that employ comparison–contrast and other types of structures. After reading a text that has an explanation–process structure, students might write an explanation of a process they find intriguing. Over time, they should have the opportunity to practice with all the major types of structures.

Students might also use photos or drawings to help them grasp a selection's organizational pattern. For time sequence, they might sequentially arrange photos of a vacation trip they have taken with their family. For explanation–process, they might create a series of drawings showing how to plant tomato seeds. They might use a series of photos to compare or contrast two vehicles, two countries, or two animals. After arranging the graphics, students can add a title, headings, and captions.

When asked inferential questions during the reading of a story, students generated inferences and included this information in a later retelling. The inferences they generated became a part of their memory for the story (Sundbye, 1987). Through questioning, they had constructed an elaborated version of the tale.

Using Narrative and Expository Text for Mutual Support

If students are about to read expository text on a difficult topic, arrange for them to read an informative narrative piece on the subject first. Before students read about Pearl Harbor, they might build their background knowledge by reading *A Boy at War, A Novel of Pearl Harbor* (Mazer, 2001). Before reading the novel *The New Land* (Reynolds, 1997), students might read an informational selection about emigration from Europe.

THE ROLE OF QUESTIONS IN COMPREHENSION

Questions play a central role in facilitating comprehension. They can be used to develop concepts, build background, clarify reasoning processes, and even lead students to higher levels of thinking. In one study, students became more adept at making inferences simply by being asked inferential questions (Hansen & Pearson, 1980).

Questions foster understanding and retention. When questions are asked about information in text, that information is remembered longer. Asking higher-level questions is especially helpful. Questioning that demands integrating information in a text "will promote deeper processing, and therefore more learning and better remembering than questions that require recall of specific facts only" (Sundbye, 1987, p. 85). As Wixson (1983) put it, "What you ask about is what children learn" (p. 287). If you ask questions about trivial facts, then those facts are what children will focus on and remember. The questions we ask shape students' comprehension and also their concept of what is important in a text.

> Asking "Why?" can increase retention of information (Menke & Pressley, 1994). One group of students was given paragraphs about animals and told to study the information in the paragraph. A second group was given the same paragraphs but was instructed to ask "Why?" after each piece of information. The group that asked why remembered significantly more.

Planning Questions

Because of their importance, questions need to be planned carefully. They should be used to establish the main elements in a story or the main concepts in a nonfiction selection (Beck, Omanson, & McKeown, 1982). Poor readers benefit from questions that elicit the basic elements in a selection (Medley, 1977). Once the basic plot of a story or the main facts in an article are established, students can be led to a deeper understanding of the material. It is important to ask questions that help students see relationships among ideas, relate new information to their background of experience, and modify their schema. Students must also have opportunities to respond in a personal way to literary pieces—to judge the material and apply the information they gather to their own lives.

Placement of Questions

The placement of questions has an impact upon their effect. Questions asked before reading help readers activate schema and set a purpose (Harris & Sipay, 1990). They guide readers into the text and tell them what information to seek. Questions that are asked after reading help readers organize and summarize the text. Questions asked during reading help readers process text. During-reading questions are especially helpful when used with struggling readers. Teachers may stop the reading of a selection halfway through or even at the end of each page and pose questions. Such questioning can clarify any confusing elements in text just read and prepare students to read the upcoming segment.

Types of Questions

One way of looking at questions is to examine the kinds of thinking processes involved in asking and answering them. An arrangement of skills from least demanding

■ A **taxonomy** is a classification of objectives, types of questions, or other items.

One of the simplest taxonomies is that which describes comprehension in terms of the reader's interaction with the text: literal, interpretive, and applied. Literal comprehension entails comprehending the basic meaning of the text. Interpretive comprehension entails making inferences by putting together several pieces of information or combining information from the text with the reader's knowledge. In applied comprehension, the reader makes use of ideas found in the text.

ADAPTING INSTRUCTION for _STRUGGLING READERS and WRITERS_

There is a tendency to give struggling readers mostly lower-level questions. Be sure to include some higher-level questions, but provide scaffolding and prompts as necessary.

to those that require the highest mental powers is known as a **taxonomy.** The following taxonomy or levels of questions is based on Weinstein and Mayer's (1986) system, which has also been used to classify the comprehension strategies described in this text. However, the first level, comprehending, is drawn from Bloom's (1957) taxonomy.

Comprehending. Students understand prose on a literal level. They can recite five facts stated in a selection, name the main characters, and indicate dates and places. This level also includes having students put information in their own words.

Organizing. Students select important details from the selection and construct relationships among them. This involves identifying or constructing main ideas, classifying, noting sequence, and summarizing.

Elaborating. Elaborating entails making connections between information from the text and prior knowledge and includes a wide range of activities: making inferences, creating images and analogies, and evaluating or judging.

Monitoring. Monitoring involves being aware of cognitive processes. It entails knowing whether a selection makes sense and knowing what steps might be taken to repair comprehension.

Listed below are examples of each type of question. They are drawn from _Supergiants: The Biggest Dinosaurs_ (Lessem, 1997).

Comprehending

Which of the dinosaurs was the biggest? When was the biggest dinosaur discovered? Which of the dinosaurs was the longest?

Organizing

In what ways were the biggest dinosaurs alike? In what ways were they different?

Elaborating

How do you know that Professor Rodolfo is determined and hard-working? In your mind, picture Argentinosaurus. What does Argentinosaurus look like? What is the area where Argentinosaurus lives like? What sounds do you hear?

Monitoring

Did you find any confusing parts? Did you run into any words that you couldn't read or whose meanings you didn't know? If so, what did you do? Can you summarize each dinosaur's main characteristics? If you forget some important details, what might you do?

Using Wait Time

■ **Wait time** is a period of silence between asking a question and repeating or rephrasing the question, calling on another student, or making some sort of comment.

One way of extending responses is to make use of **wait time.** Teachers often expect an immediate answer and, when none is forthcoming, call on another student. Waiting five seconds results in longer, more elaborative responses, higher-level thought processes, and fewer no-responses and I-don't-knows. Teachers who use wait time become more proficient at helping students clarify and expand their responses (Dillon, 1983; Gambrell, 1980). It would be difficult to find a better instructional use of five seconds of silence.

Silence after an answer is given also helps. Used to rapid-fire responding, teachers tend to call on another pupil the second the respondent stops talking. Often, however, students have more to say if given a few moments to catch their mental breath. Dillon (1983) suggested waiting from three to five seconds when a student pauses, seems to be unable to continue, or seems to be finished speaking. Often the student will resume talking and may even supply the most thoughtful part of the response at that point. Such postresponse wait time must be a genuine grace period. Maintain eye contact and do not turn away. Failing to maintain eye contact and turning away are cues that your attention is being diverted and will shut down any additional response that the student is about to make (Christenbury & Kelly, 1983).

> Wait time requires practice and patience; you will have to make a conscious effort to implement it. Try counting to five thousand by thousands after asking a question or after a student has halted an initial response. Ask a colleague to evaluate your beginning attempts.

Classroom Atmosphere

Even more important than using wait time or asking thought-provoking questions is establishing the right classroom atmosphere. The spirit of inquiry and exploration should be obvious. The teacher must be warm and accepting, so students will feel free to speculate, go out on an intellectual limb, or take an unpopular stand without being criticized. Criticism by teachers or classmates actually leads to lowered performance. Less emphasis should be placed on the rightness or wrongness of an answer and more on the reasons supporting the response.

Questions should be democratic, with everyone's contribution valued. That means calling on slower students as often as brighter ones and giving introverts as much opportunity to respond as extroverts. Ironically, research suggests that not only are bright students asked more questions than are slow students but also they are given more prompts (Brophy & Good, 1970). All too often, the teacher calls on another student as soon as a slower learner begins to falter. Thus, the ones who would profit the most from prompting receive the least.

> Teacher's guides may include an excessive number of questions. If so, ask only the most relevant ones. Note the major concepts or ideas that you want students to take away from their reading and then restrict questions to the ones that lead to those learnings.

Techniques for Asking Questions

Discussions should be considered opportunities to expand students' background and enhance their verbal and thinking skills. All too often, however, discussions become oral quizzes with a focus on correct answers; emphasis should instead be on helping the student. If a student is unable to provide an answer, it may be the fault of the question—rephrase it, or ask an easier one (Pearson & Johnson, 1978). Some students, because of shyness or because they come from an environment that does not prepare them for the types of questions asked in school, have difficulty answering higher-level questions (Heath, 1991). They may know the answers but must be prompted to help shape their responses. Questioning procedures that make effective use of prompts are described below.

> Searfoss and Readence (1994) caution against asking questions that are too diffuse. A question such as: "What is the main idea of the selection?" is so general that it fails to provide the kind of structure that helps prompt a response. Rather than asking a single general question, it would be better to ask several questions that are more specific and provide better support.

■ FELS

A useful, research-based technique for using questions to evoke higher-level thinking processes was devised by Taba (1965). Known by the acronym FELS, it consists of asking questions and using prompts and probes that are focusing, extending, lifting, and substantiating.

Hyman (1978) describes a technique similar to FELS as being the plateaus approach. Using this technique, the questioner asks at least three questions on one level of cognition, thereby establishing a plateau, before asking a higher-level question and moving to a higher plateau.

Focusing questions, as the name implies, direct the student's attention to a particular topic—for example, the peculiar behavior of Sam, a character in a story. The teacher asks literal questions designed to help students describe that behavior.

Extending questions are designed to elicit clarification and elaboration. By extending the student's thoughts on the same level, they might seek additional information about a character or event and clear up points of confusion. Extending is important because it prepares students for the next step and also provides slower students with an opportunity to become involved.

Lifting is the crucial stage. Through questioning or other means, the teacher lifts the discussion to a higher level. Through focusing and extending, the teacher has established that Sam refused to go into the reptile house on the class trip to the zoo, would not get out of the car when the family stopped for a picnic in the woods, and has not visited his friend Joe since Joe obtained a pet snake. The teacher asks, "What do all these actions tell us about Sam?" Now, instead of just giving factual responses, students are asked to draw the conclusion that Sam is afraid of snakes.

Substantiating questions ask students what evidence they found or what standards or criteria they used to draw a conclusion, make a judgment, or prove a point—for example, the evidence that Sam is afraid of snakes.

The following example shows how FELS might be used to build higher-level comprehension. The questions are based on a selection about Andrea, a knowledgeable backpacker who is trekking through the forest.

Focusing

Teacher: Where was Andrea?
Student: Forest.
Teacher: What did she watch out for?
Student: Snakes.
Teacher: What was she wearing?
Student: Shirt and jeans.

Extending

Teacher: What else did she watch out for besides snakes?
Student: I don't know.
Teacher: Let's look back over the story.
Student: Oh, I see. She was watching out for poison ivy.
Teacher: What kind of shirt was she wearing?
Student: Old.
Teacher: What kind of sleeves did it have?
Student: Long.

Lifting

Teacher: We usually judge people by their actions. Think over Andrea's actions. What do they tell us about her? What kind of person does she seem to be?
Student: Careful.

BUILDING LANGUAGE

Probing and prompting students' responses helps them to use higher-level language and more elaborated language.

Substantiating

Teacher: Which actions led you to believe that Andrea is careful?

Student: She watched out for snakes and poison ivy. She wore a shirt with long sleeves so she wouldn't get poison ivy or insect bites.

Taba (1965) cautioned that FELS should be used with care. Frequent shifting from level to level may produce a lack of sustained achievement at any level and result in a return to a more basic level. It is also important for teachers to encourage students to reason out and substantiate their answers. If teachers do the students' thinking for them, the strategy is ineffective. Timing and pacing are also important. The teacher has to know, for example, when to proceed to a higher level. Moving to lifting before building a solid understanding of the selection through focusing and extending hinders students' progress. It is also important that the FELS procedure be individualized, as some students require more time on a level than others (Taba, 1965).

> All too often, our responses to questions correctly answered are a lukewarm "That's right" or "Uh-huh." Try using a stronger response such as "You're absolutely right!" or "That's a very thoughtful observation!" (Hyman, 1978).

■ Responsive Elaboration

Despite use of a carefully constructed questioning procedure such as FELS, students' thought processes sometimes go astray. They may have misinterpreted instructions or may be misapplying a strategy. A procedure that works well in these instances is **responsive elaboration** (Duffy & Roehler, 1987). Responsive elaboration is not an introduction to or a new explanation of a strategy or skill but an elaboration. It is responsive because it is based on students' answers, which are used as guides to students' thought processes.

> ■ **Responsive elaboration** is a process of asking a student to tell why an idea or concept is true or why something works the way it does.

To use responsive elaboration, teachers listen to answers to determine how students arrived at those responses. Instead of asking, "Is this answer right or wrong?" they ask, "What thought processes led the student to this response?" And, if the answer is wrong, "How can those thought processes be redirected?" Instead of calling on another student, telling where the answer might be found, or giving obvious hints, teachers ask questions or make statements that help put students' thinking back on the right track. The key to using responsive elaboration is asking yourself two questions: "What has gone wrong with the student's thinking?" and "What can I ask or state that would guide the student's thinking to the right thought processes and correct answer?"

The following is a scripted example of how a teacher might use responsive elaboration with a student who has inferred a main idea that is too narrow in scope:

Student (giving incorrect main idea): Getting new words from Indians.

Teacher: Well, let's test it. Is the first sentence talking about new words from the Indians?

Student: Yes.

Teacher: Is the next?

Student: Yes.

Teacher: How about the next?

Student: No.

Teacher: No. It says that Indians also learned new words from the settlers, right? Can you fit that into your main idea?

Student: The Indians taught the settlers words and the settlers taught the Indians words.

Teacher: Good. You see, you have to think about all the ideas in the paragraph to decide on the main idea. (Duffy & Roehler, 1987, p. 517)

■ Other Probes and Prompts

In addition to the probes and prompts recommended in FELS and responsive elaboration, there are several additional ones that can be used to foster students' thinking. If students' answers are too brief, use an elaboration probe: "Would you please tell me more?" If a response is unclear, you might use a restating–crystallizing probe. In this probe, you restate what you believe the student said and then ask whether your restatement is correct: "You seem to be saying that Gopher should have told someone about his problem. Is that right?" The purpose of a restating-crystallizing probe is to help the speaker clarify her or his thoughts. It can also be used to keep the speaker on track if she or he has gotten off the subject (Hyman, 1978).

FRAMEWORKS FOR FOSTERING COMPREHENSION

Asking the right kinds of questions, building background, activating schema, learning to use strategies, and monitoring one's cognitive processes are all essential elements in fostering comprehension. Systematic but unified approaches that incorporate all these elements are required so that building background and vocabulary and prereading and postreading questions are all related to the selection's major concepts and the students' needs. Three such frameworks are guided reading, the directed reading activity, and the directed reading–thinking activity.

Guided Reading

■ **Guided reading** is an instructional framework within which the teacher supplies whatever help or guidance students need to read a story successfully.

Guided reading is a framework within which the teacher supplies whatever assistance or guidance students need in order for them to read a selection successfully (Fountas & Pinnell, 1996; Fountas & Pinnell, 2001). Guided reading is used with individuals or groups who are on approximately the same level of reading development. Selections are provided that match the students' level of development. Students should know most but not all of the words (at least 95 percent). Selections should contain some challenge so that students could apply strategies but should not contain so many new words or unfamiliar concepts as to be overwhelming. "The ultimate goal in guided reading is to help children learn how to use independent reading strategies successfully" (Fountas & Pinnell, 1996, p. 2). This includes both word recognition and comprehension strategies. Students read silently and, as they progress in skill, they read increasingly more difficult selections or whole books.

The amount of guidance provided varies depending on students' abilities and the complexity of the selection to be read. For struggling readers, the guidance might consist of going through the text page by page and discussing the selection and highlighting unfamiliar expressions, unknown concepts, and difficult words. This is known as a text walk. For achieving readers, guidance may consist of a directed reading activity, a directed reading–thinking activity, or KWL.

To be effective, guided reading must be organized. Although organized instruction is not necessarily effective, a lack of organization will derail even the most potentially effective lesson. Guided reading instruction is best held around a u-shaped or round table so that you are facing all the students. Place nearby in a box, crate, or rolling cart needed supplies: paper, magic marker, easel with white board, pocket chart, audiovisual materials, dictionary, copies of the selection to be read, and whatever other materials are needed (Fountas & Pinnell, 2001). Try to meet with groups every day. If this is not possible, try to schedule meetings on several consecutive days. For the sake of continuity, it is better to meet three consecutive days than it is to meet every other day (Fountas & Pinnell, 2001). For struggling readers and those who have difficulty sustaining attention, plan to read texts that can be completed in one or two sessions.

While students are reading silently, you can work individually with members of the group, or you may work with another group until the original group finishes reading silently. Usually students can read a 1,000-word selection in about ten minutes. However, rate of reading varies greatly. Some students might read the selection in five minutes, others might take fifteen. Students who finish early might complete a story map, character web, or literary sociogram, or engage in a similar activity. Or they might respond in their journals or read from one of their independent reading books.

> See Chapter 9 for suggestions for managing guided reading and providing the rest of the class with useful activities while you are working with groups.

> **ADAPTING INSTRUCTION for *STRUGGLING READERS and WRITERS***
> Although originally used with young readers, the text walk technique can be used with older students who are struggling with reading.

Directed Reading Activity

The **directed reading activity** (DRA) is probably the most widely used and the most highly respected instructional procedure used in reading and is a form of guided reading. A flexible procedure, the DRA is the basis for a number of teaching techniques, including the directed reading–thinking activity and the instructional framework. The traditional DRA has five steps: preparation or readiness, silent reading, discussion and skill development, rereading, and follow-up. Today's DRA also incorporates schema theory, metacognition, and text analysis (Adoption Guidelines Project, 1990) and may also include strategy review (Gaskins, 1998).

> ■ **Directed reading activity** is a traditional five-step lesson plan designed to assist students in the reading of a selection.

■ Steps in a Directed Reading Activity
An updated DRA proceeds as follows.

Preparation.   Through discussion, demonstration, use of audiovisual aids, and/or simulations, students are given guidance in the following areas:

- *Experiential background or concepts.* Experiential gaps that impede understanding of the selection's major concepts are filled in. If students are about to read a piece about solar power but have no experience with the subject, the teacher might demonstrate the workings of a solar toy. Concepts or ideas crucial to understanding the selection are also developed. Batteries would be an important concept in this instance; however, in the discussion, students might indicate that they know that batteries are necessary to make certain devices run, but they do not know why. The battery's use as a device for storing energy would then be discussed.

■ *Critical vocabulary*. Vocabulary necessary for understanding the selection is presented. For a factual article about Australia's animals, the words *kangaroos*, *marsupials*, and *herbivores* are presented. Care is taken to show how these words are related to each other.

■ *Reading strategies*. Students have to know how a selection is to be read. Most selections require a mix of preparational, organizational, and elaboration strategies. However, some strategies work better than others with certain kinds of materials. An editorial, for example, requires evaluation. A fictional story might require students to visualize the setting. At times, the format might be unfamiliar. For example, before tackling a play, students should be given tips on techniques for reading stage directions and dialogue. Because teaching a strategy is time consuming, it would be best if the needed strategy were taught beforehand and then briefly reviewed during the preparatory discussion.

■ *Purpose for reading*. Whether set by the teacher or the class, the purpose for reading usually embraces the overall significance of the selection. It may grow out of the preparatory discussion. Students discussing hearing-ear dogs might want to find out how they are chosen, and that would become the purpose for reading. On other occasions, the teacher might set the reading purpose.

■ *Interest*. Last but not least, the teacher tries to create interest in the selection. To do this in a piece about an explorer lost in a jungle, the teacher might read the portion of the selection that describes the dangers the explorer faced.

For the purpose of clarity, the elements in the preparation step have been described separately, but in actual practice they are merged. For instance, background concepts and the vocabulary used to label them are presented at the same time. The purpose for reading flows from the overall discussion, and throughout the discussion, the teacher tries to create an interest in the selection. Reading strategies might become a part of the purpose: "Read the story straight through, but read it carefully, to find out how the Great Brain solved the mystery" (reading purpose); "Look for clues as you read the story and try to figure out what they mean" (reading strategy).

Silent reading. The first reading is usually silent. Silent reading is preferred because reading is a meaning-obtaining process rather than a speech activity. What a student understands is more important than how the selection's words are pronounced. During silent reading, a student might reread a difficult portion of text, get help from an illustration, use context, look up a word in the glossary, or take other steps to foster comprehension. Normally, none of these steps would be taken during an oral reading (Hammond, 2001). During the silent reading, the teacher should be alert to any problems that students might be having. If the class is listless, the piece may be too difficult or too boring. If it is humorous and no one is chuckling, perhaps the humor is too sophisticated or too childish. Finger

pointing and lip movement are signs that individuals are having difficulty with the selection. The teacher should also be available to give assistance as needed, making note of who requested help and what kinds of help were supplied. Those students can then be scheduled for added instruction or practice in those areas. Reading speed should also be noted. Very fast reading with good comprehension might be a sign that materials are too easy. Very slow reading might be a sign that they are too difficult.

During the silent reading, students should monitor their comprehension to check whether they adequately understand what they are reading and, if necessary, take appropriate steps to correct the difficulties. The teacher should note these monitoring and repair strategies. In some classrooms, steps for attacking unfamiliar words or repairing comprehension failure are posted in prominent spots.

Discussion. The discussion complements the purpose for reading. Students read a selection for a specific purpose; the discussion begins with the purpose question. If the students read about how hearing-ear dogs are trained, the purpose question is "How are hearing-ear dogs trained?" During the discussion, concepts are clarified and expanded, background is built, and relationships between known and unknown, new and old are reinforced.

Difficulties applying comprehension and word-attack strategies are corrected spontaneously, if possible. The teacher also evaluates students' performance, noting whether they were able to consider evidence carefully and draw conclusions and noting weaknesses in concepts, comprehension, word attack, and application. Any difficulties noted provide direction not only for immediate help for those that can be resolved on the spot, but also for future lessons for those that require more work. Although the discussion is partly evaluative, it should not be regarded as an oral quiz. Its main purpose is to build understanding, not test it. Questioning techniques, such as probes, prompts, FELS, and wait time should be used. Part of the discussion might also be devoted to asking students to describe their use of strategies, with a focus on the strategy being emphasized.

Rereading. In most lessons, rereading blends in naturally with the discussion. It may be done to correct misinformation, to obtain additional data, to enhance appreciation or deepen understanding, and to give students opportunities for purposeful oral reading. During the discussion of hearing-ear dogs, students might indicate that they believe the dogs are easy to train (a mistaken notion). Students can then be directed to locate and read aloud passages that describe how long training takes. If students disagree as to what main character traits such dogs should possess, they can be asked to locate and read orally passages that support their assertions.

On occasion, rereading may be an entirely separate step. For instance, students might dramatize a story that has a substantial amount of dialogue or reread a selection to gain a deeper appreciation of the author's style. A separate reading is generally undertaken for a new purpose, although it may be for a purpose that grows out of the discussion. Rereading is not a necessary step. Some selections are not worth reading a second time, or students might grasp the essence in the first reading.

In the rereading stage, oral reading should not be overemphasized. Unless a selection is being dramatized, it is generally a poor practice to have students reread an entire selection orally. Oral rereading should be for specific purposes: to clarify a point, to listen to a humorous passage or enjoy an especially vivid description, and to substantiate a conclusion or an answer to a question.

Follow-up.   Follow-up or extension activities offer opportunities to work on comprehension or word-attack weaknesses evidenced during the discussion phase, to provide additional practice, to extend concepts introduced in the selection, or to apply skills and strategies. These activities may involve any or all of the language arts or creative arts. Students might read a selection on the same topic or by the same author, draw illustrations for the selection, hold a panel discussion on a controversial idea, create an advertisement for the text, or write a letter to the author. The possibilities are virtually limitless, but the follow-up should grow out of the selection and should encompass worthwhile language or creative arts activities. As with rereading, it is not necessary to have follow-up or extension activities for every reading. In fact, follow-up activities should be conducted sparingly. "Extending every book (brief books that can be read in a single sitting) through art, writing, or drama is impractical and could interfere with time needed to read widely" (Fountas & Pinnell, 1996, p. 3).

■ Preparing a Directed Reading Activity

Creating a DRA starts with an analysis of the selection to be read. After reading the selection, the teacher decides what she or he wants the students to learn from it. Content analysis of fiction may result in statements about plot, theme, charac-

> The directed reading activity is probably the most widely used instructional technique. A flexible procedure, the DRA is the basis for a number of teaching techniques, including guided reading, the directed reading–thinking activity, and the instructional framework.

*D*uring a directed or guided reading activity discussion, students may be asked to go back to the text to find support for a statement.

ter, setting, or author's style. For nonfiction, the statements concern the main principles, ideas, concepts, rules, or whatever the students are expected to learn. After analyzing the selection, the teacher chooses two or three ideas or story elements that she or he feels are most important. The piece may be saturated with important concepts; however, more than two or three cannot be handled in any depth at one time and could diffuse the focus of the activity. Even if an accompanying teacher's guide lists important concepts or provides key story events, the teacher should still complete a content analysis. That way, the teacher, not the textbook author, decides what is important for the class to learn. For example, for a piece entitled "Dream Cars for the 2000s," the teacher composes the following major learnings. These will provide the focus for prereading and postreading activities and strategies for prereading, during reading, and postreading.

> The T-2008 will be easier to care for, repair, and guide.
> The T-2008 will be safer and more flexible.
> The Express will be faster.

After selecting these major ideas, the teacher lists vocabulary necessary to understand them. If the list contains a dozen terms, the teacher knows that is too many to attempt to cover. As a rule of thumb, no more than five or six vocabulary words should be chosen. An excessive number of difficult words may be a sign that the selection is too difficult.

The teacher selects the words that will be difficult for the students. From the list of difficult words, those most essential to an understanding of the selection are chosen. For example, the following words are chosen as most essential to understanding the three learnings listed for the dream cars selection and as being ones that students are likely to find difficult: *turbine engine, protective devices, sensors, communicate,* and *satellites*. Examining these words gives the teacher a sense of what prior knowledge or schema the passage requires. A mental assessment of the students helps the teacher decide whether additional background has to be built. For example, poor urban children whose families do not own a car may have very limited experience with cars and so would require more background than middle-class children whose families own one or two cars.

Once the major understandings and difficult vocabulary words have been chosen, the teacher looks over the selection to decide what major cognitive and reading strategies are necessary to understand it. For the dream cars selection, visualizing and using illustrations would be helpful strategies. Comprehension should be improved if students visualize the futuristic vehicles and their major capabilities and characteristics. In addition, the photos illustrating the cars being described should help students understand the text.

Building background and vocabulary, activating schema, piquing interest, setting purposes, and giving guidance in reading and cognitive strategies are all done in the preparatory segment of the lesson. Generally, this takes the form of a discussion. Key vocabulary words are written on the board. When discussing each word, the teacher points to it on the board so that students become familiar with it in print. Lesson 6.1 presents a sample DRA for "Dream Cars for the 2000s."

A sample DRA

Step 1. Preparation

The DRA in Lesson 6.1 is just one of many possible lessons. Another teacher might choose to stress different understandings and would tailor discussion and other activities to match her or his teaching style and the abilities, backgrounds, and interests of the students. The teacher might also choose different purposes for rereading or elect not to have any follow-up.

(During the discussion, the teacher introduces vocabulary words and concepts that might be difficult for students. These are italicized. As the teacher mentions the words, she or he points to each, which has already been written on the board.) To start the discussion, the teacher asks, "What is your favorite car? What do you like best about that car? If you were a designer of cars for the future, what kind of a dream car would you build? What kind of an engine would you put in it? A *turbine engine*? Why or why not? (Explain that a turbine engine is used on jets.) How many passengers would your car hold? What kind of *protective devices* would it have? Protective devices are things like air bags and seat belts that help keep passengers safe in case of a crash. Would you have any devices that would help you *communicate*? What do we do when we communicate? Would your car make use of *satellites*? What are satellites, and how might they help car drivers in the future? What kind of *sensors* might the car have? What do sensors do? (Although judged to be difficult for students, the key words *module* and *guidance system* are not introduced because it is felt that they are adequately explained in the selection.) Now that we have talked over some of the parts of a future car, put all your ideas together, close your eyes, and picture your dream car and its main parts. (Students are given a few minutes to picture their dream cars.) What do your dream cars look like? (Students discuss possible dream cars.) Read 'Dream Cars for the 2000s.' Find out what two of tomorrow's dream cars, the T-2008 and the Express, are like. As you read, use the imaging strategy that we have been studying. (Teacher briefly goes over the steps of the strategy, which are posted in the front of the room.) Try to picture in your mind what the car or car part looks like or what's happening in the car. Also look at the pictures of the T-2008 and Express. They will help you to understand the selection."

Step 2. Silent reading

During silent reading, the teacher looks around to get a sense of the students' reactions to the story. Their silence suggests that they are intrigued. She notes that most of them are glancing at the photos as they read. One student raises his hand and asks for help with the word *ambulance*. The teacher suggests that he look for pronounceable word parts and put them together; when he is unable to do so or use an analogy or contextual strategy successfully, she asks whether the word *ambulance* or *animal* would fit the sense of the selection. Another student has difficulty with *anniversary*, a third with *efficiently*, and a fourth with *kilometers*. The teacher makes a note to work with polysyllabic words in the future.

Step 3. Discussion

The teacher begins the discussion with the purpose question "What are the T-2008 and Express like?" Additional questions flow from the students' responses; however, the teacher keeps in mind the three major understandings that she wants students to learn and will make sure that they are explored: "Why might a variety of people buy the T-2008? What could an owner who needed more passenger room do? How many passengers will the T-2008 hold?" There is some disagreement, and the teacher asks the class to go back over the story to find a passage that will answer the question. Then she asks, "How will the T-2008 use a satellite link?" The class seems confused. Satellite link is an important concept. The teacher decides that it is worth some in-depth teaching. She directs the class to go back over the part that tells about it. She reminds students to try to picture in their minds how the satellite link operates and suggests that after rereading the section, they make a drawing showing how it works. The drawings are discussed, demonstrating students' improved understanding. The teacher asks further questions: "How will the driver and the car use the satellite link? Why will the T-2008 be hard to steal? Why do you think there will be fewer accidents with a T-2008? In case of an accident, would the passengers be safer than if they were in a regular car? What is the Express like? Which car do you like better? How do these cars compare with your dream car?

"What strategies did you use to help you read the story? How did the pictures help? How did imaging help? Which parts of the selection did you image? What did your image look like? Did it have sounds? What were the sounds like?"

Step 4. Rereading

During the discussion, the teacher notes that the students had difficulty scanning through the selection to find facts that would justify their responses. The next day, she reviews the skill of scanning. She models the process and explains why it is important and when it is used. She gives the class a series of questions whose answers are numerals, alerting them to this fact so they know to look for numerals rather than words. The questions are "What does T-2008 stand for? How fast does the Express go? When will cars like the Express be seen?"

The teacher also reviews methods for attacking multisyllabic words and stresses the importance of both syllabication and context. Students scan to find the words *information, ambulance, notified, location, kilometers,* and *anniversary,* which are examined in context. Students use both syllabication and context clues to figure them out. As a review of vocabulary, students create and then discuss semantic maps for words they learned in "Dream Cars for the 2000s."

Step 5. Follow-up

Some students design their own dream cars and create ads for them. Others read books about transportation in the future or other books about cars. Still others elect to read about satellites. A few write to auto manufacturers to obtain information about the newest experimental cars. One group checks the Internet for information about experimental cars. They look under the heading "Concept Cars." The class also makes plans to visit the auto show.

■ A **story elements map** lists the key components of a story: theme, problem, plot, and needed concepts. One way of creating a story elements map is to begin by noting the problem or the conflict. Then list the major events leading up to the resolution. At that point, use that information to compose the story's theme or moral. You might also list the key characters and also identify and list any vocabulary or concepts needed to understand the key elements of the story. Then create questions that focus on the central elements of the story.

■ **DRA for Fiction**

The sample DRA in Lesson 6.1 was written for informational text. A lesson for a piece of fiction would incorporate the same features; however, it might use a **story elements map** instead of a list of main concepts as the framework. Created by Beck, Omanson, and McKeown (1982), story elements maps result in better questions and improved comprehension. Basically the teacher asks him- or herself, "What is the core of this story?" and then gears questions for students to it. To reach the core, the teacher decides what the starting point of the story is and then lists "the major events and ideas that constitute the plot or gist of the story, being sure to include implied ideas that are part of the story though not part of the text, and the links between events and ideas that unify the story" (Beck, Omanson, & McKeown, 1982, p. 479). A sample story elements map is presented in Figure 6.5.

A story elements map provides a sense of the most important elements in a story, allowing the teacher to gear preparatory and postreading activities to understanding those elements. Preliminary questions lead up to the story; postreading questions enhance understanding of its main elements. Questions about style and questions that lead to appreciation of the author's craft are asked after the reader has a grasp of the essentials. However, some provision should be made for eliciting a personal response.

Directed Reading–Thinking Activity

■ **Directed reading–thinking activity (DR–TA)** is an adaptation of the directed reading activity in which readers use preview and prediction strategies to set their own purposes for reading.

The DRA is primarily a teacher-directed lesson. The **DR–TA (directed reading–thinking activity)** has been designed to help students begin to take responsibility for their own learning. Although based on the DRA, the DR–TA puts the ball in the students' court. The teacher leads them to establish their own purposes for reading, to decide when these purposes have been fulfilled, and to attack unfamiliar words independently. The DR–TA works best when students have background knowledge to bring to the selection and can attack difficult words independently. If students are lacking in background or have weak word analysis skills, then the DRA is a better choice.

Stauffer (1970), the creator of the DR–TA, based the approach on our penchant for predicting and hypothesizing. By nature, we have an innate tendency to look ahead. We are also decision-making creatures who need opportunities as well as the freedom to make decisions. Building on these propensities, Stauffer structured a predict–read strategy that has the following facets:

- *Setting purposes.* Students have to know how to ask questions about text they are about to read.
- *Obtaining information.* Students have to know how to sift through reading material to get the information they need to answer a question.
- *Keeping goals in mind.* Students must be able to work within the constraints of their goals, noting information that fits in with these goals and not being led astray by information that does not.
- *Keeping personal feelings in bounds.* Students have to be able to suspend personal judgments when reading a piece that contains ideas with which they might

FIGURE 6.5

A Story Elements Map

Title: *Earthquake Terror*

Author: Peg Kehret

Theme: It's important to keep calm in time of danger.

Problem: When his parents leave the campsite because his mom has broken her ankle, Jonathan takes care of his partially paralyzed little sister in a time of danger.

Plot: Jonathan's mom breaks her ankle while the family is camping in the woods of Magpie Island.

Jonathan's dad drives his mom to town.

Jonathan takes care of his little sister who is partially paralyzed.

An earthquake strikes.

Jonathan and his sister take cover under a large fallen tree.

Jonathan's sister is hurt.

Jonathan calms his sister.

Ending: Jonathan gets to the mainland.

Needed Concepts or Ideas: During an earthquake it is important to follow safety rules such as finding a shelter that is safe from falling trees and to stay calm.

not agree, at least until they have finished the piece and have a good grasp of what the author is trying to say.

■ *Considering options.* Students must be able to consider a number of choices as they make their predictions and also be flexible enough to change or refine a prediction in the light of new information.

Like the DRA, the DR–TA has five steps, as outlined in Lesson 6.2. The major difference is that students are given a more active role in the DR–TA (Stauffer, 1969).

A DR–TA

LESSON 6.2

Step 1. Preparation

Students are led to create their own purposes for reading. The title of the selection, headings and subheads, illustrations, and/or the beginning paragraph are used to stimulate predictions about the content of the selection. For example, in preparation for reading "Live Cargo!" which is the first chapter of *Misty of Chincoteague* (Henry, 1947), the teacher might have the

One problem with using the DR–TA is that developing students' background knowledge and vocabulary prior to reading a selection might be neglected (Tierney, Readence, & Dishner, 1995). To build background, spend additional time with the predicting phase. While discussing the title and illustrations and other elements needed to make predictions, build essential background and vocabulary. One indicator that students may not have adequate background is difficulty in making reasonable predictions.

students examine the first illustration—a Spanish galleon. After discussing it, the teacher would have the students read the title of the chapter and then ask them what they think the chapter might be about. Responses, which might include slaves, prisoners, horses, and cattle, would be written on the board. Because the DR–TA is an active process, all students are encouraged to make a prediction or at least to indicate a preference for one of the predictions made by others. The teacher reads the predictions aloud and asks students to raise their hands to show which one they think is most likely.

Step 2. Silent reading

Students read silently until they are able to evaluate their predictions; this might entail reading a single page, several pages, or a whole chapter. Students are encouraged to modify their initial predictions if they find information that runs counter to them.

Step 3. Discussion

This stage is almost identical to Step 3 of the DRA, except that it begins with the consideration of the class's predictions. After reading a portion of "Live Cargo!" students evaluate their predictions and identify which ones were correct and which required rethinking. Additional questions flowing from the sense of the selection are then asked: "Where were the ponies being taken? Why was the captain headed for trouble? What is a stallion?" During the discussion, students offer proof of the adequacy of their predictions or clarify disputed points by reading passages orally. As in the DRA, the teacher develops comprehension, background, and concepts as the need arises and the opportunity presents itself. The discussion also leads students into making further predictions, as the teacher asks, "Why do you think the captain is angry with the stallion? What do you think will happen next?" If students do not respond to these prediction-making questions, the questions should be rephrased or altered. For instance, after getting no response to the question "What do you think will happen next?" the teacher might ask, "What do you think will happen to the stallion and the ponies?" The teacher might also read a few paragraphs aloud to stimulate predictions. As in Step 1, predictions are written on the board and students select the ones they believe are best or most probable.

Step 4. Rereading

This is the same as Step 4 of the DRA (see p. 255).

Step 5. Follow-up

This is the same as Step 5 of the DRA (see p. 255).

    The DR–TA should be used with both fiction and nonfiction. If students apply the strategies of surveying, predicting, sifting, and verifying to fiction only, they may not develop the ability to transfer these to nonfiction. In time, the strategies practiced in the DR–TA should become automatic.

KWL, an approach introduced in the next chapter, is useful when you want to assess and make use of students' backgrounds.

THE CLOZE PROCEDURE

Another approach used to foster comprehension is cloze; it is illustrated in the following exercise. As you read the paragraph, supply the missing words.

> If we see a part of a person or object, we tend to fill in the missing portions. If someone omits the final word of a sentence, we supply it _____ her or him. There is something about the human _____ that can't _____ incompleteness. This tendency to fill in what's _____ is the basis of cloze, a technique by which readers achieve closure by filling in the _____ words in a selection. Based on the concept of gestalt _____, cloze was first proposed as a _____ for measuring the difficulty _____ of reading material. Today it is also used to test reading ability and to build comprehension.

Cloze is an excellent device for building comprehension. Filling in missing words forces a reader to use semantic and syntactic clues together with symbol–sound information and to predict meaning. It also activates the reader's background knowledge. The reader's knowledge of the world must be used to figure out which words should be put in the blanks. Cloze works especially well with students who are concentrating so hard on sounding out words that they fail to read for meaning.

> ■ **Cloze** is a procedure in which the reader demonstrates comprehension by supplying missing words. Cloze is short for "closure," which is the tendency to fill in missing or incomplete information.

Classic Cloze

In classic cloze, the teacher deletes words at random from a narrative or expository passage. The first and last sentences are left intact, and no proper nouns are removed; otherwise, every fifth, sixth, seventh, eighth, ninth, or tenth word is deleted. (Generally, the interval for word deletion should be no more than every fifth and no fewer than every tenth.)

The teacher explains the purpose of cloze, gives tips such as the following for completing the exercise, and models the process of completing a cloze activity.

- ■ Read the whole exercise first.
- ■ Use all the clues given in a passage.
- ■ Read past the blank to the end of the sentence. Sometimes the best clues come after a blank.
- ■ If necessary, read a sentence or two ahead to get additional clues.
- ■ Spell as best you can. You lose no points for misspelled words.
- ■ Do your best, but do not worry if you cannot correctly complete each blank. Most readers will be able to fill in fewer than half the blanks correctly.
- ■ After you have filled in as many blanks as you can, reread the selection. Make any changes that you think are necessary.

> ▌Dewitz, Carr, and Patberg, (1987) theorize that completing cloze exercises is similar to drawing inferences. After learning to complete cloze exercises, the students then applied the technique to intact social studies passages. After the students read a passage, they used the same strategies they had used to complete the cloze exercises. The students were shown how to use their prior knowledge and clues in the passage just as they had done when completing the cloze exercises.

Scoring Cloze

■ Exact Replacement

There are two ways of scoring a cloze exercise. When it is used as a test, only exact replacements are counted as correct. Otherwise, marking becomes both time consuming and subjective. Scores are noticeably lower on cloze exercises than they are on multiple-choice activities; a score of 50 percent is adequate. Criteria for scoring a cloze procedure using exact replacement are shown below:

Level	Percentage
Independent	> 57
Instructional	44–57
Frustration	< 44

■ Substitution Scoring

When cloze is used for instructional purposes, substitution scoring is generally used. A response is considered correct if it fits both semantically and syntactically. Thus, the following sentence would have a number of correct responses, such as *wagon, toy, ball, bike, coat,* and *dress:*

The child pointed to the red _____ and cried, "I want that!"

Discussion for Comprehension

Discussion enhances the value of cloze as a comprehension building technique (Jongsma, 1980). Discussions can be led by the teacher or pupils. During the discussion, participants talk over their responses and give reasons for their choices, thus justifying their responses and clarifying their thinking processes. They also compare their answers; in the process, they broaden vocabulary, concepts, and experience and learn to consider and value different perspectives.

Constructing Cloze Exercises

Before students guide discussions, the teacher should model how to do it, and ground rules should be established. Discussion groups should be large enough to encompass several perspectives but small enough to allow plenty of opportunity for each member to participate (Rye, 1982).

The first rule for constructing cloze exercises is to choose selections that are interesting so that students will be motivated to complete them. It is best to start with easier exercises and progress to more difficult ones. In general, the following items affect the difficulty of a cloze exercise (Rye, 1982):

- *Number of deletions.* The fewer the deletions, the easier the task.
- *Types of words deleted.* Content words such as nouns, verbs, adverbs, and, to a lesser degree, adjectives are more difficult to replace than structure words such as articles, prepositions, and conjunctions.
- *Location of deletion.* Deletions in the beginning of a sentence are more difficult to replace than those in the middle or end.

In early exercises, the teacher may want to delete just one word out of ten—mainly structure words that occur in the second half of a sentence. In time, the number of deletions can be increased, more content words can be omitted, and a proportion of words can be taken out of the beginnings of sentences. The kinds of deletions will be dictated by instructional objectives. If the teacher wants students to work on seeing relationships, she may delete structure words such as *if, then, and, but, moreover,* and *however.* Deleting nouns and verbs and, to a lesser extent, adjectives and adverbs will place the focus on content. Deleting adjectives and adverbs could be a device for having students note how modifiers alter a selection.

Modified Cloze

Traditional cloze exercises are not recommended until students have achieved a fourth-grade reading level. However, modified cloze activities can be used with students reading below that level. In modified cloze, each blank is accompanied by answer choices so that students do not have to supply the word; they simply identify the best of three or four possible choices. This is a format employed by a number of commercial workbooks and some tests. Although they provide valuable practice, these exercises shift the focus from predicting a word to considering which alternative is best. The task is changed from being one of constructing meaning to recognizing meaning, a subtle but significant alteration. However, modified cloze can be good preparation for completing classic cloze exercises.

CRITICAL READING

Critical reading is an affective as well as a cognitive skill. To read critically, students must be able to suspend judgment and consider other viewpoints. Generally, people tend to interpret what they read in light of their beliefs. Some readers, and

■ **Critical reading** refers to a type of reading in which the reader evaluates or judges the accuracy and truthfulness of the content.

*T*oday's students should be taught how to read advertisements critically.

TABLE 6.1 Critical reading skills
Distinguishing between facts and opinions
Identifying words that signal opinions
Verifying factual statements
Identifying the uses of words (e.g., to describe, to judge)
Recognizing denotations and connotations
Identifying persuasive language
Identifying an author's purpose
Drawing logical conclusions
Supporting conclusions
Judging sources of information
Identifying slanted or biased writing
Identifying major propaganda techniques
Recognizing assumptions

this seems to be especially true of poor readers, reject information that contradicts their beliefs. On the other hand, some readers suffer from a malady that one educator called the "Gutenberg syndrome" (J. Rothermich, personal communication, January 1980): If a statement appears in print, it must be true. Students have to challenge what they read and realize that a printed statement might be erroneous or simply be someone else's opinion.

To encourage critical reading, the teacher must create a spirit of inquiry. Students must feel free to challenge statements, support controversial ideas, offer divergent viewpoints, and venture statements that conflict with the majority view. When they see that their own ideas are accepted, they are better able to accept the ideas of others. The program, of course, must be balanced. The idea is not to turn students into mistrustful young cynics but to create judicious thinkers.

There are dozens of critical reading skills. The suggested skills listed in Table 6.1 are based on examination of professional materials and analysis of critical reading tasks. No timetable is suggested for these skills.

Uses of Language

BUILDING LANGUAGE

Examine stories and trade books that students are reading. Call attention to words that make a person or thing sound worse and those that make a person or thing sound better.

A good starting point for a study of critical reading is to examine how language is used. What do words do? What functions do statements fulfill? Words are used in four main ways: to describe, to evaluate, to point out, and to interject (Wilson, 1960). The words *car, take,* and *dog* describe bits of reality. The words *evil* and *stupid* evaluate, going beyond mere description to judgment. Some words both describe and evaluate: *jalopy, steal,* and *mutt* describe objects and actions, but they also incorporate unfavorable evaluations. A key strategy in critical reading is to note whether words offer neutral descriptions, evaluations, or both. To introduce the concept of the uses of words, write a series of sentences similar to the following on the board:

> The horse weighs 950 pounds.
> The horse is black with white spots.
> The horse is lazy.
> The horse is wonderful.

Discuss which words just tell about the horse and which judge it. Guide students as they locate words in their texts that describe, judge, or do both. While discussing selections that students have read, note words that are used to judge. To extend the concept of uses of words, introduce the concept of connotations; have students note words that have favorable connotations (*thrifty, slim*) and those that have unfavorable ones (*selfish, skinny*). For younger students, you may want to use phrases like "sounds better" and "sounds worse," instead of "favorable connotations" and "unfavorable connotations."

Introduce the concept of persuasive language by bringing in ads and package labels. Have students locate words that sell or persuade in television and print ads—*fresh, delicious, new,* and *improved.* They can even compose their own persuasive advertising.

Understanding Factual Statements and Opinions

Factual statements are ones that can be verified through objective evidence or through analyzing language. The statement "It is raining" can be verified by looking outside. Even if the sun is shining, the statement is a factual one rather than an opinion because it can be verified. In this case, the statement is verified to be inaccurate. The statement "A hurricane is called a *typhoon* when it occurs over the Pacific Ocean" cannot be verified by observing hurricanes or typhoons. It is verified by analyzing the statement to see whether the language is being used accurately. Analytic statements of this type are frequently verified by using a reference. Because the word *fact* suggests something that is true, it is better to use the term *factual statement* rather than *fact.* To introduce the concept of factual statements and opinions, place sentences similar to the following on the board:

> We have twenty-five players on our soccer team.
> We have won twelve games in a row.
> Our uniforms are red.
> Soccer is the best sport.

Show students that the first three sentences can be proved in some way, but the last one cannot. It is simply an opinion, a statement that tells how someone feels. Help students locate statements of fact and opinion in their texts. To reinforce and extend this concept, plan lessons and activities such as the following.

REINFORCEMENT ACTIVITIES **Identifying factual and opinion statements**

- Present words that signal opinions, such as *good, bad, worse, terrible, wonderful,* and *awful.* Ask students to use these and other signal words in differentiating between factual statements and opinions.
- Introduce the concept of verifying factual statements. Explain to students that factual statements can be proved in some way—by measuring, weighing, observing, touching, hearing, counting, and so on. Bring in a kiwi or other unusual fruit, and encourage students to make factual statements about it—for example, "The kiwi is brown" and "It has fuzzy skin." Discuss how each statement might be proved. Bring in a scale and a measuring tape so that the kiwi can be weighed and measured. Have students make other factual statements and tell how they might prove them—that

is, whether they would mainly count, measure, weigh, touch, listen, or observe to prove the statements.

■ Let students examine an object and make at least five factual statements about it based on counting, measuring, weighing, touching, listening, observing, or checking a reference book. Then ask them to write down their personal opinions about that object. This might be an opportunity for them to be especially imaginative and creative.

■ Ask students whether a statement in a reading selection is a factual one or an opinion. Take special note of opinions that might be mistaken for facts.

Recognizing the Author's Purpose

In addition to being a key critical reading skill, recognizing the author's purpose is an essential general comprehension skill. According to Spearitt (1972), it is one of only four distinct skills involved in comprehension.

The three main purposes for writing are to inform, entertain, and persuade. Recognizing which one applies to a particular selection enables students to match their strategy to their reading. For example, knowing that a writer is attempting to persuade, they will look at the piece with a critical eye. To introduce the concept of purpose, read aloud an ad or an editorial, an encyclopedia article, and a short story, and discuss each author's purpose. Help students suggest other writings that are designed to inform, entertain, and persuade.

To extend the concept, have students predict the author's purpose before reading a selection and then discuss their predictions after reading. For each book report that students complete, have them identify the author's purpose. Students can also decide what their own purpose is before writing a piece. Let them write editorials for the school newspaper or letters to the editor. Bring in persuasive pieces, and discuss them with the class. Help the class see what persuasive techniques are being used.

Drawing Logical Conclusions

Drawing a conclusion is a type of inference. It usually entails examining several facts or details and coming to some sort of conclusion based on the information. In critical reading, stress is placed on drawing conclusions that are logical, have sufficient support, and consider all the evidence. In many instances, different conclusions can be applied to a set of facts. Students should be shown that they should reach the most likely conclusion while keeping an open mind because other conclusions are possible.

To introduce drawing logical conclusions, model the process and provide guided practice. Have students apply the skill to all content areas, drawing conclusions about the main character in a piece of fiction, about experiments in science, and about historical events and figures in social studies. Stress the need to consider the evidence very carefully.

Judging Sources

Because students tend to believe everything they read, whether it be in print or on a computer screen, they should understand that some sources are better than others. Three main criteria are used to judge a source: whether it has expert knowledge about the subject, whether the information is up to date, and whether the source is unbiased.

Encourage students to examine their textbooks to see whether they are written by experts and are up to date. When students read nonfiction, have them note who wrote the information and then examine the book jacket or another source of information to see whether the author seems to be an expert. For a Web site, students should see whether the author's name is given and whether the author's credentials are provided. Students should also check the date of publication. When examining Web sites, students can note when the site was last updated. Also, discuss the issue of author bias. For instance, talk over why a book or Web site on coal mining written by someone who works for a coal company might be considered to be written by an expert but could be biased in favor of the coal industry.

When using the Internet, students might also determine what the URL tells them about a site. Students can tell whether the site is educational (.edu), governmental (.gov), an organization (.org), or commercial (.com) (Caruso, 1997). One might have more trust in a site sponsored by a library, university, or government agency than in one sponsored by a commercial entity or individual.

■ Slanted Writing

Slanted, or biased, writing uses emotionally toned words and specially chosen details to create an unfairly favorable or unfavorable impression about a person, place, object, or idea. It is found in political speeches, personal opinion columns in magazines and newspapers and Internet sites, sports articles, biographies and autobiographies, and history texts.

Show students how words and details can be selected in such a way as to shape readers' opinions. Discuss why it is important to recognize slanted writing. Assign selections, some of which are slanted and some of which are neutral, and ask students to decide which are which. They should take note of techniques used to slant writing. Most important, they must be able to detect it in their reading. To reinforce this skill, keep a file of examples of slanted writing, and from time to time, share and discuss some of them with the class. Encourage students to bring in examples of slanted writing, and discuss these also. Have students look for examples of slanted writing in their own written pieces.

*W*hen using a Web site, students should evaluate the accuracy and fairness of information.

Judging sources

Once students seem to grasp the concept of judging sources for fairness, help them develop a set of questions that they might use to assess printed sources and Web sites they consult:

Is the source up to date?
Who is the author?
Is the author an expert?
Is the author unbiased? Is there any reason that the author would be in favor of one side or one position?
Is the writing fair, or does it seem to be slanted?
Does the author give enough proof for all conclusions?

You might post the questions as a reminder for students to use them when they are reading. In adapted form, the questions might also be used for evaluating speeches and informational TV programs.

HELP FOR STRUGGLING READERS AND WRITERS

Achieving readers often pick up strategies on their own. Struggling readers and writers have a greater need for structure and explicit instruction. They also need to have materials on the appropriate level of difficulty. In an experiment with a class of thirty-two fourth-graders in an elementary school that was part of a public housing project, Mosenthal (1990) noted that all thirty-two youngsters received whole class instruction and read from a text that was on grade level, even though some children were reading below grade level. Selecting the seven lowest-achieving students, Mosenthal and the children's teacher, who was highly experienced, obtained materials on a second-grade level and provided the children with supplementary comprehension instruction that consisted of directed reading–thinking activities and written retellings. Retellings were chosen because they offered insights into the children's changing ability to comprehend narrative text.

Over a period of three months, the students' retellings improved dramatically. They became more complete and began to reflect the most important elements in the tales that had been read. Although instruction and practice were undoubtedly essential factors in the children's improvement, setting may have been even more important than the quality of instruction. As the students' teacher noted, "I know at times in the beginning that they (the students in the reading and writing group) were elated that they were part of a small group. I think the stories helped. They were stories they could read and they could enjoy" (Mosenthal, 1990, p. 282). Although reluctant to write at first, the children's attitude changed because they were praised for their efforts. Over time, they also felt better about themselves. As their teacher remarked, "They saw improvement and I think they felt better about what they were doing" (Mosenthal, 1990, p. 283).

As the researchers noted, improved learning environment interacted with direct instruction in reading and writing. Being given materials they could read; tasks they could perform; and a positive, can-do atmosphere, students were able to make the most of instruction.

ESSENTIAL STANDARDS

Fourth through eighth grades
Students will

- use their knowledge of story grammar to help them understand narratives.
- grow in their ability to use retelling procedures to build and demonstrate comprehension.
- use expository text structures to foster comprehension of informational text.
- distinguish between factual statements and opinions.
- identify persuasive and slanted language.
- identify an author's purpose.
- draw conclusions.
- judge sources of information.
- identify slanted or biased writing.

ACTION PLAN

1. Gear instruction to students' level of cognitive development. With skills such as retelling, begin with supported retelling and gradually lead students to independent retelling.
2. Guide students in the use of text structure to help them comprehend narrative and expository selections.
3. Create a classroom atmosphere that values inquiry and discussion but in which the students feel safe to venture opinions and conjectures.
4. Ask questions on a variety of levels. Use wait time, prompts and probes to build students'

confidence and comprehension. Use QAR as needed.
5. Use frameworks such as text walk, guided reading, DRA, and DR–TA to foster comprehension. Adapt techniques to the needs of the students. Use a DRA or guided reading for students who need maximum structure and DR–TA or KWL for those who need less structure.
6. Incorporate activities and ask questions that lead students to evaluate what they read.

**ASSESSMENT**

Through observation and discussion and oral or written retellings, note students' ability to use story grammar and knowledge of text structure to foster comprehension. Using these same assessment techniques, note students' ability to think, read, and write critically. Use techniques such as responsive elaboration to both assess and guide students' thinking and processing of text. Through assessment, obtain information that you can then use to improve instruction. See Chapter 2 for additional information on assessing comprehension.

SUMMARY

1. Through hearing stories, reading, and writing, students develop a schema for narrative tales.
2. Generally, expository works are harder to read than narratives. Major types of text structures are enumeration–description, time sequence, explanation–process, problem–solution, comparison–contrast, and cause–effect.
3. Questions play a vital role in facilitating comprehension. A taxonomy is a useful guide for constructing questions on a variety of thinking levels and for judging questions that have already been created. Establishing an accepting atmosphere enhances students' responses.
4. Guided reading and the DRA (directed reading activity) are highly useful frameworks for conducting reading lessons. The DR–TA (directed

reading–thinking activity) gives students more responsibility for their learning.
5. Cloze is valuable for building comprehension because it forces students to read for meaning, use context, and make predictions.
6. An affective as well as a cognitive skill, critical reading involves willingness to suspend judgment, consider another point of view, and think carefully about what one reads. Thoughtful reading and discussion also promote critical thinking.
7. The total class setting has an impact on comprehension. Students do better when materials are on the proper level of difficulty, when assignments seem doable, and when there is a positive can-do atmosphere.

EXTENDING AND APPLYING

1. Collect samples of biased writing from children's periodicals and textbooks.
2. Examine a lesson from a basal series that is no more than three or four years old. Examine the questions for three selections, and classify them according to Weinstein and Mayer's taxonomy. What percentage are on a comprehension level? Organizing level? Elaboration level? Monitoring level?
3. Plan a DRA or similar guided reading lesson for a chapter of a children's book, a short story, an

informational piece, or information from a Web site. Teach the lesson and evaluate its effectiveness.
4. Create and teach a cloze lesson. Evaluate its effectiveness.
5. Try out the FELS system for asking questions with a class. Also use wait time, and create an accepting atmosphere. Do this for a week. Have a colleague observe your performance and give you objective feedback.

DEVELOPING A PROFESSIONAL PORTFOLIO

Look over the comprehension standards issued by the state or district where you are teaching or plan to teach. Also look at the tests or other devices used to assess comprehension. How well are the two aligned? In your portfolio, note any work you have done or plan to do so that your instructional program in comprehension is aligned with state or district standards and the assessment measures.

DEVELOPING A RESOURCE FILE

Maintain a file of different types of text structures so that these can be used to illustrate ways in which ideas can be presented. Also maintain a file of passages, selections, and Web sites that can be used to provide practice with fact and opinion, drawing conclusions, and evaluation of sources.

7

Reading and Writing
in the Content Areas
and Study Skills

ANTICIPATION GUIDE

For each of the following statements related to the chapter you are about to read, put a check under "Agree" or "Disagree" to show how you feel. Discuss your responses with classmates before you read the chapter.

	Agree	*Disagree*
1 Content-area textbooks should be simplified.	_____	_____
2 The strategies that are most effective in promoting comprehension of content-area material are those that are used after the text has been read.	_____	_____
3 When teaching reading of content-area material, the teacher should stress content rather than strategies.	_____	_____
4 Content-area teachers should be responsible for teaching the reading skills necessary to use their subjects' texts.	_____	_____
5 Content-area information should be presented to poor readers through discussions, experiments, and audiovisual aids rather than through texts that might be too difficult for them.	_____	_____
6 Most students learn effective study techniques without any formal instruction.	_____	_____

USING WHAT YOU KNOW

Chapters 5 and 6 presented a variety of strategies for improving comprehension of narrative and expository text. This chapter focuses on applying those strategies to improve literacy in the content areas. Additional aids to comprehension are introduced, and some special difficulties inherent in reading in the content areas are explained. It also explores studying and techniques for remembering content-area and other material.

Before reading this chapter, reflect on your knowledge of reading in science, history, and other content areas. Do you use any special strategies to comprehend what you read in the content areas? If so, what are they? How well do they work for you? Do you have any problems reading in the content areas? Do you have any problems studying? How might you improve your comprehension and retention of the material? How might you help students improve their reading in the content areas? How might you help them improve their studying?

OVERALL GOALS OF LITERACY INSTRUCTION IN THE CONTENT AREAS

Peer interaction helps students organize and evaluate information from content-area texts. It enhances their understanding and motivates them to read more (Alvermann, O'Brien, & Dillon, 1990).

The overall goal of content-area instruction is to help students construct their own understanding of key concepts. Students bring their own unique backgrounds and perspectives to each reading selection and use them to create an understanding of the content area. No longer are students seen as passive recipients of knowledge. Rather, they actively seek to make sense of new information by relating it to what they know about a topic. This type of learning requires time to discuss and reflect. In addition to thoughtful demonstrations and explanations by the teacher and in the text, the students need opportunities to interact with the information, to mull it over, talk about it, and make it their own. This is in stark contrast to the concept of coverage in which topics are presented but not explored and reflected upon, leaving students without the opportunity to interact with the information, discuss it, see its implications for their lives, and, if appropriate, apply it (Brandt, 1992).

ADAPTING INSTRUCTION for *STRUGGLING READERS and WRITERS*

The typical sequence for handling the reading of content-area texts is read-listen-discuss. Students read a chapter, perhaps for homework, which the teacher then explains. After the explanation, the class discusses the text. A more effective sequence might be listen-read-discuss, in which the teacher gives a five- to fifteen-minute explanation of the material, directs the students to read it, and then has the class discuss it. Because the explanation precedes the reading of the text, the students are better prepared to read it.

USING CONTENT-AREA TEXTBOOKS

Although children's books are being used with increasing frequency to present and reinforce concepts in the content areas, content-area textbooks account for an

*A*s students move through the grades, reading and writing in the content areas take on more importance.

estimated 75 to 90 percent of the learning that takes place in subject-matter classes. However, students may be poorly prepared to learn from content-area texts. Stories are emphasized in the early years, so students may have little experience with informational text. Often, the informational text that they do read in their basals has a strong narrative thread. Content-area text has a different, more complex structure. Instead of following a narrative, readers must understand complex processes and identify causes and effects as well as problems and solutions.

Readers must also cope with increased density of ideas and technical vocabulary and concepts for which they may have a very limited background. However, what really sets content-area reading apart from other reading is its purpose, which is to learn and, ultimately, to be able to apply what is learned.

Fortunately, content-area textbooks offer plenty of comprehension aids: chapter overviews; headings that outline the text; helpful graphics such as maps, charts, tables, graphs, diagrams, photos, and drawings; difficult words defined in context; summaries; and review questions. Also on the positive side, research suggests that students' reading of content-area materials can be improved. In a review of the research, Wade (1983) concluded that students perform better in both social studies and reading when provided with an instructional program that includes an active teacher and varied activities and materials.

As teachers provide instruction in the use of social studies materials, they should build independent learning strategies. As Herber (1970) commented,

> If we fail to help students develop skills for independent learning, then "education" will cease when they leave school. This understanding sets the teaching of reading in content areas in its proper perspective. Its purpose is to help students acquire the skills they need for adequate study of all materials required in their subjects. Using subject-related material, regularly assigned, as the vehicle for this instruction, content teachers can provide for the simultaneous teaching of reading skills and course content. Neither has to be sacrificed to the other. (p. v)

Choosing Materials

The first order of business is to decide what content to teach. The teacher should decide on his or her objectives and the topics to be covered and then select the materials. Typically, a single textbook is the major source and sometimes the only one. It should be supplemented with informational children's books, periodicals, primary sources, audiovisual aids, computer software, and, possibly, information from the Internet.

■ Textual Features That Foster Learning

From a reading standpoint, a number of features promote learning from a textbook. As noted in Chapter 5, the five major groups of strategies (excluding rehearsal) are preparing to read; selecting and organizing relevant information; elaborating on the information once it has been selected, which means integrating the new information with existing knowledge structures or schemata; monitoring for meaning; and affective or motivational strategies. Table 7.1 presents textual features that foster these processes.

USING TECHNOLOGY

700+ Sites: Planet Earth and Beyond lists a variety of sites that explore science topics, such as animals, earth, and weather. **http://www.ala.org/ parentspage/ greatsites/earth.html**

History/Social Studies Web Site provides help for using the Web as a resource for teaching history and social studies. **http://www.execpc. com/~dboals/boals. html**

See also Internet Resources for K–8 Students: Update 2000. ERIC Digest at **http://ericir.syr.edu/ ithome.**

When comparing math and science texts with those used in other countries, Olson (1994) found that U.S. texts covered more topics but covered them in less depth. Breadth rather than depth is definitely emphasized. The typical U.S. science text covers between fifty-three and sixty-seven topics. Other countries' texts cover between 8 and 17 topics (Science and Engineering Indicators, 2001).

TABLE 7.1	Textual features that foster use of learning strategies	
Benefit	**Examples**
Help students prepare	Chapter overview that lets student activate schema
	Semantic maps or other graphic organizers
	Heading and illustrations to make predictions
	Key terms and explanations
	Glossary
Help readers select relevant information and organize it	Introduction and summaries to highlight important information
	Headings and subheadings highlighting main ideas
	Details that clearly support main ideas
	Topics developed in sufficient detail but not so much as to overwhelm readers
	Clear, well-written text with connectives and transitions where needed
	Graphic aids
	Questions and activities at the end of the chapter
	Explanations to relate new knowledge to readers' background
Help readers elaborate or integrate important information	Questions or activities that help readers relate what they have read to their prior knowledge or experience
Help students monitor reading	Questions at the end of the chapter or interspersed throughout the chapter that ask students to check their understanding
Foster motivation	Illustrations and other graphic devices that give the text an appealing look
	Interesting style that engages the reader; use of anecdotes
	Relationships drawn between content and students' lives

Adapted from *Textual Features That Aid Learning from Text,* unpublished manuscript by B. Armbruster, 1987. Champaign, IL: Center for the Study of Reading.

The best of today's content-area texts provide a wealth of support for the reading and writing skills needed to comprehend and remember key concepts. They build background and vocabulary and provide previews, overviews, lots of helpful graphics, review questions, and activities. In one recently published social studies program, students are taught a target reading strategy that will assist them as they read the chapter (Boyd et al., 2003). In a chapter on the American Revolutionary War, students are taught to recognize cause and effect structure and to make use of this structure to comprehend the text. After being taught the skill in the context of an article on events leading up to the Revolutionary War, they apply the skill throughout the chapter. Questions build on the skill and lead students to apply it. For instance, students are asked questions such as: What effect did the Sons of Liberty have on the Stamp Act? What caused British leaders to pass the Townshend Acts? Graphic organizers also reinforce skills as students fill in missing causes on a cause-effect organizer.

Writing is used to foster learning. Students are asked to pretend that they are a member of the Virginia House of Burgesses and write a speech opposing the Stamp Act.

Assessment is tied to instruction. For instance, if students are unable to tell how the Townshend Act was similar to but different from the Stamp Act, it is suggested that the teacher guide students as they create a graphic organizer designed to show differences and similarities.

The best content texts are so carefully designed that they are potentially more effective for building literacy skills than many of the literacy programs designed specifically to develop skills. This doesn't mean that the history teacher has become a teacher of reading and writing. It means that the teacher is helping students learn skills needed to learn history. Through acquiring effective learning strategies, students learn more content.

■ Estimating Readability

As with all reading, it is important to provide students with texts they can read. Readability levels of textbooks are available from publishers. The readability levels of many textbooks can be found on the following Web site: http://www. tasaliteracy.com. Readabilities for informational trade books are available on a piece of easy-to-use software, *BookLink* (TASA), and also on the Web sites for Renaissance Learning http://www. renlearn.com (click on Quizzes) and metametrics http://www.lexile.com. If readabilities are not available, you can use one of the formulas described in Chapter 2, the benchmark passages presented in that chapter, or the *Qualitative Assessment of Text Difficulty* (Chall, Bissex, Conard, & Harris-Sharples, 1996), which contains benchmark passages in social sciences, science, and literature.

In many classrooms, the whole class usually reads the same textbook, generally one designed for the average student. In the average class, however, such a book will be too difficult for approximately one child out of four or more. Singer and Donlan (1989) claimed that in the upper grades, as many as 50 percent of students may have difficulty with their textbooks. Also, some students will be able to use a more challenging book. Some provision has to be made for these varying reading abilities, especially for students reading significantly below the level of the textbook.

The teacher's editions of today's content-area text provide a wealth of suggestions for adapting texts to meet varying levels of ability. Many of today's texts have audio versions so that students can listen to the text as they read it. The best of them also have suggestions for scaffolding the learning for all readers but especially for struggling readers and ELL. Some program also provide a brief, easy-to-read summary so that below-level readers will have access to information that they call read and study. The summaries are written two or three grade levels below the level of the text.

If texts are simply too difficult for your class, consider using texts that are designed for below-level readers. Some easy-to-read content-area textbooks are listed below. If you do use an easy-to-read textbook, make sure that it covers all the essential content. If not, supplement the book you do use with easy-to-read children's books, discussions, audio-visual aids, and simulations.

America's Story. Bernstein, V. Austin, TX: Steck-Vaughn. Although designed for high school students, this text, which is written on a second- to third-grade level, could be used with upper elementary and middle school students.

Science in Action Series. Upper Battle River, MN: Globe Fearon. A series of twelve short texts that present major science topics on reading levels 2.5 to 4. Designed

> See Chapter 2 for additional information on readability. In addition to considering readability estimates yielded by a formula or supplied by a publisher, consider subjective factors, especially those discussed in Chapter 2 and noted in Table 7.1.

USING TECHNOLOGY
Mount Vernon features an easy-to-read biography of Washington.
**http://www.
mountvernon.org/
education/biography/
gwbio1.asp**

for middle school and high school students, they may be adapted for poor readers in the upper elementary grades.

Steck-Vaughn Social Studies. Austin, TX: Steck-Vaughn. Covering content traditionally presented in elementary social studies, this recently published series of six texts is written significantly below the grade levels for which they were intended.

The Wonders of Science. Gottlieb, J. Austin, TX: Steck-Vaughn. This six-book series is written at grade level two to three and designed for middle school and high school students; many of the topics covered are presented in the upper elementary grades. Titles in the series include *The Human Body; Water Life; The Earth and Beyond; Land Animals; Matter, Motion and Machines;* and *Plant Life.*

World History. Hart, D. Upper Battle River, MN: Globe Fearon. Although designed for middle and high school students, this text, which is written on a third- to fourth-grade level, may be used with upper elementary students.

TRADE BOOKS IN THE CONTENT AREAS

There are a number of series books that would help young readers better understand past eras. These include the *American Girls Collection* (Pleasant Company), *Dear America* (Scholastic), and *Her Story* (Silver), which are written on a third- to fourth-grade level.

In addition to or instead of using content-area textbooks with poor readers, you might use easy-to-read trade books written on the topic being studied. For instance, when studying the Civil War or Abraham Lincoln, students might read *Just a Few Words, Mr. Lincoln* (Fritz, 1993), which is written on a third-grade level, but would appeal to older students. When studying ancient Egypt, students might read *Tut's Mummy Lost . . . And Found* (Donnelly, 1988), which is also written on a third-grade level but is of high interest. Additional excellent sources of brief, heavily illustrated, easy-to-read children's books are the Harper's Trophy series and Random House's *Step into Reading* series, which feature a variety of lively, easy-to-read books on dinosaurs, whales, dolphins, sharks, and historical figures. Books in the *Picture Biography* series by Adler (Holiday House), which are written on a third-grade level and are brief and heavily illustrated, or the *First-Start Biography* series (Troll), written on a second-grade level, portray a number of famous Americans and the times in which they lived. Other easy-to-read informational books include the following:

Appendix A lists a number of easy-to-read books that cover content-area topics.

Biographies from American History. Upper Battle River, MN: Globe Fearon. Thirty historical biographies written on a second-grade level. Subjects range from Susan B. Anthony to Frank Lloyd Wright.

Colonial Leaders, Revolutionary War Leaders, Famous Figures of the Civil War Era. New York: Chelsea House. Fifty historical biographies written on a grade three to four level.

Rookie Read-About Science. Chicago: Children's Press. Easy readers that cover a wide range of topics, including seasons, weather, the five senses, mammals, and plants. Written on a first- and second-grade level.

Trade books aren't just for struggling readers. There are a multitude of trade books written for achieving readers as well as struggling readers. Trade books fully develop topics that are barely mentioned in today's overcrowded social studies and science texts. Trade books can make difficult concepts clear and bring to life important discoveries and events. They can also be motivational. They can make students want to learn more about a topic (Gunning, 2003). From a pragmatic point of view, there is probably no better way to build background knowledge and vocabulary than reading informational trade books. In their desire to improve performance on high-stakes tests in reading, some administrators and teachers have reduced the amount of time spent teaching social studies and science. Ironically, the challenging reading required in these areas is just the kind of reading that is very effective in developing a host of essential reading skills.

To locate titles of suitable books on a variety of topics and a variety of levels use BookLink software or the Web sites for Renaissance Learning or Metametrics (Lexile Framework). Books can be searched by title, author, subject, maturity level, or readability level.

Talking CD-ROM Books

A number of informational books are accompanied by a CD-ROM that contains a spoken version of the text. The CD-ROM in the *Factfinders Series* (Smithmark) presents information from the text and also reads it; highlights key bits of information; has animation, sound, and quizzes; and has a notetaking feature. CD-ROM books should improve the involvement and understanding of all students but would be especially helpful for struggling or reluctant readers. Some titles in the series include: *Ancient Times, Bugs, Dinosaurs, The Earth, Outer Space, The Sea,* and *The Weather.*

Using Trade Books to Provide Better Coverage

Children's books can also be used to provide in-depth coverage of key topics. In general, content-area texts provide a survey of an area. Important events or phenomena may receive only passing treatment because there is so much to cover. When topics are not covered in sufficient detail, they are hard to understand and easy to forget. One way to rectify this problem is to look over your content-area curriculum and decide which topics are most important and should be covered in greater detail. Then obtain multiple copies of children's books on those topics so that students can explore them more fully. Today, interest in nonfiction topics is booming. Often lavishly illustrated, nonfiction books are attracting young readers in record numbers. Today's nonfiction books are also easier to read. Increasingly, informational books are assisting their readers by incorporating such features as headings, subheads, diagrams, photos, glossaries, sidebars, and bibliographies, including listings of Web sites. In addition, there are more informational books than ever. More than half the 4,000-plus children's books published each year are nonfiction (Helper, 1998). A number of nonfiction books for elementary and middle school students are listed in Appendix A. An excellent source of information on selecting

USING TECHNOLOGY
An excellent software series that explores a variety of science topics is the *Magic School Bus* (Scholastic).

The most extensive list of nonfiction books can be found in *The Elementary School Library Collection* (22nd ed.) (Homa, 2000).

A good source of current high-quality materials in social studies is the annual listing of "Notable Children's Trade Books in the Field of Social Studies," which is published in the April/May issue of *Social Education* and can also be found online (http://www.ncss.org/resources/notable/). A list of excellent science books is published each year in the March issue of *Science and Children.*

Exemplary Teaching

Using Literature in the Content Areas

*T*o make history come alive in her multicultural sixth-grade classroom in New York City, Lila Alexander, working with Queens University associate professor Myra Zarnowski, used literature sets. The sets incorporated five issues: poverty, human rights, immigration, the environment, and civil rights. The literature sets included novels, photo essays, picture books, and informational texts.

Each of the five sets of books was discussed, and students chose which set they wanted to read. Students read their books and kept journals in which they recorded interesting information and their feelings about this information. Meeting in groups of five several times a week, they discussed their journal entries and related questions. During discussions, Alexander and Zarnowski moved among the groups. As active participants, they encouraged children to raise important questions and make connections among the books read. They expanded students' understanding of the issues under consideration. In the following exchange, for instance, Alexander helped the group investigating immigration construct an important generalization about the way immigrants were treated:

Paula: I was reading about the Irish. If America is the land of freedom, why are immigrants treated so badly?

Bruce: They don't shoot them.

Alexander: Paula's point was that they were badly treated.

Ellen: The same thing happened to the Chinese.

John: The West Indians—it was the same.

Alexander: Is there a pattern here? (Zarnowski & Gallagher, 1989, p. 38)

With a little prodding and through the reading and discussion of a number of texts on the same theme, students were able to construct their own understandings of immigration, past and present. Their comprehension of immigration was richer, deeper, and far more personal than it would have been if they had simply read a brief textbook account of immigration.

and using nonfiction books is *Making Facts Come Alive: Choosing Quality Nonfiction Literature K–8* (Bamford & Kristo, 1998).

Adding a Multicultural Perspective

USING TECHNOLOGY

Making Multicultural Connections through Trade Books offers many resources for using multicultural books:
http://www.mcps.k12.md.us/curriculum/socialstd/MBDBooks_Begin.html

Trade books can also add a multicultural perspective to content-area study. When exploring inventions, students who read a biography of Thomas Edison have a deeper understanding of the process of inventing. However, along with reading about inventors traditionally presented in textbooks, students might read about African American inventors in Haskin's (1991) *Outward Dreams: Black Inventors and Their Inventions* or when studying whaling, they might read *Black Hands, White Sails: The Story of African-American Whalers* (McKissack & McKissack, 1999). When studying explorers, include a biography of DuSable along with those of Columbus and Magellan (Sims, 1994). Be sure to discuss multicultural perspectives. What was the impact of the Westward Movement on Native Americans? What is their perspective on this historical event? When studying math look at the number systems created by other cultures. Look, too, at the contributions made in science by other cultures (Sims, 1994).

TABLE 7.2	Social studies periodicals	
Periodical	**Appropriate Grades**	**Content**
Ask	3–5	Social studies and science
Calliope	4–8	World history
Cobblestone	4–9	American history
Faces	4–8	Geography and world cultures
Footsteps	4–8	African-American history
Junior Scholastic	6–8	Current events and general social studies topics
Current Events	7–10	Current national and world events
Faces: The Magazine about People	4–9	People from diverse lands and cultures
Know Your World Extra	5–8	Social studies, science, general interest. Easy to read
Scholastic News	K–6	Social studies, science, and other topics of interest to children
Time for Kids	4–6	Current events
*U*S* Kids*	1–5	Children in other lands
Weekly Reader	K–6	Social studies, science, and other topics of interest to children

Using Periodicals

Living in such a fast-changing world, keeping up to date means reading periodicals as well as books. Periodicals are especially important in social studies because they usually present current events; Table 7.2 shows some examples. Table 7.3 lists periodicals that explore science topics. For a more complete listing of periodicals for young people, see *Magazines for Kids and Teens* (2nd ed.) (Stoll, 1997), which is published by the International Reading Association.

Scholastic provides stories from current and past issues of *Scholastic News Senior,* a number of interesting activities, and links to other sites: http://teacher.scholastic.com/scholasticnews/.

TABLE 7.3	Science periodicals	
Periodical	**Appropriate Grades**	**Content**
Child Life	1–4	General interest, with focus on health
Children's Digest	1–6	General interest, with emphasis on health
Children's Playmate	1–6	General interest and health topics
Current Health I	4–7	Health topics typically taught in schools
Current Science	5–8	General science
Dolphin Log	2–8	Emphasis on marine sciences
Explore	5–8	Science and technology
Muse	5–8	Science, nature, music, general interest
National Geographic World	3–6	General interest, with emphasis on nature and ecology
Odyssey	3–8	Emphasis on astronomy and space
Owl Magazine	4–7	General science, with emphasis on nature
Ranger Rick	1–6	Wildlife and ecology
Science Weekly	1–8	General science and math
Superscience	3–6	General science

Online magazines include:

Dragonfly, which features a number of intriguing activities:
http://miavx1.acs. muo-hio.edu/~ dragonfly/.

Consumer Reports for Kids, which features articles on school lunches, clothing, toys, and other areas of interest to young consumers:
http://www.zillion.org.

See Tables 7.2 and 7.3 for a listing and description of young people's periodicals.

GROUP INVENTORY PLACEMENT

In order to provide students with the proper level of textbook, it is important to know what each student's reading level is. In a typical class, there is a wide range of abilities. Although most students may be reading on or near grade level, some may be reading two or more years above grade level and some may be reading two or more years below grade level. The best technique for matching students with textbooks they can handle is to try out the books. This can be done through administering individual informal reading inventories (as explained in Chapter 2). Group inventories (Johnson, Kress, & Pikulski, 1987) and cloze tests (Singer & Donlan, 1989) based on the target textbooks can also be employed.

INSTRUCTIONAL TECHNIQUES

The first principle of content-area reading instruction is to help students build conceptual understanding. In their study of upper elementary school students reading a U.S. history text, researchers McKeown, Beck, and Sandora (1991) found that students took "one swift pass through the words on a page, and then formed them into a shallow representation of the text" (p. 101). They didn't seek out key ideas or relate what they were reading to what they already knew. Conceptual understanding means going beyond the facts or the events and building a deeper understanding.

Building conceptual understanding requires that the teacher decide what major concepts she wishes her students to learn and then designing learning activities that will help students construct those concepts. For instance, as a result of studying World War II, the teacher might want students to understand that excessive national pride, economic needs, and conflicting ideologies lead to wars. Activities need to be designed that lead to these understandings. Simply answering factual end-of-chapter questions will lead to shallow understanding. Through careful reading, discussions, and questions that help students see the big picture, a conceptual understanding can be formulated.

It is also important that students make connections. Concepts are stored in networks. Students can understand and retain new information better if they relate it to already existing schemata. For instance, if students have a well-developed schema for World War I, they are better able to understand how economic hardship and the humiliation of the Treaty of Versailles set the stage for Germany's aggression and the beginning of World War II. Instead of being isolated bits of knowledge, information about the two wars becomes a part of a larger web of knowledge about wars. Going beyond dates of battles and names of countries and leaders, looking at the big picture, including the underlying causes and effects of the war, will also foster a deeper understanding. Questions and activities that involve students in making comparisons, connecting bits of information, and drawing conclusions help students construct a conceptual understanding. For instance, students might compare World War II with recent wars and current conflicts and draw conclusions about wars in general.

Because the text is a key source of information in the content areas, being able to use effective reading and learning strategies will help students acquire the information that forms a base for building a conceptual understanding. Techniques for helping students get more out of their content-area reading fall in one or more of the following categories: before reading, during reading, and after reading.

Before Reading

In preparing to read a text, strategic readers survey the selection, activate appropriate prior knowledge, predict what the text will be about, set goals, and decide how to read the material. To help the reader learn and apply these strategies independently, the teacher uses the DRA, DR–TA, ReQuest, Reciprocal Teaching, or Questioning-the-Author techniques, which were introduced in Chapters 5 and 6. The following instructional procedures can also be used: PReP, anticipation guides, and structured overviews.

■ PReP

The **prereading plan (PReP)** is both a diagnostic and an instructional device. It helps the teacher diagnose students' prior knowledge and provide necessary instruction to prepare them for comprehending the main concepts in an upcoming selection (Langer, 1981). For students who already know a great deal about the topic, PReP can help them determine which information is relevant. For those who do not realize that they are familiar with the subject, PReP can help them activate prior knowledge. For students who have a limited background, the technique can be used to expand what knowledge they do have. It can also help the teacher decide whether the students have adequate knowledge to bring to a selection or whether some additional concept building is required (Tierney, Readence, & Dishner, 1995). PReP has four main steps, which are described in Lesson 7.1.

> ■ The **prereading plan (PReP)** is an instructional technique designed to help the teacher build background knowledge.

LESSON 7.1   Using PReP

Step 1. Preparation

Examining the text, the teacher decides on the key concept that she or he wishes to stress. The teacher then chooses a word, phrase, or picture to initiate a discussion. In preparation for reading the cloud section of *Can It Really Rain Frogs? The World's Strangest Weather Events* (Christian & Felix, 1997), for example, the teacher might decide that the concept to be stressed is that clouds are formed in three main ways.

Step 2. Initial association

The teacher invites the class to brainstorm the topic. She says, "Tell what comes to mind when you hear the word *clouds.*" Responses are written on the board. Brainstorming enables students to make associations between their prior knowledge and the key concept. Associations might include *sky, rain, fluffy,* and *fog.*

Step 3. Reflections

Students reflect on their initial associations. The teacher asks what it was that made them think of these words. In this second stage of the discussion, students "develop awareness of their network of associations" (Langer, 1981, p. 154). They also listen to the responses of others. This helps them evaluate and organize their associations and, perhaps, think of additional ones.

Step 4. Reformulation

Students refine and expand their concepts. The teacher asks whether, based on the discussion, students have any new ideas about clouds. Responses are generally clearer and more fully developed. Students have had a chance to search their memories for related knowledge and to learn from their peers.

■ An **anticipation guide** is an instructional technique designed to activate and have students reflect on background knowledge.

Throughout the discussion, the teacher uses directed questions to help students clarify and elaborate responses and make connections. The teacher also evaluates students' prior knowledge to determine whether it is adequate to build a bridge between what they know and the content of the text. If it is adequate, the discussion can lead into a purpose for reading, one that builds on students' knowledge. In this instance, the teacher judges the students' background to be adequate and has them read the selection. The teacher's purpose question is "What are the three main ways in which clouds are formed?" If students' background seems inadequate, the teacher might decide to do some spot teaching or decide that more extensive preparation is needed.

■ Anticipation Guides

There is nothing like a good old-fashioned debate to perk up a class. Everyone, young and old, enjoys expressing opinions on controversial subjects. One device that capitalizes on this predilection is the **anticipation guide**—a simple listing of three or more debatable statements about a topic that students indicate whether they agree with before they read about the topic. (An adapted anticipation guide introduces each chapter in this book.)

*T*aking part in hands-on activities and watching demonstrations before reading the science text help make key concepts covered in the text more understandable.

Besides building interest, the anticipation guide activates prior knowledge. Readers have to activate information that they possess to decide whether they agree or disagree with each statement. The guide also gives students a purpose for reading: to evaluate their responses. In addition, it opens the students' minds. Some students, especially those who are younger and poor readers, tend to reject statements in print that contradict concepts they might have (Lipson, 1984; Maria &

MacGinitie, 1987). By comparing their responses with what the author said and by listening to the class discussion of the statements, they can correct and clarify these ideas.

The anticipation guide can be used with any age group and works best when students have some familiarity with the subject. If they do not know anything about it, they do not have much to agree or disagree with. The guide is also most effective when used with subjects about which students have misconceptions—for example, diet, pollution, legal rights, snakes, and insects. The recommended steps for constructing an anticipation guide are described in Lesson 7.2 (Head & Readence, 1986).

LESSON 7.2 Using an anticipation guide

Step 1. Identification of major concepts

List two to four major concepts that you wish students to learn.

Step 2. Determination of students' background

Consider the experiential and cultural backgrounds of your students. Ask yourself how their backgrounds will affect their knowledge and beliefs about the topic under study. What misconceptions might they have?

Step 3. Creation of statements for the guide

Write three to five statements (or more) that are sufficiently open-ended or general to encourage a discussion. Do not choose simple, factual statements. Instead, think of those that might touch on students' misconceptions or involve areas in which students have partial knowledge. The statements can be arranged in the order in which the concepts they reflect appear in the selection or from simplest to most complex. They may be written on the chalkboard or on paper.

Step 4. Introduction of the guide

Introduce and explain the guide, and have students respond to the statements. Emphasize that they should think about their responses because they will be asked to defend them.

Step 5. Discussion of responses

Talk over each statement. You might begin by having students raise their hands if they agree with it. Ask volunteers to tell why they agreed or disagreed.

Step 6. Reading of the text

Sum up the main points of the discussion and have students read the text to compare their responses with what the material states. In some instances, the text may contain information that proves or disproves a statement. However, if the statements have been constructed carefully, they will be sufficiently open-ended

> The anticipation guide should help students refine erroneous concepts because it involves confronting erroneous beliefs.

that students will find information that may support a position but will not prove it one way or another.

Step 7. Discussion of text and statements

Talk over each statement in light of the information in the text. Ask students whether they changed their responses because of information in the text. Ask what that information was and why they changed their minds. Responses can be discussed in small or large groups. If small groups are used, bring the whole class together for a summary after the groups have finished their discussions. At this point, you might want to go over at greater length any statements that seem especially controversial or confusing.

The anticipation guide can be extended. In an extended anticipation guide, students note next to each response whether or not they have found support for their responses. If the text contains information that runs counter to a response, they then write a summary statement of that information next to their response. This helps students to correct misconceptions.

■ Structured Overviews

Students learn new concepts more easily if they can relate them to old ones. It is also helpful if students have an overview of what is to be learned so that they can see this relationship and how the new concepts are related to each other. For example, it is easier to understand the new concepts gavials and caimans once one sees that these creatures are related to alligators and crocodiles and that they all belong to the group known as crocodilians.

■ The **structured overview** is a technique designed to help students relate new words and concepts to known words and concepts.

Adapting a strategy devised by Ausubel (1960) known as the advanced organizer, Barron (1969) created the **structured overview,** which uses vocabulary words to relate new materials to old materials and to show interrelationships among both old and new concepts. The overview should provide a structure "so that it does not appear to students that they are being taught a series of unrelated or equally important words" (Estes, Mills, & Barron, 1969, p. 41). To construct an overview, follow the six steps listed below (Barron, 1969):

1. *Selection of concepts.* Analyze the selection to be read or unit to be introduced, and select two to four concepts that you think are important.

2. *Analysis of vocabulary.* Analyze and list the vocabulary necessary to understand the concepts.

3. *Arrangement of words.* Arrange the list of words into a diagram that shows their interrelationships.

4. *Addition of known words.* Add vocabulary words that you think students already understand so that they can see how the new words relate to them.

5. *Evaluation of overview.* Evaluate the overview. Ask whether the major relationships are clearly shown. Can the overview be simplified and still do a good job?

6. *Introduction of overview.* Introduce students to the learning task. Display the structured overview, and explain why you arranged the words the way you

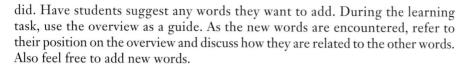

did. Have students suggest any words they want to add. During the learning task, use the overview as a guide. As the new words are encountered, refer to their position on the overview and discuss how they are related to the other words. Also feel free to add new words.

A fifth-grade class has just finished a unit on invertebrates and is now tackling a unit on vertebrates. The teacher examines the textbook chapter and thinks about what students already know about vertebrates and what he would like them to learn. The teacher decides to emphasize the following concepts:

1. Vertebrates have a skeleton.
2. There are seven main groups of vertebrates.

The teacher then lists the following words that he thinks would be necessary to understand the two concepts about vertebrates:

vertebrates	fish	reptiles	amphibians	warm-blooded
backbone	jawless fish	lizards	newts	cold-blooded
mammals	cartilage fish	turtles	metamorphosis	
birds	bony fish	crocodilians		

The teacher organizes the words in a structured overview. He then examines the overview and adds *animals, invertebrates,* and *no backbones,* so that students can see how the information on vertebrates fits in with the information on invertebrates. Believing that the word *amphibian* would be unknown, the teacher adds *frogs* to the list so that students will have an example of an amphibian. The teacher evaluates the overview. The words *metamorphosis* and *newts* are important; however, they seem to be making the display too complex, so he removes them. The revised structured overview is shown in Figure 7.1.

The teacher presents the overview. The class discusses the fact that there are two main types of animals: vertebrates and invertebrates. Various interrelationships are discussed. A question is raised about *cartilage;* its meaning is discussed.

The overview becomes a unifying element for the unit. As each group of vertebrates is discussed, the class refers to the overview. It is expanded to include other examples of amphibians, reptiles, birds, mammals, and the three kinds of fish. Students are thus able to see how these new words relate to the ones already contained in the structured overview.

As students gain skill in seeing relationships, they take part in constructing the overviews. They might construct overviews in cooperative learning groups. Eventually, they should be guided to use these tools as a study aid. Although designed to be used at the beginning of a unit or lesson, overviews can also be used as a summary at its conclusion.

During Reading

During reading, strategic readers construct meaning. They distinguish between important and unimportant details, organize information from text, summarize sections, and generate questions. They also integrate information from text with prior knowledge, make inferences, check predictions, seek clarification, and, per-

Note that some strategies, such as summarizing, question generating, and imaging, can be used during and after reading.

FIGURE 7.1

A Sample Structured Overview

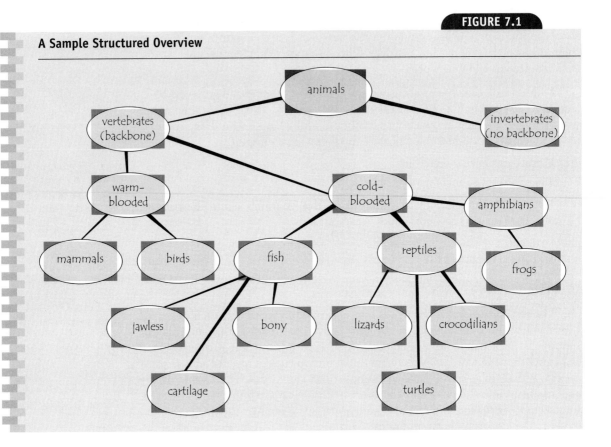

haps, create images of scenes and events portrayed by the text. They use the structure of the text as an aid to comprehension. Strategic readers also regulate their rate of reading and monitor their understanding of the passage. They may reread or seek clarification if their comprehension breaks down.

During-reading strategies include using chapter organization, text structure, and think-alouds. Study guides and glosses, which are teacher-created devices designed to foster comprehension, are also presented.

■ Chapter Organization and Text Structure

Along with visuals, numerous typographical aids are generally included in most content-area textbooks to assist the reader in determining organization and noting important points. These include the title, subheads, colored panels, sidebars, bullets, use of color type, and words printed in italics or boldface. Questions might also be posed in the margins. Although typographical aids are often used to preview a chapter, they should also be used as the reader interacts with the reading. Personal observation and experience suggest that they are given only limited attention, however. Perhaps students do not realize their full value. With the help of a textbook that makes especially good use of these elements, explain the purpose and value of each one. Then model how you might use them to aid your understanding of the content.

■ Think-Alouds

Think-alouds are just what their name suggests. The teacher models a silent reading strategy by thinking aloud as she or he processes a text, thus making explicit skills that normally cannot be observed. Originally a research technique for studying reading processes, think-alouds are used to model comprehension processes, such as making predictions, creating images, linking information in text with prior knowledge, monitoring comprehension, and using a fix-up strategy when there is a problem with word recognition or comprehension. In addition to being a demonstration technique, think-alouds can be used by students to become more aware of their reading processes and to make needed changes in the way they read.

Lesson 7.3 illustrates how the technique is put into operation as a repair strategy when comprehension has failed.

■ **Think-alouds** follow the expert–apprentice model. As the expert, the teacher demonstrates how she reads text so the pupil-apprentice can gain insight into the process. Cooperative learning is also involved as students work on their think-alouds with partners.

Think-alouds

Step 1. Modeling

The teacher reads a brief passage aloud, showing what her or his thoughts are when the text does not make sense and what repair strategies she or he might implement:

> Like a camera, the picture of the outside world which lands on the retina is upside down. The brain turns it the right way up as it interprets the messages from the retina. (Baldwin & Lister, 1984, p. 9)

Then the teacher thinks aloud, "I don't get this. I don't know where the retina is. I'll take a look at the diagram. There it is; it's the lining at the back of the eyeball, and there's the optic nerve. The optic nerve goes from the retina to the brain. Now I understand."

Step 2. Working with partners

Students take turns reading brief passages orally to each other. The selections should be fairly difficult or contain problems. The reader thinks aloud to show what processes he or she is using, what problems he or she is encountering, and how he or she is attempting to solve those problems. The partner is encouraged to ask questions: "Are you trying to picture the main character as you read? Do you see any words you don't know?"

Step 3. Practicing

Students practice thinking through materials as they read them silently. Self-questionnaires or checklists are used to encourage readers to use active processes and to monitor their reading. A sample self-questionnaire, in which students may answer the questions orally or in writing, is shown in Figure 7.2.

Think-alouds indicate the difficulty level of text. Think-alouds by several students on the same text may indicate that the text is hard to understand because the author didn't include enough information to enable the reader to make necessary inferences (Trabasso & Magliano, 1996).

As an alternative to a self-questionnaire, you might use a checklist such as the one in Figure 7.3. It assesses use of before-, during-, and after-reading strategies. When using a checklist, include only strategies that have been introduced. Also model the use of the self-questionnaire and checklist before using it. An even simpler device is to have students place a sticky note next to passages that pose problems. Problem passages can be discussed later.

Step 4. Applying think-alouds

Students apply the strategy to everyday and content-area material. During post-reading discussions, the teacher asks students to tell about their comprehension processes. "What pictures did you create in your mind as you read? Were there any confusing passages? How did you handle them?" Discussing strategies helps the student responding to clarify his or her use of strategies. It also helps the members of the class learn how others process text.

In addition to yielding information about comprehension processes, think-alouds foster improved comprehension. Think-alouds demand more focused attention and deeper processing. Through talking about the text, the reader makes connections among ideas, constructs explanations, and makes more predictions. Thinking aloud also promotes monitoring. When students think aloud, they note difficult or confusing passages. This monitoring helps the teacher understand the reader's processes and shows the teacher where to provide assistance.

■ Study Guides

■ **A study guide** is a teacher-prepared set of questions or other activities designed to foster understanding of a selection that the student reads independently.

Study guides are flexible, time-tested devices that help students during as well as after reading. They can take a variety of forms, such as asking students to respond mentally to a series of questions; to match items; to indicate whether statements are true or false; to fill in blanks; to complete a time line, a semantic map, a structured overview, or a comparison–contrast chart; to list the steps of a process; or to work a crossword puzzle. The best guides help students organize information and reflect on it. Procedures for creating a study guide are outlined below:

1. Analyze the selection to be read. Note the major concepts or principles that you think students should learn. Make a note of the sections that students must read to grasp the concepts. The chapter may cover concepts that you do not think are important. Indicate those pages so that students can skip unnecessary parts.

2. Consider elements of the text that might pose problems for students, such as difficult vocabulary, figurative language, confusing explanations, or complex organization.

3. Assess the organizational patterns of the chapter, such as enumeration–description, sequential, explanation/process, or other (see Chapter 6 for a description of patterns). Keep in mind that more than one pattern may be used.

4. Note strategies or skills that students might use to get the most out of their reading.

FIGURE 7.2

A Think-Aloud Self-Questionnaiare

A. Before reading
   1. How do I prepare for reading?
B. During reading
   1. What do I do to improve my understanding of what I am reading?
   2. What do I do if I come across a word I don't know?
   3. What do I do if the selection doesn't make sense?
C. After reading
   1. Do I do anything special with the information I just read? If so, what?

5. Construct a study guide that leads students to critical content, aids them in overcoming potential hindrances to comprehension, and directs them in the use of appropriate strategies and skills.

Pattern Guides

Detecting the pattern of writing in a piece fosters both understanding and retention (Herber, 1970). For example, if readers realize that the author is using a comparison pattern to discuss U. S. Presidents Harry Truman and Franklin D. Roosevelt, they can mentally sort the information into the proper categories. If readers know

Study guides can be constructed for a wide variety of purposes: fostering comprehension, highlighting key concepts, providing extra help for poor readers, examining both sides of a controversial subject, and so on.

FIGURE 7.3

Think-Aloud Checklist

Put a check next to the things you did before, during, and after you read.

Before Reading

Surveyed title, headings, illustrations _____
Thought about what I know about the topic _____
Predicted what the text might be about or what might happen _____
Made up a question to answer _____
Other (describe) _____

During Reading

Predicted what might happen next _____
Inferred ideas not stated _____
Got main idea of section _____
Got important details _____
Summarized each section _____
Created images about parts of the selections _____
Thought about what I had read _____

Judged whether information was true or the story seemed real _____
Made up questions to be answered _____
Checked to make sure I was understanding what I read _____
Repaired by rereading puzzling parts, getting meaning of hard words, etc. _____
Other (describe) _____

After Reading

Summarized what I had read _____
Thought about what I had read _____
Connected what I had read to what I already knew _____
Applied what I had learned in the selection _____
Other (describe) _____

that a piece has a main idea–details organization, they can mentally file the details under the main idea.

A pattern guide can take various forms. It may be a partially completed outline in which just the main ideas are included. Or it may involve matching causes and effects or a compare–contrast pattern (Estes & Vaughn, 1985). The sample pattern guide in Figure 7.4 not only helps students obtain essential information from the section, it also assists them in organizing that information so they can note the main ideas and see how the details relate to them.

ADAPTING INSTRUCTION for *STRUGGLING READERS and WRITERS*
Maps, graphs, tables, and other information can be part of a fix-up strategy. The reader who doesn't understand the verbal part of the text may be able to use graphic information to aid comprehension.

Levels of Thinking Guide

Levels of thinking guides are designed to promote comprehension at a variety of levels (Herber & Herber, 1993). To construct a levels guide, create questions or activities that involve literal comprehension, drawing conclusions, evaluating, and/or applying. As an alternative, use the QAR taxonomy and ask questions that are right there, putting it together, on my own, and writer and me.

After students complete the guides, they meet in groups of four or five and discuss their responses. Emphasis is on explaining and supporting responses. Where possible, students should be prepared to go back to the text to support their responses.

FIGURE 7.4

A Pattern Guide on Food Makers

All living creatures must have food to stay alive, even plants. Plants make food for themselves, for animals, and for us. Read "Food Makers," pp. 350–353. Find out where plants store their food, what kinds of food-producing plants there are, and what forms of food plants make. After reading the section, complete the outline by listing supporting details under main ideas.

A. Where food is stored in plants
   1. Roots—carrots
   2.
   3.
B. Types of food producers in a water community
   1. Plants with roots—cattails
   2.
   3.
   4.
C. Types of food producers in a forest community
   1. Ground layer—mosses
   2.
   3.
D. Forms of food made by plants
   1. Starch—beans
   2.

Guide designed for use with *Holt Science 4* (pp. 350–353), by J. Abruscato, J. Fusco, D. Peck, and J. Strange, 1989, New York: Holt, Rinehart and Winston.

After small groups have completed their discussions, the class meets as a whole. A representative from each group summarizes his or her group's discussion. Students also ask questions at this point and any confusing points are clarified.

■ Gloss

A gloss is a special kind of aid in which technical items or difficult concepts are explained in marginal notes. An easy way of creating a gloss is to photocopy one or more pages and write explanatory notes in the margins and distribute copies to students. Or line up a sheet of paper next to the text and write your gloss notes next to the target text. Make copies and distribute to students.

The gloss may define hard words, explain a key idea, paraphrase a difficult passage, tap prior knowledge, or point out a key idea (Gunning, 2002). Various kinds of questions might be included: those that help a student relate new information to old, those that help a student use a key comprehension strategy, or those that help a student set a purpose for reading (Richgels & Hansen, 1984).

A gloss can be particularly helpful for poor readers. If a text is too difficult, the gloss may summarize key information in simpler language and direct the student to illustrations, charts, maps, and other graphic aids which are easy to read but contain key information. As you write your gloss, think of terms or concepts or passages that may pose problems for your students. Provide the kinds of explanations or guidance that would help students cope with these items.

> If you are photocopying significant parts of the text, secure permission from the publisher.

> In using a gloss, key in on a few major points. A gloss becomes overwhelming if it has more than three or four items per page (Stewart, 1993).

After Reading

After completing reading, strategic readers reflect on what they have read, continue to integrate new information with old information, may evaluate the new information or use it in some way, and may seek additional information on the topic. To help students learn to use after-reading strategies, the teacher can apply several instructional procedures in addition to summarizing, retelling, and other postreading strategies covered in previous chapters. These additional procedures include constructing analogies, creating graphic organizers, and applying and extending.

■ Constructing Analogies

Analogies can foster comprehension and are frequently used in the content areas, especially in science. Students better understand an article about the game of cricket when given analogies between cricket and baseball or other information from which they can construct their own analogies (Hayes & Tierney, 1982). An analogy between the functioning of cells in the body and the operation of a factory will also lead to improved comprehension.

Recognizing and constructing analogies is one way of helping students bridge the gap between the new and the old. Point out analogies when they appear. Traditional analogies include the eye and a camera, the heart and a pump, the brain and a computer, and memory and a file cabinet. The best analogies are those in which the items being compared share a number of features, which is why the analogy between the eye and a camera is especially effective. However, it is important that the item that is the basis for comparison (the camera) be familiar. If students don't know how a camera works, the analogy won't be very helpful (Glynn, 1994). Help students create their own analogies by comparing old information and new concepts. You might ask, for instance, "How is the eye like a camera? How is memory like a file cabinet?" Self-created analogies are generally more effective than those made up by others.

For best results in using analogies, discuss the analogy thoroughly. After introducing the target concept, explain the analogy, identifying both similarities and differences between the target concept and the analog. Clarify any confusions that students might have (Glynn, 1994).

■ Creating Graphic Organizers

■ **Graphic organizers** are visual devices designed to help the reader note relationships between key concepts or events in a selection.

One of the most effective ways to understand and retain complex content-area information is to use some sort of **graphic organizer** to represent key concepts, main points, or basic steps. In addition to highlighting essential information, graphic organizers show how ideas are interrelated. The content and structure of material and the teaching–learning purpose dictate the type of organizer used: structured overview, time line, or an organizer that highlights the steps in a process, contrasts elements, or identifies causes. Whatever form it takes, the visual display should focus on the most essential information and do so vividly. Key concepts should "jump out at the students as soon as their eyes meet the page" (D. H. Robinson, 1998, p. 100).

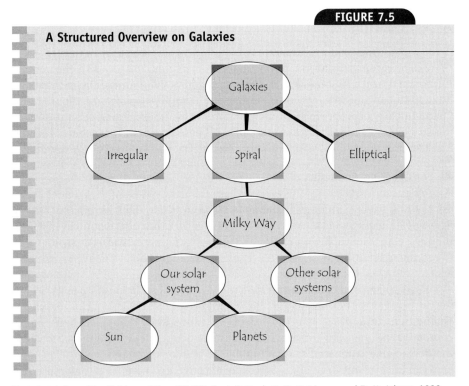

FIGURE 7.5

A Structured Overview on Galaxies

Text drawn from *Merrill Science 5* (pp. 98–99), by J. K. Hackett, R. H. Moyer, and D. K. Adams, 1989, Columbus, OH: Merrill.

One of the most useful graphic organizers is the structured overview because it shows subordinate relationships. Figure 7.5 shows a structured overview for the concept of galaxies. Earlier in this chapter, the structured overview was presented as a device for preparing students to read. It also can be created or added to as an after-reading strategy. It then becomes a method to enhance understanding and retention, especially if students play an active role in creating it. After the selection has been read, its elements would be discussed again. Information obtained from reading might be placed on lines beneath each element. For example, a brief definition of the word *galaxy* might be given, together with descriptions of irregular, spiral, and elliptical galaxies.

If given their own copies of the overview, students can add information about the elements as they read. They can also use drawings to illustrate concepts, such as irregular, spiral, and elliptical galaxies. In time, they can aid in constructing overviews or make their own. Through creation of graphic organizers, students achieve better understanding of essential processes and concepts. Retention is also aided. A structured overview may also be created in its entirety after a selection has been read, in which case it functions as a summary of major concepts.

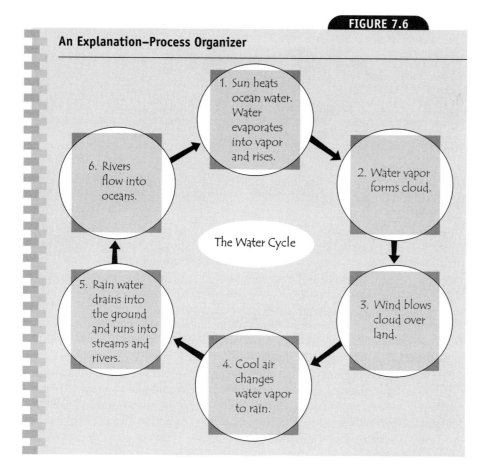

FIGURE 7.6

An Explanation–Process Organizer

The Water Cycle

1. Sun heats ocean water. Water evaporates into vapor and rises.

2. Water vapor forms cloud.

3. Wind blows cloud over land.

4. Cool air changes water vapor to rain.

5. Rain water drains into the ground and runs into streams and rivers.

6. Rivers flow into oceans.

Graphic organizers may also lead to dual encoding. They may be encoded and stored in memory verbally and visually. This dual encoding would make the information easier to recall (Robinson, 1998).

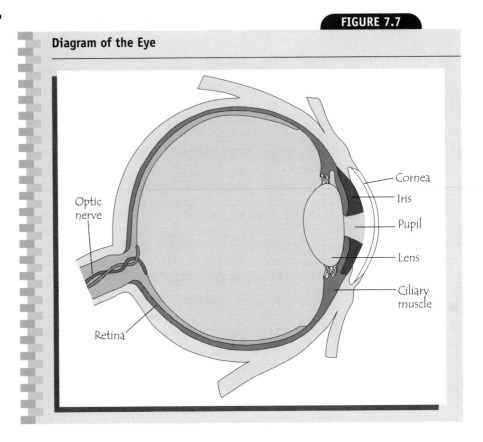

FIGURE 7.7

Diagram of the Eye

Another kind of graphic organizer that can be used as a postreading aid was presented in Chapter 6—an organizer that reflects the actual structure of the text (enumeration–description, time sequence, explanation–process, comparison–contrast, problem–solution, or cause–effect). Building as it does on structure, this kind of organizer enhances understanding of the interrelationships of the ideas covered in the text or the process being explained. For instance, an explanation–process organizer can be used to show how an engine operates, how solar cells turn sunlight into energy, how the water cycle operates, or how numerous other systems work (see Figure 7.6). Boxes or circles containing explanatory text show the steps in the process, with arrows indicating the flow of the process.

For some elements, the best graphic organizer is a diagram. For example, a diagram is the best way to show the parts of the eye (see Figure 7.7). Initially, a diagram can be drawn or traced by the teacher. However, having students create their own diagrams makes reading an active process.

For reading material that has a chronological organization, a time chart is a useful way to highlight major events (see Figure 7.8 for an example). A time line serves the same function and may be used instead of a time chart. Often, two or

FIGURE 7.8

A Time Chart

1524—Verrazano explored the eastern coast of North America.

1535—Jacques Cartier sailed up the Saint Lawrence River and claimed that area for France.

1608—Samuel de Champlain founded Quebec, the first permanent French colony in the Americas.

1673—Father Marquette and Louis Joliet set out on a journey that took them to the Mississippi River.

1682—Robert de La Salle reached the Gulf of Mexico after canoeing down the Mississippi River. He claimed the area for France.

more kinds of graphic organizers can be combined. For instance, a map showing the voyages of the French explorers might be used together with the time chart in Figure 7.8.

■ Applying and Extending

A particularly effective way of deepening comprehension is to reflect on one's own reading, which often results in a sense of not knowing enough or wanting to know more. Encourage students to use and extend what they know by expanding their knowledge. They can do this by reading books that explore a particular topic in detail or ones that provide enjoyment while increasing knowledge—for example, a book of math puzzles, one on bird watching, or a piece of historical fiction.

REINFORCEMENT ACTIVITIES   After-reading strategies

■ Putting knowledge to use expands and enhances it. After completing a unit on the heart and circulation, encourage students to exercise regularly and eat a balanced diet. A unit on geology may encourage some children to become rock collectors. A unit on weather could provide the impetus for some readers to set up a weather-watchers' club. A study of plants may inspire others to become novice gardeners. Provide encouragement and printed materials that explain how to turn interests into hobbies.

■ Provide students with project book kits. Combine an informational book with the tools needed to complete projects related to the topic of the book. Possibilities for project kits include a book on magnets and a set of magnets, a book on plants with packets of seeds and soil in a tray, a book on stamp collecting and some canceled stamps, and a book on robots and a kit for building a model robot.

KWL Plus: A Technique for Before, During, and After Reading

■ **KWL Plus** (Know, Want to know, and Learn) is a technique designed to help readers build and organize background and seek out and reflect on key elements in a reading selection.

A lesson designed to give students an active role before, during, and after reading is **KWL Plus:** Know, Want to know, and Learn. According to Ogle (1989), KWL evolved as she and a number of classroom teachers searched for a way to "build active personal reading of expository text" (p. 206).

The before-reading stage of KWL consists of four steps: brainstorming, categorizing, anticipating or predicting, and questioning. Brainstorming begins when the teacher asks the class what they know about a topic. If they are about to read a selection about camels, for example, the teacher asks what they know

Exemplary Teaching

CORI: A Motivational Content-Area Theme Unit

*A*ll too often, students read to complete an assignment rather than to learn. Their goal is to get to the end of the chapter rather than to construct meaning. Students need to be engaged in the reading task. Using a framework known as CORI (Concept Oriented Reading Instruction) with fifth-grade students in a Title 1 program, Anderson and Guthrie (1996) established a teaching unit that builds strategies and intrinsic motivation. CORI incorporates four main elements.

1. *Observing and personalizing.* To initiate a unit of study, students observed some material phenomenon. This ranged from observing crickets, the life cycle of caterpillars, and the phases of the moon to the social environment. Students' observations were discussed, and, in a KWL-type activity, they noted what they knew about the topic and what they wanted to learn. Topics of interest and questions to be answered were listed. Observations were recorded.

2. *Searching and retrieving.* Through brainstorming sources of information, students learned where to go to get information to answer their questions and to search for subtopics related to their general area of interest. Students learned how to locate appropriate trade books, to make appropriate scientific observations, and to use globes and other sources of information. In addition to discussion, direct

instruction was used to show students how to use the table of contents and index to locate relevant information.

3. *Comprehending and integrating.* Students learned how to identify important ideas and how to take notes to summarize what they had read and synthesize information. They also learned how to combine information from several sources, including both informational and fiction books and real-life sources. Technical vocabulary was developed. During this and other stages, peer interaction was encouraged.

4. *Communicating to others.* Students learned to use the process approach to compose a report. Typical reporting activities included sketching and labeling the parts of the creature or element being studied, inventing an insect, creating habitat posters, creating fictional pieces based on facts they researched, and creating other types of reports (Guthrie & McCann, 1997).

As a result of combining strategy instruction with elements, such as building on student's choices, the CORI program produced students who were intrinsically motivated and carefully taught, and who, as a result, read more, understood what they read better, and were better able to transfer both their knowledge and strategies to solve new problems.

about camels. Responses are written on the board and discussed. If a disagreement occurs or students seem puzzled by a statement, this cognitive conflict can be used to create a what-we-want-to-know question. The group brainstorming activates prior knowledge so that students become more aware of what they know. The students would then write about their personal knowledge of camels in the first column of a KWL worksheet.

Next, in a step similar to semantic mapping, students categorize their prior knowledge. The process of categorization is modeled. Brainstormed items already written on the board are placed in appropriate categories. Students then label the items in the "what we know" column with letters that indicate category names as shown in Figure 7.9: H = habitat, C = characteristics, and F = food. Students also anticipate what categories of information the author will provide. This helps them both anticipate the content of the text and organize the information as they read it. The process of anticipating categories is modeled. The teacher might ask, for example, what kinds of information an author might provide about camels. Students then write these items at the bottom of the KWL worksheet.

The categorizing and anticipating categories steps in KWL are frequently skipped and can be considered optional.

KWL is excellent preparation for writing a report. If details are classified, each group could be written as a separate paragraph.

FIGURE 7.9

KWL Plus

Name: _____   Topic: ___Army ants___   Date: _____

What we know	What we want to know	What we learned	What we still want to know
H Live in the jungle	How large a group do army ants form?	Tens of thousands form a group.	Do army ants harm people?
C Are fierce	Why are there so many army ants in a group?	The queen lays 100,000 to 300,000 eggs at a time.	What are larvae and pupae?
H Live in the ground	Why do the ants form armies?	Form armies to get food for larvae and pupae	
F Eat plants	What do army ants eat?	Kill other insects and small animals and take them back to their home.	
C Work together		Live in the ground or in trees in the jungles of South America.	
F Eat insects			

Categories of information we expect to see

Habitat	Society
Food	Travel
Characteristics	Appearance

Insofar as possible, help students relate what they are studying to their personal lives. For example, make the Bill of Rights provisions more concrete by having students write about how they exercise their rights every day or about an incident that made them appreciate their freedom to use their rights.

In the third step, questions are created. As a group, the class discusses what they want to know about camels. Questions are written on the chalkboard. Each student then records in the second column of the worksheet her or his personal questions.

With these questions in mind, the class reads the text. After reading, students discuss what they learned and the teacher writes their responses on the chalkboard. Information is organized, misconceptions are clarified, and emerging concepts are developed more fully. After the discussion, students enter what they learned personally in the third column. In light of this information, they cross out any misconceptions that were written in the first column. They may find that they still have questions about the topic, so a fourth column—with the heading "what we still want to know"—could be added to the worksheet. You might also discuss with the class how they might go about finding the answers to the questions they still have. A completed KWL worksheet is presented in Figure 7.9. Ogle (1989) presents a fuller description of KWL, including a sample lesson.

WRITING TO LEARN

Writing is a way of learning as well as a method of communication. Zinsser (1988), a professional writer and teacher of writing, observed,

> We write to find out what we know and want to say. I thought of how often as a writer I had made clear to myself some subject I had previously known nothing about by just putting one sentence after another—by reasoning my way in sequential steps to its meaning. (pp. viii–ix)

However, some kinds of writing are better than others for learning. Different kinds of writing lead students to think in different kinds of ways. Writing short answers aids recall over the short term. However, activities in which students manipulate information lead to increased recall over a longer period of time and deeper understanding. Writing that involves comparing, contrasting, concluding, and evaluating has a greater impact than writing that requires only restating. Writing in which students have a sense of ownership and in which they see value because it fosters their learning and which they feel competent to undertake seems to work best (Langer & Applebee, 1987).

Writing activities, such as the following, can help clarify complex topics:

- Comparing, contrasting, or evaluating key points in a chapter
- Writing critical reports on famous people or events or taking on the role of the famous person or describing the key event as though one were there
- Interpreting the results of a science experiment conducted in class
- Writing an essay on a social studies or science topic: What does the Bill of Rights mean to me? What can we do to clean up our home, the earth?

Students' writing in the content areas often consists of simply retelling information. One solution is to have them conduct firsthand investigations and report the results. They might undertake activities such as the following:

- Writing observations about a natural phenomenon (for example, changes in plants that are being grown from seed)
- Describing birds that visit a bird feeder, changes in a tree from season to season, or changes in a puppy or kitten as it develops over a period of months
- Summarizing and interpreting the results of a classroom poll
- Interviewing older family members about life when they were growing up

A writing activity that can be used in any content-area class is having students explain a process to someone who has no knowledge of it. Processes include finding the area of a rectangle, how magnets work, how the president is elected, and how to find a particular state on a map. Students might also use graphics to help explain a process. Where appropriate, the explanation might be oral, instead of written.

Other kinds of writing-to-learn activities include the following (Noyce & Christie, 1989):

- Writing letters to convey personal reactions or request information on a topic
- Writing scripts to dramatize key events in history
- Writing historical fiction
- Writing a children's book on an interesting social studies or science topic
- Writing an editorial or commentary about a social issue
- Writing an illustrated glossary of key terms
- Creating captions for photos of a scientific experiment
- Creating a puzzle for key terms

Learning Logs

One easy device that combines personal reaction with exploration of content is the **learning log.** It consists of a notebook that is

> . . . informal, tentative, first draft, and brief, usually consisting of no more than ten minutes of focused free writing. The teacher poses questions and situations or sets themes that invite students to observe, speculate, list, chart, web, brainstorm, roleplay, ask questions, activate prior knowledge, collaborate, correspond, summarize, predict, or shift to a new perspective: in short, to participate in their own learning. (Atwell, 1990, p. xvii)

The class can discuss their learning logs, or the teacher can collect them and respond to them in writing. Following is a learning log from a student who drew up a summary based on the teacher's reading of *Squirrels* (Wildsmith, 1988):

> Squirrels nests are called dreys. Squirrels tails are used for leaps, a parachute, change directions, swim, balance, blanket. Sometimes squirrels steal eggs. (Thompson, 1990, p. 48)

The main purpose of logs is to have students examine and express what they are learning, not to air personal matters (Atwell, 1990). Logs can also be used to ask questions. Calkins (1986) suggested that before viewing a film or reading a selection, students might record the questions they have about that topic. Later,

---

For suggestions for guiding the writing of reports, see chapter 10.

USING TECHNOLOGY
Kids Connect
By filling out a form, students can get help researching a school report or project. Help is provided by a volunteer librarian, but students have to allow two days for a response.
http://www.ala.org/ICONN/AskKC.html

For immediate information, students can use the Kids Connect Favorite Sites for K–12 Students, which contains an extensive list of resources.
http://www.ala.org/ICONN/kcfavorites.html

- A **learning log** is a type of journal in which students record and reflect upon concepts that they are studying.

The major advantage of learning logs is that they provide students with the opportunity to reflect on their learning and raise questions about concepts that puzzle them and issues that are of concern.

they can evaluate how well their questions were answered. On other occasions students might record what they know about a topic before reading a selection or undertaking a unit of study.

Whether students pose a question, jot down a reaction, or create a semantic map, the writing stimulus should help them think as scientists, historians, or mathematicians and think about what they are learning. At times, they can draft free responses in their learning logs; at other times, the teacher might want to provide prompts. Log-writing prompts for a unit on weather might include the following, only one of which would be provided for any one session:

- What do I know about weather forecasting?
- What questions do I have about weather?
- What is the worst kind of storm? Why?
- What kind of weather do I like best? Least? Why?
- How does weather affect my life?
- What kinds of people might be most affected by the weather?
- What causes fog?
- What are some of the ways in which people who are not scientists predict the weather?

Prompts that foster reflection, manipulation of information, evaluation, and relating information to one's personal life also foster higher-level thinking skills.

Students can also write prelearning and postlearning entries in their logs. Before studying snakes, they might write what they know about snakes and then share their knowledge with a partner. Talking to a partner helps them to elicit more information. Students then read the selection and make journal entries indicating what they know now. Prelearning and postlearning entries help students become more metacognitive, more aware of what they know and are learning (Santa, 1994).

SHELTERED ENGLISH FOR ENGLISH LEARNERS

Introduced in the 1980s by Krashen (1991), **sheltered English** is a way of fostering English through the study of content areas. As students learn science and social studies, they develop English language skills. Sheltered English is generally taught by content-area specialists who have training in teaching English, but some of the techniques employed in sheltered English can be adapted by classroom teachers.

Sheltered English is student centered. There are high levels of student interaction, with much of the work being done in cooperative learning groups. Hands-on activities are stressed. Making the input comprehensible to students is also emphasized.

The following steps might be taken to make content understandable:

- Your presentation should be as understandable as possible. Speak at a slower pace with deliberate enunciation. Use simple, straightforward language.

Avoid figurative language, idioms, and cultural references that students might not recognize (Gunning, 2003).

■ Use visuals to support the verbal. Use audiovisual aids, gestures, facial expressions, and demonstrations to make the language more meaningful. When introducing a new word, show a picture of it, if possible, and write it on the board. When mentioning a place, write its name on the board and show it on a map. Pantomime actions and demonstrate processes. Use timelines, graphs, videos, and filmclips on CD-ROM. Use manipulatives such as globes.

■ When giving directions, show students what to do in addition to telling them. If possible, model the process for them. Then ask students to carry out directions or apply a concept under your guidance. Provide additional help as needed.

■ Plan lots of hands-on activities, drawings, webs, maps, and other graphic organizers so that students can use techniques that are less language dependent to extend their understanding and express their knowledge.

■ Use brainstorming, quick write, and similar techniques to activate background knowledge. In a quick write, students are given two or three minutes to sum up what they have just learned.

■ Modify use of text. Conduct text walks or read and explain portions of the text. Make generous use of the text's illustrations. Also point out cognates. You might use Questioning the Author or reciprocal teaching to help students construct meaning.

■ Obtain texts that use a simpler language.

■ Make use of the students' native language. Provide explanations of complex concepts in the students' native language. If you are unfamiliar with their native language, ask another student who knows the language to provide the explanation. Encourage students to discuss content in their native language as well as in English.

■ Scaffold instruction. Provide prompts and other assistance as needed. Use prompts that encourage students to clarify or expand responses: "That's interesting. I'd like to hear more about that. Can you explain that? Can you tell us more? So what happened next?"

■ Plan opportunities for students to talk over ideas. This could be in whole-class discussions, pairs, or small groups. This gives English language learners (ELLs) the opportunity to use academic language as they engage in activities and discuss procedures and findings. ELLs are more willing to engage in discussions in small groups than they are in larger groups.

■ Use real-world materials such as signs, recycling and nutrition labels, menus, job applications, and bank deposit slips.

■ Provide wait time. Instead of requiring students to answer as soon as you pose a question, wait a few seconds. This is helpful to all students (Lake, 1973; Rowe, 1969) but is especially beneficial to ELLs because, being less familiar with the language, they need extra time to formulate their responses.

■ When assessing students' work, allow students to demonstrate their knowledge in multiple ways. If possible, include ways that don't rely so heavily on language. Students might conduct an experiment, draw a diagram, or complete a project.

In addition to teaching content-area vocabulary, it is also important to teach academic language, the language of instruction, so students understand what they are to do when they are asked to *compare, contrast, discuss, illustrate, predict, summarize,* or *give examples.* When giving directions, use visual aids and, if you are talking about a multistep process, model the process and walk students through each of the steps. Here is how one teacher combined instruction in content vocabulary with instruction in school language while introducing the concept of buoyancy (Echeverria, Vogt, & Short, 2000). Mr. Lew explained that the purpose of the unit was to find out why some objects float and others sink. As he said the word *float,* he pointed to an orange floating in a tank. As he said the word *sink,* he placed a peeled orange in the tank and the class watched as it sank. He also told the students that at the end of the unit, they would be able to calculate and predict whether an object would be buoyant enough to float. The words *float, sink, buoyant, calculate,* and *predict* were written on the board. Mr. Lew used the word *calculate* on purpose. He could have used the word *figure,* but he believed that *calculate* might be more readily recognized by the students because it is a cognate for *calcular* in Spanish and most of his students were native speakers of Spanish.

Throughout the unit, Mr. Lew used visuals, demonstrations, hands-on activities, and understandable language to convey the concept of buoyancy. Academic tasks were introduced in step-by-step fashion and were modeled. For instance, Mr. Lew carefully explained how they were to get into groups and make boats out of aluminum foil, calculate the object's mass, and determine the boat's buoyancy. They were to write summaries describing the results and create graphs. After carefully explaining each step, Mr. Lew then demonstrated the process. After that he asked the students to assemble in their groups, and start on their assignment. Circulating among the groups and answering questions, he noted that all the groups but one were on the right track. He asked one of the successful groups to show and explain what they had done so that the students in the struggling group could see what they should do (Echeverria, Vogt, & Short, 2000). The lesson was successful for all. Because of the careful explanations, demonstrations, use of visuals, small-group work, careful guidance, and use of comprehensible language, the students were able to grasp what they were supposed to do and complete the assignment, which enabled them to apply an important concept.

READING TO REMEMBER

Marge, a fifth-grader, is feeling anxious. She has been told to study the chapter on the Revolutionary War for a unit test the next day. Marge is a good reader and usually does well in school, but she is having trouble with history. She understands what she reads, but she does not remember the dates and names that the tests ask for. She remembers most of the main ideas but not the details. Marge's problem is a common one. She knows how to read for understanding, but she has no strategies for reading for retention. Marge has another problem, too. Whereas she reads for main ideas, the test will concentrate on details. Marge has to gear her studying for the type of test she will be given. Research suggests that knowing the type of test to be taken is an important factor in effective studying (Anderson & Armbruster, 1984).

Some students seem to learn on their own how to study for different types of tests, while others require instruction. Teachers should let students know what types of tests they intend to give and should explain how to study for each one. For example, essay tests require knowing the main ideas of the material; objective tests require more attention to details. Teachers should also discuss the difference between studying for multiple-choice tests, which require only that one recognize correct answers, and studying for fill-in-the-blank exams, which require recalling names, dates, or terms. Recognizing is, of course, far easier than recalling.

Studying also has an affective component. Up to 75 percent of academic failure is attributed to poor study habits or strategies. However, a number of studies conducted over the years indicate that when students are taught these skills, their performance improves significantly (Richardson & Morgan, 1994). A key element is motivation. When students are convinced of the value of study skills, they are more likely to use them (Schunk & Rice, 1987). Another crucial element in study strategy instruction is proving to students that these strategies work—they need to see that better studying leads to better grades.

Study habits develop early, and effective study skills take many years to learn. Locating, organizing, and taking steps to retain information should be an integral part of the elementary and middle school curriculum. From the very beginning, students should be taught how to preview a book to get an overview of its contents and how to use the table of contents. Students should also be taught in the earliest grades how to preview a section of text, make predictions, create questions, summarize, and then apply what they read. Instruction in these strategies will help build a solid foundation for effective study skills. This instruction will pave the way for the teaching of more formal study strategies such as SQ3R.

> The five basic principles of effective studying are: attention, goal orientation, organization, practice, and encoding specificity (Readence, Bean, & Baldwin, 1992). If students fail to pay attention to key ideas, they will learn the wrong material. Students must also have as a goal the intention to learn and remember material. If they simply read to complete an assignment, they will fail to use strategies that foster understanding and retention. Students are better able to learn material when they organize it in some way. Learning new material requires actual time spent practicing or studying the material. Encoding specificity means that the students learn the material in much the same way as they will be tested on it.

> Understanding content material isn't sufficient. Because students must also be able to retain and retrieve new information, study skills are an essential part of the elementary and middle school literacy curriculum.

FOSTERING RETENTION

Knowing how the memory works is the key to devising techniques to improve retention. Memory has three stages: encoding, storing, and retrieving. Encoding should be clear and purposeful; text that is vaguely understood will be quickly forgotten. Storage works best when the material is meaningful. Students will remember a piece of information better if they concentrate on its meaning rather than on the exact words used, which is why it is best to respond to questions in one's own words. Retrieval, or remembering, works best when the material is carefully encoded.

To get a sense of how memory works, read the following paragraph and see how much you can remember of it.

> With hocked gems financing him, our hero bravely defied all scornful laughter that tried to prevent his scheme. "Your eyes deceive," he had said. "An egg, not a table

correctly typifies this unexplored planet." Now three sturdy sisters sought proof. Forging along, sometimes through calm vastness, yet more often over turbulent peaks and valleys, days became weeks as many doubters spread fearful rumors about the edge. At last, from nowhere a welcomed winged creature appeared, signifying momentous success. (Carlson & Buskist, 1997, p. 247)

How much of this paragraph do you remember? Most people don't remember very much because the paragraph is not very meaningful to them. Unable to make connections, they can process it only on a shallow level. But now give the paragraph a title, "Columbus Discovers America." Read the paragraph again. Now how much do you remember? In experiments, people who were told the title before reading remembered significantly more (Dooling & Lachman, 1971). Improving encoding by making the material more understandable improves memory just as activating schema improves students' understanding and memory of a selection to be read.

Elaborating information also aids memory. For example, a student reads and might want to remember the following three facts from a selection about anteaters:

1. They have a long, thin snout.
2. They have sharp claws.
3. They have sticky tongues.

The student then elaborates on the text by asking herself or himself why anteaters have a long and thin snout, sharp claws, and a sticky tongue, and determines that it can use its long snout to poke into underground ant nests, its claws can rip open the nests, and it can pick up the ants with its sticky tongue. This elaboration aids long-term storage and retrieval.

The more connections that are constructed between items of information in memory, the greater the number of retrieval paths (Atkinson, Atkinson, Smith, & Hilgard, 1987). "Questions about the causes and consequences of an event are particularly effective elaborations because each question sets up a meaningful connection, or retrieval path, to the event" (p. 269).

Principles for Improving Memory

The following principles are based on the way that memory is believed to work and should aid retention:

- Get a clear, meaningful encoding of the material to be learned.
- Have a purposeful intention to learn. Activate strategies that will aid retention.
- Organize and elaborate information so that it will have a greater number of meaningful connections and thus will be easier to store and retrieve. Creating outlines, summaries, and maps; taking notes; reflecting; and applying information promote retention.
- Overlearning aids retention. **Overlearning** means that a person continues to study after the material has been learned. This extra practice pays off in

■ **Overlearning** refers to the practice of continuing to study after the material has been learned in order to foster increased retention.

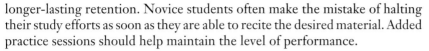

longer-lasting retention. Novice students often make the mistake of halting their study efforts as soon as they are able to recite the desired material. Added practice sessions should help maintain the level of performance.

- When it is not possible to structure meaningful connections between material to be learned and prior knowledge, use mnemonic and other memory devices to create connections. Some popular memory, or rehearsal, devices are described in the following section.

- Give your mind a rest. After intensive studying, take a break, rest, and get enough sleep. Sleep, it is believed, gives the brain the opportunity to organize information.

Memory Devices

■ Conceptual Understanding

The best way to remember new material is to achieve conceptual understanding. Bransford (1994) gives an example of a student who is studying arteries and veins for a test: The student knows that one type of blood vessel is thick and elastic, and one is thin and nonelastic, but he is not sure which is which. He can use a number of strategies to help him remember. He could use simple rehearsal and just say, "artery, thick, elastic" over and over. But a far better approach would be to seek conceptual understanding and ask, "Why are arteries thick and elastic?" The student has read that blood is pumped from the heart through the arteries in spurts and reasons, therefore, that the arteries must be elastic so that they can contract and expand for pumping. They have to be thick because they must withstand the pressure of the blood. If the explanation that enables the learner to see the significance of the information is not provided in the reading, the learner must seek it out.

■ Rehearsal

The simplest memory device of all is **rehearsal.** Rehearsal may be used when conceptual understanding is not feasible or possible. For instance, one has to memorize a list of arbitrary dates. In its most basic form, rehearsal involves saying the item to be memorized over and over again. It is the way students learn the names of the letters of the alphabet, the names of the vowels, and their home addresses and telephone numbers. Rehearsal works because it focuses the learner's attention on the items to be learned and transfers material into long-term memory (Weinstein & Mayer, 1986).

■ **Rehearsal** refers to the process of memorizing information.

■ Mnemonic Method

Rehearsal is an inefficient way to remember material. If at all possible, a more meaningful approach should be used. If conceptual understanding is not possible, learners might use a mnemonic method that constructs connections that are artificially meaningful. **Mnemonics** are artificial memory devices, such as using verses to remember how many days there are in each month ("thirty days has September, April, June, and November"). Mnemonics are used when it is not possible to create more meaningful connections. One especially useful mnemonic device is the key word technique.

■ **Mnemonics** refers to devices such as a rhyme used to aid memory. Mnemonics represent a level of processing deeper than simply saying an item over and over.

■ The **key word technique** is a memory device in which the learner associates a new word with a key word and a visual image that incorporates the key word and a portion of the target word.

The key word technique. The **key word technique** uses visual images to build associations. This technique was explained in Chapter 4 as a device for remembering vocabulary; however, it can also be used to remember facts (Peters & Levin, 1986).

To use the key word technique, students follow a two-step procedure. First, they create a key word that sounds like the item they wish to remember. For instance, to remember the name of James Smithson, who helped establish the Smithsonian Institution, students might choose the word *smile*. Then, students create an interactive image that involves both the key word and the person's accomplishment. For Smithson, the interactive image might be of a family smiling as they view the dinosaur exhibit in a museum. The dinosaurs are also smiling (Peters & Levin, 1986). The key word technique aids memory because when students see the name *Smithson*, they think of *smile*, which begins like *Smithson*, and picture people and animals smiling in a museum. Conversely, when students see the word *museum*, they think of people smiling in a museum and then think of *Smithson* because it has the same beginning letters and sounds as *smile*.

▎Try the key word technique with some difficult terms that you have to learn for this or another class. Note any difficulties that you encounter. Assess the effectiveness and utility of the technique.

Other mnemonic devices. An assortment of devices are used to aid in the memorization of facts and details. Many traditional rhymes were written specifically to help school children with memory tasks:

> In fourteen hundred and ninety-two
> Columbus sailed the ocean blue. . . .
>
> Use *i* before *e* except after *c*
> or when sounded like *a* as in *neighbor* and *weigh*.

■ An **acronym** is a word made up of the first letter of each of a series of words.

Acronyms. Words made from the first letters of a series of words are often used to assist memory. Common **acronyms** include *roy g. biv* for the colors of visible light in the order in which they appear in the spectrum (red, orange, yellow, green, blue, indigo, violet); and *homes* for the Great Lakes (Huron, Ontario, Michigan, Erie, and Superior).

■ An **acrostic** is a device in which the first letters in a series of words spell out a word or phrase or correspond to the first letters in another series of words to be memorized.

Acrostics. In **acrostics**, a simple phrase is used to learn a series of words or letters. For instance, *Every Good Boy Does Fine* has long been used as an aid in memorizing the letters of the string chords (E, G, B, D, and F) and *My Very Educated Mother Just Served Us Nine Pizzas* to help remember the names of the nine planets (Mercury, Venus, Earth, Mars, Jupiter, Saturn, Uranus, Neptune, Pluto). Acrostics and acronyms work because they provide a way to organize information whose natural organization is essentially random.

The best mnemonic devices are those that students create for themselves. Help the class create rhymes or other assists for remembering important dates, names, rules, or other items that have to be memorized.

▎Used to learning most material with ease, bright students may balk at memorizing and/or stop as soon as they can recite the information they have been studying. Demonstrate the benefits of using these strategies.

■ Flash Cards

Memorizing dates, names, formulas, or terms is essential but can be tedious. In addition, some students simply do not know how to memorize. To use flash cards as an aid to memorization, have students put each item to be learned on one side of a three-by-five card and its explanation or definition on the other. Students can make a game of memorizing by studying the items and then testing themselves, with the goal of getting all items correct. They should not attempt to learn too many items at one time. For some, five might be plenty; others may be able to handle eight to ten. Students' performance should be the guide as to how many items they attempt to learn at one sitting. As additional motivation, students can work with partners and take turns testing each other.

Metacognitive Awareness

In addition to learning how to use memory techniques, students must be able to recognize which techniques work best in certain circumstances. Acronyms and acrostics, for example, work best when memorizing lists of items. The key word technique works best for single words. Seeking conceptual understanding works best with meaningful material, such as key concepts. All strategies should be adapted to students' individual learning styles.

Distributed versus Massed Practice

Generally speaking, short practice sessions work better than long ones, especially when students are memorizing. Brief reviews are also important to forestall forgetting.

Distributed practice, or studying that is spread over a number of sessions, is often preferred over massed practice. Concentration can be best maintained for short periods, and there is less chance for the student to become bored. This is especially true when the student is engaged in rote tasks, such as studying spelling words or a list of dates. **Massed practice,** or studying for extended periods of time, works best when the material has a wholeness that would be lost if it were split into separate segments. Reading a long story or writing an essay would fall into this category. Lengthier study periods also seem to work better for students who have difficulty settling down and tend to fritter away the first fifteen minutes of a study session.

SQ3R: A THEORY-BASED STUDY STRATEGY

A five-step technique known as SQ3R—Survey, Question, Read, Recite, and Review—implements many of the principles presented in the previous section. Devised in the 1930s, it is the most thoroughly documented and widely used study technique in the English language. SQ3R, or a method based on it, appears in nearly every text that discusses studying. It is very effective when properly applied (Caverly & Orlando, 1991).

> "When students commit information to memory, the very act of knowing something increases their confidence, and often their self-image. This is especially important for students who may have gotten the idea that they do not know anything and that what they say has no value. The chief benefit of mnemonics and memory training is that, by making difficult study easier, they can kindle in the student a desire to learn" (Richardson & Morgan, 1994, p. 354).

Effective studying requires: task, strategy, and performance awareness. Task awareness means that the student is aware of what is to be studied—which chapters in the text, notes, etc. Strategy awareness means that the student has command of study strategies and knows which ones to use in a particular situation. Performance awareness means that the student can gauge when the material is mastered or to what extent it is mastered (Alvermann & Phelps, 1994).

■ **Distributed practice** refers to studying or doing practice exercises at intervals.

■ **Massed practice** refers to studying or doing practice exercises all at one time.

Principles of SQ3R

Although procrastination is natural and so we put off studying until the evening before the test, distributed practice or spreading out our studying over a period of time is more effective than is massed practice or cramming.

SQ3R is based on the following principles, derived from F. P. Robinson's (1970) review of research on studying:

- Surveying headings and summaries increases speed of reading, helps students remember the text and, perhaps most importantly, provides an overview of the text.
- Asking a question before reading each section improves comprehension.

SQ3R cannot be mastered in a day or even a month. Each element requires extensive practice and guidance. Students also have to be able to recognize whether they are applying the technique correctly and, if they are not, what they can do about it.

- Reciting from memory immediately after reading slows down forgetting. If asked questions immediately after reading, students are able to answer only about half of them. After just one day, 50 percent of what was learned is forgotten. Students are then able to answer just 25 percent of questions asked about a text. However, those who review the material have a retention rate of more than 80 percent one day later. In another study, students who spent 20 percent of their time reading and 80 percent reciting were able to answer twice as many questions as those who simply read the material (Gates, 1917).
- Understanding major ideas and seeing relationships among ideas helps comprehension and retention.
- Having short review sessions, outlining, and relating information to students' personal needs and interests are helpful.

Applying any one of Robinson's (1970) principles should result in more effective studying. However, Robinson based SQ3R on all of them. SQ3R consists of the procedure described in the following Student Strategy box, which prepares students to read and helps them organize, elaborate, and rehearse information from text.

STUDENT strategies **Applying SQ3R**

Although devised a half century ago, SQ3R incorporates many strategies recently recommended by cognitive psychologists: predicting or surveying, setting goals, constructing questions, summarizing, monitoring for meaning, and repairing.

1. *Survey.* Survey the chapter that you are about to read for an overall picture of what it is about. Glance over the title and headings. Quickly read the overview and summary. Note what main ideas are covered. This quick survey will help you organize the information in the chapter as you read it.
2. *Question.* Turn each heading into a question. The heading "Causes of the Great Depression" would become "What were the causes of the Great Depression?" Answering the question you created gives you a purpose for reading.
3. *Read.* Read to answer the question. Having a question to answer focuses your attention and makes you a more active reader.
4. *Recite.* When you come to the end of the section, stop and test yourself. Try to answer your question. If you cannot, go back over the section and then try once again to answer the question. The answer may be oral or written. Note, however, that a written answer is preferable

because it is more active and forces you to summarize what you have learned. The answer should also be brief; otherwise, SQ3R takes up too much time.

Do not take notes until you have read the entire section. Taking notes before completing the section interrupts your reading and could interfere with your understanding of the section. Repeat steps 2, 3, and 4 until the entire selection has been read.

5. *Review.* When you have finished the assignment, spend a few minutes reviewing what you read. If you took notes, cover them up. Then, asking yourself the questions you created from the headings, try to recall the major points that support the headings. The review helps you put information together and remember it longer.

In general, special elements should be treated the same way as text. For graphs, tables, and maps, the title is turned into a question and the information in the graph, table, or map is then used to answer the question (Robinson, 1970). A diagram may be as important as the text and merit special effort. After examining the diagram carefully, students should try to draw it from memory and then compare their drawings with the diagram in the book (Robinson, 1970). Drawing becomes a form of recitation.

Teaching SQ3R

Although originally designed for college students, SQ3R works well with elementary school students. In fact, if SQ3R or some of its elements are not taught in the early grades, college may be too late. By the upper elementary and middle school years, unless students have learned otherwise, they may have acquired inefficient study habits that are resistant to change (Walker, 1995). Very young readers can and should be taught to survey material, make predictions, and read to answer questions they have composed or to check how accurate their predictions were. Answering questions and reacting to predictions is a form of recitation. Once students are reading large amounts of text (in fourth grade or so) and are expected to remember information for tests, they should be introduced to all the principles of SQ3R or some other effective study strategy. If students are to be tested, they must know how to prepare for tests.

Teaching SQ3R requires a commitment of time and effort. Each step must be taught carefully, with ample opportunity provided for practice and application. Early and Sawyer (1984) recommended spending at least a semester using it with older students. Slower students require additional instruction and practice time (Caverly & Orlando, 1991). Even after it has been taught carefully and practiced conscientiously, SQ3R requires periodic review and reteaching.

To use SQ3R fully, students should be able to generate main ideas. It also helps if they have some knowledge of text structures (Walker, 1995).

In addition to needing a great deal of opportunity for application, students using SQ3R require individual feedback so that they can make necessary adjustments in the way the technique is applied.

"SQ3R is hard to teach because it requires not only the development of component skills but the replacement of old habits. Consider that most students—even the best of them—turn to the first page of a chapter and begin at the first word. It's the student in a hurry, sometimes the less conscientious one, who is sensible enough to turn first to the questions at the end to see what the authors consider important. The survey step requires skimming and scanning, which many students, again the better ones, shun" (Early & Sawyer, 1984, p. 422).

Numerous adaptations have been made to SQ3R. A step that several practitioners advocate adding is reflecting (Pauk, 1989; Thomas & Robinson, 1972; Vacca & Vacca, 1986). After reading, students are encouraged to think about the material and how they might use it. Before reading, students reflect on what they already know about the topic.

TEST-TAKING STRATEGIES

In addition to teaching students study strategies, teach them how to take a test. Of course, the best way to prepare for a test is to study conscientiously and strategically and to be fully aware of what will be tested and how it will be tested. A systematic way of teaching test-taking strategies is to implement PLAE: Preplanning, Listing, Activity, and Evaluating (Nist & Simpson, 1989).

■ *Preplanning.* In the preplanning stage, students describe the study task, asking questions such as these: What will the test cover? What kind of questions will be asked? What will be the format of the questions?

■ *Listing.* Based on preplanning information, students list the steps they will take to prepare for the test. They will answer the following or similar questions: How will I get ready for the test? When will I study? How long will I study? Which study strategies will I use?

■ *Activity.* Students activate their plans and monitor them. They ask whether they are using the right strategies and spending the right amount of time studying. They might ask the following or similar questions: Am I following my plan? If not, why not? Is my plan working? Am I learning what I need to learn? If not, what changes do I need to make in my plan? Am I using the best study strategies?

■ *Evaluating.* Based on their performance on the test, students evaluate the effectiveness of their study plans. They might ask questions such as these: Which questions did I miss? Why? Did I study all the material that the questions were based on? Did I remember the material? How could I have studied to get more questions right?

To help students develop realistic study strategies, arrange for practice study sessions and practice tests. Focus on the kinds of tests that students are most often required to take. Choose a selection that is representative of the type of material they will be tested on. Discuss the criterion task—the topic of the test to be given—and ways in which the material might be studied. Also discuss how students can self-test to assess how well they have studied (performance awareness). Then administer the test, and discuss the results. Discuss with students how effective their studying was and what might be done to improve it. Provide practice with several test formats, and acquaint students with any formats, such as cloze, that may be unfamiliar to them.

Test-Taking Tips

In addition to learning a test-taking strategy such as PLAE, students should be advised to get a good night's rest the night before a test, eat a good breakfast, and bring all necessary supplies. Other test-taking strategies include the following:

■ Surveying the test to see what is involved

■ Reading directions carefully

■ Using time well and not spending too much time on any one item

- Doing known or easy items first
- In a multiple-choice test, making careful guesses, especially if points are taken off for wrong answers

Preparation for High-Stakes Tests

As discussed in Chapter 2, beginning in 2005, students in grades three through eight must be assessed in reading and other areas each year. Results of the tests will be used to judge the proficiency of students and the effectiveness of school. States and local school districts may also decide to give additional tests. The best way to prepare students for high-stakes tests of this type is to have in place a high-quality literacy program and intervention programs for students who need them. In addition, students also need to know how to take tests. In their study of standardized test-taking among elementary school students, Calkins, Montgomery, and Santman (1998) found that a number of students had poor test-taking skills. They failed to follow directions, did not take guesses when it was to their benefit to do so, did not look back over a passage to find the right answer, did not check answers, and often used background rather than text knowledge to answer questions.

A program of test preparation should include:

- Teaching the language of tests and teaching students how to read and follow directions
- Teaching students how to use lookbacks, use their time well, and check answers
- Teaching students to read intensively and with full concentration as they take a test
- Teach students to answer questions on the basis of information in the test passage rather than one's personal experience or opinion

To gain insight into students' test-taking skills, observe them as they take a test. Note their test-taking strategies and how they use their time. Discuss with them their test-taking strategies. Model test-taking strategies. Show how you go about taking a test. Explain your thinking processes as you read and follow directions. Show how you answer the easiest items first and go about eliminating answer choices when you are not sure of an answer. Model the process of checking answers and pacing yourself. Provide extra coaching for students whose responding style lowers their scores: those who work too rapidly and fail to check answers as well as those who work too slowly and are overly concerned with making a mistake. Provide students with strategies for reading difficult passages and answering tough questions. Also explain the correction factor. On some tests, students lose a quarter of a point for wrong responses, and so are better off leaving an answer blank if they have no idea which of the answer options is correct. However, if they eliminate more than one of the options, the odds of getting the right answer are in their favor. If there is no penalty for guessing, students should make their best guess.

Test preparation should be ethical. Providing students with items from the actual test is unethical. It is also unethical to raise students' scores without also increasing their underlying knowledge and skill (Popham, 2000). The goal of test preparation is to instruct students so that they have the test-taking skills to enable them to show what they know and can do. Test-taking preparation should not be so extensive that it displaces other valuable literacy activities.

STUDY HABITS

Some people have such intense powers of concentration that they seem to be able to study almost anywhere. As a child, the Nobel Prize–winning scientist Madame Curie became so engrossed in a book that she was not aware that her siblings had constructed a pyramid of chairs over her until she had completed her reading, bumped into the chairs, and the pyramid collapsed (Curie, 1937). Most students do not have such a remarkable ability to concentrate and will study best under certain controlled conditions. Ideally, each student should have a quiet place to study that is free of distractions. The area should be well lit, contain a desk or other writing surface, and be supplied with paper, pens, pencils, and a few basic reference books, such as a dictionary and an almanac. Of course, not every child has the luxury of such a retreat, but children should be advised to find the best study spot they can. In even the most crowded homes, there is a time when quiet prevails. One member of a ten-person family did his studying early in the morning while everyone else was asleep.

Studying, however, is more a matter of attitude than place. Research and common practice suggest that students study best when they meet the following conditions:

- They know how to study.
- They know why they are studying. The assignment has value and the students understand what that value is.
- They know what type of test they are studying for and how to adjust their efforts to meet its demands.
- They have a routine. Studying requires discipline. Students should determine the best time for them to study and then study at that time every day. Generally, study should precede recreation.
- Studying is active and purposeful. An hour of concentrated study is better than two hours of studying in which the student takes many breaks and lets her or his attention wander.

Another condition that fosters effective studying includes rewarding oneself. Suggest that students reward themselves for a job well done. For instance, they might treat themselves to a snack or to watching a favorite TV show after forty-five minutes of concentrated study. Having an interest in the material also makes it easier to study and learn. Some material is intrinsically interesting; in other cases, interest has to be built. Students should be encouraged to envision how a certain subject might fit in with their personal needs and goals. If that fails, they can remember the extrinsic rewards—studying the material will result in a higher grade, for example.

■ Discuss study habits and strategies with the class. Invite students to tell how, when, and where they study. Highlight successful strategies and habits.

■ Unless steps are taken to prevent it, the rate of forgetting is rapid. Within days, we forget 60 percent of what we have learned. Students may believe that forgetting is a sign of a lack of ability. Explain to students that forgetting is natural, but we can enhance our memories through studying (Richardson & Morgan, 1994).

*A*lthough having a quiet place to study helps, studying is more a question of attitude than location.

Students need to see a payoff for studying. Those who study hard but get poor grades on tests will become discouraged. In order to increase the chance that their studying will pay off in higher grades, students should be told exactly what type of test they will be given and how to study for that test. Tests should reflect the content that has been emphasized and should take the form that you, as the teacher, indicated they would take. They should contain no trick questions.

Introducing Study Strategies and Habits

Discuss with students the importance of studying and the specific payoffs it has. Also discuss the results of not studying. Talk over hindrances to studying and how these might be overcome. You might also model how you go about studying for a test and then provide guided practice. Observe students as they study and discuss the procedures that they use. Lead them to use efficient study strategies. Also help students make a detailed study plan. This should include not only what they will study and why, but where, when, how long, and under what circumstances. Study plans should be individualized, so encourage students to try different techniques. Part of learning to study is discovering how, when, and where one studies best.

❚ Learning a new habit takes about three months or more (Prochaska, Norcross, & DiClemente, 1994). Provide ongoing instruction, practice, and encouragement.

EXPRESSIVE STUDY SKILLS

A key part of studying is recording information in some way. This might take the form of traditional or simplified notes or various kinds of graphic organizers.

Taking Notes

Taking notes is an essential study skill. It is also a very practical one. Writing telephone messages is a form of note taking, as is jotting down a series of complex de-

❚ Taking notes is better than highlighting. In taking notes we think more deeply about the information, so we understand it better and remember it longer (Carlson & Buskist, 1997).

tails. Teaching students how to take phone messages provides them with a practical skill and can also be an effective introduction to note taking. Model the process of taking messages. Emphasize that it is necessary to obtain only the essential information: who called, whom the call was for, and the caller's message. Pretend that you are a caller and have students take notes. Discuss the clarity and conciseness of their notes. Have pairs of students role-play, with one student playing the part of the caller, the other the message taker. Also discuss real-life cases in which students have taken notes.

As students begin writing expository reports, a natural need arises for note taking. They have to have some method for preserving information drawn from a variety of sources. As they prepare to write reports, share with them experiences you have had taking notes. Model how you might take notes from an encyclopedia or other source. Teach students a tried-and-true procedure that might include the steps outlined in the Student Strategy below.

 Taking notes

1. Write the name of the topic on the top line of the card: for example, "Camels—how they help people." Turn the topic into a question: "How do camels help people?"

2. Search for information that answers the question. You do not have to read every word of each article that you locate on your topic. You can skim through to find the relevant facts, and you can skip parts that do not contain what you are looking for.

3. Take notes on details that answer your question. Put the notes in your own words. The best way to do this is to read a brief section and write the important facts from memory. To save time and space, leave out words that are not important like *the*, *a*, and *an*. Write in phrases instead of sentences, and do not bother with punctuation except in quotations.

4. Check back over the section. Make sure that you have taken all the notes that answer your question and that you have put them in your own words. Sometimes, you may want to quote someone's exact words. Maybe a famous scientist said something interesting about camels. If you use exact words, make sure that you put quotation marks around them. Also make sure that you write exactly what the person said.

5. Fill in identifying information. At the bottom of the card, write the page number where you got your information. At the top, write the author's name, title of the article, title of the book or periodical, volume number if it has one, publisher's name, place where the publisher is located, and date of publication. (Younger students may use a simplified bibliographic reference.) The finished notes might look like those in Figure 7.10.

A major problem with elementary and middle school students' research reports is that often they are verbatim copies of encyclopedia articles. Having students take notes in their own words is one way to eliminate this. Another is to request that students obtain information from at least two sources. Actually, encyclopedias should be only a starting point. Their information is limited and often dated. Encourage students to find other sources from the large number of high-quality informational books published each year and high-quality Web sites. Students should also be encouraged to think over the information they have collected and to select only the most essential details for inclusion in their reports. The ultimate solution to this problem is to have students explore areas in which they have a genuine interest. Calkins and Harwayne (1991) called this "writing with voice": "We will write with voice when we have read, questioned, dreamed, argued, worried, wept, gossiped, and laughed over a topic" (p. 201).

If students are using an electronic source, such as a CD-ROM encyclopedia, they may be able to make use of special note-taking features. The program will probably allow them to cut and paste so that they do not have to copy all of the information by hand. They will also be able to copy charts and graphs. The electronic encyclopedia *Encarta* (for instance), uses both "Notemarks" and "Notecards" to help students take notes from text. "Notemarks" serve the same purpose as sticky notes do. Students can mark a page or passage or write brief notes about a passage. The notes can be collected in a list, edited, and printed out. "Notecards" function in the same way as traditional notecards. *World Book Multimedia Encyclopedia*, which has similar features, will allow students to look just at headings so that they get an outline view of an article or topic. This outline might be used as headings for their notes. Both encyclopedias offer students opportunities to seek out related information on the Web.

Encarta also walks students through the process of taking notes and has a feature, called "Source Wizard," that helps them document the source of the information as well as an outline feature that helps students organize their notes. One additional advantage of electronic references is that most of them have a speech component so that students can have words, phrases, or whole articles read to them. This plus the generous use of graphics is an aid to struggling readers and ELLs.

FIGURE 7.10

Example of Note Taking

Camels—how they help people

Dagg, Ann Innis. Camel. *World Book Encyclopedia*, Vol. 3, Chicago: World Book, 2000, pp. 75–78.

Pull plows
Turn water wheels to work pumps
Carry grain to market
Carry people and their goods
Meat of young camels is eaten—can be tough
Fat from hump used as butter
Can drink camel's milk and make cheese
Camel's milk is very rich
Hair made into cloth and blankets
Skin used to make tents
Skin used to make leather for shoes, saddles, saddlebags
Bones used for decorations and as cooking and eating utensils

---

USING TECHNOLOGY

Most of the CD-ROM encyclopedia programs incorporate note-taking features, as does the *Factfinders* series. Because of the novelty and ease of use of note-taking features in computer programs, they can be used to encourage note taking.

Outlining

A complex skill, outlining requires that students note the relative importance of major and minor details. As Anderson and Armbruster (1984) observed, "A potential problem with outlining as a study aid is that it is very time consuming to think through the logical relationships in text and represent the meaning in outline form" (p. 673).

If full outlining is beyond the capabilities of your students, try simple outlining. Simple outlining can be a valuable study aid. Santa (1988) devised proposition-support and opinion-proof outlines (see Figure 7.11) that may be used with students. In these two-level outlines, students state a proposition or an opinion and then list supporting statements. The main steps in introducing this procedure are detailed in Lesson 7.4.

 Introducing simple outlining

Step 1. Explain and model the procedure. Read a brief selection and construct a proposition or thesis. Then search out proof or supporting details. Place the proposition and proof on the chalkboard or an overhead projector, explaining the process as you go along.

Step 2. Have students divide their papers into two columns as in Figure 7.11, or supply sheets on which columns have been created.

Step 3. After reading a brief selection, help students develop a proposition.

Step 4. Help students find proof for the proposition and list the proof in the support portion of the outline.

Step 5. Check over the outline to ensure that all the important supporting details have been included and that the outline is clear. As an extension, students might use their outlines as a basis for drawing conclusions or writing expository pieces.

Step 6. Have students develop proposition-support outlines independently.

Using the Internet to Obtain Information

According to Google.com, the Web has close to two billion sites. With all those sites, searching efficiently is a key skill in today's information age. Just as with a traditional library search, an efficient Web search starts with a careful delineation of the topic and the questions that the students hope to answer. Student researchers must compose a topic statement or question(s) to be answered. A key

FIGURE 7.11

A Simplified Two-Level Outline

Proposition	Support
Animals help the disabled.	Guide dogs for the blind Hearing-ear dogs for the deaf Aid dogs for the physically handicapped
Animals help the elderly.	Keep them company Keep them active Give them an interest in life

skill is narrowing the topic so that it has reasonable limits. A student interested in robots, for instance, might limit her topic to a history of industrial robots, robots in the automobile industry, robots of the future, fire fighting robots, or rescue robots. Simply typing in *robots* using a Googgle search turned up more than a million references.

■ Using Subject Directories and Indexes

Subject directories and indexes are often overlooked as sources of information. Indexes or directories arrange information by categories. They can be searched by examining and clicking on categories or entering keywords. Directories are arranged in hierarchical fashion. For instance, in Yahooligans, *alpaca* is listed under *farm animals*, which is listed under *animals*, which is listed under *science and nature*. Students can start with *science and nature* and work their way on to *alpacas* or simply type in the keyword *alpacas*. One advantage of directories is that students need have only a general idea of what they're looking for. They need not know the precise terms. A second advantage of directories is that they are compiled by humans so items are placed in a category because they belong there, not simply because they contain certain words. Other useful subject directories are listed below:

About.com: http://www.about.com

Librarians' Index: http://lii.org

Open Directory Project: http://dmoz.org/

WWW Virtual Library: http://www.vlib.org/

■ Search Engines and Directories for Students

A number of search engines and directories have been specially designed for student use. Sites have been inspected by librarians or other professionals to make sure that they are appropriate for students. Some of the most widely used include:

- *AOL NetFind Kids Only:* Contains links to sites that are safe for students.
- *Awesome Library:* Provides links to 22,000 carefully reviewed resources for students of all ages. The browser is available in a number of languages and has

a translation feature so that users can browse in Spanish and more than a dozen other languages.

http://www.awesomelibrary.org/

- *Ask Jeeves for Kids:* Uses questions rather than keywords to conduct a search. The reader types in a question, and the engine responds by listing the writer's question and/or similar questions and sites that provide possible answers.

    http://www.ajkids.com/

- *KidsClick!* Web search for kids by librarians. Lists about 5,000 Web sites. Gives estimated readabilities of sites.

    http://sunsite.berkeley.edu/KidsClick!/

- *Yahooligans!* Launched in 1996 and designed for young people from seven to twelve, Yahooligans is the oldest major directory for students.

    http://www.yahooligans.com/

One problem with search engines for students is that they will turn up only a very limited number of sites. The problem with general search engines is that they locate inappropriate material. However, many general search engines have filtering devices. Filtering systems are mechanical. They may exclude sites that should be included and fail to block some that are objectionable. The advantage of general searches is that they locate many more sites. Google located 12,000 sites in response to a quest for a history of robots. Search engines for students located only one or two.

■ Obtaining Articles

Also available on the Internet are computerized searches of periodicals and general references that include the text, so that students can view the references and obtain the articles. One such service is Infotrac, which has several versions designed specifically for students. The general student edition contains nearly 2 million articles. Libraries subscribe to the service and then offer it to patrons. Patrons use their library bar codes or some sort of password to access the services from their home or school computer.

■ Preparing and Conducting a Search

In preparation for a student search of the Internet, discuss students' topics and their key questions. After students have established their questions, they might then decide what key or concept words will enable them to obtain answers to their questions. For instance, a student interested in ways in which robots are used to manufacture cars might frame her questions as: How are robots used to manufacture cars? Possible keywords might include: *robots, cars, manufacture* and synonyms of these words. A sample worksheet for searching the Internet is presented in Figure 7.12.

After locating sources of information, students need to sift through and locate sources that are offering pertinent information. Overloaded with information, it is important that today's students learn how to select the best data. Model

FIGURE 7.12

Internet Search Form

Internet Search Form

What question do you want answered? Be as specific as you can.

How are robots used to manufacture cars?

What are the keywords in your question? What are synonyms for your keywords?

Keywords	Synonyms
car	auto, vehicle
robot	
manufacture	assemble

Using only key words, what will you ask the search engine to find?

(car OR auto OR vehicle) AND robot AND (manufacture OR assemble)

Put parentheses around synonyms and join them with OR. Put AND between keywords.

Adapted from Creighton University (2001). *Conducting an Internet Search.* Available online at http://www.creighton.edu.

and discuss with students techniques for selecting material that provides answers to their questions. Demonstrate how you use titles or brief annotations or quickly skim articles to decide whether a source is pertinent. In addition to assessing the source to see whether it contains pertinent information, students must also evaluate the source to see whether the information is reliable, as was explained in Chapter 6.

METACOGNITIVE STUDY STRATEGIES

The key to teaching children how to direct their study is to present metacognitive study strategies within the context of material to be read or a project to be undertaken. Although presented in context, the strategies must be taught in such a way that they transfer to other texts and other situations. As with the comprehension strategies introduced in earlier chapters, it is essential that the metacognitive demands be presented and integrated with cognitive and affective factors.

Metacognitive strategies that apply to virtually all study tasks are listed in Table 7.4 (Nisbet & Shucksmith, 1986). Students involved in writing reports and other long-term projects should learn to go through the six stages: asking questions, planning, monitoring, checking, revising, and self-testing, as shown in the table. These stages, in adapted, abbreviated form, can also be used in studying for tests and completing daily homework assignments. Initially, you should walk the students step by step through these stages. Gradually, they should assume responsibility for each stage on their own; ideally, this will become automatic.

TABLE 7.4	Metacognitive study strategies
Strategy	**Examples**
Asking questions: What do I want to learn?	This includes setting up hypotheses, setting aims, defining boundaries of area to be explored, discovering audience, and relating task to previous work.
Planning: How will I go about the task?	This includes deciding on tactics and subdividing the overall task into subtasks.
Monitoring: Am I answering my questions?	This is a continuing attempt to see whether the results of one's efforts are matching the questions posed or purposes set.
Checking: How have I done so far?	This is a preliminary check to assess results and tactics.
Revising: What do I have to change?	Tactics, results, or goals may have to be changed.
Self-testing: How did I do? What did I learn?	In this final evaluation, both the results and method of achieving them are assessed.

Along with responding to these metacognitive questions, students also need to use self-regulatory behaviors to complete academic tasks. They must use self-discipline and perseverance in order to overcome obstacles and forge ahead. Students work best when they understand why they are undertaking a project, understand what they are to do, feel that the task is doable, and have the necessary materials and strategies. Encourage students to tell you of any obstacles that they encounter. Discuss ways in which they might overcome these obstacles. Provide guidance and encouragement as needed (Gensemer, 1998).

HELP FOR STRUGGLING READERS AND WRITERS

ADAPTING INSTRUCTION for *STRUGGLING READERS*

For students who have severe reading difficulties, obtain tape versions of their texts and review ways of studying information from an oral source. Recordings for the Blind and Dyslexic (20 Roszel Road, Princeton, NJ 08540) provides taped versions of school textbooks for students with reading problems. Taped periodicals and children's books are available from Talking Books, National Library Service for the Blind and Physically Handicapped (includes dyslexia), Library of Congress, Washington, DC 20542.

Struggling readers and writers can be helped in a number of ways to cope with content-area materials. An attempt should be made to provide materials that are as close as possible to students' reading levels. This might entail obtaining easy-to-read texts or easy-to-read trade books that cover key social studies topics. Some such trade books are listed in Appendix A. You might make the text more accessible by providing extra help with key words and concepts, reading all or parts of it with students, making or obtaining tapes of the text, or creating a gloss. You might also use a language experience approach. You read portions of the text to students or discuss key concepts and then discuss the information. After the discussion, students, aided by your prompts, dictate a summary, which you write on the chalkboard or overhead transparency. After the summary has been composed, you read it and then volunteers read it and discuss it. The summary is duplicated and given to students to read on their own. A collection of these summaries might be assembled and used as a content-area text.

Completing hands-on activities, conducting experiments and demonstrations, and viewing filmstrips and videos also provide students with content-area concepts. While engaging in these activities, emphasize building background, vocabulary, and reasoning skills. The activities will help build students' competence in comprehending the content areas.

ESSENTIAL STANDARDS

The essential standards translate the information presented in this chapter into relatively specific student objectives so that you will be better able to apply the instructional program discussed. However, the objectives are flexible. Feel free to add or modify objectives or move objectives from one grade level to another. The objectives should be tailored to meet the needs of your particular teaching situation.

Fourth through eighth grades
Students will

- use a variety of strategies to learn from informational text.
- use various types of writing to learn content-area information.
- use text features such as headings, maps, charts, and graphs to foster understanding.
- use understanding, rehearsal, and mnemonics to remember information.
- take notes from text and interviews.
- identify questions to be explored, use multiple sources, including electronic texts, and present reports that use visuals to support the report.
- plan and complete short-term and long-term assignments.
- select an appropriate place to study and develop appropriate study habits.
- use effective test-taking strategies.

ASSESSMENT

Using observations, quizzes, tests, samples of students' work, and discussions, note how well students are able to comprehend content-area materials. Assess, in particular, how effectively they use appropriate strategies. Assess, too, whether students are using study strategies and whether or not they have good study habits. One way of determining this is to analyze their test grades and the quality of their projects.

ACTION PLAN

1. Decide what content you want to teach.
2. Select appropriate materials, including texts, trade books, periodicals, CD-ROMs, and Web sites.
3. Use group or individual inventories to help you determine students' reading levels.
4. Match materials to students' level of reading ability. Make adjustments in materials and approaches and provide additional help as needed.
5. Use PReP, Anticipation guides, the survey technique, structured overviews, and other techniques to prepare students for their reading.
6. Guide students in the use of chapter organization, text structure, think-alouds, study guides, and glosses to foster comprehension during reading.
7. Use analogies, graphic organizers, reflection, and application to extend and deepen students' understanding after they have finished reading.
8. Use approaches such as KWL to foster understanding before, during, and after reading.
9. Teach content knowledge and guide students through conceptual change.
10. Use reports, logs, and journals to foster students' learning.
11. Use sheltered English or a similar approach to help ELL learn English as they learn content.
12. Guide students in the use of study techniques such as SQ3R and mnemonic devices.
13. Teach students test-taking skills but do not overemphasize them.
14. Build effective study habits and metacognitive awareness of study skills.
15. Teach outlining, note taking, I-Charts, and other expressive study skills.
16. Guide students in the use of the Internet to obtain information.
17. Monitor the progress of students and make adjustments as necessary.

SUMMARY

1. Content-area textbooks, which account for most of the teaching and learning of subject matter, pose special problems because they are more complex than narrative materials and may contain a high proportion of difficult concepts and technical vocabulary. In addition, they require reading to learn, which is a step beyond reading to comprehend. Children's books enliven content-area instruction and can be used along with or instead of content-area textbooks.
2. Numerous strategies can be used to prepare students for content-area textbooks: PReP, anticipation guides, and structured overviews. During-reading strategies include imaging, graphic aids, textual aids, think-alouds, and study guides. After-reading strategies feature construction of analogies, graphic organizers, and application and extension. KWL Plus can be used during all three phases of reading.
3. Content and strategies should be combined. The nature of the content determines choice of strategies. Increased content knowledge also makes strategies easier to apply.
4. In sheltered English, students learn content and English.
5. Concepts that run counter to students' commonsense ideas pose a special problem. To counter misconceptions, it is important to teach for conceptual change.
6. Writing is a powerful way to promote learning in the content area.
7. Studying requires remembering in addition to understanding material. Retention of important information is improved by understanding, organization, and elaboration.
8. Rehearsal is an appropriate strategy for learning materials that lack meaningful connections. Memory devices such as the key word technique,

rhymes, acronyms, and acrostics should be used with materials that lack meaningful connections.

9. A study strategy that has been effective with a variety of students is SQ3R (Study, Question, Read, Recite, Review). An effective technique for taking tests is PLAE (Preplanning, Listing, Activity, and Evaluating).

10. Good study habits include finding an appropriate time and place to study and studying purposefully as part of a regular routine.

11. Expressive study skills include taking notes, outlining, composing reports, and conducting efficient Internet searches.

12. Metacognitive strategies essential to studying include asking questions, planning, monitoring, checking, revising, and self-testing.

13. Help for struggling readers and writers includes making the content information accessible to students and providing hands-on experiences.

EXTENDING AND APPLYING

1. Examine an up-to-date content-area book. Using the Fry readability graph (Figure 2.11) or the Qualitative Assessment of Texts (Chall, Bissex, Conard, & Harris-Sharples, 1996) on at least three separate passages of one hundred words or more, obtain an estimate of the readability of the book. Also note textual features such as those listed in Table 7.1. How does the book shape up? What are its strengths and weaknesses?

2. Try out one of the strategies described in this chapter for at least a week. Use a learning log to keep a record of your experience. How well did it work? How hard was it to use? How practical is it?

3. Create a lesson showing how you would introduce KWL or another strategy to a class. If possible, teach the lesson and evaluate its effectiveness.

4. Prepare a study guide or gloss for a chapter in a science or social studies textbook or children's book. If possible, use the guide with a class. Have students react to the guide, telling how it helped them and how it might be changed to make it better.

DEVELOPING A PROFESSIONAL PORTFOLIO

Include items that demonstrate your ability to teach content area literacy skills or study skills. The items might be a taped lesson, lesson or unit plans, or examples of students' work, such as a learning log or completed KWL chart. Be sure to describe and reflect on items included.

DEVELOPING A RESOURCE FILE

1. Collect and/or create mnemonic devices for learning key facts in a subject matter or skill area that you teach.

2. Start a collection of bibliography cards or database entries on books that might supplement or replace the textbook in the content area that you teach or plan to teach. Try to locate books on easy, average, and challenging levels.

8

Reading Literature

*F*or each of the following statements related to the chapter you are about to read, put a check under "Agree" or "Disagree" to show how you feel. Discuss your responses with classmates before you read the chapter.

		Agree	*Disagree*
1	A literature program for the elementary and middle school should emphasize the classics.	_____	_____
2	The main danger of a literature approach to reading is that selections will be overanalyzed.	_____	_____
3	Students need to rely on the teacher for an accurate interpretation of literature.	_____	_____
4	Students should have some say in choosing the literature they read.	_____	_____
5	It does not really matter what children read just as long as they read something.	_____	_____
6	Setting aside a period each day for voluntary reading is an excellent use of time.	_____	_____

USING WHAT YOU KNOW

*H*ow do you go about reading a piece of literature? Do you read it in the same way that you read a popular novel? If your approach is different, how is it different? When reading literature, students use many of the same processes that they use when reading more mundane materials; word-attack and comprehension strategies and skills are necessary. However, reading literature involves going beyond mere comprehension. The focus is on appreciation, enjoyment, and reader response. This chapter explores ideas for building understanding and appreciation of folklore, myths, poems, plays, and novels and ends with suggestions for promoting voluntary reading.

What are your favorite kinds of literature? What experiences have you had that created a love of literature? What experiences have you had that may have created negative feelings about literature? How might literature be taught so that students learn to understand and appreciate it without losing the fun of reading it? What might be done to make students lifelong readers of high-quality novels, poetry, plays, and biographies?

EXPERIENCING LITERATURE

Reading literature involves a dimension beyond reading ordinary material. If read properly, a classic tale draws out a feeling of wholeness or oneness, a carefully drawn character or situation evokes a feeling of recognition, and a poem that speaks to the heart engenders a feeling of tranquility. Louise Rosenblatt (1978) called this the **aesthetic** response: "In aesthetic reading, the reader's attention is centered directly on what he is living through during his relationship with that particular text" (p. 25).

In contrast to aesthetic reading is **efferent reading,** in which the reader's attention is directed to "concepts to be refined, ideas to be tested, actions to be performed after the reading" (Rosenblatt, 1978, p. 24). In efferent reading, the reader "carries away" meaning. In aesthetic reading, the reader is carried away by feelings evoked by the text. Text can be read efferently or aesthetically, depending on the reader's stance. For example, we could read an essay efferently for ideas or information, but if we respond to its biting satire or subtle humor, our stance becomes aesthetic. Thus, it is not an either/or proposition but falls on a continuum, with the reader moving closer to one stance or the other depending on her or his expectations and focus (Dias, 1990). As Rosenblatt (1991) explained, "We read for information, but we are conscious of emotions about it and feel pleasure when the words we call up arouse vivid images and are rhythmic to the inner ear" (p. 445).

Rosenblatt cautioned that it is important to have a clear sense of purpose when asking students to read a particular piece. The purpose should fit in with the nature of the piece and the objective for presenting it. By its nature, for instance, poetry generally demands an aesthetic reading. But if the focus of the reading is on literal comprehension, then the experience will be efferent. The reading is aesthetic if the focus is on experiencing the poem or story and savoring the sounds, sights, and emotions that the words conjure up.

How might students' responses be fostered? The research suggests several possibilities. Students might be allowed to choose the form of their response: It could be a poem, a story, a letter, a journal entry, or, simply, an oral reaction. It is important that students be encouraged to make connections with their personal lives and other texts that they have read. Students also need time to respond, with ample opportunity to share and discuss. As Cox and Many (1992) commented, "A lot of groping goes on during this talking and again seems necessary to provide for quick flashes of personal understanding that come suddenly and quickly during informal, open discussions" (p. 32). Individual response is at the heart of reading literature.

■ **Aesthetic reading** refers to experiencing emotions evoked by a piece of writing.

■ **Efferent reading** means reading to comprehend the information conveyed by a piece of writing.

Students interpret literature in terms of their own experience. For instance, in their discussions of *Maniac Magee* (Spinnelli, 1990), a tale of a homeless boy and race relations in a small town, students spoke of how characters in the books remind them of family members (Lehr & Thompson, 2000). They made connections between events in their lives and what was happening to the characters in the book. One student, who had been shuffled between his mother's house and grandmother's, identified with Maniac Magee's satisfaction at finally having an address.

Reader Response Theory

To illustrate **reader response theory,** Probst (1988) described observing a class discussion of a story about a student who, feeling pressured to succeed, yielded to a temptation to cheat on a test. The tale hit home. Not even waiting for the teacher to initiate the discussion, one student remarked, "I know exactly how he felt" (p. 32). The student then explained how, because of parental pressure to achieve, she might cheat if she felt she were going to fail a test. A lively, spontaneous discussion erupted. However, the teacher's purpose for the lesson was to review with her class the literary devices for revealing character. Persisting with her question, "Now there are three ways an author reveals character—can you tell me what they are?" (p. 33), the teacher succeeded in quelling the discussion and extracting the correct answer from the subdued group. The teacher missed a wonderful opportunity to lead the students to experience the power of literature and how its themes often relate to their lives. Ironically, she could also have fostered a deeper understanding of literary techniques, including ways to reveal character, thereby achieving her original purpose. If she had allowed the students to respond fully to the piece, they would have been more interested in how the author had crafted such a gripping tale.

As Probst (1988) pointed out, the teacher had an erroneous vision of the purpose of literature. To her, it was a series of technical terms and techniques to be grasped, which is a little like trying to understand the workings of the mind by memorizing the parts of the brain. However, the ultimate purpose of literature is to touch our inner lives in some way. Unless we feel that touch, we do not truly experience literature. Rosenblatt (1990) explained that there are a number of practices that hinder an aesthetic response:

> The habit of explaining the literary qualities of the work by pointing to elements in the text (such as rhythm, imagery, metaphor, and departures from ordinary diction) has prevented the realization that the reader must first of all adopt what I term an "aesthetic stance"—that is, focus on the private, as well as the public aspects of meaning. Reading to find the answer to a factual question requires attention only to the public aspects of meaning, and excludes, pushes into the periphery, any personal feelings or ideas activated. (p. 104)

The teacher's first purpose, then, should be to evoke a response. Because literature is a **transaction** between reader and writer, that response must be personal. Using a poem, story, novel, or other literary work as a blueprint, readers can create their own work. A class of twenty-five students reading *The Lion, the Witch, and the Wardrobe* (Lewis, 1950) will create twenty-five different versions of that classic story. This does not mean that readers are free to interpret a literary selection in any way that they want. Their interpretations must be based on the blueprint, which is the text. However, to build from that blueprint, readers bring their life experiences, perspectives, experiences in reading literature, cognitive ability, attitudes, and values, all of which become part of the final meaning that they construct. As a practical matter, readers often agree on some common meaning in their response to a piece of literature. However, there is also considerable personal interpretation and reaction (Beach & Hynds, 1991).

To promote aesthetic reading, "teachers should recognize, support, and further encourage signs that the reader's focus of attention is on the lived-through experience of the literary evocation. . . . [T]he signs of the aesthetic response may include: picturing and imagining while reading or viewing; imagining themselves in a character's place or in story events; questioning or hypothesizing about a story; making associations with other stories and their own life experiences; and mentioning feelings evoked" (Cox & Many, 1992, pp. 32–33).

■ **Reader response theory** is a view of reading in which the reader plays a central role in constructing the meaning of a text. The meaning is not found in the text or the reader but is found in the relationship or transaction between the two.

Huck (1989) stated, "Most of what children learn in school is concerned with knowing; literature is concerned with feeling" (p. 254).

■ **Transaction** is the process whereby the reader is part of the reading act so that the reader is affected by the text and the text, in turn, is affected by the reader. Reader, text, and the act of reading all have an impact on each other and are, in turn, impacted.

Readers who make aesthetic responses enjoy a richer experience and produce more elaborated written responses. When elementary school students write from an aesthetic stance, the students' responses are more fully developed and more likely to show connections between the text and their lives. Efferent responses are more likely to consist of a bare-bones retelling of the tale and a brief evaluation of literary elements (Many, 1990, 1991).

Essentially, therefore, teaching literature is a matter of planning activities in which students respond to a selection and then clarify the impact of the selection in terms of itself and its meaning in their lives. It is important to create an environment in which students feel free to deal with their own reactions first and then work out, through reflection and discussion, a personal meaning for the piece. Although in the early stages the reader's response to literature may be highly personal, readers gradually learn to become more evaluative. As Rosenblatt (1991) explained, personal response becomes the basis for "growth toward more and more balanced, self-critical, knowledgeable interpretation" (p. 100).

How does one go about eliciting reader response? Probst (1988) described the following general steps:

1. *Creating a reader response environment.* Establish a setting in which students feel free to respond and each response is valued so that students are free of worry about rightness or wrongness.

2. *Preparing to read the literary piece.* Preparation for reading a literary piece is basically the same as that for reading any text: A DRA framework might be used. In the preparatory stage, a schema is activated, new concepts and vocabulary words are taught, interest in reading the selection is engendered, and a purpose is set. The purpose generally is open-ended, to evoke a response. As an alternative, the teacher might read aloud and discuss the first portion, especially if it is a chapter book or novel.

3. *Reading the literary piece.* The work is read silently by students. However, if it is a poem, you may elect to read it aloud, as the sound of poetry is essential to its impact.

4. *Small-group discussion.* The literary piece is discussed by groups consisting of four or five students. In small groups, each student has a better opportunity to express her or his response to the piece and compare it with that of others. Discussion is essential because it leads to deeper exploration of a piece.

Students need assistance in holding discussions. Set ground rules, and have a group role-play the process.

To foster a fuller discussion, students might be asked to take a few moments to jot down their responses before they discuss them. Writing facilitates careful consideration. Questions that might be used to evoke a response include the following, some of which were suggested by Probst (1988). Select from the questions. Four or five questions should be sufficient to evoke a full discussion.

This is a menu of questions. Choose ones that are most appropriate for your circumstances, but do not attempt to ask them all.

- Which part of the selection stands out in your mind the most?
- Picture a part of the piece in your mind. Which part did you picture? Why?
- Was there anything in the selection that bothered you?
- Was there anything in it that surprised you?
- What main feeling did it stir up?
- What is the best line or paragraph in the piece?
- Does this selection make you think of anything that has happened in your life?
- As you read, did your feelings change? If so, how?
- Does this piece remind you of anything else that you have read?
- If the author were here, what would you say to her or him?

- What questions would you ask?
- If you were the editor, what changes might you suggest that the author make?
- What do you think the writer was trying to say?
- What special words, expressions, or writing devices did the author use? Which of these did you like best? Least?
- If you were grading the author, what mark would you give her or him? Why? What comments might you write on the author's paper?

5. *Class discussion.* After the small groups have discussed the piece for about ten minutes, extend the discussion to the whole class. The discussion should center on the responses, beginning with those made in the small groups. Ask each group, "How did your group respond to the piece? In what way were responses the same? Is there anything about the work that we can agree on? How were the responses different? Did your response change as your group discussed the piece? If so, how?"

Throughout the discussion, you, as the teacher, must remain neutral and not intervene with your interpretation. Students have to be empowered to construct their own interpretations, and they need opportunities to develop their interpretive skills. Lesson 8.1 shows how a reader response lesson might be presented using the poem "Today" (Carlyle, 1885).

> Rosenblatt (1991) comments: "Textbooks and teachers' questions too often hurry students away from the lived-through experience. After the reading, the experience should be recaptured, reflected on. It can be the subject of further aesthetic activities—drawing, dancing, miming, talking, writing, role-playing, or oral interpretation. It can be discussed and analyzed efferently. Or it can yield information. But first, if it is indeed to be literature for these students, it must be experienced" (p. 447).

LESSON 8.1   Reader response

Step 1. Preparing to read the literary piece

Ask students to tell what the expression, "Tomorrow is a new day," means to them. Talk over times when they are glad when a new day comes. Have them read or listen to the poem to find out what advice the author has for them.

Step 2. Reading the literary piece

Have students read "Today" or listen as you read it. Their purpose should be to see what feelings, thoughts, or pictures the poem brings to mind.

> Today
> By Thomas Carlyle
> So here hath been dawning
>   Another blue Day;
> Think, wilt thou let it
>   Slip useless away?
> Out of Eternity
>   This new Day is born;
> Into eternity,
>   At night will return.
> Before it aforetime
>   No eye ever did;
> So soon it for ever
>   From all eyes is hid.

> Refrain from asking "Why?" after a reader has described his response. "Why?" implies that the youngster must justify his reaction to a piece. It tends to make him defensive. Instead of asking "why?", request that the student "tell me more about how you're thinking" (McClure & Kristo, 1994, p. xvi).

> In her study of students' reading stance, Cox noted that the students had a variety of ways of responding aesthetically (Cox & Zarillo, 1993). They talked about their favorite part, discussed what pictures the selection brought to mind, or made connections between the piece and their own lives or between another piece that they had read.

> Here hath been dawning
> Another blue Day;
> Think, wilt thou let it
> Slip useless away?

Step 3. Responding to the piece

Have students write a brief response to each of the following questions, using their thoughts and feelings:

- What do you think the poet is trying to say in this poem?
- What feelings, thoughts, or pictures come to mind as you read the poem?
- After reading the poem, what stands out most in your mind?
- Was there anything in the poem that bothered you or surprised you?
- Does the poem remind you of any thoughts or feelings you have had?

Step 4. Small-group discussion

Students talk over their responses in groups of four or five. Each question should be discussed. Students will have been taught previously to accept everyone's responses, but they can ask for explanations or elaborations. Each group should have a discussion leader and a spokesperson. The leader keeps the discussion moving and on track. The spokesperson sums up the group's reactions.

Step 5. Whole-class discussion

Have the whole class discuss the responses. Being careful not to inject your own interpretation, guide the discussion to obtain a full range of responses, thereby making it possible for students to hear them all. You can first take a quick survey of reactions by calling on the spokespeople for each group. Probe and develop those responses by calling on other members of the class. Encourage students to justify their responses by reading phrases or lines from the poem. As the opportunity presents itself, discuss how the language of the poem helps create feelings, images, and thoughts.

Step 6. Extension

Have students read other poems about the pasage of time and compare them with "Today."

> Notice how the questions are geared to the readers' feelings or affective responses. Instead of asking typical comprehension questions, such as, "What did the boy do?" the questions ask the students to tell about what they pictured or felt as they read or to tell what impact the poem had upon them.

> Type of selection read has an impact on literature discussions. Works that embody powerful themes result in the most sustained and deepest discussions and most insightful responses (Eeds & Wells, 1989).

■ Using Journals to Elicit Responses

Response journals, or literary logs, can also be used to evoke responses to literature. After reading a chapter in a novel, students might write their thoughts and reactions in a literary log. These responses could be open-ended or could be the result of a prompt. Parsons (1990) suggested the following types of questions, some of which have been altered slightly:

> ■ A **response journal** is a notebook in which students write down their feelings or reactions to a selection they have read. They may also jot down questions that they have about the selection.

- What surprised you about the section that you read today? How does it affect what might happen next in the story?

■ As you read today, what feelings did you experience in response to events or characters; for example, did you feel anger, surprise, irritation, or disappointment? Why do you think you responded that way?

■ What startling, unusual, or effective words, phrases, expressions, or images did you come across in your reading that you would like to have explained or clarified?

■ What characters and situations in the story reminded you of people and situations in your own life? How are they similar, and how do they differ?

Two other response prompts that might be used are "What if . . . " and "If I were in the story . . ." In the "What if . . . " response, readers speculate what might have happened if a character had taken a different course of action or if a key event in the story had been different. In the "If I were in the story . . . " response, readers tell what they would have done if they had been a part of the story's action (Raphael & Boyd, 1997).

Generally, students would be provided with just one or two prompts but should feel free to respond to other concerns or situations. Gradually, the prompts should be faded so that students can come up with their own concerns. Responses in the logs become the basis for the next day's discussion of the selection read. In supplying prompts for literary journals, Meyers (1988) took a different tack. She supplied students with a list of twenty questions, similar to those listed above and earlier in this chapter. They were free to choose two or three questions from the list.

Two other kinds of journals include the literary and the dialogue journals. In the literary journal, the student assumes the role of one of the characters in a selection and writes as though he or she were that character. A student assuming the role of Carlie in *The Pinballs* (Byars, 1977) might tell how she felt when she saw how sick Harvey had become. In dialogue journals, students write to the teacher and the teacher responds, or pairs of students might write to each other.

One problem with using literary logs or journals is that students may fall into a rut. When this happens, provide creative prompts that invite students to see selections in new ways. Also, share entries from your journal so that you can model "new ways of thinking about literature" (Temple, Martinez, Yokota, & Naylor, 1998, p. 463).

Although students should be given choices in their written responses to literature, assigned writing can sometimes lead students to investigate themes and issues that they might not have considered (Lehr & Thompson, 2000). In one study of literature discussions, students were asked to write a letter from the main character's eyes. The assignment gave the students the opportunity to role-play, see life through a character's perspective, and problem solve.

*D*uring a discussion of a literary work, emphasis is placed on eliciting an aesthetic response.

Dialogue journals help the teacher keep close contact with her students and also extend their understanding of selections. The journal writing should be a genuine exchange between teacher and student and not simply a means for checking on students' reading. If viewed as a checking device, journals may lose their vitality. In a study by Bagge-Rynerson (1994), responses showed more life after the teacher modeled the kinds of responses that might be written and also made her responses to the journal entries more personal and more affirming.

■ Other Forms of Response

Having students respond in a variety of imaginative ways builds interest and motivation. It also gives students multiple ways of responding and so builds multiple skills. For instance, by responding both visually and verbally, students are building both areas. In addition, some selections lend themselves to one mode of response but not to another. Listed below are some creative but effective response activities. Most have been drawn from the California Literature Project (1992).

> Responses need not be written. Young children may respond by drawing their favorite character, favorite part of the story, funniest or scariest event, and so on. The drawings become a basis for response-oriented discussions.

- *Open mind.* Open mind is a visualization activity in which an individual or small group analyzes a character in depth, and, using an outline drawing of the back of a head, which signifies an open mind, represents what a character in a story is thinking and feeling or what the character's motivations might be or how the character sees himself or others. The open mind might be divided into two halves to show a conflict that the character is experiencing or the pros and cons of a decision that the character is making. Students may draw pictures or paste in pictures or symbols in a kind of collage format to show what the character is feeling and thinking or imagining. Words or phrases might also be used. Happiness may be signified with bright sunshine, sadness with a gray cloud (Arciero, 1998).
- *Postcard.* A character from a story writes a postcard to another character or to the reader. The front of the postcard is illustrated and the back has a stamp and a dated postmark.
- *Duologue.* Pairs of students select a scene from a story and then have a conversation of the type that two characters from the story might have had.
- *Press conference.* One or more characters from a novel or the subject of a biography holds a press conference to announce a new discovery, invention, retirement, or other momentous news. Other students function as reporters.
- *Story rap.* Students summarize the whole selection or a portion of it in a rap.

> Questions designed to elicit a genuine response from a reader are much like those that might occur in a conversation between two adults discussing a book. Thus, a conversation about Patricia MacLachlan's *Sarah, Plain and Tall* (1985) might go like this: "Sarah made me think of the time I moved to the Midwest from New England. I missed the ocean and landscape, much as Sarah did. Have any of you had a similar kind of experience?" (McClure & Kristo, 1994, pp. xv–xvi).

Using Literature Discussion Groups to Elicit Responses

One effective technique for fostering a genuine response to literature is to form a literature discussion group, an interpretative community that shares a text much as a group of adults might do. This sharing can be both formal and informal. It can take place in whole-class discussions, small groups, or between partners.

Discussion groups, which are also known as literature circles, literature study groups, conversational discussion groups, and book clubs, are an attempt to improve upon the quiz-type formats that are typical of many traditional discussions. In traditional discussions, the teacher's questions follow an IRE (Initiate, Respond, Evaluate) format, in which the teacher initiates a question, the student responds, and the teacher evaluates the response. Literature discussion groups allow students to describe responses, compare impressions, contrast interpretations, and, in general, engage in the same type of talk that we might have with peers when we talk about books that we have read. The discussions, which have been termed "grand conversations," feature a natural give-and-take and a freedom to offer one's interpretation with the expectation that it will be respected (Eeds & Wells, 1989). In preparation for meeting with their discussion group, students read the selection and might jot down a response in a log or journal. The ultimate intent of literature discussion groups is to lead students to engage in higher-level talk, not just more talk.

Students find literature discussion groups to be valuable in fostering deeper comprehension of material that they have read (Alvermann et al., 1996). However, groups need to be carefully prepared and monitored. Proficient discussion groups are especially effective at staying on task and sticking with a topic long enough to develop it fairly fully (Almasi, O'Flahavan, & Arya, 2001). They are effective at making connections between the current topic and points made earlier in the discussion or in previous discussion. The teacher's role is crucial. Although the teacher needs to provide direction, especially in the early stages, it is important that the teacher gradually turn over responsibility to students. Students need to learn how to manage group processes. If the teacher becomes the one who provides directives for staying on task, the students will not take ownership of the procedure. Deprived of the opportunity to think through problems, students fail to learn how to conduct discussions. Through scaffolded instruction, the teacher must lead students to recognize when procedural problems arise and to resolve them. However, over time, the teacher must assign this responsibility to students. As Almasi, O'Flahavan, and Arya (2001) noted, "By failing to give students the opportunity to monitor their own discussion, teachers may hinder students' ability to operate in the group independent of the teacher" (p. 118).

Based on their study of fifty-eight eighth-grade classrooms, Nystrand and Gamoran (1991) concluded that the following elements are essential for a productive discussion: open-ended questions to which there was no preconceived answer; uptake, in which the teacher's response to students' contributions included the students' words and ideas; and affirmation, in which the teacher made positive comments about students' responses and used those responses as a platform for moving the discussion forward.

■ Book Club

In Book Club, a carefully researched form of discussion group, the following procedures are used (McMahon, 1997):

- *Books are selected.* The class might read the same book or choose from a selection of three or four books related to a common theme. Books could be on different levels of difficulty to accommodate varying levels in a typical class.
- *Students are organized in groups of four or five.* Small groups foster more interaction and individual participation. Groups should be balanced on the basis

> When working with a group of youngsters discussing a literary piece, the most difficult part of initiating reader response might be refraining from taking over. "The real work of adults in the group is to LISTEN, LISTEN, LISTEN. The children are working at creating meaning for themselves. By listening carefully, our own reflections can be carefully phrased to stimulate higher levels of thinking or at least more informed reflections" (Borders & Naylor, 1993, p. 27).

> Only about one teacher out of every three uses peer discussions on a regular basis. It takes time for students to learn how to conduct discussions. Almasi, O'Flahavan, and Arya (2001) found that it takes at least five meetings before students learn to function together.

of factors, such as interests, communication skills, and leadership. All the leaders shouldn't be in the same group.

■ *Procedures are explained.* Students are given explicit instruction about the nature of a literate or grand conversation, providing opportunities for all members of the group to participate, and about how to encourage others to participate. Sample discussions are modeled. Basic rules for conducting the discussion should also be set:

> Sit in a circle so that everyone can see each other.
> Only one person talks at a time.
> Listen to each other.
> Stay on the topic. (McGee, 1995, p. 113)

■ *Students are taught how to respond to their reading.* After reading a segment of text, students complete a response log. This response might be triggered by a teacher prompt: "How did Jennifer react to the witch's offer? If you had been Jennifer, what would you have done?" Responses might also be unprompted. Students can simply write their reaction to what they read. Responses might be in the form of a sentence or a paragraph, but they could also be diagrams of plots or a web of character interactions or a drawing of the main character.

■ *Book Club discussions are held.* The teacher might start the discussion by asking students to share their responses, or the teacher might ask a general question, such as "What was the most important thing that happened in Chapter 5?" or "Was there anything in Chapter 5 that puzzled or surprised you?" It's important to create the kind of atmosphere and ask the kinds of questions that motivate students to respond to books in a thoughtful but relaxed way, much the same way that you might respond if you were sitting with a group of friends discussing a favorite book.

Literature discussion groups meet for about twenty minutes. Discussions might be student led, teacher led, or a combination of the two (Temple, Martinez, Yokota, & Naylor, 1998). Students feel freer to express themselves when the teacher isn't present, but the teacher can provide expert assistance. Even if the discussion is student led, in the beginning the teacher should be there to assist the group in getting started and might model the literary kinds of questions that students are learning to ask. The teacher should also monitor the group to make sure they are on task and everyone is participating. From time to time, the teacher might drop in to model higher-level questioning or to perk up a flagging group.

■ **Literature Circles as Cooperative Learning Groups**

A second kind of literature discussion group, known as literature circles, incorporates the principles of cooperative learning to provide more structure (Bjorklund, Handler, Mitten, & Stockwell, 1998). The circles are composed of five or six students who have chosen to read the same book. Students choose from six books the three that they would most like to read. Books could cover the same theme or topic, be in the same genre, or have the same author. They might all be biogra-

BUILDING LANGUAGE

Introduce concepts and words such as *theme, moral, point of view, realistic characters,* and *suspense* that enable students to judge and talk about literary selections. From time to time, join in the groups' discussions. Provide prompts that help the students engage in thoughtful discussions.

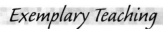

Exemplary Teaching

Literature Circles

At the Sandy Hook School in Connecticut, the fourth- and fifth-grade teachers fostered appreciation through the use of literature circles. Students were given a choice of six books to read. The books might explore a common question or topic—survival, for instance—or they constituted an author study: All the books were written by the same author. Students listed three books they would most like to read, and based on their choices, groups were formed. The groups were heterogeneous, so that all the poorest readers or all the best readers didn't end up in the same group. However, the teacher matched up books and students so that all students, including below-level readers, had books they could handle.

After the groups were formed and jobs were assigned (jobs included discussion leader, summarizer, literacy reporter, illustrator, word chief, and connector), students were given a calendar and asked to make up a schedule for reading their novel and completing their jobs. Students were required to complete the book in two weeks, but they decided how many pages they would read each night. They could choose to do the most reading on days when they had few afternoon activities. After the schedule was created, students were given two copies of it, one for home and one to be kept at school.

Students seldom missed their assignments. Having been able to choose their reading and set up their schedules, they were committed to completing their assignments. Besides, there was considerable peer pressure. If they didn't complete an assignment, they were letting the group down. If students did miss their assignments, they were not allowed to take part in the circle. Instead, they worked by themselves to complete the missed work.

Each day, just two of the four groups met for discussion. The other two groups worked on their assignments. By having just two groups meet each day, the teacher was better able to oversee their discussions and provide any needed help. But mostly, the teacher took on the role of participant. To be a realistic participant, the teacher responded to the story in her journal and then brought her journal to the circle. In that way, she was a genuine participant and not just someone who came to direct or assess.

Students were enthusiastic about their circles, and they also improved their ability to appreciate and respond to literature. By year's end, they also incorporated the six roles into their reading so that, as they read, they were asking themselves questions, summarizing, visualizing, appreciating the author's craft, making connections, and noting difficult words and confusing passages.

What was the secret of the teachers' success? Through careful planning and implementation, they let the students know what was expected of them and they set them up for success. The teachers also were caring and enthusiastic (Bjorklund, Handler, Mitten, & Stockwell, 1998).

---

phies, or they might all have survival in the wilderness as a theme, for instance. The books should represent a range of interests and difficulty levels so that students have a genuine choice and there are books that are appropriate for average, below-average, and above-average readers.

The books are presented. The teacher provides an overview of each one, and students are invited to examine the books. Students are invited to look over the books to see whether they are interesting and whether they are on the right level of challenge. Students are urged to read two or three pages at scattered intervals in order to judge the difficulty level of the book. Students then list their top three choices.

Based on the students' choices, the teacher forms four or five groups. The teacher tries to get a mix of students in each group so that a number of perspectives are represented and a number of personalities are included. The teacher also tries to match below-average readers with books that they can handle.

Once the groups have been formed, roles are assigned by the teacher or the group decides who will fulfill which role. Key roles are the discussion leader, summarizer, literacy reporter, illustrator, word chief, and connector. The discussion leader develops questions for the group and leads the discussion. The summarizer summarizes the selection. The literacy reporter locates passages that stand out because they are funny, sad, contain key incidents, or feature memorable language. The reporter can read the passages out loud, ask the group to read them silently and discuss them, or, with other members of the group, dramatize them. An illustrator illustrates a key part of the selection with a drawing or graphic organizer. The word chief locates difficult words or expressions from the selection, looks them up in the dictionary, and writes down their definitions. At the circle meeting, the word chief points out and discusses the words with the group. The connector finds links between the book and other books the group has read or with real events, problems, or situations. The connector describes the connection and discusses it with the group. Although each student has a certain role to fulfill in the circle, any student may bring up a question for discussion, a passage that stands out, a confusing word, a vivid figure of speech, or a possible connection.

The roles reflect the kinds of things that students should be doing as they read a text. They should be creating questions in their minds, making connections, visualizing, summarizing, noting key passages, coping with difficult words and confusing passages, and appreciating expressive language and literary techniques. Students switch roles periodically so that each student has the opportunity to carry out each of the roles.

To help students fulfill their roles, they are given job sheets. A sample job sheet for a discussion leader is shown in Figure 8.1. Each of the jobs is also modeled and discussed. The class, as a whole, also practices each of the jobs by applying it to a brief, relatively easy selection. Creation of questions is given special attention. Questions that lead to in-depth sharing of responses are stressed. Discussions are modeled. The teacher might do this by training a group and then having them demonstrate before the class. Students are given two or three weeks to complete a book. After a group has been formed, the group meets and sets up a schedule for how much reading they will do each evening. A written schedule is created and pasted to the inside cover of the response journal. If students are doing some or all of their work in school, they meet every other day. Days they don't meet are used to complete their reading and tasks.

The teacher visits each group and in the early stages might model asking questions or responding to a selection. As students become more adept, the teacher takes on the role of participant.

Whole-class sessions are held each day so that groups can share with each other. This is also a good time to present minilessons or perhaps read aloud a selection that pertains to the theme or topic of the books being read.

ADAPTING INSTRUCTION for *STRUGGLING READERS and WRITERS*

Although similar to Book Clubs, literature circles provide students with choice and also can be organized according to cooperative learning principles, with each student having a well-defined role. Because students have a choice of materials, struggling readers can select books that are closer to their level. Struggling ELL students and many members of minority groups do better in cooperative learning groups.

If there are more roles than students, some students may fulfill more than one role or roles may be combined.

FIGURE 8.1

Discussion Leader Job Sheet

The discussion leader's job is to ask a series of questions about the part of the book that your group will be discussing. Ask questions that will make the other students in your group think carefully about what they read and walk in the shoes of the main characters. Some possible questions are:

How do you feel about this part of the story?

Was there anything that bothered or surprised you?

What would you have done if you had been the main character?

What do you think will happen in the next part of the story?

Write your questions on the lines below.

1. _____

2. _____

3. _____

4. _____

Adapted from Daniels, H. (1994). *Literature Circles, Voice and Choice in the Student-Centered Classroom.* York, ME: Stenhouse.

After the books have been completely read and discussed, students meet in groups according to the roles they fulfilled. All the discussion leaders meet, as do all the sumarizers, connectors, illustrators, word chiefs, and literary reporters. In these groups, students give an overview of the book they read and their opinion of the book. They also discuss the books they read from the point of view of their roles. In this way, all of the students become acquainted with the books read in other groups.

Each group also makes a brief presentation of its book. This might be in the form of an ad, a skit based on the book, a panel discussion, an interview of the main character, or a dramatization of a key passage. Literature circles can also be organized in a less structured way so that students meet to discuss their reading but don't have specific roles. However, teachers who have used this structured approach find that in time, students automatically carry out the various roles as they read.

Although student discussions about literary works can be fruitful, teacher guidance is essential in some situations. When reading fiction in which historical events play an important role, as in Mildred Taylor's (1987) *The Friendship*, it is important that the teacher play an active role. In their study of fifth-graders, Lehr and Thompson (2000) found that many of the students were misinformed about key historical events. Because of a lack of knowledge of history, they had difficulty interpreting the novel, which deals with civil rights in the 1930s. Students needed teacher guidance to help them correct their misconceptions. Students also needed the teacher to guide them to a higher level of understanding. Students' initial responses were on a literal level. They seemed to need to know who did what before they could begin to interpret the characters' actions.

Developing Aesthetic Judgment

As children gain depth in their response to literature, they should also develop standards by which to judge what they read. For a piece of fiction, they should judge the quality of the character development, plot, theme, author's style, and setting.

- *Character development.* In most pieces of fiction, character development is key. As Lukens (1995) explains, well-developed characters are rounded; they are not flat or one-dimensional, nor are they all good or all bad. They seem real enough to us so that we can identify with their struggles, bemoan their defeats, and glory in their victories. Most of all, they are memorable—they stay with us long after the final page has been read.
- *Plot.* Children thrive on action and adventure, so well-plotted stories will gain and maintain their interest. Twists and turns in a story grab children's attention, and plot developments must be plausible and have a measure of originality. Predictable plots are boring, but contrived plots leave readers feeling tricked or cheated.
- *Theme.* The theme may be implicit or directly stated, but as the main idea or central meaning of a work, it provides coherence to a story that otherwise would simply be a collection of episodes. Themes are most evident in traditional tales in which love conquers all, virtue is rewarded, and evil is punished. However, a theme should not be preachy. A tale written to demonstrate the evils of drugs or selfishness falls flat. Genuine themes arise out of the credible actions of believable characters (Lukens, 1995).
- *Author's style.* Style is simply the way an author writes. Authors may have a simple style, an ornate or flowing style, a plodding style, or a brisk style. Good writing is distinguished from poor writing by its forcefulness and originality of style, including choice of words, aptness of description, presence of original figures of speech, and imagery used to create pictures in our minds.
- *Setting.* Setting includes the time and place of a story and the mood that the author creates. For example, in a horror story, the author must create a sense of impending supernatural occurrence as well as depict a deserted castle in a far-off place. When the setting is an integral part of a story, as it would be in a survival tale set in the Arctic, the author must make the setting come alive.

TYPES OF LITERATURE

Folklore

A good place to start the study of literature is with folklore, which includes folktales, myths, rituals, superstitions, songs, and jokes. **Folklore** follows an oral

ADAPTING INSTRUCTION for *STRUGGLING READERS and WRITERS* Although ELLs in your class may have acquired a good store of everyday words and expressions, they may have difficulty with the more formal language of instruction. When introducing new words and concepts, make generous use of audiovisual aids to foster students' understanding.

- **Envisionment** is the understanding that a reader has of a text. The understanding may change with reflection, additional reading, or discussion.

- **Folklore** refers to the tales, rituals, superstitions, nursery rhymes, and other oral works created by people.

tradition. As M. A. Taylor (1990) put it, "The tales of the tongue are a good introduction to the tales of the pen." Having stood the test of time, folklore has universal appeal.

Every culture has produced its own **folktales.** Students can investigate those drawn from the culture of their ancestors. African American students might look into Virginia Hamilton's (1985) *The People Could Fly: American Black Folktales.* Latino students might enjoy one of Alma Flor Ada's tales. Other outstanding sources of materials about diverse cultures are *Kaleidoscope: A Multicultural Booklist for Grades K–8* (Yokota, 2001), *Multicultural Literature for Children and Young Adults* (Kruse & Horning, 1997), and *Multicultural Teaching* (Tiedt & Tiedt, 2002). To provide follow-up after students have read and discussed a piece of folklore, use the following reinforcement activities.

■ **Folktales** are stories handed down orally from generation to generation. Folktales include fairy tales, myths, legends, and tall tales.

REINFORCEMENT ACTIVITIES Folktales

- Because folktales were meant to be told orally, have a volunteer retell a tale. Students can pretend to be members of the storyteller's family or village. They can decide when and where the tale was told and how the listeners might have reacted. Have a storytelling festival, with students retelling a tale that they located on their own.
- Have students create a semantic map of major types of folktales and their elements.
- Encourage students to ask parents and grandparents to retell favorite folktales they remember hearing. If possible, parents or grandparents might tell the stories to the class.
- Students can retell folktales through puppet shows and other dramatizations. Older students might put on shows for primary-grade students.
- Point out allusions to folktales as these occur in newspapers, magazines, or books. Discuss, for instance, terms such as *cried wolf* and *Cinderella team.*
- Above all, acquire collections of folktales for the classroom library so that students may have easy access to them. Also, continue to read folktales aloud to the class.

USING TECHNOLOGY
Cooperative Children's Book Center features a number of lists of recommended books including *Thirty Multicultural Books That Every Child Should Know.* http://www. soemadison.wisc. edu/ ccbc/

The Children's Literature Web Guides Web page provides a wealth of information about children's literature and has many links to other sites. http://www. ucalgary.ca/~ dkbrown/

To find varied versions of folktales, consult *The Storyteller's Sourcebook: A Subject, Title, and Motif-Index to Folklore Collections for Children* (McDonald, 1982).

Poetry

Research suggests that teachers' enthusiasm for particular poems can influence what children like (Terry, 1974). The first step that teachers should take is to become acquainted or reacquainted with children's poetry, as presented in the following sources:

Bauer, C. F. (1995). *The poetry break.* New York: Knopf. An annotated anthology for introducing children to poetry. More than 240 poems and suggestions for presenting them.

Reactions to poetry are very personal. One student's favorite could be another student's least liked. For example, in Terry's (1974) study of preferences, a sixth-grade boy had a special feeling for Edwin Hoey's "Foul Shot" because it reminded him of something that happened in a game in which he had played. A fourth-grade girl, however, disliked the poem because she had difficulty making shots.

Cole, J. (1984). *A new treasury of children's poetry: Old favorites and new discoveries.* New York: Doubleday. A breathtaking array of children's poems from Shakespeare to Prelutsky.

Cullinan, B. (Ed.). (1996). *A jar of tiny stars: Poems by NCTE award-winning poets.* Honesdale, PA: Boyds Mill Press. Features poems by David McCord, Aileen Fisher, Karla Kuskin, Eve Merriam, and others.

Harrison, M. & Stuart-Clark, C. (1995). *The new Oxford treasury of children's poems.* New York: Oxford. A number of classic works.

Harrison, M. & Stuart-Clark, C. (1999). *One hundred years of poetry for children.* New York: Oxford. A number of classic and contemporary works.

Hopkins, L. B. (1987). *Pass the poetry, please!* New York: Harper & Row. Good, solid information about poets and poetry and many excellent suggestions for teaching poetry.

Prelutsky, J. (Ed.) (2000). *The 20th century children's poetry treasury.* Contains more than 200 poems by 137 poets.

USING TECHNOLOGY

Children's poetry is published on the Poetry Gallery.
http://www.kidlit/ kids/artlit/poetry/

Read poems as though you were the same age as the students in your class. Read those that you most enjoy to your students. Students like poetry that has humor and a narrative element and that rhymes. Include both light verse and more thoughtful pieces. Before reading a poem to the class, practice it so that your reading is strong and dramatic. Briefly discuss vocabulary words or concepts that might interfere with students' understanding or enjoyment. Give students a purpose for listening, such as creating images in their minds, awaiting a surprise ending, or hearing unusual words.

You might emphasize questions that evoke a personal response: "What about the poem stands out most in your mind? What pictures came to mind as you listened? Which line do you like best? How does the poem make you feel? Is there anything in the poem that you do not like? Is there anything in it that surprises you?" Better yet, invite students to ask questions about anything in the poem that may have confused them. Gear discussions toward personal responses and interpretations. The emphasis should be "upon delight rather than dissection" (Sloan, 1984, p. 86).

The teacher should model how he or she reads a poem, especially one that is complex. The teacher should explain how the images create a certain mood or meaning for him or her. Much of the magic of poetry arises from its language. Read alliterative verse such as Eleanor Farejon's "Mrs. Peck Pigeon" and Rachel Field's "Something Told the Wild Geese," as well as poems that contain excellent examples of onomatopoeia, such as Rhoda Bracemesseter's "Galoshes" and David McCord's "Song of the Train." Also, help students discover how poets use sensory words, as in Mary O'Neil's "Sound of Water" and Polly Chase Boyden's "Mud." Through becoming aware of its language, students will develop an ear for poetry.

Help students discover the richness of metaphor in poetry. Discuss, for instance, how poets can use figurative language to create powerful images. Some of these are visual, as in "The Eagle" by Tennyson (Denman, 1988):

For additional ideas for poetry activities, see Bauer, C. F. (1995). *The poetry break.* New York: H. W. Wilson.

He clasps the crag with crooked hands;
Close to the sun in lonely lands,
Ringed with the azure world, he stands.
The wrinkled sea beneath him crawls;
He watches from his mountain walls,
And like a thunderbolt he falls.

Help students see the universality of images (Sloan, 1984) by using, for example, images that contain allusions to the seasons. Show students that spring is often used to symbolize new life and hope. Winter, on the other hand, is often a symbol of old age, illness, grief, or death.

Contrast the rhythms of poems such as David McCord's "Song of the Train" and "Base Stealer" by Robert Francis. Discuss how the rhythms match the poems' mood and meaning. For older students, show how free verse uses the rhythm of natural speech, whereas bound verse retains the beat of poetic patterns. Although students prefer to read bound verse, free verse may be easier to write, as it is not held to traditional formats (Calkins, 1986).

Of course, your ultimate goal is to have students sample a wide variety of poetic forms and become readers of poetry. To promote exploration, encourage students to check out books of poetry from the library and include such books in the classroom collection. If funds are limited, purchase one or two anthologies. Choose those that seem to have the greatest number of poems that might appeal to your students. Create your own anthologies by obtaining poems from basals or other sources, including selections that students bring in. Some students may want to make their own anthology or folder in which to keep their favorite poems. The following Children's Reading List presents a sampling of some of the many fine poetry anthologies available for young people.

CHILDREN'S READING LIST Poetry

Ciardi, J. (1962). *You read to me, I'll read to you.* New York: HarperCollins. Features thirty-five lighthearted poems.

Dyer, G. L., Jr. (2001). *40 Poems for "T": The fun of writing poetry.* Catskill, NY: PressTige. Letters to a young boy explain what poetry is, how to collect ideas for poems, and how to write them.

Greenfield, E. (1991). *Night on neighborhood street.* New York: Dial. A collection of seventeen poems that focuses on life in an African American neighborhood.

Hopkins, L. B. (Ed.) (1986). *Surprises.* New York: Harper. Thirty-eight easy-to-read poems on a variety of subjects ranging from pets to flying.

Hopkins, L. B. (Ed.). (2001). *My America: A poetry atlas of the United States.* Fifty-one poems celebrate different sections of the United States.

Hudson, W. (1993). *Pass it on: African-American poetry for children.* New York: Scholastic. An illustrated collection of poetry by such African American

USING TECHNOLOGY
Making Multicultural Connections through Trade Books offers many resources for using multicultural books. Provides an extensive listing of multicultural books and suggestions for content and technology connections. **http://www.mcps. k12.md.us/ curriculum/ socialstd/MBD/ Books_Begin.html**

poets as Langston Hughes, Nikki Giovanni, Eloise Greenfield, and Lucille Clifton.

Hughes, L. (1993). *The dream keeper and other poems.* New York: Knopf. A collection of sixty-six poems selected by the author for young readers, including lyrical poems and songs, many of which explore the African American tradition.

Kennedy, X. J. & Kennedy, D. M. (1999). *Knock at a star: A child's introduction to poetry.* Boston: Little, Brown. A Horn Book review praises it as one of the best introductions to poetry around.

Knudson, R. R. & Swenson, M. (1988). *American sports poems.* New York: Orchard. A collection that should be welcomed by sports fans.

Kushkin, K. (1992). *Soap soup and other verses.* New York: HarperCollins. Features a variety of easy-to-read poems.

Prelutsky, J. (1997). *The beauty of the beast.* New York: Knopf. Features a variety of poems about ants, cats, birds, dogs, fish, sharks, lizards, toads, and other creatures. Science tie-in: study of animals.

REINFORCEMENT ACTIVITIES Poetry appreciation

- Set aside time for students to talk about their favorite poems in small groups. Groups can be arranged by topic or author.
- Students can give dramatic readings of their favorite poems. These can be simply animated recitations or more elaborate events with background music and costumes.
- Arrange for choral readings for poems that lend themselves to it.
- Encourage pairs of students to read poems. Use poems that lend themselves to being read in two parts.
- Tie poetry in with the study of content-area subjects. For instance, students can read "Arithmetic" (Sandburg) in connection with the study of math. While studying insects, read poems about bugs. In *The Beauty of the Beast,* Jack Prelutsky (1997) includes a number of poems about insects.
- Last, but not least, encourage children to write poetry. An excellent guide for students in grades four through six is Ryan, M. (1991). *How to read and write poems.* New York: Watts.

Novels

In a literature-based program, novels are often set aside as a separate unit of study. Before embarking on a novel, students should receive some guidance to build background essential for understanding the text. Their interest in the book should also be piqued. Place particular emphasis on understanding the first chapter. If students, especially the poorer readers, have a thorough understanding of the first

---

Poetry Workshops
http://teacher.scholastic.com/writewit/poetry/index.htm

Poetry workshops for student poets are presented by Karla Kuskin (grades 4–8) and Jean Marzollo (grades 2–5). Writing tips are so specific that every student should be able to write a poem.

Giggle Poetry: Poetry Class
http://www.gigglepoetry.com/poetryclass.cfm

Poet Bruce Lasky has more than a dozen suggestions for writing poems.

Yahooligan School Bell: Language Arts: Poetry
http://www.yahooligans.com/school_bell/language_arts/poetry/

Links to a wide variety of sites.

chapter, they will have a solid foundation for comprehending the rest of the text. It will also build their confidence in their ability to read the rest of the book (Ford, 1994).

Generally, students are asked to read a chapter or more each day. Questions to be considered during reading can be provided, or students might make predictions and read to evaluate them. Students might also keep a response journal for their reading. Responses might be open-ended, with students jotting down their general reactions to the segment being read, or students might react to response questions posed by the teacher.

After a segment has been read, it is discussed. Students might also do some rereading to clarify confusing points or might dramatize exciting parts. A cumulative plot outline or story map could be constructed to keep track of the main events. If the story involves a long journey, the characters' progress might be charted on a map. Extension activities can be undertaken once the book has been completed. The novel might be presented within the framework of an extended directed reading activity or directed reading–thinking activity, or it might be discussed as a grand conversation in a literature discussion group. Emphasis is on building appreciation and evoking a response; skills are secondary.

Both content and form should be discussed. Design questions to help students understand what is happening in the story and to see how the setting, plot, characters, theme, point of view, and author's style work together. However, take care that you do not overanalyze a piece or ask too many questions at any one time. Balance analysis with eliciting personal responses. Response should precede analysis and general discussion. Once the reader has responded, she or he is in a better position to analyze the piece. Part of the analysis might involve discovering what elements in the piece caused the student to respond (see the earlier section on reader response for some questions). Some general questions for novels are outlined in Table 8.1. Do not attempt to ask all the questions that have been listed. Choose only those that seem most appropriate for your students.

> Through prompts, teachers can lead students to practice a variety of literacy and comprehension strategies. Prompts might ask students to predict what will happen next or make inferences about a character based on the character's actions, for instance. Or prompts might ask students to create character webs or note examples of figurative language.

■ Story Element Activities

Several activities help students gain a deeper understanding and appreciation of the story elements.

Character analysis.   A number of devices can be used to analyze characters in a story. One such device is an opinion–proof, in which readers write an opinion about a character and cite proof to back it up. The proof could be the character's actions or comments made about the person by other characters or the author (Santa, 1988). Figure 8.2 presents an opinion–proof for Jonathan from *Earthquake Terror* (Kehret, 1996).

A literary sociogram can be constructed to show how the characters relate to each other. The name of the main character is written in a circle in the middle, and other characters' names are written in circles surrounding it. Arrows are drawn between the circles. On the arrows are written words that describe how the characters feel about each other, how they get along, or how they are related (Santa,

TABLE 8.1	Possible questions for novels	
Setting	**Characters**	**Plot**
Where does the story take place?	Who are the main characters?	What event started the story?
When does the story take place?	What kinds of people are they?	What is the main problem?
How important is the setting to the story?	Do they seem like real people? Why or why not?	What is making the problem better?
Could the story have happened in a different place at a different time? Why or why not?	How does the author let you know what the main characters are like?	What is making the problem worse?
		What has been the most exciting part of the story so far?
	Did the characters change? If so, how?	Could you guess what was going to happen, or did the author surprise you? How?
When you close your eyes and imagine the setting, what do you see?	Were these changes unexpected? Did they surprise you? Why or why not?	How is the problem resolved?
	Can you picture the characters in your mind? What do they look like? What do they do? What do they say?	How does the story end?
How does the author give you a "you-are-there" feeling?	Do you know anyone like them?	
	Would you like to meet them? Why or why not?	
Point of View	**Theme**	**Style**
How is the story told?	What seems to be the main or most important idea in the story?	What are some especially well-written passages?
Is it told by a narrator who is a part of the story and who calls himself "I"?	What main idea do you take away from the story?	What are some examples of colorful words that the author uses?
Is it told in the second person, using the pronoun "you"?		Does the author use figures of speech or images? If so, give some examples.
Is the story told by someone outside, a person who can see all and tell all?		What special writing techniques does the author use? Give some examples.
		Does this story remind you of any other stories that you have read? If so, which one(s)? In what ways are they similar?
How does the author seem to feel about the characters? Who seems to be the author's favorite?		Does this author remind you of any other authors you have read? If so, who? How are they similar?
		Would you like to read another book by this same author or about this same subject? Why or why not?
		Would you recommend this book to a friend? Why or why not?
		If you could, would you make changes in this book? Why or why not? Give some changes you would make.
		Do you think this book would make a good movie or a good television show? Why or why not?

FIGURE 8.2

Opinion-Proof for Jonathan from *Earthquake Terror*

Opinion	Proof
Jonathan knew how to handle an emergency.	When the earthquake hit, Jonathan followed the safety rules he had been taught.
	Jonathan found shelter for himself and his partly paralyzed sister.
	Jonathan calmed his little sister when she was hurt.
	Jonathan planned a way to get help

1988). Figure 8.3 is a literary sociogram of the characters in *Summer of the Swans* (Byars, 1970). It represents the interrelationships that exist in the first portion of the book. For longer works, it is a good idea to draw up literary sociograms that represent interrelationships at different points in the story.

FIGURE 8.3

Literary Sociogram for *Summer of the Swans*

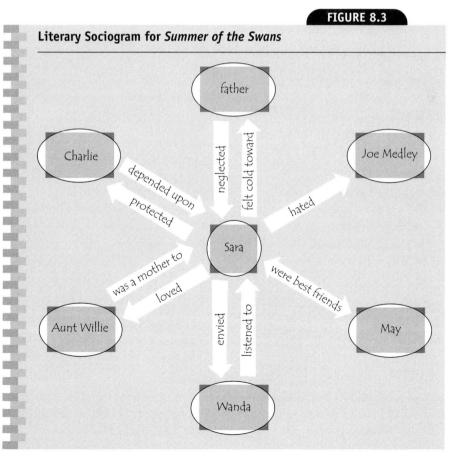

On a simplified level, a semantic map can be created for the main character. The character's name is written in the center circle, with his or her major attributes written in surrounding circles. Figure 8.4 is a semantic map for Sara in *Summer of the Swans*.

Plot analysis.   Understanding the structure of a story aids comprehension and gives students a framework for composing their own stories. A plot chart shows the story problem, the main actions or events leading up to the climax, the climax, the resolution of the problem, and the ending. It could be a series of rectangles, a diagram, or a picture.

Students might also draw the major events of a story or put the events on a time line. Acting out key scenes or putting on a puppet show would highlight the action. To help them choose the most exciting parts of the story, have students pretend that they are making a movie of the book and must decide which scenes to depict in a preview of coming attractions and which scene to show on a poster advertising the movie.

Most books lend themselves to a variety of follow-up activities. Plan activities such as the following to deepen students' understanding and appreciation of the book and to promote the development of language arts skills.

> **Remember** that the goal in reading a book is to have students understand, enjoy, and appreciate it. Do not assign so many activities that the life is squeezed out of the book. Some teachers report spending a month or more with a novel. For most books, two weeks should be adequate.

REINFORCEMENT ACTIVITIES   Chapter books and novels

- Read a sequel or another book by the same author or a book that develops the same theme or can be contrasted with the book just completed.
- Dramatize portions of the book.
- Create a print or TV ad for the book.
- Create a dust cover for the book, complete with blurbs that highlight the story and that tell about the author.
- View a movie based on the book, and then compare the two.
- Create a montage, diorama, or other piece of art related to the book.
- Write a review of the book for the school newspaper.
- Have a Characters' Day during which students dress up and act the parts of characters in the book.
- Arrange for a panel discussion of the book. The panel might be composed of the book's characters.
- Describe books on the school's or class's homepage. Include links to the author's site, if there is one.

Drama

Plays are a welcome change of pace but require some special reading skills. Although designed to be acted out or at least read orally, plays should first be read silently so that students get the gist of the work. Students need to be taught to read

FIGURE 8.4

Semantic Map for Sara in *Summer of the Swans*

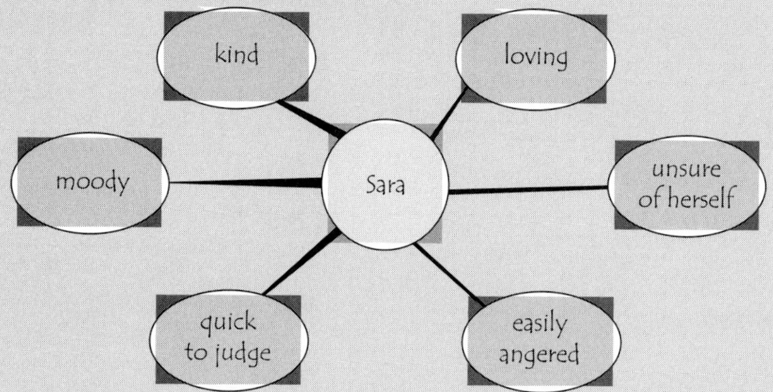

stage directions so that they can picture the setting. They also require practice in reading dialogue, which does not contain the familiar transitions and descriptive passages of their usual reading. If possible, students should see plays put on by local professional or amateur groups to give them firsthand experience with theater.

Plays are found in many basal readers and literature anthologies. Scripts from TV shows and movies are often included in children's magazines. The magazine *Plays* is, of course, an excellent source as is:

Gerke, P. (1996). *Multicultural plays for children, Volume 2: Grades 4–6*. Lyme, NH: Smith and Kraus. Features folktales from around the world and instructions for teachers for producing plays.

The following Children's Reading List identifies a number of anthologies of children's plays.

> Acting out plays provides a legitimate opportunity for students to read orally. Give them ample time to rehearse their parts, however. A drama could be presented as a radio play. Sound effects and background music might be used, but no costumes would be required. If students tape-record the play, other classes might enjoy their efforts.

CHILDREN'S READING LIST   Drama

Barchers, S. I. (2001). *From Atlanta to Zeus: Reader's theatre from Greek mythology*. Littleton, CO: Libraries Unlimited.

Blau, T. (2000). *The best of reader's theatre*. Bellevue, WA: One From the Heart Publications.

Braun, W. & Braun, C. (2000). *A reader's theatre treasury of stories*. Winnipeg, Manitoba, Canada: Portage & Main Press.

Friedman, L. (2001). *Break a leg!: The kid's guide to acting and stagecraft*. New York: Workman. A thorough introduction to acting.

USING TECHNOLOGY

Storytelling, Drama, Creative Dramatics, Puppetry, Choral Speaking & Readers Theater for Children & Young Adults has a long list of resources for drama.
http://falcon.jmu. edu/~ramseyil/ drama.htm

Kamerman, S. E. (Ed.). (1996). *Great American events on stage.* Boston: Plays. Fifteen plays celebrate America's past.

Kamerman, S. E. (Ed). (2001). *Plays of great achievers: One-act plays about inventors, scientists, statesmen, humanitarians, and explorers.* Boston: Plays. Plays that celebrate achievement.

McBride-Smith, B. (2001). *Tell it together: Foolproof scripts for story theatre.* Little Rock, AR: August House.

Tripp, V. (1995). *Five plays for boys and girls to perform.* Middletown, WI: Pleasant Company. Features a play for each of the main characters in the popular *American Girls Collection.*

Winther, B. (1992). *Plays from African tales: One-act, royalty-free dramatizations for young people, from stories and folktales of Africa.* Boston: Plays.

■ Dramatizations

To dramatize a story, actors must understand the action and must think carefully about the characters they are portraying. Instead of passive comprehension, readers as actors must put themselves into the piece. They must make the characters come alive by giving them voice, expression, and motivation. This requires that readers think carefully and creatively about what they have read.

■ **Story theater** is a form of dramatization in which participants pantomime a selection while a narrator reads it aloud.

Story theater.   In **story theater,** readers pantomime a selection—a folktale, a realistic story, or a poem—while a narrator reads it aloud. Their actions need not be limited to those performed by human characters. For example, the sun, the wind, trees swaying in the breeze, and a babbling brook can all be pantomimed. The teacher will probably have to help students organize the production, at least in the beginning. As students become familiar with the technique,

*O*ne way of interpreting literature is by dramatizing it.

they should be able to work out production details for themselves. Working out the details encourages cooperative learning and also involves all the language arts.

Reader's theater.   In **reader's theater,** participants dramatize a selection by reading it aloud. A whole selection or just one portion of it can be dramatized. Pieces having a generous amount of dialogue work best. A narrator reads the portions not spoken by characters. Parts are not memorized but are read from the text. Even though they do not have to memorize their parts, readers should spend time developing their interpretation of the dialogue and rehearsing. A reader's theater production might be implemented in the following way (Pike, Compain, & Mumper, 1994):

1. *Select or write the script.* In starting out, it might be helpful to use scripts that have already been prepared for reader's theater. Scripts can also be written by the class, but this takes more time and effort. They should include extensive dialogue, be interesting to your students, and be on the appropriate level of difficulty. The script should have from three to eight participants. Composing a script could be a fruitful cooperative learning project. However, students would need some guidance.

2. *Assign parts.* The parts can be either assigned by the teacher or decided upon by students.

3. *Rehearse the script.* Although the scripts are read aloud, they should be rehearsed. Before students rehearse the scripts, they should have read and discussed the selection. As a group, students should decide how each part is to be read. Focus should be on interpreting the character's mood and feelings. Should a character sound angry, sad, or frightened? How are these emotions to be portrayed? Students then rehearse individually and as a group.

4. *Plan a performance.* Students decide where they want to stage their performance. Although no props are needed, they may want to place their scripts in colorful folders. They may use stools if they are available, or they may stand.

Other dramatic activities.   Students might also like to try improvisation and role-playing. Using improvisation, students spontaneously dramatize a story or situation. Improvisation might be used to portray a character in a tale or extend a story. It might also be used to dramatize a concept in science or social studies.

Nonfiction

■ Biographies

Although biographies generally rank poorly when students are asked to tell what types of books they like best, the lives of interesting and relevant subjects are often runaway favorites. Biographies of sports heroes and singing stars are among some of the most heavily circulated books in the children's departments of libraries.

When properly motivated, students show an intense, long-lasting interest in historical figures. In one elementary school, students were involved in reading and

---

■ **Reader's theater** is a form of dramatization in which the participants read aloud a selection as though it were a play.

▌Prepared scripts are available from Reader's Theater Script Service (P.O. Box 178333, San Diego, CA 92117). *Spotlight on Reader's Theater* (Phoenix Learning Resources, 2349 Chaffee Drive, St. Louis, MO 63146) features a series of twenty-seven plays organized around nine themes. Designed to integrate social studies and language arts, most of the plays focus on famous people or multicultural topics. Speaking parts vary in difficulty so that even poor readers will be able to participate.

USING TECHNOLOGY
Aaron Shepard's RT Page gives an overview of reader's theater and provides a number of scripts for students in grades three and up.
http://www. aaronshep.com/rt/

Introduce students to a variety of types of reading: short stories, novels, biographies, poems, plays, and informational pieces. Students may have a favored genre or may exclude informational text from their reading. They need to experience a full range of literary types.

ADAPTING INSTRUCTION for *STRUGGLING READERS* and *WRITERS*

Several publishers have created easy-to-read biography series: *Troll's First-Start Biographies* and *Holiday House's Picture Biographies* are written on a second-grade level.

writing biographies for as long as three months. One fourth-grader, who was completing an intensive study of Benjamin Franklin, commented,

> I started writing this book in March and here I am still writing it. And believe me this is no piece of cake. I have to write it over and over to get it right. It's taking me a long time, but it's worth it. (Zarnowski, 1990, p. 18)

The key to motivating students to become interested in biography is to choose the right subject. Above all, the subject should have led an interesting life and should be someone that the students can relate to and care about. Zarnowski (1990) chose such people as Benjamin Franklin, Martin Luther King, Jr., and Eleanor Roosevelt.

In Zarnowski's (1990) study, the teacher first read biographical material aloud to give students an overview of a subject. Students then read several easy biographies that acted as stepping stones to more difficult books. Students were also introduced to primary materials, such as magazine and newspaper articles, letters, and films. As they read and wrote about their subjects, students formed a relationship with them. Entries in their journals proved that the subjects came alive. Instead of vague historical figures, they became real people with real problems that had to be overcome:

> As they read about a person, children not only learn information, they also develop feelings of sympathy and empathy, and sometimes anger and aversion. . . . As they develop both emotional and intellectual understanding, children begin to strongly connect with figures from the past. Ultimately, these connections enable children to connect with the larger scope of history. (Zarnowski, 1990, p. 5)

The following Children's Reading List provides the titles of some high-quality biographies.

Although designed for young readers, Adler's series of picture book biographies can be used with older struggling readers.

CHILDREN'S READING LIST   Biographies

Adler, D. A. (1991). *A picture book of Eleanor Roosevelt.* New York: Holiday House.

Alcott, S. (1992). *Young Amelia Earhart: A dream to fly.* Mahwah, NJ: Troll.

Anderson, W. (1992). *Laura Ingalls Wilder: A biography.* New York: HarperCollins.

Burgan, N. (2001). *Sheryl Swoopes.* New York: Chelsea House.

Engel, T. (1996). *We'll never forget you, Roberto Clemente.* New York: Scholastic.

Freedman, R. (1987). *Lincoln: A photobiography.* New York: Clarion.

Fritz, J. (1993). *Just a few words, Mr. Lincoln.* New York: Grosset & Dunlap.

Furbee, M. R. (2001). *Wild Rose: Nancy Ward and the Cherokee Nation.* Greensboro, NC: Morgan Reynolds.

Haskins, J. (1977). *The life and death of Martin Luther King, Jr.* New York: Lothrop.

Jemison, M. (2001). *Find where the wind goes: Moments from my life.* New York: Scholastic.

Kramer, S. A. (1997). *Basketball's greatest players*. New York: Random House.

Kehret, P. (1996). *Small steps: The year I got polio*. Morton Grove, IL: Whitman.

Lundell, M. (1995). *A girl named Helen Keller*. New York: Scholastic.

Meltzer, M. (1987). *Mary McLeod Bethune: Voice of black hope*. New York: Viking.

O'Connor, J. (1989). *Jackie Robinson and the story of all-black baseball*. New York: Random House.

Peare, C. O. (1959). *The Helen Keller story*. New York: Crowell.

Penner, L. R. (1994). *The true story of Pocahontas*. New York: Random House.

Schaefer, L. M. (1999). *Cesar Chavez*. Mankato, MN: Pebble Books.

Walker, A. (1974). *Langston Hughes: American poet*. New York: Crowell.

Walker, P. R. (1988). *Pride of Puerto Rico: The life of Roberto Clemente*. New York: Harcourt.

READING ALOUD TO STUDENTS

Although often associated with the primary grades, reading aloud is a valuable activity throughout all the grades. It is a valuable activity both at school and at home. Read-aloud advocate Jim Trelease (2001) testifies to the value of home and school read-alouds in his best-selling book, *The Read-Aloud Handbook* (5th ed.). As he puts it, "Every time we read aloud to a child or class, we're giving a commercial for the pleasures of reading" (p. 44). Indeed Trelease cites the case of five middle school teachers who were concerned about students' negative attitudes toward reading because they were being pressured by state standards. Although the five teachers came from five different disciplines, they decided to read to students every day. Not sure if reading aloud would restore positive feelings about reading, they measured students' attitudes. They found that the program had the following impact:

- Number of students who read at home for pleasure increased from 40 to 75 percent.
- Number of students who never read for pleasure dropped from 60 to 34 percent.
- Some 89 percent of the students reported that they like being read to. This was especially true of the lower-achieving students.

The teachers had the following suggestions for structuring a read-aloud program.

- Select books that you enjoy. Your enjoyment of the book will shine through. Also ask students to suggest titles that they would like to hear read aloud.
- If your students change classes, read aloud at the beginning of the period so the bell doesn't interrupt the reading.
- Decide ahead of time how much time you will spend reading aloud. It could be 10 or 15 minutes, or it could be longer.
- Shorter books work better than longer ones.

- Follow up with talks about books that students might enjoy reading.
- Be imaginative and creative in book selections. You might read picture or joke books on occasion.
- Read slightly above students' reading levels but not too far.
- Prepare your reading in advance. Note difficult vocabulary that might have to be discussed. Also note stopping points.

Read-alouds are also more effective if the selection you read is related to a theme or unit of study and if some time is devoted to discussing the selection (Hoffman, Rosier, & Battle, 1993). Ask open-ended questions that invite a personal response or critical thinking: Would you like to hear another book by this author? Why or why not? Are the characters in the story like anyone you know? Does this book remind you of any book that you have read? Why do you think this book is so popular with young people? Do you think the characters were realistic? What was the saddest part of the story? What message is the author trying to get across? On a scale of 1 to 10, how would you rate this book? Why? The questions that you ask will depend upon your main purpose for reading aloud. If you are reading books aloud to try to motivate students to read on their own, ask questions that focus on the enjoyment or personal satisfaction of reading. If you are trying to build thinking skills, ask questions that have them make comparisons, see similarities, draw conclusions, and make judgments.

It's important, too, to set aside routines for reading aloud, so that you read aloud at a certain time and for a designated period of time. The average for read-alouds is ten to twenty minutes. That way read-alouds aren't relegated to an activity that is undertaken when everything else is done. Read-alouds are valuable enough so that they should be regularly scheduled.

Read-alouds should be previewed. You want to prepare your read-aloud. You also want to make sure that there is nothing in the text that would embarrass students or which is not appropriate for them.

VOLUNTARY READING

The key to improved reading achievement is very simple: Encourage students to read ten minutes a day on their own. According to carefully conducted research, these extra ten minutes result in significant improvements in reading (Fielding, Wilson, & Anderson, 1986). Unfortunately, a nationally administered questionnaire revealed that fewer than half the nation's fourth-graders read for fun every day, and 13 percent never or hardly ever read for fun on their own time (Mullis, Campbell, & Farstrup, 1993). A study of fifth-graders had an even gloomier finding: Only 30 percent of the students read for ten minutes or more a day (Anderson, Wilson, & Fielding, 1988). Responding to the Motivation to Read Profile (Gambrell, Codling, & Palmer, 1996), 17 percent of the students reported that they would rather clean their rooms than read, 10 percent said that people who read are boring, and 14 percent stated that they would spend little time reading when they grew up.

According to the National Assessment of Educational Progress reading assessment results, students who are given time to read books of their own choosing in school have higher reading scores than those who don't (Donahue, Voekl, Campbell, & Mazzeo, 1999).

Students like to read about characters who are their own age or who are facing problems that are similar to theirs (Harris & Sipay, 1990). Humor is also enjoyed by students of all ages (Greenlaw, 1983). Upper-grade students have a distinct preference for mystery, adventure, and sports.

What can be done to motivate students to read? First of all, demonstrate that reading is both personally fulfilling and fun, and put students in contact with books that they will enjoy. Attractive classroom libraries attract readers. In a large-scale study of children's reading, the classroom library was the major source of books for most of the students. Students also like to choose their books and they like to talk about them with other students and the teacher. Students frequently selected a book to read because a friend or a teacher had recommended it (Gambrell, Codling, & Palmer, 1996).

Determining Interests and Attitudes

A good starting point for creating a voluntary reading program is to determine students' reading interests and their attitudes toward reading. Close observation of your students yields useful information about these areas—you probably have a good sense of who likes to read and who does not. Through observation, classroom discussions, and conversations with individual students, you probably also know who likes sports, who prefers mysteries, and who is interested in animals. An easy way to obtain an overview of the kinds of books your students might enjoy reading voluntarily is to duplicate several pages at their grade level from the catalog of a distributor of paperbacks or children's library books. Ask students to circle the ones that interest them. One experienced librarian recommended indirect questioning when exploring children's interests:

> The best way to learn what any child likes to read is to ask, but a direct question may not elicit clear information. A bit of probing may be necessary. What does he do with leisure time? What are his favorite television programs? The last good book he read? (Halstead, 1988, p. 35)

The Classroom Library

Once you have a sense of what your class might like to read, start building a classroom library and involve students in the process. Propinquity is a primary principle in promoting voluntary reading. When books are close by and easy to check out, students will read more. The goal is to build a community of readers (Fielding, Wilson, & Anderson, 1986). If students feel they have a stake in the classroom library, they will be more highly motivated to read.

Invite students, their parents, and the community at large to contribute books to your classroom library. You might also be able to obtain some volumes from the school librarian and other local librarians. Students, as they get older, find paperbacks especially appealing. Paperbacks are also cheaper to buy and to replace if lost or damaged.

■ Obtaining Books on a Variety of Levels

Students need reading material they can handle. Students are most likely to read on their own when they have books or periodicals that are interesting and when they feel competent enough to read the materials (Gambrell, Codling, & Palmer, 1996).

Surveys and questionnaires might be used to complement data from observations. Two copyright-free, useful surveys of reading attitudes are the Motivation to Read Profile (MRP) (Gambrell, Codling, & Palmer, 1996) and the Elementary Reading Attitude Survey (ERAS) (McKenna & Kerr, 1990).

Classroom libraries are powerful. Students in classes that have libraries read 50 percent more than those in classes without libraries. (Bissett, 1969, cited in Fractor et al., 1993). Although classroom libraries are popular in the early grades, fewer upper-grade classrooms have them. In the upper elementary grades and middle schools, only about one class in four has a library.

Many libraries make special provision for teachers and will loan one hundred or more books.

USING TECHNOLOGY

For information on the latest and best-selling children's books, consult the Web sites of online book stores, such as the ones listed below:

Amazon.com
http://www.amazon. com/

Barnes and Noble
http://www.bn. com/

Although students will read books that are beyond their level if they have a special interest in the subject, a steady diet of such books can be discouraging. Students are more likely to read a book all the way through if it is on their level. A study of sixth-graders found that both good and poor readers chose books on the same level; however, a higher percentage of good readers finished their books (Anderson, Higgins, & Wurster, 1985). If the less-able readers had selected books closer to their ability, perhaps they would have completed them.

■ Setting Up the Classroom Library

Make the classroom library as appealing as possible. Display books with their covers showing. You might also have special displays of books on high-interest topics. Update the collection periodically—at least once a month, add new titles to keep students interested.

One of the essentials that students learn from a classroom library is how to choose books. In informal research, P. Wilson (1992) noted that many students have difficulty selecting books during classroom visits to the library. They do not seem to know how to browse. Browsers are very selective about the books they read. They typically look through five books before choosing one and may later decide not to read the books that they have chosen. Having a classroom library with sufficient books to provide students with a genuine choice is important. Another way to promote wise selection among your students is to obtain books that students are genuinely interested in. Be sure to include informational books as well as fiction and also magazines and newspapers.

*S*tudents should have time during the day when they can read books of their own choosing.

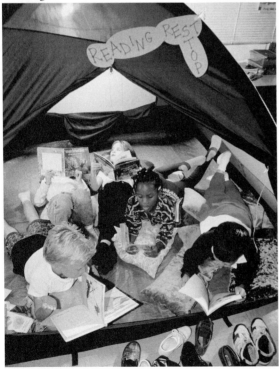

■ Managing the Classroom Library

P. Wilson (1992) suggested that the teacher involve the poorest readers in helping with the management of the classroom collection. By helping display, advertise, and keep track of the collection, poor readers become familiar with its contents.

Involve students in setting up check out procedures and rules. Keep the rules simple; if they are complicated and punitive, they will discourage borrowing (P. Wilson, 1986). Inevitably, some books will be lost or damaged. Consider this part of the cost of "doing business." Do not charge late fines or fees for lost or damaged books; these could be a genuine hardship for poor children. Instead, have a talk with students about being more responsible. If it is not a hardship, students could contribute replacement books, which do not necessarily have to have the same titles as the lost books. Put students in charge of keeping track of books; they can handle checking in, checking out, and putting books away.

Setting Aside Time for Voluntary Reading

When provided with time for recreational reading, students learn that reading is important. Initially, the time set aside for voluntary reading may be only five minutes (Fader, 1977), but it can be lengthened gradually up to twenty or thirty minutes. Some classrooms, and even entire schools, adopt a program known as SSR. Although SSR originally stood for **Sustained Silent Reading,** it should probably be changed to Self-Selected Reading. Research suggests (Manning & Manning, 1984; P. Wilson, 1992) that students get more out of their reading and read more when they can share with their peers. Students should be allowed to discuss books in small groups, read with a buddy, dramatize the reading of a book in a small group, view a CD-ROM version of a book or listen to a taped version, or silently read a book in the traditional way. Adapted rules for SSR are listed below:

■ **Sustained Silent Reading** (SSR) is a period in which all the students and the teacher in a class or everyone in a whole school reads materials of their own choosing.

Exemplary Teaching

Creating a Better Self-Selected Reading Program

*R*ealizing the importance of extensive reading, Jodi Crum Marshall (2002) initiated a SSR program. At first, she thought the program was working well. The room was quiet. There were no complaints. But then she noticed that the room was too quiet. There was no expression of excitement or enjoyment. And while there no complaints, there were no positive comments either. After discussing the SSR program with her students, Marshall concluded that she had made a series of blunders. She had failed to set expectations or goals for the program with students. They saw SSR as a free period. If they didn't raise a fuss, they could quietly do whatever they wanted. She had not included them in setting up the program or acquiring books. Although her classes were made up of sixth-, seventh-, and eighth-grade struggling readers, she had failed to acquire books on the appropriate level. Most were too difficult. And she hadn't really done anything to spark an interest in reading. Because the books were difficult and lacking in appeal, many of the students weren't really reading. Some would begin to read a book but found that it was too difficult. As one student put it, none of the books "make sense."

Marshall took a number of steps to reform the program. First of all, she had conversations with students about the program. The students wanted more books and more time to read. They also wanted to discuss their books, but they didn't want the discussions to seem like quizzes.

Responding to the issues that students raised, Marshall changed discussions so that they were more like conversations than oral quizzes. She also held individual conversations with students. And she encouraged students to keep logs of their reading. This served a practical purpose because often they forgot where they had left off reading the day before. She also began reading aloud to the class. This motivated students to read the books that she was reading to them. She also passed out book catalogs to students and had them mark the books they would like to read. These and other titles were added to the class library. But perhaps the most important thing she did was to get know her students, their reading strengths and weaknesses, and their interests. Using this knowledge, she was able to match them up with books that they could read and wanted to read. Not surprisingly, students' attitudes changed. And their gains on tests of reading comprehension and language were better than expected.

1. Each student is involved in reading.
2. The teacher reads or holds conferences or discussions with students.
3. Books to be read should be chosen before the session starts. (Students should choose two or three books, in case the original selection does not work out.)
4. A timer is used.
5. Absolutely no book reports are required.

Originally, the teacher read while her students read during self-selected reading. However, experience and interviews with a number of teachers suggests that self-selected reading is more effective when the teacher takes a more active role. Unless carefully planned and supervised, SSR can degenerate into a period where some students simply leaf through magazines, read books that are too easy or too hard, or catch up on their homework. Take a few minutes at the beginning of each SSR session to make recommendations to students, especially those who have difficulty selecting books. As the students read, provide assistance to those who seem to be having difficulty sustaining their reading. Join discussion groups and hold informal conferences with small groups and individuals. However, don't turn this into a reading workshop session. Do not teach skills. Focus on students' enjoyment. Give them suggestions for other books they might like. Help them plan ways in which they can do more reading, if they are lagging. Have them provide suggestions for books that might be added to the class library. Take a few minutes at the end of SSR to have students discuss their reading. Students might want to recommend books that they found especially enjoyable or ask others about suggestions for intriguing books.

Have students keep records of books read during SSR. Recording books read gives students a sense of accountability and accomplishment.

Modeling the Process of Selecting and Discussing Books

Read Jodi Crum Marshall's (2002) account of how she set up a SSR program for middle grade students.

Some students have little experience choosing or discussing books. From time to time, tell them how you happened to select a book that you are reading. Discuss how you got a sense of its contents by examining the cover, finding out who the author is, reading the blurb on the jacket, glancing through the book, and reading selected parts

To help students who have difficulty sharing, model the process by talking about a book that you are reading. Also ask about their books so that they realize that in a community of readers, people share their reading.

We want students to read the best that has been written. However, students must be allowed to choose what they wish to read. Once students experience the joy of reading, then, through skillful guidance, they might be led to experience high-quality literature.

Activities for Motivating Voluntary Reading

To motivate voluntary reading, be enthusiastic, accepting, and flexible. Present reading as an interesting, vital activity. Include a wide range of material from comics to classics. Do not present books as vitamins, saying, "Read them. They're good for you." Share reading with students in the same way that you might share with friends.

By doing so, you are accepting students as serious readers. Above all, be a reader yourself. Some activities for motivating voluntary reading follow.

- *Match books with interests.* Make casual, personal recommendations. For a Gary Paulsen fan, you might say, "Joe, I know you enjoy Gary Paulsen's books. The school library has a new book by him. I read it, and it's very interesting."

- *Pique students' interest.* Read a portion of a book and stop at a cliff-hanging moment; then tell students that they can read the rest themselves if they want to find out what happened.

- *Substitute voluntary reading for workbook or other seatwork assignments.* The Center for the Study of Reading (1990) made the following statement: "Independent, silent reading can fulfill many of the same functions as work-book activities—it permits students to practice what they are learning, and it keeps the rest of the class occupied while you meet with a small group of students" (p. 5).

- *Use electronic matching programs, such as* Accelerated Reading *(Advantage Learning Systems),* Electronic Book Shelf *(Scholastic), or* Book Adventure, *to foster reading.* In these systems, students select a book, read it, and then take a brief quiz on the book. Students must achieve a cutoff score in order to receive credit for having read the book. The programs have been successful in fostering voluntary reading. *Book Adventure,* which is free, is available at http://www.bookadventure.org and has a database of more than 5,000 books.

- *Use electronic databases, such as BookLink, to help students find titles which are on their level and which match their interests.* To use BookLink, students enter their level in school, interests, and reading level. (Reading level is entered in DRP units. If these are unknown, use the conversion table in Chapter 2, or obtain a score by entering a book that the student has read recently and use the DRP score for that book.)

- *Have students visit author sites on the Web to learn of the latest books by their favorite authors.*

- *Recommend books by a popular series author.* Students who have enjoyed one of Todd Strasser or Jerry Spinelli's gripping tales might not realize that these authors have a number of engaging books.

- *Book clubs that cater to school-age populations offer a variety of interesting books at bargain prices.* When students choose and pay money for a book, it is highly likely that they will read it. Make alternative provisions for economically disadvantaged children.

- *Present books as sources of interesting information.* Include the *Guinness Book of World Records* (Folkard, 2003), *Famous First Facts* (Kane, Anzovin, & Podell, 1997), *World Almanac* (Park, 2003), books on trivia, and other collections. When students disagree about the best quarterback, the tallest building, or the longest fingernails, refer them to one of these references.

- *Encourage students to build personal libraries with a few inexpensive paperbacks.* They can add to their collection by requesting books as gifts.

ADAPTING INSTRUCTION for *STRUGGLING READERS and WRITERS*

Some struggling readers select books that are too difficult because they want to read the same books that their friends are reading, even though these books may be well beyond their capability. Have available in your classroom library books that are interesting but easy. From time to time, highlight these books and allow everyone to read them so they don't become stigmatized as being "baby books."

A major benefit of sharing is that students recommend books to each other. Students are more likely to read a book when it is recommended by a friend than when it is suggested by a parent, teacher, or librarian (Gallo, 1985).

An effective reinforcer for voluntary reading is to have students keep a record of their reading. This might be a simple list, a wheel, or a graph showing number of books read, number of pages read, or number of minutes spent reading. Since students differ in reading speed, and number of words on a page varies, the fairest measurement might be number of minutes spent reading rather than number of pages read.

To help students build personal libraries, use books as awards for winners of food drives, writing competitions, and other school contests.

One problem with extrinsic motivators is that they may weaken intrinsic motivation.

- *Once a month, give students the opportunity to trade books they have read.* Before the trading session, students might want to post a list or announce titles that they will swap. You might also have a trading shelf in the classroom from which students may take any book they wish, as long as they put one in its place.
- *Suggest and have on hand books that relate to people or subjects being taught in the content areas.* Reading a brief biography of John F. Kennedy, for instance, could help shed light on his presidency and the early 1960s.
- *Use the Web.* On the class's or school's homepage, list books that parents might obtain for their children at either the local library or a bookstore.
- *The school librarian can be asked to describe new acquisitions during morning or afternoon announcements.* These descriptions could also be included in the daily bulletin. School librarian Pamela Spencer (1984) obtained five paperback copies of the title she talked about over the public address each morning so as to be prepared for the demand.
- *If all else fails, try extrinsic reinforcers.* Pizza chains, local restaurants, and fast-food establishments have supplied free pizza and other rewards to students who read a certain number of books. A teacher in New Jersey offered his students tickets to a wrestling match if they read their quota of books. In a follow-up discussion with students, the teacher discovered that the students read not for the prize but because he had tried so hard to find them books they liked (Freeland, 1986). In her study of a reading incentive program entitled Running Start, Gambrell (1996) found that providing choice and verbal praise and feedback were powerful incentives. When asked what they liked best about the program, students frequently mentioned that they enjoyed talking to the teacher about books and the praise and encouragement they were given.

Incentives seem to work best when the nature of the reward fits in with the nature of the activity and when the incentive is tied in to meeting a specific goal rather than simply engaging in the activity. In Running Start, the goal was reading twenty brief books within ten weeks. As an incentive, students could select a book to keep.

HELP FOR STRUGGLING READERS AND WRITERS

Because they are reading below grade level, struggling readers may experience difficulty handling literary selections. If they are not reading too far below the level of the selection, providing them with additional help with difficult vocabulary and concepts might make it possible for them to read the text successfully. Reading all or part of the selection to them or obtaining an audiotape or CD-ROM version of the text is another possibility. However, one reason struggling readers are behind is because they typically read less. They should also be given quality selections on their reading level so they have the experience of reading on their own. This is easier to do if you use an approach that features self-selection.

For voluntary reading, make sure you have a variety of high-interest materials on levels that would be appropriate for your struggling readers. Because some students would rather clean their rooms than read, have available intriguing, highly motivating materials: joke and riddle books; sports biographies and animal books that are heavily illustrated but have limited text; high-interest periodicals, such as *Sports Illustrated for Kids;* books on CD-ROM; and books that incorporate activities, such as a book on magnets that is accompanied by magnets.

ESSENTIAL STANDARDS

Fourth through eighth grades
Students will

- understand and appreciate a variety of types of literary selections.
- describe key elements in a selection, such as characters, setting, story problem, and plot.
- recite, read aloud with expression, or dramatize poems, stories, and plays.
- respond to literary selections in writing, art, movement, or drama, and in discussion groups.
- support responses and conclusions by referring back to the text.
- determine the underlying theme in a selection and connect ideas and themes across texts.
- learn advanced literary techniques, such as using metaphors, similes, and symbols.
- use a set of increasingly sophisticated standards to evaluate literary works.
- read and discuss to gain knowledge of their own culture, the culture of others, and the common elements of cultures.
- read and enjoy a variety of books and periodicals.
- read to acquire information that is important to them.
- read the equivalent of twenty-five full-length books. (Some standards have been adapted from the Texas, California, and New Standards.)

ASSESSMENT

Based on your observations and students' written and oral responses, assess whether they appreciate and respond on a personal and aesthetic level to works of literature. Through their responses, also determine whether or not they are becoming knowledgeable about techniques used in creating literature and whether they are

ACTION PLAN

1. Use a reader response approach to literature. Through focusing on personal response, foster in students enjoyment of and appreciation for literature.
2. Introduce students to a variety of genres and authors.
3. Use class discussions, literature discussion groups, journals, dramatizations, and art to foster responses to literature.
4. Use a unit or theme approach so that students explore themes in depth and make connections among major ideas.
5. Involve students in the establishment and management of a classroom library. Encourage students to read widely and frequently. Encourage them to share their responses to reading with friends, classmates, and family.
6. Obtain materials on a variety of levels and topics so that all students have a choice of appealing but readable materials.

acquiring standards for judging literary selections. As far as reading for enjoyment and personal satisfaction, note whether students choose to read books on their own and talk about books. Note whether they have a favorite book or a favorite author. Look over students' reading logs and journals to see how much students are reading, what they are reading, and how they are responding to their reading. You might also use the Motivation to Read Profile (Gambrell, Codling, & Palmer, 1996) or the Elementary Reading Attitude Survey (McKenna & Kerr, 1990) to obtain additional information about students' reading attitudes and habits.

SUMMARY

1. Until recently, reading was looked upon as primarily being a skills subject. Today, the emphasis is definitely on reading quality material.
2. Reading literature involves fostering appreciation and enjoyment as well as understanding. The teacher's stance becomes an aesthetic one. Focus is on eliciting a personal response and valuing students' interpretations. The reader's construction of meaning and response are part of a continuous series of processes known as envisionments.
3. Students should read a variety of types of literature: folklore, poetry, novels, plays, and biography.
4. Just ten minutes a day of voluntary reading results in significant gains in reading achievement. To promote voluntary reading, demonstrate that it is enjoyable and personally fulfilling.
5. For struggling readers, make adaptations so that they have access to literary selections that the class is reading. To foster voluntary reading, provide for students' interests and reading levels. Have available joke, riddle, and other appealing but easy-to-read books.

EXTENDING AND APPLYING

1. Read at least three current anthologies of children's poetry. Which poems did you like best? Which do you think would appeal to your students?
2. With a group of classmates, start a literature discussion group in which you discuss children's books.

3. Create a lesson in which you introduce a poem, play, or other literary piece. In your lesson, stress appreciation, enjoyment, and personal response. Teach the lesson and evaluate it.

4. Try out one of the suggestions listed in this chapter or an idea of your own for increasing voluntary reading. Implement the idea and evaluate its effectiveness.

DEVELOPING A PROFESSIONAL PORTFOLIO

Document your ability to develop an understanding and appreciation of literary works by composing a written description of a literature unit. If possible, illustrate the description with photos of students in discussion groups or photos of presentations. Also include samples of students' literature logs, dialogue journals, or other responses to literature.

DEVELOPING A RESOURCE FILE

1. Keep a card or computer database file of high-quality chapter books and novels that you feel would appeal to students you are teaching or plan to teach. Include bibliographic information, summaries of the selections, some questions you might ask about the work, and some ideas for extension activities.
2. Keep a file of activities that might be used to motivate students to read.

9

Approaches to
Teaching Reading

*F*or each of the following statements related to the chapter you are about to read, put a check under "Agree" or "Disagree" to show how you feel. Discuss your responses with classmates before you read the chapter.

	Agree	*Disagree*
1 A structured approach to reading is most effective.	_____	_____
2 Extensive reading of trade books should be a part of every elementary and middle school reading program.	_____	_____
3 Teacher and method are equally important.	_____	_____
4 A systematic skills approach to reading works best with struggling readers.	_____	_____
5 An individualized reading program would be hard to manage.	_____	_____
6 A commercial reading program, such as a basal or literary anthology, is best for new teachers because it shows them step by step how to teach reading.	_____	_____
7 Teachers should combine the best parts of each reading approach.	_____	_____
8 Teachers should be free to choose the approach to reading that they feel works best.	_____	_____

USING WHAT YOU KNOW

*T*here are two main ways of fostering reading development: by using a reading or literature anthology or by using trade books, or some combination of the two. Trade books are used in the individualized and literature-based approaches. Of course, these approaches can also be combined in various ways. Teachers who use anthologies often supplement their programs with trade books. Teachers may also use writing as a supplementary approach for developing reading skills.

Which of these approaches are you familiar with? What are the characteristics of the approaches? What are their advantages? Their disadvantages?

CHANGING APPROACHES TO TEACHING READING

In a little more than a decade, there have been two dramatic changes in reading instruction. Up until the mid-1980s, most of the nation's students were taught through basal readers. However, a holistic movement espousing the use of children's books to teach reading took hold. There was a switch from basals to children's literature and from structured teaching to a more naturalistic approach to literacy. Now, after more than a decade in which skills were downplayed in many areas, there is a movement to teach a balanced approach in which skills instruction and reading of good literature are integrated. Basal readers have also made a comeback. They are more skills oriented than ever. However, they also advocate use of high-quality literary selections and feature extensive libraries of children's literature.

Regardless of whether they are holistic or balanced, effective approaches incorporate the basic principles of teaching literacy that have been emphasized throughout this book:

- Students become readers and writers by reading and writing.
- Reading programs should include a rich variety of interesting, appropriate material and should stress a great deal of reading and writing.
- Strategies should be presented that promote independence in word recognition and comprehension.
- Reading programs should be language based. Provision should be made for developing speaking and listening as well as reading and writing skills.
- Because reading fosters writing development and writing fosters reading development, literacy programs should develop both.
- Provision should be made for individual differences. Because students differ in terms of interests, abilities, learning rate, experiential background, and culture, the approach used should take into consideration the needs of all students.
- Students' progress should be monitored, and provision should be made for helping students fully develop their potential.

This chapter examines the major approaches to teaching reading and writing. Each approach has its strengths and weaknesses. Suggestions are made for adapting each of the approaches to take advantage of its strengths and compensate for its weaknesses. For instance, suggestions are made for making the basal approach more holistic. Thus, if it has been mandated that you use a basal but you prefer a holistic approach, you can adapt your instruction to make the program more holistic and still keep within the guidelines of the school or school district that employs you.

 BASAL APPROACH

How were you taught to read? Chances are you were taught through a **basal reading program.** Basal readers are the main approach to teaching reading in the

> Until recently, reading was considered a skills subject. It did not really matter what students read. Today, content is paramount, the idea being that students' minds and lives will be greatly enriched if they read the best that has been written.

> ■ A **basal reading program** is a comprehensive program of teaching reading that includes readers or anthologies that gradually increase in difficulty, teacher's manuals, workbooks, and assessment measures. In grades seven and eight, and sometimes in grade six, there is a switch from basals to literature anthologies.

*T*oday's basals feature anthologies containing a rich variety of literary selections.

United States. A complex package based on a relatively simple concept, the basal program includes a series of readers, or anthologies, and supplementary materials that gradually increase in difficulty and act as stepping stones along a path that begins with emergent literacy and extends through sixth-grade reading. Accompanying teacher's manuals provide guidance so that the classroom teacher can lead students upward.

Basal readers have changed from the time when you were in elementary school. Costing 100 million dollars or more to produce, today's basals are created by only the largest of the educational publishers. Whereas there were more than a dozen basals just a few decades ago, today there are only five. During the 1980s and 1990s, basal readers lost some of their popularity. Many teachers began using children's books rather than basals. Basal reader publishers reacted swiftly and decisively. Today's basals feature the best in children's literature and also contain extensive libraries of trade books. Basal readers are once again being used to teach reading in more than 90 percent of America's elementary school classrooms. However, many teachers complement the use of basals with trade books.

Today's basals place greater emphasis on providing for all students. Basals of the 1990s emphasized quality literature and whole-class teaching. For struggling readers these more difficult selections were an obstacle (Hoffman et al., 1998). Today's basals have made specific provision for below-average, average, and above-average achievers. Basals have also became more language based. Today's basals generally include writing and spelling along with reading and are known as literacy, rather than reading, series.

Advantages of Basals

Basals offer teachers a convenient package of materials, techniques, and assessment devices, as well as a plan for orchestrating the various components of a total

Producing a basal program is a three-year undertaking involving fifteen to twenty program authors, consultants, editors, writers, teacher advisors, student advisors, designers, artists, and publishers' representatives and consultants (Singleton, 1997).

The latest basals, which are in a cycle of almost constant revision, attempt to implement recent research and feature the most popular young people's authors. They include high-quality literature, elaborate illustrations, and up-to-date teaching strategies.

For grades six through eight, anthologies of literature are available. Also available are a number of reading improvement programs for struggling readers.

literacy program. In their anthologies, which, for the most part, gradually increase in difficulty, basals offer students a steady progression from emergent literacy through a sixth-grade reading level. They also offer varied reading selections, an abundance of practice material, carefully planned units and lessons, and a wealth of follow-up and enrichment activities.

Disadvantages of Basals

Despite a major overhaul, basals are still driven by the same engine. The core of the basal program is the trio of anthology, workbook, and manual. Although the contents of the anthology are much improved, its function remains the same—to provide a base of materials for all students to move through. However, students have diverse interests and abilities and progress at different rates. Although basal selections are meant to be of high quality, they will not all be of interest to all students. The sports biography that delights one student is a total bore to another. A second shortcoming has to do with the way basal readers are assembled: They are anthologies and often contain excerpts from whole books. For example, the fourth-grade reader from a typical series contains "The Diary of Leigh Botts," a delightful tale of a budding young writer that is excerpted from Beverly Cleary's 1983 Newbury Award winner, *Dear Mr. Henshaw*. If reading the excerpt is worthwhile, reading the whole book should be even better.

There is also the question of pacing and time spent with a selection. Students often move through basals in lockstep fashion. Part of the problem is the nature of the teacher's guides; they offer too much of a good thing. Stories and even poems are overtaught. There are too many questions asked before a selection is read, too many asked after the piece has been read, and too many follow-up activities. A class might spend three to five days on a thousand-word story. To be fair, the guides do present activities as choices. Teachers can choose those that they wish to undertake and omit the others. Teachers may even be provided a choice of ways of presenting a story: interactively with the teacher modeling strategies, independently with the teacher providing a minimum of assistance, or with support, which means that students follow along as the teacher reads the story. All in all, the typical basal lesson has many fine suggestions, but the ideas are "canned," that is, created by someone in an editorial office far from the classroom. Designed to be all things to all teachers, the activities are not designed for a specific class of students having specific needs and interests.

Perhaps the biggest disadvantage of basals is the organizational pattern they suggest. Basal reading series have core selections in anthologies and also supplementary reading in libraries of leveled readers. The core basal selections are presented to the whole class. The selections will generally be appropriate for average students but may lack sufficient challenge for the best readers and will be too hard for as many as the one student out of four in the typical classroom who is reading below grade level. Suggestions are made for adapting instruction for all learners. This may mean reading selections to the poorest readers or providing them with audio versions of the selection so that they can read along. Only two of the basal sys-

Currently, most basals recommend that all students experience the same selection, but that steps be taken to provide extra help for those students who might find the selection to be too difficult, perhaps even reading it to them. Guided reading is also recommended. In guided reading, students are instructed in small groups and read materials on their level.

tems (Harcourt Brace & Houghton Mifflin) offer an alternative selection for struggling readers, which is related to the theme in the core selection but is easier to read. However, all of the series have sets of books on three levels—easy, average, and challenging—so that struggling readers will be reading on their level at least some of the time. Even so, this means that for series that fail to provide alternative core selections, struggling readers will be given fewer opportunities to read at their level.

Adapting Basals

Despite the criticisms voiced here and elsewhere, there is nothing intrinsically wrong with basals. Over the years, thousands of teachers have successfully used basals to teach millions of children. However, in keeping with today's research and promising practices, basals should be adapted in the following ways.

Although basal manuals have been criticized as being too didactic (K. S. Goodman, 1994), the fault may be with the professionals who use them. Manuals and, in fact, the entire basal program should be viewed as a resource. The manual is a treasure chest of ideas, and the anthologies are good, representative collections of children's literature. As professionals, we should feel free to use those selections that seem appropriate and to use the manual as a resource rather than a guide. Select only those suggestions and activities that seem appropriate and effective.

Other adaptations that might be made to make basals more effective include the following:

> Four of the five basals offer teachers a variety of instructional choices. However, one basal, Open Court, is scripted. It tells teachers what to say and offers a tightly structured sequence of teaching activities. Although novice teachers might welcome the guidance, veteran teachers may desire more flexibility, despite the good results that this series often obtains.

- *Emphasize real writing and real reading.* Many of the activities promoted in basals are practice exercises. According to Edelsky (1994), language is learned by using it for some real purpose. Because reading and writing are forms of language, they too should be learned through real use. Students should therefore read directions to find out how to operate a new computer, read a story for pleasure, make a list in preparation for shopping, or write a letter to a friend. Basal activities in which children write a letter to a storybook character or reread a story to practice reading in phrases or to reinforce new vocabulary words are exercises (Edelsky, 1994). They do not constitute reading and writing for real purposes. Where feasible, students should write letters that get mailed and respond openly to stories and poems. They should also be involved in setting their own purposes for reading and writing.

- *Workbooks should be used judiciously.* They play both management and instructional roles. Students can work in them independently while the teacher meets with a small group or individual children. Workbooks can also provide students with additional practice and yield information that the teacher can use to assess children's progress (Adoption Guidelines Project, 1990). If a workbook exercise fails to measure up, it should be skipped. The teacher should provide alternative activities, such as having the students read children's books or work in learning centers. Reading builds background and gives students an opportunity to integrate and apply skills. Instead of just practicing for the main event, they are taking part in it. In fact, students get far better practice reading children's books than they do completing workbook exercises. Writing, drawing, discussing, and preparing a presentation also provide superior alternatives to workbook exercises.

- *Emphasize wide reading of a variety of materials.* No matter how well the basal has been put together, students need to read a broader range of fiction and nonfiction materials, including books, magazines, newspapers, sets of directions, brochures, ads, menus, schedules, and other real-world materials. Make use of the extensive libraries of children's books offered by basal publishers to supplement the basal materials; excellent suggestions for additional reading are also provided in basal manuals.

- *Focus on a few key skills or strategies.* Teach and use these in context. Today's basal readers offer instruction in a wide variety of skills or strategies. In trying to cover so many areas, they typically spread themselves too thin and so fail to present crucial skills in sufficient depth. It may take twenty lessons or more before students are able to draw inferences or infer main ideas, but a basal might present just two or three lessons.

- *Provide opportunities for struggling readers to read appropriate-level material every day.* Make use of the supplementary programs or leveled libraries designed for struggling readers.

- *Gradually take control of your program.* Decide what your philosophy of teaching literacy is. List the objectives that you feel are important, aligning them, of course, with the standards set by your school and school district. If possible, work with other professionals to create a literacy program that makes sense for your situation. Consider basals as only one source of materials and teaching ideas. Basals are neither a method nor an approach to teaching reading. They are simply a carefully crafted set of materials. The core of the reading program is the teacher. It is the teacher who should decide how and when to use basals and whether to choose alternative materials.

> Reading easy books independently provides students with much needed practice. "Clocking up reading mileage on easy materials is one of the most important aspects of independent reading" (Learning Media, 1991, p. 76).

Selecting a Basal

Selecting a basal is a major decision. Ideally, the selection should be made by a committee that includes teachers, students, parents, administrators, and the school's reading/language arts specialist. The first order of business should be listing the school's or district's literacy goals and then examining materials in light of those goals. One of the best ways to assess a set of materials is to try it out before making a final decision.

Literature Anthologies

Basal readers only extend to grade six. In grade six and beyond, students use literature anthologies or sets of texts that have literary value, instead of basal readers. The main difference between basal and literature anthologies is the focus on literature. There is also an emphasis on appreciation. However, often the anthologies might also provide some coverage of reading skills. Today's literature programs are very comprehensive. The core of the program is the anthology. Anthologies typically feature a mix of contemporary works and classics. A full-length novel may accompany the anthology. The best programs provide a host of materials that teachers can use to prepare students to read the selection and to extend their appreciation and understanding. Well-designed literature anthologies also feature a program of skill development for struggling readers. In general, literature anthologies have the same advantages and disadvantages that basals have.

LITERATURE-BASED BOOK APPROACH

More and more teachers are using literature as the core of their programs. Today's basal anthologies feature high-quality selections drawn from literature. Increasingly, basals are including trade books in their entirety as an integral part of the package or a recommended component. Although there is some overlap between a basal program and a literature-based approach, the term **literature-based approach** is used here to describe programs in which teachers use sets of trade books as a basis for providing instruction in literacy. A major advantage of this approach is that teachers, independently or in committees, choose the books they wish to use with their students so the reading material can be tailored to students' interests and needs.

> ■ The **literature-based approach** is a way of teaching reading in which literary selections are the major instructional materials.

    A literature-based program may be organized in a variety of ways. Three popular models of organizing literature instruction include core literature, text sets, and thematic units.

Core Literature

Core literature is literature that has been selected for a careful, intensive reading. Core selections are often read by the whole class, but may be read by selected groups. Core literature pieces might include such children's classics as *The Prince and the Pauper* (Twain, 1881), *Treasure Island* (Stevenson, 1883), or more recent works, such as *Shiloh* (Naylor, 1991), *Number the Stars* (Lowry, 1990), or *Holes* (Sacher, 1998).

> ■ **Core literature** is a piece of literature selected to be read and analyzed by the whole class. In a core book approach, students read the same book.

    In addition to providing students with a rich foundation in the best of children's literature, the use of core selections also builds community (Ford, 1994). It gives students a common experience, thereby providing the class with common ground for conversations about selections and also a point of reference for comparing and contrasting a number of selections. The use of core literature should help boost the self-esteem of the poorer readers, who are often given less mature or less significant reading material. As Cox and Zarillo (1993) noted, in the core book model, "no child is denied access to the best of children's literature" (p. 109).

    However, there are some obvious problems with the core literature approach. Students are diverse in interests and abilities. What is exciting to one student may be boring to another. An easy read for one student may be an overwhelming task for another. Careful selection of core books with universal appeal should take care of the interest factor. It is difficult, for instance, to imagine any student not being intrigued by Sacher's *Holes* (1998). Selections can also be presented in such a way as to be accessible to all. Suggestions for presenting texts to students of varying abilities can be found in Chapter 12.

Core selections might also be overanalyzed. Move at a lively pace when working with core books. Do not move so slowly that the book becomes boring. But do not rush through the book so that slower readers cannot keep up. Do allow students to read ahead if they want to. If they finish the text early, they might read related books or books of their own choosing. Also, avoid assigning too many activities. Activities should build reading and writing skills or background knowledge and should deepen or extend students' understanding of the text. In addition, if you do use core books, make sure that students are provided with some opportunities to select books so that teacher selection of texts is balanced by student selection. Also provide for individual differences in reading ability. If core books are too difficult for some students, provide additional assistance, or, if necessary, read the books to them or obtain audiotapes of the texts. If audiotapes are available for all to use, there will be no stigma attached to using them. However, make sure that low-achieving readers have ample opportunity to read books on their level. This may entail scheduling sessions in which books on their level are introduced and discussed.

Text Sets

■ A **text set** is a series of related books. Because the books are related, reading and comparing them deepens the reader's understanding of the theme or topic of the text set.

Text sets are related books. Reading text sets fosters the making of connections. When connections are made, the reading of all related texts is enriched (Harste, Short, & Burke, 1988). In addition to deepening readers' background, text sets broaden readers' framework for thinking about literature. Having read two or more related books, they can compare and contrast them. Discussions are also enlivened because students have more to talk about. If students read books on the same topic, understanding can be developed in greater depth.

Literature Discussion Groups

In literature discussion groups, students meet and discuss pieces of literature that they have read. Students may have some choice in the books they read or the teacher may make the selections. Each group may be reading a different book, or all the groups may be reading the same text. Two types of literature discussion groups, the reading club and literature circles, were discussed in Chapter 8.

Thematic Units

■ A **unit** is a way of organizing instruction around a central idea, topic, or focus.

Another model of literature-based instruction is the **unit,** which has a theme or other unifying element. Its unifying element may be the study of a particular author, a genre—mystery or picture books, for example—or a theme. Themes might include such diverse topics as heroes, distant places, sports and hobbies, animals, survival, friendship, personal identity, or the Westward Movement. A unit's theme may involve only the language arts, or it may cut across the curriculum and include social studies, science, math, and the visual and performing arts.

Thematic organization has a number of advantages, the principal one being that it helps students make connections among reading, writing, listening, speaking, and viewing activities and among different pieces of literature. If there is integration with other subjects, even broader and more numerous connections can be constructed. However, Routman (1991) cautioned that before the language arts are integrated with content-area subjects, they should first be integrated with each other.

Routman (1991) also warned that some thematic units lack depth and "are nothing more than suggested activities clustered around a central focus or topic" (p. 277). In her judgment, this is correlation rather than integration. In order for true integration to occur, there must be some overall concepts or understandings that the unit develops, with activities designed to support those concepts or understandings. For instance, a unit may revolve around famous people, with students reading and writing about such people, but the unit would not be truly integrated unless the reading and related activities developed a genuine theme or core idea. "Famous people" is a topic rather than a theme because it does not express a unifying idea. Some unifying ideas include "Successful people have had to overcome obstacles on their way to success" or "Successful people have many characteristics in common." An excellent way to integrate such a unit is to create broad questions to be answered by students: "What are the secrets of success?" or "What are successful people like?" Ideally, these are questions that students have had a hand in creating. As part of the unit's activities, students read about successful people, then interview and write about them in order to integrate information from the unit and answer broad questions. They might also look at successful people in science, social studies, and the arts. The suggested procedure for creating and implementing a thematic unit follows:

1. *Select a topic or theme that you wish to explore.* When deciding upon a theme, select one that encompasses concepts that are an important part of the curriculum and that will facilitate the development of essential language arts goals. The theme should be significant and interesting to students. The unit "Westward Wagons" was planned by the fifth-grade teacher, the librarian, and the reading consultant in an elementary school in North Scituate, Rhode Island (DiLuglio, Eaton, & de Tarnowsky, 1988). This unit on the Westward Movement is appropriate for fifth-graders because it is a topic typically presented in that grade and it lends itself to a wide variety of language arts, science, social studies, and art activities.

2. *Involve students in the planning.* Determine through a modified KWL or similar technique what they know about the topic and what they would like to learn.

3. *State the overall ideas that you wish the unit to emphasize.* Include questions that your students might have about the topic (Routman, 1991). The teachers who created the "Westward Wagons" unit decided on four overall or big ideas: reasons for moving west, problems encountered during the move, transportation in the west, and life in a frontier settlement. Also, compose a list of language arts objectives. What literary appreciations and comprehension, study, and writing or other skills/strategies will the unit develop? These objectives should tie in with the unit's big ideas. They should help students understand the nature

For a unit on trees, the major understandings that teacher Elaine Weiner wanted to emphasize were "We cannot live on earth without trees" and "Trees provide shade, beauty, paper, homes for animals, and more" (Routman, 1991, p. 278).

As you plan a unit, focus on the theme rather than activities. Given the unit's theme and major concepts, ask: "What activities will best help students acquire an understanding of the unit's theme and major concepts?" (Lipson, Valencia, Wixson, & Peters, 1993).

of the Westward Movement. Included in the list of skill/strategy objectives are reading skills, such as summarizing, and writing skills, such as report writing, that students need in order to investigate the Westward Movement. Because the unit is interdisciplinary, objectives are listed for each content area.

> A core book, a text set, or books chosen by a literature discussion group could also be the focus of a unit. The unit would then consist of the reading of the core book, text set, or literature discussion book(s), and the completion of related activities.

4. *Decide on the reading materials and activities that will be included in the unit.* You may wish to focus on a core book that will become the center of the unit. Using a semantic map or web, show how you might integrate each of the language arts. Show, too, how you might integrate science, social studies, and other areas. Each activity should advance the theme of the unit. Activities should also promote skill/strategy development in the language arts and other areas. For instance, in the "Westward Wagons" unit, students simulated a journey west. As part of the simulation, they wrote journal entries and tracked their progress on a map.

5. *List and gather resources, including materials to be read, centers to be set up, audiovisual aids, and guest speakers or resource personnel.* Be sure to work closely with school and town librarians if students will be doing outside reading or research. In the "Westward Wagons" unit, *Sarah, Plain and Tall* (MacLachlan, 1985),

Exemplary Teaching

Implementing a Thematic Approach

*I*n a multi-year project with struggling readers and writers in grades 6 through 8, teachers in Memphis, Tennessee, implemented a thematic approach that involved cooperating across subject matter boundaries. The idea behind the project was to "move curriculum from an unlinked catalog of texts, collection of superficially related works, or sequential or chronological structure to a more integrated whole of episodes echoing one another in support of ongoing curricular conversations" (Athanases, 2003, p. 110). In other words teachers would structure activities so as to make connections among key ideas so that students would have a broader perspective of major concepts and a deeper understanding of them. Ideas introduced in language arts class would be reinforced and expanded in history and science classes. While the theme of community was being developed through reading literary works; the science teacher further developed the theme by exploring one of the theme's big ideas: interdependence. Family history was linked to science themes of nature versus nurture. Subthemes of discovery, motivation, and curiosity were developed through historical biographies of exploration and scientific experimentation.

As students were studying community, a tornado ripped through Nashville, causing enormous damage but also providing numerous opportunities for people of all economic, racial, and ethnic groups to come together and help each other out. Having studied interdependence in their community unit, students were able to come to a deeper understanding of what was happening in their city and do a better job writing about it.

At the outset, students' concepts of community were simplistic and tended to be limited to concepts of neighborhood. By year's end students' concepts of community had grown considerably in breadth and depth. They were able to use analogies and metaphors in their discussions of community. They were also able to draw from the literature they had read. As their teacher commented:

> That was exciting to me to see that all of a sudden literature wasn't just born in books that sit on the shelf. It was "literature and my life." There is some connection there and I think the themes do that . . .
> (Athanases, 2003, p. 116)

Caddie Woodlawn (Brink, 1935), *A Gathering of Days* (Blos, 1979), and other high-quality selections were listed. These texts varied in difficulty level from grades three and four to grades six and seven, so all the students might have materials on an appropriate level of difficulty.

    6. *Plan a unit opener that will set the stage for the unit.* It could be the showing of a film or video, a reading of a poem or the first chapter of the core book, or it might be a simulation. The opener might involve brainstorming with students to decide which aspect of the topic they would like to explore. For the "Westward Wagons" unit, students were asked to imagine how it might feel if they were making a long, dangerous trip across the country.

    7. *Evaluate.* Evaluation should be broad-based and keyed into the objectives that you have set for your students or that they have set for themselves in collaboration with you. It should include the unit's major concepts or understandings as well as skills and strategies that were emphasized. For example, if the ability to visualize was emphasized, it needs to be assessed. If you emphasized ability to take notes or write journals, that might be assessed through holistic evaluation of students' written pieces. As part of the evaluation, you must decide whether students learned the concepts and skills or strategies listed in the objectives. If not, reteaching is in order. In addition, you should evaluate the unit itself and determine what might be done to improve the unit. You might eliminate activities or materials that proved boring or ineffective and revise other elements as necessary.

> Units may encompass a single area, such as language arts or social studies, or they may be integrated and cut across subject matter areas. Integrated units apply the language arts to one or more content areas. The focus is on a theme, problem, or central question, such as Native Americans, friends, families, the animal world, and so on. Curriculum lines are dropped, and all activities are devoted to that topic.

Self-Selection

Reading a chapter book, novel, or full-length biography is a major commitment of time. Students will be more willing to put forth the necessary effort if they enjoy the book and have some say in its selection. Even when working with groups, it is possible to allow some self-selection. Obtain several copies of a number of appropriate books. Give a brief overview of each, and have students list them in order of preference. Group students by their preferences into literature circles or similar groups (see the discussion of literature circles in Chapter 8). You can even allow some self-selection when using a core book approach with the entire class. Give the students a choice of two or three core books from which to select. If it is necessary for the entire class to read a particular book, plan some activities in which students can select their own reading materials. You might also alternate teacher selection with self-selection: After teaching a unit that revolves around a core book, plan a unit in which students select books.

> **USING TECHNOLOGY**
> Children's Literature: Electronic Journals & Book Reviews contains a variety of sources for reviews of children's books.
> **http://www.acs. ucalgary.ca/~dkbrown/ journals.html**

Advantages and Disadvantages of a Literature-Based Approach

The primary advantage of a literature-based approach is that books can be chosen to meet students' needs and interests. The major disadvantage of a literature-based program is that fine literature may be misused, by being made simply a means for developing reading skills rather than a basis for fostering personal re-

*I*n a literature-based approach, students read whole books by well-known authors.

sponse and an aesthetic sense. A second major disadvantage is that the books chosen may not be equally appealing to all students and some books may be too difficult for struggling readers.

Adapting a Literature-Based Approach

In a literature-based approach, selections can be read in one of three ways: whole class, small group, or individually. Whole-class reading creates a sense of community and builds a common background of knowledge but neglects individual differences in reading ability and interest. Working in small groups does not build a sense of larger community but can allow for better provision for individual differences. Individualized reading, which is described in the next section, provides for individual differences and fosters self-selection but may be inefficient. If you do use whole-class reading, use it on a limited basis and complement it with small groups or an individualized approach and self-selection.

USING TECHNOLOGY
Children's Publishers on the Internet lists a variety of sites maintained by publishers of children's books. Some of the sites also include free teaching guides and other instructional resources.
http://www.acs. ucalgary.ca/~dkbrown/ publish.html

■ **Individualized reading–reading workshop** is a system of teaching reading in which students select their own reading material, read at their own pace, and are instructed in individual conferences and whole-class or small-group lessons.

INDIVIDUALIZED READING–READING WORKSHOP

The **individualized reading–reading workshop** approach is designed to create readers who can and do read. Each student chooses her or his own reading material and has periodic conferences with the teacher to discuss it. The most popular form of individualized reading is known as **reading workshop.** Reading workshop is similar to writing workshop, but the focus is on reading. Reading workshop has three major components: preparation time, self-selected reading and responding, and student sharing (Atwell, 1987; Cooper, 1997; Reutzel and Cooter, 1991).

Preparation Time

Reading workshop begins with preparation time, which includes a state-of-the-class conference and a minilesson. The state-of-the-class conference is a housekeeping procedure and can be as brief as a minute or two. During this time, the schedule for the workshop is set, as students note what they will be doing. In the minilesson, the teacher presents a skill/strategy lesson based on a need evidenced by the whole class. It could be a lesson on making inferences, predicting, using context clues, deciphering multisyllabic words, or interpreting metaphors. Or it could be a lesson on selecting a book, finding more time to read, or how to share a book with a partner (Calkins, 2001). The minilesson might be drawn from the basal reader or literature resource book or might be created by the teacher (Cooper, 1997). It should be presented within the framework of a story or article that students have read or listened to, and it should be applicable to the reading that they will do that day. The minilesson should last approximately ten minutes, but could be longer.

Although brief, minilessons should be memorable and effective. Calkins (2001) has found a five-part lesson to be effective. The parts are connection, teaching, active involvement, link, and follow-up. The connection explains why a particular strategy or topic was chosen. For instance, the teacher might say, "When I'm reading a book about a new topic, I use the pictures to help me. Yesterday, I was reading about robots. I don't know much about robots, but the illustrations really helped." The teaching is the actual instruction. The teacher shows specifically how the illustrations and diagrams added to his understanding of robots and clarified some ideas that weren't clear. Active involvement means that at least for a few minutes, students try out the strategy or a portion of it. The teacher gives students a handout that describes several unusual animals but contains no illustrations. The teacher then gives students the same handout with illustrations. The students briefly discuss how the second handout helped them better understand the selection. The link connects the strategy with a story that the students are about to read. Students are reading informational books of their own choosing. The teacher suggests to students that they use the illustrations to help them better understand the topics they are reading about. In a follow-up, students are asked to tell or demonstrate how they applied the strategy. During the sharing, the teacher asks students to tell how illustrations helped them better understand the articles they read.

Self-Selected Reading and Responding

At the heart of the workshop is the time when students read self-selected books, respond to their reading, or engage in group or individual conferences. Self-selected reading may last approximately thirty minutes or longer. If time is available, this period can be extended. If students have difficulty reading alone for that period of time, a portion of the period might be set aside for reading with a partner or in a small group. Because students will be reading their self-selected books independently, they should be encouraged to use appropriate strategies. Before reading, they should survey, predict, and set a purpose for reading. As they read, they should use summarizing, inferencing, and imaging strategies—if appropriate— and should monitor for meaning. As they read, students can use sticky notes to indicate a difficult word or puzzling passage. Or, as suggested by Atwell (1987), they can record difficult words and the page numbers of puzzling passages on a bookmark. A full bookmark could be a sign that a book is too difficult. After reading, students should evaluate their original prediction and judge whether they can retell the selection and relate it to their own experiences.

Response time may last from fifteen to thirty minutes or longer. During response time, students may meet in a literature discussion group to discuss their reading, write in their journals, work on an extension activity, plan a reader's theater or other type of presentation, work at one of the classroom's centers, continue to

■ **Reading workshop** is a form of individualized reading in which students choose their own books and have individual or group conferences but may meet in groups to discuss books or work on projects. There may also be whole-class or small-group lessons.

▌Pinnell and Fountas (2002) recommend that guided reading be a part of reading workshop for students in grades three and beyond.

▌Minilessons may not allow sufficient time for instruction in complex skills. When introducing a skill, especially a complex one, you may need to extend the lesson. Shorter lessons might suffice when you are reviewing a skill.

read, or attend a conference. During response time, hold individual and/or group conferences. If time allows, circulate around the room, giving help and guidance as needed. Visiting literature circles should be a priority.

Conferences

Just as in writing workshop, conferences are a key part of reading workshop. Both individual and group conferences are recommended, each having distinct advantages.

■ Individual Conferences

In the original version of individualized reading, teachers held individual conferences with students. In reading workshop, teachers hold group as well as individual conferences.

Although time consuming, the individual conference allows each student to have the teacher's full attention and direct guidance and instruction for at least a brief period. It builds a warm relationship between teacher and student and provides the teacher with valuable insights into each student and her or his needs. While individual conferences are being held, other students are engaged in silent reading. No interruption of the conference is allowed, and those involved in silent reading are not to be disturbed.

An individual conference begins with some questions designed to put the student at ease and to get a general sense of the student's understanding of the book. Through questioning, the teacher also attempts to elicit the student's personal response to the text and encourages the student to relate the text to her or his own life. The teacher poses questions to clear up difficulties and to build comprehension—and concepts, if necessary—and reviews difficult vocabulary. In addition, the teacher assesses how well the student understood the book, whether she or he enjoyed it, and whether she or he is able to apply the strategies and skills that have been taught. The teacher notes any needs the student has and may provide spontaneous instruction or give help later. To prepare for individual conferences, students choose a favorite part of the book to read to the teacher and also give a personal assessment of the book, telling why they did or did not like it or what they learned from it. Students also bring words, ideas, or items they want clarified or questions that they have about the text. In addition, students may be asked to complete a generic response sheet or a specific response sheet geared to the book they have read. Figures 9.1 and 9.2 present generic response forms that include items designed to elicit a personal response from students. To avoid having students do an excessive amount of writing, you might focus on just a few of the personal response questions or have students respond to the questions orally rather than in writing.

Another way that students can prepare for an individual conference is to keep track of their reading in journals. Students note the date and title and author of the book and their personal response to the piece, answering questions such as these: How does the selection make me feel? What will I most remember about it? Was there anything in it that bothered me (Gage, 1990)? Did it remind me of a person or event in my life? Do I have any questions about the piece (Parsons, 1990)? For an informational book, students answer such questions as these: Which details did I find most interesting? How might I use the information? What questions do I

BUILDING LANGUAGE

In conferences, ask open-ended questions, such as "Tell me about your book. What do you like best about it?" Use wait time to help students develop their responses more fully. Model the use of literary language as you ask such questions as, "How did the author build suspense in the story? How did she develop the characters? How did she make them seem real?"

FIGURE 9.1

Response Sheet for Fiction

Name: _____   Date: _____

Title of book: _____   Publisher: _____

Author: _____   Date of publication: _____

Plot

      Problem: _____
                  _____

Main happenings: _____
                  _____

      Climax: _____
                  _____

     Outcome: _____
                  _____
                  _____
                  _____

Answer any three of the following questions:

1. What did you like best about the book?

   _____
   _____

2. Is there anything in the book that you would like to change? If so, what? Also tell why you would like to make changes.

   _____
   _____

3. Is there anything in the book that puzzled you or bothered you?

   _____
   _____

4. Would you like to be friends with any of the characters in the book? Why or why not?

   _____
   _____

5. If other students your age asked whether you thought they might like to read this book, what would you tell them?

   _____
   _____

FIGURE 9.2

Response Sheet for Informational Books

Name: _____   Date: _____

Title of book: _____   Publisher: _____

Author: _____   Date of publication: _____

Topic of book: _____

Main things I learned: _____

_____

_____

_____

Most interesting thing I learned: _____

_____

Questions I still have about the topic: _____

_____

_____

_____

Recommendation to others: _____

_____

_____

still have about the topic? Questions should not be so time consuming or arduous that students avoid reading so they will not have to answer them. As an alternative, you might have students keep a dialogue journal as described later in this chapter.

Students should keep a record of all books that they read. While helping the teacher keep track of students' reading, such records are also motivational. Students get a sense of accomplishment from seeing their list grow. A simple record such as that in Figure 9.3 would suffice.

Individual conferences can last anywhere from five to ten minutes. At least one individual or group conference should be held for each student each week. Not every book needs a conference. A student who is reading two or three books a week should decide on one book to talk about. On the other hand, if the student is a slow reader, a conference may be held when she or he is halfway through the book. Conferences should be scheduled. A simple way to do this is to have students who are ready for conferences list their names on the chalkboard. The teacher can then fill in the times for the conferences.

After the conference is over, the teacher should make brief notes in the student's folder, including date, title of book read, assessment of student's understanding and satisfaction with the book, strategies or skills introduced or reinforced, student's present and future needs, and student's future plans. A sample conference report form is presented in Figure 9.4.

ASSESSING STUDENTS' PROGRESS

After holding a conference, be sure to summarize it. Include date, selection read, and student's reaction to the text. Does she enjoy it? Is she able to respond to it? Can she cope with the book? Is it too difficult or too easy? Does she select books wisely? Did you note any needs? If so, how will these be provided for? What are her plans for the future? Will she engage in an extension or enrichment activity? Will she read another book?

FIGURE 9.3

A Reading Log

Name: _____

Title of book: _____

Author: _____

Publisher: _____

Date of publication: _____

Number of pages: _____

Subject: _____

Date started: _____

Date completed: _____

Recommendations to others: _____

_____

_____

_____

■ Group Conferences

Group conferences are an efficient use of time and can be used along with or instead of individual conferences. The teacher has the opportunity to work with five or six students rather than just one. Conferences can be held to discuss books by

Teachers might hold conferences during silent reading and during response time.

FIGURE 9.4

An Individualized Reading Conference Report

Name: *Althea S.*   Date: *10/19*

Title: *Island of the Blue Dolphins*   Author: *Scott O'Dell*

Understanding of text and personal response:	*Discussion of Ch. 3 of text: Was able to retell major events. Remembered a time when she was chased by a vicious dog and the fear that she felt.*
Oral reading:	*Fairly smooth. Good interpretation. Some difficulty reading hard words. 97% accuracy.*
Needs:	*Needs to learn to use morpheme analysis and context to decode hard words and check glossary later on.*
Future plans:	*Plans to finish book within two weeks. Will join Literature Circle and compare books. Will share most exciting incident with whole class.*

the same author, those with a common theme, or those in the same genre. Group conferences work best when students have read the same book. If several copies of a book are available, they can be given to interested students, who then confer.

A group conference includes three types of questions: an opening question to get the discussion started, following questions to keep the discussion moving, and process questions to "help the children focus on particular elements of the text" (Hornsby, Sukarna, & Parry, 1986, p. 62). Process questions focus on comprehending and appreciating a piece and are similar to those asked in the discussion and rereading portions of a DRA. They are often related to reading strategies and might ask students to summarize a passage, compare characters, predict events, clarify difficult terms, or locate proof for an inference. Students should also have the opportunity to respond personally to the text. Process and response questions might be interwoven. The teacher should lead the discussion, although students eventually may take on that role. Just as in individual conferences, the teacher evaluates students' performance, notes needs, and plans future activities based on those needs. Along with or instead of a group conference, students might take part in a literature discussion group.

Using Dialogue Journals

■ A **dialogue journal** is a journal in which the students react to or make observations about their reading or other topic and the teacher responds by writing in the journal.

If you are working with older students, you might try **dialogue journals** as an alternative to conferences or along with conferences. After Nancy Atwell (1987) instituted self-selection and time to read in her classroom, her students read an average of thirty-five books. She commented, "Last year's average of thirty-five books per student grew as much from students' power to choose as from the time I made for them to read. I heard again and again from students of every ability that freedom of choice had turned them into readers" (p. 161). Although providing students with time to read and freedom to choose started them reading, Atwell was not satisfied. She realized that response was needed to allow students to reflect on their reading and deepen their understanding and appreciation. Because individual conferences were so brief, they did not lend themselves to an in-depth discussion of the text. To provide the framework for response, Atwell used dialogue journals to initiate an exchange with the students.

Having the opportunity to write about their reading gave students time to reflect and led to deeper insights. With the give and take of dialogue, they were led to develop their thoughts and reconsider interpretations. Atwell commented:

BUILDING LANGUAGE

In dialogue journals you can ask students to expand on responses, perhaps asking a student who said that he liked *Heads or Tails: Stories from the Sixth Grade* (Gantos, 1994) because it was funny to tell what made it funny or to tell what the funniest part was.

I initiated written dialogues about literature because I had some hunches about the combined possibilities of writing as a way of reflecting on reading, and teacher–learner correspondence as a way of extending and enriching reflection through collaboration. I suspected kids' written responses to books would go deeper than their talk; that writing would give them time to consider their thinking and that thoughts captured would spark new insights. I also suspected that a written exchange between two readers, student and adult expert, would move readers even deeper inside written texts, with the give and take of the dialogue helping them to consider and develop their thoughts. Finally, I believed this special context—a teacher initiating and inviting first-draft chat—would provide a way for me to be responsive to every reader as well as creating a specific occasion for them to write and reflect: a genuine and genuinely interested audience who was going to write back. (p. 165)

In addition to providing students with an opportunity to respond, dialogue journals yield insight into students' growth as readers. Thus, they offer the teacher a rich source of ideas for teaching lessons. Although, at first, the dialogue was between teacher and individual students, Atwell discovered students passing notes about poems they had read. She extended an invitation for students to dialogue with a partner, and students began exchanging their responses. Because responding to each student's journal on a daily basis could be overwhelming, you might want to have one-fifth of the class turn in their journals each day. That way you respond each day to just a few students, but you see each student's journal once a week.

Student Sharing

During the student-sharing portion of reading workshop, which should last from ten to twenty minutes, students share their reading with the entire class. They might give the highlights of a book they especially enjoyed, read an exciting passage, share a poem, make a recommendation, enact a reader's theater performance, or share in some other way. "Sharing time advertises and promotes the excitement of literacy learning and helps to promote the class as a community of readers" (Cooper, 1997, p. 491). As an alternative to whole-class sharing, the teacher might arrange for small-group sharing with four or so students in each group. The teacher can then visit with the groups as a participant or observer (Cooper, 1997).

Organizing the Program

The classroom must be organized carefully. Just as in a library, it should have an inviting browsing area where students can choose books and settle down comfortably to read. Routines should be established for selecting books, keeping track of books circulated, taking part in conferences, and completing independent activities. The nature of the activity should determine the types of rules and routines. Because they are expected to follow these procedures, students should have a role in formulating them. The teacher might describe the situation and have students suggest ways to make it work.

The following basic conditions must be managed: (1) the teacher must be able to hold individual or group conferences with students that are free from interruptions; (2) students must be able

> One of the primary advantages of dialogue journals is that teachers can model and scaffold more mature expression (Atwell, 1987). Through thoughtful comments and careful questioning, they can elicit lengthier, more elaborated responses and they can direct students to look at essential aspects of the texts being discussed. Closed questions such as, "Which character did you like best?" would tend to elicit a limited response. However, open questions such as "The story sounds interesting. Tell me about it," would tend to bring forth a fuller response.

During reading workshop, students might share their response journals with a partner.

An approach that features self-selected reading requires a large collection of materials. As a rule of thumb, there should be at least three times as many books as students in the class, with more books being added over time. School and local libraries might loan a classroom collection, students might bring in books from home, or the community might be asked to contribute. Old basals can be a part of the collection.

to work on their own without disturbing others; and (3) students must be responsible for choosing books on their own and reading them. Some commonsense rules and routines might include the following:

- *Book selection.* The number of students choosing books at one time is limited to five; students may select two books at one time; students may make one exchange. Some students, especially those who are struggling with their reading, may waste a great deal of time choosing books. Instead of having students select books during reading workshop, you might have students gather books to be read from the school or classroom library prior to reading. Younger students might gather four or five books that they intend to read. Older students might gather two or three. These can be kept in book boxes or accordion folders or oversized envelopes along with students' reading logs and conference sheets and any other reading aids, such as a model words chart (Calkins, 2001).
- *Circulation.* Students are responsible for the books they check out; a card, sign-out sheet, or computerized system is used to keep track of books; students are in charge of the circulation system; books may be taken home.
- *Conference time.* No one may interrupt the teacher during conferences; students must come prepared to conferences; students (or the teacher) must arrange for periodic conferences.

A main reason that teachers found individualized reading unmanageable in the past was the demand that conferences made on their time. However, with group conferences and the experience gained by holding writing conferences, this should no longer be a major hindrance.

Advantages and Disadvantages of Reading Workshop

Self-selection, moving at one's own pace, using group processes, and relating reading and writing are the major advantages of reading workshop. Disadvantages include potential neglect of skills and the possibility that the teacher might spread himself too thin in an attempt to meet with a variety of groups and individuals and respond to students' journal entries. Also, reading workshop might be unsuitable for students who have a difficult time working independently or whose skills are so limited that there are few books they can read on their own.

ADAPTING INSTRUCTION for *STRUGGLING READERS and WRITERS*

Because students select their own books and read at their own pace, individualized reading–reading workshop works extremely well with students reading below grade. No longer are they stigmatized by being put in the low group or forced to read material that is too difficult for them.

Adapting Reading Workshop

Reading workshop can be used instead of a basal series or along with it. For instance, you might use a basal three days and reading workshop two days. Or you might use a basal for a part of the day and reading workshop for a portion. Use whole-class instruction as appropriate. For instance, teach book selection and strategies needed by all students to the whole class. Use small-group instruction for those children who evidence a specific need for additional help. Obtain multiple copies of selected titles, just as you might do for a literature-based approach, and periodically invite students to choose one of the titles and read it as part of a small group–guided reading lesson. Use efficient management techniques, and do not overextend yourself. If you use reading workshop with students whose writing skills are still rather limited, gradually lead them into the use of dialogue journals.

LANGUAGE-EXPERIENCE APPROACH

In the **language-experience** approach, students use writing as a means for developing reading skills. Students have an experience. This might be conducting a science experiment, going on a field trip, recounting a frightening or humorous experience, engaging in a simulation, viewing a video, creating a list, planning a celebration, or summarizing a selection that was read to them. The experience is discussed. The students then decide how they are going to organize the experience and, with the help of teacher prompts, dictate an account of it. The teacher, acting as a scribe, takes down their dictation. Stories may be dictated by individuals, by small groups, or by the whole class. The dictated story then becomes a source of reading material and/or a model for writing.

■ **Language experience** is an approach to teaching reading in which students dictate a story based on an experience they have had. The dictated story is written down by a teacher or aide and used to instruct the students in reading.

The language-experience approach is most frequently used as a supplement to other reading programs and is especially useful in the beginning stages of learning to read. However, the language-experience approach can also be used with older students. It can be used with students who are reading on such a low reading level that it is difficult to find suitable reading materials. If content-area texts are too difficult, it can be used to summarize key concepts. It can also be used with English language learners. Because both the language and the experience are familiar, the language-experience approach presents fewer difficulties for students who are struggling with reading or the English language. The language-experience approach can also be used to foster writing skills. By participating in the writing of a language-experience story, students learn how to compose similar pieces.

The language-experience approach integrates thinking, listening, speaking, reading, and writing. Through discussion, the teacher can lead students to organize and reflect on their experiences. If time order is garbled, the teacher can ask, "What happened first? What happened next?" If details are scant, the teacher can request the students to tell more or can ask open-ended questions, such as "How do you think the dinosaur tracks got there? What do the tracks tell us about dinosaurs?" Through comments that show an interest in the students and the topic, the teacher affirms them and encourages them to elaborate.

Whereas the teacher should affirm, support, encourage, and scaffold, she needs to be careful not to take over. The teacher should draw language from the students, not put words in their mouths. When recording students' stories, it is important to write their exact words. Rephrasing what they have dictated shows a lack of acceptance for the language used. In addition, if the story is expressed in words that the student does not normally use, the student may have difficulty reading it. For instance, if the student dictates, "I been over my grandma's house," and the teacher rewords it as "I have been to my grandma's house," the student might stumble over the unfamiliar syntax. As Cunningham and Allington (1999) have observed,

> If language-experience is being used with an individual child to help the child understand what reading and writing are and that the child can write and read what he or she can say, then the child's exact words must be written down. To do anything else will hopelessly confuse the child about the very things you are trying to clarify by using individual language-experience. (p. 92)

However, when a group story is being written, the situation is somewhat different. The story and the way it is written reflect the language structures that the group typically uses. To record a nonstandard structure might confuse some members of the group and result in criticism for the child who volunteered the structure. Displaying group stories containing nonstandard structures might also result in protests from parents and administrators (Cunningham & Allington, 1999). Lesson 9.1 describes the steps for a group language-experience story.

LESSON 9.1 Group language-experience chart

Step 1. Building experiential background for the story

The students have an experience that they share as a group and that they can write about. It might be a field trip, a science experiment, the baking of bread, summary of a content area selection that you read aloud, or a similar experience.

Step 2. Discussing the experience

Students reflect on their experience and talk about it. During the discussion, you help them organize the experience. In discussing a visit to a science museum, you might ask them to tell what they liked best so that they do not get lost in details. If they baked bread, pose questions in such a way that the students list in order the steps involved.

Step 3. Dictating the story

The students dictate the story. Write it on large lined paper, an overhead transparency, or the chalkboard, or you might even type it on a computer that has an attachment to magnify the input and project it on a screen. Read aloud what you are writing so that students can see the spoken words being written. Then read each sentence to make sure it is what the student who volunteered the sentence wanted to say.

Step 4. Reviewing the story

After the whole story has been written, read it aloud once more. Students listen to see that the story says what they want it to say. Invite them to make changes. After the story has been edited, reread it. Have students read along with you to see if they are satisfied with the changes. Make any additional changes that are called for. These multiple rereadings help students become familiar with the text.

Step 5. Reading of story by teacher and students

If students are struggling readers, reread the story, running your hand under each word as it is read. The students read along with you.

Step 6. Discussion

Discuss the content of the selection with students. As part of the discussion, have students read sentences that help answer questions that are posed. If students, for instance, are asked to tell why oil floats on water, you might request that they

ADAPTING INSTRUCTION for *STRUGGLING READERS and WRITERS*

The language-experience approach is most often used in the beginning stages of reading and is usually combined with another approach. However, it can be very useful when working with older students reading on a very low level. Instead of using books that are "babyish," students can read their language-experience stories.

read the sentence that explains why. This helps you to check whether they are able to read the experience story on their own. Go over any words that students might be having difficulty reading. If working with struggling readers, spend more time on word recognition skills. You might focus on phonics, syllable patterns, or morphemic elements, for instance.

Take a look at the sample experience story in Figure 9.5. It is drawn from a summary of a ection of a sixth-grade science text, *Discovery Works* (Badders et al., 1999). The text was too difficult for one group of students to read on its own, so the teacher read it out loud instead. The group then composed an experience story summarizing the segment. The segment was revised and edited. Once the class had finished editing the selection and the teacher had reread it to them, they discussed it. They discussed what density is and why it could be used to predict whether something would sink or float. To make sure that students could read key words in the selection, the teacher asked them to read sentences orally. They were asked to read the sentence that tells what density is and also the sentence that tells what the density of water is. They also discussed what a gram is and what a milliliter is. To develop word analysis skills, you might work on the prefix *milli-* and the suffix *-ity* by looking at other words that contain these elements.

Copies of the story were printed so that each student would have one. They were placed in binders that contained other summaries, so that students had material to review or to use to study for a test.

An Individual Approach

Individual language-experience stories are similar to group stories, except that they are more personalized. Just as in the group approach, the student dictates a story and the teacher, an aide, or a volunteer writes it down and uses it as the basis for teaching reading.

If your students are creating individual language-experience stories, it's helpful if you have an aide or volunteers to assist with dictation. First explain the process to your helpers and let them observe you until they feel they can undertake the procedure on their own.

FIGURE 9.5

Group Experience Story: Summary of Segment of Science Text

Density and Rotten Eggs

Knowing about density can keep you from eating a rotten egg. A fresh egg has a smaller density than a rotten egg. Density is the amount of matter in space. Pick up a piece of wood and a piece of iron that are the same size. The piece of iron is heavier. That is because iron has more matter in the same amount of space than a piece of wood.

Density can tell you whether something will sink or float. If an object has a greater density than water, it will sink. If it has a density that is less than that of water, it will float. Water has a density of 1.0 g/mL. That means it has one gram of matter for each milliliter of space. A fresh egg has a density of about 1.2 g/mL. A rotten egg has a density of about 0.9 g/mL. That is why a rotten egg will float. So if you are going to boil an egg for breakfast and it floats, throw it away!

When dictating a language-experience story, a student may bring up experiences that are highly personal or that reveal private family matters. Affirm the student's feelings, but suggest a more appropriate way for the student to relate the experience. "I'm pleased that you trusted me enough to share that with me, but I think maybe you should tell your mom or dad about it." If the situation warrants it, make a referral to the school counselor or social worker. If the student uses language that is unsuitable for the classroom, have her or him use more appropriate language: "Can you think of another way to say it?" (Tierney, Readence, & Dishner, 1995). Maintaining the student's dignity and self-concept is of primary importance. Handle delicate situations with sensitivity and careful professional judgment.

> If you are not sure how to handle information that a student has revealed, have a conference with the school counselor or social worker. Discuss ways in which revelatory information might be handled and steps that might be taken to affirm or assist the student.

The Language-Experience Approach and ELL Students

> **ADAPTING INSTRUCTION for** *ENGLISH LANGUAGE LEARNERS*
> Because the language-experience approach is based on students' language, it is a very effective technique to use with students who are still learning English.

Because it uses a student's own language and can draw on aspects of the student's culture, the language-experience approach can be especially helpful for ELLs. However, even a bilingual student who has learned enough English to read a little may have difficulty with idiomatic expressions, many syntactical structures, and, of course, some words.

Teachers often wonder whether they should edit an ELL's dictation if it contains unconventional or nonstandard items. As with native speakers of English, the best advice is to accept the students' language and show that it is valued. If the teacher edits it, it becomes the teacher's language, not the student's. This is especially true when students are in the initial stages of learning to read. In general, students' words should be written exactly as they are dictated; however, even if mispronounced, they should be spelled correctly, for example:

> *Dictation:* I happy. My dog do'an be sick.
> *Written:* I happy. My dog don't be sick.

As students grow in language, they will have opportunities to develop fuller knowledge of verbs, contractions, and pronunciation. The teacher might work on these patterns at appropriate times or consult with the ESL teacher if the student is taking part in such a program. However, focus at this point should be on introducing reading in English. Because the student is demonstrating a basic grasp of English, waiting for further refinement is an unnecessary delay.

> Because language experience is based on students' individual backgrounds, it allows each student to share her culture, experience, and mode of self-expression. It has the power to promote understanding and community among students whose backgrounds may differ.

Variant Dialects

> ■ A **dialect** is a variety of a language that may differ somewhat in pronunciation, grammar, and vocabulary.

Some students may speak a **dialect** that is somewhat different from that typically expected by the school. It is important to accept that language: It will be confusing if the students say one thing and you write another, and constant correction will turn them off. At this point, students are rapidly acquiring vocabulary and developing their understanding of increasingly complex constructions. The last thing a teacher wants to do is to cut off the flow of language and risk interfering with their development. Introducing a standard dialect and correcting variant English should not be a part of reading instruction.

The Language-Experience Approach in the Content Areas

Science and social studies textbooks might be too difficult for some students. Discussion, projects, filmstrips, and experiments can be used to present the subject matter. Language-experience stories can be used to summarize key topics so that students have a text—their own—to read. Group-experience stories can be used to summarize main concepts or events. After studying mammals, for example, the teacher can discuss the main ideas and have the class dictate an experience story that highlights them. Duplicated copies of the stories can be distributed and collected into a science booklet; students can then illustrate their booklets.

Other Uses for the Language-Experience Approach

The language-experience approach does not have to be confined to narratives or summaries of content-area textbooks. Thank-you notes to a visiting author, a letter to a classmate who is hospitalized, an invitation to a guest speaker, recipes, a set of directions for the computer, class rules, charts, lists, captions, diaries, booklets, plays, and similar items are suitable for the language-experience approach. When possible, the pieces should be written for real purposes.

Shared writing is another way in which the language-experience approach might be used. Shared writing is a cooperative venture involving teacher and students. In a regular language-experience story, the teacher records students' exact words. In shared writing, the teacher draws from the students the substance of what they want to say but may rephrase it (Cunningham & Allington, 1999). For instance, at the end of the day, the teacher may ask the students what they learned that day. Summarizing the contributions of many students, the teacher records the day's highlights. In doing so, the teacher is modeling how spoken language is transformed into written language.

Advantages and Disadvantages of the Language-Experience Approach

The major advantage of the approach is that it builds on students' language and experience and can be especially effective when used with struggling readers and ELLs. A major disadvantage of using it as the sole approach to teaching reading is that the students' reading will be limited to their own experiences.

Adapting the Language-Experience Approach

Because it neglects published reading materials and because it limits students' reading experiences, language experience should not be the sole approach to reading instruction. However, it makes an excellent supplement to any of the other approaches presented in this chapter.

How to handle dialect is a controversial issue. Shuy (1973) made the point that it is developmentally inappropriate to introduce another dialect to a young student. The student would be confused and wouldn't pick up the second dialect. As students grow older, they may choose to use other dialects to be able to communicate more effectively with diverse groups. This does not mean that they will surrender their home dialect.

Group language-experience stories can be used beyond the beginning or early reading level to demonstrate writing techniques. One way of showing students how to write a letter to the editor, a persuasive essay, or a story is to arrange for the class to compose these items as group experience stories.

WHOLE LANGUAGE

■ **Whole language** has been described as a grass roots movement. It's a movement that classroom teachers across the land embraced and pushed forward. To help each other apply a whole language approach, a number of vigorous support groups sprang up. These include national networks, such as TAWL (Teachers Applying Whole Language).

Described as a philosophy of learning rather than a teaching approach, **whole language** incorporates a naturalistic, organic view of literacy learning. The basic premise is that children learn to read and write in much the same way that they learn to speak. Oral language is learned by being used for real purposes, not by completing artificial practice exercises that present it piecemeal—work on adjectives today, nouns tomorrow, verbs the day after. Because theorists see reading and writing as a part of the whole, they reason that they should be learned in the same way oral language is learned—through use and for real purposes. The basic belief underlying whole language is acquisition of all aspects of language, including reading and writing, "through use not exercise" (Altwerger, Edelsky, & Flores, 1987, p. 149).

Because whole language is not a prescribed program or method, its implementation varies from setting to setting and is expected to evolve and change as more is learned about how literacy is acquired. Basically, it embodies the following principles.

▌In whole language classes, students take responsibility for their own learning. As Crafton (1991) explains, "When learners of any age initiate their own learning, the intent and purpose of the experience are clear. With self-initiation comes a greater degree of ownership, involvement, and commitment to the activity" (p. 16).

First, reading is best learned through actual use. Students learn by reading whole stories, articles, and real-world materials. Because of the richness of these materials, students are able to use their sense of language and the three cueing systems of semantics, syntax, and letter–sound relationships to grow in reading.

In a whole language classroom, students read and write for real purposes. There are no letters written to aunts who do not exist, thanking them for gifts that were not sent, just so that students can practice the format of the friendly letter. They write letters to real people for real reasons and mail them.

According to the whole language philosophy, literacy is a social undertaking best learned in the context of a group. Therefore, in whole language classrooms, one sees writing workshops, group conferences, peer editing, and other examples of cooperative learning.

GUIDED READING

▌Whole-to-part learning, an important element in a holistic approach, is a form of instruction in which students experience the skill or strategy to be learned in the context of a reading or writing selection or other activity, then focus on the skill or strategy, and apply or encounter the skill or strategy in a new reading selection or other context.

Guided reading is a way of organizing reading instruction that uses grouping. In guided reading, students are grouped and instructed according to their level of development (Fountas & Pinnell, 1996, 2001). The groups meet on a daily basis for ten to thirty minutes or more. The teacher may organize as many groups as she believes are necessary, but the more groups assembled, the less time there is for each one. As a practical matter, three or four groups are the most that can be handled efficiently. Grouping, however, is flexible. When appropriate, students are moved into other groups.

What does the rest of the class do while the teacher is working with guided reading groups? While the teacher is working with guided reading groups, students can engage in a number of independent activities. These activities should provide students with the opportunity to apply and extend their skills. One of the best activities for developing reading skills is, of course, to read. Students can

- read independently in the reading corner.
- read along with an audiotape or CD-ROM.
- meet with a literature circle.
- meet with a cooperative learning group.
- work on a piece of writing.
- research a project in the library or on the Internet.
- work on a carefully chosen Web site that fosters literacy.

Advantages and Disadvantages of Guided Reading

A key advantage of guided reading is that students are instructed on their level and are given the support and instruction they need. The approach works especially well if the grouping is flexible and students not meeting in groups are provided with worthwhile activities.

AN INTEGRATED APPROACH

A large-scale comparison of approaches to teaching reading in the 1960s came up with no clear winner (Bond & Dykstra, 1967, 1997). All of the approaches evaluated were effective in some cases. However, some students experienced difficulty with each one. The study suggested that the teacher is more important than the method and that a method successful in one situation may not be successful in all. Combinations of approaches were recommended.

Another interpretation of the research strongly suggests that what is really most effective is using the best features of all approaches. Draw from holistic literature-based approaches the emphasis on functional–contextual instruction, the use of trade books, and integration of language arts. From basal programs, adopt some of the structure built into the skills/strategies components. From individualized approaches, take the emphasis on self-selection of students' reading material. From the language-experience approach, adopt the practice of using writing to build and extend literacy skills.

Above all else, use your professional judgment. This book presents a core of essential skills and strategies in word recognition, comprehension, reading in the content areas, and study skills. Use this core of skills as a foundation when implementing your literacy program, regardless of which approach or approaches you use. If a skill or strategy is omitted or neglected, then add it or strengthen it. For instance, not all basals recommend the use of pronounceable word parts or analogy strategies. If you are using a basal and these elements are missing, add them.

USING TECHNOLGY

Whole Language Umbrella provides an overview of whole language and links to related organizations. **http://www.ncte.org/wlu**

To join a group discussing whole language, you can sign up with the listserv: TAWL@Listserv.Arizona.Edu

ACTION PLAN

1. Become acquainted with the major approaches to reading.
2. Whatever approach you use, incorporate principles of effective literacy instruction. Make sure that students are reading on their levels, are reading widely, are being taught skills in a functional fashion, and that progress is being monitored.
3. If students don't learn with one approach, try to find out why this is so and make adjustments. If the approach fails to work despite your best ef-

forts, try another approach. Also match approaches to students' needs. Most students will learn regardless of what approach you use. But some students will only be successful when certain approaches are used. That is why it is necessary for you to have command of several approaches. If you are in a situation where an approach is mandated, make modifications so that the program is as effective as it can be.
4. Monitor the effectiveness of your program and make adjustments as necessary.

HELP FOR STRUGGLING READERS AND WRITERS

No one of the approaches described is necessarily best for struggling readers and writers. A program, such as reading workshop, that implements self-selected reading would be less likely to stigmatize poor readers because students would be able to choose materials on their level. A basal program would offer the structure that struggling readers and writers need. However, it would be imperative that poor readers be given materials on the appropriate level of challenge, perhaps in a guided reading format. A literature-based program would work well, too, as long as students were given the skills instruction they needed and books on the appropriate level. The language-experience approach works well with struggling readers because it is based on their language. When obtaining suitable reading material is a problem because the struggling reader is older but is reading on a very low level, language-experience stories can be used as the students' reading material.

If you are using a twenty-first century basal, take advantage of the materials and techniques suggested for use with students who are struggling. If you are using an older basal and it seems too difficult for your struggling readers, provide books that the students can handle successfully. Working with students who were struggling with literary selections, Cole (1998) used books from easy-to-read series, such as *Step into Reading* (Random House), and *All Aboard Reading* (Grossett & Dunlap). Books from these and other easy-to-read series can be found in Appendix A.

Regardless of approach used, it would be most helpful if struggling readers and writers were given extra instruction, perhaps in a small group. For students in grades four through eight, there is a program known as Project Success (Soar to Success) that features graphic organizers, discussion, and the reading of high-interest informational books. The program can be taught within the classroom by the classroom teacher or by a specialist (Cooper, 1996). Literacy programs for struggling readers are discussed in Chapter 12.

SUMMARY

1. There are a number of approaches to teaching reading. Approaches that use a textbook to teach reading include basal and literature anthologies. The literature-based approach and reading workshop use trade books, as does whole language, which is more a philosophy than a method. Language experience uses writing to teach reading. Each approach has advantages and disadvantages and may be combined with other approaches and/or adapted.
2. Guided reading is a way of grouping and instructing students according to their needs. Whole language is a holistic, functional philosophy for teaching literacy.
3. According to research, no one approach to teaching reading yields consistently superior results. A combination is probably best. Teachers should use their professional judgment and know-how to adapt programs to fit the needs of their students.
4. Struggling readers need materials on their level and may benefit from additional instruction.

EXTENDING AND APPLYING

1. Examine your philosophy of teaching literacy. Make a list of your beliefs and your teaching practices. Also note the approach to reading that best fits in with your philosophy of teaching reading. Do your practices fit in with your beliefs? If not, what might you do to align the two?
2. Examine a current basal series or literature anthology. Look at a particular level and assess the interest of the selections, the kinds of strategies and teaching suggestions presented in the manual, and the usefulness of the workbook exercises. Summarize your findings.
3. Observe a series of reading workshop lessons. Note the structures and techniques used to make the approach effective.
4. Adapt a lesson in a basal reader or literature anthology to fit the needs of a group of students you are teaching. Teach the lesson and assess its appropriateness. In what ways was the manual a helpful resource? What adaptations did you have to make?

DEVELOPING A PROFESSIONAL PORTFOLIO

If possible, videotape the adapted reader lesson described in Item 4 of Extending and Applying. Place the videotape and/or a typed copy of the plan for the lesson in your portfolio. Summarize the plan and note adaptations you made to the lesson as described in the basal reader manual. Explain why adaptations were made and reflect on the effectiveness of the lesson.

DEVELOPING A RESOURCE FILE

Prepare conference cards or database entries for three trade books that you might use to teach reading. Include bibliographic information, a summary of the selection, a series of questions that you might ask about the book, and a description of some possible extension activities.

10

Writing and Reading

ANTICIPATION GUIDE

*F*or each of the following statements related to the chapter you are about to read, put a check under "Agree" or "Disagree" to show how you feel. Discuss your responses with classmates before you read the chapter.

		Agree	*Disagree*
1	Reading and writing are two sides of the same coin.	____	____
2	Struggling writers should write short pieces to keep their mistakes to a minimum.	____	____
3	Students should be allowed to choose their own topics.	____	____
4	Completing endings for unfinished stories written by others is good practice for budding fiction writers.	____	____
5	The most time-consuming part of the writing process is revising.	____	____
6	Teachers should mark all uncorrected errors after a piece has been edited by a student.	____	____
7	Emphasis in a writing program for elementary and middle school students should be on content rather than form.	____	____

USING WHAT YOU KNOW

*W*riting and reading are related processes that are mutually supportive. Reading improves writing, and vice versa. The last two decades have witnessed a revolution in writing instruction, which today is based on the processes that expert student and professional writers use as they compose pieces.

What is your writing process? What steps do you take before you begin writing? What elements do you consider when you choose a topic? How do you plan your writing? How do you go about revising and editing your writing? How are your reading and writing related? What impact does your reading have on your writing? What impact does writing have on your reading?

THE ROOTS OF WRITING

In any one class, students might vary greatly in their writing development. Some may be grappling with basic expression. Others may be well on their way to becoming proficient writers. It is important to determine where students are on the writing continuum to know how best to help them. Writing development generally follows the stages listed in Figure 10.1. However, it should be noted that students can and do move back and forth between stages and that the stages overlap. In addition, students may be in one stage for narrative writing and another for expository.

Although the description of the stages of writing may not indicate it, all acts of writing are not the same. Writing a poem or essay relies on more complex processes

FIGURE 10.1

Developmental Stages/Scoring Guidelines

Stage 1: The Emerging Writer

- Little or no topic development, organization, and/or detail.
- Little awareness of audience or writing task.
- Errors in surface features prevent the reader from understanding the writer's message.

Stage 2: The Developing Writer

- Topic beginning to be developed. Response contains the beginning of an organization plan.
- Simple word choice and sentence patterns.
- Limited awareness of audience and/or task.
- Errors in surface features interfere with communication.

Stage 3: The Focusing Writer

- Topic clear even though development is incomplete. Plan apparent although ideas are loosely organized.
- Sense of audience and/or task.
- Minimal variety of vocabulary and sentence patterns.
- Errors in surface features interrupt the flow of communication.

Stage 4: The Experimenting Writer

- Topic clear and developed (development may be uneven). Clear plan with beginning, middle, and end (beginning and/or ending may be clumsy).

- Written for an audience.
- Experiments with language and sentence patterns. Word combinations and word choice may be novel.
- Errors in surface features may interrupt the flow of communication.

Stage 5: The Engaging Writer

- Topic well developed. Clear beginning, middle, and end. Organization sustains the writer's purpose.
- Engages the reader.
- Effective use of varied language and sentence patterns.
- Errors in surface features do not interfere with meaning.

Stage 6: The Extending Writer

- Topic fully elaborated with rich details. Organization sustains the writer's purpose and moves the reader through the piece.
- Engages and sustains the reader's interest.
- Creative and novel use of language and effective use of varied sentence patterns.
- Errors in surface features do not interfere with meaning.

From Georgia Department of Education, *Developmental Stages/Scoring Guidelines for Writing,* Atlanta, GA: 2000.

than writing a friendly letter. Processes also develop and change with age and experience. Novice writers use a knowledge-telling process in which writing is similar to telling a story orally or providing an oral explanation. It requires "no greater amount of planning or goal setting than ordinary conversation" (Bereiter & Scardamalia, 1982, p. 9). Novice writers use a what-next strategy in which they write from one sentence to the next without having an overall plan for the whole piece (Dahl & Farnan, 1998). The sentence currently being written provides a springboard for the next sentence.

Gradually, writers acquire a knowledge-tranforming ability in which they alter their thoughts as they write. As they compose, their writing affects their thinking, and their thinking affects their writing. Instead of merely summarizing thoughts, writers are reconsidering and drawing conclusions, which are reflected in their writing. Thus, as students progress, some of the writing activities provided should go beyond having them merely list or summarize and should ask them to compare, contrast, conclude, and evaluate.

GUIDED WRITING

Just as reading instruction should be geared to the students' level of reading development, writing instruction should be geared to students' level of writing development. Although some skills can be taught to the whole class, students' specific needs can be more directly targeted if students are members of small groups. To estimate where students are in their writing development, examine sample pieces of their writing, using Figure 10.1 as a guide. The teacher meets with one or two groups each day and conducts a writing process or strategy lesson. Grouped by their level of development, students are given instruction geared to their stage. For the focusing writer, instruction might stress using appropriate organizational patterns. For the experimenting writer, the focus of instruction might be on using examples or details to develop a topic (Davis, Jackson, & Johnson, 2000). As part of guided writing, students need to be taught specific strategies for writing. Teaching students writing strategies has four steps:

1. Identifying a strategy worth teaching.
2. Introducing the strategy by modeling it.
3. Helping students try the strategy out with teacher guidance.
4. Helping students work toward independent mastery of the strategy through repeated practice and reinforcement. (Collins, 1998, p. 65)

To identify a strategy that needs teaching, examine students' writing. You might also discuss their writing with them. Note areas that are posing problems or that they are having difficulty with. Choose a strategy such as adding interesting examples that would seem to be of most benefit to them in terms of their level of development. The strategy can be introduced to a whole class, to a guided writing group, or to an individual. After the strategy has been introduced, students should have ample opportunity to apply it. As you work with students, help them adapt the strategy so that it becomes a part of their writing repertoire. Provide opportunities for students to use the strategy in a number of situations so that they attain independent mastery of it. Guided strategic writing is presented within the framework of a process writing approach.

THE PROCESS APPROACH TO WRITING

■ The **writing process** is an approach to teaching writing that is based on the way students and professionals write.

In the **process approach,** writing instruction is based on writing processes that professional writers and students actually use. From the research of D. H. Graves (1983), Emig (1971), and others, a series of steps has been described that attempts to explain how writers write. The steps are prewriting, composing, revising, editing, and publishing. However, these steps are not linear. They are recursive. Writers may engage in prewriting activities after composing and may be revising while composing. Based on National Assessment data, students who use a process approach write better than those who don't. "It appears that the process approach to writing, in which planning, writing, and revision through several drafts are practiced, gives students the opportunity to write more and to employ editing strategies, which in turn affords them the opportunity to improve their mastery of the writing conventions" (Ballator, Farnum, & Kaplan, 1999). Despite overall improvement in writing, about 16 percent of elementary and middle school students are unable to write at a basic level (Greenwald, Persky, Campbell, & Mazzeo, 1999).

▌ Writing is not a linear process. We don't plan and then write and then revise. As we write, we plan and revise.

Implicit in the process approach is the role of writing in the writer's life. Each of us is a writer. We have written letters, essays, lists, notes, plans, goals, diary and journal entries, term papers, and stories and poems. Part of teaching the writing process is helping students see the power and importance of writing in their lives. As teachers, we need to set up an environment in which writing has meaning for students so that they will want to write (Calkins, 1994). This is best done by showing rather than telling. We need to show students the part that writing plays in our lives and encourage them to share the role that writing plays in their lives. We might share how, through writing, we keep in touch with friends, explore topics of interest, record the everyday events of our lives, or entertain or enlighten others and invite our students to do the same.

▌ The writing process approach needs to be applied flexibly. Writing a friendly letter, for instance, would require a bare minimum of planning and doesn't usually involve revising and editing. A letter to the editor, however, might require very careful planning, revising, and editing.

Although some students enjoy writing, others see it as a chore and as little more than an exercise undertaken for the teacher. Once students see that they have stories to tell, that their unique observations of life have value, writing will take on a new meaning for them.

Prewriting

Easily the most important step, prewriting encompasses all necessary preparation for writing, including topic selection, researching the topic, and gathering information.

■ Topic Selection

Topic selection is the hallmark of the process approach. In the past, students were supplied with topics and story starters. The intent was to help, but the result was writing that was wooden, contrived, and lacking in substance and feeling because the topics were ones in which the students had no interest. Letting students choose their own topics is one of the keys to good writing because there is a greater chance that students will invest more of themselves in a piece that means something to them. When students were allowed to choose their topics, they wrote four times as much as a peer group that was assigned subjects (D. H. Graves, 1975).

D. H. Graves (1982) recounted the story of a teacher who left Graves's weekly workshop filled with enthusiasm for the process approach but returned to the next session angry and discouraged. The problem? Hearing that they were to choose their own topics, the students demanded that the teacher supply them with suitable subjects. They felt that it was bad enough they had been asked to write; having to decide on their own subject matter was adding insult to injury. According to Graves, these students were unable to choose topics because they had never been taught how to do so. In previous years, well-meaning teachers had always provided them with topics. There was an implicit message in this: These students had nothing worth writing about and thus had to be fed a diet of story starters, topic sentences, finish-the-story exercises, and other canned activities. Undoubtedly, some of these topics were quite creative. However, the best writing is about something that matters to the writer—a question that the writer wants to answer, a discovery or adventure that the writer wants to share, or a humorous episode that the writer wants to recount.

Murray (1989) suggested that teaching writing is mainly a matter of helping students discover what they have to say and how to say it. The teacher should model the process of selecting a topic and begin by discussing what he or she has done, seen, or knows that he or she would like to tell others. The teacher then jots down three or four topics on the chalkboard. They might be similar to the following:

I saw a real whale close up.
I saw the tallest building in the world.
I saw the longest baseball game ever played.

As the class listens, the teacher goes through the process of choosing a topic. The teacher rejects the first two because many people have seen whales and the tallest building, but only a handful of fans watched the longest game ever played. Most important, that is the topic that holds the greatest interest for the teacher.

Once the teacher has demonstrated the process, he or she asks the class to **brainstorm** topics and then lists them on the board. This helps others discover subjects of interest. After a discussion, each student lists three or four tentative topics and, later, chooses one to develop. In group discussions and one-on-one conversations or conferences with the teacher, students discover additional topics. With the teacher's questioning as a stimulus, they find subjects in which they have expertise, that they would like to explore, and that they would like to share.

Knowing that they will be writing nearly every day and so must have many subjects to write about, students search for topics continuously. They find them on television, in their reading, in their other classes, in their homes, in writing notebooks, and in outside activities. They can keep lists of topics in their folders or in special notebooks or journals (Calkins, 1994; Calkins & Harwayne, 1991).

It isn't necessary for students to have a piece blocked out in their minds before they begin writing. In a way, writing is an exploration. Writers may not be sure what they want to say until they've said it.

Canned topics have been repackaged as writing prompts. Pressured to prepare students for upcoming competency tests, teachers require students to write to test-type prompts. While it is important to prepare students for tests, practice should not be excessive. Students' abilities are best developed through a balanced program of writing instruction.

■ **Brainstorming** is a process in which members of a group attempt to accomplish a task by submitting ideas and writing spontaneously.

Students might also keep a list of questions. Questions to be answered are an excellent source of topics. They might have personal questions, questions about sports or hobbies, or questions about a topic they are studying or an interesting fact that they heard (Spandel, 2001).

Journals are a favorite repository for writers' observations and ideas. In their writing journals, students can list topic ideas, outline observations they have made, or explore ideas. They can also record passages from their reading that were especially memorable or that contained distinctive language. Students might also use their journals to test out writing techniques or experiment with story ideas. Journals keep ideas germinating until they are ready to flower. When students keep writing journals or notebooks, prewriting might consist primarily of selecting an anecdote or question from the notebook to explore or elaborate.

> Over time, journal writing can deteriorate. Routman (2000) suggests that journal writing can become more worthwhile if teachers encourage students to "write for several days on a topic they care very much about and if they teach students how to write with detail and voice" (p. 235).

With students, establish guidelines for journals. If you plan to read the journals, make that known to students so that the journals do not become private diaries. Reading students' writing journals has several advantages. It makes the journals part of the writing program and encourages students to make entries. It also provides you with the opportunity to gain insight into students' thoughts about writing and to respond. Students could highlight any items that they would like you to focus on, and they can mark as private or fold over a page containing any item that they do not want you to see. Journals are not graded, and corrections are not made, because doing so will shut off the flow of ideas. However, you should write a response.

One of the shortcomings of journals is that they can, over time, become a diary of mundane events. Encourage students to take a broader look at the world and also to dig beneath the surface. The student's journal entry "I struck out three times in the Little League game" might draw the following responses from the teacher: "What happened because you struck out? How did you feel? Why do you think you struck out? What might you do about it? Could this be the start of a story?" You might also encourage students to write for several days on a topic they care about (Routman, 2000). From time to time, model the process of composing journal entries. Show students how you develop topics or try out new techniques in your journal.

> An excellent repository of topics is the idea folder. Idea folders hold newspaper clippings, notes, or magazine articles that could become stories. For example, intriguing newspaper articles about flying snakes or the return of monarch butterflies can be stored for future reference.

Time expended on collecting and selecting topics is time well spent. Students discover that they have stories to tell. Their writing becomes better and less time-consuming to produce. In one study, as students learned to choose and limit topics, fewer drafts were required (D. H. Graves, 1983).

■ Planning

Research and preparation are also essential parts of prewriting. Preparation might take the form of discussing, brainstorming, creating semantic maps or webs, reading, viewing films or filmstrips, or devising a plot outline or general outline. Drawing might be used with older students who have difficulty expressing themselves verbally. Visual details in the drawings can prompt students to include these deatails in their writing.

A particularly effective prewriting strategy is to have students brainstorm words that they think they might use to develop their topics. Brainstorming is a free-flowing, spontaneous activity. All ideas should be accepted and recorded but not critiqued.

Everyone should contribute. After brainstorming, ideas generated can be discussed, elaborated on, and clarified. Related ideas can also be introduced.

Brainstorming helps students note details to include in their pieces (Bereiter & Scardamalia, 1982). D'Arcy (1989) recommended several different kinds of brainstorming. The simplest form involves writing down names—of birds, famous people, or mystery places, for example. Students jot down the results of their brainstorming rather than simply think aloud. This gives them a written record of their associations as well as concrete proof of the power of brainstorming to draw out items. Students then share their lists with partners, which may result in additional items. At this point, students might circle the name of a bird, famous person, or place that they know the most about and brainstorm that item. Later, they brainstorm questions about the item they have chosen: Where do bald eagles live? What kinds of nests do they have? Are they in danger of becoming extinct? What do they eat? How fast do they fly? The questions can be the basis for exploring and writing pieces about the topic.

Memories, feelings, images, and scenes can also be brainstormed. For instance, students might go down their lists of items and note the one that drew the strongest feelings or created the sharpest image. Words to describe the feelings or details that describe the image could be brainstormed and listed.

Clustering and freewriting are versions of brainstorming. **Clustering** is a kind of mapping in which students jot down the associations evoked by a word. Lines and circles are used to show relationships. In **freewriting,** students write freely for approximately ten minutes on an assigned or self-selected topic, about a real event or an imagined one. The idea is to have students catch the flow of their thoughts and feelings by writing nonstop. Ideas or themes generated can then become the basis for more focused work. In some instances, freewriting might be an end in itself—an exercise that promotes spontaneity in writing.

To help students flesh out their writing and determine what kinds of details they might include, model how you might brainstorm possible questions that the readers of your article might have. For instance, if students plan to write about flying snakes, they might brainstorm questions such as:

How do the snakes fly?
Where do they live?
Are they poisonous?
How big are they?
What do they eat?
Why do they fly out of trees?

Orally sharing ideas is another form of preparing for writing. Discussing helps students "order their thoughts and generate many more ideas and angles for writing" (Muschla, 1993, p. 37). This technique is especially effective when students work in pairs. After students have generated ideas through brainstorming, clustering, or some other method, have them talk over their ideas with their partners. The listener should summarize what the speaker has said, ask the speaker to clarify any parts that are not clear, and answer questions that the speaker might have, thereby helping the speaker shape and clarify his ideas.

▌Distressed that a number of her students typically produced brief paragraphs almost totally devoid of detail, J. L. Olson (1987) encouraged them to draw a picture of their subjects. After discussing the drawings with her, the students then wrote. The improvement was dramatic; the resulting pieces were rich in detail. Drawing helped students retrieve details about their subjects.

■ **Clustering** is a form of brainstorming.

■ **Freewriting** is a form of writing in which participants write for a brief period of time on an assigned or self-selected topic without prior planning and without stopping. Freewriting can be used as a warm-up activity or a way of freeing up the participant's writing ability. One danger of freewriting is that students might get the mistaken idea that writing is an unplanned, spontaneous activity.

Role-playing can be an effective way to draw out ideas (Muschla, 1993). Students can role-play fictional or real-life events, including historical happenings or events that they have personally experienced. Role-playing can also help students elaborate on and clarify what they want to say. For instance, if students are about to write a letter to a classmate who has moved away, they might divide up into pairs and role-play the writer of the letter and the intended receiver. Students might role-play situations that they intend to write about: persuading the town to fix up the park or requesting that the local health department get rid of rats in the neighborhood. Students might also role-play Washington's crossing of the Delaware, the landing of astronauts on the moon, or other historical occasions. Or they could role-play a Little League coach giving her team a pep talk, the principal confronting two students who have been arguing, or a zookeeper answering questions about the newly acquired giraffe.

Actually beginning to write is another way of getting started. "Writing is generative. The hardest line to write is the first one" (Spandel, 2001, p. 135). Often, after writers get that first sentence down, the ideas begin to flow.

■ Rehearsing

■ **Rehearsing** is that part of the writing process in which the writer thinks over or mentally composes a piece of writing.

Experienced writers do a substantial amount of **rehearsing,** or writing in their heads, composing articles, stories, and even parts of books at odd moments during the day or before going to sleep. Professional writers, if they can avoid it, do not write "cold." They are ready to write down ideas that they have been rehearsing in their minds when they finally sit down at their desks. How important is rehearsal? Donald Murray (1989), Pulitzer Prize–winning journalist, commented, "When the writing goes well, it usually means I have mulled over the idea and the material for quite a long time" (p. 250).

In a way, rehearsing is a way of looking at life. Throughout the day, the writer is aware of episodes or objects that might become a topic for writing or an element in a story. An item in a newspaper or an overheard conversation might trigger a story. A puzzling question might set off an exploration and result in an essay or informational book. Throughout the day, students should be alert to possible sources of writing topics and record these in their journal notebooks.

Composing

■ **Composing** is that part of the writing process in which the writer creates a piece.

Composing is the act of writing a piece. The idea is for the writer to put her or his thoughts down on paper without concern for neatness, spelling, or the mechanics. A writer who is concerned about spelling is taking valuable time away from the more important job of creating. Reassure students that they will have time later to revise and edit. Model how you go about composing a piece. As you compose your piece, explain what is going on in your mind so that students can gain insight into the process.

Instruction might begin with narrative writing. Because it has the familiar flow of a story, narrative writing is easier for students who have difficulty with writing or for English language learners who are in the early stages of learning to write in English. A number of techniques can be used to foster narrative writing. You might model the process of writing a narrative about a humorous or frightening experience that you have had. You might also lead the class in the writing of a group account of an experience that the class has had. Reading first-person narratives provides students with models and possible topics. After reading or listening to *Where the Red Fern Grows* (Rawls, 1961), they might write about a time when they wanted a pet or something else that was special to them. After reading or listening to *Heads or Tails: Stories from the Sixth Grade* (Gantos, 1994), they might write about some humorous experiences that they have had.

Once students have some experience writing first-person narratives, they might try their hands at writing fictional pieces. Just as with first-person narratives, model the process, compose group stories, and use pieces of fiction as models for ideas and composition. You might also have students use visuals to help them organize their stories. Cut out a series of pictures and have students sequence the pictures and create a story to accompany the pictures. This could be a whole-group or small-group activity. Students might also create a storyboard. A storyboard is a series of drawings used by creators of ads, TV shows, and movies to show the plot of their work. The storyboard might show the main scenes, actions, or events.

Composing is not a smooth process. If a writer is primed and the ideas flow, her or his pen might race ahead and produce page after page of text, in seemingly effortless, almost automatic fashion. Or the writer may simply stare at the page for endless moments before finally producing a tortured paragraph. Or the writer may write in fits and starts. An initial burst of writing is usually followed by intense reflection, which is then followed by another burst of writing.

Preparation can help the composing process, but perseverance is required. A writer must be prepared to overcome various obstacles and blocks. By using strategies that experienced writers employ, the writer can avoid certain pitfalls. A key pitfall for many students is believing that the first draft is the last draft, thereby blocking their writing with an overconcern with correctness and neatness. As Calkins (1986) commented,

> By the time many unskilled writers have written three words . . . they already believe they have made an error. . . . They continually interrupt themselves to worry about spelling, to reread, and to fret. This "stuttering in writing" leads to tangled syntax and destroys fluency. (p. 16)

Students need to know that their first writing is a draft and that the focus should be on getting thoughts down. There is plenty of time for revising and correcting later.

Beginnings are often the most difficult part of a piece to create. If students are blocked by an inability to create an interesting beginning, advise them to write down the best beginning they can think of and then return to it after they have completed their first **draft.** This same principle applies to other aspects of composing. If students cannot remember a fact, a name, or how to spell a word, they can leave a blank or insert a question mark and come back later. Nothing should interrupt the forward flow of the composing process.

Some students freeze at the sight of a blank piece of paper. Discuss some possible opening sentences. If nothing else works, suggest to the students that they

---

■ Composing is difficult because the writer must compose the whole message without the prompts supplied in conversation, must also create a context so the message is understandable, and must compose for an unseen audience. Prewriting activities and conferences help supply some of the support that is provided in conversation but not composition.

■ Because much of the writing students will be asked to do in life and in content-area subjects will be expository, the program should include a balance of narrative and expository writing. One way of achieving this balance is to include writing in all areas of the curriculum.

■ Composing is an uneven process. We sometimes can't get our ideas down fast enough. At other times, we labor to get a few words down so the paper won't look so blank.

■ A **draft** is the writer's first copy and is not intended to be a finished product.

just start writing. Their first sentence might simply be a statement that they are having difficulty getting started. As they continue to write, it is very likely that other thoughts will kick in.

■ Focusing on Audience

Although we make lists or diary entries strictly for ourselves, most of our writing is geared toward an audience. A sense of audience helps shape our writing. As we write, we consider the backgrounds and interests of our readers. We try to think of ways of making our writing appealing as well as informative. Student writers typically lack a sense of audience and may assume that the readers already know whatever the writers know. A first step in writing is to define whom one is writing for. To help students write for a particular audience, help them ponder the following questions (Learning Media, 1991):

> What is my topic?
> Why am I writing this piece?
> Who will read my piece?
> What might they already know about the topic?
> What do they need to know?

The answers to these questions should help sharpen students' focus and provide them with a plan for gathering information. As they look over what they need to know and what they want to tell their audience, students can begin collecting information from books, family members, Web sites, computer databases, or experts. They might then use semantic webs or other diagrams to help them organize their information. Again, audience comes into play as students ask themselves, "How can I present this information so that my audience will understand it?" Teacher modeling, minilessons, and conferences with teacher and peers might be used to help students organize their material.

To help students gain a sense of audience, have them share what they have written. Students should focus on communicating with others rather than writing to meet a certain standard of performance or earn a certain grade. As they get feedback, they can clarify confusing details or add examples if that is what their audience seemed to need. The teacher can model sharing by reading pieces she has written and inviting students to respond.

Revising

For many students, revising means making mechanical corrections—putting in missing periods and capital letters and checking suspicious spellings. Actually, **revising** goes to the heart of the piece and could involve adding or deleting material, changing the sequence, getting a better lead, adding details, or substituting more vivid words for overused expressions. Revising means rethinking a work and can, in fact, lead to a total reworking of the piece. Revision may be aided by a peer conference or a conference with the teacher.

Sidebar notes:

Composing requires focus, discipline, and time. Make the writing period as long as possible, and if your schedule permits, allow students whose writing is flowing to continue for a longer stretch of time.

Once students gain a sense of audience, their writing becomes more restricted. They begin to worry whether their peers will approve of their writing.

■ **Revising** is that part of the writing process in which the author reconsiders and alters what she has written.

■ Modeling the Revision Process

One way of conveying the concept of revision is for the teacher to model the process. The teacher puts an original draft that he or she has written on the chalkboard or overhead. She or he poses pertinent questions such as: "Does this piece say what I want it to say? Have I fully explained what I want to say? Is it clear? Is it interesting? Is it well organized?" The teacher can then show how to add details, clarify a confusing passage, or switch sentences around. The teacher might also model some highly productive revising routines. Essential routines include rewriting for clarity, rewriting beginnings and endings to give them more impact, substituting more vivid or more appropriate words, rearranging sentences or paragraphs, and adding additional examples or details.

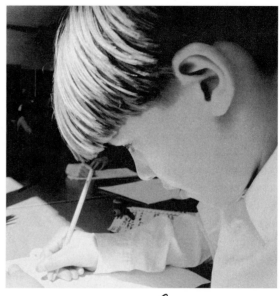

*C*omposing a first draft is a key element in the writing process.

Another helpful approach is to use samples of published pieces and students' writing to demonstrate effective writing. When working on improving leads, for instance, show students a variety of pieces in which writers have composed especially effective openings. Also encourage students to note particularly creative leads in their reading. Do the same with endings and also middles. Summarize by looking at pieces that do all three well.

To dramatize the power of good leads, share a piece that has an especially good opening, but omit the opening. Instead have students select from three leads the one they think the author wrote. Do the same with conclusions.

Over a series of lessons, the teacher shows students how to make revisions, as indicated by the kinds of writing challenges that students are meeting. One group might be grappling with lead sentences, whereas another group might not be fully developing ideas. In time, students can demonstrate to their peers how they successfully revised a piece. Having professional writers such as children's authors and newspaper reporters visit the class to demonstrate how they revise will emphasize the importance of revision and the fact that virtually everyone who writes must do it.

Have students practice revising by revising someone else's paper. The paper could be one that you have composed for this purpose or it could be from a published source or one that was done by a student in a former class. The author, of course, should be anonymous. Start with papers that obviously need revising but aren't so hopelessly bad that they would overwhelm students. Revise some of the papers as a group exercise. Allow students to add or delete details or examples so they aren't just rewording the piece. After students have caught onto the idea of revising, have them work in pairs and then individually. When working in pairs, they should discuss the reasons for any changes they made. As they work individually, they revise their own writing. However, after revising a paper, they might then confer with a partner.

▌ Show students how you read and reread a draft and decide what changes need to be made. With the class, devise a revision checklist. A key question to ask is: Does it sound right? Students should develop an "ear" for good writing.

> ### FIGURE 10.2
>
> ### A Sample Revision Checklist
>
> _____ Does the piece say what I want it to say?
> _____ Will the audience understand it?
> _____ Is it interesting?
> _____ What might I do to make it more interesting?
> _____ Did I give enough details or examples?
> _____ Does it sound right?

Instruction should also include the mechanical techniques of revision. Students can cross out, cut and paste, and use carets to insert to their hearts' content. Long insertions may be indicated with an asterisk and placed on a separate sheet of paper. Students should be encouraged to revise as much as they feel they have to. To remind students of the kinds of things they should be doing when they revise, you might develop a revision checklist. Figure 10.2 presents a sample checklist.

Conferences help students move beyond mechanical revisions. "Revisions that children make as a result of the conference can be at a much higher level than those made when the child is working and reading alone" (D. H. Graves, 1983, p. 153). This is an excellent manifestation of Vygotsky's (1987) concept of zone of proximal development, which states that with the support of adults, children can operate on a higher level and, ultimately, perform higher-level tasks on their own. In other words, what students ask for help with now they will be able to do on their own in the future.

> **Revising takes objectivity.** To distance themselves from their writing, professional writers usually let a piece sit for at least twenty-four hours and then take a good, hard look at it.

During the revision process, focus on one element. Revision is more effective when the focus is on just one element at a time—the lead, details, word choices, or concluding sentence (Spandel, 2001).

■ Tools of Revision

In his publications, _After the End_ (Lane, 1993) and _The Reviser's Tool Box_ (Lane, 1998), Barry Lane proposes the use of five tools for helping students revise the substance of their pieces: questions, snapshots, thoughtshots, exploding a moment, and building a scene.

> **Revising should not be neglected, but there is some danger in overemphasizing it. Although all pieces should be reread carefully, they may not have to be revised or may require only minor changes. This is especially true if the writer is experienced and has prepared carefully before writing. Knowing when to revise and when not to revise is an important skill.**

Questions. Listeners jot down any questions they have as the author reads his piece. The author answers these questions and then decides whether he wants to include any of the answers in his story. The answer to a key question may result in a substantial expansion of the piece or may help the writer redirect his piece.

Snapshots. With a zoom lens, the writer uses details to bring a character or event into focus. This is more than just adding an adjective or two; it's making a character or event come alive by showing what the character does or the particulars of the event.

Thoughtshots. In expository writing, the thoughtshot is the main idea of the piece. The writer asks: "What point am I trying to get across here?" In fiction or biographical writing it's the thinking of the characters or subjects. To create thoughtshots, students ask themselves: "What might the main character be thinking? If I were the main character, what would I be thinking?"

Exploding a moment. Novice writers will often finish off an exciting moment with a sentence or two. What should have been a climatic event will lack the nec-

Exemplary Teaching

Revising

*W*orking with a class composed primarily of ESL students, Laura Harper (1997) feared that her lessons on revising weren't having much impact. Their revisions consisted of a few changes here and there and recopying the piece in neater handwriting. She decided to use the revising tools described by Barry Lane (1993) in *After the End*.

After explaining Questions, Harper had pairs of students ask questions about pieces they had written. The students then selected the most appealing questions about their drafts and freewrote on them. As she revised, one student, Elena, rethought her draft and transformed it from a lifeless description of her aunt to a poignant account of her relationship with her aunt.

After discussing Snapshots, students created Snapshots of each other, writing a description of what they saw or drawing a picture. Working in pairs, students looked for places in each other's drafts that were difficult to visualize. Using the technique, Amber vividly described the experience of getting an unusual haircut.

Using Thoughtshots, Maria described the thought processes she went through and her actions as she decided whether she should face up to a scolding her parents were sure to deliver or hide with her little brother. Using Exploding the Moment, Felicia was able to recreate the terror she felt when she was locked inside the trunk of a car. Using Building a Scene, Monica added dialogue to make her description of a house robbery come alive.

As a result of their training, students became better writers and better conference partners. As one student, Tait, put it, "I used to think revision was just a waste of time. But now I see what revision can do to a story" (p. 199).

essary build-up. Read exciting passages from trade books to students and discuss how the author built suspense. Writers might use the prompts, "How can I show the reader what happened? How can I build excitement and suspense?" Exploding a moment might include both thoughtshots and snapshots.

Building a scene. The writer combines dialogue with snapshots and thought-shots to build a scene.

Editing

In the **editing** stage, students check carefully for mechanical errors, adding commas and question marks and correcting misspelled words. Ideally, all mechanical errors should be corrected. Realistically, the teacher should stress certain major elements. For some students, correcting all errors could be a very discouraging process. The degree of editing depends on students' maturity and proficiency.

Just as with revision, editing should be modeled. Students should also have access to its tools: pencils, a dictionary, easy style guides, and editing checklists. Such checklists help support students' evolving executive function and encourage them to focus on the conventions of writing, which require looking at writing objectively and abstractly. Such a checklist should be geared to the students' expertise and experience; a sample is presented in Figure 10.3. Peer editing can also be employed. However, this is just an additional check. The authors should realize that, ultimately, it is their own responsibility to correct errors.

■ **Editing** is that part of the writing process in which the author searches for spelling, typographical, and other mechanical errors.

FIGURE 10.3

A Sample Editing Checklist

_____ Is my story clear? Will readers be able to understand it?

_____ Did I write in complete sentences?

_____ Did I capitalize the first word of every sentence?

_____ Did I capitalize the names of people, cities, towns, and other places?

_____ Did I end each sentence with a period, question mark, or exclamation point?

_____ Did I spell all the words correctly?

USING TECHNOLOGY

With talking word processing programs, students can listen as the program recites their pieces. Hearing their pieces read, they are better able to note dropped *ing*s and *ed*s, omitted words, and awkward expressions.

As part of learning the editing process, students should be introduced to the use of a writer's indispensable tool—the dictionary. Although students may understand that the dictionary is used to look up the meanings and spellings of unfamiliar words, they may not realize that dictionaries can be used to check capitalization and usage and that most dictionaries contain sections on grammar, punctuation, forming endings, ways to address dignitaries, and correct forms for business and friendly letters and thank-you notes. Model the various ways in which the dictionary can be used in editing and, as the need arises, encourage and guide students in their use of the dictionary. If possible, each student should have a copy of a dictionary on the appropriate level. Also model and encourage the use of style guides and thesauruses. If these tools are available on word processing programs used by the class, show how the computerized versions are used. An especially useful device, especially for struggling readers and writers, is a talking word processing program.

When deciding which editing skills to introduce, examine students' current writing and see what is most needed. Sometimes, the nature of the writing will dictate the skill. If students are writing pieces in which they will be talking about titles of books, introduce italicizing and underlining. After you have taught a skill, have students add it to their editing checklists. Also display a brief explanation or example of the skill's use on the bulletin board, as shown in Figure 10.4, so that students have a reminder of it (Muschla, 1993).

As a final editing check, the teacher should examine the piece before approving it for copying onto good paper or typing. The teacher might decide to note all errors for an advanced student and focus on only one or two areas for a less advanced student. If the piece is to be published, however, all errors should be corrected. The corrections should be handled in such a way that the child is not deprived of pride in his product. Making such corrections must be recognized for the lower-level, mechanical skill that it is.

FIGURE 10.4

Editing Reminder

Underline the titles of books, magazines, newspapers, and movies:
The Paper Chase, My Friend Rabbit, Sports Illustrated for Kids.
(If you are using a word processor, italicize instead of underlining. Underlining is used to tell whoever is printing the piece to use italics.)

The writing process has been described step by step to make it more understandable; however, in reality, many steps may be operating at the same time, and the steps are not necessarily executed in order. For example, writers mentally plan and revise and edit as they compose (Scardamalia & Bereiter, 1986). Books designed to assist young writers are listed in the following Children's Reading List.

CHILDREN'S READING LIST Books for young writers

Bentley, N., & Guthrie, D. (1996). *Putting on a play.* Brookfield, CT: Millbrook Press. Explains how to write and put on a play. Provides sample scripts for practice.

Guthrie, D., Nancy, B., & Arnsteen, K. (1994). *Author's do-it-yourself book: How to write, illustrate, and produce your own book.* Brookfield, CT: Millbrook Press. Discusses how to write a story and provides possible topics.

Livingstone, M. C. (1991). *Poem-making: Ways to begin writing poetry.* New York: HarperCollins. Discussion of poetry and how to write it by a poet.

New Moon Books Girls Editorial Board (2000). *New moon writing: How to express yourself with passion and practice.* Duluth, MN: The New Moon Books Girls Editorial Board.

Otfinoski, S. (1993). *The Scholastic guide to putting it in writing.* New York: Scholastic. Examples, models, and advice for writing letters to friends, relatives, and businesses and preparing school reports.

Ryan, E. A. (1992). *How to be a better writer.* Mahwah, NJ: Troll. Suggestions for practical techniques for improving one's writing.

> Collect trade books and periodicals that provide good models for writing. For instance, when introducing a question-and-answer format, use *What Food Is This?* (Hausher, 1994), *Ask Me Anything about Dinosaurs* (Phillips, 1997), or similar question-and-answer texts as models.

USING TECHNOLOGY
One way of publishing students' work is to post it on the class's homepage. Internet in the Classroom provides useful directions and resources for creating a Web site for your class. **http://seamonkey.ed. asu.edu/~hixson/ index/class.html**

Writing by Children
For a list of sites that publish children's writing, see **http://www.ala.org/ parentspage/ greatsites/amazing. html**

Publishing

As Emig (1971) noted in her landmark study, students all too often write for an audience of one—the teacher—which limits their style. Students tend to write in a way they think will be most appealing to the teacher and so never gain a true sense of audience. In the writing process approach, the emphasis is on writing for real purposes and real audiences and on going public with the works. Poems are collected in anthologies. Stories are bound in books, which are placed in the library. Essays and reports are shared and placed on classroom and school bulletin boards or on the class or school Web site. Scripts are dramatized. Essays and stories are entered in contests and printed in class and school publications or submitted to Web sites and children's magazines that print young people's works. Other ways of **publishing** include creating charts, posters, ads, brochures, announcements, sets of directions, book reviews, and video- or audiotapes.

To emphasize the importance of the writer, the teacher might arrange to have a student share his or her writing orally through use of the **author's chair.** Seated in this special chair, the author reads her or his piece to the class and invites com-

■ **Publishing** is that part of the writing process in which the author makes her writing public.

■ **Author's chair** is the practice of having a student author share her work with the rest of the class.

ments. Special assemblies are also held to honor authors. Professional writers are invited to share with the other writers in the class. With publication and celebration, students put their hearts into their writing.

Conferences

■ A **conference** is a conversation between teacher and student(s) or among students designed to foster the development of one or more aspects of the writing process.

Wanting to improve her writing, Lucy McCormick Calkins (1986) wrote to Donald Murray, a well-known writing teacher, and asked if he could help her. Murray agreed to hold **conferences** with her once a month. For two years, Calkins made the five-hour round trip from Connecticut to the University of New Hampshire each month for a fifteen-minute conference, which was primarily a conversation about her writing. Was the drive worth it? According to Calkins, yes: "He taught me I had something to say" (p. 124).

If a conference does not show writers that they have something to say, it fails to achieve its purpose. Through encouraging, careful questioning and responding, the teacher tells the writer, "You have a story to tell!" A conference is an affirmation. A belief in young people is the only unbreakable rule for conducting conferences. If we have a fundamental faith that everyone has a story to tell, we do not supply topics. Students must search within themselves and their experiences for subjects to write about. If we start directing and shaping, we are taking over the topic. Written under our direction, the piece may actually sound better, but it will be our piece—we will have stolen it from the student. Through careful questioning and responding, help students discover their stories and techniques for telling them. According to Turbill (1982), the teacher "is advised to develop the art of questioning; instead of telling what to do, [the teacher] uses questions to move the child to find answers" (p. 35).

■ Conference Questions

■ In helping young writers, teachers tend to stress content, which is as it should be. However, some attention has to be paid to form, especially when children are exploring new modes, such as a first attempt to write an informational piece or a mystery.

In a typical conference, three types of questions are asked: opening, following, and process. They are nonjudgmental and are intended to evoke an open and honest response. Opening questions might take one of the following forms: "How is it going? How is your piece coming? What are you working on today?" The student's response provides clues for following questions, which are asked to find out more about how the student's writing is progressing. Process questions such as "What will you do next?" prompt students to make plans or take action. However, do not be so concerned about asking questions that you forget to listen. Calkins (1986) cautioned, "Our first job in a conference, then, is to be a person, not just a teacher. It is to enjoy, to care, and to respond" (p. 119).

Sometimes, a human response is all that is necessary. At other times, the teacher reflects the student's line of thinking but gently nudges the student forward. The student might say, for example, "I'm not sure how to describe my dog. My dog isn't a purebred." The teacher reflects that concern by saying, "You're not sure how to describe your dog because he is just an ordinary dog?" The repetition is an expression of interest that encourages the student to elaborate and continue the flow. If that does not work, more directed responses might include such questions as "You say your dog isn't a purebred, but is there anything special about him? What does your dog look like? Can you think of anything about the way your dog acts or looks that might set him apart from other dogs?" Care must be taken that questions are not too directed, or there may be the danger that the teacher is taking over the writing. The purpose of the questioning is to have writers explore ways in which they might develop their work.

If a piece is confusing, the teacher might say, "I liked the way you talked about the funny things your dog did, but I don't understand how you taught him to roll over." The student will then tell how she or he taught the dog to roll over and most likely realize that this is an element to be included in the piece.

If a student has not developed a piece adequately, the teacher might say, "You said your dog was always getting into trouble. Can you tell me what kind of trouble he gets into?" Often, the response will be an oral rehearsal for what to write in the next draft. "They tell me what they are going to write in the next draft, and they hear their own voices telling me. I listen and they learn" (Murray, 1979, p. 16).

Through our questioning, we come to an understanding of the writer. Using this understanding, we are better able to supply the guidance that will best help the writer develop. We ask ourselves, "Of all that I could say to this student, what will help her most?" (Calkins, 1994). Questions are geared to the nature and needs of the student. Table 10.1 presents some common writing difficulties that students encounter and teacher prompts that might be used to help them focus on these difficulties. At times, students will reject the teacher's hints or suggestions, preferring to take a piece in a different direction. That is their prerogative. After each conference, note the student's writing strengths, needs, plans, and other pertinent information. A sample writing conference summary sheet is shown in Figure 10.5.

■ Peer Conferences

Conferences with peers can also be very helpful. Group discussions in which students weigh alternatives lead students to plan on a deeper level and weigh suggestions (Bereiter & Scardamalia, 1982).

Effective peer conferencing is a learned behavior. Discuss the ingredients of a successful conference and then model and supervise the process. In addition to being

> **ADAPTING INSTRUCTION for *ENGLISH LANGUAGE LEARNERS***
>
> If ELLs can write in their home language, they will be able to transfer many writing skills to English. However, in addition to learning English vocabulary and syntax, these students may also be faced with learning a new orthography. For some, it might mean learning the entire alphabet.

> Highly effective teachers carefully instruct students in the art of conducting successful writing and reading conferences. They might even have a group of students from a previous year model a conference. They also continue to monitor conferences so that they can lend their expertise to making sure that conferences are as productive as they can be (Wharton-McDonald, 2001).

TABLE 10.1 Teacher prompts for common writing difficulties

Writing Difficulty	Teacher Prompts
Topic is too broad or lacks focus	What is your purpose in writing this? What's the most important or most interesting idea here? How might you develop that?
Piece lacks details or examples	I like your piece about _____. But I don't know very much about _____. Can you tell more about it?
Needs a beginning sentence	How might you start this off? What might you say to pull your reader into this story?
Inadequate conclusion or lack of ending	How might you sum up what you've said? What thought or idea do you want your reader to take away from this?
Lack of coherence or unity	What is your main purpose here? Do all your ideas fit? Are your ideas in the best order?

Adapted from *Writing Workshop Survival Kit* by G. R. Muschla, 1993, West Nyack, NY: The Center for Applied Research in Education.

FIGURE 10.5

Writing Conference Summary

Name	Date	Topic	Strengths	Needs	Plans
Angel	11/15	Football game	Exciting opening.	Key part not clear.	Tell how he caught pass.
Amy	11/15	Taking care of a horse	Interesting subject.	Not developed enough.	Give examples of pet's tricks.
James		Little sister			
Keisha		Making friends			
Maria		Dream vacation			
Marsha		Recycling trash			
Robert		Letter to sports star			
Stephanie		Caught in a hurricane			

Adapted from *Writing Workshop Survival Kit* by G. R. Muschla, 1993, West Nyack, NY: The Center for Applied Research in Education.

effective and producing improved writing, conferences must be humane and should build a sense of community and respect. Some general principles of conferencing include the following:

- Students should learn to listen carefully.
- Students should lead off with a positive comment about the piece.
- Students should make concrete suggestions.
- Suggestions should be put in positive terms.

Working with a student, model a peer conference and show how suggestions can be used to make revisions.

■ Authors' Circle

One form of peer conference is the **authors' circle.** When students have pieces they wish to share, they gather at an authors' table and read their works to each other.

■ An **authors' circle** is a form of peer conferencing in which students meet to discuss their drafts and obtain suggestions for possible revision.

The teacher may also join the circle. The only requirement is that everyone in the circle have a work he or she wishes to read (Harste, Short, & Burke, 1988).

The authors' circle is designed for rough drafts rather than edited pieces. By seeking and listening to the reactions of others, students can determine whether their works need clarification and which parts might have to be revised. Both authors and listeners benefit from the circle. Harste, Short, and Burke (1988) commented:

> As they shared their stories with others through informal interactions and authors' circles, the children shifted from taking the perspective of an author to taking the perspective of reader and critic. These shifts occurred as they read their pieces aloud and listened to the comments other authors made about their stories. As children became aware of their audience, they were able to see their writing in a different light. (p. 32)

The ultimate purpose of conferences is to help writers internalize the process so that they ask themselves such things as: "How is my writing going? What will I do next? How do I like what I have written? Is there anything I would like to change?"

> Discussions help students become better writers. As students share where they get ideas, how they compose topic sentences, how they develop their ideas, and how they revise, they learn from each other (Dahl & Farnan, 1998).

WRITING WORKSHOP

Just as students learn to read by reading, they learn to write by writing. The **writing workshop** is a way of providing students with the opportunity to try out newly introduced strategies under the teacher's guidance (Collins, 1998). Through individual or small-group conferences, the teacher can help students adapt and implement strategies that were taught in whole-class or guided writing sessions. Writing workshop consists of the following elements: minilessons, guided writing, writing time, conferences, and sharing. If possible, the workshop should be held every day.

> ■ **Writing workshop** is a way of organizing writing instruction that includes a minilesson, time for students to write, individual and group conferences, and whole-class sharing.

Minilesson

Minilessons are generally presented to the whole group. The purpose of the **minilesson** is to present a needed writing skill or concept. The minilesson lasts for only about ten minutes, so the skill should be one that is fairly easy to understand. The skill could be capitalizing titles, selecting topics, using correct letter form, or any one of a dozen fairly easy-to-teach skills. Minlessons can also be used to explain workshop procedures.

> Daily writing keeps the writer connected to the piece that he is developing. If several days pass without engagement with the piece, the writer loses the flow of the writing.

> ■ The **minilesson** is a brief lesson on a needed writing or reading skill. The skill is usually applied in the following writing or reading workshop.

Guided Writing/Strategic Writing

During guided writing, students are taught writing strategies in small groups according to their stage of writing development. To teach a writing strategy, provide examples of the target strategy as it appears in selections that students are reading and also in pieces written by their peers and you. Just as in other sample lessons, discuss the strategy and how it will help their writing. Model the use of the strategy, showing, for instance, how you might write an interesting lead. Provide guided practice and have students apply the skill by using it in their own writing. Revision and evaluation should focus on the element introduced. The skill should be reviewed and reintroduced in conferences and follow-up lessons until it becomes virtually automatic. Here is a sample strategic writing lesson. Notice that this lesson is more extensive than a minilesson and may take ten to twenty minutes to teach.

 Writing strategy: Adding specific details

Step 1. Show a paragraph, such as the following, that calls out for elaboration. Do not use a student's paragraph, as this will embarrass the writer.

> The Strange Day
> I turned on the radio. The announcer said to stay inside. She said that the streets were very dangerous. My father said that the announcement was a joke. But it wasn't.

Invite students to read the paragraph. Ask students whether they have questions that they might like to have answered. Write students' questions on the board. Discuss the author's failure to include needed details.

Step 2. Show the students how you can make the piece come alive by adding details. Add needed details and compare the revised paragraph with the original.

> The Strange Day
> On my way to my place at the breakfast table, I switched on the radio. My favorite song was being played. Suddenly, the music stopped. "We have an important news flash for our listeners," the announcer said. "A monkey stole keys from the zoo keeper and opened all the cages. The streets are now full of dangerous, wild animals. The elephants have already smashed five cars. Stay in your homes. If you spot any wild animals, call the police immediately. But do not let the animals into your home."
>
> "Hey, Mom and Dad," I shouted. "Come quick. There's trouble in the streets." When I told them what I had heard, they started laughing. Dad pointed to the calendar. "Don't you remember what day this is? It's April first. It's April Fool's Day. Somebody is playing a trick on the town."
>
> Dad was still laughing when he headed out the door for work. But he wasn't laughing seconds later when he rushed back inside and slammed the door shut. "Call 911!" he shouted. "There's a tiger sitting on the roof of my car."

Step 3. Guided practice

Provide one or two practice paragraphs that are lacking in details. Working with students, add needed details.

Step 4. Application

Encourage students to flesh out their stories by adding needed details. During the ensuing workshop session, provide any needed assistance.

Step 5. Extension

As a follow-up, have volunteers show how they added details to their stories. In subsequent lessons, discuss the many ways in which writing can be elaborated.

Step 6. Assessment and review

In conferences and while looking over various drafts of students' writings, evaluate whether they are fully developing their pieces. Provide additional instruction as needed.

Writing Strategies

There are dozens of writing strategies. Listed below are the ones that seem most essential for students. The strategies are listed in approximate order of difficulty. However, some strategies are taught at every level. For instance, writing an interesting lead would be a concern throughout the elementary and middle school grades but would be a more complex undertaking in the upper grades than it would be in the lower ones.

■ **Expository Writing**
- Writing clear, complete sentences.
- Writing a lead or beginning sentence. The lead or beginning sentence often gives the main idea of a piece and should grab the reader's interest and entice her or him to read the piece.
- Developing informational pieces. Informational pieces can be developed with details, including facts, opinions, examples, and descriptions. Failure to develop a topic is a major flaw in students' writing.
- Writing an effective ending. An effective ending should provide a summary of the piece and or restate the main point of the piece in such a way that it has an impact on the reader.
- Using precise, varied, and vivid words, using substitutes for *said* or *good*, for instance.
- Using a thesaurus to help achieve a varied vocabulary.
- Gathering appropriate and sufficient information for a piece. Writers do their best work when they are overflowing with information and can't wait to put it down on paper.

USING TECHNOLOGY

Young Writers' Clubhouse is an informative site for young writers that features author information, writing guidelines and hints, and book reviews. **http://www.realkids. com/club.shtml**

Biography Maker provides step-by-step directions for composing biographies. **http://www.bham. wednet.edu/bio/ biomak2.htm**

Open Directory Project Kids and Teens:School Time: English:Writing **http://dmoz.org/ Kids_and_Teens/ School_ Time/English/ Writing**

Lists a number of sites that assist students with their writing.

- Using figurative language, including similes and metaphors.
- Using advanced writing devices such as alliteration and rhetorical questions.
- Using varied sentence patterns.
- Combining short sentences into longer ones.
- Writing in a variety of forms: poems, stories, plays, letters, advertisements, announcements, expository pieces, newspaper articles, essays.
- Writing for a variety of purposes and audiences.
- Providing transitions so that one thought leads into another and the writing flows.
- Creating headings and subheadings for longer pieces.
- Eliminating details that detract from a piece.

■ Narrative or Fictional Writing

- Writing a story that has a well-developed beginning, middle, and end.
- Developing believable characters by using description, action, and dialogue.
- Creating a setting.
- Developing an interesting plot.
- Creating an interesting ending, including surprise endings.
- Writing dialogue that sounds natural.
- Creating a title that makes the reader want to read the piece.
- Building suspense.
- Using advanced fiction techniques, such as flashback or starting in the middle of the story (*in media res*).

Writing Time

"Time is an important element in writing workshop. If students are going to become deeply invested in their writing . . . and if they are going to let their ideas grow and gather momentum, if they are going to draft and revise, sharing their texts with one another as they write, they need the luxury of time" (Calkins, 1994, p. 186).

Writing time, which is the core of the workshop, lasts for thirty minutes or longer. During that time, students work on their individual pieces, have peer or teacher conferences, meet in small groups to discuss their writing, or meet in their guided writing groups. Before beginning this portion of the lesson, you may want to check with students to see what their plans are for this period.

As students write, hold one or two guided writing sessions. As time allows, circulate in the classroom and supply on-the-spot help or encouragement as needed. You might show one student how to use the spell checker, applaud another who has just finished a piece, encourage a third who is searching for just the right ending, and discuss topic possibilities with a student who cannot seem to decide what to write about. You might also have scheduled conferences with several students or sit in on a peer conference that students have convened.

In peer conferences, students can meet in pairs or in small groups of four or five. In these conferences, one or more students may read their drafts and seek the comments and suggestions of the others.

■ Group Sharing

At appropriate times, such as the end of the day, students gather for group sharing. Volunteers read their pieces. The atmosphere is positive, and other students listen attentively and tell the author what they like about the piece. They also ask questions, make suggestions, and might inquire about the author's future plans for writing. Through large-group sharing, a sense of community is built. Student writers are shown appreciation by their audience. They also have the opportunity to hear what their peers are writing about, what techniques their peers are using, and what struggles they are having.

Management of the Writing Workshop

Active and multifaceted, the writing workshop requires careful management. The room should be well organized. Professional writers have offices, studies, or at least desks at which to work.

*S*tudents should have specific plans for each day's writing workshop.

They also have access to the tools of writing. The classroom should be set up as a writer's workshop. Students can get by with pencil and paper but should have some choices, too. At times, they might feel the need to write on a yellow legal pad or with a pink magic marker. You should have a round table or two for group meetings, a word processing or editing corner, and a reference corner that contains a dictionary, style guide, almanac, and other references. Staplers, paper, and writing instruments of various kinds should be placed in the supply corner. Writing folders or portfolios should be arranged alphabetically in cartons. Involve students in helping with housekeeping chores. They can take turns seeing that materials are put away and that writing folders are in order.

Before starting the workshop, explain the setup of the room and show where supplies and materials are located. With the class, develop a series of rules and routines. Before students engage in peer conferences or small sharing groups, discuss and model these activities.

Be aware of students' productivity. Students should have specific plans for each day's workshop: revise a piece, confer with the teacher, obtain additional information about a topic, start a new piece. Make sure that peer conferences are devoted to writing and not last night's TV programs.

Writing is a social as well as a cognitive act. Writers are influenced by the teacher's expectations and by the expectations of peers. Students try to figure out what the teacher wants and write accordingly. Writers also want approval from their peers. They may hesitate to include certain details or write on certain topics if they fear their classmates will criticize them (Dahl & Farnan, 1998).

It is important to note the social dynamics of peer group conferences. Lensmire (1994) found teasing in the peer groups in his class. And he found that students who were not socially accepted in general were mistreated in the peer conference group. Lensmire suggested that students work toward a common goal, such as investigating a particular genre. With a common goal to guide them, it was hoped that the focus would be on working toward the goal rather than on peer relationships.

BUILDING LANGUAGE

As students read and discuss their pieces, build the academic language needed to talk about writing: *writing an interesting lead, developing a topic, sticking to the topic, suppling interesting examples, using signal words*, etc.

He also recommended more teacher guidance in the workshop setting. Getting feedback from students on the impact of peer and teacher conferences and other aspects of the workshop on their development as writers would also be helpful (Dahl & Farnan, 1998).

Note students who do more conferencing than writing, those who never seem to confer, and those who have been on the same piece for weeks. You might keep a record of students' activities in a daily log. A sample daily log, adapted from Muschla (1993), is presented in Figure 10.6.

As you circulate in the room, note students' strengths and weaknesses. During the guided writing or sharing period, call attention to the positive things that you

FIGURE 10.6

Daily Log: Students' Plans for Writing Workshop

Name	Topic	M	T	W	Th	F
Angel	Football game	D-1, TC	RE			
Amy	Taking care of a horse	E, TC	PE			
James	Little sister	AC	R, TC			
Keisha	Making friends	AC	M			
Maria	Dream vacation	TC, D-2	E			
Marsha	Recycling trash	M	P, S			
Robert	Letter to sports star	AC	R			
Stephanie	Caught in a hurricane	R	D-3, TC			

Key

P: Planning	E: Editing	M: Making final copy	TC: Teacher conference
D: Drafting	PE: Peer editing	RE: Researching	AC: Author's circle
R: Revising	PUB: Publishing	PC: Peer conference	S: Sharing

Adapted from *Writing Workshop Survival Kit* by G. R. Muschla, 1993, West Nyack, NY: The Center for Applied Research in Education.

saw: Mary Lou's colorful use of language, Fred's title, Jamie's interesting topic. Needs that you note might be the basis for a future mini- or guided reading lesson or a brief, on-the-spot, one-on-one lesson or—if several students display a common need— a small-group lesson.

Most of all, serious writing demands time. Even professionals need a warm-up period to get into their writing. Once the thoughts begin to flow on paper, however, writers have to keep on writing. If possible, at least thirty minutes to an hour a day, three to five days a week, should be set aside for writing.

THINKING AND READING LIKE A WRITER

Writers use an array of tools to make their writing clear and interesting. Writers also learn from each other. When explaining their unique styles, most writers will attribute their craft to the reading of accomplished authors. Learning to write to the fullest of one's ability begins with thinking like a writer (New Standards Primary Literacy Committee, 1999). Writers listen for effective and expressive ways of saying things, internalize the rhythm of language, keep an eye or ear out for interesting new words, note scenes and events that might be used in their stories, and keep a record of observations. Learning to write also means reading like a writer, that is, reading metalinguistically. On one level, we read to enjoy, to get information. When reading like a writer, we read to learn how the writer constructed his piece. We note the use of vivid language, convincing examples, surprise endings, and intriguing plots. To foster students' ability to think as a writer, model the process. Think aloud about the author's techniques as you read a well-written excerpt to the class. As part of the discussion of selections that students have read, call attention to effective writing techniques.

IMPROVING EXPOSITORY WRITING

Although some students seem to have a natural bent for narrative and others prefer composing expository text, all students should become acquainted with all major structures, learning how each is written and developed. Part of that instruction simply involves having students read widely in order to acquire a rich background of comparison–contrast, problem–solution, and other expository and narrative structures. However, instruction should also include explaining each structure, modeling the writing of it, and having students compose similar structures.

Expository writing needs special attention. Students' early writing is primarily narrative, so that as students progress through the primary grades, there is a growing gap between narrative and expository writing. Whereas students can write fairly complex narrative structures by the time they reach fourth grade, their expository writing typically contains a simple listing of the main idea and supporting details (Langer, 1986).

In a program known as **cognitive strategy instruction in writing,** Raphael, Englert, and Kirschner (1989) combined instruction in text structure and writing strategies to improve students' composing skills. Based on tryouts and experi-

> To foster expository writing, read informational pieces aloud so that students get a feel for the language of expository prose.

ADAPTING INSTRUCTION for *STRUGGLING READERS and WRITERS*
Cognitive strategy instruction in writing is an approach to writing that emphasizes instruction in writing process and text structure and uses planning sheets as a scaffolding device. It has been especially useful for students with learning disabilities.

ments that spanned a number of years, these researchers devised strategies that help students make use of text structure to both understand and produce expository prose. In addition to instruction, scaffolding is provided through the use of a series of guides that students might use to plan, compose, and revise their pieces. These guides are dubbed "think sheets" and correspond to the major types of text organization; there are sheets for narrative pieces, compare–contrast structures, explanation, and other text forms. The think sheets are designed to be "concrete reminders of appropriate strategies to use and of the times when particular strategies might be relevant" (Raphael & Englert, 1990, p. 242).

The first think sheet (shown in Figure 10.7) prompts students to plan their writing by noting their audience and reason for writing and to list details that might be included in the piece. Students might also be asked to group ideas or show how

FIGURE 10.7

Planning Think Sheet

Author's Name: _____   Date: _____

Topic: _Echolocation_ _____

Who: Who am I writing for?
 The kids in my group. _____

Why: Why am I writing this?
 Our group is making a book on dolphins. _____

What: What is being explained?
 How dolphins find objects. _____

What are the steps?

First,   _Dolphin sends out clicks._ _____
_____

Next,   _Clicks bounce off object._ _____
_____

Third,   _Clicks return to dolphin._ _____
_____

Then,   _Dolphin senses how long it took click to return._ ___
_____

Finally, _Dophin can tell how far away object is._ _____
_____

Adapted from *Cognitive Strategy Instruction in Writing Project* by C. S. Englert, T. E. Raphael, & L. M. Anderson, 1989, East Lansing, MI: Institute for Research on Teaching.

they might be organized: steps in a process, comparison–contrast, or problem–solution, for instance. Having shown which ideas they will include and how they will organize their writing, students must then consider an interesting beginning and suitable closing. These can be created as students compose a rough draft, or they can be noted at the bottom of the planning think sheet.

After composing their pieces, students use a self-edit think sheet (shown in Figure 10.8) to assess their pieces. This think sheet prompts them through the first stage of the revising process and asks them to note whether the paper is clear, interesting, and well organized. Because the think sheet will be used by a peer editor to examine the first draft, the student also notes changes that she or he plans to make or questions for the editor. The peer editor uses the sheet to make recommendations for changes. The editor lists changes that might be made and can also offer suggestions for making the paper more interesting.

FIGURE 10.8

Self-Edit Think Sheet

Author's Name: _____   Date: _____

First, reread my paper. Then answer the following:

What do I like best about my paper? Gives a good explanation

Why? Has all the steps

What parts are not clear?

Why not?

Did I . . .

1. Tell what was being explained?	(Yes)	Sort of	No
2. Make the steps clear?	(Yes)	Sort of	No
3. Use keywords to make it clear?	(Yes)	Sort of	No
4. Make it interesting to my reader?	Yes	(Sort of)	No

What parts do I want to change?
Make a more interesting beginning

What questions do I have for my editor?
Is the explanation clear?
Is the ending OK?

Adapted from *Cognitive Strategy Instruction in Writing Project* by C. S. Englert, T. E. Raphael, & L. M. Anderson, 1989, East Lansing, MI: Institute for Research on Teaching.

After a conference with the peer editor, the student lists the editor's suggestions, decides which ones to use, lists ways of making the paper more interesting, completes a revision think sheet (as shown in Figure 10.9), and then revises the paper.

In real writing, some of the subprocesses presented separately are combined and some may be skipped. Others, such as revision, may be repeated several times. However, it is recommended that students go through all the steps of the process and use the suggested think sheets. Later, as students no longer need scaffolding to use appropriate writing strategies, they may adapt the process. Like other forms of scaffolding, think sheets are intended to be used only until students are able to use the strategies without being prompted to do so. Having incorporated the strategies prompted by the think sheets, the students will no longer need the think sheets.

FIGURE 10.9

Revision Think Sheet

Suggestions from My Editor

List all the suggestions your editor has given you:

X 1. _Use a question as a beginning sentence._

X 2. _Use more key words._

X 3. _Write a good closing._

4. _____

Put an X next to all the suggestions you would like to use in revising your paper. Also think of ideas of your own that might make your paper clearer or more interesting. Read your paper once more, and ask yourself:

Is my beginning interesting? Will it make people want to read my paper? Not exactly

Are the steps in my explanation clear? Yes

Did I write down all the steps? Yes

Are the steps in the right order? Yes

Do I have a good closing sentence? No

Returning to My Draft

On your draft, make all the changes you think will help your paper. Use ideas from the list above, those from your self-edit think sheet, and any other ideas you may have for your paper. When you are ready, you can write your revised copy.

Adapted from *Cognitive Strategy Instruction in Writing Project* by C. S. Englert, T. E. Raphael, & L. M. Anderson, 1989, East Lansing, MI: Institute for Research on Teaching.

GUIDING THE WRITING OF REPORTS

Writing reports can be a powerful learning tool. In fact, well-planned student-created reports are a characteristic of 90/90/90 schools. These are schools in which 90 percent of the students are members of a minority group, 90 percent live in poverty, but 90 percent achieve at or above grade level. An important instructional element in 90/90/90 schools is a focus on informational writing (Parker, 2002). Students are required to produce an acceptable piece of writing on a periodic basis. After being provided with thorough guidance and instruction, students write an informative piece and then are required to revise and edit as much as necessary to produce an acceptable piece. Students turn in one such report each month.

In their informational pieces students must include information that they do not already know so that the project becomes a genuine quest for new knowledge. The format can vary and might include reports, a persuasive editorial, a biography, or an explanation of a process in science. In writing their pieces, students not only increase content knowledge, they also develop thinking and writing skills (Knox, 2002).

Instruction is both whole group and small group. The whole class is instructed in procedures or skills that all need to learn. Small-group instruction is used to teach groups of students who have common needs.

Writing is a whole-school activity and is assessed using a common rubric. The rubric highlights key characteristics of effective writing. The principal and teachers regularly discuss and share students' writing to maintain their focus on key characteristics of students' writing.

In writing reports, students differ greatly in the degree of elaboration and the organization of the report. Writing an organized report involves analyzing the information and classifying it by category. Analyzing and classifying information is easier if students are writing about a familiar topic. If students are writing about an unfamiliar area, they will have difficulty highlighting important information. Because the information is new to them, they won't be able to distinguish important ideas from trivial details. Organization will also be a problem. They will lack the understanding needed to create categories of information and will probably simply use the headings contained in their source material.

Part of students' difficulty in writing about an unfamiliar topic may be rooted in their reading. Because the material is new, their understanding may be so limited that they are forced to use the author's words. Chances are they will not understand the material well enough to put it into their own words. Reports in which students use a few phrases of their own to string together material taken directly from their source material is known as "patch" writing. Building a deeper understanding of background material can foster more effective report writing. Students do best when they have a depth of understanding of their material and when they are provided with the type of guidance that helps them select relevant information and organize it (New Standards Primary Literacy Committee, 1999).

Even older students may not understand what is involved in writing a report. In a study of eleven- and twelve-year-olds assigned to research and write on a topic related to Word War II, the students perceived the task in one of three ways: accumulating information, transferring information, or transforming information (Many, Fyfe, Lewis, & Mitchell, 1996). Those who interpreted the assignment in terms of accumulating or transferring information took a task-completion approach. Their goal was to fill up the twelve-page booklets that they had been given. There was little thought given to considering the audience or even sticking to the topic.

Although they had created planning webs at the beginning of the project, the information accumulators paid little attention to them. They included in their reports any information that was interesting, even though it did not support their specific topic. They chose resource materials on the basis of availability, even if they weren't appropriate. Their reports consisted primarily of paraphrased information.

Students who saw the task as a transferring process sought out pertinent materials and recorded that information in their own words. However, although they may have used multiple sources, they failed to synthesize information. Instead, they used one source for one subtopic and another source for a second subtopic, and so forth.

Information transformers saw their task as compiling information for a specific audience—in this case, students their own age. They reviewed and revised their work in light of their planning and their audience. They synthesized information from multiple sources and reflected on the information they presented. Instead of focusing on filling up the pages, their goal was to convey accurate information in an interesting, understandable fashion.

The availability of appropriate resources was a major factor in the nature and quality of the reports. When the references were difficult to read, even the most capable writers relied on paraphrasing or word-for-word copying. To help all students become information transformers, try the following:

- Make sure that students understand the nature and purpose of the assignment. With as much student input as possible, compose a rubric so that students have a clear idea of what is expected.
- If possible, students should be given a choice of topics so that they have a sense of ownership. They will then be willing to invest the time and energy needed to create a thoughtfully composed report. Before students make a final choice of a topic, encourage them to do some preliminary exploration so that they are better able to determine whether this is a topic that interests them and that there is enough information available for them to develop the topic. The information should not be so difficult or complex that students would not be able to understand it.
- With your help, students select sources of information. Make sure that you have materials on a variety of levels so that below-level readers have accessible sources. Finding relevant information is surprisingly complex (Gans, 1940). Model the process and provide guided practice. Pose questions or topics

and have students search through indices and tables of content to locate what seem to be relevant passages. Then have the class read the passages and decide whether the passages are relevant. You might also distribute copies of selected passages and have the class decide whether they pertain to a particular topic (Singer & Donlan, 1989).

- Students complete a planning guide that includes a brief description of the audience, the topic, key supporting subtopics, and a list of sources of information.

- Students compile relevant information. Because younger students and less-expert writers have a tendency to copy, they need instruction in taking notes. Students might be taught a paraphrasing strategy in which they read a relevant passage, recall what they have read, and summarize what they have read in their own words on real or electronic note cards.

- Students organize their information by grouping actual or electronic cards that contain information on the same subtopic. Groups of cards are then placed in sequential or some other kind of logical order.

- Using information they have compiled, students compose their reports. When using multiple sources, students use a cut-and-paste synthesis or a discourse synthesis. In a cut-and-paste synthesis, students simply jot down information from one source and then information from a second source. In discourse synthesis, students integrate the information from two or more sources. To help students use a discourse synthesis, model the process and provide guided practice.

- Students review their reports to make sure they are accurate and contain sufficient information (Many, Fyfe, Lewis, & Mitchell, 1996). Students also examine their reports to make sure they are interesting and that the mechanics are correct.

Because report writing is complex, you might do a shared report involving the whole class or guided writing groups. The next step would be to have cooperative groups compose reports. If available, provide students with sample reports written by former students. To make the task of writing a report more manageable, you might also break it down into segments. The first segment might be topic selection, preliminary exploration, and completion of a planning guide. The second segment might be the first draft. Segment three could be revising and editing. The final segment might be the finished report.

ASSESSING AND IMPROVING WRITING: THE KEY TRAITS APPROACH

Improving writing requires having a concept of what good writing is, being able to explain to and show students the traits of good writing, and having an assessment system that enables students and teachers to judge whether a piece of writing contains those characteristics. The last part of the piece is devising a

Classroom teachers at all levels are invited to join the Profiles Network. Details are available at **http://www.misd.net.** Type in "Profiles Network" under Search.

The Six Traits Plus analytical model for assessing and teaching writing is made up of: Ideas, the heart of the message; Organization, the internal structure of the piece; Voice, the personal tone and flavor of the author's message; Word Choice, the vocabulary a writer chooses to convey meaning; Sentence Fluency, the rhythm and flow of the language; Conventions, the mechanical correctness; and Presentation, how the writing actually looks on the page.

Voice is the distinctive style or personality that writers put into their work. To foster voice, Simmons (1996) suggests that we read and respond as readers and not as teachers. Our initial reading should be directed to what the student is saying and how he is saying it. Students also need to see models of pieces that have a distinctive voice and time to develop voice.

plan for teaching students how to revise their writing so as to strengthen key characteristics (Spandel, 2001). In a sense, it's creating a rubric that students can use to plan their writing, assess their writing, and revise their writing. The teacher can use this same rubric, or perhaps a more elaborated form, to plan instruction and assess students' writing. Such a system enables a teacher to base instruction on assessment.

Describing key characteristics of good writing is somewhat subjective. First of all, you as a teacher need to have a sense of the characteristics of good writing at your grade level. One way of doing this is to examine the best pieces of writing in your class to determine what traits make these pieces of writing especially effective. Although you can do this for your class, it is even more effective when done on a schoolwide or districtwide basis. To help you with the process, visit the Web site of Profiles Network. Profiles Network has a system for examining students' writing, one that teachers at all levels can participate in. Profiles Network also provides a list of traits for several different kinds of writing, along with student samples at each grade level.

The main element in effective writing as determined by Profiles Network and Six Traits Plus, a popular writing assessment system, is content. These are the ideas or information that the piece conveys or, for narrative, the story that it tells. The remainder of the characteristics have to do with form, the way the content is presented. Form can be subdivided into organization, word choice, sentence construction, and mechanics. A final element is voice, which reflects the individual personality of the author.

To help students become aware of the components of good writing, invite them to tell what they think these components are. Write their responses on the board and create a web of the elements. Their responses will tell you what they think the important elements are and, by implication, where they put their efforts when they are writing. Share samples of good writing with students. Discuss with students what it is about these pieces that makes them effective. This will help students broaden their concept of what good writing is (Spandel, 2001). Provide an overview of the characteristics, but then focus on them one by one. You can start with any trait that you want, but because content is key, most teachers start with that one.

To help students become familiar with the traits and to provide practice for assessing writing, have students assess the writing of unknown writers. You might start with published writers who have works on the students' level. One good source would be from periodicals designed for young people. For fifth- or sixth-graders, for instance, look at samples from *Weekly Reader Senior* and *Scholastic News Senior*, or *Time for Kids*. If you don't subscribe to these and they are not available in your school library, sample articles are usually available on the publishers' Web sites. Collect pieces of writing that illustrate key elements in writing. Collect both good examples and bad examples so that you can show how the two differ. After students have had some practice assessing the writing of others, have them assess their own writing (Spandel, 2001). The key characteristics should be translated into a rubric (see Figure 2.8 in Chapter 2). Although a generic rubric is helpful, rubrics geared to each major kind of writing would be more

Exemplary Teaching

The Profiles Network

*T*he Profiles Network is an organization of teachers who ask students in K through twelfth grade to write to a common prompt. They seek out the best pieces and then analyze these pieces to extract attributes of effective writing. This helps teachers better understand the writing process, and it also provides them with a basis for instruction. Using feedback from their analysis and model pieces, they instruct their students.

Implementing the Profiles approach, teachers in Hamtramck, Michigan, had their students write to the prompt "What I do best." Teachers met and analyzed their papers in order to determine what kinds of things students could do well in their writing and what kinds of things they had difficulty with. On the basis of this analysis, they set general goals and grade-level objectives. By analyzing the best papers, they

were able to select strategies that the best students used and also used these as model pieces of writing.

Teachers also filled out a form for students that told them what was good about the writing and what they might do to improve. In order to help them focus their instruction, teachers also answered a series of questions about students' writing:

- What knowledge and skills are reflected in the students' writing?
- What challenges does the student face?
- What areas does she/he need to develop more fully?
- What interventions or supports would assist this student in meeting the challenges she/he faces? (What can the teacher do to help the student grow as a writer?) (Weber, Nelson, & Woods, 2000, p. 45)

---

effective because they would offer more specific guidance. In addition, different types of writing have different demands. Focusing on key elements, the most effective rubrics are concise and contain only three to six evaluative criteria. Each evaluative criterion must encompass a teachable skill. For instance, evaluative criteria for a how-to piece might include clear description of steps; list of needed materials; effective, sequential organization; and correct use of mechanics. All of these criteria are teachable.

If possible, students should be involved in constructing rubrics. This gives them a sense of ownership and a better understanding of what is expected of them. In one study, students involved in rubric creation improved in both their writing and their ability to apply criteria to their own writing and that of their writing partners (Boyle, 1996).

So that they can more readily assess their progress over time, students should have a place to store and keep track of their completed works, works in progress, and future writing plans. File folders make convenient, inexpensive portfolios. Two for each student are recommended—one for completed works and one for works in progress. The works-in-progress folder should also contain a listing of the key characteristics of good writing, an editing checklist, a list of skills mastered, a list of topics attempted, and a list of possible future topics.

The works-completed folder, or portfolio, provides a means for examining the student's development. If all drafts of a piece are saved, the teacher can see how the student progressed through the writing steps. A comparison of current works with beginning pieces will show how the writer has developed over the course of the year. Careful examination of the portfolio's contents should reveal strengths and weaknesses and provide insights into interests and abilities. While reading through the portfolio, the teacher might try to ascertain whether a student is finding his or her own voice, has a pattern of interests, is showing a bent for certain kinds of writing, is applying certain techniques, and is being challenged to grow and develop. The teacher then decides what will best help the student progress further.

Students should also examine their portfolios with a critical eye. What have they learned? What topics have they explored? What pieces do they like best? What kinds of writing do they enjoy most? What are some signs of growth? What questions do they have about their writing? What would help them become better writers? Are there some kinds of writing that they have not yet attempted but would like to try? Of course, teacher and student should confer about the portfolio, reviewing past accomplishments, planning future goals, discussing current concerns, and setting up future goals and projects. (For more information on portfolio assessment, see Chapter 2.)

TECHNOLOGY AND WRITING

Word processing makes students' text readily visible, so it is easier for the teacher to take a quick look at students' work. This visibility makes peer conferencing and collaboration easier (Zorfass, Corley, & Remy, 1994).

Generally, it is advisable for students to compose their first drafts with pencil and paper because they are faster at writing than they are at typing.

The invention of the printing press revolutionized the world's reading and writing habits. To a lesser extent, so did the availability of cheap paper and the invention of inexpensive, easy-to-use writing instruments, such as pencils with erasers and ballpoint pens. Today, the computer is making significant changes in the ways in which we record our ideas. Using a computer results in better writing, especially for less accomplished writers (Bangert-Downs, 1993). Less adept writers seem to be motivated by the added engagement that a word processing program offers.

Using a computer may also lead to more collaboration. Because it makes the student's writing more visible, this seems to lead to discussions about writing between the teacher and student and among students (Farnan, 1998; Dahl & Dickinson, 1986). Word processing programs have taken the drudgery out of revising. No longer is it necessary to recopy a piece just because a revision has been made. Computer editing programs allow the user to move words, phrases, sentences, or whole passages; eliminate unwanted words and other elements; and revise elements with a minimum of effort. Many programs also contain spell checkers that alert students to possible spelling and typing errors. Some programs include a thesaurus so student writers can seek substitutes for overworked words. The more sophisticated programs will even check grammar, indicate average sentence length, and note certain characteristics of style that might require alteration, such as overusing certain words and writing mostly in simple sentences.

Text-to-speech word processing programs such as *Write: Outloud* (Don Johnston), *Dr. Peet's Talk/Writer* (Interest-Driven Learning), or *Special Writer Coach* (Tom Snyder) say the words that students type in. These programs are especially helpful for students with impaired vision. They can also be used by students who have difficulty detecting errors in their writing. Students who reread a written piece without detecting a dropped *-ed* or *-ing*, missing words, or awkward phrases often notice these errors when they hear the computer read the piece aloud. *Write: Outloud* is doubly helpful because it has a talking spell checker.

Desktop Publishing

As the last step in the writing process, publishing is often ignored. However, it is the step that gives purpose to writing. **Desktop publishing,** as its name suggests, provides publishing opportunities where none existed before. With it, students can produce high-quality posters, banners, signs, forms, brochures, résumés, classroom or school newspapers, and newsletters for clubs. They can also illustrate stories or write stories based on illustrations. In some programs, they can insert background music, sound effects, animation, and speech. One such program is the Ultimate Writing and Creativity Center (The Learning Company). Based on the writing process, it has suggestions for prewriting activities and tips for editing, revising, and composing. It provides photos, art, music, and sound effects that can be added to stories. It also has a presentation feature and a speech capability that reads stories.

E-Mail

One of the most popular features of the Internet is e-mail. Surprisingly, e-mailing friends is a favorite activity for young people. Being an immediate form of communication, e-mail is motivating to students. It is also a critical skill as more and more adults use it to keep in touch with friends and to communicate at work. When discussing e-mailing, compare it to the traditional postcard and letter. Share with students how you go about composing an e-mail. Note that e-mail is less formal, but that the correct use of the mechanics and spelling are still important.

Discuss the use of a subject heading for e-mail and the importance of typing the address accurately and the convenience of the address book. Discuss, too, including digital photos or illustrations and attachments. Emphasize the importance of courtesy and safety. With parental permission, you might have students e-mail you and each other. E-mail might be used for practical purposes, such as communicating with members of the literature circle or submitting a project or homework assignment. You might also arrange for students to have keypals in other schools. Sources of keypals are listed below.

IECC-Intercultural E-mail ClassroomConnections
    http://www.iecc.org
ePALS Classroom Exchange
    http://www.epals.com/
Mighty Media Keypals Club
    http://www.mightymedia.com/keypals/

> **USING TECHNOLOGY**
> Kidspiration (Inspiration) uses questions and illustrations to prompt students' writing. It also has a speech component that reads students' writing.

■ **Desktop publishing** is the combining of word processing with layout and other graphic design features so that the user can place print and graphic elements on a page.

Electronics is changing the way we communicate. Web sites and e-mail lend themselves to brief communication. Web sites also lend themselves to careful organization and linking of information. Web sites and, to a lesser extent, e-mail use graphics as part of the message. Today's students need to learn how to incorporate graphics into research reports and other kinds of writing which were previously totally verbal. Along with deciding what kind of information to include in a report and how to compose that information, students need to determine ways in which graphics will support the information in their report.

READING HELPS WRITING

INVOLVING PARENTS

Prepare a handout providing parents with some specific things they might do to foster their children's writing development. They can provide the tools of writing and a place to write; explain the kinds of writing they do; share in a writing task, such as writing a note to a relative or sending an e-mail; act as a helpful resource and answer questions about style and format; provide research resources by taking their children to the library; and explain how the Web might be used as a resource. Most important of all, parents can affirm their children's efforts.

In *Dear Mr. Henshaw* (Cleary, 1983), Leigh Botts keeps a diary in which he pretends to write his favorite author. This could be a model for keeping a diary and letter writing.

Frequent reading is associated with superior writing. This fact was borne out by the results of several studies reviewed by Stotsky (1983). Students who were assigned additional reading improved as much or more in expository writing as those who studied grammar or were assigned extra writing practice. It should be noted that the students who improved did engage in writing tasks. Improved writing resulted only when students also engaged in writing.

One of the most fundamental ways in which reading enhances writing is by providing a model of form. Students' writing reflects the forms with which they are familiar. Calkins (1986) described how a group of sixth-graders moved from reading mysteries to writing their own. Through a discussion of the books they were reading, they came to understand and appreciate the components of a mystery and believed that the authors were showing them how to write in this genre.

In addition to being a source of ideas, books and articles can also provide model formats. For instance, *Cinderella's Rat* (Meddaugh, 1997) models telling a story from another point of view. Using this format, students might tell about themselves from the point of view of their dog, a neighbor, a peer, or sibling. After reading *Spider Boy* (Fletcher, 1997), in which the main character keeps a journal, students might keep journals of their own. Reading can also help with topic selection. For instance, reading about some funny incidents that happened to Jack in *Heads or Tails: Stories from the Sixth Grade* (Gantos, 1994), may remind students of humorous happenings in their lives.

Students have a better chance of learning about writing through reading if they "read like a writer," which means that as they read, they notice the techniques the author uses to create a story. This process is enhanced if students respond to their reading in journals. As they begin to look at character's motives and other story elements, they might then begin to incorporate them in their own writing (Hiebert et al., 1998). It also helps if students take note of authors' techniques during discussions of books read. Teachers might make specific recommendations of pieces that students could use as models or sources of techniques. For example, one of Beverly Cleary's or Betsy Byars's works might help a student who is attempting to write conversational prose.

TABLE 10.2	Suggested writing activities	

Academic

Book review/book report
Essay test
State competency test
Web site

Business/economic

Business letter
Consumer complaint
Correcting a mistake
Seeking information
Ordering a product

Civic/personal development letters

Letter to the editor
Making a suggestion
Protesting a government decision
Requesting help
Seeking information

Everyday/practical

Directions
List
Message (computer, telephone)
Notice
Sign

Social

E-mail
Friendly letter
Postcard
Thank-you note
Get-well card and note
Special occasion card and note
Invitation
Fan letter

General communication

Announcement
Newsletter

Newspaper

Ad
Editorial
Feature
Letter to editor
News story
Photo essay/caption

Creative

Story
Poem/verse
Essay (humorous or serious)
Play/script

Personal

Diary
Journal

Writing to learn

Descriptions of characters, persons, places, events, experiments
Comparisons of characters, places, events, issues, processes
Explanation of processes, events, movements, causes, and effects
Diary of events
Journal of observation
Summary of information
Synthesis of several sources of information
Critique of a story, play, movie, or TV program

 ## A FULL MENU

Students should engage in a full range of writing activities. With guidance, everyone can and should write poetry, plays, and stories. How can we tell what our limits are unless we try? Exploring a new genre helps students understand that particular form and provides them with a different kind of writing experience. Another advantage is that the skills learned in one mode often transfer to other modes. Writing poetry improves word choice and figurative language. Writing plays helps improve dialogue when writing fiction. Fictional techniques enliven expository writing.

Budding writers need a full menu of writing experiences. They should write everything from postcards and thank-you notes to poetry, the most demanding kind of writing. Table 10.2 contains some of the kinds of writing activities that might be introduced in an elementary or middle school. It is not a definitive list and of-

USING TECHNOLOGY

National Writing Project Provides suggestions for professional development. Has a number of useful links.
http://www. writingproject.org

fers only suggestions. It should be adapted to fit the needs of your students and your school district's curriculum.

HELP FOR STRUGGLING READERS AND WRITERS

Although word processing programs offer assistance to all writers, they are particularly helpful to struggling readers and writers, especially if they have text-to-speech capability. Hearing their compositions read out loud helps students note errors or awkward portions of their pieces that they may not otherwise have detected. For students who have serious writing problems, prediction software such as *Co: Writer* (Don Johnston) can be highly beneficial. *Co: Writer*, which is designed to be used with word processing software, predicts what the writer will say next. For instance, after a letter or two have been typed, *Co: Writer* lists words beginning with that letter. The student can select the whole word and it will be inserted. If the student can't read the words, *Co: Writer* will pronounce them. After the first word has been inserted, *Co: Writer* will predict the next word. *Co: Writer* is helpful for students who have physical difficulty typing in words and struggling readers who know what they want to say but who have serious writing and reading difficulties.

Struggling writers also benefit from suggestions provided in teacher and peer conferences. These serve as scaffolds directing them where and how to revise (Dahl & Farnan, 1998).

Think sheets, as explained earlier in the chapter, would also be of benefit to struggling writers, as would direct instruction in writing techniques and the use of frames. Frames are partly written paragraphs, which the students complete. A frame

TABLE 10.3   Sample comparison/contrast frame paragraphs

African and Asian elephants have many similarities.

Both African and Asian elephants are _____.

Both _____.

However, there are several differences between African and Asian elephants.

African elephants _____,

but Asian elephants _____.

African elephants _____.

However, Asian elephants _____.

As you can see, African and Asian elephants differ in the way they look and how they act.

for comparison–contrast paragraphs is presented in Table 10.3. As struggling writers gain in skill, frames can be faded.

All too often, struggling writers judge that they have nothing worth putting down on paper. To show struggling writers that they have something to say, find out in which areas they are experts. Do they know a lot about raising a puppy, making cookies, or playing basketball? Encourage them to read to find out about favorite topics and to write in their areas of expertise (Hiebert et al., 1998).

ESSENTIAL STANDARDS

The essential standards translate the information presented in this chapter into relatively specific student objectives so that you will be better able to apply the instructional program discussed. However, the standards are flexible. Feel free to add or modify standards or move standards from one grade level to another. The standards should be tailored to meet the needs of your particular teaching situation.

Fourth through eighth grades
Students will

- write letters, directions, explanations, reports, opinions, narratives, and responses to literature.
- write narratives that have more complex plots and more fully developed characters.
- use varied sentence patterns.
- use descriptive words and vivid verbs.
- follow basic rules of capitalization and punctuation.
- use story-telling techniques, such as building suspense and writing a surprise ending.
- use a number of details and/or examples to develop an idea.
- write mulitparagraph pieces that contain an introduction, development, and conclusion.
- use dialogue, figurative language, and other stylistic devices.
- show increased sense of audience.
- revise text by adding, deleting, rearranging, and expanding text.
- use a rubric to evaluate and revise their writing.

ASSESSMENT

In addition to the assessment measures discussed in this chapter, use the devices presented in Chapter 2. The portfolios and holistic and analytic devices described in that chapter should prove to be especially useful. Also, observe students in writing workshop. Note how they approach writing and carry out their

ACTION PLAN

1. Use writing samples and observations of students at work to asses students' current writing development and needs.
2. Based on students' needs, provide guided writing instruction to students.
3. Use discussion, brainstorming, clustering, freewriting, and other techniques to prepare students for writing. Also encourage students to collect topic ideas in journals.
4. Model and discuss the process of composing. Use conferences, wordless books, drawings, models of stories, student research, reading, or other devices to aid students as they compose. If necessary, use frames or specific guidelines, such as those provided in Cognitive Strategy Instruction in Writing, but fade their use as students grow more proficient.
5. Model the process of revising and editing. Provide practice by having students analyze and revise sample pieces. Provide guidance for peer revising and self-revising. Stress revising to make pieces more interesting and more informative. Encourage the use of devices such as questions, snapshots, thoughtshots, exploding a moment, and building a scene.
6. Provide opportunities to publish so that students are motivated to write and gain a sense of audience.
7. Model and explain the process of composing reports. Provide extensive guidance.
8. Guide students as they use word processing programs and construct multimedia presentations.
9. Plan a full-range of writing activities. Create a program that balances students' need to engage in a variety of writing tasks with their need to write on topics of personal interest.
10. Prepare students for local, state, and national assessments. However, don't spend an excessive amount of time practicing for the kinds of writing they will be tested on. Remember that a well-rounded writing program is the best preparation for any writing assessment.
11. Use portfolios and observations to monitor students' progress and make adjustments as called for. Involve students in the creation of rubrics so they have an understanding of writing assignments and a sense of participation in the assessment process.
12. Monitor the effectiveness of your program and make adjustments as necessary.

writing activities. Do they have strategies for getting started and developing their pieces? Do they see themselves as competent writers? If not, what might be done to build their sense of competence?

SUMMARY

1. Instruction should be geared to students' stage of writing development. Needed writing strategies should be identified, presented, practiced, and applied.
2. Once viewed primarily as a product, writing today is viewed as both process and product. Major processes involved in writing include prewriting (topic selection, planning, and rehearsing), composing, revising, editing, and publishing.
3. Essential techniques for teaching writing include modeling, conferencing, sharing, and direct teaching of skills and strategies.
4. Improving writing requires knowing what the characteristics of good writing are. Characteristics of good writing can be translated into rubrics or checklists that help students better understand the requirements of a piece of writing and provide guidance for assessment and revision. Portfolios

in the form of file folders are recommended for storing students' writing and keeping track of it.

5. Although the emphasis in writing instruction is on content, form is also important. Good form improves content. A balanced writing program should include instruction and exploration of a variety of narrative and expository forms.

6. Instruction in composing and mechanical skills should be geared to students' current needs and should be continuing and systematic, including daily instruction as well as on-the-spot aid when problems arise.

7. Good readers tend to be good writers, and vice versa. Also, students who read more tend to be better at writing. Their writing reflects structures and stylistic elements learned through reading. Through reading, they also pick up ideas for topics.

EXTENDING AND APPLYING

1. Observe a group of elementary or middle school students as they write. Note how they go about prewriting, composing, revising, and editing. What strategies do they use? How effectively do they employ them? What other strategies might they use?

2. Try writing for a short period of time three to five days a week to gain insight into the process. If possible, have conferences with a colleague. Note your strengths and areas that need work.

3. Examine a student's permanent writing folder. Track the student's growth. Note gains and needs as well as the types of topics the student has explored and the kinds of writing the student has done. With the student, make plans for future activities.

4. Plan a writing lesson. Using the process approach, focus on topic selection and planning. If possible, teach the lesson. Give an overview of the results of the lesson.

DEVELOPING A PROFESSIONAL PORTFOLIO

Keep a portfolio of your writing, especially professional pieces such as articles that you have written and class newsletters or other student projects that you have guided. Also include a videotape and/or copy of a lesson plan completed for Item 4 in Extending and Applying above or another writing lesson. Keep documents for any special writing projects that you conducted with your students.

DEVELOPING A RESOURCE FILE

Maintain a collection of published and unpublished pieces that might be used to illustrate various writing techniques. Also collect pieces of writing that might be used by students to practice assessing or revising writing. Maintain a list of possible topics and rubrics.

11

Dichotomous Key for the Dogs of
1a IF THE DOG IS A SOLID COLOR, GO TO 2.
1b IF THE DOG IS NOT A SOLID COLOR, THEN GO TO 4.
2a IF THE DOG IS BLACK, IT IS A NEWFOUNDLAND.
2b IF THE DOG IS NOT BLACK, GO TO 3.
3a IF THE DOG HAS A BROWN BODY AND BLACK FACE, IT IS A PUG.
3b IF THE DOG HAS A BROWN BODY AND ONLY BLACK ON NOSE, IT IS A COCKER SPANEL.
4a IF THE DOG IS BLACK, WHITE, BROWN, & HAS LONG EARS, IT IS A BASET HOUND.
4b IF THE DOG HAS NO BROWN, GO TO 5.
5a IF THE DOG IS SPOTTED, IT IS A DALMATIAN
5b IF THE DOG HAS ALL WHITE LEGS AND BLACK EARS,

Diversity in the Classroom

ANTICIPATION GUIDE

*F*or each of the following statements related to the chapter you are about to read, put a check under "Agree" or "Disagree" to show how you feel. Discuss your responses with classmates before you read the chapter.

	Agree	*Disagree*
1 By and large, techniques used to teach average students also work with those who have special needs.	_____	_____
2 Labeling students as reading disabled, learning disabled, or at risk is harmful.	_____	_____
3 It is best to teach English-as-a-second-language students to read in their native language.	_____	_____
4 Even students with serious reading or other learning disabilities should be taught in the regular classroom.	_____	_____

USING WHAT YOU KNOW

*O*ur nation is the most culturally diverse in the world. Dozens of languages are spoken in our schools, and dozens of cultures are represented. Adding to that diversity is the trend toward inclusion. Increasingly, students who have learning or reading disabilities, visual or hearing impairments, emotional or health problems, or other disabilities are being taught in regular classrooms. Because these children have special needs, adjustments may have to be made in their programs so that they can reach their full potential. Adjustments also need to be made for children who are economically disadvantaged or who are still learning English. The gifted and talented also have special needs and require assistance to reach their full potential.

What has been your experience teaching students from other cultures or students who are just learning to speak English? What has been your experience with students who have special needs? Think of some special needs students you have known. What provisions did the school make for these students? Could the school have done more? If so, what? What are some adjustments that you make now or might make in the future for such students?

TEACHING ALL STUDENTS

Increasingly, the success of the nation's schools depends on the way that we plan for all our children. As a first step, we can put children at the center of the learning process (Crawford, 1993). If, as educators, we focus on all children and use caring and common sense in dealing with their needs, we will have gone a long way toward establishing equity in our schools.

STUDENTS AT RISK

■ **At risk** refers to students who have been judged likely to have difficulty at school because of poverty, low grades, retention in a grade, excessive absence, or other potentially limiting factors.

At-risk students have been identified as those who are likely to fail either at life or in school (Frymier & Gansneder, 1989; Strickland, 1998). This group includes 25 to 35 percent of the country's schoolchildren. Students have been said to be at risk if they are identified as having any six of some forty-five factors. The list includes such diverse factors as parents or peers who use drugs and alcohol, retention in a grade, low marks, low scores on standardized tests, IQ below 90, membership in a special education class, negative self-image, illness, excessive absence from school, frequent changes of schools, and a home where English is not the principal language. Poverty and attending a substandard school are also key risk factors (Snow, Burns, & Griffin, 1998).

Although widely used, the term *at-risk* is avoided by some because it has a negative connotation.

> By focusing primarily on characteristics of the students, their families and their communities, the accompanying responsibility and blame for the at-risk condition is placed on the population themselves. . . . Instead . . . attention should be focused on the educational situation and on the sociocultural factors that have contributed to the at-risk condition. (García, Pearson, & Jiménez, 1994, p. 4)

A single classroom may include a number of cultural groups.

Moreover, if educators blame the victims or their backgrounds, they may lower their expectations for these students. Slavin (1997–1998) suggests that we start looking at these students as having promise and give them the kinds of high-quality programs that foster success.

Ironically, in their desire to provide at-risk children with an effective program, educators may offer a program that focuses on lower-level skills. In her study of fifth-grade classes, Anyon (1980) found that instruction in low-income schools emphasizes rote learning, minimal student involvement, and low expectations, whereas the programs in more affluent schools stress higher-level skills, student involvement, and high expectations. Studies of lower-achieving readers have found that these students read less, are less likely to be taught comprehension strategies, and are not assigned out-of-class reading because the teachers feel they would not do it (García, Pearson, & Jiménez, 1994).

However, when poor and middle-class African American and white students are given similar reading instruction, their achievement is similar. Neither race nor socioeconomic status is a factor. This is a key point that cannot be overemphasized. When carefully taught with effective methods and materials, the vast majority of students learn to read and write (Snow, Burns, & Griffin, 1998). This has been proved dramatically and conclusively by intervention programs, which are described later in the chapter. At-risk students have also been highly successful in regular classes in which explicit instruction, a great deal of real reading and writing, and a genuine interest in each student were emphasized (Baumann & Ivey, 1997).

Economically Disadvantaged Students

Poverty in and of itself does not mean that students cannot and will not be successful in school. However, it does make getting an education more difficult, and many students who live in poverty experience lowered achievement in literacy skills. Only 42 percent of fourth-graders eligible for free lunch read at or above a basic level. However, 73 percent of those not eligible for a free lunch read at or above the basic level (Donahue et al., 1999). By age seventeen, **economically disadvantaged** children lag about four years behind more affluent students (Langer, Applebee, Mullis, & Foertsch, 1990). Even so, many children do achieve success despite poverty, especially if their homes are achievement oriented (Dave, 1964) and they are given effective instruction (Snow, Burns, & Griffin, 1998).

■ Principles for Teaching the Economically Disadvantaged

Build background.   It is important that background in reading be developed for all students. For some economically disadvantaged students, this background will have to be extensive. Limited incomes generally mean limited travel and lack of opportunity for vacations, summer camps, and other expensive activities. However, the teacher should not assume that students do not have the necessary background for a particular selection they are about to read. One teacher was somewhat surprised to learn that a group of low-income sixth-graders with whom she was working had a fairly large amount of knowledge about the feudal system (Maria, 1990).

One way to close the achievement gap between at-risk and other students is to provide smaller class size. Smaller classes (about fifteen students in a class) result in increased achievement for all students but are especially beneficial for poor students. In smaller classes teachers are more likely to work more intensely with parents and struggling students (Achilles, Finn, & Bain, 1997–1998).

Among the poorest of the poor are the homeless. The 1987 Stewart B. McKinney Homeless Assistance Act and amendments in 1990 and 1994 provide special school safeguards for homeless children and are intended to ensure rapid placement in school, an equitable education, and access to all the services that a student with a permanent residence might have.

■ **Economically disadvantaged** are those people whose lives and opportunities are limited or put at risk by having insufficient economic resources.

Poor children are three
times as likely to drop out
of school (García, Pearson,
Jiménez, 1994).

Middle-class children also
need this instruction, but
economically disadvantaged
children must be given
extra or more thorough
instruction in this area
because they are less likely
to get help at home.

Use a technique such as brainstorming or simple questioning to probe students' background to avoid making unwarranted assumptions about knowledge.

Create an atmosphere of success. As teachers, we sometimes emphasize problems, not successes. MacArthur Award recipient L. D. Delpit (1990) said that teachers must maintain visions of success for the disadvantaged. We have to help them get *A*s, not just pass. Because the disadvantaged often fall behind, they must catch up and then move ahead.

Make instruction explicit. Middle-class students are more likely to be taught strategies at home that will help them achieve success in school and are more likely to receive help at home if they have difficulty or fail to understand implicit instruction at school. Low-income students need direct, explicit instruction. If they do not learn skills at school, the home will be less likely to supply or obtain remedial help for them. The disadvantaged must have better teaching and more of it (Delpit, 1990).

Provide a balanced program. Because the economically disadvantaged as a group do less well on skills tests, teachers may overemphasize basic skills (García, 1990). The disadvantaged need higher-level as well as basic skills and strategies. These skills should be taught in context with plenty of opportunity to apply them to high-quality reading materials and real life.

Provide access to books and magazines. One of the most powerful determiners of how well students read is how much they read. Unfortunately, poor children often have few books in their homes. In one study poor children, on average, had fewer than three books in their homes. What's more, their classroom, school, and public libraries had far fewer books than did more affluent areas (Krashen, 1997–1998). However, the number of books a student reads is related to the number of books available and having a quiet, comfortable place to read (Krashen, 1997–1998).

Counteract the fourth-grade slump. In their study of children of poverty, Chall, Jacobs, and Baldwin (1990) observed a phenomenon known as the fourth-grade slump. Students perform well in second and third grades on measures of reading and language, although form lags behind content in writing. However, beginning in fourth grade, many students slump in several areas. They have particular difficulty defining abstract, more academically oriented words. In addition to vocabulary, word recognition and spelling scores begin to slip. These are the skills that undergird achievement in reading and writing. They are also the skills for which the schools bear primary responsibility.

From fourth grade on, the school's role in the development of low-income children's literacy capabilities becomes especially important. The school must teach the vocabulary and concepts necessary to cope with subject matter texts. Chall, Jacobs, and Baldwin (1990) recommended the use of trade books, both informational and fictional. "Exposure to books on a variety of subjects and on a wide range of difficulty levels was particularly effective in the development of vocabulary" (p. 155).

Added opportunity for writing and reading in the content areas was also recommended. The researchers noted that children who wrote more comprehended better, and those who were in classes where the teachers taught content-area reading had higher vocabulary scores. It also helps to "overdetermine success." Overdetermining success "anticipates all the ways children might fail and then plans how each will be prevented or quickly and effectively dealt with" (Slavin, 1997–1998). This means making arrangements for tutoring, counseling, and family support.

Linguistically and Culturally Diverse Students

Understanding students' cultural background can lead to more effective teaching. Cultural groups might socialize their children in such a way and have expectations that put children at a disadvantage when they attend school. For instance, children of Mexican immigrants are taught to be passive around adults. They are also discouraged from showing off what they know (Valdes, 1996). However, in the typical public school classroom, students are expected to be assertive and demonstrate their knowledge. As a result of a lack of assertiveness and a failure to display what they know, children of Mexican immigrants were judged to be lacking in skills and background knowledge and were placed in lower reading groups.

■ Making Use of Diverse Ways of Responding

Culture is not just content. It determines how we respond and express ourselves, and even how we learn. In the typical classroom, the teacher asks a question, calls on a student, and the student responds. Emphasis is on the individual. In some cultures, however, students use a shared response style in discussion. Hawaiian children, for example, use a discussion style known as story talk in which two or more respond to a question simultaneously (Au & Mason, 1981). When a teacher allows students to respond in story talk, their time is spent more productively. Discussions center on the story and are much more effective than those led by a teacher who uses traditional structure and devotes much time to management issues such as keeping students from "talking out of turn." When this same program was used on a Navajo reservation, the program was adjusted to fit the turn-taking styles of the students. One of the secrets of the success of the program, which is known as KEEP, is providing a culturally responsive environment in which activities are geared to students' ways of learning and communicating. As students see that familiar ways of learning and responding are used, they feel accepted and affirmed (Erickson, 1963).

■ Accepting the Student's Language

A student's language is part of who she or he is. Rejecting it is interpreted as a personal rejection. Everyone speaks a dialect, which is determined by place of birth, socioeconomic status, and other factors. Some African American children speak a dialect known as Black English. It is very similar to standard English. The differences between the two dialects are minor and include features such as dropping

Strickland (1998) recommends using talk to foster students' understanding. "Engage students in literature study groups, group discussion, partner activities, and research groups. Plan activities where talk is used along with reading and writing as a tool for learning" (p. 402).

Schools in the United States are highly individualistic in their teaching and learning styles, evaluation procedures, and norms. Many students, particularly African Americans, Hispanics, and American Indians, are group oriented (Banks & Banks, 1997). Cooperative learning might help these students learn more effectively.

As is true of a number of dialects, some African American English pronunciations can cause some slight difficulty in phonics. Students might not perceive some final consonant clustering and may confuse word parts, as in *toll* and *told,* and *coal* and *cold.* The use of context and added work on auditory discrimination will help take care of this minor interference.

ADAPTING INSTRUCTION for *ENGLISH LANGUAGE LEARNERS*

If students are taught in their native language as they are learning English, they can also get the assistance of their families. Parents will be able to help students with their assignments when the instruction is in their native language (Freeman & Freeman, 1998).

the suffixes *-ing* and *-ed,* omitting the word *is* ("He busy"), and some variations in pronunciation such as "pin" for *pen* (Shuy, 1973).

No research suggests that Black English hampers a child's reading in any significant way (Goodman & Goodman, 1978; Melmed, 1973). In fact, the opposite might be true. Stopping a discussion to correct a student's dialect may cause the student to reduce her or his participation in class. In their study of minority-group students, Au and Mason (1981) mentioned that the students who were superior responders were given "breathing room": "The term *breathing room* referred to a teacher's willingness to let the children respond as best they could at the moment, without criticism that reflected on their abilities. Responses given in dialect were always accepted, as long as their content was appropriate" (p. 124).

Dialect, then, has no negative effect on reading achievement, with the possible exception of teacher attitude (Goodman & Goodman, 1978). Teachers who form unfavorable opinions on the basis of variant dialects can convey those feelings and associated lowered expectations to students. If they constantly correct language, teachers might also be hindering communication between themselves and their students. J. J. Brown (1988) warned,

> When students are told constantly that their verb forms are incorrect, their syntax is awkward, their modifiers are misplaced, or their speech is unacceptable for school, they decide that the risks associated with attempts to communicate with teachers outweigh the benefits. This decision results in limited interacting with teachers and ultimately, limited opportunities to engage actively in planned learning experiences. (p. 13)

Even when reading orally, a student who uses a variant dialect should not be corrected. In fact, translation of printed symbols into one's dialect is a positive sign (Goodman & Goodman, 1978). It indicates that the student is reading for meaning and not just making sounds.

Teachers should use standard English, thus providing a model for students who speak a variant dialect. Although all dialects are equally acceptable, the use of standard English can be a factor in vocational success. Rather than correcting or eradicating the variant dialect, J. J. Brown (1988) recommended that standard English be presented as a second dialect that students may use if they wish. The New Standards Speaking and Listening Committee (2001) suggests that students who have been in school a few years should be expected to use standard English for academic purposes but not necessarily in social situations. "All students should learn the shared rules of standard English—but not in ways that tread on their heritage" (p. 24).

Bilingual Learners

There are currently more than 4.5 million public school children in the United States whose native language is not English (U.S. Department of Education, 1998). Moreover, that number is increasing rapidly. More than 10 percent of all elementary school students have been classified as being Limited English Proficient (Kindler, 2002). Limited English Proficient (LEP) is "the legal term for students who were not born in the United States or whose native language is not English and who cannot participate effectively in the regular curriculum because they have difficulty speaking, understanding, reading, and writing English" (Office of Bilingual Education, 1998, p. 3). However, this text will use the term ELL (English language learner). About 75 percent of ELLs attend high-poverty schools. For many ELL students, schooling is a struggle.

Overview of a Program for English Language Learners

The classroom teacher's role is to support the efforts of these bilingual and/or ESL professionals by meeting regularly with them and mutually planning activities that will enhance students' progress. Even after students have finished the ESL program, they still require special language-development activities. Some adjustments that might be made to adapt the classroom instruction to ELL's needs are described in the paragraphs that follow.

Build language. The ELL students' greatest need is to develop skills in understanding and using English. Special emphasis should be placed on school-type language. As students learn English, they first acquire functional structures that allow them to greet others, make conversational statements, and ask questions. This type of everyday communication is heavily contextualized and is augmented by gestures, pointing at objects, and pantomiming. It takes approximately two years for students to become socially proficient in English (Cummins, 2001). However, schooling demands academic language, which is more varied and abstract and relatively decontextualized. This is the language in which math procedures and subject matter concepts are explained. Proficiency in academic English may take up to five years or more. Even though ELL students may seem proficient in oral English, they may have difficulty with academic language. Mastery of conversational English may mask deficiencies in important higher-level language skills (Sutton, 1989). Because of the time required to acquire academic language, English learners may not demonstrate their true abilities on achievement and cognitive ability tests administered in English.

Increasing the amount of oral language in the classroom enhances English speaking. Structure conversations at the beginning of the school day and at other convenient times to talk about current events, weather, hobbies, sports, or other topics of interest. Encourage students to participate in discussions and provide opportunities for them to use "language for a broad variety of functions, both social and academic" (Allen, 1991, p. 362).

A reading program for ELL students should include trade books. "Children's books can provide a rich input of cohesive language, made comprehensible by patterned language, predictable structure, and strong, supportive illustrations" (Allen, 1994, pp. 117–118). Children's books can be used as a stimulus for discussion, show objects that ELL students may not be familiar with, and build concepts. Books that are well illustrated and whose illustrations support the text are especially helpful.

To facilitate understanding of oral language, add illustrative elements to discussions. Use objects, models, and pictures to illustrate vocabulary words that might be difficult. Role-play situations and pantomime activities. When talking about rocks in a geology unit, bring some in and hold them up when mentioning their names. When discussing a story about a tiger, point to a picture of the tiger. When intro-

English learners should be involved in reading and writing English as soon as possible. "Written language is fixed. It does not speed past the way oral language does. (Freeman & Freeman, 1998, p. 412).

ADAPTING INSTRUCTION for *ENGLISH LANGUAGE LEARNERS*
See pp. 444–445 for suggestions for using the language-experience approach to teach ELLs.

ADAPTING INSTRUCTION for *ENGLISH LANGUAGE LEARNERS*
The social environment of a classroom is important for language learning. Wong (1991, cited in Cummins, 1994) recommends: "Those situations that promote frequent contacts are the best, especially if the contacts last long enough to give learners ample opportunity to observe people using the language for a variety of communication purposes. Those which permit learners to engage in the frequent use of the language with speakers are even better" (p. 54).

ADAPTING INSTRUCTION for *ENGLISH LANGUAGE LEARNERS*
See the discussion of sheltered learning on p. 300 for suggestions for using content to foster language development.

Shared readings from a book, choral readings, and songs can be used to develop oral-language fluency. Scripts, dramatized stories, and readers' theater might also be used.

Before students read a piece, activate their prior knowledge. Because of cultural and linguistic differences, students might not realize that they have background to bring to a story or article. Also, emphasize comprehension over pronunciation (Chamot & O'Malley, 1994).

ducing a unit on magnets, hold up a magnet every time you use the word; point to the poles each time you mention them. Supplement oral directions with gestures and demonstrations. Think of yourself as an actor in a silent movie who must use body language to convey meaning.

Use print.   Use print to support and expand the oral-language learning of English learners. Label items in the room. Write directions, schedules, and similar information about routines on the chalkboard. As you write them, read them orally (Sutton, 1989). Also encourage students to write:

> Provide experiences in which language is greatly contextualized (as, for example, a field trip, a science experiment, role playing, planning a class party, solving a puzzle). Use print materials with these activities as a natural extension of the oral language generated: write a class language experience report about the field trip; record information on a science chart; write dialogues or captions for a set of pictures; make lists of party items needed; follow written directions to find a hidden treasure. (p. 686)

Adapt instruction.   Compare the student's native language with English and note features that might cause difficulty; then provide help in those areas. For example, some major differences between Spanish and English are noted in Table 11.1 (O'Brien, 1973). Other differences between Spanish and English include a lack of contractions in Spanish and confusion caused by idiomatic expressions, such as "shoot down the street," and "call up a friend." Another difference has to

TABLE 11.1   Areas of special difficulty for native speakers of Spanish

Phonological	Morphological	Syntactical
Fewer vowel sounds: no short *a* (*hat*), short *i* (*fish*), short *u* (*up*), short double *o* (*took*), or *schwa* (*sofa*)	*de* (of) used to show possession: *Joe's pen* becomes *the pen of Joe*	use of *no* for *not*: He no do his homework.
Fewer consonant sounds: no /j/ (*jump*), /v/ (*vase*), /z/ (*zipper*), /sh/ (*shoe*), /ŋ/ (*sing*), /hw/ (*when*), /zh/ (*beige*)	*mas* (more) used to show comparison: *faster* becomes *more fast*	no *s* for plural: my two friend
Some possible confusions:		no auxiliary verbs: She no play soccer.
/b/ pronounced /p/: *cab* becomes *cap*		adjectives after nouns: the car blue
/j/ pronounced /y/: *jet* becomes *yet*		agreement of adjectives: the elephants bigs
/ŋ/ pronounced as /n/: *thing* becomes *thin*		no inversion of question: Anna is here?
/ch/ pronounced as /sh/: *chin* becomes *shin*		articles with professional titles: I went to the Dr. Rodriguez.
/v/ pronounced as /b/: *vote* becomes *boat*		
/y/ pronounced as /j/: *yes* becomes *jes*		
/sk/, /sp/, /st/ pronounced as /esk/, /esp/, /est/: *speak* becomes *espeak*		
/a/ pronounced as /e/: *bat* becomes *bet*		
/i/ pronounced as /ē/: *hit* becomes *heat*		
/ē/ pronounced as /i/: *heal* becomes *hill*		
/u/ pronounced as /o/: *hut* becomes *hot*		
/o͞o/ pronounced as /o͞o/: *look* becomes *Luke*		

Adapted from C. A. O'Brien, *Teaching the Language-Different Child to Read,* Columbus, OH: Merrill, 1973.

do with relationships between speakers and listeners. In Hispanic cultures, for example, it is customary to avert one's eyes when speaking to persons in authority. However, for many cultural groups, the opposite is true. Students learning English should learn the cultural expectations of the language along with vocabulary and syntax.

Adapt lessons to meet the needs of English learners. For example, when teaching phonics, start with sound–symbol relationships that are the same in both languages. For Spanish-speaking children, you might start with long *o*, since that sound is common in both English and Spanish. Before teaching elements that are not present in Spanish—short *i*, for instance—make sure that these elements have been introduced in the ELL class. For easily confused auditory items—long *e* and short *i*, for example—provide added auditory-discrimination exercises. Also use the items in context or use real objects or pictures to illustrate them. When discussing shoes, for example, point to them.

When teaching a reading lesson, examine the text for items that might cause special problems. Pay particular attention to the following items:

- *Vocabulary.* What vocabulary words might pose problems for ELLs? Unfamiliar vocabulary is a major stumbling block for ELLs. There may be a number of common English words that ELLs may not be familiar with.

- *Background of experience.* What background is needed to understand the selection? Coming from diverse lands, ELLs may not have the experiences assumed by the selection to be read.

- *Syntax.* Does the selection use sentence patterns that the student might have difficulty with? Is there a heavy use of contractions?

- *Semantics.* Might certain figures of speech or idiomatic expressions cause confusion?

- *Culture.* What cultural items might cause problems in understanding the selection? For instance, some ELL students from traditional cultures might have difficulty understanding the casual relationship that children in the mainstream culture have with authority figures.

The teacher does not have to attempt to present all potentially confusing items. Those most important to a basic understanding of the selection should be chosen. Some potentially difficult items might be discussed after the story has been read.

Of course, as with any group of students, care must be taken to explain to English learners concepts and vocabulary that could hinder their understanding, as well as to build background and activate schemata. Before students read a piece, activate their prior knowledge.

The first reading of a selection should be silent. Because English learners are still learning English, the temptation is to have them read orally. However, this turns the reading lesson into a speech lesson. Plan legitimate activities for purposeful oral rereading after the selection has been read silently and discussed.

Chances are English Language Learners will read more slowly than native speakers of English. Because they are learning the language, it will take longer to process. In addition, until their recognition of English words becomes automatic, they may have to translate words from English into their native tongue. Seeing the

ADAPTING INSTRUCTION for *ENGLISH LANGUAGE LEARNERS*

Because of limited English, ELLs may have difficulty fully explaining what they know about a selection they have read. They may mispronounce words whose meanings they know. The key element is whether students are getting meaning from these words, not whether they are pronouncing them correctly. In one study, students who were good readers in Spanish and were becoming proficient readers in English were not given instruction in comprehension because the teachers wrongly believed that their mispronunciations were a sign of weak decoding skills (Moll, Estrada, Diaz, & Lopez, 1980, cited in García, Pearson, & Jiménez, 1994).

USING TECHNOLOGY
National Clearinghouse for English Language Acquisition provides a wealth of information on bilingual education and includes excellent links to useful sites. http://www.ncela.gwu.edu/

Dr. Mora's Web site is also an excellent source of information about bilingual education. http://coe.sdsu.edu/people/jmora/

BUILDING LANGUAGE
Keep a file of pictures and artifacts that might be used to help explain a topic. For instance, maintain a file of minerals that might include pictures of minerals or actual samples. When you mention the mineral, hold up an illustration of it or the real mineral. This helps all learners, but is especially helpful to ELLs. Your picture file might be electronic and stored on your hard drive or a disk. When needed, it can be flashed on a screen or printed out and held up.

word *cow*, the student may have to search his lexicon for the Spanish equivalent of *cow*, *vaca*. The extra step slows down the reading.

Use cooperative learning and peer tutoring strategies. Working with peers provides excellent opportunities for ELLs to apply language skills. In a small group, they are less reluctant to speak. In addition, they are better able to make themselves understood and better able to understand others.

Also plan strategic use of the students' native language. Use that level of English that students are familiar with. However, for developing complex concepts, use the students' native language, if possible, or ask another student to provide a translation. That way the student doesn't have the burden of trying to understand difficult concepts expressed in terms that may be hard to understand.

Use a language-experience approach. A language-experience approach avoids the problem of unfamiliar syntax and vocabulary because students read selections that they dictate. Some students might dictate stories that contain words in both English and their native tongue. This should be allowed and could be an aid as the student makes the transition to English.

Although students are learning to read in English, they should still be encouraged to read in their native tongue if they are literate in that language. In the classroom library, include books written in the various languages of English learners. Because Spanish is spoken by a large proportion of the U.S. population, a number of books are published in Spanish, including both translations and original works. Most of the major educational and children's book publishers offer translations of favorite books.

Fortunately, ELLs have several strategies they can use to foster comprehension. One strategy is the use of cognates. Cognates are words that are descended from the same language or form. The word for *electricity* in Spanish is *electricidad*. Seeing the word *electricity*, the Spanish-speaking reader realizes that it means the same thing as *electricidad*. Native speakers of Spanish may not realize how many Spanish words have English cognates. You might model the process by demonstrating how cognates help you to read Spanish words. A listing of common cognates is presented in Figure 4.7.

Another strength that ELLs may possesses is enhanced metacognitive awareness. Learning a second language has provided them with greater insights into language on an abstract level (García, Pearson, & Jiménez, 1994). ELLs can also use their native language to foster comprehension by activating prior knowledge in both languages. Another useful strategy is translating difficult passages, especially when they are in the earlier stages of learning English. Transferring prior knowledge, translating passages into their native language, and reflecting on text in their native or stronger language has the potential for improving comprehension (Jiménez, 1997).

When responding to questions or retelling a story, students should be encouraged to use their native language if they cannot respond in English. Being able to use their native language helps students to express ideas that they might not have the words for in English. If you don't speak the student's native language, you might ask the student to translate for you. If the student is unable to translate, perhaps another student in the class can do so (Kamil & Bernhardt, 2001). One way of building vocabulary is to create a word wall or charts of words in English and Spanish or other languages. If the class is about to read a selection about snakes, you might list key words such as *snakes, poisonous, prey, fangs,* and *skin* in English and in the native language of the ELL students. The ELL students can help you with the words in their native language (Kamil & Bernhardt, 2001).

Informational text, by the way, may be easier for English Language Learners to read than narrative text. This is especially true if the informational text is developing topics with which ELL students are familiar. In addition, informational text tends to be more culture free than narrative text, so ELLs are not puzzled by unfamiliar customs (Kamil & Bernhardt, 2001).

After two to three years of exposure to English, ELLs achieve at approximately the 10th percentile as a group (Thomas & Collier, 1999). Native English-speaking peers score at the 50th percentile, which is an average performance. This puts ELLs significantly behind in reading. Sixth graders reading at the 10th percentile would reading at an ending third or beginning fourth-grade level. They are nearly three years behind in reading. To close this 40-percentile gap, ELLs must make more than a year's progress in a year's time. They must accelerate their progress so that they are gaining 15 months for each 10-month school year. They need to gain a year and a half for five or six years in a row.

Although ELLs may be three or more years behind in reading, they should not be regarded as being remedial. Remedial readers are students who were given the opportunity to learn but failed to do so adequately. ELLs are below grade level because language differences have limited their opportunity to learn to read in English. If sixth-grade ELLs had only been exposed to English for two years, it would be unrealistic for them to be expected to read on a sixth-grade level. ELLs need an enriched program that accelerates their progress. They would benefit by being scheduled for extra instruction before and after school, on Saturdays, and during the summer. They should be encouraged to do extra reading on their own to help them catch up. Some ELLs who experience difficulty learning to read in English, might be given remedial assistance if that difficulty is not caused by a lack of proficiency in English. A certain percentage of ELLs may indeed experience some difficulty learning to read just as a certain percentage of native speakers struggle with reading.

Because learning an academic language takes a considerable amount of time, it is the responsibility of every teacher to modify instruction to meet the needs of these students. Much of that modification will simply be good commonsensical teaching in which you do whatever it takes to convey concepts and strategies. In fact, programs designed to assist ELLs in mainstream classes incorporate the kinds of procedures that benefit all students.

If possible, team teach with an ESL or bilingual teacher, or at least confer with the specialists so that you are able to structure an effective program for your English language learners. If you have grade level or subject-matter meetings, invite the ESL teacher to be a member or a least a resource. Collaboration is the key to closing the gap.

Using Technology

Software programs and Web sites that have a speech component can be helpful to ELLs. *Usborne's Animated First Thousand Words* has a dictionary that illustrates words and says them in both English and Spanish. Printed words also appear in English and Spanish. *Usborne's Animated First Thousand Words* has a variety of challenging games and activities for learning and reinforcing words. Students select any one of thirty-five scenes and have a choice of five games for each of the scenes. Students can hear words read aloud, see them depicted with illustrations, match words to pictures, sort words, and practice saying words by having a word read, recording the word, and comparing their recording to the original version. *Usborne's Animated First Thousand Words* provides excellent practice for both struggling readers and ELLs.

STUDENTS WITH LEARNING DISABILITIES

One of the largest categories of special needs students is represented by the group identified as learning disabled. Nearly 5 percent of all students have been determined to be learning disabled (U.S. Department of Education, 2000). About 80 percent of those diagnosed as having a learning disability have a serious reading problem. The learning disability group is also the most controversial; experts disagree as to what constitutes a learning disability. The most widely followed definition is that used by the federal government and which is contained in the Individuals with Disabilities Education Act, or IDEA (PL 101–476):

> Specific **learning disability** means a disorder in one or more of the basic psychological processes involved in understanding or in using language, spoken or written, which may manifest itself in an imperfect ability to listen, think, speak, read, write, spell, or to do mathematical calculations. The term includes such conditions as perceptual handicaps, brain injury, minimal brain dysfunction, dyslexia, and developmental aphasia. The term does not include children who have learning problems which are primarily the result of visual, hearing, or motor handicaps, of mental retardation, or of environmental, cultural, or economic disadvantage. [PL 94–142, section 5(b)(4)]

■ **Learning disability** is a general term used to refer to a group of disorders that are evidenced by difficulty learning to read, write, speak, listen, or do math. These speaking and listening difficulties are not caused by articulation disorders or impaired hearing.

Accompanying regulations further define a student with learning disabilities as one who evidences a serious discrepancy between ability and achievement. In other words, a learning-disabled child has adequate intellectual ability but displays a significant gap between level of ability and achievement. Moreover, as far as can be determined, this gap is not caused by mental retardation, emotional problems, physical handicaps, or poverty.

Increasingly, classroom teachers are becoming more involved in the instruction of students with special needs. In the 1997 reauthorization of PL 94–142 (Education of All Handicapped Children Act), there is a call for improved programs in regular education so that there will be fewer unnecessary referrals for learning disabilities placement. In Connecticut, for instance, schools must show that students have been provided with an adequate program of instruction and have been given extra help before they can be referred for placement in a learning disabilities program.

■ Characteristics of Students with Learning Disabilities

Because of the vague definition, the learning-disabled group is quite heterogeneous. It includes students who have visual- or auditory-perceptual dysfunction, difficulty paying attention, memory deficits, problems using language to learn, or all of these conditions. Students may have an underlying problem that manifests itself in all school subjects, or the problem may be restricted to a single area, such as reading, writing, or math. The most common reason for referral is a reading problem. About 80 percent of students classified as learning disabled have a reading difficulty.

In general, a learning disability can be caused by a weakness in the information processing system. Key information processing skills include visual perceptual skills, auditory processing and language skills, and attention and motor skills.

■ Literacy Program for Students with Learning Disabilities

Based on the major behavioral and academic characteristics noted, a literacy program for learning-disabled students should include several important features. These students should be provided with reading materials at their instructional level so that they can experience success and begin to see themselves as learners.

Learning-disabled students, especially those with reading difficulties, often experience problems with basic decoding skills. Having difficulty with phonemic awareness, these students might miss out on rudimentary phonics instruction when it is provided in primary grades. As they move through the grades, it might be assumed that they have mastered these skills. Through an IRI, a word-list test, or observation, find out where struggling readers are and provide instruction in basic decoding skills if necessary. Word building, discussed in Chapter 3, is a very thorough approach. Relate the skills taught to books and stories students are reading. Provide plenty of reinforcement in the form of books and materials that incorporate the phonics elements or patterns you have taught.

Some disabled readers have been taught a full range of decoding skills but at too rapid a pace, so the skills never became automatic. What these students need is ample opportunity to apply their skills with texts that are relatively easy for them to read. Some students need more practice time than others, perhaps because they never got sufficient opportunity to apply their skills. If students do not respond to your best efforts, seek help from the reading teacher or specialist in learning disabilities.

■ Materials for Students with Learning Disabilities

Because they frequently read below grade level, students with learning disabilities often need high-interest, low-readability books. There are also periodicals specifically designed for older disabled readers:

For a list of easy-to-read books, see Appendix A. For each grade level, books that are of grade-level interest but are written below grade level are listed under Easy Reading Level.

Know Your World Extra (Stamford, CT: Weekly Reader Corporation). Written on grade levels two to four, this is designed for poor readers in grades five and up. It is a well-rounded periodical that includes news and science articles, recreational features, puzzles, and word games.

Scholastic Action (New York: Scholastic). Written on grade levels four to five, this periodical is designed for poor readers in grades seven and up. It features news and recreational and general interest features and often contains a TV script.

Impact of No Child Left Behind Act of 2001

The purpose of Title 1 of the No Child Left Behind Act of 2001 is

> to ensure that all children have a fair, equal, and significant opportunity to obtain a high-quality education and reach, at a minimum, proficiency on challenging State academic achievement standards and state academic assessments. (No Child Left Behind Act of 2001, Sec 1001)

Title 1 is designed to close

> the achievement gap between high- and low-performing children, especially the achievement gaps between minority and nonminority students, and between disadvantaged children and their more advantaged peers... (No Child Left Behind Act of 2001, Sec 1001)

Title 1 includes provisions for assessment, teacher training, and creation of effective programs based on scientifically validated approaches and materials. All students in grades three through eight must be assessed in reading and math beginning with the 2005–2006 school year. This includes students who have disabilities as well as those who have been classified as Limited English Proficient. Students classified as having a disability may be given alternate assessments. Data from the tests will be reported by poverty levels, race, ethnicities, disabilities, and limited English proficiencies of students. The data will show how all the students in a school are doing. It will also show how each group is progressing. The purpose of disaggregated data is to make sure that each of these groups is making progress.

The English proficiency of LEP students will be assessed on a yearly basis. LEP students who have been attending U.S. schools for 30 consecutive months, except those living in Puerto Rico, will be required to participate in reading assessments in English.

States are required to set annual objectives to measure progress of schools and districts to ensure that all groups of students—including low-income students, students from major racial and ethnic groups, students with disabilities, and students with limited English proficiency—reach proficiency within twelve years. Schools that fail to meet improvement targets will be given additional help. Parents of children in underperforming schools will be given the option of transferring their children to other schools. They will also be offered the opportunity to obtain tutoring services for their children.

Because of the assessment and performance provisions of No Child Left Behind, greater attention will be paid to instructing at-risk students. Helping at-risk students reach proficiency will require the best efforts of both resource and classroom teachers. Although No Child Left Behind will place pressure on schools and teachers, it should also result in a higher level of achievement for at-risk students.

Title 1 and Remedial Programs

Increasingly, Title 1 and remedial specialists are moving toward an inclusive model, which means that remedial instruction is often conducted within the classroom instead of in a resource room. To obtain the best results for the students in Title 1 or remedial programs, it is important for teachers and specialists to confer regularly. All involved benefit from these conferences. The classroom teacher obtains insight into the student's problem and techniques for later use in the classroom; the specialist learns information about the student's functioning in a group and can enlist the classroom teacher's help in providing opportunities for having the student apply skills. The student, of course, benefits by getting the best from both professionals. Conducting remediation in the classroom has many advantages. The classroom teacher is less isolated and spends more time working with other professionals. In addition, disabled readers prefer working in the regular classroom and spend more time reading books and less time on worksheets. Having additional assistance in the classroom also means greater individualization (Gelzheiser & Meyers, 1990).

Today's basals and anthologies make provisions for struggling readers. One advantage of these programs is that they are closely tied to the core program. The core program and the intervention program are mutually reinforcing so that struggling readers are given maximum assistance. Harcourt (Farr et al., 2001) provides a parallel intervention program that follows the same theme as the anthology and introduces some of the same vocabulary. However, the intervention reader is written on a lower level and stresses word recognition. Each lesson is accompanied by instruction in a key skill and practice and application activities. Directed reading lessons are specially geared to struggling readers. The selection is read in short chunks with lots of guidance by the teacher.

Intervention Programs

Elements of Literature (Holt, Rinehart and Winston), a widely used literature anthology series, has a program of skill development for struggling readers. The program builds skills that students need to read the selections. Auditory versions of the selections are available for students who are unable to read the selections on their own or who might benefit by listening to the selections. Selections are coded as being easy, on-level, and challenging. If you have a number of struggling readers, you might have them read the easy selections and skip the hard ones or read those later in the year. Extensive suggestions are also provided for ELLs. Included are selections that have been translated into Spanish.

Bridges to Literature (McDougal Littell) uses high-interest literature selections, combined with instruction in reading and vocabulary skills, to help prepare less-proficient readers so that they would be able to handle the on-level anthologies. Bridges to Literature includes selections with readability levels that are designed for students reading one to three years below level. The reading level of the selections gradually increases in difficulty so that students can make the transition into a traditional anthology.

Reading selections are broken down into manageable chunks to increase comprehension. Guides appear throughout the text to help students apply effective reading strategies. Vocabulary terms are previewed at the beginning of each selection and reinforced at point-of-use.

In addition to programs accompanying traditional basals and anthologies, there are a number of programs specifically created to assist older struggling readers

To provide students with disabilities with a high-quality education, federal law requires that students with disabilities be included in state- and districtwide assessments, with or without accommodations. Alternate assessments must be developed for students who cannot participate in regular assessments. The IEP was also changed to ensure that students with disabilities would have access to the regular education curriculum (Individuals with Disabilities Act Amendments of 1997).

The intent of many remedial programs is to help students catch up so that they can then learn with their peers. However, some practices represent a slow-it-down, make-it-more concrete approach. Having a low estimate of students' ability to progress, the pace of the work is slowed down and students might even be retained (McGill-Franzen, 1994).

(see Table 11.2). Programs range from those designed for students who are virtual nonreaders to programs that bolster weak comprehension skills.

HELP FOR STRUGGLING READERS AND WRITERS

As you have undoubtedly noticed, most of the techniques presented in this chapter are the same as those discussed in previous chapters. In general, the techniques that work with achieving readers also work with students who are at risk. The chief difference in working with achieving and at-risk students is making appropriate adaptations and modifications. Based on the major principles covered in this chapter and the intervention programs reviewed, the following framework for an intervention program has been created. This framework has been designed to provide a basis for planning an intervention program that can be taught by the classroom teacher. The program is flexible and can be used with students who are experiencing difficulty with word recognition, comprehension, study skills, writing, or all four.

■ **Building Literacy: A Classroom Intervention Program**

Goals and objectives.   Objectives should be those that are most likely to result in maximum improvement in literacy.

Direct, systematic instruction.   Struggling readers and writers need direct, systematic instruction geared to their strengths. High-quality instructional techniques emphasized in this text feature word building, guided reading, language experience, use of graphic organizers, ReQuest, reciprocal teaching, and Questioning the Author.

Selecting students.   Select students with the greatest needs in reading and writing. Depending on students' levels, use an informal reading inventory and/or assessment devices from Appendix B. Also use observation, samples of students' work, and portfolios, if available.

Size of group.   A group of six or seven is the maximum size that can be taught effectively. However, the more serious the difficulties, the smaller the group should be.

Scheduling instruction.   Intervention instruction is most beneficial when it's in addition to the instruction already provided. Students who are behind need more instructional time if they are expected to catch up. Before school, after school, Saturday, and summer programs are recommended. However, if this is not practical, arrange intervention sessions when they would best fit into the daily schedule. You might hold intervention sessions when the rest of the class is engaged in sustained reading, working at learning centers, or working on individual or group projects. Intervention groups should be scheduled every day, if possible, but not less than three times a week. Sessions can last from twenty to forty-five minutes, with forty minutes being the recommended duration.

▌Mature but easy-to-read books are available from High Noon, Globe Fearon, Perfection Learning, EMC Publishing, American Guidance Services (AGS), Lake Education, Sundance, and Steck-Vaughn.

TABLE 11.2	Programs for older struggling readers			
Title	Publisher	Interest Level	Grade Level	Overview
Breaking the Code	SRA	4–12	1–3	Intensive scripted program for older students who lack basic decoding skills.
Contemporary Reader	Jamestown	7–12	2.5–5	Features informational selections and comprehension exercises.
Corrective Reading	SRA	4–12	1–5+	Scripted presentation approach. Includes both a decoding and a comprehension component. Part of the REACH System, which includes Reasoning and Writing and Spelling through morphographs (morphemic elements).
Fast Track Reading	Wright Group McGraw Hill	4–8	1–5+	Uses a magazine format. Combines direct, explicit skills and phonics instruction with comprehension coaching and fluency practice. Word Work strand features explicit phonics and skills instruction and decodable books and plays.
Focus on Reading	SRA	5–12	2.5–6.0	Fictional and informational selections, some by well-known writers. Comprehension and vocabulary exercises.
Great Series	Steck-Vaughn	6–12	2–4	Each text features great escapes or great rescues or other events. Comprehension and vocabulary exercises.
High Noon Reading	High Noon	3–12	1–4+	Features systematic instruction in decoding and comprehension.
High Point	Hampton Brown	4–12	1–6	Includes instruction in reading, writing, vocabulary, language, and grammar. Theme-based. Features high-interest, multicultural selections written by award-winning authors. Consists of a variety of components including teacher's manuals, student anthologies, practice books, theme libraries, tapes and CDs of selections, tests, and a number of other supplementary components. Designed for ELLs.
Language	Sopris West/ Glencoe/ McGraw Hill	4–12	1–9	Comprehensive literacy intervention curriculum designed for students reading two or more years below grade level or at the 30th percentile or below. Features 540 lessons in 18 strands, that include reading, writing, spelling, vocabulary, and grammar. Has a special component for ELLs.
Reading Skills for Life	American Guidance Service	6–12	1–6	Includes worktexts, easy readers, and extra practice on CD-ROM.
Read 180	Scholastic	4–8	1.5– 8.9	Includes software, student books, audiobooks, and paperbacks for independent reading. Is a high-tech program.
Reading XL	Scholastic	6–8	4–7	Includes reading of trade books and anthologies.
Soar to Succes	Houghton Mifflin	3–8	2–8	Features cooperative groups, reading of trade books, and teaching of comprehension strategies.

Materials.   Use high-interest materials. Make sure that materials are on the appropriate level of difficulty. Books listed in Appendix A, especially those listed under the Easy category, could be used as a starting point. Or you could use one of the comercial programs listed in Table 11.2 or the intervention program that accompanies your basal reader or literature anthology. Also, have students use technology, such as talking software, to help them overcome learning difficulties.

Assessment.   Continuously monitor students' progress. Keep records of books read and conduct a running record or modified IRI monthly or weekly, if possible. Observe and make note of student's daily progress. Maintain a portfolio of work samples. Periodically, at least once a month, review each student's progress and make any necessary adjustments.

Parental involvement.   Let the parents know about the program. Keep them informed about the students' progress. Also, enlist their support. Students in the program should read twenty minutes a night at least four times a week. Discuss with parents how they might help their children fulfill this requirement. Parents might also volunteer to help out. They might work with the rest of the class while you are teaching the intervention group.

Professional support.   Discuss your program with the principal and enlist her or his support. Also, talk it over with other professionals. They may have suggestions for improvement or may provide assistance should serious problems arise.

Parts of a building literacy lesson.   A Building Literacy lesson should include certain key elements. At a minimum, there should be a review of past material, an introduction or extension of a new skill or strategy, and opportunity to apply that skill or strategy by reading a selection. If time allows, there should be a writing activity. Conclude the session with a brief activity chosen by the student: a game, computer time, or reading from a book of jokes or riddles or fascinating facts, for instance. Students should also have a take-home activity, such as a book or periodical to read or reread.

ACTION PLAN

1. Plan and implement a program that provides for all students.
2. Modify assignments as necessary to meet any special needs that students have.
3. Provide extra instruction or alternate instruction for students who are not making progress.
4. For English language learners, build language as you build literacy. Build on background knowledge and skills that students bring to class. Make use of cognates, for instance. Be aware of differences between English and the students' native language so special attention can be paid to elements that are likely to pose problems.
5. If students are struggling, intervene early. If intervention programs are not available, create your own. Set aside a period of the day when you can work with struggling readers.
6. Monitor the progress of students who are not achieving adequately and make adjustments as necessary.

SUMMARY

1. Because of the multicultural nature of our nation and the trend to include disabled students in the regular classroom, schools are becoming increasingly pluralistic and require a focus on the diverse backgrounds and needs of all children.
2. Between 25 and 35 percent of U.S. schoolchildren are at risk of failing either in life or in school. These include economically disadvantaged children, linguistically and culturally diverse children, and students with learning disabilities.
3. There are more than 4.5 million public school students whose language skills are so limited that they will have difficulty learning in classrooms in which English is spoken. Instruction should be adapted to promote understanding and foster language development.
4. Increasingly, students with a range of learning disabilities will be taught within the classroom. Working closely with special education resource personnel, the classroom teacher should make adjustments in the program so that these students learn to read and write to their full capacities.
5. A number of intervention programs are available for older struggling readers. You might also construct your own.

EXTENDING AND APPLYING

1. Interview the special education, Title 1, or remedial reading specialist at the school where you teach or at a nearby elementary school or middle school. Find out what kinds of programs the school offers for special education, Title 1, and remedial students.
2. Observe a classroom in which remedial or special education instruction is offered according to the inclusion model. What arrangements have the specialist and the classroom teacher made for working together? What are the advantages of this type of arrangement? What are some of the disadvantages?
3. Investigate the culture of a minority group that is represented in a class you are now teaching or that you may be teaching in the future. Find out information about the group's literature, language, and customs. How might you use this information to plan more effective instruction for the class? Plan a lesson using this information. If possible, teach the lesson and evaluate its effectiveness.
4. Plan a reading lesson for a student with a reading disability. Obtain material that is of interest to the student but that is on his or her reading level. If possible, teach the lesson and evaluate its effectiveness.

DEVELOPING A PROFESSIONAL PORTFOLIO

Teach a lesson as suggested in Item 4 of Extending and Applying above and record it on a video or CD-ROM and/or keep a copy of the plan for the lesson. Reflect on the effectiveness of the lesson. Experiment with the language-experience approach, sheltered instruction, cooperative learning, or other techniques and approaches that have been shown to be effective with ELL students. Summarize and reflect on your use of the techniques.

DEVELOPING A RESOURCE FILE

Maintain a bibliography of books and other materials that you might use to teach students who have special needs. Also maintain a bibliography of multicultural literature that would be appropriate for the age level that you teach.

12

Creating and Managing a Literacy Program

For each of the following statements related to the chapter you are about to read, put a check under "Agree" or "Disagree" to show how you feel. Discuss your responses with classmates before you read the chapter.

	Agree	*Disagree*
1 Students should be heterogeneously rather than homogeneously grouped for reading instruction.	_____	_____
2 Teaching small groups of students with common needs is just about the best way to provide for individual differences.	_____	_____
3 Ultimate responsibility for the progress of struggling readers rests with the classroom teacher.	_____	_____
4 Without parental support, literacy programs have a greatly diminished chance for success.	_____	_____
5 Instruction in the use of the Internet should be a part of the literacy program.	_____	_____
6 Educators have been oversold on the educational value of technology.	_____	_____

USING WHAT YOU KNOW

The best teachers are caring individuals who have solid knowledge of their field, broad knowledge of children and how they learn, and a firm grasp of effective teaching strategies. In addition, they must be skilled managers. They must have goals and objectives and the means to meet them. They must make wise and efficient use of their resources: time, materials, and professional assistance. They must also have positive interactions with students, administrative and supervising staff, resource personnel, parents, and the community at large. Clearly, a tall order.

Think of some teachers you have had who were excellent managers. What management strategies did they use? What routines did they devise to keep the class running smoothly? As you read this chapter, try to visualize how you might implement those strategies and principles. Also think about the components of a successful literacy program. What elements would such a program have?

CONSTRUCTING A LITERACY PROGRAM

Previous chapters provided the building blocks for a literacy program. Constructing a program means assembling the blocks in some logical way and then reassembling them when necessary. Effective programs have some common features, such as a philosophy that all students can learn, high expectations for students, objectives that are specific and clearly stated, varied and appropriate materials, effective teaching strategies, motivation, building a sense of community, efficient use of time and increased time on task, continuous monitoring of progress, involvement of parents, cooperation among staff, a consistent program that builds on past learnings, prevention and intervention as necessary, and a process for evaluating the program (Hiebert et al., 1998; Hoffman, 1991; Samuels, 1988).

Construction of a literacy program starts with the students. The program should be built on their interests, their cultures, their abilities, and the nature of the community in which they live. To build an effective program, you need to ask: "What are the students' needs? What are their interests? What aspirations do their parents have for them? What literacy skills do they need in order to survive and prosper now and in the future?"

After acquiring as much information as you can about your students and their community, you should consider your philosophy of teaching reading and writing. Do you prefer a top-down or a bottom-up approach, or an interactive approach? Will you use direct systematic instruction, an opportunistic approach, or a combination of approaches? Will you use a basal, anthologies, trade books, or some sort of combination? What role will technology play in your program?

Setting Goals

Once you have acquired some basic information about students and have clarified your philosophy of teaching reading and writing, you can start setting goals. In setting goals, you might consider the objectives set forth in this text, the school and school district's curriculum framework, and state and national standards. Setting goals should be a collaborative activity among the staff in a school. Teachers need to create a shared vision of what they want their literacy program to do and what shape it will take. Once they agree on common objectives, they can begin planning activities that help them meet those objectives and select the kinds of assessment devices that will keep them aware of how they are doing and flag problem areas.

Although research suggests that literacy programs should have specific objectives, teachers should take a broad view of literacy and also set broad goals (Au & Mason, 1989). These goals should include reading for enjoyment as well as building reading and writing skills to meet the demands of school and society. In addition, specific objectives should be established that lead to fulfilling the goals.

Ultimately, goals and objectives will be determined by the needs of the students. A goal for fifth-graders who will be reading a great deal of content-area material,

"A clear understanding of a school's shared goals is the cornerstone to successful reading programs" (Hiebert et al., 1998, p. 3).

USING TECHNOLOGY

Developing Educational Standards offers a wealth of information about curriculum frameworks and standards and provides links to each state so that you can examine your state's standards. Also has links to national standards in all subject fields.
http://edstandards. org/Standards.html

for example, may be to have them learn and apply study strategies. A goal for fourth-graders who are reading at a slow rate and need to stop to decode the more difficult words might be to have them improve their automatic application of skills.

Choosing Materials

Goals and philosophy lead naturally into a choice of materials and activities. For instance, one teacher may elect to use children's books together with a holistic approach that makes generous use of literary discussion groups to foster comprehension. A second might use a more structured approach that uses a basal and systematic explicit instruction in comprehension strategies. Both approaches have the same general goals but reflect different philosophies.

Regardless of philosophy, materials should be varied and should include children's books, both fiction and informational. Because students' interests and abilities are diverse, the selection should cover a wide variety of topics and include easy as well as challenging books. There should also be reference books, children's magazines and newspapers, pamphlets, menus, telephone books, and directions for activities as diverse as planting seeds and operating the classroom computer.

Supplementary materials, such as a VCR and videocassette library, DVD player and DVD library, tape recorders and audiocassettes, and computers and software, should also be available. There should also be access to the Web. (Additional information on the use of computers and today's technology in a literacy program is offered at the end of this chapter.) Basals and other commercial materials should be on hand if the teacher chooses to use them.

Exemplary Teaching

Organizing for Self-Regulated Learning

*I*n an intensive study of ten fourth- and fifth-grade literacy classes, Ms. Kurtz's students stood out. Although the atmosphere in her class was friendly, it was also purposeful. Students were actively engaged in their learning, were seldom seen to be wasting time, were highly motivated, and had excellent work habits.

What was the secret of Ms. Kurtz's success? Involvement and instruction. Whenever possible, she gave students choices, and she also actively involved them in planning activities. Ms. Kurtz's instruction was organized around thematic units, with theme topics including survival, mysteries, the Revolutionary War, and others. After a unit was planned, she provided students with a list of unit activities and let them decide when to complete the activities. Instead of leaving them to their own devices, she actively promoted self-regulated learning. She assisted students with decision making and helped them plan their assignments. Students were also encouraged to reflect on and evaluate their work.

She expected students to be independent, but she taught them how to work on their own. Having been given the tools to become independent and the motivation to use them, the students lived up to expectations (Pressley, Wharton-McDonald, Mistretta-Hampston, & Echevarria, 1998).

Teachers' knowledge of techniques should be metacognitive. Not only should they know how to teach the techniques, they should also know where and when to use them. For example, a group of students who need a maximum of structure and assistance should be taught within a DRA framework. As their work habits improve, the DR–TA can be introduced to foster independence. Later, reciprocal teaching might be employed.

Selecting Techniques and Strategies

The heart of the instructional program is the quality of the teaching. Effective teachers will have mastered a variety of techniques that they can adapt to fit the needs of their students. Some basic techniques for teaching literacy are listed in Table 12.1.

Teachers must also decide when it is time to substitute one technique or approach for another. For instance, if discussion techniques such as KWL or Questioning the Author aren't working, the teacher might try direct, explicit teaching of strategies. The important point is that the teacher chooses the techniques to be used and makes adjustments when necessary.

Some key student strategies are listed in Table 12.2. It is important to teach students a variety of strategies: Research suggests that, because of the novelty factor, changing strategies enhances achievement.

Building Motivation

Strategy instruction should also include affective factors so that students become engaged learners. Engaged learners possess the necessary cognitive tools, but they are also excited about learning. Without motivation, "the difficult work of cognitive learning does not occur rapidly, if it occurs at all" (Guthrie & Wigfield, 1997,

---

TABLE 12.1 Essential techniques for teaching literacy

Technique	Appropriate Grade Level
Reading to students	All grades
Language experience	All grades
Word building	Remedial
Pattern approach to syllabication	Grades 4–5/remedial
Morphemic analysis	All grades
Direct instructional lesson for skills and strategies	All grades
Modeling	All grades
Think-aloud lesson	All grades
DRA	All grades
DR–TA	All grades
Guided reading	All grades
Text walk	All grades
Cooperative learning	All grades
Literature discussion groups	All grades
ReQuest	All grades
Reciprocal teaching	All grades
KWL Plus	All grades
Questioning the Author	All grades
Responsive elaboration	All grades
Process approach to writing	All grades

TABLE 12.2	Learning strategies and related instructional techniques	
	Student's Learning Strategies	**Integrating word-attack skills** **Teacher's Instructional Techniques**
Preparational	Activating prior knowledge	
	Previewing	Brainstorming
	Predicting	Discussion
	Setting purpose	KWL
	SQ3R	DRA and DR–TA
		Guided reading
		Text walk
		Discussing misconceptions
		Modeling
		Direct instruction
		Questioning the Author
		Reciprocal teaching, ReQuest
		Think-alouds
		Responsive elaboration
Selecting/organizing	Selecting important or relevant details	
	Main idea	Think-alouds
	Summarizing	DRA and DR–TA
	Questioning	Guided reading
	Using graphic organizers	Modeling
	SQ3R	Direct instruction
		Reciprocal teaching
		KWL
		Discussing
		Questioning the Author
		Study guide
		Responsive elaboration
Elaborational	Inferring	
	Evaluating	Direct instruction
	Applying	DRA and DR–TA
	Imaging	Guided reading
	SQ3R	Modeling
		Think-alouds
		Reciprocal teaching
		Questioning the Author
		Discussing
		Study guide
		KWL
		Responsive elaboration
Monitoring/metacognitive	Monitoring for meaning	
	SQ3R	Think-alouds
	Using fix-up strategies	Modeling
		Reciprocal teaching
		Direct instruction
		Study guide
		Questioning the Author
Affective	Attending/concentrating	
	Staying on task	Think-alouds
	Self-talk	Modeling
		Discussing
		Encouraging

(continued)

TABLE 12.2	Learning strategies and related instructional techniques *(continued)*	
	Student's Learning Strategies	**Teacher's Instructional Techniques**
Rehearsal/study	Using understanding Using mnemonic devices Rehearsing SQ3R	Modeling Think-alouds Direct instruction
Word recognition	Using pronounceable word parts Using analogies Using context Using morphemic analysis Using syllabic analysis Using the dictionary	Modeling Word building Think-alouds Responsive elaboration

Adapted from Jones, Palincsar, Ogle, & Carr, 1986.

p. 3). To foster engagement, the teacher involves students, helps them set goals, provides them with choices, and, in general, helps them understand what they are doing and why so that they are motivated to apply strategies.

In a series of studies on effective instruction, Pressley (2001) discovered that motivation had a significant impact on students' learning. Motivation, the researcher discovered, is mainly a matter of creating a positive and encouraging but challenging environment. Students get the feeling that they're valued and competent and that they are engaged in interesting, worthwhile learning activities. The following characteristics are also featured (Boothroyd, 2001):

- Variety of techniques are used. Techniques are matched to students' needs.
- Routines and procedures are well established. The classroom is orderly.
- Effort is emphasized. Praise and reinforcement are used as appropriate.
- The teacher builds a sense of excitement and enthusiasm.
- Cooperation rather than competition is emphasized.
- Manipulatives and hands-on activities are prominent. However, the activities are minds-on and have legitimate learning goals.

Building a Sense of Community

It is essential that teachers build communities of learning so that we learn from each other as we learn about each other (Peterson, 1992).

In an effective literacy program, the teacher focuses on building a community of learners. Traditionally, the focus in schools has been on the individual. As the importance of learning from others through scaffolding, discussion, cooperative learning, and consideration of multiple perspectives has become apparent, we see that the focus must be on group learning and building a community of learners. In an ideal community of learners, all students' contributions are valued. Activities and discussions are genuine because students feel that they are a valuable part of the learning community.

MANAGING A LITERACY PROGRAM

A teacher of literacy must be an efficient manager, determining how to handle physical set-up, materials, time, paid classroom assistants, and volunteers. With the current emphasis on inclusion and collaboration, the teacher must also co-ordinate his or her efforts with a number of specialists: the special education teacher, Title 1 personnel, the reading consultant, and the bilingual and ESL teachers. The teacher must consult with the school social worker, nurse, vice principal, principal, and supervisory personnel and enlist the support of parents.

Using Time Efficiently

Research clearly indicates that the more time students spend engaged in learning activities and the more content they cover, the more they learn (Berliner, 1985; Brophy & Good, 1986; Rosenshine & Stevens, 1984). The amount of time spent on reading varies greatly; states or local districts often specify a minimum. In one study, time set aside for reading ranged from 60 to 127 minutes in fifth grade (Guthrie, 1980). Thus some students receive more than twice as much instruction as others. Aim for a minimum of 60 minutes, but 90 is more desirable.

■ Pacing

Proper pacing plays a key role in literacy achievement (Barr, 1974; Clay, 1993b). Teachers must eliminate those activities that have limited or no value. They should critically examine every activity, asking whether it results in effective learning or practice. Also, eliminate unnecessary seatwork. Use cooperative learning, have students read self-selected books, meet with their literature circle group, or work on an independent project.

Providing for Individual Differences

With inclusion, today's classrooms are more diverse than ever; in fourth grade the range of achievement could be four years or more; by eighth grade, eight years or more (Kulik, 1992). One way of providing for individual differences is to use organizational plans such as reading and writing workshop, which were explained in Chapters 9 and 10. A second technique is to give extra help to low-achieving students. They might be given one-on-one or small-group instruction before or after school, on Saturdays, or in special summer programs. A third technique is to adapt or modify the program to meet individual needs. Adaptations have been discussed throughout the text and include providing added instruction, easier materials, specialized aids to learning, changing the learning environment, or using assistive technology. A fourth technique is to use varied, **flexible grouping.** Possible groups include whole-class groups, guided reading groups, temporary skills groups, cooperative learning, study buddies, and interest groups.

One source of help for struggling readers and the rest of the class, too, is tutors. Tutors should be screened, trained, supervised, and appreciated. See the following article for excellent suggestions for using volunteers: B. A. Wasik, (1999). Reading coaches: An alternative to reading tutors. *The Reading Teacher, 52,* 653–656.

To make better use of time, avoid teaching students what they already know and stop having them practice skills they have mastered. When introducing new words for a selection, do not spend time on those that are already familiar. One study found that students already knew 80 percent of the words recommended for instruction in the basal materials (Stallman et al., 1990)

Grouping is the practice of dividing students into classes or within classes by age, ability, achievement, interests, or some other criterion.

■ Because **flexible grouping** allows students to be in a variety of groups, some based on need, some on interest, some on personal choices, they are not tracked into a low, average, or above-average group. Flexible grouping also makes it easier for specialists to work with small groups of students. While the specialist is working with one small group, the classroom teacher can be working with another group (Ogle & Fogelberg, 2001).

■ **Whole-class instruction**
is the practice of teaching
the entire class at the same
time. Although whole-class
grouping is efficient and
builds a sense of community,
it does have disadvantages.
Teaching tends to be
teacher-centered, there is
less opportunity to provide
for individual differences,
and students have less opportunity to contribute
(Radencich, 1995).

■ Whole-Class Grouping

Whole-class instruction can be efficient and build a sense of community. Reading aloud to students, shared reading, and introducing new concepts and strategies lend themselves to whole-class instruction. Reading and writing workshops begin and end with whole-class activities. As discussed in Chapter 9, some teachers also have their students read certain core texts or selections as a whole group. Preparation for reading the selection is provided to the whole class. Anticipating difficulties that students might have with the text, the teacher develops background knowledge, activates schema, builds vocabulary, sets a purpose, and creates interest in the selection. Although the initial preparatory instruction may be the same for all students, students might read the text in different ways. This is known as tiered instruction. When using tiered instruction, the same concept or skill is taught but teachers adjust the level of difficulty of materials, how the materials are to be presented, how much help is provided, or the difficulty level of the assignment. Higher-achieving students read independently. Others can receive varying degrees of assistance. The teacher might spend additional time reviewing vocabulary, reading a portion of the selection to get the students started, or guiding students through the selection section by section. For students who have more serious reading problems, the teacher might use shared or assisted reading or allow them to listen to a taped version of the selection or view it on CD-ROM.

After the selection has been read, the whole class discusses it. Having read and discussed a story together builds community among students. However, it should be emphasized that although the selection might have been easy or just slightly challenging for some students, it was probably very difficult for others. For this reason, whole-group reading of selections should be used sparingly, and some teachers might choose not to use it at all. If used, whole-group reading of selections should be balanced by providing lower-achieving students with opportunities to read on their instructional or independent levels.

■ In **tiered instruction**
(Radencich, Beers, &
Schumm, 1993), students are
exposed to the same selection in the first tier.
However, the selection might
be read aloud to students
who are unable to read the
selections on their own. In
the second tier, students are
grouped according to reading proficiency so that even
the poorest readers have material on their level.

Using **tiered instruction,** today's basals have extensive suggestions for providing for individual differences. In one basal series (McGraw Hill), the whole class experiences the main selection *Last Summer with Maizon* (Woodson, 1991) through the use of tiered instruction. There is a preparatory discussion before the selection is read. A tape is available for students who can't read the story on their own, or the teacher can read it to them. For students who are on level, there are suggestions for guided reading. The best readers read the selection on their own. After the story has been read, the class discusses it as a whole. Follow-up activities are differentiated by level. All of the activities are related to the selection. However, they differ in difficulty level. In their next lesson, students read leveled books that are related to the theme "People Teach Us." Below-level students read *A Summer Day* (Charles, 2001), average readers read *Jazzman: Louis Armstrong* (Rogers, 2001), and the best readers read *One Year in the West* (Smith, 2001).

One flaw in the system is that the lowest-level book might be too difficult for some of the students. In that case, the teacher will need to form a fourth group or differentiate instruction in some other way. The strength of this scheme is that the theme unifies the class, so when the teacher reads a story about "People Who Teach Us" to the class, all are being prepared for the selections they will read. Later, all will be able to write on related topics. Other basal series have similar plans for providing for individual differences. The trade-off of this plan is that the students who need to read the most are reading the least. The average and the above-average readers read the core selection and then in subsequent lessons read leveled books. However, the struggling readers listen to the core selection because it is too difficult for them to read, even with some guidance. As a result, they read less than the average and above-average readers. As the teacher, you would need to decide whether the benefit of being part of the whole class and listening to a high-quality selection is worth the loss in reading time.

Another series (Harcourt) offers alternative selections for poor readers. The alternative story is easier to read but incorporates some of the same vocabulary as the anthology selection. The teacher can introduce vocabulary for both selections at the same time. The alternative story also incorporates the same themes and is in the same genre as the anthology selection.

■ Guided Reading

In guided reading, students are grouped by reading proficiency (Fountas & Pinnell, 1996, 2001). The groups meet on a daily basis for ten to thirty minutes or more. The teacher may organize as many groups as she believes are necessary, but the more groups assembled, the less time there is for each one. As a practical matter, three or four groups are the most that can be handled efficiently. Grouping, however, is flexible. When appropriate, students are moved into other groups.

■ Temporary Skills Groups

In **skills** or strategies **groups,** students are grouped based on the need for a particular skill or strategy. Once the skill has been mastered, the group is disbanded. For example, if a number of students are having difficulty monitoring their comprehension, you might group them for lessons and practice sessions on how to use strategies in this area. Make sure that skills or strategies groups provide for special needs that high-achieving students have so that the groups are not stigmatized as being remedial (Radencich, 1995).

■ Study Buddies

Pairs of students can work together in a variety of ways—for example, as reading partners who take turns reading to each other, as study buddies who work on an assignment together, or as peer editors who read and comment on each other's written pieces.

■ Cooperative Learning

Another way of grouping is through **cooperative learning.** Cooperative learning seems almost too good to be true. Not only do students improve in their subject matter areas (Slavin, 1987b) but also they feel better about themselves and have the added satisfaction of working with and helping others (Johnson &

▌Ability groups tend to be inflexible. Once students have been placed in a group, they tend to stay there. This is especially true of slow learners. One group of students who were tracked into the below-average group in kindergarten stayed there throughout their elementary school years (Rist, 1970).

■ A **skills group** is a temporary group, sometimes known as an ad hoc group, that is formed for the purpose of learning a skill or strategy.

■ **Cooperative learning** is a way of acquiring skills or information in which students work together to help each other learn.

Johnson, 1987). As a bonus, they learn the interpersonal skills necessary to become leaders and cooperative workers, skills that they will need both in school and in the wider world.

■ Interest Groups

■ An **interest group** is a group formed on the basis of students' mutual interest.

In **interest groups,** students who are interested in a particular topic, author, or genre join together. For example, groups can be set up to discuss particular categories of famous people, such as inventors, entertainers, sports figures, or scientists. Students who select famous inventors would form one group. Those electing to study scientists, a second group, and so on. Each student in the group decides on a particular person to study. The group creates questions to be answered and uses trade books and other sources to gather information. The students work together in cooperative-group style. One advantage of this type of grouping is that it includes students with diverse abilities and acts as a counterbalance to ability or achievement grouping. It also provides students with choice.

■ Regrouping

▌Grouping can be harmful to self-esteem. Students who are placed in low-achieving groups see themselves as poor readers and so does everyone else, especially if the groups remain unchanged (Hiebert, 1983). Students in the low-achieving group are also deprived of peer models of high performance.

Regrouping is the practice of reassigning students from several classes on the same grade level so each teacher has students who are on the same approximate reading level. If the reading, special ed, and other specialists agree to take groups, this can result in groups that are relatively small in size. A variation of regrouping is the Joplin plan in which students from different grade levels are regrouped. Students from regular ed, special ed, and ELL programs might also be regrouped. Regrouping, when properly implemented, has been shown to increase achievement (Slavin, 1987a) and is growing in popularity. Regrouping on an informal basis can also be effective. Two fifth-grade teachers might agree that one will take the lowest-level and the other will take the highest-level students. This cuts down on the range of pupils and number of groups. Disadvantages of regrouping include time lost going from class to class and lack of flexibility in the schedule: Students must move into their groups at a certain time.

■ Balanced Grouping

Grouping patterns should be balanced and flexible. At times, it is best for the class to work as a whole; at other times, small groups or pairs work best, and students should also have some experience working individually. By employing several patterns, the teacher gives students the opportunity to mix with a greater variety of other students, and there is less of a chance that lower-achieving students will brand themselves as "slow" learners. The foundation of balanced grouping lies in the building of a sense of community. Realizing that they are valued and have a common purpose, students are better able to work with each other.

■ Advantages and Disadvantages of Grouping

Grouping reduces the variability in achievement and so makes it easier for the teacher to target instruction to the students' needs. The teacher is better able to move at a faster pace for achieving students and provide more focused and added review and practice for struggling readers. However, grouping can be harmful to the self-concepts of struggling readers, who may begin to see themselves as slow learners. Students in the lowest groups are also deprived of the opportunity to learn from the example and ideas of achieving readers. There is also a danger that low expectations will be set for struggling readers and that they will be given activities that are geared to lower-level skills so that they are deprived of opportunities to develop high-level thinking skills (Barr & Dreeben, 1991).

Continuous Monitoring of Progress

A near universal finding of research on effective teaching is that it is essential to know where students are (Hoffman, 1991). **Monitoring** should be continuous but does not necessarily entail formal testing. Observing, periodically checking portfolios, and administering informal checks can provide knowledge about students' progress. Such continuous monitoring assumes that if something is lacking in the students' learning, the program will be modified. Skills and strategies that have been forgotten will be retaught; processes that have gone off on the wrong path will be rerouted. If materials prove to be too dull or too hard, substitutions will be made. If a student needs extra time to learn, it will be supplied. Such adjustments are especially important for slow learners.

■ **Monitoring** refers to the assessment of students' progress to see whether they are performing adequately.

Involving Parents

Study after study shows that even the most impoverished and least educated parents have high aspirations for their children (Wigfield & Asher, 1984). Unfortunately, however, today's parents have less time to spend with their children. About 24 percent of U.S. families are headed by single parents, and more than 50 percent of mothers of school-age children work outside the home. According to one report, the average American mother spends less than half an hour a day talking or reading with her children; fathers spend less than fifteen minutes (U.S. Department of Education, 1986).

Parents who fail to show up for school conferences are often the ones whom the teacher wants to see because their children are having difficulty learning. Parents may well be avoiding the school because they don't want to hear bad news. What might be done to provide positive contacts with the school?

However, if systematic efforts are made, most parents will pitch in. Prior to changes made to improve the effectiveness of the program in an impoverished elementary school in Southern California, teachers incorrectly assumed that parents would lack the time, ability, or motivation to help their children (Goldenberg, 1994). Although the parents were not well educated, they had high aspirations for their children. The school sent home reading materials and suggestions for ways in which the materials might be used. Even though parents were interested and supportive, merely making suggestions at the beginning of the year wasn't enough. The teachers found that it was important to use follow-up notes, phone calls, and regular homework assignments. With follow-through and monitoring, parents began providing assistance and students' achievement increased. The lesson is clear. The school must establish and maintain contact with parents. Quarterly report cards and PTA notices are a start, but more is necessary.

A key step in communicating with parents is to keep them informed about your program when changes are made. Parents may expect instruction to be the way it was when they were in school. If they understand how a program works, they

USING TECHNOLOGY
The Partnership for Family Involvement in Education (PFIE) produces a number of publications that focus on joining together employers, educators, families, and community organizations to improve schools. Compact for Reading has specific suggestions for ways in which parents can help their children in reading. **http://ed.gov/pubs/parents/pfie.html**

"Parents are their children's first and most influential teachers. What parents do to help their children learn is more important to academic success than how well off the family is" (U.S. Department of Education, 1986, p. 7).

USING TECHNOLOGY
To increase communication with parents and to provide help with homework, supply students and parents with an e-mail address where they can get in touch with you or explain the homework assignment on the school's voice mail. Also create a Web page that contains information valuable to parents.

will be more inclined to support it, which helps ensure the program's success. The school might also hold open houses and special meetings to explain the program. Letters in which the teacher describes what students are studying and why and how parents can help should be sent home periodically. Parents want to help their children but may not know what to do. Provide suggestions specific to the current unit, as well as more general ones with more far-reaching consequences.

Working with Other Professionals

Mirroring the trend toward cooperative and group learning activities, today's model of effective literacy instruction is one of cooperation and collaboration. The classroom teacher works closely with other classroom teachers, sharing expertise, experience, and resources. In many schools, teachers meet not only to plan programs but also to support each other and to explore new developments in the field. In some schools, for instance, teachers meet to discuss the latest children's books. With the emphasis on inclusion, classroom teachers are also working more closely with the special education teacher, the reading–language arts consultant, and other specialists.

Because of the emphasis on using trade books and technology in the literacy program, it is important for classroom teachers to work with the media specialist. A well-balanced reading program must have a continuous supply of children's books. Media specialists can teach library skills, conduct book talks, help students use computers that are housed in the library, arrange special displays, and help students find appropriate books. They may even be able to provide loans to the classroom library and can keep teachers informed about the latest trade books. Classroom teachers can assist by letting the media specialist know when they plan to ask students to obtain books on certain topics or suggest that students read books by a certain author so that the necessary materials can be assembled.

Because students with special needs are being included in many classrooms, classroom teachers will be collaborating with special education teachers, reading teachers, and other learning specialists. Through collaboration, classroom teachers can obtain services and materials for special needs students and also learn teaching and management techniques that will help them more effectively instruct these students. Often, the techniques used and strategies taught work well with all students, so some of these might be used with the whole class.

Collaboration works best when the professionals involved meet regularly, establish common goals, and are flexible but work diligently to meet their common goals and make adjustments as necessary. Carefully planned and implemented collaboration can result in improved learning for both the special needs students and the rest of the class.

LITERACY AND TECHNOLOGY

Increasingly, technology is becoming a major source of information. Today, being literate means being able to use technology to gather, organize, and report information.

Using the Internet

The Internet hosts a vast reservoir of learning activities. The state of California, for instance, has produced a number of Cyberguides. Cyberguides use Web-based activities to help students extend and apply their understanding of literary selections at all grade levels. In one unit, students read *Caddie Woodlawn* (Brink, 1935) and then are asked to visit a number of sites that will provide them with information about the Westward Expansion so that they can create a brochure to convince others to join a wagon train. Students are provided with a rubric that spells out how their project will be graded (Martinez, 1998).

*G*etting information from the Internet is an essential literacy skill.

WebQuests are similar to Cyberguides. A WebQuest is an inquiry-based learning task that makes use of Internet resources (Dodge, 2001). The best WebQuests engage students as active learners and foster higher-level learning skills. Tasks range from obtaining information, answering intriguing questions, solving mysteries, synthesizing data from several sources, creating a product or plan, persuading others, building self-knowledge, analyzing events or issues, or making reasoned judgments. Typical WebQuests might include giving a PowerPoint report on the deserts of the world and offering solutions to the problem of desertification based on material found at several Web sites, comparing the biographies of two authors after visiting their sites, deciding what most likely happened to the Mayan people, creating a newspaper report of an historical event after visiting sites containing primary sources, designing an energy efficient home after visiting pertinent sites, or persuading others of your viewpoint after visiting sites that contain information about controversial issues.

Because sites are already set up for students, they make efficient use of students' time. Students don't spend a lot of time surfing the Net. Because the sites are chosen by the teacher, they are high quality and safe and geared to the teacher's instructional objectives. Listed below are suggested steps for creating a WebQuest.

In one school in Connecticut, the writing strategies taught by the learning disabilities specialist were so effective that they were adopted by the whole school. Through collaboration, classroom teachers learned about effective strategies and learning disabilities teachers increased their knowledge of the curriculum.

■ Steps in Creating a WebQuest

Step 1: Stating objectives. What is it that you want students to know or be able to do as a result of the WebQuest? You might want them to be able to write a poem, compare contrasting opinions on a timely topic, or create a Web site by following directions.

Step 2: Finding appropriate sites. Find sites that would enable students to achieve their learning objective. For instance, if the goal is to have them write a poem, you might select sites that contain a variety of poems and explain how poems are created and which provide templates for the creation of easy-to-compose poems.

ADAPTING INSTRUCTION for *STRUGGLING READERS and WRITERS*

A piece of software known as *Cast eReader* (http://www.cast.org) reads aloud and highlights text from the Internet or word-processing programs. It provides access to materials poor readers might not be able to read on their own.

USING TECHNOLOGY

A thorough but easy-to-understand explanation of techniques for searching on the Web is Worlds of Searching. **http://www.worldsofsearching.org/**

USING TECHNOLOGY

CyberGuides can be found at **http://www.sdcoe.k12.ca.us/score/cyk3.html**

Step 3: Organize the WebQuest. Create a guide that explains the purpose of the WebQuest and how to implement it. For each site that they visit, students might be provided a brief overview as well as questions to be answered or a task to be completed. The questions or tasks should foster higher-level thinking as well as basic understanding. The Quest should go beyond merely having students retell information.

Step 4: Establish outcome activities. Decide what you want students to do to use this knowledge or skill that they have gained through engaging in this WebQuest. Will they write a letter of protest? Will they create a modern-day fable? Will they share information with younger students?

Step 5: Assessing the WebQuest. Using a rubric or other assessment device, evaluate the students' learning and also the effectiveness of the WebQuest. Did they attain the Quest's learning objectives? Did the WebQuest spark interest and higher–level thinking? How might it be improved?

■ Lists of Sites

There are thousands of sites designed for elementary and middle school students. Here is a list of recommended sites:

- *Awesome Library:* Provides links to 22,000 carefully reviewed resources for students of all ages. The browser is available in a dozen languages and has a translation feature.
  http://www.awesomelibrary.org/
- *BJ Pinchbeck's Homework Helper:* Compiled by a middle school student who understands the reference needs of his fellow students.
  http://www.bjpinchbeck.com/
- *Enchanted Learning:* Features a wealth of information about animals and other topics. Also has a variety of activities and illustrations that can be printed out. Materials are in English and Spanish. Has a Little Explorer's Picture dictionary in both English and Spanish.
  http://www.enchantedlearning.com
- *Kathy Schrock's Guide for Educators: Home Page:* A popular site for teachers. Compiled by a school librarian who has also created a collection for students. http://school.discovery.com/schrockguide/
- *Kid Info/School Subjects:* Another student-created site. Arranged by subject area, and linked to many of the best educational sites on line.
  http://www.kidinfo.com/School_Subjects.html
- *PBS Teachersource:* Sites selected for curriculum content, arranged by subject areas. Click on your area of interest.
  http://www.pbs.org/teachersource/
- *700+ Great Sites from ALA:* Compiled by members of the American Library Association. For students, teachers, librarians, and parents.
  http://www.ala.org/parentspage/greatsites/

- *700+ Sites: Planet Earth and Beyond:* Lists a variety of sites that explore science topics, such as animals, Earth, and weather.
  http://www.ala.org/parentspage/greatsites/earth.html

■ Talking Web Sites

With the appropriate software, Web sites can be made to talk. Cast ereader (http://www.cast.org/) reads aloud text from the Internet or word processing programs. Awesome Talking Library (http://www.awesomelibrary.org/) also has software that reads Web sites. The software from Awesome Talking Library is free if downloaded and is very easy to use. It has variable reading speeds as well as a variety of reading voices. Students can have the whole Web site read or just portions of it. They may, for instance, just want to have a word or two spoken. Both pieces of software provide access to materials that struggling readers or novice readers might not be able to read on their own.

■ Internet Projects for the Classroom

The Internet offers a multitude of opportunities for projects. Projects that incorporate the use of the Internet in the classroom can be found on the following sites:

- *Global SchoolNet Foundation*
  http://www.gsn.org
- *Tita Mallory's Online Projects*
  http://users.techline.com/tmallory/EUI/Onlinelinks.html

■ Outstanding Internet Resource

Read Write Think (http://www.readwritethink.org/), which might just be the best literacy site on the Internet, is sponsored by the International Reading Association (IRA), the National Council of Teachers of English (NCTE), and the Marco Polo Education Foundation. The site features a wide variety of lessons in virtually every skill area and on levels from K to 8. Lessons are based on IRA/NCTE standards and integrate Internet content into the learning activity. Each lesson includes a detailed instructional plan and includes student-ready materials such as worksheets, interactives, and Web resources.

In addition to student resources the site features:

- **Instructional Resources**—sites that provide instructional resources for the teacher, such as lesson plans, classroom activities, and teaching techniques.
- **Professional Development**—sites that offer current information in the teaching profession, including research findings, teaching trends, and noteworthy events.
- **Reference Library**—sites that provide specific information or offer general reference resources.
- **Calendar**—entries provide a brief description of the event, along with related Web resources, lesson plans, and activities for your students. The resources might describe a controversial event and have students form an opinion after reading Web-based information.

> **USING TECHNOLOGY**
> Edbydesign features a number of educational activities. It provides opportunities for students to send in jokes, riddles, or other kinds of writing.
> **http://www. edbydesign.com/**

- **Web Resources Gallery**—provides links to more than 80 literacy sites on the Internet. Includes sites that provide professional information as well as sites that provide instructional resources.

■ Electronic Mail

■ **Electronic mail** (e-mail) is the sending of notes or messages by means of computer.

Because of ease and speed, **electronic mail** (e-mail) is one of the most popular features on the Internet. It benefits teachers in two ways. It's an excellent means for communicating with other professionals and it can be used to foster students' writing. Through e-mail, students can work with students in other classes and other schools and can communicate with their teachers and even submit written assignments. Students can also communicate with key-pals.

Just as letter writing is an important skill, so, too, is e-mail. In addition to the skills of traditional letter writing, students need to know the mechanics of sending e-mail, the importance of getting the address right and using an address book, and how to write a heading announcing the subject of an e-mail. For more information on composing e-mail, see Chapter 10.

■ Issues of Safety

For all its potential value, the Internet can be a source of harm to young people. Essentially, the Internet is unregulated, so objectionable material is available. Filtering software can be used to restrict access to some objectionable sites. Software that keeps track of sites that have been visited is also available. There is also the issue of security. Unfortunately, some adults have used the Internet to prey on children. The best defense is to supervise students using the Internet and to educate them and their parents about the dangers of the Internet and precautions that might be taken. In many schools, parents and students sign an agreement in which they agree to use the Internet ethically and responsibly. Students also need to be supervised when using the Internet. As a practical matter, monitors should be set up so that teachers can readily see what students are viewing.

Teachers in 94 percent of public schools monitor Internet use, and 74 percent of schools have blocking or filtering software. Nearly two-thirds of schools also have an honor code relating to Internet use. Virtually all schools have an acceptable use policy (Cattagni & Westnat, 2001).

Other Uses of Computers

With advances in technology, there have been dramatic improvements in the power of computers and quality of educational software. In addition to providing a portal to the Internet, computers have four major educational uses, which sometimes overlap. They provide practice, tutorial instruction, and simulations, and can also be used as tools.

A particularly useful tool for students is Kidspiration. Designed for students in grades K–5, Kidspiration (Inspiration) provides illustrations that students can use to brainstorm ideas or illustrate their writing pieces. It also has templates for creating semantic webs and prompts for writing. Speech capability enables students to hear what they have written.

In tutorial software, such as *Simon Spells* (Don Johnston), the student is walked through a lesson with a series of questions and answers or activities. Active participation is required. After a skill is explained, reinforcement exercises are provided. One of the best instructional uses of software is the presentation of **simulations.**

■ A **simulation** is a type of computer program that presents activities or gives the feel of the real experience.

Students can travel back in time, take journeys across country, and perform experiments without leaving their computers. For example, in *Message in a Bottle* (Brighter Child Interactive), students become paleontologists. They excavate a fossil, label its parts, and prepare a museum exhibit.

■ Using the Computer as a Tool

Computers are most powerful in literacy learning when they are used as a tool. They can help locate data, retrieve information, organize data, compose information, and present information.

Word processing.   Computers are most frequently used as an aid to composition. The major advantage of word processing software is that students can revise without rewriting or retyping the whole piece. Some software can also help with planning, checking spelling, and checking grammar and usage. Bundling word processing features, design, and illustration capabilities, desktop publishing (DTP) systems allow students to create newspapers, newsletters, brochures, and booklets. See Chapter 10 for additional information about word processing and DTP.

Databases.   Using **database** software, such as *Apple Works* (Apple) or *Filemaker Pro* (Filemaker), students can organize data and later use the data to compile a report. A database is an electronic filing system. The topic can be thought of as a file folder. The information placed in the file are records, and the categories of information found on each record are known as fields. For instance, in a project in which they are gathering information about states, students would create a record for each state. Then they would decide what kinds of information they would include. For each category of information, they would construct a field. Possible fields might include: name of state, population, geographical area, per capita income, major crops, main industries, and so on. Using their databases, students could answer such questions as: Which are the five largest states? Which states have the highest per capita income? In which states is wheat a major crop? Using the database's report function, a variety of reports could be created. If tied in to a spread sheet, this information could be used to create graphs and charts. If tied in to a DTP system, the information could be placed in an illustrated report.

■ Using the Computer as a Source of Information

With the increased storage capacity of computers, dictionaries, encyclopedias, thesauri, picture libraries, atlases, and other databases of information are now available in inexpensive CD-ROM format. They often come with features that help students locate and organize information. Many of these are also available on the Web.

Selecting Software

The key to making effective use of the computer is to obtain high-quality software. Before selecting software, decide what you want it to do and how you might use it. Decide what educational objective you wish to fulfill. In addition to being appealing and motivational, software should fulfill an educational purpose. Two print

Using a word processor results in longer, often better-written pieces and improved attitudes toward writing. A major advantage is the ease with which written pieces are revised.

■ A **database** is a collection of related data organized by a computer program or other means.

USING TECHNOLOGY

Children's Software Revue provides reviews of more than 5,000 software programs. Has links to software publishers and related sites.
http://www. childrenssoftware.com

Kids Domain Reviews Provides free reviews of more than 1,000 pieces of software.
http://www. kidsdomain.com

sources of information about educational software are *The Complete Sourcebook on Children's Software* (Buckleitner, Orr, & Wolock, 2002) and the *Educational Software Preview Guide* (ISTE). Software is regularly reviewed in the journals *Software Review, Electronic Learning,* and *Technology and Learning.*

To assess software, ask the following questions, which are adapted from Cook (1986) and Bitter (1999):

- Does it help the attainment of an educationally valid objective?
- Are its activities consistent with the way I teach reading or writing?
- Does it make use of the special capabilities of the computer—providing immediate knowledge of results, learner participation, use of graphics, use of speech, keeping track of progress, and so on?
- Does the software include learning aids, such as pronouncing and/or defining difficult words on request and providing additional information or more practice if needed?
- Is the material presented accurately and on the proper level of readability?
- Is the software reasonably easy to use?
- Can it be modified to add customized examples or exercises?

Getting the Most Out of Computers

Computer software, like other educational materials, requires teacher guidance. Students have to be prepared to complete the activity offered by the software or site they are about to visit. They must have their background knowledge activated, have a purpose for completing the assignment, and know how to read the material. Should they read it fast or slow? Should they read it in parts or as a whole? They also have to know how to use any learning aids that might be built into the program. After students have completed the activity, give them the opportunity to discuss what they have learned, clarify misconceptions, integrate new and old information, and extend and apply their learning.

In dealing with electronic media, students use many of the same basic skills and strategies that they use when engaged in traditional reading and writing. However, computers and other electronic devices demand new skills and adaptations of old ones. Given the accessibility of information, students need to be able to select information that is relevant quickly and accurately.

It is important that technology, no matter how promising or exciting or complex, be seen as a tool and not the focus of instruction. In a long-term study of the effect of technology on students, it was found that "students worked best when technology was not the topic itself but was integrated into the entire curriculum" (Bitter, 1999, p. 109).

USING TECHNOLOGY

WWW 4 Teachers provides a host of easy-to-use tools. With Quiz Star, the teacher can create online quizzes. With Web Worksheet Wizard the teacher can create Web pages. Using Project Poster, students can create Web pages. TrackStar enables teachers to create Web site projects that are based on a series of links to other sites. Teachers may customize already existing Tracks. RubiStar allows teachers to customize any one of several dozen rubrics. NoteStar is designed to help students take notes from online sources.
http://4teachers. org/

■ Teacher Tools

Technology has also created a variety of valuable tools for the teacher. For instance, using *Wynn Reader* (Arkenstone) the teacher can make adaptations in electronic text. Text can be added, deleted, or simplified. Study aids, such as voice notes, and a built-in dictionary are available. *Worksheet Magic Plus* (Teacher Support Software) makes it possible to create fifteen different kinds of practice activities including crossword puzzles and word searches. *Inspiration* (Inspiration Software) can be used by both students and teachers to make graphic organizers. The software includes 35 graphic organizer templates and 1,250 pieces of clip art. Presentation software such as *PowerPoint* (Microsoft) or *Keynote* (Apple) can be used by both teachers and students to make slides, transparencies, and computer presentations. Software such as *Front Page* (Microsoft) can be used in the construction of Web pages.

Other Technologies

Audio and audiovisual technologies can be used to motivate students to read or to expand students' understanding and appreciation of a selection. For poor readers, audiovisual aids may provide access to a piece of literature that they would not be able to read on their own.

■ Audio Technologies

Audio versions of books have three advantages (Rickelman & Henk, 1990). Although warmth and interaction are missing in an electronic reading, it can be played over and over by the student. In addition, it often includes sound effects, may be dramatized, and may even have been recorded by the author of the work. Because of their superior sound quality, CD versions are preferred to taped ones but may not be available for certain titles.

■ Audiovisual Technologies

Films and video cassettes are available for a wide variety of children's books. There are hundreds of children's books on video, including *Why Don't You Get a Horse, Sam Adams?* (Weston Woods/Scholastic), *Rikki-Tikki-Tavi* (Weston Woods/Scholastic), *Call It Courage* (Disney), and *Following the Drinking Gourd* (SRA Group).

LITERACY IN TODAY'S AND TOMORROW'S WORLD

Increasingly, literacy will include the ability to use computers and other high-technology devices. Students need to know how to use resources such as the Internet and how to construct multimedia reports. They also need to understand how to get the most out of interactive encyclopedias and other sophisticated sources of information. Computer literacy still requires traditional skills: the ability to read with understanding, to write coherently, and to think clearly. However, today's technology also requires a higher level of literacy. Internet searches allow students to obtain greater amounts of data on a particular topic, including data published that day. Students need the skills to skim and scan data so that they can quickly select information that is relevant and important. A key reading skill for the era of the information superhighway is the ability to decide quickly and efficiently whether an article, study, or other document merits reading. With so much more information available, it is essential that time is not wasted reading texts that are not pertinent or worthwhile.

Having more data to work with means that students must be better at organizing information, evaluating it, drawing conclusions, and conveying the essence of the information to others. They also need cognitive flexibility to make use of the growing amounts of information in proposing diverse solutions to the increasingly complex problems sure to arise in the coming years.

PROFESSIONAL DEVELOPMENT

To keep up with the latest developments in the fields of reading and writing instruction, it is necessary to be professionally active—to join professional organizations, attend meetings, take part in staff-development activities, and read in the field. The International Reading Association (100 Barksdale Road, Newark, DE 19714) and the National Council of Teachers of English (1111 Kenyon Road, Urbana, IL 61801) are devoted to professional improvement in reading and the language arts. For elementary school teachers, the IRA publishes the widely read periodical *The Reading Teacher* and the NCTE publishes *Language Arts*. For middle school teachers, IRA publishes the *Journal of Adolescent and Adult Literacy*; NCTE publishes the *English Journal*. Both organizations have local and state chapters and sponsor local, state, regional, and national conferences.

As with any other vital endeavor, teachers should set both long-term goals and short-term professional objectives, asking such questions as the following:

- Where do I want to be professionally five years from now?
- What steps do I have to take to get there?

*D*uring inservice sessions, teachers learn about the latest developments in literacy instruction.

FIGURE 12.1

Checklist for an Effective Literacy Program

Directions: To read each question, insert the phrase "Do I" before it (e.g., Do I read aloud regularly?). Then circle the appropriate response. If you are not in the teaching situation described, respond as though you were. When finished, analyze your answers. What are your strengths? What are some areas in which you might need improvement?

Teaching Practices: General	Never	Seldom	Often	Usually
Read aloud regularly	1	2	3	4
Directly teach key strategies and skills	1	2	3	4
Model reading and writing processes	1	2	3	4
Use think-alouds to make reading and writing processes explicit	1	2	3	4
Provide adequate guided practice	1	2	3	4
Provide opportunities for application	1	2	3	4
Integrate reading, writing, listening, and speaking	1	2	3	4

Teaching Practices: Comprehension/Study Skills				
Build background and activate prior knowledge	1	2	3	4
Set or encourage the setting of purposes	1	2	3	4
Present a variety of comprehension strategies	1	2	3	4
Teach monitoring/strategic reading	1	2	3	4
Provide adequate practice/application	1	2	3	4

Teaching Practices: Word Recognition				
Provide systematic instruction in major skill areas: phonics, context clues, syllabication, morphemic analysis, dictionary skills	1	2	3	4
Provide systematic instruction in use of major cueing systems: phonics, syntactic, semantic	1	2	3	4
Encourage the use of a variety of decoding strategies	1	2	3	4
Provide opportunities for students to read widely so skills become automatic	1	2	3	4

Teaching Practices: Content Area				
Use high-quality content-area texts	1	2	3	4
Supplement content-area texts with informational books and nonprint materials	1	2	3	4
Provide texts on appropriate levels of difficulty or make adjustments	1	2	3	4
Present skills and strategies necessary to learn from informational texts	1	2	3	4

Teaching Practices: Writing				
Encourage self-selection of topics	1	2	3	4
Use a process approach	1	2	3	4
Provide guided instruction in writing strategies	1	2	3	4

(continued)

FIGURE 12.1

Checklist for an Effective Literacy Program *(continued)*

	Never	Seldom	Often	Usually
Provide frequent opportunities for writing	1	2	3	4
Provide opportunities to compose in a variety of forms	1	2	3	4

Materials

	Never	Seldom	Often	Usually
Use a variety of print materials	1	2	3	4
Children's books, fiction and nonfiction	1	2	3	4
Supplementary materials	1	2	3	4
Basal series	1	2	3	4
Periodicals	1	2	3	4
Real-world materials	1	2	3	4
Pamphlets, brochures	1	2	3	4
Pupil-written works	1	2	3	4
Use a variety of nonprint materials	1	2	3	4
Tape recorder/CD player	1	2	3	4
VCR/DVD	1	2	3	4
Videodiscs	1	2	3	4
Computer software	1	2	3	4
Web sites	1	2	3	4
Games	1	2	3	4
Adapt materials to students' needs	1	2	3	4
Provide materials for slow as well as bright students	1	2	3	4
Evaluate materials before using them	1	2	3	4

Evaluation

	Never	Seldom	Often	Usually
Set goals and objectives (standards) for the program	1	2	3	4
Align standards (objectives) and assessment	1	2	3	4
Collect formal and informal data to use as a basis for evaluating the program	1	2	3	4
Encourage self-assessment	1	2	3	4
Assess data-collection instruments in terms of validity and reliability	1	2	3	4
Assemble a portfolio for each student	1	2	3	4
Share assessment data with students and parents	1	2	3	4
Use assessment data to improve instruction for each student and to improve program	1	2	3	4

Organization/Management

	Never	Seldom	Often	Usually
Provide for individual differences	1	2	3	4
Use a variety of grouping strategies	1	2	3	4
Use time and materials efficiently	1	2	3	4

- What are my strengths and weaknesses as a teacher of reading and writing?
- How can I build on my strengths and remediate my weaknesses?
- What new professional techniques/skills or areas of knowledge would I most like to learn?

The answers should result in a plan of professional development.

Filling out the checklist in Figure 12.1 will help you create a profile of your strengths and weaknesses as a reading/writing teacher. The checklist covers the entire literacy program and incorporates the major principles covered in the text. As such, it provides a review of the book as well as a means of self-assessment.

> **USING TECHNOLOGY**
>
> An excellent source of Internet sites for professional development is *The Prentice Hall Directory of Online Resources* (Bigham & Bigham, 1998).

ESSENTIAL STANDARDS

Fourth through eighth grades
Students will

- operate a computer to run basic and advanced educational software.
- use a word-processing system and a desktop publishing system.

ACTION PLAN

1. Obtain basic information about your students' culture, their literacy strengths, and needs.
2. Construct a program based on the nature of students that you will be teaching. Set goals and objectives.
3. Obtain materials and select teaching techniques and activities that will help you reach those goals.
4. Build motivation by helping students experience the joy of successful learning. Build a classroom community in which students help each other learn.
5. Use time efficiently and provide for individual differences. Use a variety of types of grouping. However, make sure that grouping is flexible so that students can move back and forth between groups and there is no stigma to being in certain groups.
6. Make sure that students, especially the struggling readers, are given materials and instruction at their level each day.
7. Continuously monitor progress with both formal and informal instruments. Make sure that instruction is guided by assessment.
8. Involve parents in their children's learning. Use a variety of techniques to keep them informed about their children's progress. Provide specific suggestions for things they might do to help their children. Make use of their talents and knowledge in the classroom by having them give presentations and help out through tutoring, translating, or performing other tasks.
9. Work cooperatively with the media specialist, the learning disabilities teacher, the reading teacher, and other professionals. Coordinate efforts so that students receive maximum benefit.
10. Make use of technology to foster literacy and guide students so that they learn to use technology as a literacy tool.
11. Evaluate your program and make adjustments as needed.
12. Create a plan for professional development. Include long-term goals and short-term objectives. Keep up with the professional literature, take courses, attend workshops and conferences, observe highly effective teachers, and join a study group to further your professional development.

- use a database to organize information.
- compose e-mail and communicate with other students.
- use CD-ROM and online encyclopedias, databases, and other electronic reference sources.
- use a variety of Internet sites to gather information.
- use audio tape recorders to play and record information.
- use technology ethically and responsibly.

SUMMARY

1. The construction of a literacy program starts with consideration of the needs and characteristics of students, the parents' wishes, and the nature of the community. General goals and specific objectives are based on these factors and the school district's curriculum or standards.

2. Other elements in the construction of a literacy program include: high-quality teaching, use of varied materials, continuous monitoring of students' progress, involvement of parents, efficient management of time and resources, provision for individual differences, and collaborating with other professionals.

3. Technology should be integrated into the literacy program. Effective use of the Internet requires instruction in efficient searching techniques and the ability to judge the relevance and reliability of information. In addition to yielding a connection to the Internet, computers provide practice, tutorial instruction, and simulations and are a powerful literacy tool. Word processing and DTP systems can help students present information. Audio and audiovisual technologies can be used to motivate students.

EXTENDING AND APPLYING

1. Set up goals and objectives for a reading/language arts program that you are now teaching or plan to teach. Discuss your goals and objectives with a colleague or classmate.

2. Complete the checklist in Figure 12.1. If you are not teaching now, answer it on the basis of how you believe you will conduct yourself when you are a teacher. According to the results, what are your strengths and weaknesses?

3. Respond to the questions about professional goals and objectives on page 474 and 477. Based on these responses and your responses to the checklist in Figure 12.1, plan a series of professional development activities.

4. For a week, keep a record of the activities in your reading/language arts class. Which seem to be especially valuable? Which, if any, seem to have limited value or take up excessive amounts of time? Based on your observations, construct a plan for making better use of instructional time. If you are not teaching now, arrange to observe a teacher who has a reputation for having a well-managed classroom. Note the strategies that the teacher uses to keep the class running smoothly and to make efficient use of time.

5. Assess the parental involvement component of your literacy program. Based on your assessment and the suggestions made in this chapter, make any changes that seem to be needed.

DEVELOPING A PROFESSIONAL PORTFOLIO

Keep a record of experiences that you have had with technology. This might include Web sites that you set up or helped set up, video productions that you have supervised, or audio tapes that you or your students have created. Note any special training that you have had with technology. Also include lesson plans in which you made effective use of technology.

DEVELOPING A RESOURCE FILE

Start and maintain a file of Internet sites or titles of software and other technological devices that seem to be especially valuable for the grade level that you teach or plan to teach.

Appendix A
Graded Listing of 800+ Children's Books

• Designates outstanding books.
N Designates nonfiction.

Impey, Rose. *Desperate for a Dog.* Dutton, 1988, 62 pp.

•James, Ellen Foley. *Little Bull, Growing Up in Africa's Elephant Kingdom.* Sterling, 1998, 48 pp.

Johnson, Dolores. *Grandma's Hands.* Marshall Cavendish, 1998, 30 pp.

Johnston, Marianne. *Rhinos.* Rosen, 1998, 24 pp. **N**

Kalbacken, Joan. *The Food Pyramid.* Children's Press, 1998, 48 pp. **N**

Karas, G. Brian. *The Nature of the Beast.* Tambourine, 1996, 30 pp.

Kessler, Cristina. *Konte Chameleon, Fine, Fine, Fine!* Boyds Mill Press, 1997, 28 pp.

Kimmel, Eric A. *Easy Work! An Old Tale!* Holiday House, 1998, 30 pp.

Kirkwood, Jon. *Fire Fighters.* Copper Beech Books, 1997, 32 pp. **N**

Lafferty, Peter. *Why Do Balls Bounce? First Questions and Answers about How Things Work.* Time Life, 1995, 48 pp. **N**

Leedy, Loreen. *Mapping Penny's World.* Holt, 2000, 30 pp.

Levitin, Sonia. *Boom Town.* Orchard Books, 1998, 30 pp.

Lindbergh, Reeve. *Nobody Owns the Sky.* Candlewick Press, 1996, 22 pp. **N**

•Llewellyn, Claire. *I Didn't Know That Some Birds Hang Upside Down.* Copper Beech Book, 1998, 32 pp. **N**

Malone, Peter. *Star Shapes.* Chronicle Books, 1997, 22 pp. **N**

Manning, Mick. *My Body, Your Body.* Franklin Watts, 1997, 32 pp. **N**

•Markle, Sandra. *Outside and Inside Bats.* Atheneum, 1997, 40 pp. **N**

McCourt, Lisa. *The Goodness Gorillas.* Health Communications, 1997, 29 pp.

McCourt, Lisa. *The Never-Forgotten Doll.* Health Communications, 1997, 29 pp.

Meddaugh, Susan. *Cinderella's Rat.* Houghton Mifflin, 1997, 32 pp.

Meddaugh, Susan. *Martha Walks the Dog.* Houghton Mifflin, 1998, 32 pp.

Medina, Tony. *Deshawn Days.* Lee & Low, 2001, 30 pp.

Mitchell, Rhonda. *The Talking Cloth.* Orchard, 1997, 26 pp.

Naylor, Phyllis Reynolds. *I Can't Take You Anywhere.* Atheneum, 1997, 32 pp.

Onyefulu, Ifeoma. *Chidi Only Likes Blue.* Dutton, 1997, 18 pp.

Osborne, Mary Pope. *Ghost Town at Sundown.* Random House, 1997, 73 pp.

Petersen, P. J. *The Sub.* Dutton, 1993, 86 pp.

Peterson-Fleming, Judy, & Fleming, Bill. *Kitten Care and Critters, Too.* Tambourine, 1994, 40 pp. **N**

Peterson-Fleming, Judy, & Fleming, Bill. *Puppy Training and Critters, Too.* Tambourine, 1996, 40 pp. **N**

Petricic, Dusan, & Gryski, Camilla. *Let's Play, Traditional Games of Childhood.* Kids Can Press, 1998, 48 pp. **N**

Philip, Neil (Retold by). *Fairy Tales of the Brothers Grimm.* Viking, 1997, 140 pp.

Polacco, Patricia. *Aunt Chip and the Great Triple Creek Dam Affair.* Philomel, 1996, 36 pp.

Reynolds, Marilynn. *The New Land.* Orca, 1997, 30 pp.

Riggio, Anita. *Secret Signs along the Underground Railroad.* Boyds Mill Press, 1997, 28 pp.

Ripley, Catherine. *Why Does Popcorn Pop? And Other Kitchen Questions.* Firefly Books, 1997, 32 pp. **N**

Sanders, Scott Russell. *A Place Called Freedom.* Simon & Schuster, 1997, 28 pp.

Sathre, Vivian. *Leroy Potts Meets the Crooks.* Delacorte, 1997, 48 pp.

Shannon, David. *The Rain Came Down.* Scholastic, 2000, 30 pp.

Shannon, George. *This Is the Bird.* Houghton Mifflin, 1997, 30 pp.

•Silverstein, Shel. *Where the Sidewalk Ends.* HarperCollins, 1974, 166 pp. **N**

Slepian, Jan, & Seidler, Ann. *The Hungry Thing Goes to a Restaurant.* Scholastic, 1992, 30 pp.

Soto, Gary. *Big Bushy Mustache.* Knopf, 1998, 30 pp.

Speed, Toby. *Whoosh! Went the Wish.* Putnam's, 1997, 30 pp.

•Stefoff, Rebecca. *Octopus.* Marshall Cavendish, 1997, 32 pp. **N**

Stewart, Dianne. *Gift of the Sun: A Tale from South Africa.* Farrar, Straus & Giroux, 1996, 24 pp.

Stille, Darlene R. *Helicopters.* Children's Press, 1997, 48 pp. **N**

Stolz, Mary. *King Emmett the Second.* Greenwillow, 1991, 56 pp.

Teague, Mark. *The Secret Shortcut.* Scholastic, 1996, 24 pp.

Van Leeuwen, Jean. *Fourth of July on the Plains.* Dial, 1997, 30 pp.

Vizurraga, Susan. *Our Old House.* Holt, 1997, 30 pp.

Warner, Gertrude C. *The Boxcar Children: Mystery Behind the Wall.* Albert Whitman, 1973, 127 pp.

Wohl, Lauren L. *Christopher Davis's Best Year Yet.* Hyperion, 1995, 60 pp.

Wood, Audrey. *The Flying Dragon Room.* Scholastic, 1996, 28 pp.

Yezerski, Thomas F. *Together in Pinecone Patch.* Farrar, Straus & Giroux, 1998, 30 pp.

Yolen, Jane. *Sleeping Ugly.* Coward, McCann & Geoghegan, 1981, 64 pp.

Zoehfeld, Kathleen Weidner. *How Mountains Are Made.* HarperCollins, 1995, 32 pp. **N**

Fourth-Grade Books

Easy Reading Level: Grade 1 (Interest Level: Grade 4)

Schwartz, Alvin. *In a Dark Dark Room.* HarperCollins, 1984, 62 pp.

Easy Reading Level: Grade 2 (Interest Level: Grade 4)

•Bulla, Clyde Robert. *Shoeshine Girl.* Crowell, 1975, 84 pp.

•Shea, George. *Amazing Rescues.* Random House, 1992, 48 pp. **N**

Easy Reading Level: Grade 3 (Interest Level: Grade 4)

Abbott, Tony. *Danger Guys.* HarperCollins, 1994, 69 pp.

Adler, David A. *Calculator Riddles.* Holiday House, 1995, 32 pp. **N**

Adler, David A. *Lou Gehrig, The Luckiest Man.* Harcourt Brace, 1997, 30 pp. **N**

•Avi. *Man from the Sky.* Knopf, 1980, 117 pp.

Ballard, Robert. *Finding the* Titanic. Scholastic, 1993, 48 pp. **N**

•Berends, Polly. *The Case of the Elevator Duck.* Random House, 1973, 60 pp.

Blume, Judy. *Blubber.* Dell, 1974, 153 pp.

Bulla, Clyde Robert. *Pirate's Promise.* HarperCollins, 1958, 87 pp.

Bunting, Eve. *Train to Somewhere.* Houghton Mifflin, 1996, 32 pp.

Clymer, Eleanor. *The Trolley Car Family.* Scholastic, 1947, 216 pp.

Danziger, Paula. *Amber Brown Goes Fourth.* Putnam, 1995, 101 pp.

DiCamillo, Kate. *Because of Winn-Dixie.* Candlewick Press, 2000, 182 pp.

Donnelly, Judy. *The* Titanic *Lost and Found.* Random House, 1987, 48 pp. **N**

Donnelly, Judy. *Tut's Mummy Lost . . . and Found.* Random House, 1988, 48 pp. **N**

Fritz, Jean. *Just a Few Words, Mr. Lincoln.* Grossett, & Dunlap, 1993, 48 pp. **N**

Giff, Patricia Reilly. *Shark in School.* Delacorte, 1994, 103 pp.

Hall, Lynn. *Barry, The Bravest Saint Bernard*. Random House, 1973, 48 pp. **N**

Haviland, Virginia. *Favorite Fairy Tales, Book 16, Told in Norway*. Beech Tree Books (William Morrow),1961, 1996, 96 pp.

Hest, Amy. *When Jessie Came across the Sea*. Candlewick Press, 1997, 36 pp.

Hooks, William H. *The Girl Who Could Fly*. Macmillan, 1995, 51 pp.

Kallen, Stuart. *Mutts*. Abdo Consulting Group, 1996, 24 pp.

Kroeger, Mary Kay, & Borden, Louise. *Paperboy*. Clarion, 1996, 31 pp.

Kroll, Virginia. *Faraway Drums*. Little, Brown, 1998, 30 pp.

Kunhardt, Edith. *Pompeii . . . Buried Alive*. Random House, 1987, 48 pp. **N**

Lears, Laurie. *Ian's Walk, A Story about Autism*. Whitman, 1998, 28 pp.

Little, Emily. *The Trojan Horse, How Greeks Won the War*. Random House, 1992, 48 pp. **N**

Louie, Ai-Ling. *Yeh-Shen: A Cinderella Story from China*. Philomel, 1982, 28 pp.

•Lundell, Margo (Retold by). *Lad, a Dog*. Scholastic, 1997, 44 pp.

MacLachlan, Patricia. *Skylark*. HarperCollins, 1994, 87 pp.

Milton, Joyce. *Mummies*. Grossett & Dunlap, 1996, 48 pp. **N**

Moore, Floyd C. *I Gave Thomas Edison My Sandwich*. Whitman, 1995, 30 pp.

Mora, Pat. *Tomás and the Library Lady*. Random House, 1997, 28 pp.

O'Connor, Jim. *Comeback! Four True Stories*. Random House, 1992, 48 pp. **N**

•Penner, Lucille Recht. *Twisters*. Random House, 1996, 46 pp. **N**

Pinkwater, Daniel. *Mush: A Dog from Space*. Atheneum, 1995, 40 pp.

Prelutsky, Jack. *The Beauty of the Beast*. Knopf, 1997, 100 pp. **N**

Rylant, Cynthia. *Best Wishes*. Richard C. Owen, 1992, 32 pp. **N**

•Sachar, Louis. *Wayside School Is Falling Down*. Avon, 1989, 179 pp.

Sachar, Louis. *Wayside School Gets a Little Stranger*. Avon, 1995, 168 pp.

•Shuter, Jane. *The Ancient Egyptians*. Heinemann, 1997, 32 pp. **N**

•Shuter, Jane. *The Ancient Greeks*. Heinemann, 1997, 32 pp. **N**

Sobol, Donald J. *Encyclopedia Brown Saves the Day*. Bantam, 1970, 114 pp.

Steptoe, John. *Creativity*. Houghton Mifflin, 1997, 28 pp.

•Wells, Robert E. *What's Faster than a Speeding Cheetah?* Whitman, 1997, 29 pp. **N**

Willis, Meredith Sue. *Marco's Monster*. HarperCollins, 1996, 118 pp.

Wilson, Nancy Hope. *Old People, Frogs, and Albert*. Farrar, Straus & Giroux, 1997, 58 pp.

Wroble, Lisa A. *Kids in Colonial Times*. Rosen, 1997, 24 pp. **N**

Average Reading Level: Grade 4 (Interest Level: Grade 4)

Aardema, Verna. *Why Mosquitoes Buzz in People's Ears*. Dial, 1975, 21 pp.

•Ada, Alma Flor. *The Gold Coin*. Atheneum, 1991, 32 pp.

Allen, Eugenie. *The Best Ever Kids' Book of Lists*. Avon, 1991, 117 pp. **N**

Arnold, Eric. *Volcanoes! Mountains of Fire*. Random House, 1997, 64 pp. **N**

•Atwater, Richard, & Atwater, Florence. *Mr. Popper's Penguins*. Little, Brown, 1938, 139 pp.

•Banks, Kate. *The Bunnysitters*. Random House, 1991, 63 pp.

Ben-Ezer, Ehud. *Hosni the Dreamer*. Farrar, Straus & Giroux, 1997, 28 pp.

Blume, Judy. *Blubber*. Dell, 1974, 153 pp.

Brown, Don. *Alice Ramsey's Grand Adventure*. Houghton Mifflin, 1997, 32 pp. **N**

Brown, Jeff. *Flat Stanley*. HarperCollins, 1964, 44 pp.

•Bunting, Eve. *Nasty, Stinky Sneakers*. HarperCollins, 1994, 105 pp.

Burnie, Richard. *Masterthief: Catch the Crook and Solve the Crime*. Johnathan Cape, 2000, 30 pp.

•Butterworth, Oliver. *The Enormous Egg*. Little, Brown, 1956, 169 pp.

Choi, Yangsook. *The Name Jar*. Knopf, 2001, 30 pp.

Christopher, Matt. *The Dog That Pitched a No-Hitter*. Little, Brown, 1988, 32 pp.

Christopher, Matt. *The Hit-Away Kid*. Little, Brown, 1988, 60 pp.

•Christopher, Matt. *Baseball Turnaround*. Little, Brown, 1997, 122 pp.

Clement, Frank. *Counting on Frank*. Gareth Stevens, 1991, 30 pp.

•Clifford, Eth. *Help! I'm a Prisoner in the Library*. Scholastic, 1979, 96 pp.

Cooper, Floyd. *Coming Home: From the Life of Langston Hughes*. Philomel, 1994, 30 pp. **N**

•Coote, Roger. *The Earth*. Zigzag

Multimedia (Smithmark), 1997, 32 pp. **N**

Costain, Meredith, & Collins, Paul. *Welcome to China*. Chelsea House, 2002, 32 pp. **N**

Curtis, Gavin. *The Bat Boy and His Violin*. Simon & Schuster, 1998, 28 pp.

Dadey, Debbie, & Jones, Marcia Thornton. *Martians Don't Take Temperatures*. Scholastic, 1996, 67 pp.

Dean, Harvey. *Secret Elephant of Harlan Kooter*. Houghton Mifflin, 1992, 130 pp.

Donati, Annabelle. *Animal Record Holders*. Western, 1993, 32 pp. **N**

Earle, Sylvia. *Hello, Fish*. National Geographic Society, 1999, 30 pp. **N**

Earth Works Group. *50 Simple Things Kids Can Do to Save the Earth*. Andrew and McMeel, 1990, 156 pp. **N**

Engel, Trudie. *We'll Never Forget You, Roberto Clemente*. Scholastic, 1996, 106 pp. **N**

•Facklam, Margery. *Creepy, Crawly Caterpillars*. Little, Brown, 1996, 32 pp. **N**

Fisher, Leonard Everett. *Cyclops*. Holiday House, 1991, 28 pp.

Flournoy, Valerie. *The Patchwork Quilt*. Dial, 1985, 29 pp.

Fritz, Jean. *The Cabin Faced West*. Puffin, 1958, 124 pp.

Fritz, Jean. *And Then What Happened, Paul Revere*. Coward, McCann & Geoghegan, 1973, 48 pp. **N**

•Gardiner, John Reynolds. *Stone Fox*. HarperCollins, 1980, 71 pp.

Gavin, Jamila. *Children Just Like Me, Our Favorite Stories*. Dorling Kindersley, 1997, 48 pp.

Gregory, Christiana. *The Winter of the Red Snow: The Revolutionary War Diary of Abigail Jane Stewart*. Scholastic, 1996, 167 pp.

Gutelle, Andrew. *Baseball's Best*. Random House, 1990, 48 pp. **N**

•Hanly, Sheila. *The Big Book of Animals*. Dorling Kindersley, 1997, 48 pp. **N**

Harrison, David L. *Rivers: Nature's Wonderous Waterways*. Boyds Mill Press, 2002, 30 pp.

Hermes, Patricia. *The Starving Time. Elizabeth's Diary, Book Two*. Scholastic, 2001, 110 pp.

Hopkinson, Deborah. *Birdie's Lighthouse*. Atheneum, 1997, 29 pp.

Hughes, Carol. *Toots and the Upside-Down House*. Random House, 1996, 143 pp.

Hurwitz, Johanna. *Aldo Applesauce.* Morrow, 1979, 127 pp.

James, Mary. *Shoebag Returns.* Scholastic, 1996, 144 pp.

Kenah, Katharine. *Eggs over Easy.* Dutton, 1993, 84 pp.

•Kerr, Daisy. *Knights & Armor.* Franklin Watts, 1997, 39 pp. **N**

•Kerr, Daisy. *Medieval Town.* Franklin Watts, 1997, 39 pp. **N**

Kimmel, Eric A. *Ten Suns, A Chinese Legend.* Holiday House, 1998, 30 pp.

Kirk, Daniel. *Humpty Dumpty.* Putnam, 2000, 32 pp.

Koller, Jackie French. *Dragons of Krad.* Simon & Schuster, 1997, 88 pp.

Koralek, Jenny (Retold by). *Treasury of Stories from the Brothers Grimm.* Kingfisher, 1996, 157 pp.

Kramer, S. A. *Basketball's Greatest Players.* Random House, 1997, 48 pp. **N**

Kramer, S. A. *Wonder Women of Sports.* Grossett & Dunlap, 1997, 48 pp. **N**

•Krumgold, Joseph. *And Now Miguel.* Crowell, 1953, 245 pp.

Krupinski, Loretta. *The Bluewater Journal, Voyage of the* Sea Tiger. HarperCollins, 1995, 26 pp.

Lauber, Patricia. *You're Aboard Spaceship* Earth. HarperCollins, 1996, 32 pp. **N**

Lears, Laurie. *Becky the Brave.* Whitman, 2002, 28 pp.

Levy, Elizabeth. *A Mammoth Mix-up.* HarperCollins, 1995, 87 pp.

Lindgren, Astrid. *Pippi Longstocking.* Puffin, 1950, 160 pp.

Lottridge, Celia Barker. *The Wind Wagon.* Silver Burdett, 1995, 56 pp.

•MacLachlan, Patricia. *Sarah, Plain and Tall.* HarperCollins, 1985, 58 pp.

McGinty, Alice B. *The Jumping Spider.* Rosen, 2002, 24 pp.

•Mead, Alice. *Junebug.* HarperCollins, 1995, 102 pp.

Minahan, John A. *Abigail's Drum.* Pippin, 1995, 64 pp.

•Moss, Cynthia. *Elephant Woman: Cynthia Moss Explores the World of Elephants.* Atheneum, 1997, 42 pp. **N**

Murphy, Elspeth Campbell. *The Mystery of the Eagle Feather.* Bethany House, 1995, 62 pp.

Murphy, Jim. *West to a Land of Plenty, The Diary of Teresa Angelino Viscardi.* Scholastic, 1998, 204 pp.

Nathan, Emma. *What Do You Call a Group of Hippos? And Other Animal Groups.* Blackbirch, 2000, 24 pp. **N**

Nixon, Joan Lowery. *If You Say So, Claude.* Penguin, 1980, 44 pp.

O'Connor, Jim. *Jackie Robinson and the Story of All-Black Baseball.* Random House, 1989, 48 pp. **N**

•Petty, Kate. *I Didn't Know That the Sun Is a Star and Other Amazing Facts about the Universe.* Copper Beech Books, 1997, 32 pp. **N**

Phillips, Louis. *Keep 'em Laughing. Jokes to Amuse and Annoy Your Friends.* Viking, 1996, 60 pp. **N**

Press, Judy. *The Kids' Natural History Book.* Williamson Publishing, 2000, 144 pp. **N**

Pryor, Bonnie. *Poison Ivy and Eyebrow Wigs.* Morrow, 1993, 162 pp.

Richards, Julie. *Howling Hurricanes.* Chelsea House, 2002, 32 pp. **N**

•Rylant, Cynthia. *The Van Gogh Cafe.* Harcourt, 1995, 53 pp.

•Sachs, Marilyn. *The Bears' House.* Puffin Books, 1971, 67 pp.

Saunders, Susan. *The Curse of the Cat Mummy.* HarperCollins, 1997, 83 pp.

Seabrooke, Brenda. *The Care and Feeding of Dragons.* Dutton, 1998, 120 pp.

Shreve, Susan. *Joshua T. Bates in Trouble Again.* Knopf, 1997, 90 pp.

Simon, Seymour. *Seymour Simon's Book of Trucks.* HarperCollins, 2000, 32 pp. **N**

Singer, Beth Wolfensberger. *Lefty, a Handbook for Left-Handed Kids.* Addison Wesley Longman, 1997, 64 pp. **N**

Sinykin, Sheri Cooper. *The Secret of the Attic.* Magic Attic Press, 1995, 75 pp.

Soto, Gary. *The Cat's Meow.* Scholastic, 1987, 78 pp.

Spinner, Stephanie, & Weiss, Ellen. *The Weebie Zone.* HarperCollins, 1996, 76 pp.

Spyri, Johanna (Retold by Krupinski, Loretta). *Heidi.* HarperCollins, 1996, 30 pp.

•Stoops, Eric D., Martin, Jeffrey L., & Stone, Debbie Lynne. *Whales.* Sterling, 1995, 80 pp. **N**

Taylor, Mildred D. *The Gold Cadillac.* Dial, 1987, 43 pp.

Turner, Ann. *Finding Walter.* Harcourt, Brace, 1997, 161 pp.

Van Laan, Nancy. *In a Circle Long Ago.* Knopf, 1995, 128 pp.

•Walker, Jane. *Fascinating Facts about Volcanoes.* Millbrook Press, 1994, 32 pp. **N**

Wallner, Alexandra. *Laura Ingalls Wilder.* Holiday House, 1997, 32 pp. **N**

Warnock-Kinsey, Natalie, & Kinsey,

Helen. *The Bear That Heard Crying.* Cobblehill/Dutton, 1993, 28 pp.

•White, E. B. *Charlotte's Web.* HarperCollins, 1952, 184 pp.

•Wilder, Laura Ingalls. *Little House in the Big Woods.* HarperCollins, 1932, 238 pp.

•Wilkinson, Philip. *Spacebusters: The Race to the Moon.* Dorling Kindersley, 1998, 48 pp. **N**

Woodruff, Elvira. *Awfully Short for the Fourth Grade.* Bantam Doubleday Dell, 1989, 142 pp.

Challenging Reading Level: Grade 5 (Interest Level: Grade 4)

Avi. *The Barn.* Orchard, 1994, 106 pp.

•Awan, Shaila. *The Burrow Book.* Dorling Kindersley, 1997, 19 pp. **N**

Bateman, Teresa. *The Ring of Truth.* Holiday House, 1997, 28 pp.

Baum, L. Frank. *The Wizard of Oz.* Puffin, 1900, 1988, 188 pp.

Bernhard, Emery, & Bernhard, Durga. *Prairie Dogs.* Harcourt, 1997, 29 pp. **N**

Bishop, Nic. *Animal Flight.* Houghton Mifflin, 1997, 32 pp. **N**

•Dahl, Roald. *James and the Giant Peach.* Puffin, 1961, 126 pp.

•Facklam, Margery. *The Big Bug Book.* Little, Brown, 1994, 32 pp. **N**

Fritz, Jean. *Why Don't You Get a Horse, Sam Adams?* Coward, McCann & Geoghegan, 1974, 48 pp. **N**

Gutman, Bill. *Becoming Your Dog's Best Friend.* Millbrook Press, 1996, 64 pp. **N**

•Henry, Marguerite. *Benjamin West and His Cat Grimalkin.* Macmillan, 1947, 147 pp.

Kipling, Rudyard. *The Jungle Book.* Weathervane Books, 1893, 1964, 213 pp.

Mahy, Margaret. *The Five Sisters.* Viking, 1997, 80 pp.

McCully, Emily Arnold. *The Bobbin Girl.* Dial, 1996, 30 pp.

•McKay, Hilary. *Dog Friday.* Simon & Schuster, 1994, 133 pp.

Palin, Nick. *Nick Palin's Hidden Pictures.* Millbrook Press, 1996, 37 pp. **N**

•Price, Susanna, & Stephens, Tim. *Click! Fun with Photography.* Sterling, 1997, 48 pp. **N**

San Souci, Robert D. *Kate Shelley, Bound for Legend.* Dial, 1995, 28 pp. **N**

Sipiera, Paul P. *Galaxies.* Children's Press, 1997, 48 pp. **N**

•Taylor, Mildred. *Roll of Thunder, Hear My Cry.* Puffin, 1976, 275 pp.

- World Almanac. *The World Almanac for Kids.* World Almanac Books, 2004. **N**

Fifth-Grade Books

Easy Reading Level: Grade 3 (Interest Level: Grade 5)

Adler, David A. *Jeffrey's Ghost and the Fifth-Grade Dragon.* Holt, 1985, 52 pp.

Blatchford, Claire H. *Going with the Flow.* Carolrhoda, 1998, 40 pp.

Bulla, Clyde Robert. *White Bird.* Random House, 1966, 1990, 63 pp.

Cole, Joanna, & Calmeson, Stephanie. *Yours Till Banana Splits.* Morrow, 1995, 64 pp. **N**

Giovanni, Nikki. *Spin a Soft Song* (Rev. ed.). Farrar, Straus, & Giroux, 1985, 57 pp. **N**

Haas, Jessie. *Beware the Mare.* Greenwillow, 1993, 66 pp.

Hamilton, Virginia. *The People Could Fly.* Knopf, 1985, 173 pp.

- Peck, Robert Newton. *Banjo.* Knopf, 1982, 80 pp.

Slote, Alfred. *Finding Buck McHenry.* HarperCollins, 1991, 250 pp.

Easy Reading Level: Grade 4 (Interest Level: Grade 5)

Armstrong, Jennifer. *Black-Eyed Susan.* Crown, 1995, 120 pp.

Banim, Lisa. *A Spy in the King's Colony.* Silver Moon Press, 1994, 76 pp.

Belton, Sandra. *Ernestine, & Amanda, Members of the C. L. U. B.* Simon & Schuster, 1997, 161 pp.

- Bledsoe, Lucy Jane. *Tracks in the Snow.* Holiday House, 1997, 152 pp.

Boyd, Candy Dawson. *Chevrolet Saturdays.* Penguin, 1995, 176 pp.

Bryan, Ashley. *Ashley Bryan's ABC of African American Poetry.* Atheneum, 1997, 26 pp. **N**

Bunting, Eve. *The In-Between Days.* HarperCollins, 1994, 119 pp.

- Byars, Betsy. *The Pinballs.* HarperCollins, 1977, 136 pp.

Byars, Betsy. *Cracker Jackson.* Puffin, 1985, 146 pp.

Clyne, Densey. *Flutter by, Butterfly.* Gareth Stevens, 1998, 32 pp. **N**

Cohen, Barbara. *Thank You, Jackie Robinson.* Lothrop, Lee & Shepard, 1974, 125 pp.

Coville, Bruce. *I Left My Sneakers in Dimension X.* Pocket Books, 1994, 180 pp.

DeClements, Barthe. *Nothing Is Fair in Fifth Grade.* Penguin, 1990, 137 pp.

DeClements, Barthe. *The Bite of the*

Gold Bug, A Story of the Alaskan Gold Rush. Viking, 1992, 56 pp.

England, Linda. *3 Kids Dreamin'.* Simon & Schuster, 1997, 30 pp.

Etra, Jonathan, & Spinner, Stephanie. *Aliens for Lunch.* Random House, 1991, 64 pp.

Gilson, Jamie. *Wagon Train 911.* Lothrop, Lee & Shepard, 1996, 189 pp.

Greenburg, Dan. *The Zack Files: My Son the Time Traveler.* Grossett & Dunlap, 1997, 57 pp.

Gutman, Dan. *Honus & Me.* Avon, 1997, 138 pp.

Haas, Jessie. *Be Well, Beware.* Greenwillow, 1996, 66 pp.

Hamm, Diane Johnston. *Daughter of Suqua.* Whitman, 1997, 154 pp.

Hendry, Diana. *Kid Kibble.* Candlewick Press. 1992, 1994, 80 pp.

Herman, Hank. *Super Hoops Rebound!* Bantam, 1998, 85 pp.

Hest, Amy. *Private Notebook of Katie Roberts, Age 11.* Candlewick Press, 1995, 75 pp.

Hildick, E. W. *The Case of the Absent Author.* Simon & Schuster, 1995, 151 pp.

Hoobler, Dorothy, & Hoobler, Thomas. *Julie Meyer: The Story of a Wagon Train Girl.* Silver, 1997, 124 pp.

Howe, James. *Bunnicula.* Avon, 1979, 98 pp.

Hurwitz, Johanna. *The Up and Down Spring.* Morrow, 1993, 103 pp.

Kalman, Esther. *Tchaikovsky Discovers America.* Orchard, 1994, 32 pp.

Klise, Kate. *Regarding the Fountain, A Tale in Letters, of Liars and Leaks.* Avon, 1998, 138 pp.

- Levy, Elizabeth. *My Life as a Fifth-Grade Comedian.* HarperCollins, 1997, 184 pp.

Lowell, Susan. *I Am Lavina Cumming.* Milkweed Editions, 1993, 198 pp.

Marschall, Ken. *Inside the* Titanic. Little, Brown, 1997, 31 pp. **N**

McSwigan, Marie. *Snow Treasure.* Scholastic, 1942, 156 pp.

Moiss, Marissa. *Rachel's Journal, The Story of a Pioneer Girl.* Harcourt, 1998, 44 pp.

- Myers, Walter Dean. *Mop, Moondance, and the Nagasaki Knights.* Bantam Doubleday Dell, 1992, 150 pp.

- Naylor, Phyllis Reynolds. *Shiloh.* Dell, 1991, 144 pp.

- O'Dell, Scott. *Island of the Blue Dolphins.* Houghton Mifflin, 1960, 192 pp.

Oliver, Diana. *McCracken's Class,*

Tough Luck, Ronnie. Random House, 1994, 124 pp.

Paulsen, Gary. *Mr. Tucket.* Delacorte, 1994, 166 pp.

- Paulsen, Gary. *My Life in Dog Years.* Delacorte Press, 1998, 137 pp. **N**

- Pearson, Kit. *Awake and Dreaming.* Viking, 1996, 228 pp.

Pfeffer, Susan Beth. *Devil's Den.* Walker, 1998, 115 pp.

Phillips, Louis. *School Daze. Jokes Your Teacher Will Hate.* Viking, 1994, 58 pp. **N**

Porter, Tracey. *Treasures in the Dust.* HarperCollins, 1997, 148 pp.

Prelutsky, Jack. *A Pizza the Size of the Sun: Poems by Jack Prelutsky.* Greenwillow, 1996, 159 pp. **N**

Roop, Peter, & Roop, Connie. *Ahyoka and the Talking Leaves.* Lothrop, Lee & Shepard, 1992, 60 pp.

Sachar, Louis. *There's a Boy in the Girls' Bathroom.* Random House, 1987, 195 pp.

- Spinelli, Jerry. *Wringer.* HarperCollins, 1997, 229 pp.

Strasser, Todd. *Kidnap Kids.* Putnam, 1998, 166 pp.

Tamar, Erika. *The Junkyard Dog.* Knopf, 1995, 185 pp.

Thomas, Joyce Carol. *I Have Heard of a Land.* HarperCollins, 1998, 27 pp.

Van Leewen, Loretta. *Blue Sky, Butterfly.* Dial, 1996, 125 pp.

- Walton, Darwin McBeth. *Dance, Kayla!* Whitman, 1998, 155 pp.

- Willner-Pardo, Gina. *Jason and the Losers.* Clarion, 1995, 120 pp.

Average Reading Level: Grade 5 (Interest Level: Grade 5)

Anderson, William. *Laura Ingalls Wilder: A Biography.* HarperCollins, 1992, 240 pp. **N**

Armstrong, Jennifer. *Black-Eyed Susan.* Crown, 1995, 120 pp.

Arnold, Caroline. *Did You Hear That?* Charlesbridge, 2001, 30 pp. **N**

Arnosky, Jim. *All about Rattlesnakes.* Scholastic, 1997, 22 pp. **N**

Arnosky, Jim. *Watching Water Birds.* National Geographic, 1997, 28 pp. **N**

Auch, Mary Jane. *Journey to Nowhere.* Holt, 1997, 202 pp.

Avi. *Poppy.* Camelot, 1995, 160 pp.

Banks, Lynne Reid. *The Indian in the Cupboard.* Doubleday, 1980, 181 pp.

Barrett, Tracy. *Growing Up in Colonial America.* Millbrook Press, 1995, 96 pp. **N**

Barrie, J. M. *Peter Pan.* Bantam, 1911, 168 pp.

- Bentley, Nancy, & Guthrie, Donna.

Putting on a Play. Millbrook Press, 1996, 64 pp. **N**

Betancourt, Jeanne. *My Name is Brain Brian.* Scholastic, 1993, 128 pp.

Birdseye, Tom. *Just Call Me Stupid.* Holiday House, 1993, 181 pp.

•Brink, Carol Ryrie. *Caddie Woodlawn.* Macmillan, 1933, 275 pp.

Bryan, Jenny. *Your Amazing Brain.* Joshua Morris Publishing, 1995, 17 pp. **N**

•Byars, Betsy. *The TV Kid.* Puffin Books, 1976, 123 pp.

•Byars, Betsy. *The Pinballs.* HarperCollins, 1977, 136 pp.

Christopher, Matt. *Baseball Jokes and Riddles.* Little, Brown, 1996, 45 pp. **N**

Cleary, Beverly. *The Mouse and the Motorcycle.* Morrow, 1965, 160 pp.

•Cleary, Beverly. *Dear Mr. Henshaw.* Morrow, 1983, 133 pp.

Conrad, Pam. *Pedro's Journal: A Voyage with Christopher Columbus, August 3, 1492–February 14, 1493.* Boyd's Mill Press, 1991, 81 pp.

Coville, Bruce. *Jennifer Murdley's Toad.* Harcourt Brace, 1992, 148 pp.

Cummings, Pat. *Talking with Artists, Volume Two.* Simon & Schuster, 1995, 96 pp. **N**

Curtis, Christopher Paul. *Bud, Not Buddy.* Delacorte, 1999, 245 pp.

Dahl, Roald. *Charlie and the Chocolate Factory.* Penguin, 1964, 162 pp.

Dudley, Karen. *Giant Pandas.* Raintree Steck-Vaughn, 1997, 64 pp. **N**

Engel, Dean, & Freedman, Florence B. *Ezra Jack Keats, A Biography with Illustrations.* Silver Moon Press, 1995, 81 pp. **N**

Fitzgerald, John D. *The Great Brain.* Bantam Doubleday Dell, 1967, 174 pp.

Fleschman, Sid. *The Whipping Boy.* Greenwillow, 1986, 89 pp.

•Ford, Harry, & Barnham, Kay. *Outer Space.* Zigzag Multimedia (Smithmark Publishers), 1997, 32 pp. **N**

Fritz, Jean. *Homesick: My Own Story.* Putnam, 1982, 163 pp. **N**

•Giff, Patricia Reilly. *Lily's Crossing.* Delacorte, 1997, 180 pp.

•Greenberg, Keith. *Risky Business, Storm Chaser: Into the Eye of a Hurricane.* Blackbirch Press, 1998, 32 pp. **N**

Greenlaw, M. Jean. *Welcome to the Stock Show.* Lodestar, 1997, 48 pp. **N**

Henkes, Kevin. *Sun and Spoon.* Greenwillow, 1997, 135 pp.

Hildick, E. W. *The Purloined Corn Popper, A Felicity Snell Mystery.* Marshall Cavendish, 1997, 158 pp.

Horvath, Polly. *When the Circus Came to Town.* Farrar, Straus & Giroux, 1996, 138 pp.

Hutton, Warwick. *The Trojan Horse.* Simon & Schuster, 1992, 30 pp.

Johnson, Jinny. *Children's Guide to Birds.* Simon & Schuster, 1996, 96 pp. **N**

Johnston, Tony. *The Wagon.* Tambourine, 1996, 28 pp.

Johnstone, Michael. *The History News, Explorers.* Candlewick Press, 1997, 32 pp. **N**

•Kent, Peter. *Quest for the West: In Search of Gold.* Millbrook Press, 1997, 32 pp. **N**

Kindersley, Barnabas, & Kindersley, Anabel. *Children Just Like Me.* Dorling Kindersley, 1995, 80 pp. **N**

Kindersley, Barnabas, & Kindersley, Anabel. *Children Just Like Me, Celebrations.* Dorling Kindersley, 1997, 80 pp. **N**

•King-Smith, Dick. *Babe the Gallant Pig.* Random House, 1983, 118 pp.

•Knight, Eric. *Lassie Come Home.* Dell, 1940, 230 pp.

Konigsburg, E. L. *From the Mixed-Up Files of Mrs. Basil E. Frankweiler.* Atheneum, 1967, 162 pp.

Lasky, Kathryn. *Hercules: The Man, the Myth, the Hero.* Hyperion, 1997, 30 pp.

Lester, Julius, & Pinkney, Jerry. *Black Cowboy, Wild Horses.* Dial, 1998, 38 pp.

Lisle, Janet Taylor. *The Gold Dust Letters.* Avon, 1994, 116 pp.

Little, Jean. *The Belonging Place.* Viking, 1997, 124 pp.

Lofting, Hugh. *Voyages of Doctor Dolittle.* Bantam Doubleday Dell, 1922, 311 pp.

Lord, Betty Bao. *In the Year of the Boar and Jackie Robinson.* HarperCollins, 1984, 169 pp.

Loves, June. *Airplanes.* Chelsea House, 2001, 32 pp. **N**

Lowry, Lois. *Number the Stars.* Houghton Mifflin, 1989, 137 pp.

Macdonald, Fiona. *The World in the Time of Marco Polo.* Chelsea, 2001, 48 pp. **N**

Mann, Elizabeth. *The Great Pyramid.* Mikya Press, 1996, 48 pp. **N**

Markle, Sandra. *Outside and Inside Sharks.* Atheneum, 1996, 40 pp. **N**

Martin, James. *Tentacles, the Amazing World of Octopuses, Squid, and their Relatives.* Crown, 1993, 32 pp. **N**

McEvey, Shane F. *Beetles.* Chelsea House, 2001, 32 pp. **N**

McKissack, Patricia C. *Run Away Home.* Scholastic, 1997, 160 pp.

Myers, Jack. *Highlights Book of Science Questions That Children Ask.* Boyds Mill Press, 1995, 251 pp. **N**

Norton, Mary. *The Borrowers.* Harcourt Brace, 1953, 180 pp.

O'Brien, Patrick. *Megatooth.* Holt, 2001, 30 pp. **N**

Parker, Steve. *The Body.* Gareth Stevens, 1998, 68 pp. **N**

Polacco, Patricia. *Thank You, Mr. Falker.* Philomel, 1998, 36 pp. **N**

Rawls, Wilson. *Where the Red Fern Grows.* Doubleday, 1961, 212 pp.

•Rosen, Michael. *Walking the Bridge of Your Nose: Wordplay Poems and Rhymes.* Kingfisher, 1995, 61 pp. **N**

Ross, Michael Elshon. *Wormology.* Carolrhoda Books, 1996, 48 pp. **N**

Rudy, Lisa Jo. (Ed.). *Ben Franklin Book of Easy Incredible Experiments.* John Wiley & Sons, 1995, 131 pp. **N**

Sakurai, Gail. *Paul Revere.* Children's Press, 1997, 32 pp. **N**

San Souci, Robert D. *Young Arthur.* Doubleday, 1996, 28 pp.

San Souci, Robert D. *Young Lancelot.* Doubleday, 1996, 28 pp.

•Sewell, Anna. *Black Beauty.* Scholastic, 1877, 245 pp.

Siebold, Jan. *Rope Burn.* Whitman, 1998, 82 pp.

Simon, Seymour. *Einstein Anderson Science Detective, The On-Line Spaceman and Other Cases.* Morrow, 1997, 92 pp.

Souza, D. M. *Northern Lights.* Carolrhoda Books, 1994, 48 pp. **N**

Spyri, Johanna. *Heidi.* Scholastic, 1959, 234 pp.

Stengel, Joyce A. *Letting Go.* Poolbeg, 1997, 110 pp.

Stolz, Mary. *Stealing Home.* HarperCollins, 1992, 153 pp.

•Stoops, Eric D., Martin, Jeffrey L., & Stone, Debbie Lynne. *Dolphins.* Sterling, 1996, 80 pp. **N**

Swanson, Diane. *Buffalo Sunrise, The Story of a North American Giant.* Random House, 1996, 58 pp. **N**

Thomas, Joyce Carol. *I Have Heard of a Land.* HarperCollins, 1998, 27 pp.

Travers, P. L. *Mary Poppins.* Harcourt, 1934, 206 pp.

Tym, Wanda. *The Illustrated Rules of Tennis.* Hambleton-Hill, 1995, 32 pp. **N**

Ure, Jean. *The Children Next Door.* Scholastic, 1994, 135 pp.

Venezia, Mike. *Getting to Know the World's Greatest Composers: Ludwig Van Beethoven.* Children's Press, 1996, 32 pp. **N**

Viola, Herman J. *After Columbus: The Horse's Return to America.* Soundprints, 1992, 32 pp. **N**

Warren, Andrea. *Orphan Train Rider: One Boy's True Story.* Houghton Mifflin, 1996, 80 pp. **N**

Wechsler, Doug. *Bizarre Bugs.* Dutton, 1995, 35 pp. **N**

Williams, Nick. *How Birds Fly.* Benchmark Books, 1997, 32 pp. **N**

Woodruff, Elvira. *The Summer I Shrank My Grandmother.* Bantam Doubleday Dell, 1990, 153 pp.

Woodruff, Elvira. *The Magnificent Mummy Maker.* Scholastic, 1994, 132 pp.

Challenging Reading Level: Grade 6 (Interest Level: Grade 5)

Ballard, Carol. *The Heart and Circulatory System.* Steck-Vaughn, 1997, 48 pp. **N**

Bay, Ann Phillips. *A Kid's Guide to the Smithsonian.* Smithsonian Institution Press, 1996, 155 pp. **N**

Bray, Rosemary. *Martin Luther King.* Greenwillow, 1995, 40 pp. **N**

Christian, Mary Blount. *Sebastian (Super Sleuth) and the Copycat Crime.* Macmillan, 1993, 62 pp.

Darling, Kathy. *Komodo Dragon on Location.* Lothrop, Lee & Shepard, 1997, 40 pp. **N**

Erickson, Paul. *Daily Life in the Pilgrim Colony.* Clarion, 2001, 48 pp. **N**

Hall, Elizabeth. *Child of the Wolves.* Houghton Mifflin, 1996, 160 pp.

Issacs, Anne. *Treehouse Tales.* Dutton, 1997, 85 pp.

Johnson, Jinny. *Children's Guide to Insects and Spiders.* Simon & Schuster, 1996, 80 pp. **N**

Lewis, C. S. *The Lion, the Witch, and the Wardrobe.* HarperCollins, 1950, 189 pp.

•Markle, Sandra. *Discovering Graph Secrets.* Atheneum, 1997, 36 pp. **N**

Parsons, Alexandra. *Electricity.* World Book, 1997, 48 pp. **N**

Richards, Jon. *What If . . . Sharks?* Copper Beech Books, 1996, 32 pp. **N**

Simon, Seymour. *The Heart, Our Circulatory System.* Morrow, 1996, 29 pp. **N**

Spinelli, Jerry. *Knots in My Yo-yo String.* Knopf, 1998, 148 pp. **N**

Stein, R. Conrad. *The Pilgrims.* Children's Press, 1995, 32 pp. **N**

Taylor, Barbara. *Animal Homes.* Dorling Kindersley, 1996, 44 pp. **N**

Tesar, Jenny. *America's Top 10 Rivers.* Blackbirch Press, 1998, 24 pp. **N**

Tomecek, Steve. *Bouncing and Bending.* Freeman, 1995, 48 pp. **N**

Wallace, Barbara Brooks. *The Twin in the Tavern.* Aladdin, 1993, 177 pp.

Weitzman, David. *Old Ironsides, Americans Build a Fighting Ship.* Houghton Mifflin, 1997, 32 pp.

•Williams, Brian. *Ancient China.* Viking, 1996, 48 pp. **N**

Challenging Reading Level: Grade 7 (Interest Level: Grade 5)

•Aiken, Joan. *The Wolves of Willoughby Chase.* Dell, 1962, 168 pp.

Anderson, Dave. *The Story of Football.* Morrow, 1997, 160 pp. **N**

•Burnett, Frances Hodgson. *The Secret Garden.* HarperCollins, 1912, 224 pp.

Collier, Christopher, & Collier, James Lincoln. *The American Revolution.* Marshall Cavendish, 1998, 95 pp. **N**

Kipling, Rudyard. *Just So Stories.* New American Library, 1912, 158 pp.

Lessem, Don. *Supergiants! The Biggest Dinosaurs.* Little, Brown, 1997, 32 pp. **N**

Sixth-Grade Books

Easy Reading Level: Grade 4 (Interest Level: Grade 6)

Boulais, Sue, & Marvis, Barbara. *Tommy Nunez.* Mitchell Lane, 1998, 32 pp. **N**

•Bunting, Eve. *The Waiting Game.* Lippincott, 1981, 56 pp.

•Byars, Betsy. *Summer of the Swans.* Viking, 1970, 142 pp.

Coerr, Eleanor. *Sadako and the Thousand Paper Cranes.* Bantam Doubleday Dell, 1977, 64 pp.

Coville, Bruce. *Aliens Ate My Homework.* Simon & Schuster, Avon, 1993, 179 pp.

Fitzhugh, Louise. *Harriet the Spy.* HarperCollins, 1964, 298 pp.

Gantos, Jack. *Heads or Tails: Stories from the Sixth Grade.* Farrar, Straus & Giroux, 1994, 151 pp.

MacLachlan, Patricia. *Journey.* Delacorte, 1991, 83 pp.

•Mills, Claudia. *Losers, Inc.* HarperCollins, 1997, 150 pp.

•Paulsen, Gary. *Hatchet.* Simon & Schuster, 1987, 195 pp.

•Spinelli, Jerry. *Crash.* Knopf, 1996, 162 pp.

Stolz, Mary. *Explorer of Barkham Street.* HarperCollins, 1985, 179 pp.

Strasser, Todd. *Help! I'm Trapped in the First Day of School.* Scholastic, 1994, 114 pp.

Easy Reading Level: Grade 5 (Interest Level: Grade 6)

•Armstrong, William H. *Sounder.* HarperCollins, 1969, 116 pp.

•Balgassi, Haemi. *Tae's Sonata.* Clarion, 1997, 123 pp.

Byars, Betsy. *The Moon and I.* Julian Messner, 1991, 96 pp. **N**

Conlon-McKenna, Marita. *Fields of Home.* Holiday House, 1996, 189 pp.

Deaver, Julie Reece. *Chicago Blues.* HarperCollins, 1995, 170 pp.

Dygard, Thomas J. *Infield Hit.* Morrow, 1995, 149 pp.

Fleischman, Sid. *The Thirteenth Floor: A Ghost Story.* Greenwillow, 1995, 131 pp.

Fletcher, Ralph. *Spider Boy.* Houghton Mifflin, 1997, 180 pp.

Franklin, Kristine L. *Nerd No More.* Candlewick Press, 1996, 143 pp.

George, Jean C. *My Side of the Mountain.* Dutton, 1959, 177 pp.

Getz, David. *Thin Air.* Holt, 1990, 120 pp.

•Gipson, Fred. *Old Yeller.* HarperCollins, 1956, 158 pp.

•Haddix, Margaret Peterson. *Running Out of Time.* Simon & Schuster, 1995, 184 pp.

Harrison, Michael. *It's My Life.* Holiday House, 1997, 132 pp.

Hesse, Karen. *Out of the Dust.* Scholastic, 1997, 227 pp.

High, Linda Oatman. *Hound Heaven.* Holiday House, 1995, 194 pp.

Hurwitz, Johanna. *The Down and Up Fall.* Morrow, 1996, 165 pp.

•Kehret, Peg. *Small Steps: The Year I Got Polio.* Whitman, 1996, 179 pp. **N**

Lowry, Lois. *Anastasia, Absolutely.* Houghton Mifflin, 1995, 119 pp.

McKean, Thomas. *My Evil Twin.* Avon, 1997, 151 pp.

Merrill, Jean. *The Pushcart War.* Bantam Doubleday Dell, 1964, 223 pp.

Neufeld, John. *Almost a Hero.* Atheneum, 1995, 147 pp.

•Nixon, Joan Lowery. *Orphan Train Adventures: The Circle of Love.* Delacorte, 1997, 167 pp.

•O'Leary, Patsy Baker. *With Wings as Eagles.* Houghton Mifflin, 1997, 262 pp.

•Paulsen, Gary. *Woodsong.* Puffin, 1991, 132 pp. **N**

Pfitsch, Patricia Curtis. *Keeper of the Light.* Simon & Schuster, 1997, 136 pp.

- Slepian, Jan. *Back to Before*. Philomel, 1993, 170 pp.
- Smith, Roland. *Sasquatch*. Hyperion, 1998, 188 pp.
- Spinelli, Jerry. *Maniac Magee*. HarperCollins, 1990, 184 pp.
- Taylor, Theodore. *The Cay*. Avon, 1969, 144 pp.
- Wilson, Nancy Hope. *Flapjack Waltzes*. Farrar, Straus & Giroux, 1998, 134 pp.

**Average Reading Level: Grade 6
(Interest Level: Grade 6)**

Alcott, Louisa May. *Little Women*. Viking, 1868, 1997, 285 pp.

Applegate, Catherine. *The Story of Two American Generals, Benjamin O. Davis, Jr., Colin L. Powell*. Gareth Stevens, 1995, 108 pp. **N**

Bailey, Jill. *How Spiders Make Their Webs*. Benchmark Books, 1997, 32 pp. **N**

Birdseye, Tom. *Tucker*. Holiday House, 1990, 112 pp.

Boyd, Aaron. *Great Athletes: Tiger Woods*. Morgan Reynolds, 1997, 64 pp. **N**

Burleigh, Robert. *Black Whiteness, Admiral Byrd Alone in the Antarctic*. Simon & Schuster, 1998, 36 pp. **N**

Burton, John A. *The Changing World, Jungles and Rainforests*. Thunder Bay Press, 1996, 73 pp. **N**

Carroll, Lewis. *Alice's Adventures in Wonderland*. Holt, Rinehart & Winston, 1865, 122 pp.

Coville, Bruce. *Jeremy Thatcher, Dragon Hatcher*. Pocket Books, 1991, 148 pp.

Duffey, Betsy. *Fur-ever Yours, Booker Jones*. Viking, 2001, 100 pp.

Ellis, Veronica Freeman. *Wynton Marsalis*. Raintree Steck-Vaughn, 1997, 48 pp. **N**

Finlayson, Reggie. *Colin Powell*. Lerner Publications, 1997, 64 pp. **N**

Forbes, Esther. *Johnny Tremain*. Houghton Mifflin, 1943, 256 pp.

- Fox, Paula. *One-Eyed Cat*. Bantam Doubleday Dell, 1984, 216 pp.

Freedman, Russell. *Out of Darkness*. Houghton Mifflin, 1997, 81 pp. **N**

Fritz, Jean. *Bully for You, Teddy Roosevelt*. Scholastic, 1991, 127 pp. **N**

George, Jean Craighead. *Julie of the Wolves*. HarperCollins, 1972, 170 pp.

- Henderson, Eileen Kilgore. *The Summer of the Bonepile Monster*. Milkweed, 1995, 138 pp.

Hill, David. *Take It Easy*. Dutton, 1995, 163 pp.

Hoyt-Goldsmith, Diane. *Lacrosse, the National Game of the Iroquois*. Holiday House, 1998, 32 pp. **N**

Hudson, Wade. *Five Brave Explorers*. Scholastic, 1995, 48 pp. **N**

Jeffrey, Laura S. *Guion Bluford: A Space Biography*. Enslow, 1998, 48 pp. **N**

Jennings, Patrick. *The Beastly Arms*. Scholastic, 2001, 314 pp.

Johnstone, Michael. *The History News, Medicine*. Candlewick Press, 1997, 32 pp. **N**

Jones, Charlotte Foltz. *Accidents May Happen, Fifty Inventions Discovered by Mistake*. Delacorte, 1996, 86 pp. **N**

Juster, Norton. *The Phantom Toll Booth*. Knopf, 1961, 256 pp.

Kelley, Brent. *James Madison*. Chelsea House, 2001, 90 pp. **N**

Kelly, J. *Superstars of Women's Basketball*. Chelsea House, 1997, 64 pp. **N**

Kerrod, Robin. *Weather*. Gareth Stevens, 1998, 68 pp. **N**

King, Casey, & Osborne, Linda Barrett. *Oh Freedom!* Knopf, 1998, 137 pp.

Klise, Kate. *Trial by Jury Journal*. HarperCollins, 2001, 238 pp.

L'Engle, Madeline. *A Wrinkle in Time*. Bantam Doubleday Dell, 1962, 190 pp.

Levine, Gail Carson. *Ella Enchanted*. HarperCollins, 1997, 232 pp.

Macdonald, Fiona. *Step into the Celtic World*. Annes, 1999, 64 pp. **N**

Macdonald, Fiona. *The World in the Time of Abraham Lincoln*. Chelsea House, 2001, 48 pp. **N**

Morey, Janet, & Dunn, Wendy. *Famous Hispanic Americans*. Dutton, 1996, 190 pp. **N**

- Morley, Jacqueline, & Antram, David. *Exploring North America*. Peter Bedrick, 1996, 48 pp. **N**

Morris, Neil. *Ships*. Silver Burdett Press, 1997, 32 pp. **N**

O'Brien, Robert C. *Mrs. Frisby and the Rats of NIMH*. Aladdin, 1971, 233 pp.

O'Donoghue, Michael. *Rocks and Minerals*. Thunder Bay Press, 1994, 32 pp. **N**

Osborne, Mary Pope. *Favorite Medieval Tales*. Scholastic, 1998, 86 pp.

- Paterson, Katherine. *The Great Gilly Hopkins*. HarperCollins, 1978, 148 pp.

Paterson, Katherine. *Jacob Have I Loved*. HarperCollins, 1980, 244 pp.

Peck, Richard. *The Great Interactive Dream Machine*. Dial, 1996, 149 pp.

Pernoud, Regine. *A Day with a Noblewoman*. Lerner, 1997, 48 pp. **N**

Peterson, Melissa. *Hasta La Vista, Blarney, A Carmen Sandiego Mystery*. HarperCollins, 1997, 136 pp.

- Presnall, Judith Janda. *Circuses: Under the Big Top*. Franklin Watts, 1996, 63 pp. **N**

Regan, Dian Curtis. *Monsters in Cyberspace*. Holt, 1997, 178 pp.

Riehecky, Janet. *Irish Americans*. Marshall Cavendish, 1995, 80 pp. **N**

Rootes, David. *Exploration into the Polar Regions*. Chelsea House, 2001, 48 pp. **N**

Ross, Michael Elsohn. *Bug Watching with Charles Henry Turner*. Carolrhoda, 1997, 48 pp. **N**

- Sachar, L. *Holes*. Farrar, Straus & Giroux, 1998, 233 pp.

St. George, Judith. *Sacagawea*. Putnam, 1997, 115 pp. **N**

Savage, Jeff. *Tiger Woods, King of the Course*. Lerner, 1998, 64 pp. **N**

Simmons, Alex. *Denzel Washington*. Raintree Steck-Vaughn, 1997, 48 pp. **N**

Smith, Linda Wasmer. *Louis Pasteur, Disease Fighter*. Enslow, 1997, 128 pp. **N**

Snyder, Zilpha Keatley. *Gib Rides Home*. Delacorte Press, 1998, 246 pp.

Stanley, Diane. *The True Adventures of Daniel Hall*. Dial, 1995, 36 pp.

Stein, R. Conrad. *The Underground Railroad*. Children's Press, 1997, 32 pp. **N**

Streissguth, Thomas. *Raoul Wallenberg*. Rosen, 2001, 112 pp. **N**

Tank, Shelly. *The Buried City of Pompeii*. Heparin/Madison, 1997, 48 pp. **N**

Tashjian, Janet. *Tru Confessions*. Holt, 1997, 167 pp.

Taylor, Leighton. *Creeps from the Deep*. Chronicle Books, 1997, 45 pp. **N**

Yeoman, John. *The Seven Voyages of Sinbad the Sailor*. Simon & Schuster, 1997, 112 pp.

**Challenging Reading Level: Grade 7
(Interest Level: Grade 6)**

Aaseng, Nathan. *Meat-Eating Plants*. Enslow, 1996, 48 pp. **N**

Ash, Russell. *Incredible Comparisons*. Dorling Kindersley, 1996, 63 pp. **N**

- Blos, Joan W. *A Gathering of Days*. Aladdin, 1979, 144 pp.

Bonar, Samantha. *Comets*. Franklin Watts, 1998, 64 pp. **N**

Brook, Donna. *The Journey of English.* Clarion, 1998, 47 pp. **N**

Bumford, Sheila. *The Incredible Journey.* Bantam, 1961, 145 pp.

Burnie, David. *Dictionary of Nature.* Dorling Kindersley, 1994, 192 pp. **N**

•Christian, Spencer, & Felix, Antonia. *Can It Really Rain Frogs? The World's Strangest Weather Events.* Wiley, 1997, 121 pp. **N**

Cooper, Susan. *The Boggart.* Simon & Schuster, 1995, 196 pp.

Curtis, Patricia. *Animals You Never Even Heard Of.* Sierra Club Books, 1997, 32 pp. **N**

Dickinson, Joan D. *Bill Gates: Billionaire Computer Genius.* Enslow Publishers, 1997, 104 pp. **N**

•Freedman, Russell. *Lincoln, A Photobiography.* Clarion, 1987, 150 pp. **N**

Granfield, Linda. *In Flanders Field, The Story of the Poem by John McCrae.* Doubleday, 1995, 32 pp. **N**

Hanly, Sheila. *Amazing Bugs.* Dorling Kindersley, 1996, 44 pp. **N**

Hoobler, Dorothy, & Hoobler, Thomas. *Mexican American Family Album.* Oxford University Press, 1994, 128 pp. **N**

Hoobler, Dorothy, & Hoobler, Thomas. *Irish American Family Album.* Oxford University Press, 1995, 128 pp. **N**

Kent, Deborah, & Quinlan, Kathryn. *Extraordinary People with Disabilities.* Children's Press, 1996. 288 pp. **N**

Kessler, Brad. *Moses in Egypt.* Simon & Schuster, 1997, 33 pp. **N**

King, Martin Luther, Jr. *I Have a Dream.* Scholastic, 1997, 40 pp. **N**

Kittinger, Jo S. *A Look at Rocks, From Coal to Kimberlite.* Franklin Watts, 1997, 63 pp. **N**

•Konigsburg, E. L. *The View from Saturday.* Atheneum, 1996, 163 pp.

Langley, Andrew. *Medieval Life.* Dorling Kindersley, 1996, 64 pp. **N**

Lowry, Lois. *The Giver.* Bantam Doubleday Dell, 1993, 180 pp.

Mann, Elizabeth. *The Great Wall.* Mikya Press, 1997, 48 pp. **N**

Mason, Antony. *If You Were There, Viking Times.* Simon & Schuster, 1997, 32 pp. **N**

Medearis, Angela Shelf. *Princess of the Press, The Story of Ida B. Wells-Barnett.* Dutton, 1997, 58 pp. **N**

Meigs, Cornelia. *Invincible Louisa.* Little, Brown, 1933, 195 pp. **N**

Meltzer, Milton. *Hold Your Horses! A Feedbag Full of Fact and Fable.* HarperCollins, 1995, 133 pp. **N**

Moy, Tina. *Chinese Americans.* Marshall Cavendish, 1995, 80 pp. **N**

Murdoch, David, & Baquedano, Elizabeth. *American Peoples.* Dorling Kindersley, 1996, 128 pp. **N**

Parker, Steve. *20th Century Inventions: Satellites.* Steck-Vaughn, 1997, 48 pp. **N**

Potter, Joan, & Claytor, Constance. *African Americans Who Were First.* Dutton, 1997, 116 pp. **N**

Putnam, James, & Hart, George. *Ancient Egyptians.* Dorling Kindersley, 1996, 128 pp. **N**

•Sperry, Armstrong. *Call It Courage.* Macmillan, 1940, 95 pp.

Taylor, Barbara. *Incredible Plants.* Dorling Kindersley, 1997, 44 pp. **N**

Weber, Michael. *Battlefields across America, Yorktown.* Holt, 1997, 64 pp. **N**

Wiggin, Kate Douglas. *Rebecca of Sunnybrook Farm.* Bantam Doubleday Dell, 1903, 252 pp.

Seventh & Eighth-Grade Books

Easy Reading Level: Grade 5 (Interest Level: Grades 7–8)

Ayers, Katherine. *North by Night: A Story of the Underground Railroad.* Delacorte, 1998, 176 pp. **N**

Byars, Betsy. *Disappearing Acts.* Viking, 1998, 120 pp.

Duffey, Betsy. *Utterly Yours, Booker Jones.* Viking, 1995, 116 pp.

Easy Reading Level: Grade 6 (Interest Level: Grades 7–8)

Atkin, S. Beth. *Voices from the Fields: Children of Migrant Farm Workers Tell Their Stories.* Little, Brown, 1993, 96 pp. **N**

Collier, James L. *My Brother Sam Is Dead.* Scholastic, 1974, 216 pp.

Crist-Evans, Craig. *Moon over Tennessee: A Boy's Civil War Journal.* Houghton Mifflin, 1999, 60 pp.

Fleischman, Paul. *A Joyful Noise: Poems for Two Voices.* HarperCollins, 1993, 102 pp.

Fleischman, Paul. *Bull Run.* HarperCollins, 1995, 104 pp.

Peck, Richard. *A Year Down Yonder.* Dial Books, 2000, 230 pp.

Roop, Connie. *Girl of the Shining Mountains: Sacagawea's Story.* Hyperion, 1999, 178 pp. **N**

Average Reading Level: Grades 7–8 (Interest Level: Grades 7–8)

Armstrong, Jennifer. *Shipwreck at the Bottom of the World: The Extraordinary True Story of Shackleton and the Endurance.* Crown, 1998, 131 pp. **N**

Armstrong, Jennifer. *In My Hands: Memories of a Holocaust Rescuer.* Knopf, 1999, 276 pp. **N**

Aronson, Virginia. *Ethan Allen, Revolutionary Hero.* Chelsea House, 2001, 80 pp. **N**

Aseng, Nathan. *You Are the President II.* Oliver Press, 1994, 160 pp.

Barney, William L. *The Civil War and Reconstruction, A Student Companion.* Oxford, 2001, 368 pp. **N**

Bartoletti, Susan Campbell. *Growing Up in Coal Country.* Houghton Mifflin, 1996, 127 pp. **N**

Batten, Mary. *Anthropologist, Scientist of the People.* Houghton Mifflin, 2001, 64 pp. **N**

Bonnet, Bob, & Keen, Dan. *Science Fair Projects, Physics.* Sterling, 2000, 96 pp. **N**

Bonvillain, Nancy. *The Sac and Fox.* Chelsea House, 1995, 110 pp. **N**

Bradbury, Ray. *Dandelion Wine.* Bantam, 1957, 239 pp.

Brennan, Kristine. *Crazy Horse.* Chelsea House, 2002, 64 pp. **N**

Buller, Laura. *Native Americans, An Inside Look at the Tribes and Traditions.* Dorling Kindersley, 2001, 96 pp. **N**

Cartlidge, Cherese, & Clark, Charles. *The Central Asian States.* Lucent, 2001, 128 pp. **N**

Corrick, James A. *Life of a Medieval Knight.* Lucent Books, 2001, 95 pp. **N**

Darling, Kathy. *There's a Zoo on You.* Millbrook Press, 2000, 48 pp. **N**

De Angeli, Marguerite. *The Door in the Wall.* Scholastic, 1949, 121 pp.

DeAngelis, Gina. *Francisco Pizarro and the Conquest of the Inca.* Chelsea House, 2001, 64 pp. **N**

DeAngelis, Gina. *Jackie Robinson.* Chelsea, 2001, 104 pp. **N**

Dingle, Derek T. *First in the Field: Baseball Hero Jackie Robinson.* Hyperion, 1998, 48 pp. **N**

Frank, Anne. *The Diary of a Young Girl.* Random, 1952, 285 pp. **N**

Freedman, Russell. *Kids at Work: Lewis Hine and the Crusade against Child Labor.* Clarion, 1994, 97 pp. **N**

Goodman, Joan. *A Long and Uncertain Journey, The 27,000-Mile Voyage of Vasco da Gama.* Mikya Press, 2001, 42 pp. **N**

Hansen, Joyce. *Women of Hope: African Americans Who Made a Difference.* Scholastic, 1998, 31 pp. **N**

Henry, O. *The Gift of the Magi and Other Stories.* Creative, 1986, 32 pp.

Herriot, James. *All Creatures Great and Small*. Bantam, 1989, 499 pp. **N**

Johnson, Rebecca L. *Science on the Ice: An Antarctic Journal*. Lerner Publications, 1995, 126 pp.

Kallen, Stuart A. *The Mayans*. Lucent, 2001, 112 pp. **N**

Kipling, Rudyard. *Captains Courageous*. Doubleday, 1896, 1964, 210 pp.

Marcovitz, Hal. *John C. Fremont. Pathfinder of the West*. Chelsea House, 2002, 64 pp. **N**

Mazer, Harry. *A Boy at War: A Novel of Pearl Harbor*. Simon & Schuster, 2001, 104 pp.

Miller, Marilyn. *Words That Built a Nation*. Scholastic, 1999, 172 pp. **N**

Pinkney, Andrea Davis. *Let It Shine: Stories of Black Women Freedom Fighters*. Harcourt, 2000, 30 pp. **N**

Rice, Terence M. G. *Russia*. Gareth Stevens, 1999, 96 pp. **N**

St. George, Judith. *John & Abigail Adams*. Holiday House, 2001, 147 pp. **N**

Soto, Gary. *Jessie De La Cruz: A Portrait of a United Farm Worker*. Persea Books, 2000, 116 pp. **N**

Steffens, B., & Weaver, R. M. *Cartoonists*. Lucent, 2000, 112 pp. **N**

Tolkien, J. R. R. *The Hobbit*. Balantine, 1938, 1979, 304 pp.

Wulffson, Don L. *The Kid Who Invented the Trampoline*. Dutton, 2001, 120 pp. **N**

Challenging Reading Level: Grade 9 (Interest Level: Grades 7–8)

London, Jack. *The Call of the Wild*. Viking, 1903, 1996, 126 pp.

McKissack, Patricia C. *Black Hands, White Sails: The Story of African-American Whalers*. Scholastic, 1999, 152 pp. **N**

Rodriguez, Consuelo. *Cesar Chavez*. Chelsea House, 1991, 106 pp. **N**

Sandburg, Carl. *Abe Lincoln Grows Up*. Harcourt, 1928, 222 pp. **N**

Appendix B

Informal Assessment of Key Skills and Strategies

Name _____   Total number correct _____

Date _____   Estimated level _____

1. go ____	21. game ____	41. spark ____	61. through ____
2. me ____	22. tree ____	42. stair ____	62. straight ____
3. see ____	23. wide ____	43. shore ____	63. enough ____
4. I ____	24. road ____	44. curl ____	64. clue ____
5. no ____	25. use ____	45. steer ____	65. edge ____
6. hat ____	26. goat ____	46. park ____	66. strong ____
7. wet ____	27. save ____	47. purse ____	67. suit ____
8. sit ____	28. wheel ____	48. clear ____	68. thought ____
9. hop ____	29. mine ____	49. storm ____	69. flood ____
10. fun ____	30. cute ____	50. charge ____	70. breathe ____
11. ran ____	31. chain ____	51. chalk ____	71. calm ____
12. men ____	32. speak ____	52. brook ____	72. clothes ____
13. win ____	33. slide ____	53. crown ____	73. knock ____
14. got ____	34. toast ____	54. join ____	74. soft ____
15. bug ____	35. blind ____	55. should ____	75. fault ____
16. drop ____	36. plane ____	56. stew ____	76. tough ____
17. jump ____	37. steel ____	57. bounce ____	77. height ____
18. sand ____	38. drive ____	58. crawl ____	78. laugh ____
19. ship ____	39. broke ____	59. broom ____	79. earth ____
20. lunch ____	40. price ____	60. pound ____	80. brought ____

Directions: Give one copy of the survey to the student and keep one for marking. Mark each response + or –. Start with the first item for all pupils. Say to the student, "I am going to ask you to read a list of words to me. Some of the words may be hard for you, but read as many as you can." Stop when the student gets five in a row wrong. The survey tests four levels. Each level has twenty items as follows: 1–20: easy long-vowel and short-vowel patterns; 21–40: long-vowel patterns; 41–60: r-vowel and other vowel patterns /aw/, /o͞o/, /o͝o/, /ow/, /oy/; 61–80, irregular and low-frequency patterns. Students are proficient at a level if they get 80 percent or more correct at that level. Students should be instructed at a level if they get more than 4 out of 20 wrong at that level.

From T. Gunning (1996). *Teacher's Guide for Word Building, Book A.* New York: Phoenix Learning Resources. Reprinted by permission of Galvin Publications.

Name _____   Score _____

Date _____

Syllable Survey

1. sunup _____	18. distant _____	35. creature _____
2. inside _____	19. prevent _____	36. audience _____
3. ago _____	20. museum _____	37. pleasant _____
4. open _____	21. several _____	38. spaghetti _____
5. under _____	22. building _____	39. information _____
6. farmer _____	23. probably _____	40. voyage _____
7. finish _____	24. modern _____	41. confusion _____
8. mistake _____	25. monument _____	42. neighborhood _____
9. thunder _____	26. opposite _____	43. studio _____
10. morning _____	27. message _____	44. allowance _____
11. reward _____	28. success _____	45. microphone _____
12. famous _____	29. struggle _____	46. auditorium _____
13. mumble _____	30. repeat _____	47. available _____
14. spider _____	31. recognize _____	48. disappointment _____
15. chicken _____	32. survive _____	49. bulletin _____
16. rocket _____	33. appreciate _____	50. moisture _____
17. magnet _____	34. antelope _____	

Directions: Give one copy of the survey to the student and keep one for marking. Mark each response + or –. Start with the first item for all pupils. Say to the student, "I am going to ask you to read a list of words. Some of the words may be hard for you, but read as many as you can." Stop when the student gets five in a row wrong. A score of 45 or above indicates that the student is able to decode multisyllabic words. A score between 40 and 44 indicates some weakness in decoding multisyllabic words. A score below 40 indicates a definite need for instruction and practice in decoding multisyllabic words. A score of 5 or below suggests that the student may be deficient in basic decoding skills. Give the Word Pattern Survey.

From T. Gunning (1994). *Teacher's Guide for Word Building, Book D.* New York: Phoenix Learning Resources. Reprinted by permission of Galvin Publications.

References

Professional

Achilles, C. M., Finn, J. D., & Bain, H. P. (1997–1998). Using class size to reduce the equity gap. *Educational Leadership, 54*(8), 40–43.

Adams, M. J. (1990). *Beginning to read: Thinking and learning about print: A summary* Cambridge, MA: MIT Press.

Adams, M. J. (1994). Modeling the connections between word recognition and reading. In R. B. Ruddell, M. R. Ruddell, & H. Singer (Eds.), *Theoretical models and processes of reading* (4th ed.) (pp. 838–863). Newark, DE: International Reading Association.

Adams, M. J., & Higgins, A. W. F. (1985). The growth of children's sight vocabulary: A quick test with educational and theoretical implications. *Reading Research Quarterly, 20,* 262–281.

Adoption Guidelines Project. (1990). Workbooks. In *Adoption Guidelines Project, A guide to selecting basal reading programs.* Urbana: University of Illinois, Center for the Study of Reading.

Afflerbach, P. (1990). The influence of prior knowledge on expert readers' main idea construction strategies. *Reading Research Quarterly, 25,* 31–46.

Afflerbach, P., & VanSledright, B. (2001). Hath! Doth! What? Middle graders reading innovative history text. *Journal of Adolescent & Adult Literacy, 44,* 696–707.

Afflerbach, P. P., & Johnston, P. H. (1986). What do expert readers do when the main idea is not explicit? In J. F. Baumann (Ed.), *Teaching main idea comprehension* (pp. 49–72). Newark, DE: International Reading Association.

Ahlmann, M. E. (1992). Children as evaluators. In K. S. Goodman, L. B. Bird, & Y. M. Goodman (Eds.), *The whole language catalog: Supplement on authentic assessment* (p. 95). Santa Rosa, CA: American School Publishers.

Allen, V. (1991). Teaching bilingual and ESL children. In J. Flood, J. M. Jensen, D. Lapp, & J. R. Squire (Eds.), *Handbook of research on teaching the English language arts* (pp. 356–364). New York: Macmillan.

Allen, V. G. (l994). Selecting materials for the reading instruction of ESL children. In K. Spangenberg-Urbschat, & R. Pritchard (Eds.), *Kids come in all languages: Reading instruction for all ESL students* (pp. 108–131). Newark, DE: International Reading Association.

Allen, V. G., Freeman, E. B., Lehman, B. A., Scharer, P. L. (1995). Amos and Boris: A window on teachers' thinking about the use of literature in their classrooms. *The Reading Teacher, 48,* 384–390.

Almasi, J. F., O'Flahavan, J. F., & Arya, P. (2001). A comparative analysis of student and teacher development in more and less proficient discussions of literature. *Reading Research Quarterly, 36,* 96–120.

Altwerger, B., Edelsky, C., & Flores, B. M. (1987). Whole language: What's new? *The Reading Teacher, 41,* 144–154.

Alvermann, D. E., O'Brien, D. G., & Dillon, D. R. (1990). What teachers do when they say they're having discussions of content reading assignments: A qualitative analysis. *Reading Research Quarterly, 25,* 296–322.

Alvermann, D. E., & Phelps, S. F. (1994). *Content area reading and literacy: Succeeding in today's diverse classrooms.* Boston: Allyn & Bacon.

Alvermann, D. E., Young, J. P., Weaver, D., Hinchman, K. A., Moore, D. W., Phelps, S. F., Thrash, E. C., Zaleewski, P. (1996). Middle and high school students' perceptions of how they experience text-based discussions: A multicase study. *Reading Research Quarterly, 31,* 244–267.

American Academy of Pediatrics. (2000). Clinical practice guideline. Diagnosis and evaluation of the child with attention deficit/hyperactivity disorder. *Pediatrics, 105,* 1158–1170.

American Educational Research Association. (2000). *Policy statement on high-stakes testing.* Available online at http://www.aera.net/about/policy/ stakes.htm

American Psychiatric Association. (1994). *Diagnostic and statistical manual of mental disorders* (4th ed.). Washington, DC: Author.

Anderson, C. W. (1987). Strategic teaching in science. In B. F. Jones, A. S. Palincsar, D. S. Ogle, & E. G. Carr (Eds.), *Strategic teaching and learning: Cognitive instruction in the content areas* (pp. 73–91). Alexandria, VA: Association for Supervision and Curriculum Development.

Anderson, G., Higgins, D., & Wurster, S. R. (1985). Differences in the free-reading books selected by high, average, and low achievers. *The Reading Teacher, 39,* 326–330.

Anderson, L. (1981). *Student responses to seatwork: Implications for the study of students' cognitive processing* (Research Series No. 102). East Lansing: Michigan State University, The Institute for Research on Teaching.

Anderson, R. C. (1984). Role of the reader's schema in comprehension, learning, and memory. In R. C. Anderson, J. Osborn, & R. J. Tierney (Eds.), *Learning to read in American schools: Basal readers and content texts* (pp. 469–482). Hillsdale, NJ: Lawrence Erlbaum.

Anderson, R. C. (1990, May). *Microanalysis of classroom reading instruction.* Paper presented at the annual conference on reading research, Atlanta.

Anderson, R. C., Hiebert, E. H., Scott, J. A., & Wilkinson, I. A. G. (1985). *Becoming a nation of readers: The report of the commission on reading.* Washington, DC: National Institute of Education.

Anderson, R. C., Wilson, P. T., & Fielding, L. G. (1988). Growth in reading and how children spend their time outside of school. *Reading Research Quarterly, 23,* 285–303.

Anderson, T. H., & Armbruster, B. B. (1984). Studying. In P. D. Pearson, R. Barr, M. L. Kamil, & P. Mosenthal (Eds.), *Handbook of reading research* (pp. 657–679). New York: Longman.

Andre, M. E. D. A., & Anderson, T. H. (1978–1979). The development and evaluation of a self-questioning study technique. *Reading Research Quarterly, 14,* 605–623.

Anthony, H. M., Pearson, P. D., & Raphael, T. E. (1989). *Reading comprehension research: A selected review* (Technical Report No. 448). Champaign: University of Illinois, Center for the Study of Reading.

Anyon, J. (1980). Social class and the hidden curriculum of work. *Journal of Education, 162*(1), 67–92.

492

Applebee, A. N. (1978). *The child's concept of story: Ages two to seventeen.* Chicago: University of Chicago Press.

Applebee, A. N., Langer, J. A., & Mullis, I. V. S. (1988). Who reads best? *Factors related to reading achievement in grades 3, 7, and 11.* Princeton, NJ: Educational Testing Service.

Arciero, J. (1998, October). *Strategies for shared text reading responses.* Paper presented at the Connecticut Reading Association meeting, Waterbury.

Armbruster, B. B., & Anderson, T. H. (1981). *Content area textbooks* (Technical Report No. 23). Champaign: University of Illinois, Center for the Study of Reading.

Asch, S., & Nerlove, H. (1967). The development of double function terms in children: An exploratory investigation. In J. P. Cecco (Ed.), *The psychology of thought, language, and instruction* (pp. 283–291). New York: Holt, Rinehart & Winston.

Ashcraft, M. H. (1994). *Human memory and cognition.* New York: HarperCollins.

Athanases, S. Z. (2003). Thematic study of literature: Middle school teachers, professional development, and educational reform. *English Education, 35,* 107–121.

Atkinson, R. L., Atkinson, R. C., Smith, E. E., & Hilgard, E. R. (1987). *Introduction to psychology* (9th ed.). New York: Harcourt Brace Jovanovich.

Atwell, N. (1987). *In the middle.* Portsmouth, NH: Boynton/Cook.

Atwell, N. (1990). *Coming to know: Writing to learn in the intermediate grades.* Portsmouth, NH: Heinemann.

Au, K. H. (1994). Portfolio assessment: Experiences at the Kamehameha elementary education program. In S. W. Valencia, E. H. Hiebert, & P. P. Afflerbach (Eds.), *Authentic reading assessment: Practices and possibilities* (pp. 103–126). Newark, DE: International Reading Association.

Au, K. H., & Mason, J. M. (1981). Social organization factors in learning to read: The balance of rights hypothesis. *Reading Research Quarterly, 17,* 115–151.

Ausubel, D. P. (1959). Viewpoints from related disciplines: Human growth and development. *Teachers College Record, 60,* 245–254.

Ausubel, D. P. (1960). The use of advance organizers in the learning and retention of meaningful verbal material. *Journal of Educational Psychology, 51,* 267–272.

Badders, W., Bethel, L. J., Fu, V., Peck, D., Sumners, C., & Valentino, C. (1999). *Discovery works 6.* Parsippany, NJ: Silver Burdett Ginn.

Bader, L. A. (2002). *Reading and language inventory* (4th ed.). Upper Saddle River, NJ: Prentice Hall.

Bagge-Rynerson, B. (1994). Learning good lessons: Young readers respond to books. In T. Newkirk (Ed.), *Workshop 5: The writing process revisited* (pp. 90–100). Portsmouth, NH: Heinemann.

Baker, L., & Brown, A. L. (1984). Metacognitive skills and reading. In P. D. Pearson, R. Barr, M. L. Kamil, & P. Mosenthal (Eds.), *Handbook of reading research* (pp. 353–394). New York: Longman.

Ballator, N., Farnum, M., & Kaplan, B. (1999). *NAEP 1996 trends in writing: Fluency and writing conventions.* Washington, DC: National Center for Education Statistics.

Bamford, R. A., & Kristo, J. V. (1998). *Making facts come alive: Choosing quality nonfiction literature K–8.* Norwood, MA: Christopher-Gordon.

Bangert-Downs, R. L. (1993). The word processor as an instructional tool: A meta-analysis of word processing in writing instruction. *Review of Educational Research, 63,* 69–93.

Banks, J. A., & Banks, C. A. M. (1997). *Multicultual education* (2nd ed.). Boston: Allyn & Bacon.

Barr, R. (1974). Instructional pace differences and their effect on reading acquisition. *Reading Research Quarterly, 9,* 526–554.

Barr, R., & Dreeben, R. (1991). Grouping students for reading instruction. In R. Barr, M. L. Kamil, P. Mosenthal, & P. D. Pearson (Eds.), *Handbook of reading research* (Vol. II, pp. 885–910). New York: Longman.

Barron, R. R. (1969). Research for the classroom teacher: Recent developments on the structured overview as an advanced organizer. In H. L. Herber & J. D. Riley (Eds.), *Research in reading in the content areas: The first report* (pp. 28–47). Syracuse, NY: Syracuse University, Reading and Language Arts Center.

Bartlett, F. C. (1932). *Remembering.* Cambridge, England: Cambridge University Press.

Barton, P. E. (2001). *Raising achievement and reducing gaps: Reporting progress toward goals for academic achievement.* Available online at http://www.negp.gov/issues/publication/negpdocs/negprep/rpt_barton/barton_paper.pdf

Bauman, G. A. (1990, March). *Writing tool selection and young children's writing.* Paper presented at the spring conference of the National Conference of Teachers of English, Colorado Springs, CO.

Baumann, J. F. (1986). The direct instruction of main idea comprehension ability. In J. F. Baumann (Ed.), *Teaching main idea comprehension* (pp. 133–178). Newark, DE: International Reading Association.

Baumann, J. F., Hoffman, J. V., Duffy-Hester, A. M., Ro, J. M. (2001). "The First R" yesterday and today: U.S. elementary reading instruction practices reported by teachers and administrators. *Reading Research Quarterly, 35,* 338–377.

Baumann, J. F., & Ivey, G. (1997). Delicate balances: Striving for curricular and instructional equilibrium in a second-grade, literature/strategy-based classroom. *Reading Research Quarterly, 32,* 244–275.

Baumann, J. F., Kameenui, E. J., & Ash, G. E. (2003). Research on vocabulary instruction: Voltaire redux. In J. Flood, D. Lapp, J. R. Squire, & J. M. Jensen (Eds.), *Handbook of research on teaching the English language arts* (2nd ed.) (pp. 752–785). New York: Macmillan.

Baumann, J. F., & Serra, J. K. (1984). The frequency and placement of main ideas in children's social studies textbooks: A modified replication of Braddock's research on topic sentences. *Journal of Reading Behavior, 16,* 27–40.

Beach, R., & Hynds, S. (1991). Research on response to literature. In R. Barr, M. L. Kamil, P. Mosenthal, & P. D. Pearson (Eds.), *Handbook of reading research* (Vol. II, pp. 453–489). New York: Longman.

Bear, D. (1995). *Word study: A developmental perspective based on spelling stages.* Paper presented at the annual meeting of the International Reading Association, Anaheim, CA.

Bear, D., & Barone, D. (1989). Using children's spellings to group for word study and directed reading in the primary classroom. *Reading Psychology, 10,* 275–292.

Bear, D. R., Invernizzi, M., Johnston, F., & Templeton, S. (1996). *Words their way: Word study for phonics, vocabulary, and spelling instruction.* Upper Saddle River, NJ: Merrill.

Bear, D. R., & Templeton, S. (1998). Explorations in developmental spelling: Foundations for learning and teaching phonics, spelling, and vocabulary. *The Reading Teacher, 52,* 222–242.

Beck, I. L., & McKeown, M. G. (1983). Learning words well—a

program to enhance vocabulary and comprehension. *The Reading Teacher, 36*, 622–625.

Beck, I. L., & McKeown, M. G. (2001). Text talk: Capturing the benefits of read-aloud experiences for young children. *The Reading Teacher, 55*, 10–20.

Beck, I. L., McKeown, M. G., Hamilton, R. L., & Kucan, L. (1997). *Questioning the author: An approach for enhancing student engagement with text.* Newark, DE: International Reading Association.

Beck, I. L., McKeown, M. G., & Kucan, L. (2002). *Bringing words to life: Robust vocabulary instruction.* New York: Guilford Press.

Beck, I. L., McKeown, M. G., & Omanson, R. C. (1987). The effects and uses of diverse vocabulary instructional techniques. In M. G. McKeown & M. E. Curtis (Eds.), *The nature of vocabulary acquisition* (pp. 147–163). Hillsdale, NJ: Lawrence Erlbaum.

Beck, I. L., Omanson, R. C., & McKeown, M. G. (1982). An instructional redesign of reading lessons: Effects on comprehension. *Reading Research Quarterly, 17*, 462–481.

Beers, K. (2003). *Reading strategies handbook for middle school.* New York: Holt, Rinehart and Winston.

Bereiter, C., & Scardamalia, M. (1982). From conversation to composition: The role of instruction in a developmental process. In R. Glass (Ed.), *Advances in instructional psychology* (Vol. 2, pp. 1–64). Hillsdale, NJ: Lawrence Erlbaum.

Berk, L. E. (1997). *Child development* (4th ed.). Boston: Allyn & Bacon.

Berkowitz, S. J. (1986). Effects of instruction in text organization on sixth-grade students' memory for expository text. *Reading Research Quarterly, 21*, 161–178.

Berliner, D. C. (1981). Academic learning time and reading achievement. In J. T. Guthrie (Ed.), *Comprehension and teaching: Research reviews* (pp. 203–226). Newark, DE: International Reading Association.

Berliner, D. C. (1985). Effective classroom teaching: The necessary but not sufficient condition for developing exemplary schools. In G. R. Austin & H. Gartier (Eds.), *Research on exemplary schools* (pp. 211–234). New York: Academic Press.

Biemiller, A. (1994). Some observations on acquiring and using reading skill in elementary schools. In C. K. Kinzer & D. J. Leu (Eds.), Multidimensional aspects of literacy research, theory, and practice. *Forty-third Yearbook of the National Reading Conference* (pp. 209–216). Chicago, IL: National Reading Conference.

Bigham, V. S., & Bigham, G. (1998). *The Prentice Hall directory of online educational resources.* Paramus, NJ: Prentice Hall.

Bitter, G. G. (1999). *Using technology in the classroom* (4th ed.). Boston: Allyn & Bacon.

Bitter, G. G., & Pierson, M. E. (2002). *Using technology in the classroom* (5th ed.). Boston: Allyn & Bacon.

Bjorklund, B., Handler, N., Mitten, J., & Stockwell, G. (1998, October). *Literature circles: A tool for developing students as critical readers, writers, and thinkers.* Paper presented at the forty-seventh annual conference of the Connecticut Reading Association, Waterbury.

Blachowicz, C. L. Z. (1977). Cloze activities for primary readers. *The Reading Teacher, 31*, 300–302.

Blachowicz, C. L. Z., & Fisher, P. (2000). Vocabulary instruction. In M. L. Kamil, P. B. Mosenthal, P. D. Pearson, & R. Barr (Eds.), *Handbook of Reading Research* (Vol. III, pp. 503–523). Mahwah, NJ: Erlbaum.

Bloom, B. (Ed.). (1957). *Taxonomy of educational objectives.* New York: McKay.

Blum, I. H., Koskinen, P. S., Tennant, S., Parker, E. M., Straub, M., & Curry, C. (1995). Using audiotaped books to extend classroom literacy instruction into the homes of second-language learners. *Journal of Reading Behavior, 27*, 535–564.

Board of Directors of International Reading Association (1999). High-stakes assessments in reading. *The Reading Teacher, 53*, 257–264.

Bond, G. L. & Dykstra, R. (1967). The cooperative research program in first-grade reading instruction. *Reading Research Quarterly, 2*, 1–142.

Boothroyd, K. (2001, December). *Being literate in urban third-grade classrooms.* Paper presented at the annual meeting of the National Reading Conference, San Antonio, TX.

Borders, S., & Naylor, A. P. (1993). *Children talking about books.* Phoenix, AZ: Oryx.

Boyd, C. D, Gay, G., Geiger, R., Kracht, J. B., Pang, V. O., Risinger, F. C., Sanchez, S. M. (2003). *Scott, Foresman social studies: The United States.* Glenview, IL: Scott Foresman.

Boyle, C. (1996). *Efficacy of peer evaluation and effects of peer evaluation on persuasive writing.* Unpublished master's thesis, San Diego State University, San Diego, CA.

Bradshaw, G. L., & Anderson, J. R. (1982). Elaborative encoding as an explanation of levels of processing. *Journal of Verbal Learning and Verbal Behavior, 21*, 165–174.

Brandt, R. (1992). Yes, children are still at risk. *Educational Leadership, 50* (4), 3.

Bransford, J. D. (1994). Schema activation and schema acquisition: Comments on Richard C. Anderson's remarks. In R. B. Ruddell, M. R. Ruddell, & H. Singer (Eds.), *Theoretical models and processes of reading* (4th ed.) (pp. 483–495). Newark, DE: International Reading Association.

Bransford, J. D., & Stein, B. S. (1984). *The ideal problem solver: A guide for improving thinking, learning, and creativity.* New York: Freeman.

Bransford, J. D., Stein, B. S., Shelton, T. S., & Owings, R. A. (1981). Cognition and adaptation: The importance of learning to learn. In J. Harvey (Ed.), *Cognition, social behavior, and the environment.* Hillsdale, NJ: Lawrence Erlbaum.

Brewster, P. G. (Ed.). (1952). *Children's games and rhymes.* Durham, NC: Duke University Press.

Brophy, J. E., & Good, T. L. (1970). Teachers' communication of differential expectations for children's classroom performance: Some behavioral data. *Journal of Educational Psychology, 61*, 365–375.

Brophy, J. E., & Good, T. L. (1986). Teacher behavior and student achievement. In M. E. Wittrock (Ed.), *Handbook of research on teaching* (pp. 328–375). New York: Macmillan.

Brown, A. L. (1985). *Reciprocal teaching of comprehension strategies: A natural history of one program for enhancing learning* (Technical Report No. 334). Champaign: University of Illinois, Center for the Study of Reading.

Brown, A. L., & Day, J. D. (1983). Macrorules for summarizing text: The development of expertise. *Journal of Verbal Learning and Verbal Behavior, 22*(1), 1–14.

Brown, C. S., & Lytle, S. L. (1988). Merging assessment and instruction: Protocols in the classroom. In S. M. Glazer, L. W. Searfoss, & L. M. Gentile (Eds.), *Reexamining reading diagnosis: New trends and procedures* (pp. 94–102). Newark, DE: International Reading Association.

Brown, H., & Cambourne, B. (1987). *Read and retell.* Portsmouth, NH: Heinemann.

Brown, J. J. (1988). *High impact teaching: Strategies for educating minority youth.* Lanham, MD: University Press of America.

Brown, K. J. (2000). What kind of text—For whom and when? Textual scaffolding for beginning readers. *The Reading Teacher, 53,* 292–307.

Brown, R. (1973). *A first language: The early stages.* Cambridge, MA: Harvard University Press.

Bruck, M. (1992). Persistence of dyslexics' phonological awareness deficits. *Developmental Psychology, 28,* 874–886.

Bruce, B. (1980). Plans and social actions. In R. J. Spiro, B. C. Bruce, & W. F. Brewer (Eds.), *Theoretical issues in reading comprehension* (pp, 367–384). Hillsdale, NJ: Erlbaum.

Bruner, J. (1975). The ontogenesis of speech acts. *Journal of Child Languages, 2,* 1–40.

Bruner, J. (1986). *Actual minds, possible worlds.* Cambridge, MA: Harvard University Press.

Brynildssen, S. (2000). *Vocabulary's influence on successful writing.* ERIC Clearinghouse on Reading English and Communication. Bloomington, IN: ERIC Digest D157.

Buckleitner, W. W., Orr, A. C., Wolock, E. L. (2002). *The complete sourcebook on children's software* (Vol. 10). Flemington, NJ: Children's Software Revue.

Bush, C., & Huebner, M. (1979). *Strategies for reading in the elementary school* (2nd ed.). New York: Macmillan.

Byrne, B. (1992). Studies in the acquisition procedure for reading: Rationale, hypotheses, and data. In P. B. Gough, L. C. Ehri, & R. Treiman (Eds.), *Reading acquisition* (pp. 1–35). Hillsdale, NJ: Lawrence Erlbaum Associates.

Calfee, R., & Hiebert, E. (1991). Classroom assessment of reading. In R. Barr, M. L. Kamil, P. Mosenthal, & P. D. Pearson (Eds.), *Handbook of reading research* (Vol. II, pp. 281–309). New York: Longman.

California Literature Project (1992). *Meaning-making strategies for a literature-based curriculum.* Dominguez Hills: California State University.

Calkins, L. (2001). *The art of teaching reading.* Portsmouth, NH: Heinemann.

Calkins, L., Montgomery, K., & Santman, D. (1998). *A teacher's guide to standardized reading tests.* Portsmouth, NH: Heinemann.

Calkins, L. M. (1986). *The art of teaching writing.* Portsmouth, NH: Heinemann.

Calkins, L. M. (1994). *The art of teaching writing* (new ed.). Portsmouth, NH: Heinemann.

Calkins, L. M., & Harwayne, S. (1991). *Living between the lines.* Portsmouth, NH: Heinemann.

Carlson, N. R., & Buskist, W. (1997). *Psychology: The science of behavior* (5th ed.). Boston: Allyn & Bacon.

Carnine, D., Kameenui, E. J., & Coyle, G. (1984). Utilization of contextual information in determining the meaning of unfamiliar words. *Reading Research Quarterly, 19,* 188–204.

Carnine, D., Silbert, J., & Kameenui, E. J. (1990). *Direct instruction in reading.* Columbus, OH: Merrill.

Carr, E., Dewitz, P., & Patberg, J. P. (1989). Using cloze for inference training with expository text. *The Reading Teacher, 42,* 380–385.

Carr, K. S. (1983). The importance of inference skills in the primary grades. *The Reading Teacher, 36,* 518–522.

Caruso, C. (1997). Before you cite a site. *Educational Leadership, 55*(3), 24–25.

Cattagni, A., & Westnat, E. F. (2001). *Internet access in U. S. public schools and classrooms: 1994–2000.* Washington, DC: U.S. Department of Education, National Center for Educational Statistics. Available online at http://nces.ed.gov/pubs2001/2001071.pdf

Caverly, D. C., & Orlando, V. P. (1991). Textbook study strategies. In D. C. Caverly & V. P. Orlando (Eds.), *Teaching reading and study strategies at the college level* (pp. 86–165). Newark, DE: International Reading Association.

Center for the Study of Reading. (1990). *Suggestions for the classroom: Teachers and independent reading.* Urbana: University of Illinois Press.

Chall, J. S. (1967). *Learning to read: The great debate.* New York: McGraw-Hill.

Chall, J. S. (1983a). *Learning to read: The great debate* (rev. ed.). New York: McGraw-Hill.

Chall, J. S. (1983b). *Stages of reading development.* New York: McGraw-Hill.

Chall, J. S. (1987). Two vocabularies for reading: Recognition and meaning. In M. G. McKeown & M. E. Curtis (Eds.), *The nature of vocabulary acquisition* (pp. 7–17). Hillsdale, NJ: Lawrence Erlbaum.

Chall, J. S. (1996). *Stages of reading development* (2nd ed.). Fort Worth, TX: Harcourt Brace.

Chall, J. S., Bissex, G. L., Conard, S. S., & Harris-Sharples, S. H. (1996). *Qualitative assessment of text difficulty: A practical guide for teachers and writers.* Cambridge, MA: Brookline.

Chall, J. S., & Conard, S. S. (1991). *Should textbooks challenge students? The case for easier or harder books.* New York: Teachers College Press.

Chall, J. S., & Dale, E. (1995). *The new Dale-Chall readability formula.* Cambridge, MA: Brookline.

Chall, J. S., Jacobs, V. A., & Baldwin, L. E. (1990). *The reading crisis: Why poor children fall behind.* Cambridge, MA: Harvard University Press.

Chamot, A. U., & O'Malley, J. M. (1994). Instructional approaches and teaching procedures. In K. Spangenberg-Urbschat & R. Pritchard (Eds.), *Kids come in all languages: Reading instruction for ESL students* (pp. 82–107). Newark, DE: International Reading Association.

Chan, L. K., Cole, P. G., & Barfett, S. (1987). Comprehension monitoring: Detection and identification of text inconsistencies by LD and normal students. *Learning Disability Quarterly, 10,* 114–124.

Chard, N. (1990). How learning logs change teaching. In N. Atwell (Ed.), *Coming to know: Writing to learn in the intermediate grades* (pp. 61–68). Portsmouth, NH: Heinemann.

Chicago Public Schools. (2000). *Rubrics.* Available online at http://intranet.cps.k12.il.us/Assessments/Ideas_and_Rubrics/ideas_and_rubrics.html

Children's books in print 2002 (Annual). New York: Bowker.

Christenbury, L., & Kelly, P. (1983). *Questioning: A path to critical thinking.* Urbana, IL: National Council of Teachers of English.

Clay, M. (2000). *Running records for classroom teachers.* Portsmouth, NH: Heinemann.

Clay, M. M. (1972). *Reading: The patterning of complex behavior.* Auckland, New Zealand: Heinemann.

Clay, M. M. (1982). *Observing young readers.* Portsmouth, NH: Heinemann.

Clay, M. M. (1993). *An observation survey of early literacy achievement.* Portsmouth, NH: Heinemann.

Cline, R. K. J., & Kretke, G. L. (1980). An evaluation of long-term SSR in the junior high school. *Journal of Reading, 23,* 503–506.

Cole, A. D. (1998). Beginner-oriented texts in literature-based classrooms: The segue for a few struggling readers. *The Reading Teacher, 51,* 488–501.

Collins, A., & Smith, E. (1980). *Teaching the process of reading comprehension* (Technical Report No. 182). Urbana: University of Illinois, Center for the Study of Reading.

Collins, J. L. (1998). *Strategies for struggling writers.* New York: Guilford Press.

Colorado Department of Education (2002). *Scoring rubrics.* Available online at: http://www.cde.state.co.us/cdeassess/as_rubricindex.htm

Conard, S. S. (1990). *Change and challenge in content textbooks.* Paper presented at the annual conference of the International Reading Association, New Orleans.

Constantino, M. (1999, May). *Reading and second language learners: Research report.* Olympia, WA: The Evergreen State College. Available online at http://www.evergreen.edu/user/K-12/readingSecondLangLearners.htm

Cook, D. M. (1986). *A guide to curriculum planning in reading.* Madison: Wisconsin Department of Public Instruction.

Cook, V. (2001). *Second language learning and language teaching* (3rd ed). New York: Oxford University Press.

Cooper, C. R., & Odell, L. (1977). *Evaluating writing: Describing, measuring, judging.* Urbana, IL: National Council of Teachers of English.

Cooper, P. D. (1996). *Intervention literacy instruction for hard-to-teach students in grades 3–6.* Paper presented at the annual meeting of the International Reading Association, New Orleans.

Cooper, P. D. (1997). *Literacy: Helping children construct meaning* (3rd ed.). Boston: Houghton Mifflin.

Cooper, P. D. & Pikulski, J. J. (2001). *Houghton Mifflin reading, teacher's guide, grade 5, unit 3.* Boston: Houghton Mifflin.

Courtney, A. M., & Abodeb, T. L. (1999). Diagnostic-reflective portfolios. *The Reading Teacher, 52,* 708–714.

Cox, C., & Many, J. E. (1992). Towards an understanding of the aesthetic stance towards literature. *Language Arts, 66,* 287–294.

Cox, C., & Zarillo, J. (1993). *Teaching reading with children's literature.* New York: Merrill.

Crafton, L. K. (1991). *Whole language: Getting started . . . moving forward.* Katonah, NY: Richard C. Owen.

Crawford, L. W. (1993). *Language and literacy learning in multicultural classrooms.* Boston: Allyn & Bacon.

Crawford, P., & Shannon, P. (1994). "I don't think these companies have much respect for teachers": Looking at teacher's manuals. In P. Shannon & K. Goodman (Eds.), *Basal readers: A second look* (pp. 1–18). Katonah, NY: Richard C. Owen.

Cummins, J. (1994). The acquisition of English as a second language. In K. Spangenberg-Urbschat & R. Pritchard (Eds.), *Kids come in all languages: Reading instruction for all ESL students* (pp. 36–62). Newark, DE: International Reading Association.

Cummins, J. (2001). Assessment and intervention with culturally and linguistically diverse learners. In S. R. Hollins & J. V. Tinajero (Eds.), *Literacy assessment of second language learners* (pp. 115–129). Boston: Allyn & Bacon.

Cunningham, J. W., & Foster, E. O. (1978). The ivory tower connection: A case study. *The Reading Teacher, 31,* 365–369.

Cunningham, J. W., & Moore, D. W. (1986). The confused world of main idea. In J. F. Baumann (Ed.), *Teaching main idea comprehension* (pp. 1–17). Newark, DE: International Reading Association.

Cunningham, P. M. (1978). Decoding polysyllabic words: An alternative strategy. *Journal of Reading, 21,* 608–614.

Cunningham, P. M. (1998). The multisyllabic word dilemma: Helping students build meaning, spell, and read "big" words.

Reading and Writing Quarterly: Overcoming Learning Disabilities, 14, 189–218.

Cunningham, P. M., & Allington, R. L. (1999). *Classrooms that work: They can all read and write* (2nd ed.). New York: Longwood.

Cunningham, P. M., & Allington, R. L. (2003). *Classrooms that work: They can all read and write* (3rd ed.). Boston: Allyn & Bacon.

Cunningham, P. M., & Cunningham, J. W. (1992). Making words: Enhancing the invented spelling-decoding connection. *The Reading Teacher, 46,* 106–115.

Curtis, M. E. (1987). Vocabulary testing and vocabulary instruction. In M. G. McKeown & M. E. Curtis (Eds.), *The nature of vocabulary acquisition* (pp. 37–51). Hillsdale, NJ: Lawrence Erlbaum.

Dahl, K. (1992). Kidwatching revisited. In K. S. Goodman, L. B. Bird, & Y. M. Goodman (Eds.), *The whole language catalog: Supplement on authentic instruction* (p. 50). Santa Rosa, CA: American School Publishers.

Dahl, K., & Farnan, N. (1998). *Children's writing: Perspectives from research.* Newark, DE: International Reading Association & National Reading Conference.

Dale, E., & O'Rourke, J. (1971). *Techniques of teaching vocabulary.* Chicago: Field.

D'Arcy, P. (1989). *Making sense, shaping meaning: Writing in the context of a capacity-based approach to learning.* Portsmouth, NH: Boynton/Cook.

Dave, R. H. (1964). *The identification and measurement of environmental process variables that are related to educational achievement.* Unpublished doctoral dissertation, University of Chicago.

Davies, P. (Ed.). (1986). *The American Heritage school dictionary.* Boston: Houghton Mifflin.

Davis, F. B. (1968). Research on comprehension in reading. *Reading Research Quarterly, 3,* 449–545.

Davis, G., Jackson, J., & Johnson, S. (2000, May). *Guided writing: Leveling the balance.* Paper presented at the annual meeting of the International Reading Association, Indianapolis.

Davis, Z. T., & McPherson, M. D. (1989). Story map instruction: A road map for reading comprehension. *The Reading Teacher, 43,* 232–240.

DeFord, D. E. (1985). Validating the construct of theoretical orientation in reading instruction. *Reading Research Quarterly, 20,* 351–367.

Deighton, L. C. (1959). *Vocabulary development in the classroom.* New York: Columbia University Press.

Delpit, L. D. (1990). *A socio-cultural view of diversity and instruction.* Paper presented at the Annual Conference on Reading Research, Atlanta.

Denman, G. A. (1988). *When you've made it your own—Teaching poetry to young people.* Portsmouth, NH: Heinemann.

Devine, T. G. (1986). *Teaching reading comprehension: From theory to practice.* Boston: Allyn & Bacon.

Dewitz, P., Carr, E. M., & Patberg, J. P. (1987). Effects of inference training on comprehension and comprehension monitoring. *Reading Research Quarterly, 22,* pp. 99–121.

Dias, P. (1990). A literary-response perspective on teaching reading comprehension. In D. Bogdan & S. B. Straw (Eds.), *Beyond communication: Reading comprehension and criticism* (pp. 283–299). Portsmouth, NH: Boynton/Cook.

Dillon, J. T. (1983). *Teaching and the art of questioning.* Bloomington, IN: Phi Delta Kappa.

DiLuglio, P., Eaton, D., & de Tarnowsky, J. (1988). *Westward wagons.* North Scituate, RI: Scituate School Department.

Dodge, B. (2001). *FOCUS: Five rules for writing a great WebQuest.* Available online at http://www.iste.org/L&L/archive/vol28/no8/featuredarticle/dodge/index.html

Dole, J. S., Duffy, G. G., Roehler, L. R., & Pearson, P. D. (1991). Moving from the old to the new: Research on reading comprehension. *Review of Educational Research, 61,* 239–264.

Donahue, P. A., Finnegan, R. J., Lutkus, A. D., Allen, N. R., & Campbell, J. R. (2001). *The nation's report card: Fourth-grade reading 2000.* Washington, DC: U.S. Department of Education.

Donahue, P. A., Voekl, K. E., Campbell, J. R., & Mazzeo, J. (1999). *NAEP 1998 report card for the nation and the states.* Washington, DC: U.S. Department of Education.

Donovan, C. A., &. Smolkin, L. B. (2001). Genre and other factors influencing teachers' book selection for science instruction. *Reading Research Quarterly, 36,* 421–440.

Dooling, D. J., & Lachman, R. (1971). Effects of comprehension on retention of prose. *Journal of Experimental Psychology, 88,* 216–222.

Dowhower, S. (1987). Effects of repeated reading on second-grade transitional readers' fluency and comprehension. *Reading Research Quarterly, 22,* 389–406.

Dressel, J. H. (1990). The effects of listening to and discussing different qualities of children's literature on the narrative writing of fifth graders. *Research in the Teaching of English, 24,* 397–414.

Duffelmeyer, F. A. (1985). Main ideas in paragraphs. *The Reading Teacher, 38,* 484–486.

Duffelmeyer, F. A., & Duffelmeyer, B. B. (1979). Developing vocabulary through dramatization. *Journal of Reading, 23,* 141–143.

Duffy, G. G. (2002). The case for direct explanation of strategies. In C. C. Block & M. Pressley (Eds.), *Comprehension instruction: Research-based best practices* (pp. 28–41). New York: Guilford Press.

Duffy, G. G., & Roehler, L. R. (1987). Improving reading instruction through the use of responsive elaboration. *The Reading Teacher, 40,* 514–520.

Durgunoglu, A. Y., & Oney, B. (2000). *Literacy development in two languages: Cognitive and sociocultural dimensions of cross-language transfer. A research symposium on high standards in reading for students from diverse language groups: Research, practice & policy.* Washington, DC: Office of Bilingual Education and Minority Languages Affairs, U. S. Department of Education. Available online at http://www.ncbe.gwu.edu/ncbepubs/symposia/reading/reading3.html

Early, M., & Sawyer, D. J. (1984). *Reading to learn in grades 5 to 12.* New York: Harcourt Brace Jovanovich.

Echevarria, J. (1998). *Teaching language minority students in elementary schools.* Washington, DC, and Santa Cruz, CA: Center for Research in Education, Diversity & Excellence.

Echevarria, J., & Graves, A. (1998). *Sheltered content instruction, Teaching English-language learners with diverse abilities.* Boston: Allyn & Bacon.

Echeverria, J., Vogt, M., & Short, D. J. (2000). *Making content comprehensible for English language learners: The SIOP model.* Boston: Allyn & Bacon.

Eckhoff, B. (1983). How reading affects children's writing. *Language Arts, 60,* 607–616.

Edelsky, C. (1994). Exercise isn't always healthy. In P. Shannon & K. Goodman (Eds.), *Basal readers: A second look* (pp. 19–34). Katonah, NY: Richard C. Owen.

Editorial Projects in Education. (2001). Quality counts 2001, A better balance. *Education Week on the Web.* Available online at http://www.educationweek.org/sreports/qc01

Educate the Children. (2001). *NLS activity resource sheet, Year 2, Term 2, Strand W 5.* Available online at http://www.standards.dfee.gov.uk/local/literacy/PDF/oa077.pdf

Eeds, M., & Wells, D. (1989). Grand conversations: An exploration of meaning construction in literature study groups. *Research in the Teaching of English, 23,* 4–29.

Ehri, L. C. (1991). Development of the ability to read words. In R. Barr, M. L. Kamil, P. Mosenthal, & P. D. Pearson (Eds.), *Handbook of reading research* (Vol. II, pp. 383–417). New York: Longman.

Ehri, L. C. (1994). Development of the ability to read words: Update. In R. B. Ruddell, M. R. Ruddell, & H. Singer (Eds.), *Theoretical models and processes of reading* (4th ed.) (pp. 323–358). Newark, DE: International Reading Association.

Ehri, L. C., & McCormick, S. (1998). Phases of word learning: Implications for instruction with delayed and disabled readers. *Reading and Writing Quarterly: Overcoming Learning Disabilities, 14,* 135–163.

Elley, W. B. (1989). Vocabulary acquisition from listening to stories. *Reading Research Quarterly, 24,* 174–187.

Elley, W. B. (1992). *How in the world do students read?* The Hague, The Netherlands: IEA.

Emig, J. (1971). *The composing processes of twelfth-graders.* Urbana, IL: National Council of Teachers of English.

Enz, B. (1989). *The 90 percent success solution.* Paper presented at the International Reading Association annual convention, New Orleans.

Ericson, L., & Juliebo, M. F. (1998). *The phonological awareness handbook for kindergarten and primary teachers.* Newark, DE: International Reading Association.

Erikson, E. H. (1963). *Childhood and society* (2nd ed.). New York: Norton.

Estes, T., & Vaughn, J. (1985). *Reading and learning in the content classroom* (2nd ed.). Boston: Allyn & Bacon.

Estes, T. H., Mills, D. C., & Barron, R. F. (1969). Three methods of introducing students to a reading-learning task in two content subjects. In H. L. Herber & R. F. Barron (Eds.), *Research in reading in the content areas: First-year report* (pp. 40–48). Syracuse, NY: Syracuse University, Reading and Language Arts Center.

Fader, D. (1977). *The new hooked on books.* New York: Berkley.

Farnan, N. (1996). Connecting adolescents and reading: Goals at the middle level. *Journal of Adolescent & Adult Literacy, 39,* 436–445.

Farr, R. (1991). Current issues in alternative assessment. In C. P. Smith (Ed.), *Alternative assessment of performance in the language arts: Proceedings* (pp. 3–17). Bloomington, IN: ERIC Clearinghouse on Reading and Communication Skills and Phi Delta Kappa.

Farr, R., & Carey, R. F. (1986). *Reading: What can be measured?* Newark, DE: International Reading Association.

Farr, R., & Farr, B. (1990). *Integrated assessment system.* San Antonio, TX: Psychological Corporation.

Farr, R., et al. (2001). *Collections.* Orlando, FL: Harcourt.

Ferreiro, E. (1990). Literacy development: Psychogenesis. In Y. M. Goodman (Ed.), *How children construct literacy* (pp. 12–25). Newark, DE: International Reading Association.

Fielding, L. G., Wilson, P. T., & Anderson, R. C. (1986). A new focus on free reading: The role of trade books in reading instruction. In T. E. Raphael (Ed.), *The contexts of school-based literacy* (pp. 149–160). New York: Random House.

Fillmore, L. W., & Valdez, C. (1986). Teaching bilingual learners. In M. E. Wittrock (Ed.), *Handbook of research on teaching* (pp. 648–685). New York: Macmillan.

Fischer, U. (1994). Learning words from context and dictionaries: An experimental comparison. *Applied Psycholinguistics, 15,* 551–574.

Fisher, C., & Natarelli, M. (1982). Young children's preferences in poetry: A national survey of first, second, and third graders. *Research in the Teaching of English, 16,* 339–355.

Fitzgerald, J. (1989). Research on stories: Implications for teachers. In K. P. Muth (Ed.), *Children's comprehension of text: Research into practice* (pp. 2–36). Newark, DE: International Reading Association.

Flavell, J. H. (1963). *The developmental psychology of Jean Piaget.* New York: Van Nostrand.

Flexner, S. B., & Hauck, L. C. (1994). *The Random House dictionary of the English language* (2nd ed., rev.). New York: Random House.

Flood, J., Medcaris, A., Hasbrouk, J. E., Paris, S., Hoffman, J., Stah, S., Lapp, D., Tinejero, J. V., & Wood, K. (2001). *McGraw-Hill reading, teacher's guide, level 6, unity 2.* New York: McGraw-Hill.

Foorman, B. R., Fletcher, J. M., Francis, D. J., Schatschneider, C., Mehta, P. (1998). The role of instruction in learning to read: Preventing reading failure in at-risk children. *Journal of Educational Psychology, 90,* 37–55.

Ford, M. P. (1994). *Keys to successful whole group instruction.* Paper presented at the annual conference of the Connecticut Reading Association, Waterbury.

Fountas, I. C., & Pinnell, G. S. (1996). *Guided reading: Good first teaching for all children.* Portsmouth, NH: Heinemann.

Fountas, I. C., & Pinnell, G. S. (1999). *Matching books to readers: Using leveled books in guided reading, K–3.* Portsmouth, NH: Heinemann.

Fountas, I. C., & Pinnell, G. S. (2001). *Guiding readers and writers grades 3–6.* Portsmouth, NH: Heinemann.

Fowler, A., Palumbo, L. C., Liss-Bronstein, L., Wilder, T. D., Lavalette, M., & Gillis, M. (2002). *Enhancing oral language.* New Haven, CT: RESC Alliance.

Fractor, J. S., Woodruff, M. C., Matinez, M. G., & Teale, W. H. (1993). Let's not miss opportunities to promote voluntary reading: Classroom libraries in the elementary school. *The Reading Teacher, 46,* 476–484.

Fredericks, A. D. (1986). Mental imagery activities to improve comprehension. *The Reading Teacher, 40,* 78–81.

Freeland, D. (1986, April). Perfect bribery—or how Sgt. Slaughter made 8th graders read. *Learning 86, 14*(8), 52–55.

Freeman, Y. S., & Freeman, D. E. (1998). Effective literacy practices for English learners. In C. Weaver (Ed.), *Practicing what we know: Informed reading instruction* (409–438). Urbana, IL: National Council of Teachers of English.

Fry, E. (1977a). *Elementary reading instruction.* New York: McGraw-Hill.

Fry, E. (1977b). Fry's readability graph: Clarifications, validity, and extension to level 17. *Journal of Reading, 21,* 242–252.

Frymier, J., & Gansneder, B. (1989). The Phi Delta Kappa study of students at risk. *Phi Delta Kappan, 71,* 142–146.

Gage, F. C. (1990). *An introduction to reader-response issues: How to make students into more active readers.* Paper presented at the annual meeting of the Connecticut Reading Conference, Waterbury.

Gallo, D. R. (1985). Teachers as reading researchers. In C. N. Hedley & A. N. Baratta (Eds.), *Contexts of reading* (pp. 185–199). Norwood, NJ: Ablex.

Gambrell, L. B. (1980). Think time: Implications for reading instruction. *The Reading Teacher, 34,* 143–146.

Gambrell, L. B. (1996). Creating classroom cultures that foster reading motivation. *The Reading Teacher, 50,* 14–25.

Gambrell, L. B., & Bales, R. J. (1986). Mental imagery and the comprehension monitoring performance of fourth- and fifth-grade poor readers. *Reading Research Quarterly, 21,* 454–464.

Gambrell, L. B., Codling, R. M., & Palmer, B. M. (1996). *Elementary student's motivation to read. Reading Research Report No. 52.* Athens, GA: National Reading Research Center.

Gambrell, L. B., & Javitz, P. B. (1993). Mental imagery, text illustrations, and children's story comprehension. *Reading Research Quarterly, 28,* 264–276.

Gambrell, L. B., Wilson, R. M., & Gantt, W. N. (1981). Classroom observations of good and poor readers. *Journal of Educational Research, 24,* 400–404.

Gandara, P. (2000). In the aftermath of the storm: English learners in the post-227 era. *Bilingual Research Journal, 24*(1–2), 1–13.

Gans, R. (1940). *Study of critical reading comprehension in intermediate grades: Teacher's College contributions to education, No. 811.* New York: Bureau of Publications, Teachers College, Columbia University.

García, G. E. (1990). *Response to "A socio-cultural view of diversity and instruction."* Paper presented at the annual Conference on Reading Research, Atlanta.

García, G. E., Pearson, P. D., & Jiménez, R. T. (1994). *The at-risk situation: A synthesis of reading research.* Champaign: University of Illinois, Center for the Study of Reading.

Garner, R. (1994). Metacognition and executive control. In R. B. Ruddell, M. R. Ruddell, & H. Singer (Eds.) *Theoretical models and processes of reading* (4th ed.), (pp. 715–756). Newark, DE: International Reading Association.

Garner, R., Hare, V. C., Alexander, P., Haynes, J., & Winograd, P. (1984). Inducing use of a text lookback strategy among unsuccessful readers. *American Educational Research Journal, 21,* 789–798.

Garner, R., MacCready, G. B., & Wagoner, S. (1984). Readers' acquisition of the components of the text lookback strategy. *Journal of Educational Psychology, 76,* 300–309.

Gaskins, I. W. (1998). *What research suggests are ingredients of a grades 1–6 literacy program for struggling readers.* Paper presented at the International Reading Association Convention, Orlando.

Gaskins, I. W., Ehri, L. C., Cress, C., O'Hara, C., & Donnelly, K. (1996–1997). Procedures for word learning: Making discoveries about words. *The Reading Teacher, 50,* 312–327.

Gates, A. I. (1917). Recitation as a factor in memorizing. *Archives of Psychology, 40,* 65–104.

Gelzheiser, L. M., & Meyers, J. (1990). Special and remedial education in the classroom: Theme and variation. *Reading, Writing, and Learning Disabilities, 6,* 419–436.

Gensemer, E. (1998). *Teaching strategies for taking charge of task, text, situation, and personal characteristics.* Paper presented at the International Reading Association Convention, Orlando.

Gibson, E. J., & Levin, H. (1974). *The psychology of reading.* Cambridge, MA: MIT Press.

Gibson, E. J., Osser, H., & Hammonds, M. (1962). The role of grapheme-phoneme correspondence in the perception of words. *American Journal of Psychology, 75,* 554–570.

Gibson, E. J., Osser, H., & Pick, A. (1963). A study in the development of grapheme-phoneme correspondences. *Journal of Verbal Learning and Verbal Behavior, 2,* 142–146.

Gibson, L. (1989). *Literacy learning in the early years: Through children's eyes.* New York: Teachers College Press.

Gipe, J. P. (1980). Use of a relevant context helps kids learn. *The Reading Teacher, 33,* 398–402.

Glass, G. G. (1976). *Glass analysis for decoding only: Teacher's guide.* Garden City, NY: Easier to Learn.

Glynn, S. M. (1994). *Teaching science with analogies. A strategy for teachers and textbook authors. Reading Research Report No. 15.* Athens, GA: National Reading Research Center.

Gold, J., & Fleisher, L. S. (1986). Comprehension breakdown with inductively organized text: Differences between average and disabled readers. *Remedial and Special Education, 7,* 26–32.

Goldenberg, C. (1994). Promoting early literacy development among Spanish-speaking children: Lessons from two studies. In E. H. Hiebert & B. M. Taylor (Eds.), *Getting reading right from the start* (pp. 171–200). Boston: Allyn & Bacon.

Goodman, K. S. (1974). Miscue analysis: Theory and reality in reading. In J. E. Merritt (Ed.), *New horizons in reading* (pp. 15–26). Newark, DE: International Reading Association.

Goodman, K. S. (1986). *What's whole in whole language?* Portsmouth, NH: Heinemann.

Goodman, K. S. (1994a). Forward: Lots of changes, but little gained. In P. Shannon & K. Goodman (Eds.), *Basal readers: A second look* (pp. xiii–xxvii). Katonah, NY: Richard C. Owen.

Goodman, K. S. (1994b). Reading, writing, and written texts: A transactional sociopsycholinguistic view. In R. B. Ruddell, M. R. Ruddell, & H. Singer (Eds.), *Theoretical models and processes of reading* (4th ed.) (pp. 1093–1130). Newark, DE: International Reading Association.

Goodman, K. S., & Goodman, Y. M. (1978). *Reading of American children whose language is a stable rural dialect of English or a language other than English.* Detroit: Wayne State University Press (ERIC Document Reproduction Service No. ED 182 465).

Goodman, Y. M. (1985). Kidwatching: Observing children in the classroom. In A. Jagger & M. T. Smith-Burke (Eds.), *Observing the language learner* (pp. 9–18). Newark, DE: International Reading Association.

Gordon, C. J. (1985). Modeling inference awareness across the curriculum. *Journal of Reading, 28,* 444–447.

Gordon, C. J. (1989). Teaching narrative text structure: A process approach to reading and writing. In K. P. Muth (Ed.), *Children's comprehension of text: Research into practice* (pp. 79–102). Newark, DE: International Reading Association.

Gough, P. B., & Hillinger, M. L. (1980). Learning to read: An unnatural act. *Bulletin of the Orton Society, 30,* 179–196.

Gough, P. B. (1985). *One second of reading: Postscript.* In H. Singer & R. R. Ruddell (Eds.), *Theoretical models and processes of reading* (3rd. ed.) (pp. 687–688). Newark, DE: International Reading Association.

Graesser, A., Golding, J. M., & Long, D. L. (1991). Narrative representation and comprehension. In R. Barr, M. L. Kamil, P. Mosenthal, & P. D. Pearson (Eds.), *Handbook of reading research* (Vol. II, pp. 171–205). New York: Longman.

Graesser, A. C., & Bertus, E. L. (1998). The construction of causal inferences while reading expository texts on science and technology. *Scientific Studies of Reading, 2*(3), 247–269.

Graves, D. H. (1975). Examination of the writing processes of seven-year-old children. *Research in the Teaching of English, 9,* 221–241.

Graves, D. H. (1982). Break the welfare cycle: Let writers choose their topics. *Forum, 5,* 7–11.

Graves, D. H. (1983). *Writing: Teachers and children at work.* Exeter, NH: Heinemann.

Graves, M. F. (1987). Roles of instruction in fostering vocabulary development. In M. G. McKeown & M. E. Curtis (Eds.), *The nature of vocabulary acquisition* (pp. 165–184). Hillsdale, NJ: Lawrence Erlbaum.

Graves, M. F. & Dykstra, R. (1997). Contextualizing the first-grade studies: What is the best way to teach children to read? *Reading Research Quarterly, 32,* 342–344.

Graves, M. F., & Hammond, H. K. (1980). A validated procedure for teaching prefixes and its effect on students' ability to assign meaning to novel words. In M. Kamil & A. Moe (Eds.), *Perspectives on reading research and instruction* (pp. 184–188). Washington, DC: National Reading Conference.

Graves, M. F., Juel, C., Graves, B. B. (2001). *Teaching reading in the 21st century* (2nd ed.). Boston: Allyn & Bacon.

Gray, W.S., & Holmes, E. (1938). *The development of meaning vocabulary in reading.* Chicago: Publications of the University of Chicago.

Greene, J. F. (1999). *Language.* Novato, CA: Sopris West Educational Services.

Greenlaw, M. J. (1983). Reading interest research and children's choices. In N. Roser & M. Frith (Eds.), *Children's choices: Teaching with books children like* (pp. 90–92). Newark, DE: International Reading Association.

Greenwald, E. A., Persky, H. R., Campbell, J. R., Mazzeo, J. (1999). NAEP Writing Report Card for the Nation and the States. *Education Statistics Quarterly, 1*(4), 23–28.

Griffith, P. L., & Olson, M. W. (1992). Phonemic awareness helps beginning readers break the code. *The Reading Teacher, 45,* 516–523.

Gunning, T. (1975). *A comparison of word attack skills derived from a phonological analysis of frequently used words drawn from a juvenile corpus and an adult corpus.* Unpublished doctoral dissertation, Temple University, Philadelphia.

Gunning, T. (1982). Wrong level test: Wrong information. *The Reading Teacher, 35,* 902–905.

Gunning, T. (1990). *How useful is context?* Unpublished study, Southern Connecticut State University, New Haven.

Gunning, T. (1994). *Word building book D.* New York: Phoenix Learning Systems.

Gunning, T. (1995). Word building: A strategic approach to the teaching of phonics. *The Reading Teacher, 48,* 484–488.

Gunning, T. (1996). *Choosing and using books for beginning readers.* Paper presented at the annual meeting of the Connecticut Reading Conference, Waterbury.

Gunning, T. (1998a). *Assessing and correcting reading and writing difficulties.* Boston: Allyn & Bacon.

Gunning, T. (1998b). *Best books for beginning readers.* Boston: Allyn & Bacon.

Gunning, T. (1999). *Decoding behavior of good and poor second grade students.* Paper presented at the annual meeting of the National Reading Conference, Orlando.

Gunning, T. (2000a). *Assessing the difficulty level of material in the primary grades: A study in progress.* Paper presented at the annual meeting of the National Reading Conference, Scottsdale, AZ.

Gunning, T. (2000b). *Best books for building literacy for elementary school children.* Boston: Allyn & Bacon.

Gunning, T. (2000c). *Phonological awareness and primary phonics.* Boston: Allyn & Bacon.

Gunning, T. (2001). *An analysis of second graders' attempts to read multisyllabic words.* Paper presented at the annual meeting of the National Reading Conference, San Antonio, TX.

Gunning, T. (2002). *Assessing and correcting reading and writing difficulties* (2nd ed.). Boston: Allyn & Bacon.

Gunning, T. (2003). *Building literacy in the content areas*. Boston: Allyn & Bacon.

Guthrie, J. T. (1980). Research views: Time in reading programs. *The Reading Teacher, 33*, 500–502.

Guthrie, J. T., & McCann, A. D. (1997). Characteristics of classrooms that provide motivations and strategies for learning. In J. Guthrie & A. Wigfield (Eds.), *Reading engagement, Motivating readers through integrated instruction*. Newark, DE: (pp. 128–148). International Reading Association.

Guthrie, J. T., & Wigfield, A. (1997). Reading engagement: A rationale for theory and teaching. In J. Guthrie & A. Wigfield (Eds.), *Motivating readers through integrated instruction* (pp. 1–12). Newark, DE: International Reading Association.

Hackett, J. K., Moyer, R. H., & Adams, D. K. (1989). *Merrill science*. Columbus, OH: Merrill.

Hague, S. A. (1989). Awareness of text structure: The question of transfer from L1 and L2. In S. McCormick & J. Zutell (Eds.), *Cognitive and social perspectives for literacy research and instruction* (pp. 55–64). Chicago: National Reading Conference.

Halstead, J. W. (1988). *Guiding gifted readers*. Columbus, OH: Ohio Psychology.

Hammond, D. W. (2001). *The essential nature of teacher talk and its effect on students' engagement with expository text*. Paper presented at the annual meeting of the International Reading Association, New Orleans.

Hansen, J. (1981). The effects of inference training and practice on young children's reading comprehension. *Reading Research Quarterly, 16*, 391–417.

Hansen, J., & Pearson, P. D. (1980). *The effects of inference training and practice on young children's comprehension* (Technical Report No. 166). Urbana: University of Illinois, Center for the Study of Reading.

Hansen, J., & Pearson, P. D. (1982). *Improving the inferential comprehension of good and poor fourth-grade readers* (Report No. CSR-TR-235). Urbana: University of Illinois, Center for the Study of Reading (ERIC Document Reproduction Service No. ED 215–312).

Harcourt Educational Measurement (2000). *Some things parents should know about testing: a series of questions and answers*. Available online at http://www.hbem.com/library/parents.htm

Hare, V. C., & Borchardt, K. M. (1984). Direct instruction of summarization skills. *Reading Research Quarterly, 20*, 62–78.

Harmon, J. M. (1998). Constructing word meanings: Strategies and perceptions of four middle school learners. *Journal of Literacy Research, 30*, 561–599.

Harper, L. (1997). The writer's toolbox: Five tools for active revision instruction. *Language Arts, 74*, 193–200.

Harris, A. J., & Jacobson, M. D. (1982). *Basic reading vocabularies*. New York: Macmillan.

Harris, A. J., & Sipay, E. R. (1990). *How to increase reading ability* (9th ed.). New York: Longman.

Harris, T. L., & Hodges, R. E. (1995). *The literacy dictionary, the vocabulary of reading and writing*. Newark, DE: International Reading Association.

Harste, J. C., Short, K. G., & Burke, C. (1988). *Creating classrooms for authors: The reading-writing connection*. Portsmouth, NH: Heinemann.

Hartman, D. K. (1994). The intertextual links of readers using multiple passages: A postmodern semiotic/cognitive view of meaning making. In R. B. Ruddell, M. R. Ruddell, & H. Singer (Eds.), *Theoretical models and processes of reading* (4th ed.) (pp. 616–636). Newark, DE: International Reading Association.

Harvey, S. (1998). *Nonfiction matters: Reading, writing, and research in grades 3–8*. York, ME: Stenhouse.

Hayes, D. A., & Tierney, R. J. (1982). Developing readers' knowledge through analogy. *Reading Research Quarterly, 17*, 256–280.

Head, M. H., & Readence, J. E. (1986). Anticipation guides: Meaning through prediction. In E. K. Dishner, T. W. Bean, J. E. Readence, & D. W. Moore (Eds.), *Reading in the content areas* (2nd ed.) (pp. 229–234). Dubuque, IA: Kendall/Hunt.

Heath, S. B. (1991). The sense of being literate: Historical and cross-cultural features. In R. Barr, M. L. Kamil, P. Mosenthal, & P. D. Pearson (Eds.), *Handbook of reading research* (Vol. II, pp. 3–25). New York: Longman.

Heimlich, J. E., & Pittelman, S. D. (1986). *Semantic mapping: Classroom applications*. Newark, DE: International Reading Association.

Helbig, A., & Perkins, A. (2001). *Many peoples, one land: A guide to new multicultural literature for children and young adults*. New York: Greenwood.

Helper, S. (1989). A literature program: Getting it together, keeping it going. In J. Hickman & B. Culliman (Eds.), *Children's literature in the classroom: Weaving Charlotte's web* (pp. 209–220). Needham Heights, MA: Christopher-Gordon.

Henry, M. K. (1990). Reading instruction based on word structure and origin. In P. G. Aaron & R. M. Joshi (Eds.), *Reading and writing disorders in different orthographic systems* (pp. 25–49). Dordrecht, The Netherlands: Kluwer Academic Publishers.

Herber, H. L. (1970). *Teaching reading in content areas*. Englewood Cliffs, NJ: Prentice-Hall.

Herber, H. L., & Herber, J. N. (1993). *Teaching in content areas with reading, writing, and reasoning*. Boston: Allyn & Bacon.

Herman, J. L. (1992). What research tells us about good assessment. *Educational Leadership, 49*(8), 74–78.

Herman, P. A., Anderson, R. C., Pearson, P. D., & Nagy, W. E. (1987). Incidental acquisition of word meanings from expositions with varied text features. *Reading Research Quarterly, 22*, 263–284.

Hidi, S., & Anderson, V. (1986). Producing written summaries: Task demands, cognitive operations, and implications for instruction. *Review of Educational Research, 56*, 473–493.

Hiebert, E. (1983). An examination of ability grouping for reading instruction. *Reading Research Quarterly, 18*, 231–255.

Hiebert, E. (2002). *Text matters in developing reading fluency*. Paper presented at the annual conference of the Connecticut Reading Association, Cromwell, CT.

Hiebert, E. H., Pearson, P. D., Taylor, B. M., Richardson, V., & Paris, S. G. (1998). *Every child a reader*. Ann Arbor: University of Michigan School of Education, Center for the Improvement of Early Reading Achievement.

Hiebert, E. H., Valencia, S. W., & Afflerbach, P. P. (1994). Definitions and perspectives. In S. W. Valencia, E. H. Hiebert, & P. P. Afflerbach (Eds.), *Authentic reading assessment: Practices and possibilities* (pp. 6–25). Newark, DE: International Reading Association.

Hirsch, E. D. (1987). *Cultural literacy: What every American needs to know*. Boston: Houghton Mifflin.

500

Hoffman, J. V. (1991). Teacher and school effects in learning to read. In R. Barr, M. L. Kamil, P. Mosenthal, & P. D. Pearson (Eds.), *Handbook of reading research* (Vol. II, pp. 911–950). New York: Longman.

Hoffman, J. V., Assaf, L. C., & Paris, S. G. (2001). High-stakes testing in reading: Today in Texas, tomorrow? *The Reading Teacher, 54*, 482–492.

Hoffman, J. V., McCarthney, S. J., Elliott, B., Bayles, D. L., Price, D. P., Ferree, A., Abbott, J. A. (1998). The literature-based basal in first-grade classroom: Savior, Satan, or same-old, same-old? *Reading Research Quarterly, 33*, 168–197.

Hoffman, J. V., Roser, N. L., Battle, J. (1993). Reading aloud in classrooms: From the modal toward a "model." *The Reading Teacher, 46*, 496–503.

Homa, L. L. (2000). *The elementary school library collection: A guide to books and other media, phases 1-2-3* (22nd ed.). Williamsport, PA: Brodart.

Hornsby, P., Sukarna, P., & Parry, J. (1986). *Read on: A conference approach to reading.* Portsmouth, NH: Heinemann.

Huck, C. S. (1989). No wider than the heart is wide. In J. Hickman & B. E. Cullinan (Eds.), *Children's literature in the classroom: Weaving Charlotte's web* (pp. 252–262). Needham Heights, MA: Christopher-Gordon.

Huck, C. S., Helper, S., & Hickman, J. (1993). *Children's literature in the elementary school* (5th ed.). New York: Holt, Rinehart & Winston.

Hyman, R. T. (1978). *Strategic questioning.* Englewood Cliffs, NJ: Prentice-Hall.

Idol, L., & Croll, V. (1985). Story mapping training as a means of improving reading comprehension. *Learning Disability Quarterly, 10*, 214–229.

Individuals with Disabilities Act Amendments of 1997. 20 U.S.C. 1400 et seq.

International Reading Association. (1988). *New directions in reading instruction.* Newark, DE: Author.

International Reading Association. (1999). *High stakes assessments in reading: A position statement of the International Reading Association.* Newark, DE: Author.

International Reading Association. (2002). *What is evidence-based reading? A position statement of the International Reading Association.* Newark, DE: International Reading Association. Available online at http://www.reading.org/positions/evidence_based.html

International Reading Association & National Council of Teachers of English. (1996). *Standards for the English language arts.* Newark, DE: Author.

Irwin, P. A., & Mitchell, J. N. (1983). A procedure for assessing the richness of retellings. *Journal of Reading, 26*, 391–396.

Jenkins, J. R., Matlock, B., & Slocum, T. A. (1989). Approaches to vocabulary instruction. *Reading Research Quarterly, 24*, 215–235.

Jett-Simpson, M. (Ed.). (1990). *Toward an ecological assessment of reading progress.* Schofield: Wisconsin State Reading Association.

Jiganti, M. A., & Tindall, M. A. (1986). An interactive approach to teaching vocabulary. *The Reading Teacher, 39*, 444–448.

Jiménez, R. T. (1997). The strategic reading abilities and potential of five low-literacy Latina/o readers in middle school. *Reading Research Quarterly, 32*, 224–243.

Johns, J. L. (1997). *Basic reading inventory* (7th ed.). Dubuque, IA: Kendall/Hunt.

Johnson, D. D., Moe, A. J., & Baumann, J. F. (1983). *The Ginn word book for teachers: A basic lexicon.* Lexington, MA: Ginn.

Johnson, D. D., & Pearson, J. D. (1984). *Teaching reading vocabulary* (2nd ed.). New York: Holt, Rinehart & Winston.

Johnson, D. W., & Johnson, R. T. (1994). *Learning together and alone: Cooperative, competitive, and individualistic learning* (4th ed.). Boston: Allyn & Bacon.

Johnson, J. M. (Ed). (2001). *2001 educational software preview guide.* Eugene, OR: ISTE.

Johnson, M. S., & Kress, R. A. (1965). *Developing basic thinking abilities.* Unpublished manuscript, Temple University, Philadelphia.

Johnson, M. S., Kress, R. A., & Pikulski, J. J. (1987). *Informal reading inventories* (2nd ed.). Newark, DE: International Reading Association.

Johnson, N. L. (1995). *The effect of portfolio design on student attitudes toward writing.* Unpublished master's thesis, San Diego State University, San Diego.

Johnston, F. R. (1999). The timing and teaching of word families. *The Reading Teacher, 53*, 64–75.

Johnston, F. R. (2001). The utility of phonic generalizations: Let's take another look at Clymer's conclusions. *The Reading Teacher, 55*, 132–150.

Johnston, P. (1997). *Constructive evaluation of literacy* (2nd ed.). New York: Longman.

Johnston, P. H., & Rogers, R. (2001). Early literacy development: The case for "informed assessment." In S.B. Neuman & D. K. Dickinson (Eds). *Handbook of early literacy research* (pp. 377-389). New York: Guilford Press.

Joint Task Force on Assessment. (1994). *Standards for the assessment of reading and writing.* Newark, DE: International Reading Association and Urbana, IL: National Council of Teachers of English.

Jones, B, F., Palincsar, A. S., & Ogle, D. S., &. Carr, E. G. (Eds.), (1986). *Strategic teaching and learning: Cognitive instruction in the content areas* (pp. 73–91). Alexandria, VA: ASCD.

Jongsma, E. (1980). *Cloze instruction research: A second look.* Newark, DE: International Reading Association.

Jordan, G. E., Snow, C. E., & Porche, M. V. (2000). Project ease: The effect of a family literacy project on kindergarten students' early literacy skills. *Reading Research Quarterly, 35*, 524–546.

Joyce, B., & Showers, B. (1996). Staff development as a comprehensive service organization. *Journal of Staff Development, 17*(1), 2–6.

Juel, C. (1994). *Learning to read and write in one elementary school.* New York: Springer-Verlag.

Juel, C., & Minden-Cupp, C. (2000). Learning to read words: Linguistic units and instructional strategies. *Reading Research Quarterly, 35*, 458–492.

Juel, C., & Roper-Schneider, D. (1985). The influence of basal readers on first-grade reading. *Reading Research Quarterly, 20*, 134–152.

Kameenui, E. J., Dixon, R. C., & Carnine, D. W. (1987). Issues in the design of vocabulary instruction. In M. E. McKeown & M. E. Curtis (Eds.), *The nature of vocabulary instruction* (pp. 129–145). Hillsdale, NJ: Lawrence Erlbaum.

Kamhi, A. G., & Catts, H. W. (1999). Language and reading: Convergences and divergences. In H. W. Catts and A. G. Kamhi (Eds.), *Language and reading disabilities* (pp. 1–24). Boston: Allyn & Bacon.

Kamil, M. L., & Bernhardt, E. B. (2001). Reading instruction for English language learners. In M. F. Graves, C. Juell, & B. Graves, *Teaching reading in the 21st century* (pp. 460–503). Boston: Allyn & Bacon.

Keene, E. O., & Zimmermann, S. (1997). *Mosaic of thought: Teaching reading comprehension in a reader's workshop.* Portsmouth, NH: Heinemann.

Kibby, M. W. (1989). Teaching sight vocabulary with and without context before silent reading: A field test of the "focus of attention" hypothesis. *Journal of Reading Behavior, 21,* 261–278.

Kimmel, S., & MacGinitie, W. H. (1984). Identifying children who use a perseverative text processing strategy. *Reading Research Quarterly, 19,* 162–172.

Kindler, A. L. (2002). *Survey of the states' limited English proficient students and available educational programs and services 2000–2001 summary report.* Washington, DC: National Clearinghouse for English Language Acquisition & Language Instruction.

King-Sears, M. E., & Cummings, C. S. (1996). Inclusive practices of classroom teachers. *Remedial and Special Education, 17,* 217–225.

Kintsch, W. (1989). Learning from text. In L. B. Resnick (Ed.), *Knowing, learning, and instruction: Essays in honor of Robert Glaser* (pp. 25–46). Hillsdale, NJ: Lawrence Erlbaum.

Kintsch, W. (1994). The role of knowledge in discourse comprehension: A construction-integration model. In R. B. Ruddell, M. R. Ruddell, & H. Singer (Eds.), *Theoretical models and processes of reading* (4th ed.) (pp. 951–995). Newark, DE: International Reading Association.

Kletzien, S. B. (1991). Strategy use by good and poor comprehenders reading expository text of differing levels. *Reading Research Quarterly, 26,* 67–86.

Knox, C. M. (2002). *Accelerated literacy for English language learners (ELLs): A field-tested, research-based model of training and learning.* Paper presented at the annual conference of the International Reading Association, San Francisco.

Koskinen, P. S., Gambrell, L. B., Kapinus, B. A., & Heathington, B. S. (1988). Retelling: A strategy for enhancing students' reading comprehension. *The Reading Teacher, 41,* 892–896.

Krashen, S. (1991). Sheltered subject matter teaching. *Cross Currents, 18,* 183–189.

Krashen, S. (1993). *The power of reading: Insights from the research.* Englewood, CO: Libraries Unlimited.

Krashen, S. (1997–1998). Bridging inequity with books. *Educational Leadership, 55*(4), 18–21.

Kucan, L., & Beck, I. L. (1996). Thinking aloud and reading comprehension research: Inquiry, instruction, and social interaction. *Review of Educational Research, 67,* 271–299.

Kulik, J. A. (1992). *An analysis of the research on ability grouping: Historical and contemporary perspectives.* Storrs: The National Research Center on the Gifted and Talented, University of Connecticut. (ERIC Document Reproduction Service No. ED 350 777).

Kutpier, K., & Wilson, P. (1993). Updating poetry preferences: A look at the poetry children really like. *The Reading Teacher, 47,* 28–35.

Laberge, D., & Samuels, S. J. (1974). Toward a theory of automatic information processing in reading. *Cognitive Psychology, 6,* 293–323.

Lake, J. H. (1973). *The influence of wait time on the verbal dimensions of student inquiry behavior.* Dissertations Abstracts International, 34, 6476A. (University Microfilms No. 74–08866).

Landau, S. I. (1984). Dictionaries: *The art and craft of lexicography.* New York: Scribner.

Lane, B. (1993). *After the end: Teaching and learning creative revision.* Portsmouth, NH: Heinemann.

Lane, B. (1998). *The reviser's toolbox.* Shoreham, VT: Discover Writing Press.

Langer, J. A. (1981). From theory to practice: A prereading plan. *Journal of Reading, 25,* 152–156.

Langer, J. A. (1986). Reading, writing, and understanding: An analysis of the construction of meaning. *Written Communication, 3,* 219–266.

Langer, J. A. (1999). *Beating the odds: Teaching middle and high school students to read and write well.* Albany, NY: National Research Center on English Learning and Achievement. (ERIC Document Reproduction Service No. ED 435 993).

Langer, J. A., & Applebee, A. N. (1987). *How writing shapes thinking.* Urbana, IL: National Council of Teachers of English.

Langer, J. A., Applebee, A. N., Mullis, I. V. S., & Foertsch, M. A. (1990). *Learning to read in our nation's schools: Instruction and achievement in 1988 at grades 4, 8, and 12.* Princeton, NJ: Educational Testing Service.

Laufer, B., & Sim, D. D. (1985). Measuring and explaining the reading threshold needed for English for academic purposes texts. *Foreign Language Annals, 18,* 405–411.

Law, B., & Eckes, M. (2002). *The more than just surviving handbook: ESL for every classroom teacher.* Winnipeg, Canada: Portage & Main Press.

Learning Media. (1991). *Dancing with the pen: The learner as writer.* Wellington, New Zealand: Ministry of Education.

Lehr, S., & Thompson, D. L. (2000). The dynamic nature of response: Children reading and responding to *Maniac Magee* and *The Friendship. The Reading Teacher, 53,* 480–493.

Lensmire, T. (1994). *When children write: Critical re-visions of the writing workshop.* New York: Teachers College Press.

Leseman, P. P. M., & deJong, P. F. (1998). Home literacy: Opportunity, instruction, cooperation and social-emotional quality predicting early reading achievement. *Reading Research Quarterly, 33,* 294–318.

Leslie, L., & Caldwell, J. (2001). *Qualitative reading inventory-3.* New York: Addison Wesley Longman.

Leu, D. J . (2000). Exploring literacy on the Internet. *The Reading Teacher, 53,* 424–429.

Linden, M., & Wittrock, M. C. (1981). The teaching of reading comprehension according to the model of generative learning. *Reading Research Quarterly, 17,* 44–57.

Lipson, M. Y. (1984). Some unexpected issues in prior knowledge and comprehension. *The Reading Teacher, 37,* 760–764.

Lipson, M. Y., Valencia, S. W., Wixson, K. K., & Peters, C. W. (1993). Integration and thematic teaching and learning. *Language Arts, 70,* 252–263.

Lipson, M. Y., & Wixson, K. K. (1997). *Assessment and instruction of reading disability: An interactive approach* (2nd ed.). New York: HarperCollins.

Lukens, R. J. (1995). *A critical handbook of children's literature* (5th ed.). New York: HarperCollins.

Maclean, M., Bryant, P., & Bradley, L. (1987). Rhymes, nursery rhymes, and reading in early childhood. *Merrill Palmer Quarterly, 33,* 255–281.

Madden, N. (2000, February). Meeting the expository challenge with SFA. *Success Stories,* p. 6. Available online at http://www.successforall.net/current/newsletters.htm

Manning, G. L., & Manning, M. (1984). What models of recreational reading make a difference? *Reading World, 23,* 375–380.

Many, J., Fyfe, R., Lewis, G., & Mitchell, E. (1996). Traversing the topical landscape: Exploring students' self-directed reading-writing-research processes. *Reading Research Quarterly, 31,* 122–135.

Many, J. E. (1990). The effect of reader stance on students' personal understanding of literature. In J. Zutell & S. McCormick (Eds.), *Literacy theory and research: Analyses from multiple paradigms* (thirty-ninth yearbook of the National Reading Conference) (pp. 51–63). Chicago: National Reading Conference.

Many, J. E. (1991). The effects of stance and age level on children's literary responses. *Journal of Reading Behavior, 21,* 61–85.

Manzo, A. V. (1969). The ReQuest procedure. *Journal of Reading, 13,* 123–126.

Manzo, A. V., & Manzo, V. C. (1993). *Literacy disorders.* Fort Worth, TX: Harcourt Brace Jovanovich.

Maria, K. (1990). *Reading comprehension instruction: Issues and strategies.* Parkton, MD: York Press.

Maria, K., & MacGinitie, W. (1987). Learning from texts that refute the reader's prior knowledge. *Reading Research and Instruction, 26,* 222–238.

Marshall, S. C. (2002). *Are they really reading? Expanding SSR in the middle grades.* Portland, ME: Stenhouse.

Martinez, E. (1998). *CyberGuide for* Caddie Woodlawn. San Diego: San Diego County Office of Education. Available online at http://www.sdcoe.k12.ca.us/score/caddie/caddiesg3.html

Marzano, R. J., & Marzano, J. S. (1988). *A cluster approach to elementary vocabulary instruction.* Newark, DE: International Reading Association.

Mastropierei, M. A., & Scruggs, T. E. (1994). Text verus hands-on science curriculum: Implications for students with disabilities. *Remedial and Special Education, 15*(2), 72–85.

Matthews, J. K. (1990). From computer management to portfolio assessment. *The Reading Teacher, 43,* 420–421.

McArthur, T. (Ed.). (1992). *The Oxford companion to the English language.* New York: Oxford University.

McClure, A. A., Harrison, P., & Reed, S. (1990). *Sunrises and songs: Reading and writing poetry in an elementary classroom.* Portsmouth, NH: Heinemann.

McClure, A. A., & Kristo, J. V. (Eds.). (1994). *Inviting children's responses to literature.* Urbana, IL: National Council of Teachers of English.

McCormick, S. (1992). Disabled readers' erroneous responses to inferential comprehension questions: Description and analysis. *Reading Research Quarterly, 27,* 55–77.

McCoy, K. M., & Pany, D. (1986). Summary and analysis of oral reading corrective feedback research. *The Reading Teacher, 39,* 548–554.

McCracken, R. A. (1991). *Spelling through phonics.* Grand Forks, ND: Pegusis.

McGee, L. M. (1995). Talking about books with young children. In N. L. Roser & M. G. Martinez (Eds.), *Book talk and beyond* (pp. 105–115). Newark, DE: International Reading Association.

McGee, L. M., & Tompkins, G. E. (1981). The videotape answer to independent reading comprehension activities. *The Reading Teacher, 34,* 427–433.

McGill-Franzen, A. (1994). Compensatory and special education: Is there accountability for learning and belief in children's potential? In E. H. Hiebert & B. M. Taylor (Eds.), *Getting reading right from the start: Effective early literacy interventions* (pp. 13–35). Boston: Allyn & Bacon.

McKenna, M. C., & Kerr, D. J. (1990). Measuring attitude toward reading: A new tool for teachers. *The Reading Teacher, 43,* 626–639.

McKeown, M. G. (1993). Creating effective definitions for young word learners. *Reading Research Quarterly, 28,* 16–32.

McKeown, M. G., Beck, I. L., & Sandora, C. A. (1996). Questioning the author: An approach to developing meaningful classroom discourse. In M. F. Graves, P. Van den Broek, & B. M. Taylor, (Eds.), *The first R, every child's right to read* (pp. 97–119). New York: Teachers College Press.

McLaughlin, B., August, D., Snow, C., Carlo, M., Dressier, C., White, C., Lively, T., & Lippman, D. (2000). *Vocabulary knowledge and reading comprehension in English language learners. Final performance report.* Washington, DC: Office of Educational Research and Improvement. Available online at http://www.ncela.gwu.edu/ncbepubs/symposia/reading/6ugust.PDF

McMahon, S. (1997). Book clubs: Contexts for students to lead their own discussions. In S. I. McMahon & T. E. Raphael (Eds.), *The book club connection: Literacy learning and classroom talk* (pp. 89–106). New York: Teachers College Press.

McMaster, J. C. (1998). "Doing" literature: Using drama to build literacy. *The Reading Teacher, 51,* 574–584.

McNamara, T. P., Miller, D. L., & Bransford, J. D. (1991). Mental models and reading comprehension. In R. Barr, M. L. Kamil, P. Mosenthal, & P. D. Pearson (Eds.), *Handbook of reading research* (Vol. II, pp. 490–511). New York: Longman.

McNeil, J. D. (1987). *Reading comprehension: New directions for classroom practice* (2nd ed.). Glenview, IL: Scott, Foresman.

Medley, D. M. (1977). *Teacher competence and teacher effectiveness: A review of process-product research.* Washington, DC: American Association of Colleges for Teacher Education.

Melmed, P. J. (1973). Black English phonology: The question of reading interference. In J. L. Laffey & R. Shuy (Eds.), *Language differences: Do they interfere?* (pp. 70–85). Newark, DE: International Reading Association.

Menke, P. J., & Pressley, M. (1994). Elaborative interrogation: Using "why" questions to enhance the learning from text. *Journal of Reading, 37,* 642–645.

Meyer, B. J. F., & Rice, G. E. (1984). The structure of text. In P. D. Pearson, R. Barr, M. L. Kamil, & P. Mosenthal (Eds.), *Handbook of reading research* (pp. 319–351). New York: Longman.

Meyers, K. L. (1988). Twenty (better) questions. *English Journal, 77*(1), 64–65.

Mills, E. (1974). Children's literature and teaching written composition. *Elementary English, 51,* 971–973.

Modiano, N. (1968). National or mother language in beginning reading: A comparative study. *Research in the Teaching of English, 2,* 32–43.

Moldofsky, P. B. (1983). Teaching students to determine the central story problem: A practical application of schema theory. *The Reading Teacher, 38,* 377–382.

Moore, D. W., & Moore, S. A. (1986). Possible sentences. In E. K. Dishner, T. W. Bean, J. E. Readence, & D. W. Moore (Eds.), *Reading in the content areas: Improving classroom instruction* (2nd ed.) (pp. 174–179). Dubuque, IA: Kendall/Hunt.

Moore, D. W., Moore, S. A., Cunningham, P. M., & Cunningham, J. W. (1986). *Developing readers and writers in the content areas.* New York: Longman.

Morrow, L. M. (1985). Reading and retelling stories: Strategies for emergent readers. *The Reading Teacher, 38,* 871–875.

Morrow, L. M. (1997). *Literacy development in the early years: Helping children read and write* (3rd ed.). Boston: Allyn & Bacon

Morrow, L. M., & Asbury, E. B. (2001). Patricia Loden. In M.

Pressley, R. L. Allington, R. Wharton-McDonald, C. C. Block, & L. M. Morrow (Eds.), *Learning to read: Lessons from exemplary first-grade classrooms* (pp. 184–202). New York: Guilford Press.

Mosenthal, J. H. (1990). Developing low-performing, fourth-grade, inner-city students' ability to comprehend narrative. In J. Zutell & S. McCormick (Eds.), *Literacy theory and research: Analyses from multiple paradigms* (thirty-ninth yearbook of the National Reading Conference) (pp. 275–286). Chicago: National Reading Conference.

Moustafa, M., & Maldonado-Colon, E. (1999). Whole-to-part phonics instruction: Building on what children know to help them know more. *The Reading Teacher, 52*, 448–458.

Mullis, I. V. S., Campbell, J. R., & Farstrup, A. E. (1993). *Executive summary of the NAEP 1992 reading report card for the nation and the states.* Princeton, NJ: Educational Testing Service.

Murphy, L. L., Plake, B. S., Impara, J. C., & Spies, R. A. (Eds.). (2003). *Tests in print VI.* Lincoln: University of Nebraska Press.

Murray, D. (1979). The listening eye: Reflections on the writing conference. *College English, 41*, 13–18.

Murray, D. M. (1989). *Expecting the unexpected: Teaching myself—and others—to read and write.* Portsmouth, NH: Boynton/Cook.

Muschla, G. R. (1993). *Writing workshop survival kit.* West Nyack, NY: Center for Applied Research in Education.

Muter, V., & Snowling, M. (1998). Concurrent and longitudinal predictors of reading: The role of metalinguistic and short-term memory skills. *Reading Research Quarterly, 33*, 320–337.

Muth, K. D. (1987). Teachers' connection questions: Prompting students to organize text ideas. *Journal of Reading, 31*, 254–259.

Nagy, W., García, G. E., Durgunoglu, A., & Hancin-Bhatt, B. (1993). Spanish-English bilingual students' use of cognates in English reading. *Journal of Reading Behavior, 25*, 241–259.

Nagy, W. E. (1988). *Teaching vocabulary to improve reading comprehension.* Newark, DE: International Reading Association.

Nagy, W. E., & Anderson, R. C. (1984). How many words are there in printed English? *Reading Research Quarterly, 19*, 304–330.

Nagy, W. E., Anderson, R. C., & Herman, P. A. (1987). Learning word meanings from context during normal reading. *American Educational Research Journal, 24*, 237–270.

Nagy, W. E., & Herman, P. A. (1987). Breadth and depth of vocabulary knowledge: Implications for acquisition and instruction. In M. G. McKeown & M. E. Curtis (Eds.), *The nature of vocabulary acquisition* (pp. 19–35). Hillsdale, NJ: Lawrence Erlbaum.

Nagy, W. E., & Scott, J. A. (2000). Vocabulary processes. In M. L. Kamil, P. B. Mosenthal, P. D. Pearson, & R. Barr (Eds.), *Handbook of Reading Research* (Vol. III, pp. 269–284). Mahwah, NJ: Erlbaum.

Nation, P. (2001). *Learning vocabulary in another language.* Cambridge: Cambridge University Press.

National Assessment Governing Board. (2001). *Reading framework for the national assessment of educational progress: 1992–2000.* Washington, DC: Author. Available online at http://www.nagb. org/pubs/read92-2000.pdf

National Center on Education and the Economy & The University of Pittsburgh. (1997). *Performance standards, Vol. 1, Elementary school.* Washington, DC: New Standards.

National Center on Education and the Economy & The University of Pittsburgh. (2001). *Speaking and listening for preschool through third grade.* Washington, DC: New Standards.

National Institute of Environmental Health Sciences (2002). National Institute of Environmental Health Sciences kids' Pages. Available online at http://www.niehs.nih.gov/kids/home.htm

Nessel, D. (1987). The new face of comprehension instruction: A closer look at questions. *The Reading Teacher, 40*, 604–606.

New Standards Primary Literacy Committee (1999). *Reading and writing grade by grade: Primary literacy standards through third grade.* Washington, DC: National Center on Education and the Economy & The University of Pittsburgh.

Nisbet, J., & Shucksmith, J. (1986). *Learning strategies.* London: Routledge & Kegan Paul.

Nist, S. L., & Simpson, M. L. (1989). PLAE, a validated study strategy. *Journal of Reading, 33*, 182–186.

No Child Left Behind Act of 2001, Public Law PL 107–110, Sec. 1001.

Noyce, R., & Christie, J. F. (1989). *Integrating reading and writing instruction in grades K–8.* Boston: Allyn & Bacon.

Nystrand, M., & Gamoran, A. (1991). Instructional discourse, student engagement, and literature achievement. *Research in the Teaching of English, 25*, 261–292.

Oakhill, J., & Yuill, N. (1996). Higher-order factors in comprehension disability: Processess and remediation. In C. Cornoldi & J. Oakhill (Eds.), *Reading comprehension difficulties: Process and intervention* (pp. 69–92). Mahwah, NJ: Erlbaum.

O'Brien, C. A. (1973). *Teaching the language-different child to read.* Columbus, OH: Merrill.

O'Donnell, M. D. (1997). Boston's Lewenberg Middle School delivers success. *Phi Delta Kappan, 78*, 508–512.

Ogle, D., & Fogelberg, E. (2001). Expanding collaborative roles of reading specialists: Developing an intermediate reading support program. In V. J. Risko & K. Bromley (Eds), *Collaboration for diverse learners: Viewpoints and practices.* Newark, DE: International Reading Association.

Ogle, D. M. (1989). The know, want to know, learn strategy. In K. D. Muth (Ed.), *Children's comprehension of text* (pp. 205–223). Newark, DE: International Reading Association.

Olson, J. L. (1987). Drawing to write. *School Arts, 87*(1), 25–27.

Oregon Department of Education. (2001). *Frequently asked questions: Test administration.* Available online at http://www. ode.state.or.us/asmt/faqs/

O'Rourke, J. P. (1974). *Toward a science of vocabulary development.* The Hague: Mouton.

Palincsar, A. S., & Brown, A. L. (1986). Interactive teaching to promote independent learning from text. *The Reading Teacher, 39*, 771–777.

Palincsar, A. S., Winn, J., David, Y., Snyder, B., & Stevens, D. (1993). Approaches to strategic reading instruction reflecting different assumptions regarding teaching and learning. In L. J. Meltzer (Ed.), *Strategy assessment and instruction for students with learning disabilities: From theory to practice* (pp. 247–292). Austin, TX: Pro-Ed.

Paris, S. G., Wasik, B. A., & Turner, J. C. (1991). The development of strategic readers. In R. Barr, M. L. Kamil, P. Mosenthal, & P. D. Pearson (Eds.), *Handbook of reading research* (Vol. II, pp. 609–640). New York: Longman.

Parker, D. (2002). *Accelerated literacy for English language learners (ELLs): A field-tested, research-based model of training and learning.* Paper presented at the annual conference of the International Reading Association, San Francisco.

504

Parsons, L. (1990). *Response journals.* Portsmouth, NH: Heinemann.

Pauk, W. (1989). The new SQ3R. *Reading World, 23,* 386–387.

Pearson, P. D. (1985). Changing the face of reading comprehension instruction. *The Reading Teacher, 38,* 724–738.

Pearson, P. D., & Camperell, K. (1994). Comprehension of text structures. In R. B. Ruddell, M. R. Ruddell, & H. Singer (Eds.), *Theoretical models and processes of reading* (4th ed.) (pp. 448–568). Newark, DE: International Reading Association.

Pearson, P. D., & Gallagher, M. C. (1983). The instruction of reading comprehension. *Contemporary Educational Psychology, 8,* 317–345.

Pearson, P. D., & Johnson, D. D. (1978). *Teaching reading comprehension.* New York: Holt, Rinehart & Winston.

Peters, E. E., & Levin, J. R. (1986). Effects of a mnemonic imagery strategy on good and poor readers' prose recall. *Reading Research Quarterly, 21,* 179–192.

Peterson, R. (1992). *Life in a crowded place: Making a learning community.* Portsmouth, NH: Heinemann.

Petty, W., Herold, C., & Stoll, E. (1968). *The state of the knowledge of the teaching of vocabulary* (Cooperative Research Project No. 3128). Champaign, IL: National Council of Teachers of English.

Pike, K., Compain, R., & Mumper, J. (1994). *New connections: An integrated approach to literacy.* New York: HarperCollins.

Pinnell, G. S., & Fountas, I. C. (1998). *Word matters.* Portsmouth, NH: Heinemann.

Pinnell, G. S., & Fountas, I. C. (2002). *Leveled books for readers grades 3–6.* Portsmouth, NH: Heinemann.

Pinnell, G. S., Pikulski, J. J., Wixson, K.K., Campbell, J. R., Gough, P. B., & Beatty, A. S. (1995) *Listening to children read aloud.* Washington, DC: U.S. Department of Education, National Center for Education Statistics.

Plake, B. S., Impara, J. C., & Spies, R. A. (Eds.). (2003). *The fifteenth mental measurements yearbook.* Lincoln: University of Nebraska Press.

Popham, W. J. (2000). *Modern educational measurement: Practical guidelines for educational leaders.* Boston: Allyn & Bacon.

Prawat, R. S. (1989). Promoting access to knowledge, strategy, and disposition in students: A research synthesis. *Review of Educational Research, 59,* 1–41.

Pressley, M. (1994). *What makes sense in reading instruction according to research.* Paper presented at the annual meeting of the Connecticut Reading Association, Waterbury.

Pressley, M., Allington, R. L., Wharton-McDonald, R., Block, C. C., & Morrow, L. M. (2001). The nature of first-grade instruction that promotes literacy achievement. In M. Pressley, R. L. Allington, R. Wharton-McDonald, C. C. Block, & L. M. Morrow (Eds.), *Learning to read: Lessons from exemplary first-grade classrooms* (pp. 48–69). New York: Guilford Press.

Pressley, M., Borkowski, J. G., Forrest-Pressley, D., Gaskins, I. W., & Wiley, D. (1990). *Cognitive strategy instruction that really improves children's academic performance.* Cambridge, MA: Brookline Books.

Pressley, M., Borkowski, J. G., Forrest-Pressley, D., Gaskins, I. W., & Wiley, D. (1993). Closing thoughts on strategy instruction for individuals with learning disabilities: The good information-processing perspective. In L. Meltzer (Ed.), *Strategy assessment and instruction for students with learning disabilities: From theory to practice* (pp. 355–377). Austin, TX: Pro-Ed.

Pressley, M., Johnson, C. J., Symons, S., McGoldrick, J. A., &

Kurita, J. A. (1989). Strategies that improve children's memory and comprehension of what is read. *Elementary School Journal, 89,* 3–32.

Pressley, M., Levin, J. R., & McDaniel, M. A. (1987). Remembering versus inferring what a word means: Mnemonic and contextual approaches. In M. G. McKeown & M. E. Curtis (Eds.), *The nature of vocabulary acquisition* (pp. 107–127). Hillsdale, NJ: Lawrence Erlbaum.

Pressley, M., Levin, J. R., & Miller, G. E. (1981). How does the keyword method affect vocabulary comprehension and usage? *Reading Research Quarterly, 16,* 213–226.

Pressley, M., Ross, K. A., Levin, J. R., & Ghatala, E. S. (1984). The role of strategy utility knowledge in children's strategy decision making. *Journal of Experimental Child Psychology, 38,* 491–504.

Pressley, M., Wharton-McDonald, R., Mistretta-Hampston, J., & Echevarria, M. (1998). Literacy instruction in 10 fourth- and fifth-grade classrooms in upstate New York. *Scientific Studies of Reading, 2,* 159–194.

Probst, R. (1988). Dialogue with a text. *English Journal, 77*(1), 32–38.

Prochaska, J. O., Norcross, J. C., & DiClemente, D. C. (1994). *Changing for the good.* New York: Avon.

Radencich, M. C. (1995). *Administration and supervision of the reading/writing program.* Boston: Allyn & Bacon.

Radencich, M. C., Beers, P. G., & Schumm, J. S. (1993). *A handbook for the K–12 resource specialist.* Boston: Allyn & Bacon.

Ramos, F., & Krashen, S. (1998). The impact of one trip to the public library: Making books available may be the best incentive for reading. *The Reading Teacher, 51,* 614–615.

Raphael, T. E. (1984). Teaching learners about sources of information for answering questions. *The Reading Teacher, 28,* 303–311.

Raphael, T. E. (1986). Teaching question/answer relationships, revisited. *The Reading Teacher, 39,* 516–522.

Raphael, T. E., & Boyd, F. B. (1997). When readers write: The book club writing component. In S. I. McMachon & T. E. Raphael (Eds.), *The book club connection: Literacy learning and classroom talk* (pp. 69–88). New York: Teachers College Press.

Raphael, T. E., & Englert, C. S. (1989). Integrating reading and writing instruction. In P. Winograd, K. K. Wixson, & M. Y. Lipson (Eds.). *Improving basal reading instruction* (pp. 231-255). New York: Teachers College Press.

Raphael, T. E., & Englert, C. S. (1990). Writing and reading: Partners in constructing meaning. *The Reading Teacher, 43,* 388–400.

Raphael, T. E., Englert, C. S., & Kirschner, B. W. (1989). Acquisition of expository writing skills. In J. M. Mason (Ed.), *Reading and writing connections* (pp. 261–290). Boston: Allyn & Bacon.

Rashotte, C. A., & Torgesen, J. K. (1985). Repeated reading and reading fluency in learning disabled children. *Reading Research Quarterly, 20,* 180–188.

Readence, J. E., Bean, T. W., & Baldwin, R. S. (1992). *Content area literacy: An integrated approach* (4th ed.). Dubuque, IA: Kendall/Hunt.

Reeve, J., Bolt, E., & Cai, Y. (1999). Autonomy-supportive teachers: How they teach and motivate students. *Journal of Educational Psychology, 91,* 537–548.

Reinking, D., & Rickman, S. S. (1990). The effects of computer-mediated texts on the vocabulary learning and comprehension of intermediate-grade readers. *Journal of Reading Behavior, 22,* 395–411.

Reutzel, D. R., & Cooter, R. B. (1991). Organizing for effective instruction: The reading workshop. *The Reading Teacher, 44*, 548-555.

Reutzel, D. R., & Cooter, R. B. (1992). *Teaching children to read: From basals to books.* New York: Macmillan.

Rhodes, L. K. (1990, March). *Anecdotal records: A powerful tool for ongoing literacy assessment.* Paper presented at the National Council of Teachers of English spring conference, Colorado Springs, CO.

Richardson, J. S., & Morgan, R. F. (1994). *Reading to learn in the content areas* (2nd ed.). Belmont, CA: Wadsworth.

Richgels, D. S., & Hansen, R. (1984). Gloss: Helping students apply both skills and strategies in reading content texts. *Journal of Reading, 27*, 312–317.

Richgels, D. S., McGee, L. M., & Slaton, E. A. (1989). Teaching expository text structure in reading and writing. In K. D. Muth (Ed.), *Children's comprehension of text* (pp. 167–184). Newark, DE: International Reading Association.

Richgels, D. S., & Wold, L. S. (1998). Literacy on the road: Backpacking partnerships between school and home. *The Reading Teacher, 52*, 18–29.

Rickelman, R. J., & Henk, W. A. (1990). Reading technology: Children's literature and audio/visual technologies. *The Reading Teacher, 43*, 682–684.

Rimer, S. (1990, June 19). Slow readers sparkling with a handful of words. *The New York Times*, pp. B1, B5.

Rinehart, S. D., Stahl, S. A., & Erickson, L. G. (1986). Some effects of summarization training on reading and studying. *Reading Research Quarterly, 21*, 422–438.

Rist, R. (1970). Student social class and teacher expectations: The self-fulfilling prophecy in ghetto education. *Harvard Educational Review, 40*, 411–451.

Robinson, D. H. (1998). Graphic organizers as aids to text learning. *Reading Research and Instruction, 37*, 85–105.

Robinson, F. P. (1970). *Effective study* (4th ed.). New York: Harper & Row.

Rodriguez, T. A. (2001). Teaching ideas: From the known to the unknown: Using cognates to teach English to Spanish-speaking literates. *The Reading Teacher, 54*, 744–746.

Rose, M. C., Cundick, B. P., & Higbee, K. L. (1983). Verbal rehearsal and visual imagery: Mnemonic aids for learning disabled children. *Journal of Learning Disabilities, 16*, 352–354.

Rosenblatt, L. (1978). *The reader, the text, the poem.* Carbondale: Southern Illinois University Press.

Rosenblatt, L. (1991). Literature—S. O. S.! *Language Arts, 68*, 444–448.

Rosenblatt, L. M. (1990). Retrospect. In E. S. Farrell & J. R. Squire (Eds.), *Transactions with literature: A fifty-year perspective* (pp. 97-107). Urbana, IL: National Council of Teachers of English.

Rosenblatt, L. M. (1994). The traditional theory of reading and writing. In R. B. Ruddell, M. R. Ruddell, & H. Singer (Eds.), *Theoretical models and processes of reading* (4th ed.) (pp. 1057–1092). Newark, DE: International Reading Association.

Rosenshine, B., & Meister, C. (1994). Reciprocal teaching: A review of the research. *Review of Educational Research, 64*, 479–530.

Rosenshine, B., Meister, C., & Chapman, S. (1996). Teaching students to generate questions: A review of the intervention studies. *Review of Educational Research, 66*, 181–221.

Rosenshine, B., & Stevens, R. (1984). Classroom instruction in reading. In P. D. Pearson, R. Barr, M. L. Kamil, & P.

Mosenthal (Eds.), *Handbook of reading research* (Vol. II, pp. 745–798). New York: Longman.

Rosier, P. (1977). *A comparative study of two approaches introducing initial reading to Navajo children: The direct method and the native language method.* Unpublished doctoral dissertation, Northern Arizona University, Flagstaff.

Routman, R. (1991). *Invitations: Changing as teachers and learners K–12.* Portsmouth, NH: Heinemann.

Rowand, C. (2000). Teacher use of computers and the Internet in public schools. *Education Statistics Quarterly, 2*(2), 72–75. Available online at http://www.asd.com/asd/

Rowe, M. B. (1969). Science, silence, and sanctions. *Science for Children, 6*(6), 11–13.

Ruddell, M. R. (1992). Integrated content and long-term vocabulary learning with the vocabulary self-collection strategy. In E. K. Dishner, T. W. Bean, J. E. Readence, & D. W. Moore (Eds.), *Reading in the content areas: Improving classroom instruction* (3rd ed.) (pp. 190–196). Dubuque, IA: Kendall/Hunt.

Ruddell, R. B. (1995). Those influential literacy teachers: Meaning negotiators and motivators. *The Reading Teacher, 48*, 454–463.

Ruddell, R. B., & Boyle, O. F. (1989). A study of cognitive mapping as a means to improve summarization and comprehension of expository text. *Reading Research and Instruction, 29*(1), 12–22.

Rumelhart, D. (1980). Schemata: The building blocks of cognition. In R. J. Spiro, B. C. Bruce, & W. F. Bruner (Eds.), *Theoretical issues in reading comprehension* (pp. 33–58). Hillsdale, NJ: Lawrence Erlbaum.

Rumelhart, D. (1984). Understanding understanding. In J. Flood (Ed.), *Understanding reading comprehension* (pp. 1–20). Newark, DE: International Reading Association.

Ryder, R. J., & Graves, M. F. (1994). Vocabulary instruction presented prior to reading in two basal programs. *Elementary School Journal, 95*, 139–152.

Rye, J. (1982). *Cloze procedure and the teaching of reading.* London: Heinemann.

Sadow, M. K. (1982). The use of story grammar in the design of questions. *The Reading Teacher, 35*, 518–522.

Sadowski, M., & Paivio, A. (1994). A dual coding view of imagery and verbal processes in reading comprehension. In R. B. Ruddell, M. R. Ruddell, & H. Singer (Eds.), *Theoretical models and processes of reading* (4th ed.) (pp. 582–601). Newark, DE: International Reading Association.

Salinger, T. (2001). Assessing the literacy of young children: The case for multiple forms of evidence. In S. B. Neuman & D. K. Dickinson (Eds), *Handbook of early literacy research* (pp. 390–418). New York: Guilford Press.

Samuels, S. J. (1979). Decoding and automaticity: Helping poor readers become automatic at word recognition. *The Reading Teacher, 41*, 756-760.

Samuels, S. J. (1988a). Characteristics of exemplary reading programs. In S. J. Samuels & P. D. Pearson (Eds.), *Changing school reading programs: Principles and case studies* (pp. 3–9). Newark, DE: International Reading Association.

Samuels, S. J. (1988b). Decoding and automaticity: Helping poor readers become automatic at word recognition. *The Reading Teacher, 41*, 756–760.

Samuels, S. J. (1994). Toward a theory of automatic information processing in reading revisited. In R. B. Ruddell, M. R. Ruddell, & H. Singer (Eds.), *Theoretical models and processes of reading* (4th ed.) (pp. 816–837). Newark, DE: International Reading Association.

Santa, C. (1989). *Comprehension strategies across content areas.* Paper presented at the annual conference of the New England Reading Association, Newport, RI.

Santa, C. (1994, October). *Teaching reading in the content areas.* Paper presented at the International Reading Association's Southwest Regional Conference, Little Rock, AR.

Santa, C. M. (1988). *Reading opportunities in literature.* Unpublished manuscript.

Scardamalia, M., & Bereiter, C. (1986). Research on written composition. In M. C. Wittrock (Ed.), *Handbook of research on teaching* (pp. 778–863). New York: Macmillan.

Schatz, E. K., & Baldwin, R. S. (1986). Context clues are unreliable predictors of word meanings. *Reading Research Quarterly, 21*, 439–453.

Schiefele, U. (1999). Interest and learning from text. *Scientific Studies of Reading, 3*, 257–279.

Schnorr, J. A., & Atkinson, R. C. (1969). Repetition versus imagery instructions in the short- and long-term retention of paired associates. *Psychonomic Science, 15*, 183–184.

Schulz, J. B. (1993). Teaching students with disabilities in the regular classroom. In J. A. Banks & C. A. M. Banks (Eds.), *Multicultural education: Issues and perspectives* (2nd ed.) (pp. 262–278). Boston: Allyn & Bacon.

Schunk, D. H., & Rice, J. H. (1987). Enhancing comprehension skill and self-efficacy with strategy value information. *Journal of Reading Behavior, 19*, 285–302.

Schunk, D. H., & Zimmerman, B. J. (1997). Developing self-efficacious readers and writers: The role of social and self-regulatory processes. In J. T. Guthrie & A. Wigfield (Eds.), *Reading engagement: Motivating readers through integrated instruction* (pp. 34–50). Newark, DE: International Reading Association.

Schickedanz, J. A. (1999). *Much more than the abcs: The early stages of reading and writing.* Washington, DC: National Association for the Education of Young Children.

Scott, T. (1998). *Using content area text to teach decoding and comprehension strategies.* Paper presented at the annual meeting of the International Reading Association, Orlando.

Searfoss, L. W., & Readence, J. E. (1994). *Helping children learn to read* (3rd ed.). Boston: Allyn & Bacon.

Shearer, B. (1999). *The vocabulary self-collection strategy (VSS) in a middle school.* Paper presented at the forty-ninth annual meeting of the National Reading Conference, Orlando.

Shefelbine, J. (1990). A syllabic-unit approach to teaching decoding of polysyllabic words to fourth- and sixth-grade disabled readers. In J. Zutell & S. McCormick (Eds.), *Literacy theory and research: Analyses from multiple paradigms* (thirty-ninth yearbook of the National Reading Conference) (pp. 223–229). Chicago: National Reading Conference.

Shefelbine, J., & Calhoun, J. (1991). Variability in approaches to identifying polysyllabic words: A descriptive study of sixth graders with highly, moderately, and poorly developed syllabication strategies. In S. McCormick & J. Zutell (Eds.), *Learner factors/teacher factors: Issues in literacy research and instruction* (pp. 169–177). Chicago: National Reading Conference.

Shefelbine, J., & Newman, K. K. (2000). *SIPPS (systematic instruction in phoneme awareness, phonics, and sight words): Challenge level.* Concord, CA: Developmental Studies Center.

Short, K. G. (1990, March). *Using evaluation to support learning in process-centered classrooms.* Paper presented at the spring conference of the National Council of Teachers of English, Colorado Springs, CO.

Shuy, R. (1973). Nonstandard dialect problems: An overview. In J. L. Laffey & R. Shuy (Eds.), *Language differences: Do they interfere?* (pp. 3–16). Newark, DE: International Reading Association.

Silvaroli, N. J., & Wheelock, A. (2001). *Classroom reading inventory* (9th ed.). New York: McGraw-Hill.

Simmons, J. (1990a). Portfolios as large-scale assessment. *Language Arts, 67*, 262–268.

Simmons, J. (1990b). What writers know with time. *Language Arts, 73*, 602–605.

Simmons, J. (1996). What writers know with time. *Language Arts, 73*, 602–605.

Sims, R. S. (Ed.). (1994). *Kaleidoscope, A multicultural booklist for grades K–8.* Urbana, IL: National Council of Teachers of English.

Sinatra, G. M., Brown, K. J. & Reynolds, R. E. (2002). Implications of cognitive resource allocation for comprehension strategy instruction. In C. C. Block & M. Pressley (Eds.), *Comprehension instruction: Research-based best practices* (pp. 62–76). New York: Guilford Press.

Sinatra, R. C., Stahl-Gemeke, J., & Berg, D. N. (1984). Improving reading comprehension of disabled readers through semantic mapping. *The Reading Teacher, 38*, 22–29.

Sinatra, R. C., Stahl-Gemeke, J., & Morgan, N. W. (1986). Using semantic mapping after reading to organize and write original discourse. *Journal of Reading, 30*, 4–13.

Singer, H., & Donlan, D. (1989). *Reading and learning from text* (2nd ed.). Hillsdale, NJ: Lawrence Erlbaum.

Singleton, S. (1997). The creation of a basal program: A collaborative effort. In J. Flood, S. B. Heath, & D. Lapp (Eds.), *Handbook of research on teaching literacy through the communicative and visual arts* (pp. 869–871). New York: Simon & Schuster Macmillan.

Skillings, M. J., & Ferrell, R. (2000). Student-generated rubrics: Bringing students into the assessment process. *The Reading Teacher, 53*, 452–455.

Slater, W. H., & Graves, M. F. (1989). Research on expository text. Implications for teachers. In K. D. Muth (Ed.), *Children's comprehension of text* (pp. 140–166). Newark, DE: International Reading Association.

Slavin, R. E. (1987a). Ability grouping and student achievement in elementary schools: A best-evidence synthesis. *Review of Education Research, 57*, 293–336.

Slavin, R. E. (1987b). Cooperative learning and the cooperative school. *Educational Leadership, 45*(3), 7–13.

Slavin, R. E. (1997–1998). Can education reduce societal inequity? *Educational Leadership, 55*(4), 6–10.

Sloan, G. D. (1984). *The child as critic* (2nd ed.). New York: Teachers College Press.

Snider, M. A., Lima, S. S., & DeVito, P. J. (1994). Rhode Island's literacy portfolio assessment project. In S. Valencia, E. H. Hiebert, & P. P. Afflerbach (Eds.), *Authentic reading assessment: Practices and possibilities* (pp. 71–88). Newark, DE: International Reading Association.

Snow, C. E. (Ed.) (2002). *Reading for understanding: Toward a research and development program in reading comprehension, MR–1465.* Santa Monica, CA: Rand Cooperation. Available online at http://www.rand.org/

Snow, C. E., Burns, M. S., & Griffin, P. (1998). *Preventing reading difficulties in young children.* Washington, DC: National Academy Press.

Spandel, V. (2001). *Creating writers through 6-trait writing assessment and instruction.* New York: Longman.

Spandel, V., & Stiggins, R. J. (1997). *Creating writers: Linking writing assessment and instruction* (2nd ed.). New York: Longman.

Spearitt, D. (1972). Identification of subskills and reading comprehension by maximum likelihood factor analysis. *Reading Research Quarterly, 8*, 92–111.

Spencer, P. G. (1984). Booktalking seventeen hundred students at once—Why not? *English Journal, 73*, 86–87.

Spires, H. A., & Donley, J. (1998). Prior knowledge activation: Inducing engagement with informational texts. *Journal of Educational Psychology, 90*, 249–260.

Squire, J. R. (1994). Research in reader response, naturally interdisciplinary. In R. B. Ruddell, M. R. Ruddell, & H. Singer (Eds.), *Theoretical models and processes of reading* (4th ed.) (pp. 637–652). Newark, DE: International Reading Association.

Stahl, S. A. (1998). Teaching children with reading problems to decode: Phonics and "not-phonics" instruction. *Reading and Writing Quarterly: Overcoming Learning Disabilities, 14*, 165–188.

Stahl, S. A., & Fairbanks, M. M. (1986). The effects of vocabulary instruction: A model-based meta-analysis. *Review of Educational Research, 56*, 72–110.

Stahl, S. A., Osborne, J., & Lehr, F. (1990). *Beginning to read: Thinking and learning about print: A summary*. Urbana: Center for the Study of Reading, University of Illinois at Urbana-Champaign.

Stahl, S. A., Richek, M. A., & Vandeiver, R. J. (1991). Learning meaning vocabulary through listening: A sixth-grade replication. In J. Zutell & S. McCormick (Eds.), *Learner factors/teacher factors: Issues in literacy research and instruction* (pp. 185–192). Chicago: National Reading Conference.

Stallings, J. A., & Stipek, D. (1986). Research on early childhood and elementary school teaching programs. In M. E. Wittrock (Ed.), *Handbook of research on teaching* (pp. 727–754). New York: Macmillan.

Stallman, A. C., Commeyras, M., Ken, B., Jiminez, R., Hartman, D. K., & Pearson, P. D. (1990). Are "new" words really new? *Reading Research and Instruction 29*, 12–29.

Stauffer, R. G. (1969). *Directing reading maturity as a cognitive process*. New York: Harper & Row.

Stauffer, R. G. (1970). *Reading-thinking skills*. Paper presented at the annual reading conference at Temple University, Philadelphia.

Stecher, B. M., Barron, S., Kaganoff, T., & Goodwin, J. (1998). *The effects of standards-based assessment on classroom practices: Results of the 1996–97 RAND survey of Kentucky teachers of mathematics and writing*. CSE Technical Report 482.

Steinmetz, S. (Ed.). (1999). *Random House Webster's unabridged dictionary of the English language* (2nd ed.). New York: Random House.

Sternberg, R. J. (1987). Most vocabulary is learned from context. In M. G. McKeown & M. E. Curtis (Eds.), *The nature of vocabulary acquisition* (pp. 89–105). Hillsdale, NJ: Lawrence Erlbaum.

Sternberg, R. J., & Powell, J. S. (1983). Comprehending verbal comprehension. *American Psychologist, 38*, 878–893.

Stewart, R. A., & Cross, T. L. (1993). A field test of five forms of marginal gloss study guide: An ecological study. *Reading Psychology, 14*, 113–139.

Sticht, T. G., & James, J. H. (1984). Listening and reading. In P. D. Pearson, R. Barr, M. L. Kamil, & P. Mosenthal (Eds.), *Handbook of reading research* (pp. 293–317). New York: Longman.

Stoll, D. R. (1997). *Magazines for kids and teens* (2nd ed.). Newark, DE: International Reading Association.

Stotsky, S. (1983). Research of reading/writing relationships: A synthesis and suggested directions. *Language Arts, 60*, 568–580.

Strickland, D. S. (1998). Educating African-American learners at risk: Finding a better way. In C. Weaver (Ed.), *Practicing what we know: Informed reading instruction* (pp. 394–408). Urbana, IL: National Council of Teachers of English.

Sundbye, N. (1987). Text explicitness and inferential questioning: Effects on story understanding and recall. *Reading Research Quarterly, 22*, 82–98.

Sutherland, Z., & Arbuthnot, M. H. (1986). *Children and books* (7th ed.). Glenview, IL: Scott, Foresman.

Sutton, C. (1989). Helping the nonnative English speaker with reading. *The Reading Teacher, 42*, 684–688.

Sweet, A. P. (1997). Teacher perceptions of student motivation and their relation to literacy learning. In K. Guthrie & A. Wigfield (Eds.), *Reading engagement: Motivating readers through integrated instruction* (pp. 86–101). Newark, DE: International Reading Association.

Taba, H. (1965). The teaching of thinking. *Elementary English, 42*, 534–542.

Taylor, D., & Dorsey-Gaines, C. (1988). *Growing up literate: Learning from inner-city families*. Portsmouth, NH: Heinemann.

Taylor, K. K. (1986). Summary writing by young children. *Reading Research Quarterly, 21*, 193–208.

Taylor, M. A. (1990, March). *Exploring mythology and folklore: The macrocosm and microcosm*. Paper presented at the spring conference of the National Council of Teachers of English, Colorado Springs, CO.

Temple, C., Martinez, M., Yokota, J., & Naylor, A. (1998). *Children's books in children's hands: An introduction to their literature*. Boston: Allyn & Bacon.

Terry, A. (1974). *Children's poetry preferences*. Urbana, IL: National Council of Teachers of English.

Tetewsky, S. J., & Sternberg, R. J. (1986). Conceptual and lexical determinants of nonentrenched thinking. *Journal of Memory and Language, 25*, 202–225.

Thomas, E. L., & Robinson, H. A. (1972). *Improving reading in every class: A sourcebook for teachers*. Boston: Allyn & Bacon.

Thomas, W. P., & Collier, Virginia P. (1999). Accelerated Schooling for English Language Learners. *Educational Leadership, 56*, 46–49.

Thompson, A. (1990). Thinking and writing in learning logs. In N. Atwell (Ed.), *Coming to know: Writing to learn in the intermediate schools* (pp. 35–51). Portsmouth, NH: Heinemann.

Thorndike, R. L. (1973). Reading as reasoning. *Reading Research Quarterly, 9*, 135–147.

Thorndyke, P. (1977). Cognitive structures in comprehension and memory of narrative discourse. *Cognitive Psychology, 9*, 77–110.

Tiedt, P. M., & Tiedt, I. M. (2002). *Multicultural teaching: A handbook of activities, information, and resources* (6th ed.). Boston: Allyn & Bacon.

Tierney, R. J., Carter, M. A., & Desai, L. E. (1991). *Portfolio assessment in the reading-writing classroom*. Norwood, MA: Christopher-Gordon.

Tierney, R. J., & Readence, J. E. (2000). *Reading strategies and practices: A compendium* (5th ed.). Boston: Allyn & Bacon.

Tierney, R. J., Readence, J. E., & Dishner, E. K. (1995). *Reading strategies and practices: A compendium* (4th ed.). Boston: Allyn & Bacon.

Tompkins, G. E., & Yaden, D. B. (1986). *Answering questions about words.* Urbana, IL: National Council of Teachers of English.

Topping, K. (1987). Paired reading: A powerful technique for parent use. *The Reading Teacher, 40,* 608–609.

Topping, K. (1989). Peer tutoring and paired reading: Combining two powerful techniques. *The Reading Teacher, 42,* 488–494.

Topping, K. (1998). Effective tutoring in America Reads: A reply to Wasik. *The Reading Teacher, 52,* 42–50.

Torgesen, J. K., Wagner, R. K., & Rashotte, C. A. (1994). Longitudinal studies of phonological processing and reading. *Journal of Learning Disabilities, 27,* 276–286.

Touchstone Applied Science Associates (1994). *DRP handbook.* Brewster, NY: Author.

Touchstone Applied Science Associates. (1997). *Text sense, summary writing, teacher's resource manual.* Brewster, NY: Author.

Trabasso, T., & Magliano, J. P. (1996). How do children understand what they read and what can we do to help them? In M. F. Graves, P. van den Broek, & B. M. Taylor (Eds.), *The first R, every child's right to read* (pp. 160–188). New York: Teachers College Press & International Reading Association.

Trelease, J. (2001). *The new read-aloud handbook* (5th ed.). New York: Penguin.

Trussell-Cullen, A. (1994). *Celebrating the real strategies for developing non-fiction reading and writing.* Paper presented at the annual meeting of the Connecticut Reading Association, Waterbury.

Tunnell, M. O., & Jacobs, J. S. (1989). Using "real" books: Research findings on literature-based reading instruction. *The Reading Teacher, 42,* 470–477.

Turbill, J. (1982). *No better way to teach writing!* Rozelle, Australia: Primary English Teaching Association.

Tyson, E. S., & Mountain, L. (1982). A riddle or pun makes learning words fun. *The Reading Teacher, 36,* 170–173.

U.S. Department of Education. (1986). *What works: Research on teaching and learning.* Washington, DC: Government Printing Office.

U.S. Department of Education. (1991, September 16). *Memorandum: Clarification of policy to address the needs of children with attention deficit disorders within general and/or special education.* Washington, DC: Author.

U.S. Department of Education (Office of Bilingual Education and Minority Languages Affairs). (1998). *Facts about limited English proficient students.* Available online at http://www.ed.gov/offices/OBEMLA/index.html

U.S. Department of Education (Office of Special Education and Rehabilitative Services). (2000). *Twenty-second annual report to Congress on the implementation of the Individuals with Disabilities Education Act.* Washington, DC: Government Printing Office.

U.S. Department of Education (2002). *The No Child Left Behind Act of 2001.* Available online at http://www.ed.gov/legislation/ESEA02/

Vacca, R. T., & Vacca, J. L. (1986). *Content area reading* (2nd ed.). Boston: Little, Brown.

Valdes, G. (1996). *Con respeto: Bridging the distance between culturally diverse families and schools: An ethnographic portrait.* New York: Teachers College Press.

Valencia, S. W. (1990). Assessment: A portfolio approach to classroom reading assessment: The whys, whats, and hows. *The Reading Teacher, 43,* 338–340.

Valencia, S. W., & Place, N. A. (1994). Literacy portfolios for teaching, learning, and accountability: The Bellevue literacy assessment project. In S. W. Valencia, E. H. Hiebert, & P. P. Afflerbach (Eds.), *Authentic reading assessment: Practices and possibilities* (pp. 134–156). Newark, DE: International Reading Association.

Valencia, S. W., & Wixson, K. W. (2001). Inside English/language arts standards: What's in a grade? *Reading Research Quarterly, 36,* 202–217.

van den Broek, P., & Kremer, K. E. (2000). The mind in action: What it means to comprehend during reading. In B. Taylor, M. F. Graves, & P. van den Broek (Eds.), *Reading for meaning: Fostering comprehension in the middle grades* (pp. 1–31). New York: Teachers College Press.

Vardell, S. M. (2002). *Scaffolding ESL students' oral language development.* Paper presented at the annual conference of the International Reading Association, San Francisco.

Venezky, R. L. (1965). *A study of English spelling-to-sound correspondences on historical principles.* Unpublished doctoral dissertation, Stanford University, Stanford, CA.

Verhallen, M., & Schoonen, R. (1993). Vocabulary knowledge of monolingual and bilingual children. *Applied Linguistics, 14,* 344–363.

Vygotsky, L. S. (1962). *Mind and society: The development of higher psychological processes.* Cambridge, MA: MIT Press.

Vygotsky, L. S. (1978). *Thought and language.* Cambridge, MA: MIT Press.

Vygotsky, L. S. (1987). The development of scientific concepts in childhood. In R. F. Rieber & A. S. Carton (Eds.), *The collected works of L. S. Vygotsky* (N. Mnick, Trans.) (Vol 1, pp. 167–241). New York: Plenum.

Wade, S. E. (1983). A synthesis of the research for improving reading in the social studies. *Review of Educational Research, 53,* 461–497.

Walker, M. L. (1995). Help for the "fourth-grade slump"—SRQ2R plus instruction in text structure or main idea. *Reading Horizons, 36,* 38–58.

Weaver, B. (1992). *Defining literacy levels.* Charlotteville, NY: Story House.

Weaver, C. K., & Kintsch, W. (1991). Expository text. In R. Barr, M. L. Kamil, P. Mosenthal, & P. D. Pearson (Eds.), *Handbook of reading research* (Vol. II, pp. 230–245). New York: Longman.

Weber, E., Nelson, B., & Woods, R. (2000). *Into the millennium, Profiles in writing.* Clinton Township, MI: Macomb Intermediate School District.

Weber, E., Reed, B., & Woods, R. (1997). *Profiles: Windows on writing.* Flint, MI: Genesee Intermediate School District.

Weinstein, C., & Mayer, R. (1986). The teaching of learning strategies. In M. C. Wittrock (Ed.), *Handbook of research on teaching* (pp. 315–327). New York: Macmillan.

Westby, C. E. (1999). Assessing and facilitating text comprehension problems. In H. W. Catts and A. G. Kamhi (Eds.), *Language and reading disabilities* (pp. 154–223). Boston: Allyn & Bacon.

Wharton-McDonald, R. (2001). Teaching writing in first grade, instruction, scaffolds and expectations. In M. Pressley, R. L. Allington, R. Wharton-McDonald, C. C. Block, & L. M. Morrow (Eds.), *Learning to read: Lessons from exemplary first-grade classrooms* (pp. 70–91). New York: Guilford Press.

White, T. G., Power, M. A., & White, S. (1989). Morphological analysis: Implications for teaching and understanding vocabulary growth. *Reading Research Quarterly, 24,* 283–304.

White, T. G., Sowell, J., & Yanagihara, A. (1989). Teaching elementary students to use word-part clues. *The Reading Teacher, 42,* 302–308.

Wigfield, A. (1997). Children's motivations for reading and writing engagement. In J. Guthrie & A. Wigfield (Eds.), *Motivating readers through integrated instruction* (pp. 14–33). Newark, DE: International Reading Association.

Wigfield, A., & Asher, S. R. (1984). Social and motivational influences on reading. In P. D. Pearson, R. Barr, M. L. Kamil, & P. Mosenthal (Eds.), *Handbook of reading research* (pp. 423–452). New York: Longman.

Williams, J. P. (1986a). Identifying main ideas: A basic aspect of reading comprehension. *Topics in Language Disorders*, 8, 1–13.

Williams, J. P. (1986b). Research and instructional development on main idea skills. In J. F. Baumann (Ed.), *Teaching main idea comprehension* (pp. 73–95). Newark, DE: International Reading Association.

Wilson, J. (1960). *Language and the pursuit of truth*. London: Cambridge University Press.

Wilson, P. (1986). *Voluntary reading*. Paper presented at the annual convention of the International Reading Association, Philadelphia.

Wilson, P. (1992). Among nonreaders: Voluntary reading, reading achievement, and the development of reading habits. In C. Temple & P. Collins (Eds.), *Stories and readers: New perspectives on literature in the elementary classroom* (pp. 157–169). Norwood, MA: Christopher-Gordon.

Winne, R. H., Graham L., & Prock, L. (1993). A model of poor readers' text-based inferencing: Effects of explanatory feedback. *Reading Research Quarterly*, 28, 536–566.

Winograd, P. N. (1984). Strategic difficulties in summarizing text. *Reading Research Quarterly*, 19, 404–425.

Withers, C. (Ed.). (1948). *A rocket in my pocket: The rhymes and chants of young Americans*. New York: Holt.

Wixson, K. K. (1983). Questions about a text: What you ask about is what children learn. *The Reading Teacher*, 37, 287–293.

Wixson, K. K., & Dutro, E. (1998). Standards for primary-grade reading: An analysis of state frameworks (CIERA Report #3-001). Available online at http://www.ciera.org/ciera/publications/report-series/

Wolf, M., & Katzir-Cohen, T. (2001). Reading fluency and its intervention. *Scientific Studies of Reading*, 5, 211–238.

Wong, B. Y. L., & Wong, R. (1986). Study behavior as a function of metacognitive knowledge about critical task variables: An investigation of above average, average, and learning disabled readers. *Learning Disabilities Research*, 1, 101–111.

Wood, W. D., & Baker, S. A. (1999). Preferences for parent education programs among low socioeconomic status, culturally diverse parents. *Psychology in the Schools*, 36, 239–247.

Worthy, J., & Broaddus, K. (2001). Fluency beyond the primary grades: From group performance to silent, independent reading. *The Reading Teacher*, 55, 334–343.

Worthy, J., Broadus, K, & Ivy, G. (2001). *Pathways to independence*. New York: Guilford Press.

Yokota, J. (Ed.). (2001). *Kaleidoscope, a multicultural booklist for grades K–8* (3rd ed.). Urbana, IL: National Council of Teachers of English.

Yopp, H. K. (1988). The validity and reliability of phonemic awareness tests. *Reading Research Quarterly*, 23, 159–199.

Zarnowski, M. (1990). *Learning about biographies: A reading-and-writing approach for children*. Urbana, IL: National Council of Teachers of English.

Zarnowski, M., & Gallagher, A. F. (Eds.). (1993). *Children's literature and social studies: Selecting and using notable books in the classroom*. Washington, DC: National Council for the Social Studies.

Zeno, S. M., Ivens, S. H., Millard, R. T., & Duvvuri, R. (1995). *The educator's word frequency scale*. Brewster, NY: Touchstone Applied Science Associates.

Zinsser, W. (1988). *Writing to learn*. New York: Harper & Row.

Zorfass, J., Corley, P., & Remy, A. (1994). Helping students with disabilities become writers. *Educational Leadership*, 51(7), 62–66.

Zumwalt, M. (2003). Words of fortune. *The Reading Teacher*, 56, 439–441.

Zwaan, R. A., & Graesser, A. C. (1998). Introduction to special issue of SSR: Constructing meaning during reading. *Scientific Studies of Reading*, 2(3), 195–198.

Zwaan, R. A., Radvansky, G. A., Hilliard, A. E., & Curiel, J. M. (1998). Constructing multidimensional situation models during reading. *Scientific Studies of Reading*, 2(3), 199–220.

Children's Books and Periodicals

Aardema, V. (1975). *Why mosquitoes buzz in people's ears: A West African folk tale*. New York: Dial.

Aiken, J. (1962). *Wolves of Willoughby Chase*. New York: Dell.

Arnold, C. (2001). *Did you hear that?* Watertown, MA: Charlesbridge.

Avi. (1994). *The barn*. New York: Orchard.

Baldwin, D., & Lister, C. (1984). *Your five senses*. Chicago: Children's Press.

Bang, M. (1985). *The paper crane*. New York: Greenwillow.

Blos, J. W. (1979). *A gathering of days: A New England girl's journal*. New York: Scribner's.

Brink, C. (1935). *Caddie Woodlawn*. New York: Macmillan.

Burchard, P. (1999) *Lincoln and slavery*. New York: Antheneum.

Burnford, S. (1961). *Incredible journey*. New York: Bantam.

Byars, B. (1970). *Summer of the swans*. New York: Viking.

Byars, B. (1977). *The pinballs*. New York: Harper & Row.

Charles, S. (2001). *A summer day* (Leveled Readers in McGraw-Hill Reading). New York: McGraw-Hill.

Christian, A., & Felix, A. (1997). *Can it really rain frogs? The world's strangest weather events*. New York: John Wiley & Sons.

Cleary, B. (1983). *Dear Mr. Henshaw*. New York: Morrow.

Cole, J. (1992). *Magic school bus on the ocean floor*. New York: Scholastic.

Curie, E. (1937). *Madam Curie: A biography* (V. Sheehan, trans.). New York: Doubleday.

Dalgliesh, S. (1954). *Courage of Sarah Noble*. New York: Scribner's.

Donnelly, J. (1988). *Tut's mummy lost . . . and found*. New York: Random House.

Egan, R. (1997). *From wheat to pasta*. Danbury, CT: Children's Press.

Fletcher, R. J. (1997). *Spider boy*. New York: Clarion.

Folkard, C. (2003). *Guinness book of world records*. New York: Bantam.

Friedman, I. (1984). *How my parents learned to eat*. New York: Houghton Mifflin.

Fritz, J. (1975). *Where was Patrick Henry on the 29th of May?* New York: Coward, McCann & Geoghegan.

Fritz, J. (1982). *Will you sign here, John Hancock?* New York: Coward.

Fritz, J. (1993). *Just a few words, Mr. Lincoln*. New York: Grosset & Dunlap.

Gantos, J. (1994). *Heads or tails: Stories from the sixth grade*. New York: HarperCollins.

Gershator, D., & Gershator, P. (1997). *Palampam Day*. New York: Marshall Cavendish.

Gibbons, G. (1992). *Recycle! A handbook for kids*. Boston: Little Brown.

Giff, P. R. (1997). *Lily's crossing*. New York: Delacorte Press.

Grote, J. A. (2000). *Patrick Henry: American statesman and speaker*. New York: Chelsea House.

Hamilton, V. (1985). *The people could fly*. New York: Knopf.

Haskins, J. (1991). *Outward dreams: Black inventors and their inventions*. New York: Crowell.

Haushner, R. (1994). *What food is this?* New York: Scholastic.

Henry, M. (1947). *Misty of Chincoteague*. New York: Rand McNally.

Kallen, S. A. (2001). *Patrick Henry*. Edina, MN: ABDO Publishing.

Kane, J. N. (1981). *Famous first facts* (4th ed.). New York: Wilson.

Kehret, P. (1996). *Earthquake terror*. New York: Cobblehill Books.

Kukla, A. J. (2002). *Patrick Henry: voice of the revolution*. New York: Rosen Publishing Group.

L'Engle, M. (1962). *A wrinkle in time*. New York: Farrar, Straus & Giroux.

Lessem, D. (1997). *Supergiants: The biggest dinosaurs*. Little Brown.

Lewis, C. S. (1950). *The lion, the witch, and the wardrobe*. New York: Macmillan.

Locker, T. (1997). *Water dance*. San Diego, CA: Harcourt.

Lowry, L. (1990). *Number the stars*. Boston: Houghton Mifflin.

Lutz, N. J. (2001). *Frederick Douglas*. Broomall, PA: Chelsea House.

Macdonald, F. (2001) *The world in the time of Marco Polo*. Broomall, PA: Chelsea House.

MacLachlan, P. (1985). *Sarah, plain and tall*. New York: Harper & Row.

Mason, A. (1997). *If you were there, Viking times*. New York: Simon & Schuster.

Mazer, H. (2001). *A boy at war, a novel of Pearl Harbor*. New York: Simon & Schuster.

Meddaugh, S. (1997). *Cinderella's rat*. Boston: Houghton Mifflin.

Mora, P. (1997). *Tomas and the library lady*. New York: Random House.

Naylor, P. (1991). *Shiloh*. New York: Atheneum.

Naylor, P. (1996). *Fear Place*. New York: Alladin.

Neff, M. M. (1990). Legends: How Gordie Howe was a hockey star in his youth and also when he was a grandpa. *Sports Illustrated for Kids, 2*(2), 48.

Park, K. (2003). *The world almanac and book of facts*. New York: World Almanac Books.

Paulsen, G. (1991). *Woodsong*. New York: Puffin.

Rawls, W. (1961). *Where the red fern grows*. New York: Doubleday.

Reynolds, M. (1997). *The new land*. New York: Orca.

Richards, J. (2002) *Howling hurricanes*. Broomall, PA: Chelsea House.

Rogers, S. (2001). *Jazzman: Louis Armstrong* (Leveled Readers in McGraw-Hill Reading). New York: McGraw-Hill.

Rolfer, G. (1990). Game day. *Sports Illustrated for Kids, 2*(8), 25.

Sachar, L. (1998). *Holes*. New York: Yearling.

Shuter, J. (1997). *The ancient Egyptians*. Portsmouth, NH: Heineman.

Sims, W. (1999). *The tug*. Novato, CA: High Noon.

Smith, G. (2001). *One year in the west* (Leveled Readers in McGraw-Hill Reading). New York: McGraw-Hill.

Sobol, D. (1961). *The Wright brothers at Kitty Hawk*. New York: Dutton.

Souza, D. M. (1998). *Fish that play tricks*. Minneapolis: Carolrhoda.

Speare, E. (1958). *The witch of Blackbird Pond*. Boston: Houghton Mifflin.

Spinnelli, J. (1990). *Maniac Magee*. New York: HarperCollins.

Stevenson, R. L. (1883/1986). *Treasure island*. New York: Signet.

Stevenson, R. L. (1885/1985). *A child's garden of verses*. London: Longman.

Stolz, M. (1992). *Stealing home*. New York: HarperCollins.

Stone, L. M. (1985). *Antarctica*. Chicago: Children's Press.

Stone, L. M. (1998). *Brown bears*. Minneapolis: Lerner.

Taylor, M. (1987). *The friendship*. New York: Dial.

Taylor, M. (2003). Song of the trees. In Holt, Rinehart and Winston (Ed.), *Elements of literature first course* (pp. 29–40). New York: Author.

Thompson, S. E. (1998). *Built for speed: The extraordinary, enigmatic cheetah*. Minneapolis: Lerner.

Twain, M. (1881/2001). *The prince and the pauper*. New York: Bantam.

White, E. B. (1952). *Charlotte's web*. New York: Harper & Row.

Whitebird, M. (2001). Ta-Na-E-Ka. In J. Flood, A. Medcaris, J. E. Hasbrouk, S. Paris, J. Hoffman, S. Stahl, D. Lapp, J. V. Tinejero & K. D. Wood. *McGraw-Hill reading, level 6, unit 2*. New York: McGraw-Hill.

Wilder, L. I. (1932). *Little house in the big woods*. New York: HarperCollins.

Wilder, L. I. (1941). *Little house on the prairie*. New York: HarperCollins.

Wildsmith, B. (1988). *Squirrels*. New York: Oxford University Press.

Woodson, J. (1991). *Last summer with Maizon*. New York: Dell.

Young, M. (1999). *Guinness book of world records*. New York: Sterling.

Index

Note: Page numbers followed by *f* or *t* indicate figures or tables, respectively.

Photo Credits